Materials management and purchasing

Materials management and purchasing

Dean S. Ammer, Ph.D.

President
Hospital Purchasing Institute, Inc.

1980   Fourth edition

RICHARD D. IRWIN, INC.   Homewood, Illinois   60430
Irwin-Dorsey Limited   Georgetown, Ontario   L7G 4B3

ISBN 0-256-02146-5
Library of Congress Catalog Card No. 79-88788

Printed in the United States of America

1 2 3 4 5 6 7 8 9 0 MP 7 6 5 4 3 2 1 0

Preface

Materials management problems are common to every organization. To a great extent, these problems are being solved by executives with titles like Materials Manager or Director of Materials. This was not true even in most large manufacturing organizations in 1958 when I began research on my doctoral dissertation, which was concerned with organization for materials management.

This book is inspired, in part, by that research. I have tried to make it useful both to the student who is new to the field and to the practitioner who wants to expand his or her knowledge. I treat materials management as the specialized body of knowledge that is needed to administer the overall supply process—from identification of potential vendors to ultimate delivery and use of the purchased product or service.

Despite this broad scope, I quite deliberately give more emphasis to the problems of purchasing management than to other aspects of the process. In fact, I neglect materials handling (often confused with materials management) simply because I regard it as basically an engineering skill, not a managerial one. The materials management organizations that exist in real-life organizations evolved out of purchasing departments in most cases and they are more likely to be headed by an ex-purchasing manager than anyone else. In my view, materials management is an up-to-date way to manage rationally the overall purchasing process. Thus, it is no accident that the title of this book is *Materials Management and Purchasing.*

The book is written to be teachable (although I hope it will be read by practitioners with no interest in a classroom experience). The good teacher tries to hammer home the same message three or four different ways. Cases are included as a device to permit the reader and student to see principles applied in practice. They are also, of course, a device that permits an instructor to repeat the same ideas without (it is hoped) boring students to death.

Needless to say, even the most persistent reader of this work will not acquire all of the skills required to become a purchasing manager or materials manager. The would-be purchasing manager must have some specialized technical knowledge unique to particular industries. To cite an obvious example, the hospital purchasing manager must be able to distinguish between a syringe and a catheter (knowledge that cannot be acquired from reading this book). Similarly, a buyer for DuPont could be expected to know much more about chemicals than a person picked at random off the street while, as a one-time buyer for the Ford Motor Company, I was quite familiar with the various processes for shaping metal.

I do not pretend to cover the technical skills needed for competent materials management. Nor do I cover all of the managerial skills. In fact, one major problem is that of distinguishing between skills that are unique to materials management (which I try to cover) and those that are common to all managers (which I cover, in part, especially when there may be more or less unique applications to purchasing and materials management.)

I have tried to make this book more quantitative than others I have seen—but not so much so that it presents the subject unrealistically. I hope that it is pragmatic in tone, something that is useful to my real-life practitioners.

The cases and examples reflect my own experience in the field which began in 1948. They also reflect the collective experiences of at least several hundred purchasing and materials management executives I have met in the past 30 years—particularly during the period when I was executive editor of *Purchasing* magazine. While I hope the book is more readable than the stereotype "text," its organization also undoubtedly reflects 15 years experience as a full-time academician.

I should like to acknowledge the comments—both critical and positive—from fellow instructors that have helped shape both the content and organization of this book. These include John Hoagland of Michigan State University, the late Howard Lewis of Harvard University, Harold Fearon of Arizona State University, Jack Holland of San Jose State University, and Monroe Murphy Bird of Virginia Polytechnic Institute and State University. However, I must assume responsibility for any ommissions and oversights.

January 1980   Dean S. Ammer

Contents

Organization by product or project. Span of control. Level of organization: *Materials manager's level. Within the organization.* Applying organization principles: *The Avco-Lycoming Organization. The General Electric approach. Applications to service industries.* The decentralized organization: *Staff-and-line approach. Materials staffs' activities. Results of staff-and-line organization.* The organization of the future.

jective: *Need for inventory. Nature of the problem. Inventory func-tions. Determining inventory levels.* Job-lot ordering: *Problems of control. Application of Bayesian rule. Modified job-lot control.* Or-dering for inventory: *"Perpetual" inventory control. Critical ratio.* Inventory records: *Classification. Disposition of surplus.*

data: *Applying the cost-volume principle. Buyer cost estimates. The learning curve.* Value analysis: *Definition. Organizing for value analysis. Value analysis techniques. Selling value analysis. Standardization.* Negotiating price increases: *Production versus nonproduction. Bargaining power. Justifying the increase. Cost analysis. Error in supplier pricing.*

List of cases

1

Introduction to materials management

Written goals permits management by exception —

Why should anyone care about purchasing and materials management—let alone go to the trouble of reading a book on the subject? Here are a few good reasons:

1. *Our economic relationships are interdependent.* Everyone relies on someone else for materials, supplies, and services. For this reason, every organization—public or private, manufacturing or service—has someone who functions as a materials manager or purchasing manager.

2. *The supply process is not automatic or foolproof.* Genuine specialized managerial skills are required to do the job properly. Purchasing and materials management is a specialized bundle of knowledge that must be acquired.

3. *Our basic economic well-being is related to how skillfully we carry out the purchasing and materials management process.* Manufacturing companies normally spend almost twice as much on purchases as they do on payrolls so their efficiency is largely measured by how skillfully they convert something that they buy from someone else. Even organizations that are seemingly entirely service oriented are substantial buyers of supplies and services. For example, the hospital whose basic service consists of nursing services spends almost as much on purchases as it does on nursing salaries!

4. *Purchasing and materials management offers professional-level employment in almost every organization, public or private.* There are at least 100,000 directors of purchasing and materials management employed in the United States and Canada. They have uncounted thousands of subordinates. A large corporation may have as many as 5,000 persons employed in various materials management

1

activities. Even a hospital may employ 100 persons in various phases
of materials management.

What and who

Definition. It is fairly easy to define materials management quite
concisely—although it takes at least a whole book to discuss the details. Materials management is simply the process by which an organization is supplied with the goods and services that it needs to achieve
its objectives. The materials manager of a manufacturing organization
is primarily concerned with the supply of materials that the company
converts into finished products. The materials manager of a service
organization (e.g., government, airline, hospital, bank) does not buy
materials that are fabricated into products that the organization sells.
Instead, like the manufacturing organization, he or she is concerned
with thousands of purchases that are essential to operations. In every
organization, these include such basic purchases as fuel and utilities, a
myriad of paper products, and countless other supplies.

Activities. The materials management process begins with the
supplier and ends when the material is either consumed or incorporated into some product. The executives who engage in materials
management are concerned with three basic activities: buying, storage
of material, and movement. They have literally hundreds of different
job titles including purchasing or materials manager, purchasing director, traffic manager, inventory manager, and others.

BASIC ECONOMICS

Materials management is as essential to producers of services as it is
to goods. In fact, the railroads were probably the first to identify materials management as a separate activity. More recently, however, nonprofit and public institutions have begun to recognize that they, too,
are engaged in materials management, and they have established formal materials management organizations. Materials management is
common to every organization simply because none is completely
self-sufficient.

Value added by manufacture

The dependency on outside suppliers is most apparent in the manufacturing organization. Every manufacturer is a converter of materials
purchased from some outside side. Even a huge, seemingly self-
sufficient corporation like General Motors spends roughly 50 cents of
each sales dollar on purchased parts, materials, and supplies. (See
Figure 1–1.) This is almost twice as much as the company spends on
payrolls.

FIGURE 1-1
How General Motors Corporation spends its sales dollar

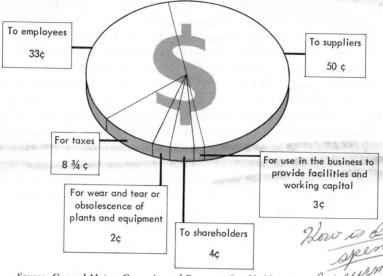

Source: General Motors Corp., *Annual Report to Stockholders.*

General Motors, like every other manufacturer, is in the business of adding value to the products it purchases. In the case of General Motors, 50 cents worth of purchased material is transformed into $1 worth of finished product, primarily by adding value through manufacture. The value that is added represents the 33 cents General Motors spends on labor, plus an additional 27 cents for taxes, depreciation, and profit.

It is fairly easy to visualize the physical process of adding value by manufacture. With automotive products, it consists of hundreds of thousands of workers shaping metal into identifiable components and then, in various stages, fastening these components together, until they become a finished automotive product.

Value added by distribution

Distribution, the other value-adding process, is harder to visualize. This is the process by which the product reaches its ultimate user; value is added by distribution when a product is packaged, stored, shipped, and sold. The distribution process begins when the last manufacturing operation is completed and continues until the product reaches the ultimate consumer. When the manufacturing is extremely simple, almost all of the value added to the product is by distribution. For example, crushed stone may sell for $1 per ton at the quarry, but by the time it is delivered, the price is $3.50. The $2.50 per ton trucking charge is a clear-cut case of value having been added by distribution. The stone is useless until it is trucked to someone who wants it.

Value is also added in less direct ways. In the course of the distribution process, material may be stored in a warehouse. Not only does the warehousing cost become value added by distribution, but so does the interest on the money that is tied up. Similarly, if merchandise is subject to spoilage or pilferage, then the loss becomes part of the value added by distribution to the products that finally do reach the user in satisfactory condition.

Value added by distribution may be roughly equal to value added by manufacture, even on complex products. For example, suppose General Motors adds $2,500 worth of value to a Chevrolet that it sells to one of its dealers for $5,000. The dealer, in turn, may sell the car to an ultimate user for $6,500. The marketing process from the end of the GM assembly line to the dealer then adds $1,500 worth of value by distribution—almost as much as that added by General Motors itself. And, as we will see later, much of the value that General Motors and other manufacturers add to their products comes from distribution, not from manufacture.

Of course, manufacturing and distribution are interrelated; one can not exist without the other. However, much of the value that is added by distribution is carried on by organizations that do no manufacturing. For example, a department store chain purchases a refrigerator from the manufacturer for $200 and sells it for $300, adding $100 worth of value by distribution to the product. Or a gas company bills a home-heating customer $150 for natural gas it may have purchased from a pipeline company for $60, thus adding $90 worth of value by distribution.

Criteria for adding value

While most distribution is carried on by nonmanufacturing organizations, manufacturers also add value by distribution. In both manufacturing and distribution, value is added under these circumstances:

1. *Costs are incurred.* Things that are free, such as the air we breathe, have value, but no value is added in the economic sense until there is cost. Thus, if a foundry spends money on pollution control, it is thereby adding value by manufacture to the castings it produces, since restoration of the air to its former pure state is (or should be) a basic part of its process. Theoretically, all costs incurred by a manufacturing firm contribute either to value added by manufacture or to value added by distribution. If they do not, then company funds are being wasted, and management should be subject to either censure or dismissal.

2. *Capital is employed.* In a modern economy, it is not possible to produce anything without some minimum stock of capital (in the

physical, not necessarily the financial sense). Investment in machinery, buildings, and in-process (also known as work-in-process) inventories is obviously essential if value is to be added by manufacture.

Capital requirements for distribution are less obvious, since the product is not transformed physically. Yet those who add value by distribution find it impossible to get along without a substantial investment in capital goods. A department store may require 50 to 75 cents worth of buildings, inventory, and other capital goods to support each $1 of sales. And, of course, the profit that is earned on sales represents the return that this capital must earn to be productive. Capital investment that does not "work" and contribute to profitability is sterile and should be eliminated. One of the major goals of materials management is to identify inventory that is not working to add value by distribution and get rid of it.

Hypothetical example

While the typical manufacturing company uses most of its capital to add value by manufacture, a substantial investment is needed to support distribution. Suppose, for example, that you are president of Appleton Corporation, a manufacturer of lighting fixtures. Your sales are $10 million per year and profits after tax are $500,000. Your most recent balance sheet, shown in Figure 1–2, indicates that you require total assets of $4 million (including $200,000 in cash) to carry on your business.

Evaluation of assets. Like every other business executive, you would be delighted to find a way to earn the same $500,000 profit with

FIGURE 1–2

APPLETON CORPORATION
Balance Sheet

Assets

Cash		$ 200,000
Accounts receivable		1,000,000
Inventory		
Purchased materials	$400,000	
In-process stocks	200,000	
Finished goods	600,000	1,200,000
Net fixed assets (land, buildings, equipment)		1,600,000
Total assets		$4,000,000

Liabilities

Current liabilities	$ 500,000
Bank loan	1,000,000
Common stock and surplus	2,500,000
Total liabilities and net worth	$4,000,000

fewer assets. However, if you try to get along with less plant and equipment, you simply will not have enough capacity to supply your customers. You would be more than happy if your customers would only pay their bills a little faster, since this would permit you to reduce your $1 million investment in accounts receivable. But if you try to force customers to pay up faster, you know that sales volume will suffer, and the decline in profits will more than offset any saving you can make. You would also like to reduce your $600,000 investment in finished goods inventory, but if you do, you know that you will not have stock on hand when customers require it. And again the loss of customer goodwill would more than offset any gain you could make by reducing finished goods stocks.

Your $200,000 investment in in-process inventory represents unfinished products awaiting further manufacturing operations. They come about naturally as a part of your process, and, if you reduce them, your production capability would be severely curtailed. Similarly, you discover that you are unable to reduce your $400,000 purchased materials inventories without adverse effects on your costs and profits. You need a stockpile of some materials to prevent your production lines from being shut down due to unexpected delays in future shipments by your suppliers. You also know that you have to buy substantial quantities of certain materials in order to purchase at the lowest price.

Thus, in your very well-run company, all assets are productive. If you try to make any reductions, you know that the benefit of lower capital investment will be more than offset by higher costs, lower sales, or both. In most cases, it is fairly easy to determine which of your assets are used to add value by manufacture and which are used to add value by distribution.

Manufacturing assets. You discover that your net investment in production equipment and machinery is $700,000 and that this investment is housed in buildings and land with a net value of $300,000. Thus, $1 million of your $1.6 million total net investment in land, buildings, and equipment is required in your manufacturing process. In addition, an investment of $200,000 is required for in-process inventory. So total assets employed in adding value by manufacture are $1.2 million ($1 million in net plant and equipment plus $200,000 for in-process inventories). Your total assets, exclusive of your cash balance of $200,000, amount to $3,800,000. Therefore, only 32 percent ($1,200,000 ÷ $3,800,000 × 100) of your "working" assets[1] are used in

---

[1] For simplicity, I am assuming that cash is not a working asset. Of course, some minimum cash balance is essential to the operation of any business, to meet unexpected increases in costs and expenses or to compensate for unexpected delays in payments of outstanding receivables. The cash is obviously needed for both the manufacturing and distribution phases of the business. In most cases, it would probably be allocated proportionately to other assets used in distribution and manufacturing. If this were done, our allocation of 32 percent of Appleton's assets to manufacturing and 68 percent to distribution would be unaffected.

adding value by manufacture. The other assets, which amount to $2.6 million, are not needed in the direct manufacturing process.

Marketing assets. Let us now examine the role these nonmanufacturing assets play. If they perform no useful economic function, they should be eliminated. Your $600,000 investment in finished goods inventory is obviously related to the distribution process; you must have it if your customers are to get your products when they need them. This finished goods inventory is stored in a company-owned warehouse with a value of $300,000, and materials handling equipment, sales offices, furniture, and so forth, account for investment of an additional $100,000. Thus, $400,000 worth of your buildings, plant, and equipment is directly associated with the marketing and distribution of your products; without these facilities, your products would never reach your customers. This is also true of your $1 million investment in accounts receivable; financing of receivables is an essential part of the distribution process in all industries where sales are not made for cash. Thus, you need a total investment of $2 million to market your product: $600,000 for finished goods stocks, $400,000 for buildings and equipment, and $1 million for accounts receivable. You therefore employ about 54 percent of your capital in the marketing process—substantially more than the 32 percent that is devoted to manufacturing.

Manufacturing companies recognize that they are usually engaged in two quite different businesses: making products and marketing them. It is not unusual for the marketing phase to be more important economically than the manufacturing aspect. Producers of packaged consumer goods, in particular, look upon themselves as being marketers much more than manufacturers. Outstanding examples of marketing-dominated manufacturers are companies such as Gillette and Revlon.

The organization structure of some companies even reflects the fact that adding value by distribution is quite different from adding value by manufacture—even though an identical product is sold. It would be easy, for example, for Appleton to reorganize itself into two separate companies: Appleton Manufacturing Company and Appleton Sales Corporation. One company would make the product, and the other would sell it. Each would employ capital and incur costs to carry on an economically useful activity.

Application to materials management

While managements have long been aware of the fact that manufacturing and marketing may be quite separate activities, they have typically been oblivious to a third basic economic activity that is carried on daily in their organizations: materials management. This activity meets the same basic value-adding criteria as marketing and manufacturing. In materials management, as in the two better known activities, *capital is employed and costs are incurred to produce something of economic value.*

Meeting value criteria. The capital that is employed in materials management is primarily purchased materials inventory, but it also includes the buildings and land needed to house this inventory, materials handling equipment that may transport it, and office space and equipment used by materials management personnel. At Appleton (see Figure 1–2), the materials management investment might include not only the $400,000 purchased materials inventory but also the $200,000 invested in land, buildings, and equipment.

Traditionally, capital employed in materials management has simply been lumped together with that used in manufacturing. While materials management existed, it was buried within the manufacturing organization. As a result, materials were often managed badly. It is fairly easy to submerge mediocre materials management activities within a rather efficient manufacturing management organization because the two functions are quite different economically. Materials management adds value by distribution. In materials management, as in marketing, products are not physically transformed but acquire additional value basically as a result of having been moved from their producer to their user. The materials management process adds value by getting material into the hands of manufacturing and other using departments; marketing takes material from manufacturing and gets it into the hands of a company customer.

Nothing for free. While materials management is a perfectly obvious example of adding value by distribution, managements persist to this day in their belief that they get something for nothing in materials management. The belief is translated into practice by the conventional cost accounting system, which assumes that purchased material has a value at the stage where it is used that is equal to the original purchase price. For example, suppose that the Appleton Corporation purchases steel at a delivered price of 9 cents per pound. If the company has a conventional cost accounting system, it will be assumed, for example, that the cost of the steel is 9 cents per pound (if there is no waste) at the point where the steel begins to be shaped into a lighting fixture by the company's presses. This means implicitly that no value has been added by distribution up to the stage of the process where value begins to be added by manufacture.

Test for added value. If no value is added to distribution prior to manufacture, why then is $600,000 invested by Appleton in inventories and various facilities related to materials management? It follows that this capital must be completely sterile. If it performs no economically useful function, it should be converted into cash and employed for something useful.

But, of course, no company can get along without a substantial investment in the assets that are essential to materials management, nor can it persuade its buyers, traffic coordinators, inventory controllers, and other materials management personnel to work without salary. Thus, value is inevitably added to purchased material in the materials management process. In a manufacturing organization, $1.00 worth of purchased material is usually worth at least $1.05 before it reaches its user; the value added by distribution in materials management then is 5 cents ($1.05 − $1.00). If the company spends 50 cents of each sales dollar on purchases, value added by materials management amounts to 5 percent of 50 cents and is therefore equal to 2½ cents of each sales dollar. Thus, in manufacturing companies, at least, materials management is never as important as marketing or manufacturing, the aggregate value added of which, in this example, would amount to 47½ cents of each sales dollar.[2]

In nonmanufacturing organizations, value added by the materials management process may be much greater. In hospitals or military organizations, there may be more than $1 of value added by materials management for each $1 of purchases. Thus, the true cost to the user of an item purchased from a supplier for $1 may become $2 or more after value is added by distribution in the materials management process.[3]

Application of principle

As president of Appleton Corporation, you have access to all of the company's accounting records. With a little work, you can calculate value added in materials management, manufacturing, and marketing. You are, of course, already familiar with the conventional income statement in which a company lumps together all of its costs, subtracts this figure from sales, and arrives at a net profit.

Five basic costs. The special income statement shown in Figure 1–3 comes out with the same net profit of $500,000 as a conventional statement would report. The main difference is that all costs and expenses are grouped into five categories:

1. Purchases. This represents what you paid to outsiders for parts and materials used in your product and is the contribution or value added by your suppliers.

---

[2] Purchases account for 50 cents of each $1 of sales. This leaves 50 cents in total value added by the company's marketing, manufacturing, and materials management activities. Value added by materials management is about 5 percent of purchases, or 5 percent of 50 cents = 2½ cents. The remainder of 47½ cents (50 cents − 2½ cents) represents value added by manufacturing and marketing.

[3] A detailed explanation of how this comes about is part of the solution of Rhode Island Hospital, Case 1–2, at the end of this chapter.

FIGURE 1–3

APPLETON CORPORATION
Adjusted Income Statement

Sales		$10,000,000
Less cost of purchases		5,000,000
Gross margin		$ 5,000,000
Less expenses		
Materials management expenses	$ 150,000	
Manufacturing payroll expenses	2,000,000	
Marketing expenses	1,000,000	$ 3,150,000
Basic operating profit		$ 1,850,000
Less executive office and staff expenses		850,000
Net profit		$ 1,000,000
Income Tax		500,000
		$ 500,000

Allocated profit	Before tax	After tax
Materials management (14%)	$ 140,000	$ 70,000
Manufacturing (32%)	320,000	160,000
Marketing (54%)	540,000	270,000
	$1,000,000	$500,000

2. *Materials management.* In the course of getting purchased material from your suppliers to the point where the material was actually used, you incurred costs of $150,000. Payrolls, mostly salaries, are the single biggest expense, but also included would be depreciation on facilities and equipment employed in materials management, your best estimate of costs of utilities, and any other expenses incurred as part of the materials management process.

3. *Manufacturing.* You estimate that you spent $2 million for wages paid to factory production workers and nonproduction employees such as supervisors, inspectors, and maintenance employees who are directly concerned with your basic process. In addition, you would include depreciation, power, and all other costs directly associated with factory operation.

4. *Marketing.* Included among marketing expenditures of $1 million would be salaries, advertising, depreciation on both office and warehouse facilities and equipment, and numerous other expenses.

5. *Executive office and staff.* Marketing, manufacturing, and materials management are the company's three "line" activities that directly add value to your product. But, of course, the company has other activities—accounting, personnel, engineering—that you cannot get along without, even though their major role is to help the "value adders" rather than to add value themselves. Since you believe that managers of the three value-adding departments should be held responsible only for costs they control, you include in this miscellaneous $850,000 expense category the budgets of all activities, including

those of the office of the president, which do not report to marketing, manufacturing, or materials management.[4]

Your total operating expenses would, of course, be identical with those shown on a conventional profit and loss statement. Both statements would show the same $500,000 aftertax profit. In the economic sense, this profit represents a reward to capital employed in adding value either by manufacture or by distribution. If we assume that Appleton's three basic value-adding activities were managed with equal proficiency, then each deserves a share of the $1 million pretax profit in proportion to its investment.

Three basic returns. As we previously calculated, your company has 32 percent of its capital in manufacturing and 54 percent in marketing. The balance of 14 percent is invested in materials management. Therefore, as shown in Figure 1–3, profits earned by materials management, manufacturing, and marketing would be $140,000, $320,000, and $540,000, respectively. The value added by each line activity is equal to expenses of that activity plus its pretax profit. Since materials management expenses are $150,000 and profit is $140,000 at Appleton, the *minimum* value added by materials management is $290,000. The *minimum* value added by manufacturing is $2,320,000 ($2,000,000 + $320,000) and that by marketing is $1,540,000. To these minimum estimates, you would have to add the contributions made by the various staff activities. While these activities do not directly add to product value, they presumably all pull their own weight in helping the line departments add value.

Adding the "helpers." Note from the adjusted income statement for Appleton that the expenses of the nonvalue adders or "helpers" amount to $850,000, while the value adders have combined expenses of $3,150,000 and their invested capital earns a combined pretax profit of $1 million. Thus, total direct value added is equal to $4,150,000. Indirect contributions of $850,000 are 20.48 percent ($850,000 ÷ $4,150,000 × 100) of direct value added. If we assume that indirect contributions can be allocated in proportion to direct contribution, then we can increase each of the three *minimum* direct contributions by 20.48 percent to get an estimate of *total* value added by each activity, as follows:

Materials management:	120.48 percent × $290,000	= $ 350,000
Manufacturing:	120.48 percent × $2,320,000	= 2,795,000
Marketing:	120.48 percent × $1,540,000	= 1,855,000
Total value added	....	$5,000,000

[4] If you wanted to be more precise, you would probably try to allocate the cost of these miscellaneous activities in proportion to the time spent with each of the line activities. For example, salaries of accounting clerks specializing in accounts payable would be allocated almost entirely to materials management, time of accounts receivable clerks would be charged to marketing, and the cost of operating the payroll department would be paid for primarily by manufacturing, which accounts for about three fourths of the company's employees.

Dividing the sales dollar. Appleton's operations can then be looked upon as a series of three steps that adds value to purchased material as follows:

	Amount	Percent of sales	Cumulative total
Purchases	$ 5,000,000	50.0	$ 5,000,000
Materials management	350,000	3.5	5,350,000
Manufacturing	2,795,000	28.0	8,145,000
Marketing	1,855,000	18.5	10,000,000
Total sales	$10,000,000		

Thus the materials management process adds 3½ cents of value to each 50 cents' worth of purchased material. Manufacturing and marketing adds 28 cents and 18½ cents, respectively, giving a total of 50 cents in value added by all three activities of 50 cents worth of purchased material for each $1 of product that is sold. Also note that material increases in value by 7 percent in materials management, by

FIGURE 1–4
Typical manufacturer's sales dollar showing value added by four basic activities

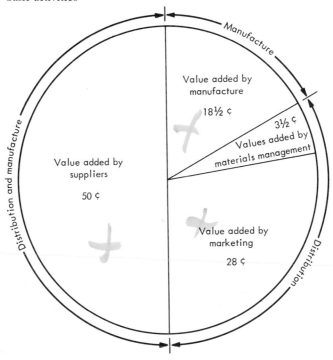

56 percent (of its original cost) in manufacturing, and by 37 percent in marketing.

As illustrated in Figure 1–4, a new type of "sales dollar" can be constructed from our estimates of value added. Instead of showing *payments*, which is essentially what is illustrated in the GM example in Figure 1–1, it shows *economic contribution.* The biggest single contribution in almost every manufacturing company is made by suppliers, and the smallest is always made by the company's own materials management process.

SCOPE OF MATERIALS MANAGEMENT

The contribution of the materials manager to the company's well-being is actually greater than Figure 1–4 suggests. In terms of basic value added to product, the materials manager is roughly but one fifth as important as the marketing manager (3½ cents of value compared with 18½ cents) and only one eighth as important as the manufacturing manager (3½ cents compared with 28 cents).

Role of purchasing

The comparison above understates the contribution that a capable materials manager should be able to make. The reason is that materials management exercises some discretion over the greatest product cost: purchases of parts and materials from outside suppliers.

Purchasing is the single most important materials management activity in most companies and institutions. If materials management adds value by distribution to purchased material, then obviously the process cannot take place unless someone buys the material. In fact, the terms "materials management" and "purchasing" are often used interchangeably. Executives whose responsibility is limited to purchasing sometimes have titles like materials manager and executives with titles like director of purchases are often given responsibilities that make them de facto materials managers.

The confusion is unfortunate, since many chief executives probably wind up believing that they are organized to do an effective job of materials management when they really are not. The fact is that purchasing is a specialized part of materials management, just as plant engineering is a specialized part of manufacturing and advertising is a part of marketing. Thus materials management is a basic function of the business that adds value directly to the product, and purchasing, such as plant engineering and advertising, is a specialized staff activity that helps a value adder but does not really add any value to the product itself.

14

Line and staff responsibilities

Line activities. To carry out its basic mission of adding value by distribution, materials management must embrace all activities that are concerned with getting purchased material from suppliers up to the stage where value begins to be added by manufacture. Included in this basic materials management activity would be not only the purchasing department but also all other activities concerned with handling, storage, or transportation of material prior to its incorporation into the manufacturing process.

When dealing with purchased material, the materials manager is a "line" executive responsible for a basic function of the business. His or her role is comparable to that of manufacturing manager or marketing manager. In many organizations, the materials manager also has a second "staff" role, comparable to that of the accountant. She is responsible for specialized services that logically fall under the control of either manufacturing or marketing. These services are delegated to materials management simply because it has skills not ordinarily associated with manufacturing or marketing.

Marketing role. It is easy to differentiate materials management skills and marketing skills. In the profit-making manufacturing or nonmanufacturing company, the basic task of the marketing manager is to sell the product. Major marketing executives invariably concentrate their efforts on sales and advertising; in most cases, their previous experience has been in these two all-important marketing activities.

While it is only rarely that a marketing manager is a specialist in something other than the art and science of persuading customers to buy company products, the scope of the marketing activity is much broader than this. The total marketing process embraces all activities necessary to get the product from the last manufacturing operation to the customer. This normally involves a great deal more than simply persuading the customer to buy the product (although that activity is by far the most important marketing activity for most products). The product must be transported and stored, going through virtually the same process that is carried on when purchased material moves from the supplier to its point of use. This process of moving goods to the ultimate consumer is called *physical distribution.*

While the technical skills involved in physical distribution are virtually identical with those associated with materials management of purchased materials, responsibility for physical-distribution policy rests with the marketing manager rather than the materials manager. For example, it is a basic part of the company's marketing strategy to decide whether to stock a particular product in the company's warehouse or to require the customer to wait for delivery. Once this and thousands of similar decisions are made, however, the marketing manager may delegate responsibility for physical distribution to the materials manager, so marketing can concentrate its efforts almost entirely on sales. The materials manager then proceeds to apply virtually the same skills to finished goods that he is already applying to purchased materials. In the latter case, he makes his own rules (consistent with overall company strategy and policy); in the former, he tries to conform to guidelines given him by the marketing manager.

Manufacturing role. The relation of the materials manager to manufacturing is more varied and complex than it is to marketing, being strongly influenced by technology. In some cases, the relationship between materials management and production is quite well defined. In an electric utility, materials management delivers fuel to the generating station, and production uses the fuel in its boilers. Similarly, in a paper company, materials management delivers purchased logs, chemicals, and other materials, and manufacturing takes over from there.

In other manufacturing companies, the relationship between materials management and manufacturing is more complex. Many manufacturers purchase materials at various stages of fabrication; materials management may supply raw material, semifinished items, and parts, and may even bypass manufacturing entirely and purchase finished products. In other cases, a company may simultaneously purchase and make identical items. A complicated system of supply inevitably draws manufacturing and materials management closer together and makes it more difficult to determine where the responsibility of one ends and the other begins.

Nevertheless, it is always possible to separate the two activities after studying a company's unique situation. In general, materials management is responsible as a line function for anything that is purchased, up to the point where value begins to be added by manufacture. In addition, materials management may also serve manufacturing in a staff capacity, just as it does for marketing.

The manufacturing manager is more difficult to stereotype than the marketing manager, simply because there are so many different manufacturing processes. Yet all manufacturing managers seem to share these two basic assignments: to keep their processes functioning efficiently and to get maximum productivity from their labor forces. The manufacturing manager is an expert at getting as much work as possible from both people and machines. The manager almost always has some combination of these people-machine skills. When the process is highly automated, the technical skills may be dominant; when the process is simple, the leadership or people skill will be what counts.

Manufacturing management is concerned essentially with keeping equipment and the labor force operating at top efficiency to produce products that marketing can sell. To carry out this basic mission, manufacturing often requires the same specialized skills as materials management. In manufacturing, as in materials management and marketing, material must be stored and moved physically from point to point. In fact, if the process is not completely automated, manufacturing is often engaged in adding value by distribution as well as adding value by manufacture. When a partially completed assembly is carried by a fork truck from one manufacturing location to another, value is being added not by manufacture but by distribution. Similarly, if a partially finished product is temporarily stored, a cost is incurred that represents value added by distribution.

While the manufacturing manager must ultimately be responsible for everything that happens during the entire manufacturing cycle, she may delegate specialized distribution tasks to the materials manager. With certain products, this delegation is all but essential if materials management is to function satisfactorily in carrying out its basic purchased materials mission. In such cases, the manufacturing process may be subject to many unexpected changes, and materials management cannot hope to achieve continuity of supply of purchased materials if it is not directly involved in all of the internal supply problems in the entire manufacturing process.

Role varies widely.   Thus, while the basic value-adding line function of materials management is universally applicable to all organizations, the staff types of activities vary widely. In organizations that produce a service, these staff activities are usually nonexistent. Materials management does its job, and other parts of the organization produce and market the service, largely on their own. At the other extreme, the staff side of materials management may be more important than the basic activity in a company that produces a bulky finished product made from its own raw materials.

HISTORY OF MATERIALS MANAGEMENT

The scope of materials management in any particular industry is at least as much a product of historical development as it is of economic logic. Organizations in which materials management plays its optimum line and staff roles have rarely been created with a single stroke of the organization planner's pen. They have evolved gradually and, in most cases, have not yet matured.

Evolutionary process

The process of development in materials management is far from uniform but seems to follow this general pattern:

Stage 1.   All materials management activities are carried on almost unconsciously, as sidelines, by executives who are primarily concerned with other activities.

Stage 2. Major materials management activities are recognized formally, but these activities report to a variety of executives and are not centralized organizationally. As a result, the only genuine materials manager in the organization is the president or general manager, who is usually preoccupied with seemingly more pressing problems.

Stage 3. Materials management activities concerned with purchased materials are grouped together under a single staff executive, who gradually begins to behave like a line manager.

Stage 4. Materials management becomes a genuine value-adding activity for purchased materials. It also provides maximum specialized staff assistance to manufacturing and to marketing in their physical distribution problems.

Slow progress. Three companies out of four have yet even to approach Stage 4 in the development of their materials management organizations. Most of those who claim to have reached this final stage in the evolution of materials management have yet to achieve the performance or play the role in general management they should ultimately be capable of.

The first factories

The concept of a separate and independent materials activity was still a novel one to most manufacturers even as late as 1900, when the United States and the leading Western European nations were already heavily industrialized. Nevertheless, since it is a basic function of the business, the materials management job was being performed. Each shop foreman or superintendent was pretty much his own materials manager. In most companies, he ran his department like a semiindependent feudal barony with remarkably loose ties (by today's standards) of allegiance to the company as a whole. The foreman scheduled his own production, bought his own supplies, and did his own hiring and firing—all with minimum interference from top management, provided he did the jobs with reasonable competence.

If someone had proposed a separate and independent materials department to the typical manager of about 1900, he probably would have been ridiculed. Why should a company incur extra overhead by hiring a purchasing agent or materials manager to do a job that could be done as well or better by the shop superintendent or foreman? Besides, favors or kickbacks from suppliers were often a substantial part of a shop superintendent's income. If they were eliminated by transferring the buying power to soneome else, the company would have to raise the salaries of its supervisors to prevent them from leaving to work for a competitor.

Specialists not needed. There is no basic need for a separate, independent materials activity if just one premise is accepted: skill in *managing* materials automatically accompanies skill in *specifying* and *using* materials. If one accepts this, one accepts the idea that a competent engineer or manufacturing manager is by definition a good materials manager, and materials automatically are managed as their specifications are developed and as they are used in operations. Thus there is no need for a materials manager.

This premise was widely accepted 50 years ago, and a few companies continue to do so today. But modern, progressive managements know it to be false. They believe there is a distinct difference between skill in specifying and using materials and skill in buying them. They know that a professional buyer trained in business management and economics and familiar with the capabilities of hundreds of suppliers can do a much better job than an engineer or supervisor whose training and orientation are less suitable for buying.

Recognition of purchasing

Outstanding purchasing managers are beginning to be recognized as top-management material—in some companies, at least. They become "second-level" executives, reporting directly to a president or general manager, and not infrequently become not only vice presidents of their companies but also serve on the board of directors. In most cases, the change in title and organization status is a formal recognition of gradual changes that have taken place in the purchasing executive's job over a period of 20 years or more. The process is initiated as top management gradually grows more confident that the purchasing agent is the logical person to make the actual buying decisions on major purchased materials and gives the agent authority to do the job.

Contributions to profit. If she is a genuine professional buyer, the purchasing agent can almost always do a better job of buying than those who formerly did it. Since purchases comprise a major part of any manufacturing company's cost, the top purchasing executive must work closely with other key managers. As the company's biggest spender, her efforts must be coordinated with the controller's department, in order to control cash. Manufacturing depends on the purchasing agent for both the production materials and the supplies it requires. Close coordination between manufacturing and purchasing is essential for solving the inevitable problems in quality and delivery of purchased materials that arise. Since practically every company relies on suppliers of parts and materials for aid in engineering and product development, the purchasing and engineering departments must work closely together on new products, in order to enlist supplier assistance.

Purchasing also has gained recognition in the nonmanufacturing company. Transportation and utility companies have long realized that they could not operate effectively without a supply function, and gradually they began to be able to distinguish between effective and ineffective purchasing and to comprehend its relation to their business success. The purchasing function evolved much later in other non-manufacturing organizations. For example, it was not until the current era of government-supported medical care that many hospitals began to approach purchasing and other materials management activities in an organized way. In the middle of the 20th century, some governmental agencies were still so ignorant of the principles of materials management that they assumed that inventory was "free" as long as there was money on hand to make a purchase.

Participation in decisions. Modern management recognizes that almost every decision made has some impact on purchasing and materials management. In addition, it is discovering that purchasing managers and materials managers can often make important contributions to problems that seemingly have nothing to do with their specialties.

Purchasing must be "in the know" regarding almost every activity in the company. It becomes almost essential that the top purchasing executive be a member of the company's key management group—its operating committee or executive committee. Because almost every major decision affects purchasing, the purchasing agent also often is a member of various other committees devoted to scheduling or production planning, make-or-buy decisions, cost reduction, standardization, and product planning, for example.

In companies with topflight purchasing departments, purchasing personnel make all major buying decisions. They also actively assist engineers by introducing them to suppliers or new products they can use, and sometimes even make specific recommendations for design changes. They assist in inventory control by buying in the most economic quantities, making special arrangements with suppliers to reduce the need for safety stocks, and so on. They assist the sales department with supplier relations programs and, in some cases, with actual sales leads.

EVOLUTION OF MATERIALS MANAGEMENT

To do its job effectively, purchasing must have a particularly close relationship with the traffic and production control departments. In most companies the three departments together control practically all materials management activities.

Production control was originally performed by the foremen, who scheduled their own production and sometimes kept records of inventories. Then parts of this job were performed by the superintendent's clerk, who kept necessary records while the superintendent continued to make the decisions. As more and more authority was stripped from line supervision and the scheduling process became more complex, the clerks eventually were superseded by a department of production control specialists.

Before the appearance of the traffic department, the traffic function usually was even more widely dispersed. Carriers were sometimes selected by suppliers, sometimes by the person responsible for the purchase, and occasionally by a top manager on the basis of personal friendship with a carrier representative. The other important functions of the traffic department were often performed casually by whoever selected the carrier, or they were not performed at all.

Managements in progressive companies realize that their purchasing, production control, and traffic departments have jobs so closely related that they can work together better to achieve common objectives if they are linked organizationally. With this integrated approach to materials management, all of the jobs encompassed by these activities would be under the overall direction of a materials manager.

Functions of materials management

There is no general agreement on what functions should be grouped organizationally for unified materials management. Most would agree, however, that in a typical manufacturing company they would embrace all activities concerned with materials *except* those directly concerned with designing or manufacturing the product or maintaining the facilities, equipment, and tooling. They would not, however, normally include receiving inspection. All large firms and many small ones routinely inspect every incoming shipment to make certain that the company is getting what it pays for. Production parts and materials are checked against blueprints and specifications. Nonproduction items are also reviewed, although most companies do not have specifications for them but simply compare the actual contents of the shipment with the description on the purchase order.

Receiving inspection. Some materials managers feel that receiving inspection should be under their jurisdiction, so that they have control over the complete materials cycle. It is wasteful, they argue, to separate receiving—where the shipment is identified and moved to an inspection area—from receiving inspection. When receiving and receiving inspection are separate activities, there is usually some duplication of work. In addition, there is a basic division of responsibility for the shipment. It is shared at this stage of the cycle by the supervisor of receiving and the supervisor of receiving inspection. One reports through channels to the materials manager; the other is responsible to the chief inspector or quality control manager. Each theoretically can pass the buck to the other should there be an error or a delay in handling the shipment.

However, most organization experts agree that quality control—including receiving inspection—should be a separate check and balance on the materials activity. It should be independent of materials management for the same reason that the accounts payable section that actually pays for the material is independent. The group that is responsible for buying the material might be subject to too many temptations if it also paid for it and inspected it. In addition, receiving inspection is a specialized skill that is naturally related to quality control, not to materials management. If the quality control department is to monitor the quality of the entire production process, its job quite naturally begins the minute incoming purchased material hits the receiving dock (and even before this in companies where quality control works with the purchasing department to monitor the quality of the supplier's process).

With the exception of receiving inspection, materials management embraces all other functions concerned with ordering, storage, and movement of material. In the typical company, it would embrace the activities performed by the following major departments: purchasing, production control, stores, traffic, and physical distribution.

The specific duties of these departments vary considerably from company to company and industry to industry. In general, however, they include the following:

1. Production and material control. The production control manager helps set the overall production schedule and is responsible for making certain that manufacturing has the parts and materials it needs to meet it. He directs five basic activities:

a. Computing detailed requirements for parts and materials—both purchased and manufactured—from up-to-date bills of material and specifications supplied by the product engineering department.
b. Scheduling production or purchase of parts and materials needed to meet overall schedules for completed end products. This involves calculation of requirements for each item, taking into account such variables as inventory, lead time, on-order positon, and so on.
c. Issuing work orders to manufacturing departments and purchase requisitions to purchasing for parts and materials needed to meet over-all production schedules. This includes following up to make certain schedules are met and revising schedules when necessary.
d. Keeping detailed records of inventory, on-order status, and potential demand for each production part and material, and making periodic physical counts of stock to verify the accuracy of records.
e. Maintaining physical inventories of all direct (i.e., production) ma-

terials[5] in various stages of fabrication, and administering controls necessary to maximize turnover and limit losses from spoilage, pilferage, or obsolescence.

2. *Nonproduction stores.* Techniques and procedures used to control nonproduction material (office supplies, perishable tools, and maintenance, repair, and operating supplies) resemble those used for production material, although they are usually less elaborate. Specifically, the stores department:

a. Maintains physical stocks of nonproduction items to be drawn on as needed for operations or maintenance.

b. Manages inventories of nonproduction materials and prepares purchase requisitions for needed material when stocks drop to the reorder point.

c. Keeps records and maintains controls to prevent duplication of inventories, minimize losses from pilferage and spoilage, and prevent stockouts.

3. *Purchasing.* The purchasing department buys material in amounts authorized by requisitions it receives from the production control and stores departments. There are four basic purchasing activities:

a. Selecting suppliers, negotiating the most advantageous terms of purchase with them, and issuing necessary purchase orders.

b. Expediting delivery from suppliers when necessary to assure delivery in time to meet schedules, and negotiating any changes in purchase schedules dictated by circumstances.

c. Acting as liaison between suppliers and other company departments, including engineering, quality control, manufacturing, production control, and finance, on all problems involving purchased materials.

d. Looking for new products, materials, and suppliers that can contribute to company profit objectives, and acting as the company's "eyes and ears" to the outside world and reporting on changes in market conditions and other factors that can affect company operations.

4. *Traffic.* While purchasing buys parts and materials, the traffic department buys transportation service. It is always concerned with

---

[5] "Direct" or "production" parts and materials are incorporated directly into the end product. "Indirect" or "nonproduction" material is consumed in making the product but does not physically become a part of it. Screws used to fasten components of a product would be direct material. If the same screws were used for a minor repair in the plant, they would be a nonproduction maintenance supply. Solvent used to wash the product would be an indirect or nonproduction material. A standard package used to ship the product would probably be considered direct material by most cost accountants.

inbound shipments of purchased materials and is frequently concerned with outbound shipments of finished products to customers. There are four basic traffic activities:

a. Selecting common or charter carriers and routines for shipments as required.

b. Tracing inbound shipments of material in short supply as requested by production control or purchasing. Assisting customers in tracing outbound shipments when asked.

c. Auditing invoices from carriers and filing claims for refunds of excess charges or for damaged shipments when required.

d. Developing techniques to reduce transportation cost. This may involve negotiation with competing shippers, special studies on selecting the most advantageous plant location for new products, analysis of tariffs, and negotiation of any number of special arrangements for handling certain traffic.

5. *Physical distribution.* Finished goods must be moved from the production line to a company warehouse and, eventually, to a customer. This process is called physical distribution. The physical distribution manager may also be responsible for the physical movement of partially finished products within the plant and may receive and transport purchased materials to storage areas and to their point of use. The traffic function may also be included in the physical distribution department, but it is independent in many companies, particularly where shipment and storage of finished goods is not especially costly.

Place in the organization

In manufacturing companies the five functions described above may be separate, but not equal, organization units. Purchasing has the highest organization status. The purchasing manager usually reports directly to the president or general manager and is on the second highest level in the organization. In some cases, she may report to the manufacturing manager or finance manager and be on the third level. Very rarely is she on the fourth level.

The production control manager and the traffic manager usually report on the third level. The traffic manager would normally report to the sales manager, purchasing manager, or manufacturing manager; the production control manager almost always reports to the manufacturing manager or works manager. Occasionally, the traffic manager reports directly to the president, and, in a few cases, so does the production control manager. Both are found more often on the fourth level of the organization than they are on the second.

Physical distribution does not exist as a separate function in many companies. When it does exist (in companies with major problems in distribution of finished products), it is very important. Some companies have vice presidents in charge of physical distribution. In most, the physical distribution manager reports directly to the materials manager.

In addition to the major activities described above, materials managers are also responsible for a variety of minor activities, such as receiving and shipping. These secondary activities hardly ever report directly to the materials manager and sometimes not even directly to one of the immediate subordinates. While they are vital parts of the material management organization, they usually do not require much management attention and, once the rules are drawn up, can largely run themselves.

Nonmanufacturing applications

While materials management is far from standardized among manufacturing companies, variations in responsibility and in organization are even greater among nonmanufacturing organizations. Such organizations always purchase material, but there is no tangible finished product. The purchasing, inventory control, and stores functions have essentially the same mission as their counterparts in manufacturing organizations. Usually there is no equivalent of production control.

Among transportation firms, as well as in military organizations, logistics management is a substitute for a physical distribution organization. The main difference is that logistics management deals with products that are going to be used, while physical distribution focuses on those that will be sold. Logistics management has much less of a marketing connotation than physical distribution has. Military problems of logistics management might include, for example, determination of the optimum number and location of specialized parts needed to repair or maintain warships or other military hardware. The peacetime version of logistics management would be an airline's distribution of key spare parts needed to service its fleet. A large airline might, for example, operate in and out of 50 different airports. Hundreds of parts can conceivably fail at any of these airports, and, obviously, the airline cannot afford to operate fully equipped maintenance bases at each of them. The basic problem in logistics management is to determine optimum investment and location of spare parts and maintenance equipment.

Hospitals also have an equivalent of a physical distribution or traffic function. Medical and surgical supplies must be transported from a central supply area to nursing stations or other points of use. Ideally, each nursing station should be stocked with exactly what is needed, but no more than that. Materials managers in hospitals and other service organizations also frequently get involved in peripheral activities—mostly because these activities have no other logical place in the organization. It is not unusual, for example, for hospital materials managers to run a laundry, to supervise the hospital's internal message service, and to operate a captive printing plant. Materials managers in industry can be involved in like activities—particularly captive printing (in companies not in the printing business) and the sale of scrap and surplus.

Cases

CASE 1–1.   GAMELIN COSMETICS CORPORATION

Defining materials management activities

Gamelin Cosmetics Corporation started operations in 1936 when Rubette Gamelin began to market on a limited scale a line of cosmetics she had originally developed almost as a hobby, while operating a highly successful beauty parlor in a large eastern city. The company gradually expanded and, by 1940, Miss Gamelin sold her beauty parlor in order to be able to devote all of her energies to the cosmetics business. By 1950, when the company became partly publicly owned, sales had grown to $2 million per year.

Sales more than tripled in the 1950s—almost entirely as a result of the company's original product line plus natural additions to it, such as a line of nail polish. Profits more than kept pace with sales. A few security analysts came to recognize Gamelin as a "growth stock" and began to acquire its shares. By 1961, the stock was selling for almost 30 times it record earnings that year. The high stock price gave Gamelin a base from which it could easily step up its rate of growth by acquiring other companies through an exchange of its stock. Gamelin sales and profits leaped ahead and by 1975, the company's sales had topped $100 million. Aftertax profits were $12 million and the company enjoyed a 38 percent aftertax return on net worth.

Despite this sparkling performance, the company was beginning to expand ahead of its cash flow. Almost all of the company's production—including that of the half dozen smaller firms that had been acquired in the last decade—were concentrated in a 60-year-old, rather ramshackle-looking factory building in an industrial suburb of a major eastern city. According to company President George Katz, "the existing facility is not only extremely expensive and costly to maintain but does not fit our image as a high-class manufacturer of cosmetics and fine chemicals."

Before starting plans for another major new building, Katz decided to have a consulting firm, the New Jersey Research Institute (NJRI) make a general study to review the company's prospects and to suggest how it should go about planning the new facility. Influenced by the NJRI study, the board authorized Katz to engage an architectural firm to design a new plant to be built on land adjacent to the company's new research and administrative facility. By 1980, it was assumed that the company would have almost $50 million invested in the new plant and related facilities and equipment. This was more capacity than the company needed at present but it was assumed that internal growth alone—without any additional acquisitions—would cause sales to increase by 20 percent per year. The company's product mix provided exceptional cyclical stability (women apparently continued to buy the company's cosmetics even when their husbands were unemployed), and, in the past, the company's record to date made a 20 percent per year growth seem realistic.

As a by-product of its study, New Jersey Research suggested that inventory reduction might be a major source of capital to finance expansion. Company inventories of all types amounted to about $50 million at the time of the study. Most of this was invested either in finished goods stocks or in raw materials. The company's processes and products were such that in-process stocks were negligible. However, there were substantial inventories of both raw materials and finished stocks. Certain raw materials were imported, and procurement lead times were sometimes long. In addition, a few critical items were refined from crops that were harvested just once a year. In such cases, the purchasing vice president had to commit for an entire year's supply, giving himself adequate reserve stocks both to ensure enough material on hand to meet demand and also to prevent being caught short should there be a partial crop failure the following year.

Finished goods inventories were made higher than normal by the nature of the company's production processes. In order to maintain complete consistency of color and/or aroma on certain product lines, machinery had to be cleaned with exceptional care between batches. Sometimes the cleaning process tied up the machine for several days. In order to minimize cleanup, the production department tried to run large batches of major materials—particularly during periods when there was no clamor from marketing to run some other product which was badly needed. Fortunately, finished product shortages were relatively rare, since inventories were usually adequate to permit the company to maintain its overnight delivery policy to customers—even on products where demand was somewhat erratic.

New Jersey Research made a few preliminary calculations to support its contention that inventories were too high. First, it estimated that the company's cost of carrying inventory must be at least 25 percent per year. Then it made rough estimates of the setup or ordering cost of a few key items—taking into account, when necessary, the need for intensive cleaning of machinery and similar problems. In a few cases, setup cost was $1,000 or more for each batch because of the cleanup problem. In most, however, it was much less than this.

New Jersey Research then calculated economic lot sizes or order quantities, using the setup and carrying costs it had estimated in addition to usage data and unit costs culled from the company's record. The formula indicated that substantial reductions would be possible in lot sizes or purchase quantities of most items, even after taking into account special costs that tended to cause production runs to be lengthened.

However, according to New Jersey Research, most of the company's inventory "fat" lay in excess safety stock. This is apparent from the company's stocking policy. In general, the company purchases and manufactures on a quarterly basis. For example, if a sales forecast indicates that 10,000 pounds of product will be required in the second quarter of the year, then manufacturing will schedule 10,000 pounds during the first quarter and purchasing will buy the necessary raw material in the fourth quarter of the previous year. But, of course, sales forecasts are sometimes less than actual demand. Safety stock is needed in order to guarantee service to customers. At Gamelin this may amount to a six- to nine-month supply. For example, the average inventory of the material with the 10,000-pound demand per quarter may be 20,000 to 30,000 pounds.

While company President Katz agrees that inventories can probably be reduced, he does not want to do anything that will impair the company's service to customers. "Our reputation is based on quality and delivery to our customers," he points out, "and it would be foolish to do anything to destroy this image." It occurs to Katz that one of the company's problems in inventory management may be organizational as much as it is procedural. He asks his planning vice president, Howard Roberts, to make a study of who actually makes inventory decisions.

Roberts and his staff trace back a variety of individual inventory decisions and also make a detailed study of the company's procedures in order to determine just who does get into inventory decisions. A few weeks later, Roberts makes his final report to Katz. In it he says:

> No one has probably ever consciously delegated inventory decisions to anyone at Gamelin. But, of course, they are made—seemingly by almost everyone. Since we do not have a formal corporate organization chart. I have attempted to construct an abbreviated version of such a chart (see Exhibit 1) in which I include everyone who seems to make these decisions. I have also included in the chart a "Materials Management Task Force," which I suggest you might consider creating to study the problem further. Obviously, if we are going to improve our procedures, we will need some sort of administrative body to recommend

28

EXHIBIT 1
Organizational relationships among activities involved in materials management

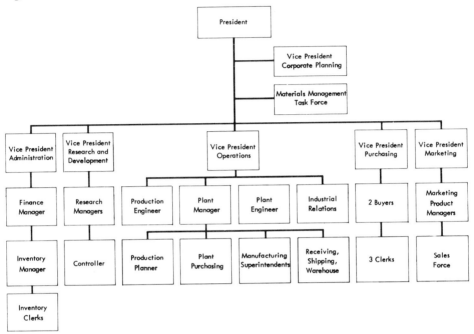

changes and, ideally, it should include representatives from all affected departments.

As you can see, my supposedly abbreviated chart of materials management decision makers includes almost every manager in the company. The president and the vice president–planning are the only ones on the chart who get into the process only indirectly in the course of drawing up and approving forecasts, plans, and budgets. The role of everyone else is more direct.

Administration. The vice president–administration and the finance manager play two major roles in materials management in their direction of the controller's office and that of the inventory manager. The controller is responsible for electronic data processing and, of course, we hope in the next few years to get our entire materials cycle on the computer. It will be the controller's responsibility to give other managers reports from the computer in a form that they need to make decisions.

The inventory manager is more dirrctly involved. She will actually use statistics generated by the controller's EDP section. The position of inventory manager, as you know, is really new to us, even though we have had someone with that title for years. In the past, it was purely a clerical operation, concerned with gathering statistics and administering the annual physical inventory. It is only recently that this activity has shown promise of broadening itself beyond a mere record-keeping function. Obviously, this department will play a key role in any aggressive plan to reduce inventories—although its present role is still at least partly influenced by its more passive tradition.

Research and Development. As you know, the research and development department—particularly the managers concerned with flavors and fragrances—is very active in selection of suppliers. They will normally test samples submitted by each supplier and then work with the supplier in developing a product that fits our needs. In the process of development they must weigh the price quoted by the supplier against the aromatic and flavor characteristics of his samples. The vice president of research and development then reviews the information on sample tests and price and suggests not only the supplier but also the purchase quantity. In some cases, he may want to leave himself flexibility to change supplier should he feel that flavor or aromatic characteristics plays a direct role in determining inventory level of certain key purchased materials. The role of the purchasing department in such cases is a mere formality.

In theory, purchasing and almost everyone else in the organization knows that research and development has no business making purchase and inventory decisions. But no one is going to do anything about it as long as the present research vice president is there. He is a very strong figure and, apparently, he cannot be faulted on his decisions—even when they fall outside what some would regard as the limits of his jurisdiction.

Operations. The production engineer and the plant engineer have some influence on materials management in their own specialties. Each deals regularly with suppliers in his particular specialty and makes purchase decisions. Their role is quite limited, however, as is that of industrial relations, which is involved with inventory only as it affects stability of employment.

The plant manager plays a much more direct role. His production planner sets lot sizes in manufacturing and thereby directly influences the level of finished goods inventory. He also works both formally and informally with the inventory manager and the purchasing vice president in ordering purchased material. Usually, this consists of estimating his materials requirements for the next quarter and then sending a requisition to purchasing. In other cases, he gives purchasing an estimate of his requirements and leaves it to them to determine how much to buy.

The plant purchasing agent's function should not be confused with that of the purchasing vice president. Plant purchasing is concerned only with supplies and other nonproduction items for the plant. In most cases, it acts upon requisitions that it gets from the operations staff functions (production engineering, plant engineering, and, occasionally, industrial relations) or from the line manufacturing organization.

The shipping and receiving department keeps a file of all open purchase orders for purchased materials and also maintains a conventional manually posted stock record for each major material and reminds the purchasing department to buy the material when stock reaches some predetermined order point. These records are maintained primarily for bulk materials which effectively are under the physical control of receiving and shipping. When inventory drops to the reorder point, shipping and receiving prepare a requisition and send it to purchasing. The bulk materials that are controlled in this way by the shipping and receiving supervisor are used in a number of products. Consequently, the production planner does not get involved in their ordering. He simply assumes they will always be on hand whenever they are needed, irrespective of what products are actually being scheduled. The inventory manager periodically compares his records (which are partially on EDP) with those of receiving and shipping. All records are revised periodically when physical inventories are taken.

Purchasing. The vice president of purchases is concerned almost entirely with production materials. He is responsible for selecting the production materials supplier in all cases except those in which research and development plays an active role. He is also sometimes influenced by reciprocal buying considerations and coordinates closely with marketing on purchases of certain chemicals, in particular. On a majority of major commodity purchases, the purchasing vice president exercises considerable discretion in determining how much to buy. He consults, of course, with marketing and with the production planner, but the ultimate inventory responsibility is his.

Marketing. Individual product managers work closely with the production planner, keeping him informed of expected changes in demand for company products. They also suggest when finished goods inventories should be increased to allow for anticipated sales gains. Marketing also works closely with research and development on new products and will, from time to time, deal directly with suppliers in development of these products. One of the marketing managers also coordinates with the purchasing department in order to make most effective use of the company's reciprocal buying power.

A few days after reading this report, Katz calls Roberts into his office and says:

The report by your department pretty much confirms what you and I already knew, but I wanted you to check it out anyway. I agree with you on the task force but, frankly, I do not think it can do much more than make suggestions; committees never actually get any work done.

One of the major jobs of the task force will be to explore ways in which we can reorganize our materials management organization in order to be able to focus our efforts more directly on inventory reduction. What I want from the task force is a consensus that reflects everyone's thinking. We do not want to get our organization all upset about a change. Our approach must be constructive. We don't want to fire anyone or, for that matter, even hurt anyone's feelings, if we can help it.

I believe in making the organization structure fit the people rather than vice versa. We already have got a comer, our new inventory manager. She is the first person in that job who has had actual training in EDP and some of those new control techniques. She is only 32 and has been with us but six months. But her department shows promise.

We can probably also make changes simply because we are growing rapidly. Our sales should double in the next five years, and this is obviously going to increase both our need for and ability to support additional first-class people.

We've also got two potential retirements to consider. Alfred Stein is 64, so we will presumably be looking for a new production planner next year. This is probably just as well, since Stein is a little inflexible. Among the older men, Jim Jenkins is a lot more adaptable. Jim is 62, so he will be around as purchasing vice president for the next three years. He has never worked in any place but purchasing but he could probably take on extra duties if we liked, at least until we could begin to groom his successor. He certainly has not done a very good job on that score, and neither has Stein. Jenkins's subordinates are competent in their present jobs but not promotable, and Stein is a lone wolf. He has virtually created his own one-man department, so we should start thinking about what to do when he's gone.

The other members of the Executive Committee are as well informed as I am on the capabilities and limitations of individual members of our staff. You should keep these personality factors in mind on your task force but, probably, not discuss them openly. What we want from the task force is some sort of plan, and then we can worry about how to fit people into it, modifying the plan if necessary.

I am going to appoint you chairman of the task force. The other nominal members of the group will be the other five vice presidents. But, except for Jenkins, who I think should be active in the group, I think the others should appoint someone to represent them. I particularly want to get Singh and Stein involved on this committee. Maybe, if we get research and development committed to its success, they will play less of a prima donna role in selecting some of these suppliers.

I want the committee to meet as soon as possible and to give me a target data for a report recommending changes in the materials management organization. I then want a target date with specific plans for inventory reduction. I will give the committee all the support it needs from the Executive Committee.

Questions

1. What factors should the task force take into consideration?
2. What recommendations do you think the task force might come up with?

CASE 1-2. RHODE ISLAND HOSPITAL

Materials management in a health care setting

Rhode Island Hospital is one of the largest and best known hospitals in New England. It is a private, nonprofit institution offering a wide range of medical and surgical services. It is also committed to a variety of medical research projects and plays a major role in a number of medical education programs, including an affiliation with Brown University's School of Medicine. In 1978, the 718-bed hospital employed 4,124 persons and had a budget of $76,034,154.

Since 1968, the hospital has had an integrated materials management department, reporting to Edward M. Boudreau. In 1972, Boudreau was appointed an assistant vice president of the hospital and, in addition to his materials management responsibilities, is in charge of the buildings and grounds, food services, office services, central transport, telephone services, and administration of the hospital capital expenditures budget.

Materials management at the hospital embraces four departments: Purchasing, General Stores and Inventory, Central Services, and Laundry. According to Boudreau:

> The Materials Management Department exists basically for the balancing and coordination of independent materials functions into a single work force. . . . The focal point of the department is transportation and processing efficiency through integration of functions and by implementing scientific application of machines for optimum utilization of personnel.
>
> Department emphasis is on creating awareness of total cost for items supplied to patients including purchase, receiving, storage processing, and final disposal. It is concerned with common materials-handling denominators in hospital operations and combined efforts to achieve economies.
>
> It is hoped that through cooperation and change, department goals of high-quality service at lowest possible cost will be achieved.

Purchasing

The hospital's purchasing expenditures total about $13,500,000 per year, or roughly 18 percent of total hospital operating costs. About $2,600,000 of these purchases are made through two purchasing cooperatives of which the hospital is a member: the Hospital Association of Rhode Island and the Hospital Bureau.

Eight persons are employed in the department, including the purchasing manager, two buyers, and five clerical employees. The department's 1978 operating budget was $112,945 per year.

In its annual report, purchasing typically reports savings of up to $325,000, part of which come from advance buying to ward off price increases. The department issues about 25–30,000 purchase orders per year. Clerical costs, as well as errors, are reduced through the use of an IBM 870 machine and related equipment to type purchase orders automatically from data generated within the purchasing department as well as that which comes from the hospital's computerized inventory control system.

General stores and inventory

The hospital's inventories are divided into 16 categories, and the hospital's stores manager reported the position shown in Exhibit 1 as of September 30, 1977.

EXHIBIT 1

	Turnover 1976–77	Number of items 1976–77	Value 1976–77	Value 1975–76
Buildings and grounds	1.51	3,631	$ 64,777	$ 54,459
Blood bank	11.51	12	10,438*	79,016
Dietary (food stores)	3.14	860	41,031	13,851
Dietary stores	4.05	51	8,113	11,430
Gift shop	0.47	26	1,595	1,854
Housekeeping	15.40	167	18,986	21,737
Laboratory	7.74	102	11,137	16,395
Linen and bedding	3.68	61	82,176	58,804
Medical and surgical	11.51	746	158,608	151,417
Medical and surgical operating room	1.01	1,473	175,090	105,403
Pharmacy	4.62	1,908	527,296*	374,862
Data processing forms	2.32	115	40,001	42,316
General forms	1.89	360	64,298	54,887
Office supplies	4.71	54	17,314	4,106
X-ray film	6.62	27	24,872	21,539
Central Services	11.30	119	51,256	44,899
Totals	91.48	9,712	$1,296,988	$1,056,975
Average turnover rate	5.72			
A net change of	$240,013, up			

* Reflects a transfer of $68,000 to pharmacy from blood bank.

The general stores and inventory department employs 16 persons and has an annual operating budget of more than $100,000. Its activities embrace not only receiving and storekeeping functions but also delivery of material to nursing stations and other points of use throughout the hospital.

Some items distributed by the stores department are for single use. The buildings and grounds department (also under Boudreau) is then responsible for their disposition. Other items are reusable, and responsibility for their recycling normally rests with the central services department.

"Hospital materials management," Boudreau explains, "begins with the purchase of material, includes not only storage but also conversion processes needed to make it useful, and doesn't end until the material is used and finally discarded."

The stores department is responsible for operations of storerooms which accommodate approximately 56 percent of the hospital's total inventory investment of $1,296,988. The exceptions are the stores areas in the dietary food and pharmacy departments. These departments operate their own storerooms primarily for convenience. For example, the dietary department naturally must have an inventory of food in close proximity to the kitchen.

When it does not control physical stocks of material, materials management is responsible for development and implementation of inventory control techniques, working with the appropriate department heads. The major exception to this is the pharmacy. The chief pharmacist both purchases the hospital's drugs and is also solely responsible for drug inventories.

In most cases, it is possible to get overnight delivery of drugs from vendor warehouses in Providence or Boston. While the hospital must be assured of a supply of any drug that is stocked, an overwhelming majority of the inventory investment is represented by relatively common drugs such as tetracycline, insulin, penicillin in various forms, barbituates, and tranquilizers.

The hospital first began using its computer for inventory control in 1966. By 1973, all inventory centers were controlled by computer with the exception of the pharmacy, whose control techniques remained essentially manual. The hospital's chief pharmacist has been reluctant to make the changeover because he believes that drug requirements change so rapidly that he doubts if it would be possible to make sufficient reductions (without impairing quality of service) in drug stocks to be worth the effort of changing over to a computerized system.

The materials management department agrees that it is no easy job to change over from a manual to a computerized inventory control system but believes it has now had enough experience with the process so that it can be carried off quite smoothly. Materials management believes that substantial improvement in inventory carrying costs can be attributed to computerization and other improvements that have been made in recent years. For example, inventories of medical-surgical supplies were cut from about $187,000 to roughly $100,000 almost immediately after the control system was computerized. With the old manual system, the materials manager never really knew what his inventory position was except just after the annual physical inventory was taken. With the computerized system, every materials transaction is keypunched and fed into the computer daily. Weekly printouts keep management up to date on the total inventory position. The reduction of about $87,000, or 47 percent, in medical-surgical inventory is essentially due to superior information provided by the computerized system.

This net reduction was made despite some increase in "official" stocks. In the past, head nurses simply requisitioned medical-surgical supplies, and each nursing station had its own inventory that was used up in accordance with patient needs. However, the hospital accounting system automatically charged the inventory to operating expense when the requisition was filled and, therefore, the inventory at the nursing stations did not officially exist.

The hospital's PAR delivery system virtually eliminates all such "unofficial" stocks. First, materials management specialists work with head nurses to determine usage of each item. For example, they might discover that a particular nursing station uses 100 disposable clinical thermometers per week. They might then establish a stock level of 150 thermometers. Each week they would check the inventory of thermometers at the nursing station, calculate the actual usage by subtracting from 150, and replenish the stock to bring it back up to 150. With this system, the nurses rarely need worry about having material on hand when needed and can concentrate strictly on nursing problems. In addition, the hospital enjoys the benefit of optimum inventories, and administrators also get a monthly printout of usage of each item by department for analysis.

Such printouts sometimes detect unusual patterns of usage. For example, the animal laboratory appeared on the inventory printout as a major user of incontinent pads. Since these pads are designed for use by human patients in medical-surgical units, materials management investigated and discovered that the pads were serving the same function that newspaper provides for the individual owner of a pet that is not housebroken. Used newspapers are free, while incontinent pads cost 14 cents each.

The animal laboratory department manager was unwilling to use newspapers because he believed that there was no convenient way in which he could get an adequate supply. The final compromise resulted in the dogs using a cheaper incontinent pad that cost 5 cents instead of 14 cents. Since hundreds of these pads are used each month, the saving was substantial.

While the materials management department expected the computer to help it police inventories, it assumed that relatively little further reductions in inventory investment could be made once the changeover to the computer was successfully completed. So far, however, the department has been able to continue to improve its inventory performance. For the last five years, investment in medical-surgical inventories has remained steady at roughly $150,000, in the face of steadily increasing usage of material and a rate of price inflation that has averaged 7–8 percent per year. Boudreau estimates that inventory turnover in physical terms has steadily improved at a rate of roughly 10 percent per year in response to a variety of techniques applied by materials management.

Much of this improvement is probably simply a result of paying more attention to inventories. "The using departments are concerned with doing their basic jobs," explains Boudreau, "and don't have time to worry about inventory levels. When we can suggest ways in which to improve performance, they are more than cooperative, but the initiative must come from a group whose primary concern is materials management performance." For example, the buildings and grounds department is primarily concerned with keeping the hospital operating under all conditions and must have materials on hand should critical operating components, such as valves, fail on a weekend or holiday when it is impossible to get deliveries from suppliers.

When the buildings and grounds department was responsible for its own inventory control, the department's focus was exclusively on having material on hand when needed. Consequently, there was a built-in tendency for stocks to accumulate simply because the department manager was fully occupied with keeping the hospital operating and did not really look upon minimizing inventory as one of his areas of responsibility or expertise.

Naturally, the buildings and grounds department became more materials management conscious when Boudreau was appointed an assistant director and buildings and grounds and materials management were linked together by a common boss. The goal of always having critical materials on hand for emergencies was not abandoned, but it proved possible to make substantial cuts in inventory without imperiling hospital operation. For example, it is conceivable that the hospital might require one or two valves of a particular type should a failure occur on a weekend. But there was no chance whatever of 12 failures on that same weekend, so it is possible to reduce the inventory of that valve from 12 units to 2 units.

Central services

The central services, or central supply, function is unique to hospital materials management. In effect, hospital inventories can be divided into two categories: sterile and nonsterile. Most of the latter are handled by the general stores department, whose operation is little different from its counterpart in a factory or nonmedical service industry.

The central services department also performs a materials management service when it maintains an inventory of sterile supplies, used primarily in the hospital's operating rooms. But, in the economic sense, it also adds value by manufacture when it sterilizes dressings and other materials, making up "kits" for the operating rooms and nursing units to use for various types of surgery and special care. For example, burn patients and some postsurgical cases require sterile kits provided by central services.

The central services department at Rhode Island Hospital is responsible not only for dressings and other sterile fabrics but also for all other sterile supplies, including surgical gloves (about 67,000 pairs per year), syringes, intravenous solutions, and a variety of miscellaneous items that must be sterile. The department employs 24 persons, has an annual budget of approximately $342,000, and requires an inventory of about $51,000.

The economic role of central services at every hospital, including Rhode Island, has been changed markedly by the introduction of disposables. In the past, almost everything handled by operating room personnel or by patients had to be processed through central services' sterilizers. Now most materials are received in sterile form from suppliers and discarded after being used just once. For example, the Rhode Island Hospital purchases and uses approximately 350,000 disposable syringes each year. Central services is concerned only with the supply of these syringes and need not sterilize them. In the past, the hospital had an inventory of nondisposable syringes which were sterilized in central services after each use.

Today, many hospitals even use disposable paper or nonwoven fabric in the operating room "packs" of sterile material that is used to drape patients and staff during surgery. However, Rhode Island Hospital continues to use conventional packs of woven cloth that is laundered and sterilized after each use. The decision to change over from nondisposables to disposables is basically economic. For example, it is apparently cheaper to purchase disposable syringes and surgical gloves than it is to sterilize and reuse nondisposables. At Rhode Island Hospital, low laundry costs are a major reason it does not pay to use disposable surgical packs which are used in some other hospitals.

Boudreau is also concerned about the increased trash problems that disposables create. The hospital is already getting rid of 10 tons of trash each day at a cost of roughly 0.4 cents per pound and would prefer to avoid any increases. Boudreau believes that analysis of the cost of any material should include not only the conventional materials management costs but also the ecological and cash cost of getting rid of used-up material.

Laundry

While a large hospital laundry uses large quantities of trisodium phosphate, this is ecologically minor compared with getting rid of an equivalent quantity of disposables. Also, manufacturers of disposables have not yet been able to match conventional linens in both quality and cost. For this reason, even hospitals that have gone in heavily for disposables still incur enormous laundry costs. Increasingly, however, this is being done by outside suppliers which can handle laundry for a number of hospitals at low cost. Thus, laundering is increasingly becoming a purchased service for hospitals. Organizationally, this is the major rationale for including the laundry—which is really a manufacturing operation and not a supply function—in the materials management department.

Several years ago, Rhode Island Hospital was considering closing its own laundry and purchasing the service. At that time, its laundry operating cost was 12 cents per pound of laundry. In contrast, the Greater Boston Hospital Council offered its cooperative laundry service to member hospitals for just 9 cents per pound. This service was available to Rhode Island Hospital, since Providence is only about 35 miles from Boston.

Shortly after being appointed materials manager, Boudreau made a detailed study of the hospital's laundry operation and proposed that $87,000 be spent for three modern washing machines, two dryers, and a materials-handling system based on conveyors and chutes to minimize handling of both dirty and clean laundry. The new equipment permitted a sharp reduction in labor hours and, by 1970, the cost of laundry had been reduced to about 8¼ cents per pound. In addition to processing almost 4 million pounds of laundry for its own needs, the improved facility is able to handle another 1 million pounds per year for a neighboring hospital.

The laundry continues to be jammed into the same building it has occupied for many years, and this creates inefficiencies which simply cannot be eliminated. Nevertheless, the hospital's own costs have been cut by a third, and no cheaper alternative exists.

Coordination between the laundry and central services has also helped eliminate duplication of work that is common to many hospitals. The laundry is responsible for washing reusable packs used in the operating rooms, and the central services department is responsible for sterilizing the material after it is laundered.

Naturally, the laundry folded each piece after it was washed. The material was then moved to central services, where it was stored until someone unfolded each item, inspected for holes, and then refolded it to be fitted in with other items in the surgical pack. If holes were found, as was often the case, the linen item was returned to the laundry for mending.

The unfolding and folding operation was eliminated by transferring seven women from central services to the laundry. This group takes material unfolded as it comes directly from the laundering operation and makes up surgical packs in a single operation. As a result, a buffer stock of unfolded laundry was eliminated, in addition to a net reduction of three employees. Boudreau estimates the saving to be at least $10,000 to $12,000 per year.

The saving would probably have been greater—or at least realized more rapidly—had there not been morale problems associated with the change. Central services is a higher status department than the laundry. Work in the former can be rationalized as "professional," even by less skilled employees, while the laundry worker suffers from no such illusions. While the actual work performed by the women who were transferred from the job did not really change, Boudreau believed that their perceptions of their jobs might well change. Consequently, he took great pains to make the group's new working area as comfortable and attractive as possible—including such a "frill" (for a laundry) as air conditioning. Air conditioning also permitted keeping the windows closed, so that flies, insects, dust and other foreign matter were kept away from the linen.

Cooperation between the laundry and central services has also helped reduce linen waste. Sheets and towels used on burn patients immediately become hopelessly stained from the silver nitrate that is used for treatment. Such linens can be reused for a while, at least, on other burn patients, but finally they become unusable for patients. They still have value within the hospital as rags (which would otherwise have to be purchased), but Boudreau discovered that hospital maintenance personnel refused to do this, preferring to use only discarded linen that was not badly stained. Apparently no one likes a bloody towel, even if he is using it as a wiping rag. The solution was to dye the stained linen a dark color. The cost of the dyeing process is only a fraction of the cost of purchased rags, and the dye makes the stained linen usable by squeamish maintenance employees.

The laundry has 59 employees, including the seven women transferred from central services. In addition to its basic laundering function, it is also responsible for delivering and picking up linen throughout the hospital. The direct operating cost of the basic laundry unit is about $320,000 per year; linen distribution also costs about $320,000. In addition, the laundry manager is responsible for a sewing room and uniform room where uniforms for hospital personnel are stored and repaired as needed. This service is budgeted at about $95,000 per year.

Questions

1. Some hospitals as large as Rhode Island Hospital operate without a formally organized materials management department. Department heads are responsible for their own purchasing and inventory management. What benefits, if any, does Rhode Island Hospital gain from its materials management organization? What are the drawbacks?
2. What materials management problem(s) does Rhode Island Hospital presently have and what, if anything, can be done to solve them?
3. Which of the departments reporting to Boudreau are "legitimate" materials management activities, in your opinion? Which do you feel are not "legitimate," and how can they be justified as part of Boudreau's operation?

2

The materials cycle

Materials management is concerned with the flow of materials to and from the manufacturing departments. The materials manager regulates this flow in relation to changes in demand for finished products, actual or predicted prices of materials, supplier performance on quality and delivery, availability of materials, and other variables. He or she bases decisions on information from other departments within the company, suppliers, and other sources, including news in business periodicals.

In its simplest form, most of materials management consists of learning how much to get, when, and from whom. Simple as this sounds, the job can be quite complex, both because of the fantastic amount of detail work involved and, as seen in Chapter 1, because of the tremendous impact of materials management decisions on a company's success or failure.

THE VACUUM CLEANER CASE

Suppose you were a materials manager for a small company making a relatively simple product such as vacuum cleaners. What would your job encompass? What would be some of the problems you would be likely to encounter?

The job would be more difficult than you might casually suppose. Even though a vacuum cleaner is not very complex, the products of almost every industry would be needed to operate a plant. The cleaner itself would probably have components made of zinc die castings; molded plastics; brushes made of wood, hog bristle, and glue; steel screws made by cold heading; sheet steel stampings; and so on.

In addition, thousands of other nonproduction items would have to be purchased before the first vacuum cleaner could be shipped to a

40

customer. Machinery, equipment, and a stock of spare parts to keep them in good repair would be needed, as would all the tools and supplies required to operate and maintain the factory and the office. These would include such diverse items as stationery, fuel for the plant's boilers, packaging supplies for the product, and countless others.

Materials management in even a small business often involves control of 8,000 to 10,000 different items, when all supplies are considered. However, the major materials management effort is directed toward the items that are "direct" material; that is, those that are incorporated directly into the product as parts, particularly the more expensive items. Usually 75 to 90 percent of the materials expenditures in a manufacturing company are for direct material, and often a few key items account for a large share of direct material expense. Needless to say, materials managers try to spend more time on these major items than on minor ones, and most of them devote 75 to 90 percent of their time to direct material[1] and concentrate a big part of it on problems involving a few key materials.

Good materials managers try to "manage by exception." They try to organize their departments so that major problems requiring decisions are promptly called to their attention, while minor problems are automatically shunted to subordinates for solution. However, some managers delegate a minimum of authority early in the materials cycle, when the product is being designed. At this stage decisions are made that have an important effect upon every succeeding stage. Sometimes they may limit the materials department's flexibility in choosing supply sources for years to come, and bad design decisions can create innumerable problems at every stage of the cycle.

THE DESIGN STAGE

Prime responsibility for design rests with the engineering department, but the purchasing department plays a vital role. No company is so big that it can afford to have on its payroll scientists and engineers who are experts in the design, application, and processing of every part and material it uses. Suppliers make enormous contributions to every company's design efforts, to a much greater extent than most people realize. For example, in a familiar product like an automobile, spring-steel bumpers, chrome-plated wheel covers, power steering, automatic transmissions, overdrives, and numerous other components were originally developed by suppliers, not by the auto manufacturers themselves.

---

[1] Naturally this is not the case in educational institutions, in governments, or in companies that sell services.

The purchasing department is the company's prime contact with supply sources. It can act as a catalyst in bringing supplier know-how to bear on the company's technical problems. Veteran materials specialists often develop an expertise of their own, both from their educational backgrounds and from their association with suppliers. In some cases, they can assist with design problems that concern their specialities. For example, in a vacuum cleaner company, the purchasing specialist who buys zinc die castings could be the best informed person in the company on die-casting technology. Engineers would be primarily interested in more critical parts of the cleaners, such as the brush action, and, especially if the company does no die casting in its own plant, their knowledge of this specialized field could be fairly limited.

Coordination of styling. Usually, the first step in creating a product whose appearance is important—such as a vacuum cleaner—is to make sketches of various styles. The final style selected would presumably offer maximum sales appeal for the lowest possible cost. Sales appeal can be determined by previous marketing experience, market research surveys, opinions of top marketing executives, and so on. Cost can be evaluated by comparison of proposed designs.

It is not easy to evaluate relative costs simply by looking at an artist's sketch of a product. At this stage, specifications for materials, dimensions, and processes have yet to be determined. The engineering approach to cost estimating, where material weights are calculated from blueprints and the like, just will not work. The cost estimate at this stage, in effect, is a well-educated guess. The company's future profits can depend on how accurate the guess is. Once a decision is made and tools are constructed to make a given design, it becomes expensive to make changes. Experienced purchasing executives can estimate relative costs with almost uncanny accuracy because they are (or should be) comparing relative values of materials as a routine part of their day-to-day jobs.

Suppose that stylists propose several different designs for the outer cover of the cleaner. Each design can be executed in a variety of ways: they could conceivably be stamped from sheet steel; die cast from zinc or aluminum; or molded from polyethylene or some other plastic. The part might be perfectly satisfactorily made by any of the processes, so the final decision would be essentially economic and not engineering. When competent purchasing experts are permitted to review stylists' sketches, they can make rough approximations of relative costs and, possibly, also suggest ways in which costs could be reduced through minor changes in the shape of the item. Preliminary reviews of this sort not only make it possible to eliminate costly features that contribute relatively little to sales appeal or utility, but also help guide engineering to the type of process (such as molded plastic) that is most economic for this particular part.

Once the style is agreed upon, engineers proceed to translate the stylists' sketches into detailed specifications to guide the manufacture of each component. Purchasing specialists also should work closely with the engineers at this stage. They can assist by proposing standard components, bringing in suppliers to aid in development work, guiding design decisions, and acquainting engineers with new materials and techniques.

Standard components. If a standard component can be used in a product, it usually costs less. In addition, there may be some saving in engineering and development cost, since the standard item is already available. Sometimes the standard item costs less than a special one, even though it may have features that are inherently more costly. For example, if the engineer's calculations in designing the vacuum cleaner indicate that a .45 hp. motor is required, what size motor should be specified? The answer is a ½ hp. motor. The slightly bigger motor is theoretically more costly, but its price would probably be lower because it is a standard size that motor manufacturers are already equipped to produce. Also, the price for the ½ hp. design may be based on relatively large production volume if other manufacturers buy a motor with the same specifications.

Supplier development. If the cleaner is a new model, the key components will probably require some engineering development before they can be produced. Because suppliers have the specialized product know-how, it is usually desirable to have them do this for the components in which they specialize. For example, the vacuum cleaner motor might be an adaptation of some supplier's standard design.

In such cases, the company may effectively commit itself to buy from a certain supplier as soon as it asks for assistance on development. The supplier will incorporate his own specifications into the adaptation, and it will not be possible to get competitive bids from other suppliers. For this reason, the purchasing department should play a strong role in choosing the suppliers needed as engineering works on new-product development.

Guiding design decisions. Engineers may have difficulty choosing from a number of acceptable designs and specifications. For example, it might be possible to make satisfactory wheels for a cleaner from wood, molded hard rubber, molded plastics, steel stampings, or die castings.

The engineer can determine which materials and processes will do the job, but he can hardly hope to be an authority on the relative cost and availability of each. Nor can he always be guided by previous design decisions. Markets change; while it may have been economic to make a component out of one material a year ago, an alternate material may be more desirable now. Relative prices and availability can change fast.

Introducing new materials. Good engineers try to keep up to date on all new products and processes that might help them. But even with a comparatively simple product such as a vacuum cleaner, there can be just too many bases for the engineer to cover. Many different industries are involved, and no single engineering department can keep up with all of them.

The purchasing specialist can help engineers by introducing them to suppliers who are promoting new ideas. For example, for the vacuum cleaner, the purchasing specialist might suggest to the engineers that they test such new materials as molded fiberglass for the exterior of the sweeper. Or the purchasing specialist might propose molded nylon or sintered metal for the wheels—or anodized aluminum (instead of stainless steel) for the decorative molding.

Minor changes. Different suppliers may use slightly different equipment and processes to make identical items. Minor changes in specifications often are necessary to adapt a design to their equipment and processes. The purchasing specialist (or buyer) must coordinate such changes with the company's engineering department. Sometimes she also becomes involved in changes to permit quality standards to be met; in this case, she must bring together the supplier with both quality control and product engineers.

THE SOURCING STAGE

The next basic stage of the materials cycle is sourcing. Since very few manufacturers start with raw materials that they mine or grow themselves, this is largely a matter of determining the stage of fabrication at which a component or material will be purchased. At one extreme, a company may buy basic raw materials and perform all manufacturing and assembly operations in its own factories. At the other extreme, it may concentrate its efforts on engineering and merchandising its products, relying on outside suppliers to produce them complete.

Most companies follow a middle course between these extremes. They fabricate some items from raw material and rely upon outside suppliers for others. For example, the typical vacuum cleaner company might buy fasteners, moldings, and die castings as finished components. It might also buy semifinished items, such as castings, forgings, copper wire, and sheet steel, which would be fabricated into parts to be assembled into finished cleaners. Since the typical company spends about twice as much on purchased parts and materials as it spends on its payroll, it can find it more advantageous to rely upon outside suppliers for many finished components and assemblies.

Make or buy. The decisions that determine which parts to make in the shop and which to buy from suppliers are by no means made exclusively by the purchasing manager or materials manager. Since they can shape the company's future for years to come, they are nearly always reviewed by all of its top managers. Among the variables that influence make-or-buy decisions are estimated manufacturing costs, purchase costs, technical skills, availability of material, and capital resources.

The materials manager plays a vital role in make-or-buy decisions. Estimates of the variables of the marketplace (present and future price and availability of materials and components) depend almost entirely upon his judgment. If he is wrong, the company may make a decision that will hurt its profits for years to come.

For example, suppose the vacuum cleaner manufacturer must make a choice between investing in facilities and equipment to make his own sheet-steel stampings or molded plastic parts. The purchasing manager would estimate current purchase prices of both types of part and try to project future price trends. These estimates would be compared with estimates of the company's own manufacturing costs for these items. The difference between the purchase price and the company's own manufacturing cost would be the company's return on investment, should it decide to make the parts. If the purchase price declines in the future because of more competitive market conditions, the company's return on investment would also decline. On the other hand, if outside market prices rise, the return will rise. With a bad make-or-buy decision, the company's funds will be invested in equipment that yields small profits or, at worst, is an actual drain on the company's earning power.

Facilities procurement. Once decisions have been made as to which products and components will be manufactured and which will be purchased, definite commitments can be made for needed facilities and equipment. Occasionally, buildings will have to be purchased. The purchasing manager would handle all dealings with contractors and subcontractors for construction.

Contracts for necessary machinery and equipment would normally be the joint responsibility of the materials manager and the chief plant or process engineer. The latter would determine the technical specifications for the equipment; the former would handle necessary negotiation with suppliers and administration of purchase contracts.

PLANNING PRODUCTION

Once a company has a product and knows what its manufacturing facilities will be, it is ready to plan production. The planning process starts with a sales forecast, which may be based on market research studies, actual orders from customers, and the judgment of the company's senior marketing executives.

The master schedule. The materials managers rarely are directly concerned with the sales forecast, but they are part of the group that translates this forecast into a master production schedule. Sometimes the schedule is identical with the market research forecast; usually it is different. The schedule must take account not only of basic market demand but of other factors. A good schedule has a minimum of fluctuations to facilitate economic operation, and it must also take into account availability of labor and materials and basic capacity.

The master production schedule influences the operation of every department in the company. For this reason, its final preparation and approval are usually a committee effort. Represented on the committee are the materials manager, marketing manager, finance manager, manufacturing manager, and other key officials.

MRP. The process of translating a sales forecast into detailed requirements for parts and materials is called *materials requirements planning* (MRP) and is a basic responsibility of the materials manager. The detailed calculations are almost always made by a computer. Suppose, for example, that 10,000 finished products are scheduled for August. A particular fastener used in assembly will be needed in August for this order and there are five fasteners for each finished product. The computer will automatically order 50,000 fasteners for July. Its order may be adjusted to take inventory changes into account. For example, if inventory is 10,000 fasteners less than deemed desirable at that time, the computer might increase the order to 60,000 fasteners.

Changing schedules. Although they can be (and are) changed, schedules introduce inflexibility into the materials cycle. Individual components and the raw materials to make them must be ordered weeks or even months before the end product is assembled. During this period, there is danger that schedules will be disrupted. The demand for end products may change. Production problems with any one component can cause scheduling and assembly problems for countless other components and end products.

Computers are quite capable of calculating what requirements will be when everything goes according to plan; materials managers must cope with the unforeseen. When one is controlling thousands of individual components, some problems are almost inevitable. There will be strikes at supplier plants, quality control problems, shortages of raw material, tooling difficulties, and so on. Materials management problems also arise when business is unusually good. If demand suddenly spurts, the flow of material must be accelerated. In such cases, materials managers look for the bottleneck items that will be most likely to prevent greater output and give them their personal attention, using techniques that will be discussed in future chapters.

THE ORDERING PROCESS

After a schedule has been determined for each item and requirements have been calculated, the ordering process begins. Requisitions and work orders are made up for each item. Typically these list unit requirements, either for a given customer's order or for total production for several months. In all but the smallest organizations, the routine ordering process is done largely with EDP. However, the computer really functions as a superclerk carrying out steps in the ordering process that were formerly done manually. In fact, in most cases, the computer prints out forms that are similar to those used in a manual ordering process.

The process traditionally begins with purchase requisitions (Figure 2–1) which provide authority to issue purchase orders (Figure 2–2) to

FIGURE 2–1
Purchase requisition form

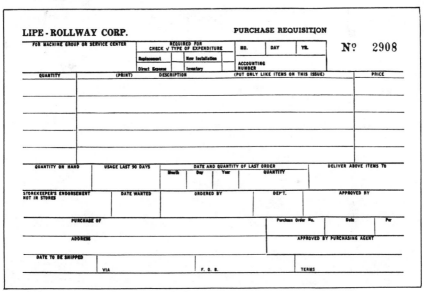

Courtesy Lipe-Rollway Corp.

The purchase requisition is the authority to buy material from an outside supplier.

outside suppliers; work orders authorize the manufacture of components made in the shop. Work orders and requisitions are interrelated. If a work order is to be carried out on schedule, the purchase requisition for the raw materials must be executed on schedule.

For example, a work order for a motor assembly for the vacuum cleaner may automatically generate a purchase requisition for the bearings used in the motor. It may also generate a second work order, for the motor's commutator assembly, which in turn might create need for a third work order for the individual components of the commutator, which in turn would generate a purchase requisition for the

48

FIGURE 2–2
Purchase order form

Courtesy Synthane Corp.

The purchase order authorizes the supplier to ship and invoice for material in accordance with its terms and provisions.

silicon steel needed. Needless to say, a single failure in supply can raise havoc with the entire operation.

To prevent supply failure, purchasing managers must exercise considerable care in selecting vendors. Before contracts are awarded, suppliers' facilities and reputations are carefully investigated. Purchasing managers also review their own records of how suppliers have handled previous orders; they naturally favor vendors who have done a good job for them in the past. But they also like to reduce prices they pay for materials, so they are prone to experiment with new suppliers who are willing to cut prices.

Placing the order. Buyers send quotation request forms (see Figure 2–3) to three or more competing suppliers when they believe they can reduce prices by competitive bidding. Often there are substantial

FIGURE 2–3
Quotation request form

Courtesy Ford Motor Co.

Quotation request forms are filled out by potential suppliers for any purchases in which there is price competition among producers.

differences between the quotes of the high and low bidders. If the high bidder has an excellent record on quality, delivery, and service, while the low bidder's record is more dubious, the purchasing manager has a problem. To whom should she award the business?

To find the answer, the purchasing manager must compare the saving made by buying from the low bidder with an estimate of the cost and greater probability of supply failure that might result from awarding the business to the low bidder. Since risks of this sort cannot be estimated precisely, such decisions are not easy to make. They depend to a great degree on the judgment and experience of the purchasing manager. They also depend on the purchasing manager's personality and the attitude of superiors. Some purchasing managers are more willing to gamble on unknown suppliers than others. Most will back their bet on a new supplier either by protecting themselves with a larger than normal inventory or with a second source of supply. When neither of these alternatives is practical, some managers refuse to gamble on a new source, regardless of the benefit. In big business and big government, the penalties for supply failure are quite real, while there may be little or no reward for brilliant success when the gamble pays off. A smart management encourages intelligent risk taking.

The purchase order formally confirms the choice of supplier. It becomes, when accepted by the supplier, a contract between buyer and seller. Before the contract is finally accepted by both parties, there may be legal problems to be ironed out. Special contract conditions may be negotiated, clauses may be added to the order, and so on. The materials manager must know enough about contract law to negotiate and write simple clauses. She must also recognize her own limitations and know when to call on an expert attorney for help with the more complex clauses that occasionally are necessary.

Follow-up. The buying job does not end with the placement of the order. Not infrequently the supplier has difficulties with specifications, tooling, and so on. Even if there are no problems, a buyer cannot just issue a purchase order for an important item and then forget about it. The buyer often follows the supplier's progress on the order in great detail, to make sure that nothing happens to prevent delivery on schedule. If the item is in particularly short supply, the buyer may even go so far as to stay in the supplier's plant and watch work on the order progress to assure that delivery will be made when promised. If the supplier has trouble getting raw material, the buyer may exert pressure along with that of the supplier's buyer on the raw-material producer. Buyers occasionally use spectacular and rather flamboyant methods to assure delivery.

Use of chartered planes is not unheard of when material is in short supply. One of the most imaginative buying feats was performed by a GM buyer during the Korean War, when nickel was in short supply.

He managed to buy substantial quantities of Chinese coins, which were then melted down, and the nickel in them presumably wound up being plated onto Chevrolet or Buick bumpers and other parts.

Shortages can also develop as a result of failures within the materials manager's own plant. Thus, real-life materials management involves continuous follow-up not only of suppliers but also of internal operations. If the manufacturing manager is immediately alerted to a problem in one of the operations, he or she may be able to solve it before the entire schedule is thrown awry.

Packaging and transportation. The materials manager is concerned with the flow of purchased material into the plant and the flow of finished products out of it. This involves her not only in the selection of carriers (trucks, trains, and sometimes planes) but also in packaging. Before the supplier can deliver, he must be given instructions as to how to package and ship. In some cases there is no problem, since the delivery may be by supplier truck and the product may require no packaging. In others, packaging specifications and transportation routing may be quite complex. Because transportation and packaging are so costly, many companies make elaborate studies of them and sometimes discover ingenious ways to reduce expenses.

Despite the most intensive cost-reduction efforts, transportation and packaging are still expensive, and if their costs are reduced too much other problems result. Service is slower, and damage in shipment is greater. As with the selection of suppliers, the materials manager must compare the savings from lower cost packaging and shipping with the greater risk of loss she assumes. Even if transportation and packaging are specified without regard to cost, there are problems. Shipments go astray or are damaged in transit, claims must be made against the carrier for damages, and bills must be audited for errors.

THE RECEIVING PROCESS

When material is shipped, the supplier encloses a packing slip. The common carrier (if one is used) encloses a bill of lading and an invoice for freight. All of these documents identify the material when it arrives at the buyer's plant. The receiving clerk checks them against the file of open purchase orders. He then physically checks the shipment to make certain that it actually contains the material indicated on the supplier's packing slip and the buyer's purchase order.

The receiving report. The receiving clerk customarily fills out a separate receiving report (see Figure 2–4) for each shipment. In it, he describes the material received, the number of the purchase order that authorized the shipment, and the name of the supplier. If there is a discrepancy between the quantity on the purchase order or supplier's packing slip and the quantity actually received, it is noted on the

52

FIGURE 2–4
Receiving report

Courtesy Cessna Corp.

The receiving report is used by the receiving department to notify interested departments of delivery of purchased material.

receiving report. Copies of the report accompany the material and also are sent separately to the purchasing department, the user of the material, and the accounting department.

Inspecting the material. The next step in the receiving process is inspection. In many companies, the quality control inspector works in the same area as the receiving clerk. The inspector compares the characteristics of incoming material with specifications and blueprints, using gauges, laboratory tests, visual inspection, and other techniques. The findings are given on an inspection report, which may be a separate form (see Figure 2–5) or part of the receiving report.

Copies of the inspection report usually go to both the buyer and the supplier (although sometimes the supplier does not get a copy if all material meets specifications), as well as to other departments in the buyer's company. If the material is rejected, the buyer will ask the supplier how it should be disposed of. The supplier may wish to have the material returned to him for either reworking or scrapping. If shipping costs are high, he will probably prefer to have the buyer either

FIGURE 2-5
Inspection report form

The inspection report indicates whether or not purchased materials conform to specifications.

scrap the material or rework it herself at the supplier's expense. Buyer and supplier often have standing agreements on how material with certain types of defects should be handled, in order to reduce the volume of letters and phone calls.

If purchased material is returned to a supplier, the buyer must prepare a shipping notice that is, in effect, a purchase order in reverse, since it calls for the supplier to buy back the material sold. If the buyer reworks or scraps the material, an agreement with the supplier on the charges or credit for scrap.

Quality problems. If an item fails to meet the buyer's specifications, the major problem usually is not administrative. Rather, the purchasing manager may, as a result of the rejection, have a shortage that can disrupt production. Suppose, for example, that a supplier of vacuum cleaner motors needs five weeks' lead time to complete each order he gets for motors. A shipment of motors arrives for the current month's production and is found defective. How does the purchasing manager prevent a shutdown of the cleaner assembly line, because of lack of motors? Sometimes she cannot prevent such a shutdown, of course, but she can usually get good motors from an alternate supply source, from inventory, by reworking the defective motors, by having suppliers work overtime at their plants (which raises the question of who pays for the premium paid to workers for overtime—the buyer or the supplier), and other measures.

Needless to say, vendors aren't happy when their shipments are rejected. If the defects are their responsibility, the loss to them can be substantial, particularly if the parts cannot be reworked and are a total loss. Occasionally, vendors will challenge the buyer's quality control procedures and maintain that specifications actually were met on the shipment. Or they will maintain that the defects were not their responsibility—either that they were not told certain specifications had to be met or that the parts were damaged after they left the supplier's plant.

The buyer must investigate all such complaints to make certain that the supplier has been treated fairly. He should always try to preserve amicable relations with suppliers, even if this sometimes means going more than halfway in reaching a compromise. He should also make certain that the supplier is familiar with the company's specifications and quality control procedures and will make an honest effort to correct quality discrepancies on future shipments.

INVENTORY CONTROL

If a shipment passes inspection, the receiving clerk usually prepares a "move" ticket that indicates to what area of the plant the material should go next. This ticket is physically attached to the shipment, along with the receiving report and the inspection report. The material is then transported either directly to the user or to a storage area. If the material goes into stores, which is true of almost all routine purchases, it becomes part of the company's inventory. It is carried on the company's balance sheet as an asset until it is incorporated into an end product that is sold to a customer.

Safety margin. Without inventories, the typical materials manager's job would be hopeless. Every minor delay in every minor component would cause a serious shortage. Production rates of components and subassemblies would have to be perfectly synchronized.

Inventories provide a safety margin for defects in scheduling and errors in forecasting the demand for and supply of materials. If its stocks are big enough, a company can operate for months without buying any raw materials at all.

For example, midwestern steel companies normally have at least six months' stock of iron ore each fall in order to avoid costly rail shipments during the winter months, when the Great Lakes freeze over and water shipments from Lake Superior ports and the St. Lawrence Seaway are cut off. Similarly, steel users always stock millions of tons of steel shortly before the contract between the steel industry and its union expires. Thus they usually are prepared to operate on inventories for two to three months if there is a strike.

In-process inventories provide a cushion between manufacturing operations. Without them, the entire plant might be shut down if a single machine tool failed to operate. In-process stocks also facilitate synchronization of production. If one machine produces 200 units per hour while another produces 400 units, production can be balanced only by building up stock from the faster machine and then shutting it down to permit the slower operation to catch up.

Cost of inventories. Although inventories solve many materials management problems, there are strong incentives for maintaining minimum stocks. Companies have a limited amount of cash to invest in inventories. Also, it costs as much as 20 to 30 percent per year to store materials. That is, an inventory with a value of $1 million may cost $200,000 to $300,000 to store.

The materials manager must have material available when needed, but he cannot afford to carry extra-large stocks just to make the job easier. He must balance the cost of carrying stock against the cost of possible shortages. His objective is the lowest overall average production cost. To achieve this, materials must flow smoothly through the plant. The proper quantities—no more, no less—of each of thousands of different items must be available at all times. Raw material stocks should be larger than the minimum only if there is some special advantage to be gained. In-process stocks should be the minimum necessary to prevent serious production problems; the tighter the scheduling and material, the smaller the protective stocks needed.

Companies with poor materials management have both big inventories and frequent shortages. Their inventories do not prevent shortages because they are not balanced. There may be enough stock of some items to last for months or even years, and no stock of one or two critical items.

THE FINAL STAGES

When material is delivered on schedule to the manufacturing organization, the materials manager has done the most important job. When manufacturing completes processing and assembles the final product, the materials cycle is almost complete. All that remain are the packaging, storage, and shipment of the end product. These final stages rarely create as many problems for the materials manager as the earlier stages.

Packaging must usually be synchronized with the production process. In such cases, the workers who do the actual packaging may be under the supervision of a supervisor or superintendent reporting to the manufacturing manager. The materials manager, however, retains responsibility for package procurement and may also be responsible for package design. The major effort on the part of the materials manager is directed toward improving packaging materials and equipment.

The storage of finished products is similar administratively to storage of raw materials. The materials manager, or the physical distribution manager, normally supervises the finished goods warehouse. As the company's experts on inventory management and warehousing, the materials manager and the physical distribution manager also regulate inventory fluctuations. They try to minimize warehouse operating costs and inventory investment levels consistent with broad company goals. The materials manager is not the company's ultimate authority on finished goods inventories, however. Both the company's marketing success and its manufacturing efficiency are directly related to finished goods inventory investment. Such stocks exist to protect customers and give them better service, and to permit more efficient operation of manufacturing plants. They also result when demand for end products is lower than anticipated when schedules were made up. Decisions concerning finished goods inventories are normally made by a top-management committee, of which the materials manager is a member.

The materials cycle for direct material ends with shipment of finished products to a customer. The materials department is always responsible for loading the finished goods into the carrier and preparing necessary shipping documents. If the customer does not have a traffic department, it may also be responsible for routing the goods to their destination.

MANAGING INDIRECT MATERIAL

The problems of managing indirect materials are similar to, but rarely as complicated as, the problems of managing direct material. The cycle for indirect material starts with the initiation of the need for the material in any department of the company—manufacturing, personnel, marketing, engineering, finance, or the materials department itself.

Nonrepetitive items. Each department needs certain materials and supplies in order to operate. It gets them by filling out a purchase requisition form if the item is not carried in stock. A buyer reviews this requisition against his purchase records, gets quotations, and issues an order to a supplier.

To this point, the materials cycle is quite similar to that for direct materials. There is one basic difference, however. Direct materials are almost always purchased in accordance with definite engineering specifications. This is not always the case with indirect materials; many are bought the way the consumer buys—by brand name. For example, if a buyer gets a requisition for a desk calculator, she does not send a set of blueprints to each calculator manufacturer. Instead, she and the user of the material evaluate various brands of calculators and compare their performance, features, and prices.

The purchase order will be for a specific brand of calculator. The materials cycle ends when the machine is delivered to the requisitioner who ordered it, and it operates satisfactorily.

Repetitive items. The conventional procedure for buying nonrepetitive items like desk calculators is wasteful if there is a continuing demand for the item. For example, it would be ridiculous to issue a separate purchase requisition and purchase order each time a light bulb burns out. Commonly used nonproduction items are bought in fairly large quantities and stocked in a storeroom. Users withdraw them from stores by presenting a stores requisition (see Figure 2-6) to the stores clerk.

FIGURE 2-6
Stores requisition form

Courtesy *International Minerals & Chemicals Corp.*

This form authorizes material to be drawn from stores and is later posted to the stores record.

The clerk (or a computer) posts withdrawals from stock to a stores record (see Figure 2-7). When stock drops to a certain reorder point, a purchase requisition is issued to authorize another buy. The purchasing procedure is similar to that for other items.

Some nonproduction items are used in sufficiently high volume to justify a lot of time and effort in their buying. Some companies even go to the trouble of making elaborate specifications for key nonproduction items. Rather than buying by brand name, they invite a number of qualified suppliers to quote in accordance with their own specifications. This usually cuts costs, as well as eliminating the problem of brand preference by users. If the materials department is forced to buy a specific brand, its efforts to get competitive bids are inhibited. In addition, inventories may be higher. If supervisor X insists on brand A, and supervisor Y insists on brand B of the same item, then the item is duplicated in inventory.

58

FIGURE 2-7
Inventory record card

INVENTORY RECORD									
Min. Point	Min. Quantity		Order Point	Order Quantity					
DATE	RECEIVED	DISBURSED	DISBURSED TO DATE	INVENTORY BALANCE	DATE	RECEIVED	DISBURSED	DISBURSED TO DATE	BALANCE INVENTORY
CODE NUMBER		ITEM							

Receipts and withdrawals from stores for each item are posted to perpetual inventory record cards.

Duplication is always a problem in nonproduction stores. It is almost impossible to draw up exact specifications for every item, and suppliers' descriptions and code numbers can be misleading. Stores personnel try to cope with these problems by using classification systems, periodic reviews of stock, standardization programs, and so on. But no system or program is foolproof. The only solution is constant vigilance by alert and intelligent materials personnel.

Cases

CASE 2-1. ZERO CORPORATION (A)

Establishing an independent materials department

Zero Corporation was founded in 1961 by George Frost, a former superintendent of a company that manufactured auto parts. The company commenced operations in a rented garage with a total of five employees. Because of its low overhead and Frost's manufacturing know-how, it was able to underbid larger competitors for contracts let by the Big Three auto manufacturers for small components used in their lower volume truck lines.

Zero grew steadily. By 1974 its annual sales were $2 million, and there were about 60 persons on the payroll. Because the company got its business by being low bidder in a very price-conscious industry with excess capacity, profits did not increase nearly so fast as sales. They were only $82,000 in 1973, the company's best year.

For all his work during this period, Frost had succeeded in paying himself only a moderate salary ($25,000 per year) and meeting obligations to his creditors. By 1974, he concluded that he was in the wrong business and began to look for a product where there was less price competition. He became acquainted with Roberta Blank, a sales representative for a firm making household refrigerators. Blank proposed to Frost that he manufacture refrigerated frozen-food display cabinets for grocery supermarkets. Although several other companies were already in the field, Blank was convinced that it was growing fast enough to support a newcomer.

Blank proposed that Frost hire her as sales manager, with a special salary and bonus arrangement. She also suggested that Frost hire Helen Brown, a young engineer who worked for the same large company as Blank, to head the design department. Frost talked to Brown, liked her, and suggested that she prepare a preliminary design proposal on a consulting basis in her spare time.

Frost then studied Brown's preliminary designs. He decided that he was equipped to produce some of the sheet-metal components of the cabinets and that he could assemble them with a minimum of additional investment—no more than $600,000 for plant, equipment, and inventory.

Meanwhile, Blank had not been idle. She discovered that a major grocery chain was contemplating a complete renovation of a number of its stores and would be in the market for as many as 10,000 cabinets. The chain planned to buy them piecemeal from a number of manufacturers. Frost suggested that Blank approach the chain's fixtures buyer and propose a contract arrangement for the entire 10,000 cabinets. The stores would not only get a lower price but would also get a design that was uniquely tailored to their needs.

The buyer was impressed with Blank's presentation and suggested that Zero Corporation present a formal proposal. Frost, Blank, and Brown went to work immediately. Working from Brown's preliminary specifications, Frost got quotations from major suppliers for such key components as compressors, electrical accessories, and steel. He then estimated his fabrication and assembly costs and added a moderate profit.

The store's buyer and director of purchases reviewed Frost's proposal and asked for additional price concessions. Frost complained that his estimated profit was already very modest and showed the buyers his unit cost estimate. A summary of the cost estimate indicated the following:

Purchased parts and materials	$505.30
Direct labor	72.60
Manufacturing overhead	90.75
Manufacturing cost	$668.65
Sales, engineering, and administrative expense	33.45
Profit	70.21
Unit selling price	$772.31

Frost pointed out that practically all of the $70.21 profit would be needed to amortize the special tooling that Zero would have to invest in for the new contract. He observed that the company would have to make an investment of $700,000 in facilities, tools, and equipment, so it would do little more than pay off this investment on the first order for 10,000 cabinets.

The prospective buyers considered this to be Frost's risk in doing business. They pointed out that about two thirds of Zero's sales dollar would go to outside suppliers. They felt that it was not enough just to solicit bids from a few leading companies when making a cost estimate. In their opinion, Zero should be able to get its material at least 10 percent cheaper by shopping around, and unit material cost should actually be no more than $450. They also suggested that since Zero had no previous experience in the field, the chain store was entitled to an extra-close price for risking its business with a new supplier. The buyers finally succeeded in persuading Frost to accept the contract at a unit price of $700, which would provide Zero with almost no profit at all unless actual costs were less than the estimate.

Frost accepted the order because without it he would find it almost impossible to raise the money to go into the refrigeration business. With the chain-store order in hand, Frost went to an investment banker and asked for help in raising the $700,000 he needed. The banker arranged a $300,000 loan and, late in 1974, another $300,000 was raised with a stock issue. Zero was in the refrigeration business.

Blank and Brown immediately became full-time employees of the company; the sales and engineering functions were well taken care of. Frost himself intended to devote his time to general management, with special interest in the finance and manufacturing areas. He already had a capable accountant and shop superintendent to assist him.

While the company was in the auto parts business, the job of materials management had been pretty much divided between Frost and the shop superintendent, Richard Howard. The job was not to complex, since the company's only product was steel stampings made to auto company specifications.

When the company quoted on a job, Frost studied the blueprint. From experience, he could readily estimate the blank size and cost of the steel sheets that were the company's major purchased material. He then determined the manufacturing operations that would be required and noted the equipment he would use if he got the order. He sent his estimated operation sheet and the blueprint to a friend of his who ran a tool shop for an estimate of the cost of the special dies that would be needed.

If he got the order, Frost ordered sufficient steel to handle the contract from a nearby mill. The superintendent scheduled production in accordance with requirements on customer orders. His system was simple. He kept a separate record for each piece of equipment and then "reserved" time on it for each job. For example, if a customer wanted 2,000 parts delivered during the month of August, the superintendent might schedule a press for the first operation on the fourth and fifth of the month, the second operation on the sixth, the third on the seventh, and so on.

Both the superintendent and the accountant purchased materials and supplies that they needed to do their work. They got Frost's approval for any unusual purchases but bought everyday items as the need arose. The accountant had a cabinet in which he stored office supplies; employees got supplies by coming to him. The superintendent had a storeskeeper who doled out material to the workers and the two job foremen as required. Materials that were bulky and not subject to pilferage were stored in open plant areas.

Frost now realizes that materials management will become more important because the company is entering the refrigeration business. It will be necessary to buy equipment and tooling to fabricate the stampings and assemble the completed units. The volume of purchases will increase and will also become more diverse. For the first time, the company will be buying components ranging from compressor assemblies consisting of several hundred components and costing about $100 to fasteners with a unit cost of a few mils.

The company will have to deal with at least 100 suppliers for production parts and materials, with plants located in many different areas. Formerly, it purchased its basic production material—steel— from two mills. Because of the wider diversity of operations, Frost believes that a greater variety of nonproduction materials will have to be purchased. Inventories of both production and nonproduction materials will increase, both because of the expected increase in volume of business and because of the greater complexity of the product.

Frost wonders if the materials management system that has worked quite well in the past will continue to work under these new conditions. He explains his doubts to his informal operating committee, consisting of the sales manager, the chief engineer, and the shop superintendent.

Both the superintendent and the chief engineer believe that the old system will continue to work best because, under it, administrative overhead will be minimized. The superintendent believes that he can schedule production and buy necessary tools and supplies just as he has done in the past. He thinks he may need a clerk to help him. The chief engineer points out that she will have to work with suppliers in developing final engineering details of the refrigeration equipment and that it will take but little effort on her part to follow through and actually place the orders for components. The sales manager disagrees with this view. She believes that materials management is a separate function of the business and should be handled by a materials manager.

Questions

1. Bearing in mind that the company wishes to keep administrative overhead at a minimum, what are some of the arguments that Blank, the sales manager, should advance for the establishment of a separate materials organization at Zero?
2. What functions should the materials department at Zero embrace? What should be the materials department's relationship with the production and engineering departments?

3

The objectives of materials management

[handwritten notes in the margin: "His job — supplying material at lowest possible total cost"]

The manager's most basic job is to focus the efforts of his or her subordinates on the objectives of the enterprise. In materials management, this boils down to supplying material at lowest possible total cost. To achieve this fundamental objective, the materials manager must take into account both the long- and the short-term effects of his actions. He must also consider the impact of his operation on the costs of other activities within the organization.

The functions of the materials manager and purchasing manager are basically economic, even in nonprofit organizations. The most fundamental objective is survival. Managers come and go, but institutions live forever. If the materials manager is successful in his economic role, he will contribute to the survival of the organization. Among private companies, at least, profits are essential to survival; in the nonprofit sector, costs cannot exceed income for any prolonged period. Every enterprise also has objectives that are seemingly noneconomic. In the long run, they are ultimately economic, however, since if they are not achieved the enterprise will fail to prosper—and may not even survive. Among these noneconomic objectives are favorable community relations, maximum service to customers, pleasant working conditions and opportunities for advancement for employees, technological leadership, and others.

Each function of the business should work to achieve those objectives. The purchasing and materials management functions are not exceptions. They contribute to survival and profits by providing materials at the lowest total cost. There are many ways they can achieve this overall objective; the most obvious is to pay minimum prices for materials. But they also help achieve this objective when they boost inventory turnover or get material of superior quality. In both cases,

64

the true cost of material is reduced, in one because of less investment and in the other because of fewer rejections due to failure to meet specifications.

GOALS OF MATERIALS MANAGEMENT

We will next examine in detail some typical objectives of materials management. Each, in some way, contributes to the achievement of some overall company objective. If the contribution is made directly by the materials function, we call it a "primary" objective. If it is indirect, and results from the materials department's assistance to another department in achieving its objectives, we call it a "secondary" objective.

Primary materials objectives

There are at least nine primary objectives in purchasing and materials management. These are low prices, high inventory turnover, low-cost acquisition and possession, continuity of supply, consistency of quality, low payroll costs, favorable relations with suppliers, development of personnel, and good records.

Low prices. Obtaining the lowest possible price for purchased materials is the most obvious purchasing objective and certainly one of the most important. If the purchasing department reduces the prices of the items it buys, operating costs are reduced and profits are enhanced. This objective is important for all purchases of materials and services, including transportation.

High inventory turnover. When inventories are low in relation to sales (inventory turnover = sales ÷ average inventories), less capital is tied up in inventories. This in turn increases the efficiency with which the company's capital is utilized, so that return on investment is higher. Also, storage and carrying costs of inventories are lower when turnover is high.

Low-cost acquisition and possession. If materials are handled and stored efficiently, their real cost is lower. Acquisition and possession costs are low when the receiving and stores departments operate efficiently. They also are reduced when shipments are received in relatively large quantities (thereby reducing the unit cost of handling), but they are increased if average inventories are boosted with the large shipments.

Continuity of supply. When there are disruptions in the continuity of supply, excess costs are inevitable. Production costs go up, excess expediting and transportation cost are likely, and so on. Continuity of supply is particularly important for highly automated processes, where costs are rigid and must be incurred even when production stops because of lack of material.

Consistency of quality. The purchasing department is responsible for the quality only of the materials and services furnished by outside suppliers. The manufacturing department is responsible for quality control of manufacturing processes. When materials purchased are homogeneous and in a primitive stage (e.g., sand and gravel), quality is rarely a big problem for purchasing personnel. But when the product is in a highly advanced stage of manufacture and specifications are a tremendous challenge for suppliers to meet consistently (e.g., components of interplanetary rockets), quality may become the single most important materials management objective.

Low payroll costs. The objective of low payroll costs is common to every organization. The lower the payroll, the higher the profits—all other factors being equal. But because no department can do its job without a payroll, the objective of low payroll must be viewed in proper perspective. It pays to spend $1.00 on additional payroll if earnings can thereby be boosted $1.01 through achieving other objectives.

Favorable supplier relations. As was pointed out in Chapter 1, businesses rely on outside suppliers to a far greater degree than is generally recognized. This makes favorable relations with suppliers extremely important. A company's standing in the business community is to a considerable degree determined by the manner in which it deals with its suppliers. A company with a good reputation in supplier relations is more likely to attract customers than one with a bad name.

Suppliers also can make a direct contribution to a company's success. Their product development and research efforts can be of tremendous assistance to their customers. Although such efforts naturally help the supplier too, it is important to remember that suppliers are human beings who respond to fair treatment. If a company has good relations with its suppliers, it will be far more successful in its efforts to stimulate superior performance from supplier personnel—extra service, cooperation on cost-reduction projects, a willingness to share new processes and ideas, and so on.

One of the major problems of materials management is sudden shifts in the demand for materials, requiring either rapid cancellation of existing commitments or extra output to prevent shortages. Cooperative suppliers can do much to help the materials manager with such problems.

Development of personnel. Every department in the company should be interested in developing the skills of its personnel. And each department head should devote special effort to locating in junior posts men and women who have the leadership potential the company needs for continued success and growth. They should try to develop these high-potential men and women as the company's future executives; the company's future profits will depend on the talents of its managers.

Good records. Good records are considered a primary objective of materials management, although paperwork is a means to an end, not an end in itself. They contribute to the role of the materials department in the company's survival and profits only indirectly. They are necessary and useful; they help materials personnel do a better job. While this can also be said of office equipment, the maintenance of the materials department's stock of typewriters, adding machines, and the like would hardly be considered a primary objective. Good records, however, are considered a primary objective in the purchasing and traffic phases of materials management for the same reason that they are a primary objective in the accounting department.

Buyers spend company money and can be subject to tremendous temptation. Suppliers may wine and dine them and give them gifts for Christmas and other holidays. Although perhaps 99 percent of all buyers are above corruption, the opportunity does exist. Good records, along with well-planned administrative controls and periodic audits, can discourage corruption. They also partly remove the onus of suspicion from a completely honest individual working at a job that is popularly associated with graft and corruption.

Secondary objectives

The secondary objectives of materials management are not nearly so limited in scope and variety as the primary objectives. Since they represent the materials department's contribution to the achievement of the primary objective of some other department, they can vary widely from industry to industry.

There are literally hundreds of possible secondary objectives in materials management. Among the more common ones are reciprocity, new materials and products, economic make-or-buy decisions, promotion of standardization, product improvement, good interdepartmental relations, accurate economic forecasts, and alertness to possible acquisitions.

Favorable reciprocal relations. When a company deliberately buys from its own customers as much as possible, it is practicing reciprocity. Sound reciprocity involves a balancing of the advantages and disadvantages of using one's buying power as an instrument for getting sales. Similarly, suppliers will use their own buying power as a sales tool.

In the consumer-goods industries, reciprocity is rarely a problem; sales are spread among many users. In producer-goods industries, however, reciprocity is a fact of business life. A firm that is a customer will inevitably want to become a supplier. The purchasing manager must work with marketing to be certain that the relationship with the customer-supplier is in the company's best interest. The problem of reciprocity is made more difficult because companies that practice it are in a "gray area" legally and may be violating antitrust laws.

New materials and products. Engineering and manufacturing managers are always interested in new products and materials that will help them operate more efficiently and thereby achieve one of their primary objectives. The purchasing department can help because it deals regularly with the suppliers responsible for the new developments.

Economic make or buy. Make-or-buy decisions are often sparked by purchasing since it is the department most intimately concerned with the selection of supply sources. By no means is purchasing solely responsible for these decisions, however. As pointed out in the previous chapter, make-or-buy decisions should be a committee effort, representing the points of view of all departments in the company. The purchasing department, in its regular views of cost and availability of materials, often will spot the need for new make-or-buy decisions and should refer them to the committee for action.

Standardization. The fewer the items that need be controlled, the simpler and more efficient the materials management process. Thus it is to the interest of materials personnel to promote standardization and simplification of specifications. The engineering groups are primarily responsible for standards and specifications, but materials management personnel can make a substantial contribution. They can periodically review stock to weed out nonstandard items; they can promote the incorporation of standard components into product designs to reduce cost; and they can promote standardization with suppliers.

Product improvement. This is perhaps the single most important objective of the engineering department. Purchasing managers can assist, however. Their economic knowledge can supplement the technical skills of the engineers on programs to boost profits through product change. The engineering of practically any product is basically a compromise between design and economic objectives. Purchasing personnel can help engineers achieve their design objectives more economically by suggesting materials or components that will do a better or equivalent job at lower cost.

Interdepartmental harmony. The materials management department deals daily with every other activity in the business. It not only can contribute to the success of every other department, but its own success depends on how successful it is in gaining the cooperation of personnel in other departments. In practice, most materials managers are fully aware of the importance of good interdepartmental relations. To prevent disputes, they are careful to define departmental responsibilities clearly (this will be discussed later in this chapter) and also try to familiarize others with materials objectives, policies, and organization.

Forecasts. To manage materials well, some conception of the future outlook for prices, costs, and general business activity is necessary. In large companies, professional economists make forecasts that are used for both sales and purchase planning. Purchasing managers translate these general forecasts into specific forecasts for purchased materials. They may also provide the economists with data for forecasts because, more than any other group in the company, they are intimately familiar with the market and general business conditions through their daily contacts with suppliers.

In the smaller company that cannot afford a staff of professionals, the materials manager may double as company economist. In such a case, good forecasts become a primary, not a secondary, objective of materials management.

Acquisitions. Most company managements are interested in growing, not only by internal expansion but also by acquiring other businesses. It is no easy job to identify a possible candidate for acquisition and then to make the necessary overtures for eventual merger. Purchasing managers can often play an important role in acquisitions, since they normally have, through dealing with many suppliers, more contacts with the outside business world than other executives in the company.

ACHIEVING OBJECTIVES

The primary and secondary objectives of materials management discussed above would be applicable to most manufacturing companies and could readily be adapted to nonmanufacturing organizations also. However, these objectives vary in relative importance from industry to industry and even among companies within an industry. One company may devote considerable effort to one objective while another may concentrate most of its efforts on a different one. Four examples which can illustrate this point are given below.

Holding down prices. In the tanning and woolen textile industries, the raw material is always available—at a price. But price fluctuations can be violent. Wool and hides (and other commodities, such as crude rubber, zinc, and copper) have been known to double or triple in price within six months or decline by a proportionate amount.

For users of the materials, the key objective is to pay minimum prices for them. It overshadows all others in importance. A shrewd materials manager can save 10—or even 100—times as much by intelligent timing of purchases as he can hope to save through achievement of other materials objectives.

Assuring reliability. In the aerospace industry, consistency of quality (i.e., reliability) is all-important. Almost any minor component can cause a $1 million missile to malfunction. The odds favor failure.

Because of the very complexity of the product, even a 99.9 percent quality standard may be inadequate. With this standard one part in 1,000 will be unsatisfactory. Since each missile contains more than 1,000 parts, it is then likely that each would contain a component that will fail.

Regulating inventory. In companies making a wide range of complicated products (instruments, machine tools, and similar items), the key problem usually is inventory turnover. Not only must the company have thousands of items available for product, but often it stocks tens of thousands of repair parts for customer service. If demand is erratic, there is always the danger that inventories will become unbalanced. The materials manager strives to prevent stockouts without tying up too much of the company's capital in inventory.

Cutting operating costs. If purchase prices are stable and inventory fluctuations are minimal, then the most important contribution the materials manager can make is to do her job at minimum cost. Her focus will be almost entirely on how to maintain the same level of basic performance at lower operating cost. In hospital materials management, for example, this may be the single most important economic objective.

Effects of business changes

Objectives also can vary within the same company. When sales are expanding, the materials manager may concentrate on continuity of supply and consistency of quality. The materials manager is less interested in inventory turnover or low prices, since the economic expansion should bring both higher sales and high prices and these objectives may be achieved automatically.

Excess inventory. But when business slumps, the story is different. Sales drop faster than output, so the materials manager is hard pressed just to keep turnover from dropping, and he must be nimble to avoid being greatly overstocked when the business cycle nears the bottom. During this period, the materials manager is also under considerable pressure to reduce purchase prices because the company may be forced to cut the prices of its end products despite slipping profit margins and lower sales volume.

Shortages. During a war or some other period of extreme scarcity, the simple act of locating sources of supply may become the single most important materials objective. This is also true when a key supplier is shut down because of labor trouble. Even under reasonably normal conditions, there can be an unpredicted upsurge in the demand for a finished product that can put considerable pressure on the materials manager to locate additional sources of supply fast enough to satisfy the demand.

No cash. In a young company that is growing rapidly, cash is perpetually short. All earnings and all borrowings are plowed back into plant and equipment. Some must be invested in inventory, of course. But the materials manager is under considerable pressure to get along with as little stock as possible in order to make cash available for other purposes. To boost inventory turnover, may buy in small quantities, even if this means he must forego quantity discounts and raise the cost of acquisition because of the greater number of receivals necessary to operate on a hand-to-mouth basis. He also may buy from suppliers with slightly higher prices, provided they will deliver with little advance notice.

Balancing of objectives

The examples above provide clues to one of the most basic parts of the materials manager's job; balancing of objectives. Objectives vary in importance. During certain periods, the materials manager may concentrate on one objective, and at other times she may concentrate on another.

Achievements bring sacrifices. Efforts to achieve one primary objective almost necessarily involve relaxation of efforts to achieve some other objective. The materials manager who concentrates on inventory turnover pays higher prices and has higher costs of acquisition because she must buy more frequently in smaller quantities. On the other hand, if she goes all out to get lower prices, the materials manager will buy in larger quantities to get quantity discounts. This will reduce inventory turnover. The higher average inventories will inevitably raise costs of possession, although unit costs of acquisition will probably decline because of the greater average size of each shipment. Continuity of supply and consistency of quality also may be affected. The materials' manager will be tempted to go to "cheap" suppliers who cut prices and also cut corners on quality and fail to live up to their delivery promises. The objective of favorable supplier relations will suffer because of the shifting of business to the "cheap" suppliers and because of the steady pressure for price reductions.

Basic principle. All materials objectives are interrelated. As illustrated in Figure 3–1, a gain in one objective means sacrifice on other objectives. In materials management you never "get something for nothing." You may, however, be getting something you do not really want or need. If an organization does not identify its material management objectives and develop a program to achieve them, it may be giving undue attention to some objectives and neglecting others.

In the organization where materials management objectives are not consciously identified, one objective—low operating cost—tends to be concentrated on to the exclusion of all others. In fact, top management

FIGURE 3–1
Interdependence and potential areas of conflict in primary objectives of materials management

Primary objective	*Other objectives adversely affected*
Low prices for purchased items	High inventory turnover, low cost of acquisition and posession, continuity of supply, consistency of quality, favorable relations with suppliers
High inventory turnover	Low cost of acquisition and possession, low prices for materials purchased, low payroll costs, continuity of supply.
Low cost of acquisition and possession	Low prices for purchased materials, high inventory turnover, good records.
Continuity of supply	Low prices for purchased materials, consistency of quality, favorable relations with suppliers, high inventory turnover.
Consistency of quality	Low prices for purchased materials, continuity of supply, favorable relations with suppliers, low cost of acquisition and posession, high inventory turnover.
Low payroll costs	Concentration on this objective can readily restrict achievement of all other objectives.
Favorable relations with suppliers	Low prices for purchased materials, high inventory turnover, continuity of supply, consistency of quality.
Development of personnel	Low payroll costs.
Good records	Low cost of acquisition and possession, low payroll costs.

often is not really aware that any other objectives exist (although it may be conscious also of the continuity-of-supply objective). In such organizations, $1 may be saved in operating cost at the cost of a $5 saving in purchase prices or inventory carrying cost. The objective in all too many organizations is to manage materials as *cheaply* as possible instead of as *profitably* as possible.

Organization limits. In many cases, organization structure inhibits achievement of a proper balance of objectives. When materials management functions are scattered throughout the organization, each materials subfunction tends to develop objectives of its own which may not be consistent with company objectives. For example, if a purchasing manager is made subordinate to a marketing manager, he begins to take on marketing objectives rather than those of materials management. Every subordinate tries to please the boss. And, in this case, the boss-pleasing effort might cause the subordinate to pay undue attention to secondary objectives like reciprocity and relatively little to more fundamental materials management objectives.

The wrong objectives get undue emphasis even in cases where the boss does not interfere. For example, a purchasing agent may give

's to the price objective and all but ignore the equally
tives of continuity of supply, inventory, and quality.
'uction control manager may be so conscious of the
_..nuity of supply that he or she all but ignores the inven-
_ujective. Materials objectives are most likely to be balanced in a
rational fashion when responsibility for achievement is clearly
delegated—preferably to a materials manager who has authority to do
the job. Even then objectives are not static. The materials manager
must always reevaluate them when business conditions change or
when they are affected by top-management decisions.

Monitoring of objectives. The basic job of the materials manager
is to translate broad company objectives into specific goals for the
department. He must regularly ask himself these questions:

1. Has there been any change in company objectives as they are
   perceived by top management?
2. Are the objectives of my department completely consistent with
   broad organizational objectives?
3. Am I giving the proper relative emphasis to my perceived objectives taking into account the current business environment and its
   effect on broad company objectives?

POLICIES AND PROCEDURES

This continuing reassessment of objectives is reflected in the materials management program. In directing the program, the materials
manager wants to manage by exception if possible. That is, she wants
to delegate the achievement of the program completely to her subordinates. If everything goes according to plan, the materials manager
does not interfere. But if something goes wrong because of a basic
defect in the plan, the materials manager wants to learn of it. She may
have to reevaluate the objectives and devise a new plan or take other
remedial steps.

Written policies and procedures permit management by exception.
They guide routine performance. With them, management decisions
are needed only when an exceptional problem arises.

Definitions. Policies are broad, overall guides to performance.
Procedures are the specific administrative actions needed to carry out
policies. Policies define in general terms the basic jobs of each department and its relation to other departments; they are derived from
the general goals and objectives of the department itself and the company as a whole. Procedures are derived from policies. They describe
routine operations in great detail.

Examples. One large aircraft and auto parts manufacturing company includes low prices and favorable vendor relations among its

materials objectives. To achieve these objectives, it has a written policy that "negotiations with vendors regarding price, terms, quality, etc. should be initiated, conducted, and concluded by the purchasing department."

This policy might be carried out with a number of procedures, such as a buying procedure whereby no purchase commitment is valid unless it is approved by a member of the purchasing department, or a procedure that prohibits anyone in departments other than purchasing from interviewing supplier salespersons without written approval of the purchasing agent.

A company with a policy of stimulating maximum competition among suppliers (in order to achieve an objective of low prices) might have a procedure calling for a minimum of three bids on each purchase.

Advantages of manuals

Progressive materials departments codify literally hundreds of policies and procedures in manuals that may include several hundred pages. They invest in hundreds of hours of high-priced specialists' time for preparing the manual. Moreover, such manuals are no good unless they are kept up to date, so frequent revisions are necessary.

After all this work, what usually happens? Nine policy and procedure manuals out of ten may not be referred to for months or even years. They just gather dust on supervisors' bookcases. Very few persons in a well-managed company ever have much need to refer to a manual. The employees know their jobs, and if they have any questions they simply ask the supervisor. New employees don't have much use for manuals, either. They normally learn their jobs by observing their fellow workers and through verbal instructions from their supervisors.

Yet the best managed companies have manuals for materials policies and procedures. They have them because manuals promote good interdepartmental relations (a secondary materials objective), make supervision easier, encourage standard practices, improve procedures, and aid in training.

Clarify interdepartmental relations. Even the best organization structure represents, to some extent, a rather artificial division of work. Departmental responsibilities overlap. Each department must work with the others if the overall job is to be done. Written policies and procedures define interdepartmental relationships. Thus they prevent many unnecessary jurisdictional disputes and also can prevent duplication of effort.

Written purchasing policies are particularly important because the purchasing department must work with other departments on problems where it is sometimes hard to determine jurisdiction. For example, although purchasing is responsible for selecting suppliers, using departments certainly have a right to receive the materials they need and to solicit suppliers for advice. Without written policies, jurisdictional disputes are almost inevitable when two departments are independently working with the same vendor on the same problem.

Make supervision easier. With written policies and procedures, a supervisor need not develop original solutions to routine problems. Nor need she even explain routine procedures to the subordinates (although she may wish to do so to make certain they understand them). The answers are in the manual. In most cases, the manual need not be referred to because employees already know what is in it. But were there no manual as a basic record, employees would gradually forget certain details of little-used procedures, and the load on supervisors would be correspondingly greater.

Develop standard practices. Without written policies and procedures, each supervisor would devise her own procedures to fit the superior's not-always-consistent instructions. As a result, eventually the same job would be performed in many different ways. Operations would be less efficient, communication slower, and supervision poorer. With written policies and procedures (called "standard practices," because that is what they are designed to promote), supervisors still deviate from routine when necessary, but they have basic guides to make them aware that they are deviating. These in themselves tend to prevent unnecessary changes in routine.

Improve procedures. When a manual is prepared, procedures are subjected to closer scrutiny than they may have received before. Improvements are almost inevitable. Unnecessary paperwork can be eliminated, and righter controls can be instituted if necessary. Periodic review and revision of the manual can prevent sloppy practices from creeping back into the system.

Aid in training. Although new employees are often lazy readers and prefer to get their training by watching and talking with fellow employees, the manual is helpful for reference. It is also useful to employees in other departments.

The job of preparing or revising a manual can be a training vehicle in itself. There is no better way to give a new high-potential employee a good grasp of the overall workings of the department and to permit the employee to apply imagination and resourcefulness to improvements in procedures.

Preparing the manual

The purchasing department probably has more need for a policy and procedures manual than any other department in the company, mainly because of its contact with outside suppliers. Almost everyone in every department likes to buy and feels particularly competent to buy the items he uses. Controllers like to buy their own accounting machines, maintenance superintendents prefer to select brands of cleaning compounds, and product engineers feel they should select suppliers of parts and materials. This results in difficulties, which make preparation of a purchasing manual an especially long and tedious job. Since most of the important policies and procedures affect other departments, the person writing the manual must submit a draft of the proposed policy to each affected department head for approval. In many cases, hours are spent discussing precisely how a given policy should be worded so that each department's prerogatives are protected.

The usual procedure in preparing a manual is to determine what is being done and then to describe each operation in writing. After existing procedures are analyzed critically, the materials manager and staff try to put down in writing what they would like to have done, as regards both policies and procedures. Existing procedures are then modified to fit these goals and drafts are submitted to all interested department heads for approval. The whole process always takes a few months and occasionally more than a year.

The effort is worthwhile, however. Written objectives, policies, and procedures provide the framework within which the materials organization does its job. But they are useless, of course, if the materials department does not also have the organization it needs to achieve the objectives. The principles of building a materials management organization will be discussed in the next chapter.

Case

CASE 3–1. LAWTON PRODUCTS COMPANY

Determining materials management objectives

The Lawton Products Company was formerly known as the Lawton Camera Corporation. The new name was adopted in 1946 to reflect the company's broadened product line. Lawton was founded in 1915 by Howard F. Lawton, Sr., to manufacture and market a relatively expensive line of cameras designed especially for the amateur photographer. The company grew at first by widening its line of photographic equipment. Home-movie cameras, movie and slide projectors, and a best selling line of 35 mm. "candid" cameras were introduced between 1920 and 1935.

The company prospered in the camera business not only because its products were of high quality and well merchandised but also because the company successfully avoided the problem of foreign competition with its products. Until World War II, the market for high-quality cameras was dominated by German manufacturers who had gained world-wide acceptance for quality and dependability. Although they were protected by an extremely high tariff, American manufacturers were hard put to compete even in their own market. Their products usually were not so widely accepted as the leading German brands. In addition, their costs were much higher; American camera workers were no more productive then German workers; but their wages were more than twice as high.

Lawton's solution to the problem of German competition was to buy major components from Japanese manufacturers, who could undersell both American and German firms. Lawton confined its efforts to design, assembly, and marketing.

The company was extremely successful, and by 1938 it had sales of $10 million, with profits of nearly $600,000 after taxes. In 1938, however, Howard Lawton became increasingly fearful of the threat to the company's survival if war should cut off his supplies of Japanese components, and so he decided to diversify. At that time, the company was doing almost no manufacturing. While Lawton desperately wanted to acquire manufacturing know-how on camera equipment, he had no desire to cut off his Japanese suppliers if he didn't have to. His solution was to buy the Abramson Company, a small manufacturer of optical instruments. In Abramson, Lawton got a profitable company with experience in optical equipment which could easily be converted to manufacture of camera components if necessary. The Abramson plant was located just a few miles from the Lawton plant, so there was no difficulty in integrating Abramson into the Lawton organization.

Pearl Harbor not only cut off Lawton's source of components, but it also cut off all manufacture of cameras for amateur photographers. The Lawton Corporation expanded its instrument line to serve the war effort. It also became one of the U.S. Navy's major contractors for optical fire-control equipment and gained considerable experience with the elaborate electric and electronic controls used in this equipment.

After the war, Lawton was able to use much of its expanded manufacturing capacity to broaden its line of photographic equipment. It also was able to apply its wartime skills in optics and electronics to a greatly expanded instrument line. In 1950 the company developed a closed-circuit television unit for industrial process control and added another line of process-control instruments to use with its TV systems. In 1951, the company reactivated its fire-control business when it got several major Navy contracts, and by 1969 the company had become a major supplier of fire-control and missile-guidance equipment for both the Navy and the Air Force.

The company's 1969 sales were $165 million, or more than 16 times as great as in 1938. Profits did not keep pace, however; they grew less than 500 percent in this period. The company's aftertax margin has deteriorated steadily since 1955, and in 1969 the company earned only 2 percent on sales and just over 5 percent on net worth. This was substantially below average aftertax returns of all durable good manufacturers (about 4 percent on sales and 8 percent on net worth).

In an effort to get to the bottom of the problem of declining profit margins, Howard Lawton, the company's president, hired the management consulting firm of Smith, Martin, and Conrad to make a broad survey of the company's organization, policies, and procedures.

The company's organization has grown a great deal since the 1930s, but its structure has changed very little. Reporting directly to Lawton are vice presidents in charge of sales, engineering, manufacturing, and finance. Reporting to the vice president of sales are an administrative assistant, advertising manager, public relations manager, sales personnel manager, general sales manager, and four product managers. The general sales manager supervises regional sales managers responsible for sales of all of the company's products except cameras.

The product managers for instruments, defense products, and electronics each supervise a small staff. They are responsible for:

1. Coordinating complaints from customers with manufacturing and engineering.
2. Liaison with engineering on new products and design changes.
3. Production and materials planning, including the breaking down of orders from customers, preparation of purchase requisitions and factory work orders for parts, and preparation of overall schedules.
4. Preparation of quotations on new business from data secured from the cost department and interested activities.

Sales of camera equipment are handled somewhat differently. Since cameras are marketed through consumer channels, an entirely separate sales force is needed. It is under the direct supervision of the camera product manager, who is also responsible for market research on cameras, styling, coordination with engineering on new-product development, and purchase of all imported purchased components and complete products.

The company's purchasing manager, who reports to the vice president in charge of manufacturing, is responsible for buying all raw materials used in the company's products, as well as all nonproduction materials. Reporting to her are two buyers (one for direct material and the other for indirect), supervisors of the storerooms for both production and nonproduction materials, and the company's general foreman in charge of receiving inspection. In addition, the purchasing manager supervises a small data processing group that keeps records of all the company's inventories, including finished goods and in-process stocks. She also is functionally responsible for the purchasing specialists in the engineering department and provides them with forms, clerical services, and so on.

Also reporting to the vice president of manufacturing are the superintendents of the company's two plants, the production planning and control manager, the traffic manager, the factory personnel manager, the master mechanic, the cost estimating manager, the work standards manager, and the quality control manager.

The planning department prepares schedules, requisitions, and work orders for cameras from sales forecasts it receives from the camera product manager. It also participates in, but is not directly responsible for, production planning for other products.

The supervisors of the shipping and receiving departments report to the traffic manager. Their activities require only a small amount of the traffic manager's time, most of which is spent on traffic problems on outgoing shipments of camera products and occasionally on assisting customers for other products when they do not specify any routing. The company has always relied on its suppliers to handle all inbound shipments. Even foreign suppliers take all responsibility for getting their shipments to Lawton and handle all details of shipping, customs, and so on.

The engineering department is organized almost entirely by product; there are chief product engineers for each of the company's lines. Reporting to each chief product engineer are various engineers who specialize in certain details of the product. Each chief engineer also has one or more buyers working for him or her who handle most routine contacts with suppliers. Individual engineers also work closely with the company's suppliers. On new products, they often rely on the supplier for substantial assistance in development. Suppliers do not charge for this service. They are rewarded indirectly, however, since the final specifications for the item usually are tailor-made to their processes, and, in some cases, they even indicate that the component should be purchased from the supplier who assisted in its development.

The engineering department is responsible for about 40 percent of the company's $110 million purchase volume. About 25 percent is spent by the camera department product manager on imported products and components, 30 percent directly by the purchasing manager, and the balance by the office manager for office supplies and by the master mechanic for machine tools and equipment.

The office manager reports to the general accounting manager, who in turn reports to the vice president in charge of finance. Also reporting to the general accounting manager are the supervisors in charge of office personnel, accounts payable, and accounts receivable. Invoices from suppliers go directly to accounts payable, where they are logged into a register and then sent for approval to the department responsible for the purchase. The department that made the purchase compares the invoice with the receiving report and the receiving inspection report and approves it if everything is in order. The approved invoice is then returned to accounts payable for payment. During an average month, accounts payable processes invoices for more than $9 million and manages to take discounts for prompt payment on all but about $500,000. Terms vary, but most suppliers offer a 1 to 2 percent discount if bills are paid within ten days.

Questions

1. Should Smith, Martin, and Conrad recommend any changes in Lawton's approach to materials management?
2. What are Lawton Products Company's probable materials management objectives?
3. How can it better achieve these objectives?

4

Organizing for materials management

Someone in every organization must make materials management decisions. Since, as noted in Chapter 3, materials objectives are interrelated, it is desirable to give one person authority over all activities concerned with materials management. Otherwise, no one—other than the president of the company—can be held responsible for materials decisions.

Suppose, for example, that materials authority is dispersed among a number of departments in a company (see Figure 4–1). A purchasing manager reporting to a finance manager is in charge of buying parts and materials. A traffic manager reporting to the sales manager buys transportation services. A production control manager reporting to the manufacturing manager schedules materials and controls inventories.

Problem of divided responsibility. Now suppose that one of the company's immediate objectives is to reduce materials cost by 5 percent. If the objective is actually achieved, the production control manager, purchasing agent, and traffic manager—and their respective bosses—all can share the credit. But who is responsible if the objective is not achieved? Each has a legitimate alibi. The production control manager is not responsible for negotiating prices of materials and services. The purchasing manager buys in amounts determined by the material control department, and his prices and bargaining power are determined by the quantities he buys. The traffic manager can't cut freight costs if purchasing insists on buying from suppliers in distant cities.

Duplication of effort. The divided materials organization not only makes it easy to pass the buck but it is wasteful. There is inevitably

80

FIGURE 4-1
Divided responsibility for materials management

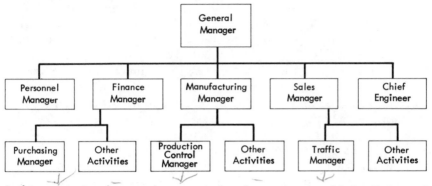

In this organization, the general manager is the only person responsible for all phases of materials management, including purchasing, production control, and traffic. Since the general manager is involved with many other problems, materials are not managed as well as they should be.

overlap of responsibility among materials functions—especially between production control and purchasing—and consequent duplication of effort. In the worst cases, production control and purchasing spend almost as much time jealously guarding their prerogatives against inroads of the rival activity as they do on the more constructive aspects of their jobs.

Sometimes the rivalry becomes genuinely destructive. In a large auto company in which I was once employed, both purchasing and production control quite correctly assumed that they were responsible for having purchased parts on hand to meet production requirements. So when a supplier failed to deliver, each activity rushed an expediter to the scene to straighten things out. There was just one difficulty. The competing expediters did not necessarily give the same instructions to the supplier. The purchasing expediter had a different set of priorities than the production control expediter did!

The difference reflected organizational level. Purchasing was centralized, and its priorities reflected what was theoretically a corporate view. The production expediter represented one of the company's major divisions, and its priorities on delivery of a wide variety of components were not the same as those of the corporate purchasing staff. The supplier presumably muddled through, trying to keep everyone happy but in reality performing less efficiently than if everyone had simply left him alone. It took the company 20 years to solve this organization problem. Today purchasing and production control are combined in a single materials management activity, so presumably the competition between the groups has been eliminated.

Lack of representation. Interfunctional rivalry can, however, be constructive, under certain conditions. Contrary to popular opinion, there is plenty of dissidence in a well-managed organization. Strong-willed executives often disagree. Each presents a point of view that reflects his or her specialty, and the decisions that result from this approach are likely to represent, on balance, the best that the organization can make at that time. For example, if engineering did not have a voice in top management, a manufacturing company might be prone to neglect research and development in order to boost short-term profit performance. On the other hand, an organization that is dominated by engineering might produce an excellent product, but it would cost too much to make and might not be marketable.

Materials management is conspicuous by its absence in the organization represented in Figure 4–1 above. If decisions reflect exclusively the viewpoints of personnel, finance, manufacturing, sales, and engineering, the best that can happen is that materials management is ignored. In the worst circumstances, however, it can be adversely affected. In one health-care organization where materials management was not represented at a high level, an expensive new facility was constructed in which almost no space was allowed for purchased materials inventory. Expensive alterations were later needed to make the facility workable.

Inventory too high. The company's loss may be more subtle than this. It can safely be assumed that purchased materials inventory will not be under tight control unless there is a strong materials manager. The reason for this is that both sales and manufacturing performance tend to be improved if there is a large purchased material inventory. The purchasing department's job is also easier. This leaves the finance manager as the only key executive with a vested interest in low inventory. She is not only outnumbered but also frequently unable to attack the problem, since her concern is entirely with dollar investment and change from some prior period.

If inventory has always been high (as it often is in the company with weak materials management), then it cannot easily be cut back. A reduction is almost certain to cause severe disruption in manufacturing or in purchasing. In fact, when inventory investment is at its optimum level, production control and purchasing personnel, in particular, may feel that they are working in a state of near chaos. They are always on the verge of running out of material—and sometimes they actually do run out. This state of affairs is rarely welcomed by the salaried employees who must cope with it. In effect, the benefits of higher return on capital go to the company's stockholders and possibly to its top management. The ulcers are awarded to those who must actually cope with the problems of tight inventory.

WHO IS MATERIALS MANAGER?

Under the conditions described above, tough inventory management must be imposed from the top, with a key executive who understands the inventory process exerting continuous pressure to keep stocks down. A materials manager is needed.

Purchasing agent as materials manager

The purchasing agent or purchasing manager may become materials manager in fact, if not in title. He gets the job through a process of evolution, gradually assuming responsibility for all phases of materials management. When the purchasing agent is given responsibility for both traffic and inventory control, he is more materials manager than purchasing agent. At this stage, responsibility for almost all of the company's materials objectives centers on a single executive, and the company's organization structure is no longer a barrier to effective materials management.

Dozens of companies do an excellent job of materials management even though they employ no official materials managers. Typically, the materials organization is headed by a vice president of purchases and traffic, who is also responsible for inventory control. This vice president is, in effect, materials management's representative in top management. His materials organization can be quite efficient. Three of the most important materials functions—purchasing, traffic, and inventory control—are linked together organizationally, and the company's efforts are consistently focused on a common set of materials objectives.

Criteria for effectiveness. The purchasing manager is most likely to make a satisfactory substitute for a materials manager in non-manufacturing organizations—especially those with minimal inventory problems. The best example of this is a construction company. Purchased material is delivered directly to the site, and there is relatively little inventory. In this extreme case, of course, the materials manager is almost exclusively concerned with purchasing.

In most other cases, purchasing is not the only skill that is required, even though the materials management process effectively ends with delivery of purchased material to the ultimate user. For example, the purchasing agent of an educational institution is really a materials manager, even if she does not have that title, because she is almost always in charge of purchased inventories.

In hospitals, the purchasing director usually has responsibilities roughly comparable to that of many industrial materials managers. When the hospital does not have a materials manager, the director of purchasing is almost always not only responsible for buying but also receiving and general stores. Thus, she not only decides from whom to buy but also how much to buy and to stock.

Purchasing agents of manufacturing companies also frequently function as materials managers, particularly if there are no major materials management problems with in-process or finished goods stocks. In the aerospace industry, for example, a purchasing manager in one company may have the same responsibilities as a materials or materiel manager in another company. In both cases, they may be responsible not only for buying but also for inbound traffic and control of purchased materials inventory. In neither case do they have much to do with in-process stocks. Since the product is extremely expensive and made to customer order, there are no conventional physical distribution problems to interest the materials manager.

Limitations. In a majority of organizations, however, the purchasing manager makes an effective materials manager only if he has both skills and authority not ordinarily associated with his specialty. Two major problems prevent the typical purchasing manager from functioning informally as materials manager.

1. *Production control and inventory control cannot be readily separated from manufacturing.* The inventory control function is pivotal. Purchasing has a legitimate interest in this function because inventory level is determined by the quantity of material purchased. (This is explained in detail in Chapter 8.) Production control is also legitimately interested, since manufacturing schedules are intimately related to inprocess and raw materials inventories.

2. *Materials functions that remain in manufacturing do not have adequate "visibility."* Receiving, shipping, warehousing, and materials handling all tend to be neglected orphans in the typical manufacturing organization. Their activities are peripheral to manufacturing's main job—making the product—and their managers typically have the feeling that manufacturing has no interest whatever in their activities. Morale and performance are often improved when these activities are transferred to materials management, an activity in which movement and handling of material are primary concerns.

Fifty years ago, it was assumed that activities such as shipping and materials handling would more or less manage themselves. In recent years, however, management has become increasingly aware that a major part of its "manufacturing" cost has nothing to do with the manufacturing process itself but is concerned with the moving and storing of materials in various stages of fabrication. New management techniques have been developed to control these moving and storing costs. These can be applied most successfully if responsibility is given to a materials manager rather than remaining in manufacturing, where management is primarily interested in the manufacturing process itself.

Dual materials management

Problems in the purchasing–materials management relationship can be solved if purchasing is not considered part of materials management. In this case, materials management consists of all of the usual activities *except* purchasing. The materials manager takes over *after* the material is bought, and purchasing functions independently of materials management. As many as one tenth of the executives with the title of materials manager or its equivalent do not include purchasing in their departments.

Physical distribution. In most cases, the division is between purchasing and a physical distribution. Purchasing buys raw materials and parts. Manufacturing and other activities take over responsibility for inventory immediately after the supplier delivers. The physical distribution department, which usually has a close relationship with marketing, is responsible for maintaining inventories and operating warehouses that are primarily filled with end products. This organization works especially well in food processing concerns where purchasing is highly skilled in buying and distribution of end products is made from a number of distribution centers throughout the country.

Politics. In some cases, the reason why purchasing and other materials management functions are separated organizationally is not economic at all. It is simply political. An ambitious executive is able to gather together all functions but purchasing, and the director of purchases is strong enough to keep his independence. Occasionally, these half-finished materials management departments will follow a more conventional pattern as soon as management finds it convenient to make further changes—often after a very senior purchasing executive retires and is replaced by a junior who is more amenable to becoming subordinate to the materials manager.

Buying power. Occasionally, the existence of materials management and purchasing departments that are independent of one another may even be justified on a logical basis. A huge, multidivision company may prefer to do almost all of its buying at the corporate level so it has a large, corporate purchasing office. Other materials management activities are completely decentralized at the division level, however, with divisional materials managers responsible for everything except purchasing.

In this organization, corporate buying power is maximized. In addition, the managers of various divisions have reasonable autonomy. They can adjust inventories up and down in order to earn maximum profits. Unfortunately, centralized buying with other phases of materials management decentralized and independent creates weaknesses within the structure. It is workable in practice only when there is very little that the corporate purchasing office can do to thwart what might be quite different objectives of the divisional materials management departments. It is hard to believe that a better way cannot be found to organize for materials management.

Materials management subordinate to manufacturing

One alternative arrangement that is quite common is simply to group together all related materials management activities under a materials manager who, in turn, reports to manufacturing. In a smaller company, a similar version of this approach is to have managers of the major materials management activities all report directly to the manufacturing manager. In this case, the manufacturing manager really has two jobs: the one implied by his title and that of materials manager.

About half of the manufacturing companies with materials managers have an integrated department reporting to manufacturing. Materials managers would undoubtedly prefer to report to top management directly rather than to be subordinate to manufacturing, and it can safely be assumed they are given no choice. Legitimate arguments can be advanced for the role of materials management as a junior partner to manufacturing, however, including expediency, indivisibility, and span of control.

Expediency. In many cases, the only way a company can get an integrated materials management activity is by making it subordinate to manufacturing. Most or even all of the key materials management functions may have been under manufacturing to start with. The main change in this case is the act of grouping them together under a materials manager. Such a change is likely to be supported by the manufacturing manager only if he continues to retain overall responsibility for materials management. In other cases there might not be a separate materials manager, and the manufacturing manager would continue to function as an effective materials manager himself.

Indivisibility. In certain types of manufacturing processes, it is extremely difficult to determine where materials management ends and manufacturing begins. In general, the materials manager is responsible for the flow of materials through the shop (adding value by distribution), while manufacturing is responsible for the workers and machines that actually make the product (adding value by manufacture). In practice, however, the production and inventory control departments may be deeply involved not only in materials management problems but also in making decisions that are definitely manufacturing responsibility. For example, a shortage of material may force production not only to reschedule equipment but also to shift workers from one production job to another. Materials management and production management decisions must then be made almost simultaneously and, since they are interrelated, should be made by the same department. Thus, in some industries, both materials management and manufacturing management can quite legitimately claim that production control belongs in their bailiwick. This ceases to be a problem if materials management is part of manufacturing to start with.

Span of control.   The general manager may be so busy she wants to limit the number of executives who report directly to her. She feels she is too busy to be involved with materials management directly. As long as materials management cannot have much impact on the company's success, this view is correct. Materials management is not always so vital to the enterprise that its chief should be on the company's second level of organization, responsible directly to top management. This is generally true of companies that do not use substantial amounts of production parts and materials. For example, materials management can quite legitimately be made subordinate to manufacturing in a mining firm where the materials management job is primarily concerned with procurement of spare parts and similar items needed to keep the mine operating.

The case for independence

Unfortunately, the materials function is still subordinate to manufacturing in many companies where it could make a greater contribution to profits if it were independent. Increasingly, however, top management are separating materials management from manufacturing. Automation is forcing the manufacturing manager to concentrate more energy on technological problems. There is less time for peripheral activities, including materials management.

EDP sharpens distinction.   In addition, electronic data processing helps sharpen the distinction between manufacturing management and materials management. The typical EDP program automatically draws all related activities of materials management together. It is only natural that the company organization chart should reflect the way in which technology has regrouped activities. One activity, headed by a materials manager, is concerned with the data on inventory, orders, shortages, and lead time that is to be fed into the computer. Another group, under a manufacturing manager, dedicates its efforts to making machines and workers meet schedules at lowest possible cost. Thus, automation in the factory and data processing are forcing many companies to integrate their materials management activities and make a single executive responsible for all materials management decisions.

88

The only way. In the overwhelming majority of independent materials management organizations, the relatively small costs are offset many times over by the results. Materials should be managed by an executive whose success or failure depends entirely on how well this job is done. If materials management is a peripheral assignment for an executive with other responsibilities, it will get peripheral treatment. If the materials organization is a subordinate function, it will inevitably take on some of the objectives of the function to which it is junior. The best results and the highest morale are achieved when the materials management department must "sink or swim" in its specialty. This environment can best be created in an organization structure resembling that in Figure 4–2, where the division of work is by function.

FIGURE 4–2
How materials management fits into the organization

The overall job of management is delegated by its major functions. Division of work at the third level is also usually functional. For example, the materials management job is divided functionally into its traffic, purchasing, and material control elements.

BUILDING THE ORGANIZATION

The materials manager requires a staff to help him achieve his objectives. Materials management is a big job. In a fairly small concern it may require 20 or 30 persons; in a big corporation, hundreds or even thousands will be needed. The overall materials job must be divided into many different jobs under some sort of organization structure. In the ideal organization, objectives are consistently attained at low cost and with a minimum of confusion. This ideal is hard to achieve, for organization is hardly an exact science. Two different managers will build entirely different organization structures, even though there are relatively few ways in which work can be divided in creating an organization. Among those that are feasible for a materials organization are division of work by: (1) function; (2) location; and (3) product or project.

Organization by function

The most widely used organization technique is division of work by function (see Figure 4–2). The principle behind it is a sound one: jobs should be organized so as to promote maximum specialization of skills. With functional specialization, jobs are broken up so that they are as narrow as possible in scope. Each employee is an expert in some highly specialized area. Materials management is itself a division of work by function.

In addition, there is considerable functional specialization in every materials organization. Breaking up the overall materials job into its components (purchasing, traffic, material control, and so on) is a form of functional specialization. Within these groups, there is even more specialization. For example, purchasing may be broken up so that one person receives purchase requisitions and prepares the records for a buyer. Another person, the buyer, contacts suppliers and actually places orders. Another specialist may do nothing but type purchase orders, and another files the necessary records. Still another specialist may follow up to make certain that the suppliers deliver on schedule. In a large purchasing organization, the buying job itself can involve as many as half a dozen different specialists, including assistant buyers, expediters, purchase analysts, and others.

Advantages. It is possible, in creating a materials organization, to divide work entirely by function. This would work fairly well in a small organization, although there might be problems in a larger one. Division of work by function is popular with good reason. It has many advantages, including the following.

1. Economic use of high-salaried help. With functional specialization, jobs can more readily be broken up into highly skilled and less skilled elements. A buyer does not type her own purchase orders (she probably wouldn't have this skill anyway); she relies on a typist whose salary is substantially lower. This permits the buyer to use her special skills more effectively. Functional specialization also makes it economic to hire specialists whom the organization could not otherwise afford.

For example, in the typical company, buyers in the purchasing department and various marketing executives all can make profitable use of periodic forecasts by a professional economist. By setting up a separate economics department to serve the entire company, each executive can get the benefit of an expert's advice. An additional function, economic forecasting, is created to serve a number of departments. Each executive served by the economist in effect delegates part of the forecasting element of the job to the economist, so that there actually has been a division of work by function.

2. *More efficient operation.* With functional specialization, it is possible to become extremely adept at one particular job. A clerk who works in a storeroom every day is bound to be able to find rarely used items much more rapidly than a temporary employee who may be forced to spending 5 or 10 minutes looking for even easy-to-find items.

3. *More flexible organization.* An organization with maximum functional specialization can adjust more readily to changes in business volume. The reason is that it makes the most effective use of a few highly skilled persons who are always needed. When volume is low, they handle both skilled and unskilled jobs. When it expands, less skilled persons can be hired to take over elements of their jobs. There is no need to hire additional highly skilled people, who might not even be available in a period of business expansion.

4. *Concentration of buying power.* In the conventional materials organization, buying assignments are normally made on the basis of commodity specialization. One buyer handles stampings, another handles office supplies, and so on. With this approach, not only does the buyer become an expert in his field, but the plant's entire buying power is concentrated for each commodity instead of being dispersed among a number of "materials specialists" or "divisional materials managers." This can make for better procurement and lower costs.

Disadvantages. Unfortunately, excessive application of the principle of functional specialization can cause serious weaknesses in the organization. Among them are the following.

1. *Employee dissatisfaction.* People get bored when their jobs become too specialized; they like variety. Also, with specialization, the general objectives of the business can become too remote from the jobs of those who are supposed to achieve them. People may become so engrossed in their specialities that they begin to regard them as ends in themselves and not as means of reaching some broader company objective.

2. *Bureaucratization.* If jobs become too specialized, everyone is liable to "pass the buck" and disclaim responsibility for solving a nonroutine problem or for committing an error. Also, as organization with a great deal of functional specialization is often "deep"—with many layers of supervision. This makes for a long chain of command and causes the decision-making process to be slow and complex.

Organization by location

In a large organization with many plants, the need for some application of the principle of organization by location is self-evident (see Figure 4–3). Each plant requires a materials organization, and at least

FIGURE 4-3
Division of work by location

When similar functions are being performed in areas remote from one another, division of work by location is desirable at some level in the organization.

part of that organization must be physically located at the plant. Therefore division of responsibility by location is essential.

Organization by location is also practical in companies that operate only one plant. Many plants have more than one receiving, shipping, or stores department. In such cases, division of responsibility usually is by location, with each unit serving a given part of the plant.

When the materials organization is by plant, materials personnel can work more closely with the other departments in that plant. They become more intimately familiar with the plant's problems. The major disadvantage of organization by plant is that it tends to disperse the materials organization. Some of the advantages of specialization are lost, and buying power is often diluted.

Organization by plant is naturally essential for some elements of the materials job, notably shipping and receiving. Organization by area served is similar. In the materials department, it is particularly applicable to field expediters and traffic clerks. Field expediters can deal with suppliers in given areas. For example, one California aerospace company has field expediters in Cleveland, Ohio, and Hartford, Connecticut, to expedite needed shipments from eastern and midwestern suppliers. If a traffic clerk specializes in shipments from a given area, she will rapidly all but memorize tariffs of carriers serving that area and so will be able to do her job more efficiently.

For other parts of the materials department, organization by location is rarer. The disadvantages of this form of organization in purchasing, for example, usually outweigh the advantages.

Organization by product or project

Since the materials organization exists to help make some product or service more profitably, breaking up materials activities by product,

FIGURE 4-4
Organization by product

There is no better way to make individuals conscious of profit margins than to give them responsibility for performing a vital function in the manufacture and marketing of that product.

process, or project is logical (see Figure 4-4). Each materials group is assigned to some product or group of products. For example, the purchasing departments of the General Motors Corporation are set up on a product basis. There is a separate purchasing department for each product division: Chevrolet, Pontiac, Frigidaire, and so on.

A project organization is a product organization with a finite life. Project organizations are temporarily set up to carry out a particular mission. When the job is done, they are either disbanded or melded into some new permanent organization. For example, a company that is contemplating manufacture of some new product would set up a project organization for that product headed by a project manager. Appropriate specialists from manufacturing, materials management, engineering, and other activities would then be assigned temporarily to that project. In many cases, they would simply return to their regular jobs when the project was completed. In others, they might form the cadre of a new permanent organization when the project organization evolved into a product organization with a permanent mission.

Within the materials department, division of work by product or commodity is quite common. Purchasing departments often are organized so that each buyer specializes in a few commodities. (This is a combination of functional specialization and product specialization.) One buyer may specialize in castings and forgings, another in sheet steel, and so on. The production control organization frequently follows the same pattern. In a cruder fashion, so do stores. Raw materials often go to one stores department, finished parts to another, and so on.

The big advantage of organization by product is that it permits personnel to become really familiar with the problems of a single group of products. As a result, they should be able to do their work more effectively. When the overall materials organization is broken up into a number of product groups, as it is at General Motors, each member's job is more closely related to the profit objectives in a particular product line.

The main disadvantage of organization by product is that it tends to disperse the overall materials effort. In a company as large as General Motors, this dispersal probably is no handicap. But it would be highly uneconomic, by contrast, to have the materials organization broken up into product groups in a company employing 1,000 persons and making 100 fairly similar products.

SPAN OF CONTROL

The three major ways in which to divide materials management work—organization by function, location and product—have been discussed above. Another fundamental principle of organizing for materials management is the concept of *span of control* which is concerned with how many divisions should be made.

In a materials organization with 100 persons, should there be one general materials manager and 99 assistant materials managers? In this case, we are assuming that the general materials manager has a span of control of 99, that is, he can effectively supervise 99 persons. Most managers would not want to have that many persons reporting directly to them. In fact, they usually prefer to have fewer than ten persons reporting directly.

For this reason, most materials organizations with a staff of 100 would more likely have half a dozen or so "assistants" reporting directly to the general materials manager. Each of the assistants, in turn, might have half a dozen persons reporting to her, and these third-level people would in turn have subordinates. So the 100 people in the materials organization might be at four distinct organization levels.

This does not mean it is desirable to have an organization with many levels. On the contrary, such an organization has many disadvantages, and there are many reasons why an organization should be kept as "flat" (i.e., with a broad span of control and relatively few levels) as possible.

The flat organization. Morale tends to be higher in the flat organization (Figure 4–5) than in the deep one. Most people are much closer to the top echelon than they would otherwise be. They are more likely to have a better grasp of the problems of the business as a whole, and they are less likely to become so immersed in their own specialities that they lose sight of overall objectives. The flat organization is relatively democratic. To a great degree, everyone is his own boss and is forced to make his own decisions.

Since people are on their own to a much greater degree, individual skills must be greater in the flat organization. And, of course, the flat

94

FIGURE 4–5
Flat organization: Purchasing agent with broad span of control

organization is a much better training ground for future top executives, since they get a chance to make decisions at a much earlier stage in their careers.

The deep organization. The deep organization (see Figure 4–6) also has advantages. In practice, most companies have fairly deep

FIGURE 4–6
Deep purchasing organization with narrow span of control

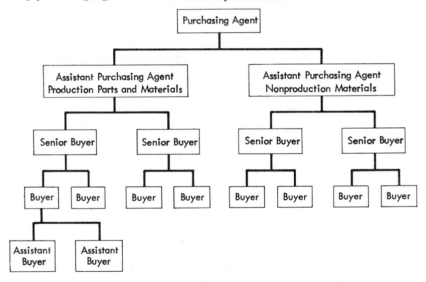

organizations, and they have them because they work. Proponents point out that there is a place for everyone in the deep organization. Highly routine, unskilled jobs can easily be found for the inexperienced and relatively inept at the bottom of the pyramid, and the skills of the highly specialized and extra talented can be utilized to a much greater degree in some position near the top. Fewer experts are needed in the deep organization. Since there is a greater breakdown of work by skill, the services of everyone in the organization are used in the most economic manner.

The deep organization has faults, too. It tends to be bureaucratic; decisions are passed upward from echelon to echelon. It can be inefficient; it requires more supervision than the flat organization does and, if carried to an extreme, this can reach the point where there are literally more chiefs than Indians. The deep organization also tends to discourage individual initiative; it is inherently more autocratic than the flatter organization. Promotions may be slow; in extreme cases, it can take exceptionally able persons years to reach jobs with sufficient responsibility for their skills to be recognized.

On the other hand, in a deep organization, supervisors are more likely to have time to train and counsel each of their subordinates on an individual basis. It is also possible to have tighter control over everyone's actions.

Wide or narrow span?   In practice, every organization structure represents a series of compromises. This is the case with span of control. Some factors tend to widen span of control; others tend to narrow it.

It is possible to have a flat organization with broad span of control when:

1. Job objectives are clearly spelled out. A person who knows exactly what is expected of him obviously requires less supervision than one who knows what she is supposed to do only by frequent contact with the boss.
2. Job performance can be measured. When there are objective measures of performance, the supervisor's job is easier. It is no problem to determine the contribution of each subordinate to the business.
3. Jobs supervised are similar and repetitious. The less complex the job, the fewer the supervisor's problems. And, of course, the supervisor's job is much simpler when she supervises persons doing almost identical jobs, all relatively unskilled, than when she supervises persons who are highly skilled, each of whom is doing a different job.
4. Supervisors and supervised both are above average in job skill and administrative skill. Exceptional supervisors can effectively handle more subordinates, and exceptional subordinates can get along with less supervision.
5. Errors are not serious. If an employee's mistakes do not have too much effect on the companys profit and survival, there is a greater inclination to put him in a spot where he can learn by making his own mistakes. If errors are too costly, supervision must be more intense.

Because errors *are* serious in a purchasing department, supervisors often have an extremely limited span of control. Each individual buyer may be spending hundreds of thousands or millions of dollars.

Obviously, the company cannot afford too many mistakes, so the buyer's work is checked and rechecked by various supervisors. On the other hand, work in a receiving department is less vital to the profits of the business. An error made on a receiving report will undoubtedly cause confusion and could be expensive, but it is unlikely to be as critical as an error in buying. Therefore it is possible to have a broader span of control in receiving.

Span of control in the ideal organization is neither too broad nor too narrow. In such an organization, the manager tries to get some of the initiative that the flat organization encourages while retaining the ease of supervision of the deep structure.

In the typical materials organizations, the span of control varies from 4 or 5 to 15 or 20. The top materials manager usually has fewer persons reporting to him than any other supervisor in the department. Receiving and shipping supervisors may supervise as many as 15 or 20 employees.

LEVEL OF ORGANIZATION

It is possible to build an effective organization simply by applying the principles of division of work to each major job within the limits of span of control. Managers whose activities embrace a big part of the organization would then report to major officials, while their subordinates would include managers with narrower responsibilities.

Materials manager's level

Ask a real-life materials manager or purchasing manager to whom he or she should report and the answer would consistently be to the chief executive officer of the organization. The reality is somewhat different. When an organization has both a materials manager and a purchasing manager, the purchasing manager is almost always subordinate to the materials manager. In fact, one job is a logical stepping-stone to the other.

However, a strong case can be made for having the chief materials executive (whether this be a purchasing manager or a materials manager) report at this second level of organization. Some of the reasons have already been discussed. But to sum up, they are as follows:

1. *Purchases account for more than half of the typical manufacturer's costs and even in service industries account for as much as one fourth of all costs.* Purchasing is simply too important an activity to be carried out at a lower level of organization. The same logic can be applied to materials management. Not only is the materials manager responsible for purchasing but his role in inventory management may also be critical. And, as has been previously pointed out, inventories may be as important an asset as plant and equipment.

2. *Purchasing and materials management should have a "voice" at the top level of the organization.* Otherwise, purchasing and materials management decisions will be made subordinate to design, marketing, and manufacturing objectives. Real-life management represents a consensus among executives with sometimes conflicting ideas. If the materials manager does not participate in arriving at this consensus, the end result will be excess inventory and less-than-optimum results.

Within the organization

While every manager would prefer to report to the president of the company, because of the limits of span of control this is seldom possible. Only those in charge of the primary functions of the business—marketing, materials management, engineering, finance, manufacturing, and personnel—customarily report to the chief executive. Similarly, only the managers of the key functions of purchasing, material control, and traffic would report directly to the materials manager.

But there are exceptions. The materials manager may have lower ranking employees reporting to her as matter of convenience. These might include a secretary or administrative assistant, for example, or the manager of some activity that provides a service to the entire materials department—perhaps a clerical group that handles filing or provides stenographic services.

The materials manager may want to have a certain executive reporting directly to her because she wishes to give particular attention to a certain area. For example, suppose a company spends a larger percentage of its purchase volume on a key raw material—crude rubber in a tire company, cloth in a clothing company, crude petroleum in an oil refining company. The materials manager may want to have the buyer of the key material report directly to him, along with the purchasing agent, traffic manager, and others. Theoretically, the buyer of the critical material should report to the purchasing agent along with the rest of the company's buyers. But the material is so important that it is worth extra attention and also may be worth the skills of an extra-talented buyer who, in salary and responsibility if not in title or nominal authority, is every bit the equal of the purchasing agent.

APPLYING ORGANIZATION PRINCIPLES

The materials organizations of the Lycoming Division of the Avco Manufacturing Company and the Jet Engine Division of the General Electric Company provide excellent examples for applying the basic principles of organization. They are similar in many ways. Both make aircraft engines. Each has a materials manager responsible for most phases of materials management. Each is too big to be typical, having several hundred persons in its materials department (although the organization structure of either could be satisfactorily adapted to a company with only a few hundred employees).

Despite these similarities, their materials organization structures are quite different. In the Avco organization, division of work by function is emphasized. In the GE organization, it is mostly by product.

The Avco-Lycoming Organization

The director of materials reports to the general manager of the Lycoming Division of Avco Manufacturing Co. (see Figure 4–7). Division of responsibility at this level is by function; the materials director is responsible for all materials management functions in the plant.

Managers of the four major materials activities at Lycoming—purchasing, expediting, traffic and transportation, and material control—report to the director of materials. Thus, division of responsibility is on a functional basis also at this level. The organization of the departments headed by these four managers is discussed below.

Purchasing. Reporting to the purchasing manager is a purchasing agent for production materials and another for nonproduction materials. One purchasing agent is responsible for all the parts and materials directly incorporated into the plant's products, the other for all the materials and services used in manufacturing and administration. Thus division of responsibility is essentially by product.

This is also true at the buyer level in the organization. The principle of commodity specialization is followed as much as possible. Each buyer handles a group of commodities (not shown on the chart in Figure 4–7). For example, one buyer may handle castings, another machined parts, and so on. With this type of organization, which is almost universally used in purchasing departments, buyers can become more familiar with suppliers, costs, manufacturing processes, and so on of the commodities in which they specialize. They can keep informed on all new technological and economic developments in their specialties.

A third person reporting directly to the purchasing manager (in addition to the two purchasing agents) is the office manager. His department handles all filing, typing, and miscellaneous clerical chores for the purchasing department. It frees the buying groups as much as possible from clerical duties, so they can concentrate their efforts on the buying process itself. Thus there is a functional division of the buying job, since much of the clerical phase is handled by a separate group. Lycoming feels this boosts efficiency. Routine clerical jobs can be more closely controlled if they are supervised by someone who is not distracted by other duties. In addition, certain records, such as copies of the purchase orders issued, must be kept centrally for the

FIGURE 4-7

Division of work in the materials department of the Lycoming Division, Avco Manufacturing Co., is almost entirely by function. Managers of the four subdepartments divide work by function; division of work at lower levels is also predominantly by function.

entire department, so the work must be organized on a department-wide basis.

Expediting. Many materials organizations do not have expediting departments. They consider expediting a basic part of the buyer's job and believe that the responsibility does not end until acceptable material is actually delivered from the supplier. Buyers retain basic responsibility for on-time delivery of purchased material at Lycoming, but a separate expediting department helps them with the clerical chores of expediting—another case of division of work by function. The expediting group is divided into three sections: vendor expediting, shop expediting on purchased parts, and office.

The division of work between vendor expediting and shop expediting is essentially by stage of manufacture. The vendor-expediting group deals with the supplier before the purchased part is manufactured or delivered. Shop expediting takes over when the part is delivered to the Avco receiving desk. If a part is on the critical shortage list, the shop expediter speeds its movement through inspection to the area in the plant where it is needed.

The office group in the expediting department is like its counterpart in purchasing. It handles typing, filing, and so on, as a functional subdivision of the overall expediting job.

Traffic and transportation. The traffic and transportation department is divided by function into its three basic sections: dispatching and drivers of company-owned cars and trucks, classifying and routing of inbound shipments from suppliers, and reservations. The first group operates the company's trucks. The second handles the conventional traffic department jobs: selecting common carriers and routes for inbound shipments and tracing shipments when necessary. The third group makes plane and hotel reservations for company executives when they travel.

Material control. The eight groups within the material control department at Avco-Lycoming reflect a combination of the stage-of-manufacture and the functional approaches to organization.

The requirements and schedules group translates customer orders into requirements for parts and materials. The planning group translates these requirements into purchase requisitions, taking account of quantities currently in inventory and on order. The receiving department unloads purchased material when it is delivered and issues a receiving report. The warehousing group stores material until it is needed. The shop-expediting group coordinates shortages that develop within manufacturing (i.e., when one manufacturing operation gets behind schedule and holds up the succeeding operation). The materials handling group is responsible for moving materials in manufacturing from operation to operation. The subcontract-materials group is responsible for seeing that major subcontracted assemblies are available on schedule for final assembly, and the shipping group is responsible for packaging and shipping the finished product.

Thus there is a separate group for each stage in the materials process. However, the organization is also functional, since each group performs a basic function in the overall materials job.

Although it is not shown on the chart, there is further functional division of responsibility within the material control department. For example, as with purchasing and expediting, separate little groups in planning and other sections within the material control department handle various specialized activities, such as typing and filing.

The General Electric approach

In most of its operating departments, General Electric Company has materials organizations that resemble Avco-Lycoming's with managers of purchasing, production control, traffic, and value analysis reporting to the plant material manager. However, General Electric used a slightly different approach to materials management in its Evendale, Ohio, jet engine plant. Reporting to the plant's materials manager were materials supervisors who were in charge of materials management for each of the plant's major products. Also reporting to him were a purchasing agent, a supervisor of shipping, receiving, and stores, and two staff supervisors (see Figure 4–8). The purchasing

FIGURE 4–8

The materials department of the Jet Engine Division of General Electric is organized by product as much as possible. Materials supervisors handled all phases of materials management for each product. Division of work at the lower levels is also by product or type of material.

agent was in charge of buying all items used throughout the plant (maintenance supplies, stationery, etc.). The staff assistants handled systems and procedures, manufacturing programming, records, and so on.

Product groups. The unique feature of this organization is division of work into product groups. Each group was responsible for all phases of materials management for a particular product including:

1. Get basic requirements and design data from engineering.
2. Locate supply sources.
3. Determine required delivery dates and purchase quantities necessary to meet the requirements of the overall program.
4. Place orders.
5. Expedite and follow up with suppliers to make sure that delivery promises are kept.
6. Maintain necessary property and inventory control records.
7. Schedule assembly buildups in the plant and handle necessary liaison on engine-test programs.

Thus each group was responsible for virtually all phases of materials management except shipping, receiving, and stores, and nonproduction buying. These remain centralized and continue to serve the entire plant.

Within the product groups, the same organization approach is used. "Materials specialists," who report to the supervisor of the product group, are responsible for various groups of commodities. Each has overall materials management responsibility and is assisted by clerical help.

The major difference between this organization and the more conventional materials organization represented by Avco is in the emphasis on functional specialization. At Avco, materials management is regarded as a series of related, but functionally distinct, activities. In the GE Jet Engine Division, materials management was regarded as a separate and almost indivisible function. Each materials specialist was a small-scale materials manager. Clerical and nonclerical phases on the job are separated when the materials specialist delegates work to clerks, but no effort is made to distinguish the functions of materials management—buying, expediting, material control, and so on.

While both the General Electric and Avco organizations have subsequently been modified to reflect changes in products, processes, and markets, each represents a model of an organizational approach that has been adopted by hundreds of other companies. The GE approach is the more innovative but the Avco example is the one that is more typical and probably works best for most organizations.

Applications to service industries

An airline. While materials management is primarily associated with manufacturing organizations such as General Electric and Avco, a surprising amount of materials management is also needed in large service organizations. For example, while United Air Lines's end product is a service, maintenance of its equipment takes on much of the character of a manufacturing operation. At its San Francisco maintenance base, United maintains an inventory of more than 100,000 different items used for both routine repairs and general overhauls of its equipment.

The materials organization (see Figure 4–9) at the San Francisco base follows roughly the same pattern as that of a manufacturing organization. The director of supply acts as materials manager. His purchasing manager heads a 127-person department that is primarily concerned with buying various types of spare parts. Buying responsibility is broken down into four product groups with separate managers for power plant parts, air frames, accessories, and equipment. The assistant to the purchasing manager is also responsible for traffic. A 291-person stores organization is responsible for receiving, storage, and shipping and a 63-person materials identification group is concerned

FIGURE 4–9

Materials management at San Francisco maintenance base of United Air Lines is organized much like a manufacturing organization, even though United's end product is transportation service.

with other problems of material control. The United materials organization is "unconventional" in just two major respects: (1) there is no production control department because the base does no manufacturing, and (2) the industrial engineering manager reports to the director of supply, whereas in a manufacturing firm he would report to the manufacturing manager.

A large hospital. The materials management organization of a hospital is also quite different from that of a typical manufacturer. Like his industrial counterpart, the hospital materials manager is responsible for conventional purchasing and stores operations, but he also adds value by manufacture to purchased material when this is necessary to put it into usable form. For example, the organization chart in Figure 4–10 indicates that the materials manager is responsible not only for purchasing and stores but also for central supply, the laundry, and the print shop. Each of these departments is a manufacturing operation in the economic sense. Central supply sterilizes dressings and other supplies that must be free from bacterial contamination. The laundry

FIGURE 4-10

Materials management in a large hospital might embrace not only the obvious supply functions but also the hospital's "manufacturing" operations. In this example, these are the print shop and the laundry.

and print shop represent "make" decisions for goods and services that would otherwise be purchased and are linked to materials management organization both because of this complementary relationship to purchasing and because there is no other organizational niche in the hospital that is more compatible than materials management.

Materials management control of transportation is also partly a matter of organizational convenience. Transportation obviously does not belong in such hospital departments as nursing, dietary, and accounting. It fits in with materials management more closely than any other major activity in the hospital, and, in fact, there is a direct relationship between the hospital transportation function and the stores activities. The stores department is normally responsible for delivering materials from the storeroom to nursing stations throughout the hospital. In some hospitals, the stores facilities may be located some distance from the hospital premises—either because the hospital is already over-crowded or because warehouse space can be rented off the hospital site at much lower cost than buildings can be constructed on the site. The materials manager with an off-premises storeroom cannot possibly operate without at least one delivery truck, and typically he finds himself in charge of all of the hospital's automotive and materials-handling equipment. In this way, the materials manager can become responsible for all hospital activities relating to transportation, including such things as the hospital's internal message and mail service.

THE DECENTRALIZED ORGANIZATION

As the above examples illustrate, the materials management organization is flexible and can be adapted to suit the specialized needs of any profit or nonprofit institution. Any of the organizational forms discussed can also be expanded almost indefinitely to fit very large as well as smaller institutions.

The expansion process is quite simple. Each supervisor adds subordinates until the limits of his span of control are reached. Then another layer of supervision is added. When these new supervisors reach the limits of their span of control, still another layer of supervision is added.

For example, the purchasing department at Avco's Lycoming Division (see Figure 4-7) can be doubled by increasing the purchasing manager's span of supervision from two purchasing agents to four. It could be redoubled by adding a new level of supervision. Each purchasing agent would hire two assistant purchasing agents, each of whom would supervise a department identical to that formerly supervised directly by the purchasing agent.

Many small firms have grown to giant corporations by following this process. Eventually they may wind up with an organization 12 or 13 levels deep. The organization becomes cumbersome and bureaucratic. It responds slowly to change, and there is ample red tape in even the simplest transactions.

Managements of giant corporations lick the problem of size with decentralization. They break up the corporation into a number of smaller divisional units, each of which operates as a semi-independent business. Decentralization has many advantages. It brings managers closer to the objectives of the business, permits tighter control of costs, and provides a better environment for training future managers. It also helps stimulate improvements in products and methods.

Diluted buying power. Decentralization, however, creates a major materials management problem: diluted buying power. One of the advantages of a big corporation over a smaller one is its greater buying power. Big buyers can purchase in carload lots; in some cases they can buy a major proportion of or even the total output of supplier factories. With this buying power, they can get big price concessions. In addition, vendors often provide superior quality, delivery, and service to their very biggest customers.

With decentralization, management faces a dilemma. Should it go only part way and continue to have a headquarters buying staff responsible for all major purchases? Or should it completely decentralize the materials activities along with the rest of the organization? With the former approach, it preserves its buying power. With the latter, it gives the managers of the decentralized "little businesses" authority over all phases of their operations, including materials management. This is consistent with the management principle that you cannot hold a manager responsible for profits unless he has authority over all phases of the operation.

Only a few giant corporations operate with a single, highly centralized buying department. A few others are highly decentralized, with a number of buying departments completely independent of one another. Usually corporations that use similar or identical parts or materials at a number of plants tend to have a centralized buying organization to exploit their buying power. For example, most chemical, steel, and petroleum companies have a centralized buying organization, both to permit corporationwide buying of key raw materials and to facilitate handling of reciprocity problems. On the other hand, those that make a number of products with little resemblance to one another tend to have a decentralized buying organization. Good examples are the Borg-Warner Corporation and American Machine & Foundry. Both companies have buying departments in each of their divisions that operate independently. It is significant that both make a wide variety of products, most of which are unrelated to one another in terms of technology and markets.

Staff-and-line approach

Most major companies compromise: they try to get the advantages of both centralization and decentralization. They do this with the so-called staff-and-line approach (see Figure 4–11). At the top of the materials management organization is a corporate staff, often headed by a corporate director of purchases or materials manager. At this level, division of responsibility is by function. The materials manager, who often is a vice president, reports to the president or executive vice president. Usually strictly a staff executive, he or she is responsible for overall materials policies and plans but has no responsibility for the basic line activities of materials management.

Directly responsible for line activities are materials managers in each plant or division. These managers usually do not report to the corporate materials executive, although they do rely on her for advice on corporate-wide buying policies and procedures and for assistance on special problems. They report directly to the general managers of their respective plants or divisions, which is consistent with the principle of making the general managers responsible for every phase of their job.

With the staff-and-line organization, most of the advantages of centralized buying are preserved. The corporate purchasing staff is able to consolidate purchases of all items used by a number of plants in order to get the lowest possible prices. Usually it makes overall contracts directly; occasionally it restricts itself only to making available information on savings that might be made if the plants choose to pool their buying power.

Materials staffs' activities

Although the corporate materials manager in a big corporation does not supervise the plant materials managers directly, he usually has a small staff under his direct supervision. The staff provides specialized

FIGURE 4–11
Staff-and-line organizations

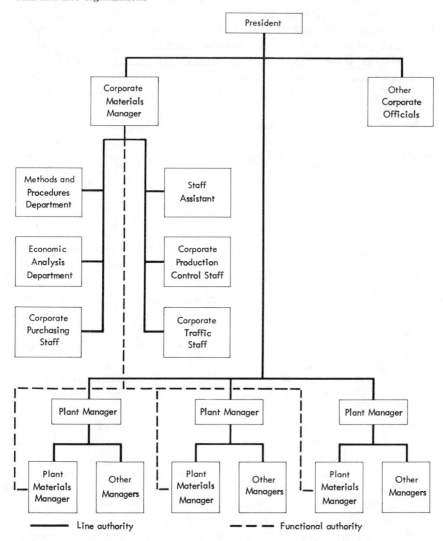

The staff-and-line approach to organization is widely used in very large corporations. A corporate materials manager coordinates policy and functionally supervises plant materials managers, who report directly to their respective plant managers.

services to both the plant materials managers and top management. Among its major services are value analysis, administrative planning, economic analysis, and electronic data processing.

Value analysis. Value analysis refers to a series of techniques that are designed to reduce costs. The value analyst is a specialist with substantial training in engineering, cost estimating, and manufacturing methods. The value analyst assists buyers and others in the materials organization with cost-reduction projects.

Administrative planning. The overall materials cycle is complex. Procedures, policies, and organization structures must be planned carefully. Records must be kept of the performance of every materials executive in every plant. Training programs must be administered. Budgetary controls are necessary. All these jobs and many others can be handled by a competent administrative assistant to the materials manager.

Economic analysis. When and how much should a company buy? How much inventory should it carry? The answers to these questions depend on more than just the company's internal costs. They depend also on the external economic environment and on the trend of both overall and individual prices and costs. Economic analysis is essential in modern materials management, and a staff economist or statistician can provide invaluable assistance to the materials manager.

Electronic data processing. It is a rare materials organization that has its own computer or even does its own programming. These responsibilities are usually delegated for the entire organization to a specialized department on the controller's staff. Nevertheless, an increasing number of materials managers have at least one computer specialist on their staff who combines knowledge of computers with materials management. This specialist can work out computer problems and also suggest new EDP applications for materials management.

Other specialists. These four types of staff specialist are the most common in industrial materials organizations. However, there are many others.

A number of big companies with thousands of suppliers have staff specialists handling vendor-relations problems. These specialists investigate complaints from suppliers who feel they have not been treated fairly by company buyers and also do everything they can to bolster supplier goodwill.

Many large companies find it convenient to have field expediters in key cities where there are a number of suppliers. These specialists expedite items in short supply for any buyer requesting their services. They investigate new suppliers, and they also help to get information about quality problems. Because they serve the entire materials department, they must report directly to the director of materials management or to one of his immediate assistants.

Results of staff-and-line organization

Breaking a department into staff-and-line activities provides additional functional specialization. Skilled specialists can be hired to serve the entire materials department. In addition, staff work provides excellent training for high-potential junior executives. They can be exposed to top-level decision making without the company's having to suffer the consequences of their mistakes.

The staff executive almost always has problems. To get anything done, she must work through line personnel and persuade them to cooperate. With strong staff employees, dual subordination frequently results, that is, the line supervisor winds up reporting to both a staff executive and a line executive. Some writers on management charge that since staff has no real responsibility to contribute directly to the objectives of the business, it is inherently wasteful.

THE ORGANIZATION OF THE FUTURE

The staff specialist often gradually takes on "line" powers. The computer has made it easier for large organizations to centralize materials management decision making. As a result, the stage is set for conflict between decentralized divisional management which is supposedly responsible for all facets of the division's operations, including materials management, a corporate materials management staff which can often buy more effectively on a corporationwide basis.

Nevertheless, materials management is still mostly a divisional-level activity in large organizations. The divisional materials manager reports either directly to the division's general manager or to some other manager who, in turn, reports to the general manager. Among manufacturing companies, about half of the divisional materials managers report (not through any choice of their own) to the manufacturing manager, while most of the others report to the general manager. Their organization structures resemble those illustrated in this chapter, with variations that primarily reflect differences in industry.

Cases

CASE 4-1. ALABAMA AIRCRAFT CORPORATION

Organizing for a new product line

Alabama Aircraft Corporation was founded in 1928. It has always specialized in fighter planes for the U.S. Air Force, and its products served the country well in both World War II and the Korean War. By 1959, the company employed 8,000 workers and its sales were almost $200 million. The company now faces one of the major turning points in its history. New orders for military aircraft are off sharply because of the growing use of missiles instead of fighter planes. Although the company may continue to produce airplanes indefinitely, management doubts that its airplane business will ever be as good as it once was. Missile orders will take up part of the slack, but the company will still be left with a tremendous unused investment in facilities and equipment to fabricate aluminum and steel.

Fortunately, the company's engineers had some advance warning of this problem and have been working for several years on a host of new products designed to fill the gap left by a slowdown of the aircraft business. Among these products are prefabricated aluminum highway bridges, house trailers, and a line of aluminum boats.

Alabama's marketing department expects that these new products will account for 25 percent of the company's sales volume almost immediately and will ultimately account for as much as 50 percent. The company already has substantial contracts with distributors and mailorder houses for some of these products, and it is convinced that the others will gain rapid acceptance. It anticipates few problems in selling products as long as its prices are competitive, but costs are a major problem. The company is used to producing aircraft-quality components where it would willingly pay as much as $1 for a simple bolt manufactured to aircraft standards. Now it must manufacture to entirely different standards and cannot afford to spend more than 5 cents for a bolt that would superficially look not much different from an aircraft bolt even if it were made from lower cost materials to looser tolerances.

Harry Spooner, the company's materials manager, anticipates that an entirely different approach to materials management may be necessary if the company is to keep its costs in line. He believes that an entirely different group of suppliers may be needed for the company's new civilian products. Aircraft suppliers are used to such high-quality standards that they may not be able to cut prices enough to compete for civilian business.

Spooner is also apprehensive about quality problems on the new line. He fears that Alabama's quality control department is so indoctrinated with aircraft quality standards that it will reject components from his new suppliers. He knows that although instruments can be used to measure quality objectively on certain dimensions, quality is at least partly a matter of the inspector's judgment. If inspectors apply their aircraft background to civilian parts, they may set such high standards that Spooner will be forced to pay higher prices. Since purchases will comprise about 60 cents out of every sales dollar on the civilian line (about the same ratio as the military line), obviously the company cannot afford to pay higher prices for components than its competitors do. On the other hand, if the company's inspectors set realistic quality standards for the new products, they may get too lax for the company's military line.

Spooner is responsible to management for meeting cost objectives on the new product line. However, he is virtually at the mercy of the quality control department in achieving them, since with a high reject rate he will have to insist that vendors institute more rigid controls over their manufacturing processes and inspect outgoing shipments more carefully. Inevitably, he will have to pay for this extra work.

Spooner believes that the best solution to the problem is to set up a separate receiving inspection department under his control that is staffed with inspectors who will work exclusively on the new product line. Currently, Spooner has a conventional materials organization. Reporting to him are managers of traffic, production control, and purchasing. The traffic department, the smallest of the three, has six transportation specialists working on routing, tracing shipments, and so on. In addition, the traffic manager supervises a foreman, who in turn supervises the company's trucks and drivers. The production control manager has seven supervisors reporting directly to him. One supervises shipping, receiving, and nonproduction storerooms; others supervise production raw materials, purchased parts, and a "bond room" in which parts are stored after they have passed inspection; and there is a supervisor in charge of in-process materials in each of the plant's main manufacturing areas. The purchasing agent supervises five senior buyers, each of whom specializes in a given group of commodities. Working for each senior buyer are three to six buyers, each of whom supervises an expediter and a secretary.

While Spooner is convinced that receiving inspection for the new line should be under his jurisdiction rather than that of the company's quality control manager, he is less certain about how he should reorganize his department to handle the new product line. Moreover, he believes that changes will be necessary, particularly in the purchasing department, where he would like buyers to be more price-conscious on the new line.

Questions

1. Should management accept Spooner's recommendation that a new receiving inspection department be established for the new line and be put under the materials manager's jurisdiction? What are the pros and cons? What are the alternatives?
2. How should the materials department be reorganized to cope with the new product? Support your recommendation with a new organization chart.

CASE 4–2. ALBERT ELECTRONICS CORPORATION

Centralized versus decentralized materials management

Albert Electronics is a New England firm that has gradually grown until it presently operates more than 20 plants from coast to coast. Last year's sales were more than $200 million, up 10 percent from the previous year. The company has hit a new sales record in nine of the last ten years, but profits have not kept pace. The company earned nearly $8 million after taxes six years ago, when its sales were only $100 million. Last year it earned only $10 million. A 100 percent increase in sales has brought a mere 20 percent increase in profits during a period when the company has also almost doubled its investment in plant and equipment.

This year the outlook is even bleaker. Dan Watson, vice president in charge of finance, predicts that profits will actually drop off a little even though sales are scheduled to rise to about $220 million. In addition, the company is going to need more money to finance the extra inventories required by expanded sales. Current inventories total about $24 million. Watson estimates that they will give rise to $27 million, and the company's cash position will tighten so much that it will have to draw on its line of credit at several large banks.

The company has grown so rapidly that it has been forced to rely on outside suppliers for an abnormally large part—68 percent—of its sales dollar. It has a small top-management staff consisting of a president, two executive vice presidents, vice presidents in charge of sales, engineering, manufacturing, personnel, and finance, and a small group to assist these top officials. The two executive vice presidents each supervise 10 of the company' 20 plant managers. The other vice presidents have no direct responsibility for operations but serve primarily in an advisory and policy-making capacity in their specialties.

Each of the company's plants is responsible for making its own purchases. Organizations within the plants vary, since Karl Albert, the founder of the company, believes in giving his plant managers maximum autonomy so long as they achieve their profit objectives. In most cases the plant materials management job is divided among a purchasing department, a traffic department, and a production control department. Typically the purchasing agent reports directly to the plant manager, while the production control manager and the traffic manager report to the plant's manufacturing manager. However, in the largest plant (the Cleveland Works), which has a purchase volume of nearly $50 million, there is a materials manager who reports to the plant manager. This materials manager supervises separate production control, purchasing, and traffic departments.

No formal efforts are made to coordinate companywide purchases. However, the Cleveland Works materials manager has made some informal efforts. Because his volume is so much greater than that of any other plant, he can sometimes get special concessions from suppliers on various mill supplies and other nonproduction materials. When he gets an especially good deal, he sends a memo to the purchasing agents of the other plants so they can call the supplier and demand the same terms on the basis of being part of the same corporation as the Cleveland Works. No one knows how many plant purchasing agents have taken advantage of these occasional opportunities.

Albert is becoming concerned because, while the company is successful in expanding its sales, its profit margin has gotten progressively narrower and now even total profits are threatening to drop off. He has engaged Merrill, Johnson & Connors, management engineers, to study the problem. In its preliminary report, Merrill, Johnson & Connors has suggested that a detailed study be made of the company's purchasing operations. Since the company spends nearly $140 million on purchases, it pointed out that relatively small improvements in this area can have a considerable effect on the company's overall profits. It believes that substantial savings could be made by consolidating purchases of certain materials.

Questions

1. Suppose you were a consultant working for Merrill, Johnson & Connors. What changes would you recommend in Albert Electronics' approach to purchasing?
2. Draw a new organization chart in which you show your suggested changes in the purchasing organization.
3. Compare the relative merits of the present completely decentralized purchasing organization at Albert Electronics with those of a completely centralized organization.

5

Legal aspects of materials management

(handwritten annotation: Company liable for mistakes not the agents)

A corporation is an artificial person. It can't talk or think. But it can own property and enter into contracts. The person who acts for the corporation is an *agent*. The directors of the corporation give power to the chief executive officer to act as the corporation's agent. Contracts involving purchases are then normally delegated to another person who is traditionally called the purchasing *agent*. This person can enter into purchase contracts on behalf of the corporation without incurring any legal liability himself. He or she deals with other agents, usually sales managers, who have been delegated power by their corporate chief executive officers to act as agents in committing their organizations to sell materials.

BASICS OF CONTRACTS

The process whereby individuals buy and sell on behalf of corporations is made legal by the law of agency, which in English-speaking countries evolved as part of the common law, a partly unwritten code that reflects over hundreds of years the decisions of sovereigns and courts. Common law, in turn, has been modified in many ways by specific statute enacted by legislative bodies. In the United States (as in every other English-speaking country), the common law as applied to business has been substantially altered by what in the United States is called the Uniform Commercial Code—a standardized set of rules governing how business is conducted in almost every state.

Uniform Commercial Code

Application. Purchasing managers are especially concerned with that part of the Code that is concerned with sales contracts. Other parts

114

of the Code cover commercial paper, bank deposits and collections, letters of credit, bulk transfers, warehouse receipts and bills of lading, investment securities, and secured transactions—sales of accounts and chattel paper. The Code is a body of law passed by state legislatures and is designed to create completely consistent ground rules for business transactions in every state. The Code varies somewhat word for word among most states but it is reasonably consistent. Differences in the Code that do exist are not significant enough to affect routine business transactions. Louisiana—whose legal tradition is French, not English—has adopted only parts of the Code.

In general, if there are no specific provisions in a contract that would override the Code or if there is no specific statute, then the Code can be presumed to apply. In the discussion that follows, we will be concerned with the law of contracts essentially as it is defined by the Code. Readers should note, however, that any government body can modify the rules for doing business within its jurisdiction provided it does not conflict with the laws of some higher government body.

Commonsense rule.   Despite the enormous progress made by the Code in creating a consistent set of rules, it is highly likely that a buyer who does business on both a national and an international scale will not be familiar with every law that can affect his or her purchases. If a contract is sufficiently important, the buyer will wish to consult with an attorney before going ahead. However, the buyer is usually on safe ground if she expresses needs in plain simple English and insists that differences in contract terms and provisions be resolved with the supplier in writing before going ahead. In most cases, only the buyer or seller trying to be too clever, or being just plain sloppy, will become embroiled in subsequent legal problems. And, of course, regardless of the law, there is no substitute for dealing with suppliers who have established their business and personal integrity.

Elements of contract

Each purchase order that the purchasing manager approves is a contract. The purchasing manager can readily get advice from the company's legal staff on any special problems that arise. But since he does approve more than 99 percent of the contracts into which the company enters, he should be familiar with the general principles of contract law.

The basic steps in making a purchase contract are quite simple:

1. Each verbal or written quotation by a supplier is an offer to sell, which is usually subject to acceptance at the time the buyer issues the purchase order.
2. Each purchase order either is an acceptance of the seller's offer, or

Both Buyer & Seller has to agree to the terms

if its terms and conditions differ somewhat from the supplier's quotation, is in effect a counteroffer. If a purchase order is simply sent to a supplier who has not made an offer, the order itself is an offer to buy subject to acceptance by the seller.

3. Each acknowledgment of a purchas order by the seller confirms the contract and makes it binding, provided that the seller accepts all of the terms and conditions of the order. If the seller takes exception to any of them, she is in effect making a counteroffer, which must be accepted by the buyer before the contract is binding. If the seller does not acknowledge the order formally, she does so informally when she complies with its terms and ships the goods or services the order calls for.

4. Every purchase order change subsequently agreed to by buyer and seller becomes a part of the purchase contract.

Possible disputes

Nonperformance. Disagreement comes about from nonperformance of any of the contract terms by either party. From the seller's point of view, the dispute is most likely to be concerned with payment, and we will discuss problems in pricing in subsequent paragraphs. From the buyer's point of view, price also can be a matter of dispute. But equally important is nonperformance arising from factors other than price. The supplier simply does not do what it allegedly agreed to do. In some cases, the material is defective. In other cases, there is no performance at all; that is, the supplier agrees to furnish some item but doesn't.

Under common law, the buyer has two choices in cases of nonperformance: suit for cash damages or suit in equity. In the former instance, a court determines the economic damage suffered by the buyer and orders the seller to pay it. For example, a court might determine that a buyer suffered a loss of $1,000 as a result of a supplier failure and therefore orders that amount to be paid by the seller to the buyer. In equity suits, the seller must somehow provide what was contracted for. For example, suppose that a supplier of widgets defaults on a contract because its machine broke down. Under common law, the court might order the seller to go out and buy widgets from someone else in order to honor the commitment made in the original contract.

The common law is modified by the Uniform Commercial Code. The seller is excused from contract obligation provided that performance becomes impossible as a result of conditions that could not be foreseen by either buyer or seller. These conditions might include such events as an outbreak of war, a natural disaster, or the like. Sellers also may explicitly protect themselves with what are called *force majeure* clauses, which relieve them of the obligation to perform on contracts under conditions where forces largely beyond their control prevent performance. For example, the Uniform Commercial Code probably would not relieve a supplier of an obligation to its customers in the event of a strike by its employees. However, companies subject to labor disputes usually insert clauses that relieve them of their legal obligations to their customers when their employees do strike.

Although buyers routinely have disagreements with their suppliers over both price and performance on contracts, they usually are resolved by amicable negotiation. If both buyer and seller try to be fair in their dealings, at least 99 percent of all possible problems are solved in advance. In fact, many organizations do not even bother to have terms and conditions in their purchase orders.

Arbitration. However, if they do disagree and cannot resolve the problem themselves, they may call on an impartial arbitrator for help, selecting him from detailed listings supplied by the American Arbitration Association. The arbitrator is sometimes an attorney but, in many cases, is simply an unbiased expert who has had substantial experience with problems similar to the issue in dispute. An arbitration hearing resembles a lawsuit in that both parties present arguments, and they are often represented by attorneys. However, arbitration is both cheaper and faster than a lawsuit. The hearings are not public, so trade secrets can be protected. In addition, complicated commercial problems can often be settled more equitably if they are reviewed by a technically qualified arbitrator than would be possible in a lawsuit where neither judge nor jury would have the technical qualifications needed for an objective evaluation of the case.

The ruling of an arbitrator is not legally binding under common law. Either party may still sue if not satisfied with the ruling. However, common law has been superseded by arbitration statutes in almost all of the major industrial states. The statutes make the arbitrator's ruling legally binding on both parties once they agree to submit their cases to an arbitrator who is mutually acceptable. Agreement to arbitrate may be reached on a case-by-case basis, but many firms include an arbitration clause in their purchase contracts. The following standard arbitration clause is recommended by the American Arbitration Association:

> Any controversy or claim arising out of or relating to this contract, or the breach thereof, shall be settled by arbitration in accordance with the Rules of the American Arbitration Association, and judgment upon the award rendered by the Arbitrator(s) may be entered in any Court having jurisdiction thereof.

Disputes with government. Contract disputes involving the federal government may also be arbitrated if both parties agree. In fact, the federal government's approach to procurement is necessarily much more legalistic than that of private firms. Procurement officials are governed by thousands of regulations (the Armed Services Procurement Regulations alone consist of more than 3,000 pages), and their every action must be within the precise letter of the law. Contractors sometimes find to their dismay that government agencies refuse to relax even the most insignificant regulations. For example, if a government invitation to bid has a deadline of noon June 21, then the firm that delivers its bid at 12:01 P.M. may find itself out of luck even if it is the low bidder.

The government is also "sovereign" and, in theory, cannot be sued. In practice, however, government purchasing officials must behave as if they were subject to the Uniform Commercial Code, and a supplier that feels it has been treated unlawfully can press its claim in the courts.

Law of agency

A corporation can sue and be sued because of the law of agency. This permits a person (or agent) to make contracts on its behalf without incurring any personal liability. The president of a corporation (both profit and nonprofit) has this power to act as agent. However, if the corporation has more than a handful of employees, the power is almost always delegated to other officials, who usually are not officers of the corporation. A purchasing agent is empowered to buy on behalf of the corporation while a sales manager is normally able to enter into agreements to sell on behalf of the corporation.

Who is agent? In numerous cases, courts have been forced to determine whether or not an enforceable contract was entered into by bona fide agents of the corporation. The general rule is to assume that the agreement is not binding until it is approved by either an officer of the corporation or the appropriate sales manager or purchasing agent. Thus, if an individual is told by an automobile salesperson that there will be a $1,000 allowance on an old car that is being traded in, this "deal" is probably not binding until it has been approved by the sales manager.

However, the courts have also held that almost anyone can be an agent who (1) behaves like an agent, and (2) that there is ample reason to believe the person is an agent because of previous behavior. The bona fide agent who meets these qualifications need not even be an employee of the organization if these criteria are met. For example, physicians are hardly ever employees of the hospitals in which they work. Yet they have been known to order equipment and supplies on behalf of the hospital, occasionally without having obtained concurrence from the hospital's administrator or purchasing manager, who are bona fide agents. Does the hospital have to accept this purchase? The answer is definitely no—provided it has never accepted the physician as a bona fide purchasing agent in the past and has given no indication that it intends to do so in the future.

Written definition.   In order to eliminate the possibility that it will be liable for contracts entered into by unauthorized persons, every corporation should define in writing precisely who is authorized to act as agent and make this information readily available to suppliers and/or customers.

If, on the other hand, a corporation tacitly accepts contracts made by persons not officially designated as its agents, it is responsible for the actions of these persons provided the other party to the contract acted in good faith. For example, corporations sometimes permit mainte-nance craftsmen to order spare parts or materials directly from suppliers without going through the purchasing department. In such cases, the craftsman becomes a bona fide agent even if the written procedures of the corporation limit purchasing authority to the pur-chasing agent.

The vendors who deal with the craftsman have accepted his orders in good faith. Their invoices have been honored, and they can quite rightly maintain that a future order should be treated as a valid contract—even if the institution has decided that it does not want the craftsman to make this particular purchase. Thus, it is important that the buying organization act promptly to restrain the unauthorized per-sons in its own organization when they attempt to enter into contracts with suppliers. The simplest procedure is simply to insist that all pur-chases be made by the officially authorized purchasing department and to adhere to this rule with no exceptions.

Control.   For this reason, it is hardly surprising that all well-run organizations take steps to prevent the power of agency from being delegated too freely. They warn suppliers that only commitments made by authorized agents will be honored and act immediately to prevent employees from functioning as unauthorized agents.

In fact, big companies usually establish internal procedures so that the power to act as buying agent is not delegated too freely even among members of the purchasing department. Typically, the proce-dure places dollar limits on the buying power of various organizational levels within the purchasing department. For example, one big com-pany permits its assistant purchasing agent to commit the company for as much as $25,000. Orders in the $25,000 to $50,000 range must be signed by the purchasing agent; those in the $50,000 to $100,000 cate-gory by the vice president of purchases; and those over $100,000 must carry the signature of the company's chief executive officer.

A company may wish to protect itself against commitments by lower echelon purchasing personnel by notifying suppliers that only certain persons have been delegated the power of agency. In practice, this may not be necessary. Lower level purchasing personnel obey the rules anyway, and suppliers are usually well informed on the real sources of buying authority.

OFFERS, ACCEPTANCE, PERFORMANCE

Consideration

Under common law, a contract is made when one party makes an offer and the other party accepts it. When the contract is in writing, it usually becomes binding when it is officially signed by both parties and the seals of the contracting parties are attached to the agreement. If the contract is oral, some form of "consideration" must pass before it is binding. As the term suggests, cash is the most common form of consideration, and sometimes oral agreements are concluded by passing a nominal amount of cash from one party to another—$1 or even 1 cent.

In some cases, courts have held that such nominal consideration is inadequate. In fact, consideration need not be cash at all. A contract has adequate consideration if something of value has been given up. For example, if a buyer calls a supplier and agrees to buy 100 feet of pipe, this commitment alone probably constitutes adequate consideration. In accepting the buyer's offer, the supplier has given up its opportunity to sell that same pipe to the next buyer who calls, and its loss could well be real if the buyer later wishes to renege on the contract.

Written versus oral contracts

Under common law, an oral contract for any amount is perfectly valid so long as (a) offer and acceptance are mirror images of one another, and (b) there is adequate consideration. The Uniform Commercial Code, however, changes the rules under which business agreements are offered and accepted in the United States, and there are comparable statutes in other countries. Moreover, any government body can pass laws that affect particular contracts that are made within its jurisdiction.

$500 oral limit. Under the Uniform Commercial Code, the Statute of Frauds provision states that a contract with a value of more than $500 is not enforceable unless there is written evidence that such a contract actually exists. However, an oral agreement with a value of over $500 may be valid under certain circumstances. Suppose, for example, that a buyer telephones a supplier with a $501 order, which the supplier than proceeds to fill without receiving written confirmation. Then suppose that either buyer or seller gets written confirmation of the contract from the other party and some key term of the agree-

ment is not acceptable. For example, the seller subsequently receives a purchase order from the buyer, and the price for the item is too low or perhaps specifications are excessively tight, from the seller's point of view. Or, more likely, the supplier simply bills the buyer, charging a price that is unacceptable. Is the contract binding? The Code says it is, provided that the other party does not object in writing within ten days.

Exception to $500 rule. The Code also says that oral contracts involving sums over $500 are binding if one of the following conditions applies:

1. The goods are made specifically to the buyer's order and are not readily salable to others. For example, suppose the buyer calls the supplier and says "make me up 100 widgets at $10 each, just like the ones you sold me last month, and start work on them right away." Then the buyer discovers that the widget business has dropped off sharply. She calls the supplier and orders work to be stopped. Her company now would be liable for the cost of work done up to that point and could not claim that the contract was not binding because it had not yet been put into writing. However, her company would not be liable for any work continued beyond the point when she advised the supplier that she was canceling the order.

2. Both parties behave as if a contract existed. Jane French, the buyer, orders over the telephone more than $500 worth of goods from Charles English, the supplier. English ships, invoices, and receives a check from French's firm. Neither French nor English can later claim that a contract did not exist because it was not in writing and its value exceeded $500. An oral contract over $500 would also be binding for the amount actually shipped if buyer or seller admits that the oral agreement was actually made.

3. The parties have always done business on an oral basis. If French consistently buys from English by telephoning an order, then neither could probably repudiate an oral agreement in excess of $500 provided the court was convinced that such a conversation did indeed take place.

Because of the difficulties in proving what was said in a conversation, the principle is obvious: there should be a written record confirming every transaction even were this not mandated by the Uniform Commercial Code.

Time constraints

Supplier's offer. However, written offers and acceptances do not have an infinite life. In most cases, a seller will specify that an offer is for immediate acceptance or set a particular time limit on its acceptance (usually 30 to 60 days). If nothing is said, however, the seller cannot assume that the offer is valid for a period of more than three months. Thus, there is no contract if French accepts on April 3 an open-ended offer made by English on January 2. English would have the option of either doing nothing or accepting what in effect has become French's offer.

Duration of contract. After buyer and seller enter into a binding contract, there still may be problems with time. If English accepts French's order and then simply does nothing, at what point in time is English in breach of contract and/or when does French have the right to cancel the order? A more common problem is that French orders 100 widgets and English ships 60. Must French accept a partial shipment? How long must she wait before she has the right to go and buy the 40 extra widgets from someone else?

The Code says (Section 2–307) that "unless otherwise agreed all goods called for by a contract for sale must be tendered in a single delivery. . . ." Thus, unless there is some specific provision to cover partial shipment, French is within her rights if she wishes to reject the shipment of 60 widgets. If she accepts the shipment, she must pay for the 60 widgets separately and not hold payment until the entire order for 100 is filled.

Partial shipments. What about the balance of the shipment? Or what happens if English does not ship at all when French expects him to? The Code says (Section 2–309) that "shipment or delivery or any other action under a contract . . . shall be [in] a reasonable time." The contract may then be terminated after some reasonable time. If English does not ship within a reasonable time, this becomes eventually a failure to perform. French may simply cancel the contract unilaterally.

Failure to perform

Buyer's remedy. The Code suggests other remedies when English fails to perform his obligations under the contract. French may (Section 2–712) "purchase goods in substitution for those due from seller" and ". . . recover from the seller as damages the difference between the cost of cover and the contract price together with any incidental or consequential damages . . . but less expenses saved in consequence of the seller's breach."

For example, if the widgets are a component of some more complex product that French's firm is committed to complete by a particular date, she has no choice but to buy these for the lowest price possible if English fails to deliver. The Code says that French then can recover from English any net excess costs incurred as a result of his failure.

Seller's loophole. English is not necessarily lost, however. His failure to perform may be due to circumstances over which he has no control. Section 2–615 of the Code gets him off the hook if performance "has been made impracticable by the occurrence of a contingency the non-occurrence of which was a basic assumption on which the contract was made . . . in good faith. . . ." Thus, English would definitely not be liable for failure to perform if subsequent governmental action made performance unlawful. This contingency would apply not only to English's ability to produce or market the widgets but also to their transport. Section 2–614 suggests that if a "commercially reasonable substitute is available" that permits English to perform, then it must be accepted by buyer or seller.

Westinghouse case.   In practice, the parts of the Code that permit nonperformance without damages have been broadly interpreted—not always successfully. For example, the Westinghouse Electric Company made contracts calling for the sale of hundreds of millions of dollars' worth of uranium to electric utilities at a price that proved to be roughly one fifth of market. Westinghouse's attorneys maintained that this enormous price change (which was a by-product of a quadrupling of crude oil prices) made performance impossible and, therefore, under the Code Westinghouse was not required to sell at what turned out to be a ridiculously low price. Westinghouse's case was never really tested in the courts. However, it was apparently strong enough so that the company was able to negotiate out-of-court settlements with the electric utilities at a fraction of the damages they claimed were the result of the breach of contract.

The moral is clear. While the buyer has the right under the Code to insist on performance of a contract except when it has become genuinely impossible, this right is not as enforceable as it appears to be—especially if the buyer's claim is so great that it imperils the economic survival of the seller.

Terms and conditions

UCC versus common law.   Every contract has a number of terms and conditions, both explicit and implicit. Under common law, as mentioned previously, the seller's offer and the buyer's acceptance must be mirror images of one another or there is no contract. Under the Uniform Commercial Code, there must be agreement on the main substance of the agreement, but other terms and conditions may be left dangling.

For example, if English offers to sell French 100 widgets at $1 each and French "accepts" English's offer and sends English a confirming order for ten widgets at $1 , English is not obliged to accept this order even if it is tendered promptly in response to his offer. There is a major difference. French's "acceptance" is really a counteroffer and would have to be acceptable to English, who could signify agreement simply by shipping the ten widgets. However, if English did not comply with this order for ten widgets, he could hardly be sued for breach of contract since no contract exists.

Additional terms. A contract may exist, however, if there are only minor differences between an offer and its acceptance. Section 2–207 of the Code says that . . . "a written confirmation which is sent within a reasonable time operates as an acceptance even though it states terms additional to or different from those offered or agreed upon, unless acceptance is expressly made conditional on assent to the additional or different terms."

The Code clarifies this by pointing out:

> The additional terms are to be construed as proposals for addition to the contract. Between merchants such terms become part of the contract unless:
> (a) the offer expressly limits acceptance to the terms of the offer;
> (b) they materially alter it; or
> (c) notification of objection to them has already been given or is given within a reasonable time after notice of them is received."

The Code also says that "conduct by both parties which recognizes the existence of a contract is sufficient to establish a contract for sale although the writings of the parties do not otherwise establish a contract."

Thus, if English received French's order for ten widgets at $1 after having quoted a price of $1 each for lots of 100, there would indeed be a contract provided he simply shipped her the ten widgets. Under common law, the price would presumably be $1. French made a counteroffer that English tacitly accepted when he shipped the ten widgets. As long as French acted in good faith, she could presumably keep the ten widgets provided she paid English $1 each for them—even though English subsequently invoices French $2 each for the widgets (maintaining that his costs were higher when shipping in small lots).

Under the Uniform Commercial Code, this outcome is less likely. There would indeed be a contract for ten widgets. But the question of price would have to be resolved. Obviously, if there was disagreement, the easiest solution (for which one does not need an attorney!) is simply for French to return the widgets to English and the contract would be terminated by mutual agreement.

Whose terms apply? Let's suppose, however, that French's company has incorporated the widgets into some end product and it is impossible to return them. English invoices for ten widgets at $2 each and the accounts payable clerk in French's company refers the invoice to her because it does not agree with the $1 unit price on the purchase order. Presumably French now would call English and say "You billed us at $2 each when my purchase order called for a price of $1 each, which is based on your quotation of $1 each." English's response might be, "I did indeed bill you for $2 each in lots of 10 and quote you $1 each in lots of 100. I charge less per unit for larger quantities and I never said I would sell you ten units for $1 each. When we got your order, we simply shipped you the ten widgets because that's what we thought you wanted and we did not think you wanted us to delay the order while we discussed price."

Does French have to pay English the $2 price or can she force him to accept the $1 price? Questions like these sometimes must be resolved by an arbitrator or a court. They, in turn, would try to arrive at a fair decision that is consistent with the law spelled out in the Code.

Here are some points that would have to be considered:

1. *Does French's action in ordering 10 widgets at $1 each really represent a material alteration to sell 100 for $1 each?* If English is a *manufacturer* of widgets made to French's specifications, the answer is almost certainly yes. Therefore, a price higher than $1 clearly would be justified and a fair price could be arrived at by negotiation between French and English. If English is a *dealer*, French's argument is stronger (provided she acted in good faith). It is unshakable, for example, if she has been buying widgets from various dealers for years and can prove that dealers set unit prices that are largely independent of quantity.

2. *Did buyer and seller act promptly in objecting to changes in terms of the contract?* In general, the courts have held that the "last piece of paper" that passes between buyer and seller sets the terms of the contract, in the absence of specific objections. If English simply ignored French's $1 price and did not protest, English would maintain that her counteroffer had indeed been accepted and English would have to prove why he could ignore this and still assume that the price was $2. Conversely, French would not have much recourse had she not promptly protested the $2 when the invoice was first called to her attention.

3. *Did French and English really agree on a price?* In some cases, this would be defined by prevailing trade practice. As suggested in (1) above, a case could be made on this basis for either the $1 price or the $2 price, depending on the nature of the item.

If the widgets had not been incorporated into an end product and could be returned, the Code is quite explicit. It says (in Section 2–305) that if the parties do not intend to be bound by the contract unless price is agreed upon, there is no contract but, of course, buyer must return goods to seller.

Since these goods cannot be returned, we must look elsewhere in the Code. Section 2–305 also says that "when a price . . . fails to be fixed through fault of one party the other may at his option treat the contract as cancelled or himself fix a reasonable price." Who failed to fix the price, French or English? We assume that each may claim the other is at fault and a third party would have to make a ruling. The final judgment would be based on a principle that is also spelled out in Section 2–305, which states that if no price has been agreed upon and the buyer is not able to return the goods, then buyer must "pay their reasonable value at the time of delivery. . . ."

The best test of "reasonable" value would be the price at which comparable widgets were being sold in comparable quantities to comparable buyers. If French could prove to English or an arbitrator that she could reasonably expect to buy widgets in lots of ten for $1 each, then there would clearly be a contract for ten widgets at $1 each. On the other hand, English might be able to prove that $2 was the going price. In this case, French would have to pay $2. Or, as a likely third alternative, some compromise price would be negotiated.

Basic principles. Section 2–207, which covers additional terms in acceptance or confirmation of a contract, suggests that these basic principles can be applied to most purchases:

1. *The first particular term that is introduced into the contract paperwork applies unless it is specifically repudiated.* For example, the supplier quotes a price of $1 but the "fine print" on the back of the quotation form says that "prices quoted herein shall be adjusted to those prevailing at time of delivery." The buyer sends supplier an order stating a price of $1 and ignores the "fine print." The supplier subsequently invoices for $1.05 and can prove that, because of inflation, prices to all customers have indeed been boosted by 5 percent. In this case, as long as the seller did not unethically sneak in the extra clause in his "fine print" about price escalation without warning the buyer, the buyer is probably obligated to pay $1.05.

However, if the buyer specifically objects to the supplier's price escalation and then sends a fixed-price order to the supplier, which the supplier tacitly accepts when he ships, the supplier can be held to the $1 price. In this instance, the buyer's specific repudiation of the seller's clause would apply, provided the supplier (a) does not specifically reject it or (b) simply did not ship.

2. *A term that "materially" alters a contract must be specifically accepted or there is no contract.* In some cases, it is hard to define a "material" alteration. However, a supplier that gets an order for brand X cannot substitute brand Y without the buyer's express permission (unless brand differentiation barely exists in the industry and it is clear from prevailing practice that no one cares). Nor can there be major changes in price. It may be reasonable, for example, for a buyer to expect a distributor to incur a 5 or 10 percent price increase from its supplier but a 100 percent price increase would certainly be a "material" alteration.

Statute of limitations

If buyer or seller believes that there has been a breach of contract, action must be taken within four years under Section 2–725 of the Uniform Commercial Code in most states. Several states (notably Mississippi, Oklahoma, South Carolina, and Wisconsin) allow more time. Iowa sets no specific time. After the statute of limitations runs out, it is not possible to initiate a suit for breach of contract. In addition, the Code sets a particular period (usually six months) before an unsuccessful breach of contract suit may be renewed.

PRICE

Price hardly ever poses a legal problem with goods available for immediate delivery. The buyer seeks quotations from one or more potential suppliers and simply issues a fixed-price order. If this confirms the seller's quotation, it becomes a contract.

Advise price orders.   However, buyers often (too often, in the writer's view) find themselves placing orders without knowing the price. In such cases, they either order the item orally or issue a purchase order that says "price advise." The vendor then invoices. If the buyer considers the price fair, the approved invoice is sent to accounts payable for payment. This procedure is perfectly legal and, of course, there can be a binding contract when the buyer (and sometimes not even the seller) does not know what the price will be at the time both parties enter into the contract.

While legal, such orders can be challenged on economic grounds. The buyer who follows this practice is not canvassing the market thoroughly and often could find a supplier who would offer a lower price if given the chance. In addition, the chosen supplier knows full well that there are no competitive pressures and is prone to charge higher prices to customers who buy on a price advise basis than would be changed to customers who are obviously seeking bids from competing suppliers.

As mentioned previously, Section 2–305 of the Code says, in effect, that the seller may charge a "reasonable" amount when price has not been specified and that either party may cancel the order if the price is deemed unreasonable. If the buyer refuses to pay this price and is unable or unwilling to return the merchandise, seller may collect (under Section 2–722) an amount equal to the market price prevailing at the time buyer repudiates the contract.

Prices change.   Unpriced orders often do lead to disputes over what price should be charged. They hardly ever lead to legal problems, however, for routine "off-the-shelf" purchases. Buyer and seller either negotiate a satisfactory price or buyer returns the goods.

Pricing problems are far more likely to arise when delivery is not "off-the-shelf" but must be made some time after the order has been placed. Prices of labor and raw material can change during this period, as can general economic conditions. In addition, if the item is made to order, the supplier's actual costs of production may be either substantially higher or lower than the estimate, so either buyer or seller may wish to change the price on the order. Neither can do so in the absence of mutual agreement or some advance provision that permits change. *A purchase order that has been unqualifiedly accepted by the seller normally legally binds both parties to the prices and quantities shown on the order, unless the order's terms and conditions specifically provide for changes.*

This is the principle under common law. As mentioned previously, the Uniform Commercial Code relieves the seller from obligations that are impossible to perform. For example, if a seller agreed on a price of $1 per pound for copper and the government added an excise tax of $5 per pound for the copper, payable by the seller, the supplier would undoubtedly successfully claim that performance is economically impossible under the Uniform Commercial Code.

As a practical matter, sellers often fail to perform on contracts that are "obsolete" from their point of view, even though they are legally obliged to do so. Thus, the ideal contract is one whose terms and conditions are in the best interests of both buyer and seller. Experience proves that buyers should be wary of deals that are too favorable; sellers simply will not perform, and it is often impractical to sue.

Many companies issue or accept purchase orders for delivery of material over a long period of time, with no provision whatever for change in prices. Occasionally they will negotiate price changes on these orders. In such cases, the provision for change is, in effect, made informally, as a result of a long-established friendly relationship.

Some private companies and all government bodies are more cautious. All orders they issue or accept have provisions for price changes incorporated in them if they anticipate the need for change. Most governments and government prime contractors employ standard provisions determined by regulation, while private firms are more flexible. The terms and conditions they use are limited only by their imagination and their acceptability to suppliers. However, these terms and conditions fall into five general categories: open-end pricing, cost plus, time and material, escalation, and price redetermination.

Open-end pricing. When there is an established free market for a material, it is possible that neither buyer nor seller will want to commit himself to a specific price for a long period of time. The purpose of the contract is to assure a supply of material for some time in the future at the prevailing market price. In such cases, the purchase order need not be priced (although it may be convenient to list the current price for reference purposes). Its terms would indicate that the supplier is to charge the "price in effect of time of delivery."

Open-end pricing is used for basic raw materials, whose prices are determined on commodity markets by impersonal supply-demand forces. It also is frequently used for other purchases simply because the producers refuse to sell unless there is open-end pricing. Producers of steel, aluminum, and other materials whose prices are not determined on commodity markets insist on open-end pricing. So do many suppliers of patented items.

Buyers avoid open-end pricing whenever possible because it limits their flexibility. With open-end pricing, the supplier gets, in effect, a blank check. In most cases, this is easy to avoid even when buying commodities where price cannot be predicted in advance. Sometimes, the price can be tied to some impartial price-reporting service. For example, a copper producer in the Philippines or Indonesia might sell to its American and Japanese customers on the basis of the current spot price for copper quoted on the London Metal Exchange. In other cases, uncertainties affecting price can be resolved by using one of the more specialized contracts discussed in the following paragraphs.

Cost-plus contracts. Sometimes a purchase contract is made for something that is so novel that neither buyer nor seller knows what the cost should be. Some sort of cost-plus contract may be the only solution. The seller agrees to do the job either at some fixed price per hour of work performed or at cost plus some extra fee as profit. Such contracts should be avoided whenever possible. Under them, suppliers have little incentive to keep down costs. In fact, waste can even become profitable for the supplier, especially if it can successfully pad its "costs" to include some profit.

When cost-plus contracts are necessary, they should be controlled and circumscribed as closely as possible. Provision should be made for a detailed audit of the supplier's costs. It also is preferable to fix the supplier's profit on such contracts, so that there is no incentive to waste time. With a cost-plus fixed-fee contract, for example, the supplier would recoup its exact cost plus some predetermined fee. With a straight cost-plus contract, it would recoup its costs plus some percentage profit on cost; the more the supplier spends, the more it makes.

Time and material. Costs can be somewhat more tightly controlled on a time and material contract. Typically, the buyer agrees to pay the supplier's material costs plus labor at some predetermined rate per hour. Time and material contracts are often used for research and development projects where neither buyer nor seller knows how long it will take to develop some particular product. Buyer agrees to pay the supplier its actual audited cost of materials plus (in some cases) a modest markup for "handling." Seller's profit and overhead are recouped from the hourly rate charged for labor. Typically, the seller will take a markup of about 100 percent on actual labor costs. Thus, an engineering firm that pays its junior engineers $10 per hour will charge $20 per hour in order to recoup overhead and earn a profit.

Needless to say, time and material contracts give the seller an incentive to make the job last. In addition, consulting firms (which frequently work on a time and material basis) have sometimes been accused of using much of the time paid for by clients in working up proposals to get more business from the client. At least one very big management consulting firm gives its engineers special incentive pay if they can persuade clients to extend the contract.

Time and material contracts are probably in the buyer's best interest with jobs where costs are so uncertain that the only alternative would be a fixed-price contract that is heavily padded by seller with allowances for uncertainties. They may also be quite satisfactory for certain professional services where the basic commodity being sold is hours of service. In general, however, time and material contracts should be avoided because they do not effectively limit the buyer's costs. They may not be desirable even when some costs are uncertain. For example, most buyers of construction services prefer fixed-price contracts, even though the seller will inevitably give itself sort of contingency allowance when bidding on a particularly tough construction job. The fixed price gives the contractor incentive to overcome its difficulties without delay. A time and material contract might make these same obstacles seem almost insurmountable.

Escalation. Almost any long-term contract should have some provision for price change. Escalation clauses in contracts permit adjustment for unforeseen changes in basic costs but otherwise require the seller to stick to its original quotation. A wise buyer (or seller) tries to define the areas of price escalation; otherwise, it is likely to lose all the benefits hoped to be gained from entering into the long-range contract. For example, buyer or seller may invest millions of dollars in plant and equipment on the strength of some long-range contract. Unrestricted escalation can make such investments unprofitable.

Escalation clauses permit a change in price if a key element of cost changes. Usually this is labor or material cost, or both. Construction contracts often permit escalation if wages paid to the various building trade workers change. Contracts issued by automobile manufacturers for electric storage batteries, on the other hand, may permit escalation if the prices of the key raw materials (lead and antimony) change. Sometimes escalation is linked to changes in some well-known price index issued by the Bureau of Labor Statistics or some other agency.

To prevent disputes, the formula for escalation should be completely clear. It should be based, whenever possible, on widely available economic information and not upon the seller's internal costs. For example, if there is an escalation clause to cover supplier wage increases, it is best to agree on a price adjustment for each cent-per-hour change in the Bureau of Labor Statistics average wage for the supplier's industry. This not only prevents arguments about the effect of a wage change on a supplier's cost but also gives the supplier an incentive to resist wage increases in collective bargaining that will make its prices higher on future bids.

When it is not feasible to base the escalation on some widely available cost data and the supplier's individual cost data must be used, then the method whereby costs are determined should be agreed upon in advance. Also, it is usually desirable to have some top limit to escalation incorporated in the contract; 10 to 15 percent of the original price is typical. However, the ceiling should be related to the term of the contract. The longer the period covered, the more flexible the contract since no one can predict what will occur far in the future.

Price redetermination.   As the term implies, price redetermination clauses permit periodic renegotiation of contract prices. They are broader than escalation clauses, since the change in price is not necessarily tied to a change in wage rates or raw material costs. The redetermination clause typically permits the price of item to be changed about once a year, to reflect both changes in basic costs and the supplier's experience in making the item. They are useful for contracts that extend over a long period or for items with which neither buyer nor seller have had much experience.

Price redetermination clauses are most frequently used in military purchasing, but they also have civilian applications. They are particularly useful when a company subcontracts an entire product. For example, a department store chain may issue a contract for its own brand of lawn mower to a manufacturer. If the supplier has never made lawn mowers before, it may not know precisely what its costs will be. It may also expect to reduce costs after it has more experience with lawn mowers, and costs will be especially low if the lawn mowers sell well. In this case, a price-redetermination contract might be ideal. Sometimes this will include an agreement permitting the buyer to audit the supplier's cost and to recoup any profits in excess of some predetermined percentage of sales. For example, Sears Roebuck reputedly allows certain suppliers an 8 percent profit on sales.

Ultimately, every contract is subject to redetermination even if there is no clause that permits it. No buyer who wants an assured source of supply can impose conditions so harsh that the supplier simply cannot meet them and stay in business. For example, the Japanese firm Mitsubishi Shoji had a fixed-price plus escalation contract with Kaiser Resources calling for delivery of millions of tons of coal from a Canadian mine over a period of years. Kaiser then discovered that the price it had agreed to was impossible to meet. In effect, bankruptcy was cheaper. So Mitsubishi had no choice but to renegotiate its seemingly fixed-price contract. Thus the terms of any contract must always be at least more favorable than the legal penalties for nonperformance. Otherwise, they may not be met at all.

OTHER ECONOMIC CONDITIONS

Payment terms

Routine purchases. The cost of materials contracted for is not determined solely by the unit price of the material and quantity. Someone, usually the buyer, must pay for transporting the material to the buyer's plant. In addition, suppliers usually offer customers a trade discount of 1 to 2 percent if they pay for the material within 10 days of its receipt instead of within the customary 30 days. The buyer should always be certain that the trade discount is included in the contract. Sometimes this discount is negotiated between buyer and seller; usually it is a standard discount that the supplier offers to all of his customers.

Payment terms can become quite complicated on construction contracts and equipment purchases. Usually suppliers insist on progress payments, to be made at specified stages. For example, on a contract to design and build a machine tool, the order might call for payments to the supplier when the design is complete, when the machine is ready to be tried out, and final payment when the machine is operating in accordance with performance specifications.

From a strictly legal point of view, payment terms pose no particular problem. The contract should describe the exact terms and, obviously, the buyer should adhere to them. If the buyer indicates preferred payment terms on a request for quotation form, these terms should be expected to apply as long as they are not specifically rejected by the seller.

Under normal conditions, it is implicitly assumed that the buyer need pay for the goods only after they arrive. Usually 30 days is allowed if the terms are net. If there is a discount, the buyer must pay in ten days or some similar period in order to earn it.

Poor credit. Selling on credit always poses some risk for the seller. The Uniform Commercial Code (Section 2–511) says that payment by check is acceptable (as distinct from cash) unless the contract specifies otherwise. However, the payment is not considered to have been completed until the buyer's bank honors the check.

If the seller discovers that the buyer is insolvent, the Code (Section 2–702) says that it may demand cash on delivery even though this was not previously a condition of the contract. The seller can reclaim goods shipped to an insolvent buyer within 10 days of their receipt except in cases where the buyer has made a misrepresentation of its solvency within the past 90 days (then the 10-day limit no longer applies).

F.o.b. point

Where title passes. Ownership of purchased material usually passes from seller to buyer at the place and time that the material is officially loaded "free on board" some common carrier. However, the Code specifically states in Section 2–401 that "title to goods passes from the seller to the buyer in any manner and on any conditions explicitly agreed on by the parties."

In the absence of specific agreement, title would normally pass:

a. At time and place of shipment if the contract requires seller to send goods to the buyer but does not require it to deliver them at destination.

b. At destination if the contract requires the supplier to deliver the goods.

However, title does *not* pass from seller to buyer if the buyer rejects the goods for any reason, whether or not justified. Thus, in most cases, the goods do not become the buyer's final property until the shipment is "signed for" by an employee of the buyer's organization.

In most cases the f.o.b. point which is a basic condition of the purchase contract determines where title passes. This point is important because it determines who is responsible for freight charges and also for damages to the goods that may occur as a result of handling.

F.o.b. destination. When this term appears on the purchase order, it means that the buyer will accept title to the shipment at the place designated in the "ship to" space on the order. In most cases, this means that the supplier is responsible for the goods until they are delivered to the buyer's receiving dock. The seller is then responsible not only for all inbound freight charges but also for any damages that occur up to the point that the merchandise is placed on the receiving dock.

Buyers will always indicate f.o.b. destination on their purchase orders if they expect the vendor to deliver in its own truck. Delivery may also be made by common carrier. The vendor may prepay the freight. If the goods arrive freight collect, the buyer may deduct the charge from the purchase price as long as the contract terms are f.o.b. destination. If the goods are damaged by the common carrier, the buyer can simply reject the shipment or seek appropriate adjustments directly from the supplier. It would be up to the supplier, in turn, to collect damages from the carrier. However, the supplier of an item damaged in an f.o.b. destination shipment would still have to "make good" with the buyer even if it was not successful in collecting its claim for damages from the carrier.

Thus, there is every reason why a buyer should strive to incorporate f.o.b. destination on every order—even if it is necessary to incorporate shipping charges into the price that is paid for the goods. If anything goes wrong with an f.o.b. destination, the supplier is responsible and not the buyer.

F.o.b. shipping point. While millions of shipments are made each day on an f.o.b. destination basis, the high-tonnage merchandise that fills most railroad cars and long-distance highway haulers has probably been shipped f.o.b. shipping point. The buyer takes title when the seller loads the goods onto a common carrier. The buyer pays transportation charges directly to the carrier and also negotiates all freight damage claims and the like with the carrier. Most companies prefer to buy major materials "f.o.b. shipping point" because then their traffic departments can completely control inbound shipments. As a result, they often can cut freight charges substantially.

In some cases, a designation of f.o.b. shipping point may be too general. Suppose, for example, that a supplier does not have a railroad siding and must truck its product to a siding. Is the shipping point then the supplier's dock or is it the rail siding? Confusion can be prevented with more specific terms. If the purchase order reads "f.o.b. San Francisco, via Southern Pacific Railroad," for example, then there is no doubt whatever that the supplier is responsible for getting the shipment to the rail siding and loading it. Conversely, if the terms are "f.o.b. supplier plant, via Southern Pacific Railroad," then the buyer takes title to the shipment at the supplier's plant and can be charged separately for getting the material to the railroad siding.

Freight equalization. Producers of uniformly priced commodities such as aluminum, steel, and cement will often equalize freight charges with competitors whose plants are located closer to customers. For example, if the freight rate is $2 per cwt. from the plant of supplier A of a given commodity and only $1.75 per cwt. from the nearest supplier, supplier A will offer a $0.25 per cwt. "freight equalization" adjustment to the buyer. The buyer's purchase order to supplier A would then read "f.o.b. shipping point; 25 cents per cwt. freight equalization adjustment allowed." The buyer would pay the common carrier the full $2 per cwt. freight charge but would deduce the 25 cents per cwt. adjustment when it paid its invoice to supplier A. If the buyer does not happen to know the amount of the freight equalization adjustment, the purchase order can read "freight charges to be equalized with (name of city and state)," and supplier must take this into account when it invoices the buyer.

Free alongside ship (f.a.s.). This term is used for export shipments and reference is made to the port of export, for example, "f.a.s. Hamburg." Buyer designates port, berth, and vessel. Vendor is responsible for getting it there and must provide a receipt indicating that goods were delivered to the ship's loading tackle in good order.

Cost, insurance, and freight (c.i.f.). This term is used in export shipment when vendor is to be responsible for getting the shipment to a dock in a port designated by the buyer. For example, if an American buys something that is shipped to him from Le Havre on a "c.i.f. New York" basis, the vendor is fully responsible up to the point that the vessel docks in New York. It is then the buyer's responsibility to see that the merchandise is unloaded from the ship and delivered to its final destination in the United States. The term c.&f. (cost and freight) is similar, except that seller does not assume any risk if merchandise is lost at sea.

REJECTION OF DEFECTIVE GOODS

The Uniform Commercial Code says that purchased goods should be "fit for the ordinary purposes for which such goods are used." This implied warranty is covered in detail in Section 2–314 of the Code. Thus, if the buyer's purchase order simply says "100-watt light bulb," there is an implied warranty that the bulb would give light when connected with a power source. Furthermore, it seems highly likely that if both buyer and seller are in the continental United States, the implied warranty would require that the bulb work on American current and seller would be in breach of contract if it shipped a light bulb that would work only on the 250-volt current that is common in the United Kingdom.

Thus, the implied warranty essentially requires the seller to give the buyer pretty much what it expects to get. It would also be a breach of implied warranty if the light bulb had a life of just 20 hours when it is common practice for such bulbs to have a life of 1,000 hours.

A judge would probably hold that it was *not* a breach of warranty for a vendor to sell a light bulb that lasted only 990 hours, however. The reason, of course, is that a 990-hour light bulb could reasonably be looked at as having been fit for the purpose for which it was intended even though it is clearly inferior to a 1,000-hour bulb. While it is not precise, the implied warranty which is unstated but nonetheless real, adequately covers a majority of the purchases that are made. The buyer is careful to describe the purpose for which the purchase is to be used and by accepting the order, the seller implicitly warrants that they shall be suitable for that purpose. A breach of contract occurs if they are not satisfactory.

Under the Code (Section 2–513) buyer has the right to inspect goods. If they are accepted, cost of inspection must be borne by buyer. If rejected, cost may be recovered from seller. In cases of dispute,

Section 2–515 of the Code provides that the goods must be preserved for inspection by the other party and that buyer and seller may agree on a third-party inspection, which may amount to arbitration of the dispute.

Buyer may reject an entire shipment, accept the shipment, or accept any commercial unit and reject the rest. This acceptance or rejection must be done within a "reasonable" time after receipt.

In most real-life disputes, the definition of "reasonable" would be closely related to the type of goods being purchased. In some cases, where desired specifications can be measured quickly and accurately, acceptance or rejection would be concurrent with delivery or take no more than a few days needed to perform certain routine tests. In other cases, the "reasonable" period could extend over a period of months. For example, a hospital could not be expected to open every sealed package holding medical-surgical supplies that were sold on the basis of their being sterile or it would defeat the purpose of its own specification. If indeed it opened a carton some months later and discovered damaged goods, the delay would almost certainly be regarded as "reasonable" within the context of the Code.

The seller who does not deliver goods suitable for the purpose for which they were intended is in breach. Buyer may simply cancel the contract. But if the seller is unwilling or unable to supply goods that do fit the implied warranty, buyer may purchase them from another supplier and recoup any premium costs that may be incurred from the original supplier. Similarly, if buyer wrongfully rejects goods that are acceptable, seller has similar privileges. The vendor may sell the goods to someone else. If there is a loss, this may be collected from the buyer.

While the principle behind the implied warranty is eminently reasonable, it takes no imagination to predict millions of contracts where seller and buyer disagree. In fact, the author predicts that every reader of this book has entered into such contracts as a consumer. In most cases, neither party to the dispute could sue and win even if it wanted to. The facts are too ambiguous. However, even if buyer or seller is clearly on the side of the angels, the loss is often not sufficient to justify the cost in terms of both money and time that a legal action would require. As a result, buyer and seller negotiate and arrive at some compromise. The seller may (in its opinion at least) go beyond the narrow requirements of an implied warranty simply to preserve goodwill or its reputation and, also, to avoid losing a customer.

Express warranty

Both buyer and seller are better off if it is possible to define explicitly seller's warranty and buyer's responsibilities in relation to it. In most cases, it is not possible for the seller to enjoy terms much weaker than those under the implied warranty. Buyers can be held to contracts only if they get goods that come reasonably close to meeting their needs irrespective of what is defined in an express warranty. How close, of course, is another matter. In general, buyer and seller should agree in advance exactly how product quality should be measured. At the very least, the order should state precisely exactly how the buyer intends to use the particular purchase. Expectations should be so well-defined that if they are not met a breach of contract is obvious to any disinterested third party who investigates.

Negligence. Well-defined purchase specifications are especially important in the purchase of equipment. Obviously, the buyer wants the equipment to do what it is supposed to do. Sometimes even more important to both buyer and seller are potential losses that may result from malfunction of the equipment. The person who is hurt by the malfunction may claim negligence. The owner of the equipment is the immediate target of a negligence action but responsibility may extend back to the manufacturer of the equipment especially if it can be proved that the equipment was designed in a fashion that made it dangerous under certain conditions.

Sellers of equipment inevitably have their lawyers insert clauses in sales agreements designed to shift responsibility for equipment malfunction to the buyer. Courts may hold otherwise if a plaintiff can prove negligence by the manufacturer. For example, if your car kills someone because a wheel falls off, the estate of the deceased would not only sue you but they, along with your attorney, would be interested in pressing a negligence case against the manufacturer if the wheel fell off because of a failure in the manufacturer's design or factory quality control.

The seller will try to avoid negligence suits through express warranty. A manufacturer may successfully escape a negligence suit, for example, if it states explicitly that a warranty is valid only if the equipment is maintained by the manufacturer's service organization. Or warranty may be invalid simply if the manufacturer's procedures on maintenance and replacement of equipment are not followed. These express conditions of warranty would be valid if a judge held them to be reasonable.

Samples. In many cases, a sample is the basis of the sale. This gives the buyer an implied warranty that the goods actually shipped must conform to the sample that was originally submitted by the seller. The Uniform Commercial Code makes this explicit when it says that "any sample or model which is made part of the basis of the bargain creates an express warranty that the whole of the goods shall conform to the sample or model."

Specifications. There is rarely a legal problem because of poor quality on purchases of standard, off-the-shelf items. In such cases the buyer's right to reject the merchandise is recognized. A company's relations with its suppliers for such materials are like a consumer's relations with a department store. If the merchandise is not satisfactory, it is returned for credit. The supplier then either sells the merchandise to another customer or returns it to the supplier.

Quality problems are not so simple when a company makes a product to the buyer's specifications. In such cases, the buyer may be the only user of the product. If buyer rejects a shipment, the supplier may suffer a substantial loss. Because of this, the buyer should incorporate specifications for the item in the purchase order. If the item is made to a blueprint, the purchase order should indicate that material is to be made in accordance with a particular blueprint number of specification accompanying the order. In such cases, the buyer need only accept the material if it meets the requested specifications.

When specifications are ambiguous or simply do not exist, the Uniform Commercial Code would hold that the goods must be suitable for the use intended. If they are not suitable, the buyer may reject them even if they have been made to order. On the other hand, if the buyer wishes to use the purchase for some application that is different from that revealed to the supplier, the goods cannot be returned for credit simply because they fail to be suitable for this new application.

Performance. With some purchases it is not possible to describe the product with detailed specifications. In buying machinery, for example, the buyer is interested not in the supplier's design of the equipment but in the performance of the equipment. So a performance specification is used. Typical is this clause incorporated into a contract issued for a machine developed for Chesebrough-Ponds Inc. by one of its suppliers:

> The machine is to be guaranteed to produce at a minimum linear speed of 240 inches per minute, using a specific material, sample rolls of which were tested by the supplier. The seals produced by the machine are to withstand a minimum of 20 inches of vacuum at 70° F. Furthermore, the machine is to be test-run, prior to shipment, with representatives of our company present. In addition, agreement is to be reached for a specific delivery date stemming from the date of final confirmation of all details.

If this machine did not actually produce at a speed of 240 inches per minute and meet all other performance specifications, then Chesebrough-Ponds would not be obliged to accept it.

Other provisions. Buyer or seller may also wish to include other explicit provisions with respect to warranty. The seller naturally likes to limit its warranty to the actual cost of the product it sells. For example, buyers of gray-iron castings sometimes do not discover that a casting is defective until some rather advanced machining operation reveals a porous section. In extreme cases, the buyer may have invested several hundred dollars of machining time into a casting that is worth no more than a few dollars. In such cases, buyer's legitimate damages are many times the cost of the casting. By trade custom, however, foundaries limit their warranty to the actual cost of the casting and normally refuse to honor claims for machining time wasted on the defective casting.

In the absence of a specific warranty, a court would always lean toward a decision that was consistent with trade custom. If a buyer wants terms superior to this, they must be included as a specific condition of the order. But, of course, the supplier is perfectly free to reject these terms or to request a price increase that more than offsets the additional risk. In most cases, it is not in the buyer's interest to insist on warranties that extend much beyond normal trade custom. The price penalty is usually greater than the value of the benefit.

The best policy is to prevent misunderstanding by explicitly defining the limits of the warranty. Inspection procedures should also be spelled out in detail. For example, an auto manufacturer may agree to accept nickel-plated parts only if a random sample of such parts can withstand 100 hours in a salt spray bath without showing any signs of corrosion.

Failure to deliver

The date that delivery is required should be clearly indicated on the buyer's order. The seller, who accepts the order, is bound to deliver by that date. What happens if the seller fails to deliver? The Uniform Sales Act says that if "seller wrongfully neglects or refuses to deliver the goods, the buyer may maintain an action against the seller for damages for nondelivery."

If the goods that a seller fails to deliver are readily available, the buyer may collect general damages. Such damages are limited to the difference between the contract price and the price the buyer must pay on the open market. Suppose, for example, that a supplier accepts an order for material at 30 cents per pound and then fails to deliver. The buyer who must pay 40 cents per pound for the material, may collect 10 cents per pound damages from the supplier who failed to deliver.

If the goods are not readily available, the buyer may recover special damages. To do so the buyer must prove that the damages suffered from nondelivery could reasonably be anticipated by both buyer and seller and be able to justify the amount of the damages.

Late delivery can often cause as much damage to buyer as no delivery. But if the buyer does not indicate a specific delivery date on the purchase order, the seller is bound to deliver only within a "reasonable" time. Courts differ in the interpretation of the word "reasonable." Many buyers protect themselves against late deliveries by inserting a clause in their purchase orders to the effect that "if shipment is not made at the time specified, buyer reserves the right to cancel the order, or any part of it, without obligation."

Public purchasing agencies sometimes require suppliers to post performance bonds. If the contract is not completed on schedule, the contractor may forfeit all or part of this bond. More frequently, both private and public purchasing agencies include penalty clauses for later delivery—particularly on construction contracts. Seller's price is automatically reduced by some predetermined rate for each week the order is behind schedule.

Sellers may refuse to accept such penalty clauses unless there is also a reward for early delivery. Military procurement officers are particularly likely to use contracts that call both for penalties and premiums based both on delivery and performance of the end product.

OTHER LAWS AND REGULATIONS

The Uniform Commercial Code is the most important body of law affecting purchase transactions. But naturally every buyer and every seller is subject to thousands of other federal, state, and local laws and regulations. In general, federal law affects only those goods and services considered to be sold in interstate commerce while the states themselves regulate intrastate commerce.

The federal laws and regulations most likely to affect purchasing managers are those concerned with regulation of freight and common carriers (discussed in detail in Chapter 16) and those concerned with antitrust and patents.

Patent infringement. Under the Uniform Commercial Code, the buyer can assume that a clear title to the purchase is conveyed unless there are terms and conditions to the contrary. If the seller infringes on a patent, the seller is liable, not the buyer. However, when there is patent infringement, the holder of the patent may sue everyone involved, not only the organization that directly infringed on the patent but also those who purchased products which incorporated features that are patented. Thus, the company that buys a patented item may be guilty of infringement, albeit innocently. It can be sued for infringement and even though it can, in turn, sue the organization that sold it the item that infringed the patent, the disadvantages of this arrangement from the point of view of the innocent buyer are obvious.

Purchasing managers sometimes try to partly protect their companies by inserting a clause in their purchase orders that might say: *Seller warrants that there has been no violation of patents or copyrights in manufacturing or distributing the items covered by this purchase order and seller agrees to hold purchaser harmless from any and all liability loss or expense occasioned by such violation.* In this case, the seller would presumably be liable for any legal costs the buyer might be forced to incur to defend itself against a patent infringement suit by a third party.

Antitrust law. The other major group of federal laws that are most likely to affect purchasing managers are those concerned with monopoly and restraint of trade. The major laws are the Sherman Act, the Federal Trade Commission Act, the Clayton Act, and the Robinson-Patman Act. In most cases, buyers are victims of the anticompetitive act by sellers. It is almost always illegal for private profit-making sellers to band together to set prices. If a buyer can prove such collision, it is possible to collect triple damages.

However, buyers themselves may also violate antitrust laws. If they use their reciprocal purchasing power in a way that restricts and limits competition, this is an antitrust violation. In addition, it is at least theoretically possible for a buyer, as well as a seller, to violate the Robinson-Patman Act. Price discrimination is illegal under the act provided that it cannot be justified by genuine differences in quality, quantity, or distribution cost and also provided that it is not required to meet competition. Thus, it may be unlawful for a company simultaneously to sell 100 widgets at $2 each to the Smith Company on the same day that it sold 100 identical widgets at 20 cents each to the Jones Company across the street. But the act is largely a paper tiger. No vendor is so eager to cut prices that it would do so were there no competitive pressure (which essentially makes the discrimination legal) and, of course, buyers (both at Jones and Smith) are supposed to try to negotiate the lowest prices they can. In fact, it would be illegal under the Sherman Act for the Jones buyer to discuss the prices paid for widgets with Smith so that Jones can readily prove it is not consciously violating Robinson-Patman when it seeks a 20 cent widget price.

In addition, nonprofit organizations are specifically exempt from the Robinson-Patman Act. It is perfectly legal for a seller to charge different prices on like sales made to different nonprofit corporations. Purchasing managers of nonprofit organizations (schools, hospitals, and so on) may also freely discuss their purchase prices with one another and sometimes band together in buying groups in order to bolster their purchasing power with suppliers. This would be a clear violation of antitrust law if done by nonaffiliated profit-making corporations.

Damages in supplier plants. Suppose that a company sends equipment or material to a supplier and it is damaged or destroyed while in the possession of the supplier. Naturally the company feels the supplier is responsible. Some companies like to clarify this situation in advance with a clause in the purchase order. For example, the B. F. Goodrich Company has a clause in its purchase orders that states: "Whenever Seller shall, by virtue hereof, have in its possession any property belonging to Buyer and/or Buyer's customer, Seller shall be deemed an insurer thereof and shall be responsible for its safe return to Buyer."

Workers' compensation and liability insurance. When a company has a contractor working on its premises, it may be liable for any injuries inflicted on others by the contractor's workers or vehicles in accidents. Therefore, it should insist in its purchase terms that contractors be covered by liability insurance. Some companies go further; they demand to see copies of the insurance policies before they will let the contractor start work. A company can also be responsible for injuries suffered by a contractor's employees. It protects itself by making certain that the contractor has workers' compensation insurance.

Tax exemption. Certain goods are subject to federal excise tax if they are used by the purchaser. But if they are purchased for further manufacture—as is the case with all production parts and materials that are incorporated into some end product—they are exempt from

FIGURE 5-1

EXEMPTION CERTIFICATE

PURCHASES FOR FURTHER MANUFACTURE
UNDER SECTION 4220 OF I.R.C.

Date: _____ 19

The undersigned hereby certifies that he is a manufacturer or producer of articles taxable under Chapter 32, sub-chapter A, of the Internal Revenue Code, as amended, and holds certificate of registry number 20 issued by the Director of Internal Revenue at Cleveland, Ohio, and that the article or articles specified in the accompanying order will be used by him as material in the manufacture or production of, or as a component part of, an article or articles enumerated in sub-chapter A to be manufactured or produced by him.

It is understood that, for all the purposes of such sub-chapter A, the undersigned will be considered the manufacturer or producer of the articles purchased hereunder and (except as specifically provided by law) must pay tax on resale or use, otherwise than as specified above of the articles purchased hereunder. It is further understood that the fraudulent use of this certificate to secure exemption will subject the undersigned and all guilty parties to revocation of the privilege of purchasing tax-free and to a fine of not more than $10,000 or to imprisonment for not more than five (5) years or both, together with costs of prosecution.

This certificate covers Purchase Order No. _____ dated _____ .

This certificate covers purchases from _____ to _____ .

THE B. F. GOODRICH COMPANY
By: _____
Title: _____

Many states have sales or use taxes, and the federal government has excise taxes on various products. Production parts and materials purchased for resale are exempt from these taxes, provided the buyer either includes the appropriate exemption certificate with the order or files it with the appropriate taxing authority. Above is an exemption certificate used by the B. F. Goodrich Company for purchases subject to federal excise tax.

tax. To avoid the tax, the buyer must add an exemption certificate to the purchase order. Figure 5–1 illustrates the certificate used by the B. F. Goodrich Company.

A company also may purchase materials for direct resale without using them in manufacture. In this case, it is also exempt from the federal excise tax and should add an exemption clause to its purchase order. A special exemption clause would also be added if the material is to be exported.

Many states also have sales or use taxes. If a material is purchased for resale, incorporation into another product, or export, it will normally be exempt from the tax, but special clauses must be added in each case in accordance with the laws of the state in which the buyer does business.

Liens. When a company has work done by a general contractor, it is potentially liable for payment of subcontractors or their employees. If the general contractor does not meet his obligations, subcontractors and employees may secure a lien against the project on which they worked. Buyers are usually careful to get waivers of lien from all subcontractors before making final payments on contracts. They are far more likely to be negligent in the purchase of major used equipment, which also may be subject to lien. The creditors of the seller of the equipment can sometimes collect from the buyer of the equipment if the seller is not able to meet her obligations. The buyer is more completely assured of a clear title to equipment if the supplier's financial condition is investigated.

CONTRACT CANCELLATION

Every purchasing manager issues purchase orders that must later be canceled because the goods are no longer needed. Contract cancellations are particularly frequent in technologically dynamic industries. Materials and components rapidly become obsolete on account of product changes. In the purchasing departments of the big aerospace companies, as many as 50 persons may be employed full time on cancellations. When a buyer cancels an order before its completion, it is called "anticipatory breach." If the merchandise for which it has contracted is salable but only at a lower price, the buyer is liable to seller for the difference between this lower price and the contract price.

A buyer who cancels an order for materials made to specification, is liable for all of the costs incurred by the seller—including the seller's liability to its suppliers—of materials and services used in carrying out the contract. In addition, the buyer is liable for the normal profit the seller would have made on the contract.

Buyers should terminate contracts without delay once they determine that the material on order is no longer needed. They are liable only for costs incurred (less salvage value) by the supplier prior to termination. Once supplier has acknowledged termination, the buyer cannot change its mind and demand reinstatement of the contract unless the supplier concurs.

All major contracts should include a termination clause. Terms of payment for all potential liabilities should be defined as clearly as possible. Procedures used to determine costs of inventories, depreciated value of special tools, and so on, should be agreed upon in advance. It is usually wise to make provision for an audit of termination costs. Both buyer and seller are protected on termination of big contracts if there is agreement when the original contract is made. And if there is no danger of unpleasant misunderstandings arising between them that will mar relations on future contracts.

It is particularly important that provision for cancellation be incorporated into purchase orders of defense contractors. Rapid changes in defense technology keep defense purchasing departments in a constant state of flux. In some firms, no more than one purchase order in two for parts and materials is even completed. Continuous design changes make it necessary to cancel an enormous number of purchase orders before they are completely filled. Military needs also sometimes change rapidly. As a result, purchasing departments in big aerospace firms sometimes are flooded with cancellations when a major contract change requires them to cancel hundreds of outstanding orders.

LETTERS OF INTENT

The letter of intent is a device that can reduce the risk of cancellation charges and misunderstandings between buyer and supplier. It is particularly useful when a buyer finds it advantageous to define purchase terms and conditions before it can formally commit to buy anything.

Typical application

Figure 5–2 shows a sample letter of intent used by the AiResearch Manufacturing Company. This letter defines price and other conditions of purchase for two parts, 259771 and 256963, for a period of one year. If the hypothetical supplier, the A.B.C. Company, acknowledges this letter of intent without qualification, then AiResearch is assured that it can buy these parts from A.B.C. in accordance with the terms of the letter of intent.

Price assured. AiResearch probably used a letter of intent for these particular parts because, at the time the letter was written, it did not

FIGURE 5–2
Letter of intent to purchase

AIRESEARCH MANUFACTURING COMPANY

A DIVISION OF THE GARRETT CORPORATION

SKY HARBOR AIRPORT · 402 SOUTH 36th STREET · PHOENIX, ARIZONA 85034

A.B.C. Company
1234 Rightway Street
Los Angeles, California 90007

Attention Mr. John Doe

Gentlemen:

This letter of intent, in response to negotiations mutually agreed upon between AiResearch Manufacturing Company and A.B.C. Company, is to confirm the pricing and conditions for manufacture of barriers, parts 259771 and 256963.

The following conditions are noted as part of this agreement:

(A) The anticipated yearly quantities of 3000 to 3500 (part 259771) and 1800 to 2300 (part 256963) are estimates only, and are not to be considered binding quantities.

(B) To allow for payment of delivered units during the period of this letter of intent, the individual purchase orders shall reflect a price of $15.50 each for part 259771, and $5.50 each for part 256963.

(C) At the end of the year's period, the buyer and seller shall adjust the final price of each purchase order issued during the year in accordance with the negotiated price established for the year's accumulative total for each part per paragraph (D) below.

(D) Firm fixed prices, based upon the accumulative quantity manufactured during the one year period of the letter are as follows:

Quantity	Unit Price	Quantity	Unit Price
500	$21.30	3501 - 4000	$13.20
1000	17.60	4001 - 4500	13.10
1500	15.50	4501 - 5000	13.05
1501 - 3000	13.50	5001 - over	13.00
3001 - 3500	13.30		

Revision of individual orders at the end of the year to the prices shown in the above aggregate quantities is based upon subsequent orders being released in a manner that will allow

(H) The minimum quantity of any order placed per this letter shall be 500 pieces.

(I) The period of this letter of intent shall be one (1) year from the date of acknowledgement.

Very truly yours,

R. D. Lutz

Max O. Mitchell
Purchasing Department

RDL:sb

Acknowledged: _____
                    A.B.C. Company

Sample letter of intent shows how AiResearch defines conditions of purchase for two parts it intends to buy, provided it gets a contract for the parts' end product.

146

have a contract for a finished product requiring them and it wanted to be assured of firm prices for purchased materials before it went ahead and quoted on a final assembly. Once AiResearch gets an order, it can then go ahead immediately with a purchase that is consistent with the terms of the letter of intent. Even though this particular letter will not necessarily lead to the purchase of anything from A.B.C., it serves useful purposes for both A.B.C. and AiResearch. Letters of intent from customers permit A.B.C. to do a better job of planning. Although A.B.C. knows that not every letter of intent will actually lead to purchase orders, there is a high probability that some percentage of them will result in firm orders. In fact, if A.B.C. needs financing, the letters can be shown to banks as evidence supporting the need for loans which will be self-liquidating from future business.

Shorter lead time. Use of the letter of intent permits AiResearch to do a much better buying job than would be possible if it were to start from scratch on subcontracts when it receives a firm prime contract. Chances are that AiResearch will get the order for the end product only if it offers to deliver promptly. This usually means that orders for purchased parts and materials must be issued almost immediately after AiResearch gets a firm order from its customer. Then there might not be sufficient time to do the best possible job of buying each component, and costs of purchased components would not be firmly pinned down. AiResearch might find itself in the unhappy position where costs or purchased materials were so high that it was impossible to make a profit on the order. Or, if purchase costs turned out to be lower than anticipated, AiResearch might never get an order for the end product because its bid was inflated by an excess allowance for cost of purchased parts and materials. Letters of intent define quite precisely what purchased costs will be and provide assurance that there will be an adequate margin between purchased materials costs and selling price. They also permit the buyer to group similar items together with the same supplier in order to get the lowest possible price.

De facto orders

While the letter of intent shown in Figure 5–2 does not commit the buyer to make any purchase, other letters of intent may become de facto purchase orders. Suppose, for example, that in the course of negotiating the terms of purchase for parts 259771 and 256963, the buyer discovers that it is impossible to get delivery until at least three months after the supplier has received a firm purchase order. He checks with production control and discovers that AiResearch will need the parts within two months after it is able to give a formal go-ahead to the supplier.

Obviously, something must give. Either AiResearch must get the parts delivered in two months instead of three months, or it must accept the risk of being late in delivering its end product. In some cases, the best solution is to authorize the supplier to do some preliminary work in the letter of intent.

For example, if the two parts are fabricated from steel, the buyer might authorize the supplier in the letter of intent to go ahead and purchase the steel but not to fabricate it. This automatically shortens the supplier's lead time and no one loses anything as long as the deal goes through. However, if the end product is not produced, the supplier will be stuck with steel he neither wants nor needs. Inevitably, the buyer would be required to compensate the supplier for any loss suffered. In this case, of course, the letter of intent becomes a partial purchase order for raw materials.

GOVERNMENT PROCUREMENT

Letters of intent and all other procedures followed by defense contractors must be consistent with Armed Services Procurement Regulations (ASPR). In addition, nondefense government agencies spend directly about one tenth of total national income for a wide variety of materials and services.

The basic principles of materials management are as applicable to government procurement as they are to private industry. In every case, materials management should be oriented toward the objectives of the organization it serves. The fundamental objective of the materials manager in government is not significantly different from that of his or her counterpart in industry. The materials manager in the private firm strives to maximize the company's profits over the long term; the public purchasing official attempts to get maximum value for the taxpayer's dollar.

Reasons for regulation

Differences between government and private industry procurement come not in basic principles but in legal environment. The private purchasing official has tremendous flexibility; the public official is regulated by a myriad of laws. Tight regulation makes public procurement inflexible and not always efficient, but it is politically essential for the two basic reasons discussed below.

1. To protect the taxpayer against corruption.   In the past, public purchasing was the means by which those in power rewarded themselves. At best, public purchases could be (and sometimes still are) diverted to business executives who support the party in power. At worst, public funds are simply misappropriated.   Contemporary public purchasing officials are at least as honest as their counterparts in private industry, but they remain circumscribed by literally hundreds of regulations designed to prevent malpractice. In some cases, these regulations protect the professional public purchaser from political pressures; in others, they simply make it difficult to do a competent job.

2. *To promote noneconomic objectives.* Legislative bodies have always assumed that public purchasing should take social as well as economic factors into account. Municipal and state purchasing officials may be forced to buy locally even when better values can be obtained from a supplier in another city or state. Similarly, the federal government is subject to regulations that discriminate in favor of American suppliers, particularly "small business" as defined by the Small Business Administration.

In addition, high-ranking officials at all levels of government often make no bones about interfering with the procurement process—particularly on major projects—in order to favor quite deliberately one group or region over another. At the local level, the town's major contractors often serve as elected or appointed officials. At state level, the party in power gets much of its financial support from those business executives who do business with the state. And, at the federal level, decisions on where to locate major government facilities are often more political than they are economic.

Advertised bidding

Government procurement officials operate in a fishbowl. Every act is a matter of public record. Local, state, and federal governments are required to advertise for bids whenever possible. Exceptions to this basic rule are possible only when the purchase is too small to be worth the time and expense of advertised bidding or when the nature of the product or service makes advertising impractical.

Mechanics of bidding. Advertised bidding requires highly detailed specifications. It is particularly useful for commodities where standards have already been set (such as foods) or for construction where detailed specifications must be drawn up anyway. Once the specifications are available, the advertised bidding process becomes highly mechanical, going through the following steps.

1. The government agency that is to do the buying gets a budget authorization and specifications from the agency that is to use the material. The buying agency must be certain that the specifications are not restrictive and lend themselves to advertising. For example, specifications for canned fruit based on the standards of the U.S. Department of Agriculture would be appropriate for advertised bidding since dozens and perhaps hundreds of canning firms are able to meet these specs. On the other hand, advertised bidding would not be appropriate for a patented item, since only the patent owner or his licensee could supply it.

2. Invitations to bid are prepared which set forth a specific place, date, and hour for opening of bids. These are sent to all qualified bidders on the procuring agency's list. In addition, the procurement may be advertised by posting it in public places or announcing it in newspapers. Federal government purchases in excess of $10,000 are also publicized in the Department of Commerce publication, *Synopsis of U.S. Government Procurement, Sales and Contract Awards.*

3. At the specified hour, bids are opened. Names of bidders and their bids are recorded on an abstract of bids which is available for public inspection. Under normal conditions, no bidder may withdraw a bid once it has been submitted. In some cases, the bidder is forced to post a performance bond which is forfeited if he refuses to accept a contract on which he is low bidder.

4. The contracting officer evaluates the bids and makes an award. Bids that do not conform in every detail to the invitation and to specifications are rejected. The contracting officer also rejects any bids that are not "responsible"—that is, those that do not come from bidders who are regular dealers or manufacturers of the item being purchased. After culling out all bids that do not qualify, the contracting officer makes the award to the low bidder.

5. The bidder is required to perform precisely in accordance with the terms of the contract. If she fails to perform, the contracting officer may be required by regulation to take legal steps needed to assure performance. For example, if the bidder fails to deliver, the contracting officer may choose to buy the item from another supplier at a higher price. She then forces the original bidder to make up the difference so that the government spends no more than what it would have under the original contract award. The contracting officer might also sue the original bidder for any losses occasioned because of late delivery.

Pros and cons. Advertised bidding guarantees reasonable impartiality in public purchasing. A recognized supplier who is willing to bid low enough can almost always get an order from a public purchasing official. In contrast, the supplier who is not "in" with many big private firms may not be able to get an order regardless of what it quotes. Almost all information on bids and so forth is held in strictest confidence in private firms. This may inhibit competition. With advertised bidding, every bidder can look at the recap and know exactly where he stands.

Despite this basic advantage, advertised bidding has rather serious weaknesses even for certain types of public purchasing. These include:

1. The contract is automatically awarded to the lowest bidder who possesses the minimum qualifications to do the job. This may not be the best firm in the business. In contrast, a purchasing official in a

private firm might not issue his order to the low bidder but prefer to do business with a supplier regarded as more reliable or superior in some other respect.

2. The public purchasing official using advertised bids tries to get bids from a maximum number of firms. In some cases, it may be necessary to evaluate several hundred bids. In contrast, the private firm rarely solicits bids from more than a half dozen suppliers. Many qualified suppliers may not be solicited at all simply because the purchasing official feels that there is already adequate competition.

3. Advertised bidding is costly and time-consuming compared with the private method of buying. It may cost several thousand dollars to prepare bids and make an award.

4. Advertised bidding does not necessarily guarantee a buyer the lowest possible price, even when a large number of bids are solicited. In many cases, one firm enjoys such an enormous advantage over its rivals that it can quote a very high price and still be low bidder. This is particularly true of engineered items where one contractor has had substantial experience.

5. Highly detailed specifications are needed. There is no margin of error with advertised bidding. If the government forgets one important specification, then the vendor is perfectly free to ignore it and cut costs in any way it can as long as it adheres to specifications. The seller cannot afford to give the government anything more than the minimum it requests; otherwise, the bid may be too high. In contrast, the atmosphere in most private procurement is considerably less formal. If a private firm buys an automobile, it can reasonably expect to get a spare tire even if it does not ask for it. Conversely, it probably will not sue a seller who fails to deliver.

6. Favoritism is not necessarily eliminated with advertised bidding. The dice can be loaded in favor of a particular seller simply by writing specifications that are best suited to that supplier's skills and equipment or insisting on special but irrelevant specifications that competing sellers are not able to meet.

Despite these serious limitations, advertised bidding is a highly effective public purchasing technique when (a) specifications are detailed, (b) there are many qualified bidders, and (c) the purchase is important enough to be worth advertising. Thus, there is good reason why most government procurement agencies will advertise except on purchases where it is clearly not workable.

Negotiated procurement

Advertised bidding in federal procurement dates back to 1809, with exceptions allowed during wartime for procurement of munitions. Negotiated procurement did not really come into its own in the federal government however, until 1947, with the enactment of the Armed

Services Procurement Act. This act authorized "negotiated" procurement for purchases where advertising is not practical or would not lead to best value for the government. At present, about 80 percent of all military procurement is "negotiated." Advertised bidding is used more frequently for nonmilitary procurement not only by the federal government but also by state and municipal governments. Almost every government purchasing office has authority to buy certain items—particularly services and small purchases of any kind—by negotiation, however.

Meaning of negotiation.   The term "negotiation" may be misleading. In federal government jargon any purchase that is not made through advertised bids is by definition negotiated. And, in fact, there is usually some discussion or negotiation with purchases that are legally negotiated. In contrast, no discussion or negotiation is necessary with advertised bidding. The seller submits a bid in writing and then is advised in writing when she gets the award.

There may be "negotiation" on even the most trivial negotiated purchase. For example, if a corner gas station repairs a flat tire on a government-owned car, payment may be made with what is legally a negotiated purchase order. The "negotiation" may consist simply asking the mechanic what he charges for fixing a flat and then paying the bill if the charge seems reasonable.

Discussions get much more involved on major negotiated purchases. In fact, competition may be keener than it is with advertised bidding because the contracting officer is less likely to accept the lowest bid that she gets. She may negotiate with one or more bidders in order to obtain even more favorable purchase terms. For example, a contracting officer may get bids of $100 million, $110 million, and $120 million for a Navy warship from three competing shipyards. Conceivably, the contracting officer could simply award the contract to the shipyard that bids $100 million. However, she may ask each of the competing shipyards to revise its bid and attempt to buy the warship for $90 million.

Truth in negotiation.   Buyers for the military services are helped a great deal in negotiation by the "Truth in Negotiation" law, which requires government contractors to reveal their cost estimates and certify their accuracy, completeness, and currency. In theory, at least, the military buyer is then at least as well informed as his suppliers and enjoys an enormous advantage over his civilian counterpart, who is not able to demand reliable supplier cost estimates. The system is by no means foolproof, however. In many cases, neither the supplier nor the buyer really knows what the item is supposed to cost, and the actual cost may turn out to be greatly in excess of the original estimate.

Favoritism of sharp practices?   In recent years, some defense contractors have had their prices hammered down in negotiation with the Pentagon and then have been stuck with contracts that, at best, yielded only nominal profits and sometimes caused major losses. Not surprisingly, both defense contractors and the congressmen who represent them have sometimes complained bitterly about his sort of negotiation, calling it "sharp practice." However, there is no doubt that government purchasers have saved taxpayers many millions of dollars through such negotiation.

The procurement officer who trades one supplier off against another is rarely accused of favoritism. There is considerably greater opportunity for favoritism—justified or unjustified—when the contracting officer must make a negotiated procurement from a single supplier. When the purchase is sufficiently small it simply isn't worth the effort to solicit bids from a number of suppliers.

However, congressmen don't complain about favoritism among corner garages fixing flat tires. The pressures come when big defense contracts are being passed out. A single contract may amount to hundreds of millions of dollars and create thousands of jobs in a congressman's district. Such procurement inherently tends to favor one supplier at the expense of another, and there is not much that can be done about it. One cannot, for example, advertise for bids for a new missile or bomber that has not yet been developed. The detailed specifications obviously do not exist, and competing aerospace firms might well propose substantially different designs to meet the same performance objective. Consequently, even if it is possible to develop detailed quotations, bids will not be comparable between competing producers, since they are not based on identical products. As a result, the contracting officer must consider qualitative factors such as design capability as well as prices and costs when he makes the award.

Rightly or wrongly, the award may also be influenced by factors that are completely noneconomic. This is often true of major military procurement. Competing firms will submit quite different design proposals. Not only must someone evaluate these designs, but political reality requires that the impact of the contract on a region's economy be taken into account. Congressmen from areas with substantial unemployment will fight hard to force the Department of Defense to favor contractors in their districts. Election results are influenced by whether or not voters feel a candidate can get more federal money for businesses in his or her district.

Favoritism without corruption. Major procurement decisions may be difficult and controversial even when there are no overt political pressures. In many cases, the government is trying to buy something that has never been made before. Competing contractors must quote a price for something that does not exist. In addition, their technical approaches are often different. If the Department of Defense wants to buy a supersonic fighter plane with certain performance characteristics, one contractor may propose a delta-wing design, another may propose wings that change position as the aircraft increases its speed, and so on. In awarding the contract, the department must take into account not only the cost of the proposed design but its practicability.

Major mistakes are inevitable when criteria for bidding are not well defined. Technical problems frequently cause costs to soar above original estimates. The competitive environment also encourages underestimating of cost. Every contractor is strongly tempted to underbid, since if his original estimate is higher than those of competitors, he probably will not get the contract. As long as the design has not been firmly established, it is usually possible to boost prices and recoup losses from underbidding. Also, if precedent is any guide to the future, the federal government will not permit a major defense contractor to go bankrupt simply because of unprofitable defense contracts.

With negotiated procurement of complex products, it is not only difficult to achieve workable competition prior to production but the government is also stuck with a single supplier even after the product has been in production for some time. For example, the F-5 fighter plane was produced for many years by the Northrup Corporation, and the Air Force has long had available highly detailed specifications for this aircraft. Theoretically, the Air Force or the Navy could send copies of these specifications to every aircraft company in the nation and solicit competitive bids on the next procurement. In practice, however, this would hardly be worthwhile. Northrup has already acquired so much experience in making this plane that its costs would be well below that of any other possible competitor. For example, if $4 million is a fair price for the plane from an experienced producer like Northrup, the lowest competitive bid might be $5 million from some other supplier who had had no experience whatever. Consequently, if the procurement were made strictly on the basis of competitive bidding, Northrup could conceivably charge $4,900,000 and still get the contract even though it made an enormous profit. Obviously, competitive bidding process just does not work when the product is very complex and a single contractor has had a great deal of experience with it.

Contract clauses

Obviously, the Department of Defense in particular must use a wide variety of contract clauses if it is to get optimum value for the taxpayer's dollar. Some defense contracts are in effect "one of a kind," developed for some particular need. However, most negotiated procurement makes use of a wide number of variations of three basic contract clauses: fixed price; cost reimbursement; and special incentive.

Fixed-price clauses.   No contract clause is needed for a firm fixed-price contract. The price on the purchase order becomes part of the contract, and the contractor is obliged to charge that price. Roughly one third of all Department of Defense purchases are for a firm, fixed price.

Escalation and redetermination. Other fixed-price contracts are not quite so fixed. The Department of Defense also uses escalation clauses on fixed-price contracts which typically permit a price to be increased as much as 10 percent for changes in wages, raw material costs, or taxes.

The department also uses price-redetermination clauses not unlike those described earlier in this chapter. A redetermination clause is ideal when the price quoted by the contractor is higher than what the government is willing to pay. The item may be so new that the contractor is often unwilling to quote the desired price because she feels she must make some allowance for contingencies. In this case, the buyer and seller negotiate a price and include a redetermination clause which permits the price to be renegotiated within some limit after the contractor has had experience with the item.

Incentive contracts. Of course, a conventional price-redetermination clause may not give the contractor much incentive to control his own costs. The contractor knows the government will reimburse him for all of his costs, so he simply spends the money. The fixed-price incentive contract may be more desirable in such cases. This contract requires the negotiation of a target cost, a target profit, a ceiling price, and a final profit formula which allows the contractor to participate in any savings.that result. For example, suppose that the buyer and seller agree that a contract should have a target price of $1 million, with costs of $920,000 and $80,000 expected profit. On the other hand, buyer and seller recognize that unforeseen contingencies may cause costs to be higher than target, and so a ceiling price of $1,250,000 is negotiated. If actual costs are less than expected costs, 20 percent of the saving goes to the contractor and 80 percent to the government. For example, suppose that the contractor's actual costs are $900,000 instead of $920,000 as indicated in the target cost. Of this $20,000 saving, the contractor gets 20 percent, bringing the total profit on the contract up to $84,000. Thus, the contractor enjoys a 20 percent profit on any savings she can make below the target cost.

Conversely, the contractor's profit is reduced by a like amount when his costs go above target. Suppose, for example, the costs of $1,100,000 are incurred on the contract. The government is then willing to pay the contractor $1,080,000—the target price plus 80 percent of the excess. The contractor's loss is $20,000 because of his 20 percent share of the cost overrun. The ceiling price of $1,250,000 cannot be exceeded in any event, regardless of the contractor's costs.

This type of contract gives the contractor incentive to keep the costs down and also avoids giving him a blank check. Such contracts must be negotiated quite carefully, since obviously the contractor has considerable incentive to inflate the original estimate as high as possible and then to come under it in order to make excess profits.

Cost-reimbursement clauses.   The government tries to make minimum use of cost-reimbursement contracts because of the obvious danger involved. However, sometimes it has no choice and roughly 5 percent of all Department of Defense procurement actions are of this type. In some cases, the contractor has a simple "cost" contract, with some allowance for direct costs and overhead but not for profit. These are most often entered into with educational and other nonprofit institutions.

Occasionally the contractor accepts a cost-sharing contract. Since the contractors stand to profit from the product that is being developed under the contract, she receives no fee and is reimbursed only for a portion of the cost. The government also issues cost plus fixed-fee contracts in which the contractor receives costs incurred along with some fee. Another variation of this is an arrangement whereby the cost plus incentive fee is increased if costs are kept under some predetermined maximum.

Special-Incentive clauses.   Occasionally, the government issues a special-incentive contract which gives the contractor an extra profit if some performance objective is exceeded. For example, suppose that the Navy issues a contract for a nuclear submarine and the specification calls for a maximum speed of at least 40 knots. Since speed is vital in nuclear submarines, the contract may carry some added provision giving the contractor extra profit if he can make the submarine go even faster (without adversely affecting other performance characteristics).

Similarly, the Bureau of Ships, in particular, has had great success with adding value engineering incentives. These contracts call for a value engineering appraisal to be made during the contract with savings to be shared between the contractor and the government. The Bureau of Ships has reportedly saved $12 for every $1 worth of value engineering that was authorized under such contracts.

Value engineering clauses and other types of incentive contracts give Department of Defense buyers considerably more flexibility than they had as recently as 20 years ago. But once the contract is signed, the defense buyer still has considerably less latitude than his counterpart in private industry.

PURCHASE ORDER "BOILER PLATE"

Almost every large private organization, such as the Department of Defense, has "fine print" on the back of its purchase orders which delineates the terms and conditions of the contract. Most large suppliers also have "fine print" on the back of their quotations and order acknowledgements. These terms and conditions are written by the organization's attorney and are basically designed to make it a "heads I win, tails you lose" proposition should unforeseen difficulties occur in the performance of the contract.

As previously mentioned, the terms and conditions of buyer and seller need not be mirror images of one another for a contract to exist and the general rule is that the last piece of paper that passes is the one that determines the agreement. Some purchasing managers give careful attention both to their own purchase order terms and to terms proposed by suppliers. This is a practice that every textbook writer must commend. Other purchasing managers are more careless. Their purchase order forms indicate the name of the supplier, what they want to buy, and not much of anything else. Is this bad practice? Maybe. But the reality is that it rarely creates any problems on routine purchases from established suppliers. Disagreements can almost always be resolved informally. If they ever got to court, the judge would rely primarily on the Uniform Commercial Code which, in effect, says that in the absence of explicit agreement, precedence based on past relations with buyer and seller would probably be the main basis for determining the terms of the contract should there be ambiguity.

Formal contract language is not even needed on large, complex contracts such as those for equipment or construction. An agreement written in plain simple English is perfectly valid. In such cases, however, the contract should normally be reviewed by the buyer's attorney simply to make certain that nothing important has been inadvertently left out. To sum up, neither buyer nor seller should try to be "clever" in devising contract terms and conditions. The objective is simply to reach an agreement that is perfectly clear and acceptable to both parties.

Yet many buyers do have boiler plate. In fact, it is essential if buyer or seller want terms and conditions that differ materially from those that are consistent with the Uniform Commercial Code. Here are some clauses used by real-life purchasing managers:

1. *Price. If price is not stated on this order, it is agreed that goods or services shall be billed at prices last quoted or prevailing market, whichever is lower.*[1] Purchasing managers are sometimes forced by expediency to issue unpriced purchase orders. Under the Uniform Commercial Code, these can lead to binding contracts under which the supplier is entitled to a "fair" price. This clause obviously prevents the supplier from being excessively "fair" to himself.

2. *Terms of payment. Cash discount period is understood to date from receipt of goods or date of invoice, whichever is later.* Suppliers

[1] This clause and some of the others that follow were originally proposed in articles written for the publication, *Hospital Purchasing Management*, by A. V. Tabaka, a Detroit attorney who has also had considerable practical experience as a purchasing manager.

commonly offer payment terms such as 2 percent 10 days, net 30 days. From the buyer's point of view, the ten-day period should not begin until buyer has both the goods and the invoice on hand.

3. **Packaging.** *It is agreed that prices listed on this order cover all containers, crates, dunnage, and other packaging materials unless otherwise stated. Seller agrees to assume all extra costs resulting from improper packing.* Clearly buyer wants the price to cover all steps needed to permit the goods to arrive in good condition.

4. **Identification.** *Packing slips must be included with all shipments and buyer's purchase order number must appear on all packages, slips, and invoices.* This should be standard practice anyway but it doesn't hurt to spell it out.

5. **Warranty.** *The buyer should strive to get the strongest warranty that the seller will accept.* In some cases, the clause that is added may be tailored to the material being ordered and might then be stronger than the implicit warranty of the Uniform Commercial Code.

6. **Delivery.** *Time is of the essence in this order. Buyer reserves the right to cancel order without obligation if delivery is not made at the time(s) specified on the face of this order.* This is stronger than the language of the Uniform Commercial Code and might therefore be unacceptable to the seller. Under the UCC, a seller who is late in delivery would probably still have a valid claim against the buyer if the order called for custom-made items not readily salable to other buyers. With this clause, the seller's case is weakened considerably should delivery be delayed.

7. **Assignment.** *Seller shall not assign any rights or claims under this purchase order without the prior written consent of the buyer.* Contracts can be assigned without the party's consent. If the Smith Company has a contract to sell widgets, it is perfectly legal to assign this contract to the Jones Company as long as Jones performs. But, of course, the buyer who orders from Smith presumably wants to do business with Smith and assignment should not be permitted unless the buyer agrees.

Most buyers would find the UCC provisions with respect to partial shipments (the buyer does not have to accept them unless there is specific agreement) and inspection (buyer has right) to be quite acceptable. However, when buying items that come in sealed containers or where there are other physical problems, the buyer may wish to strengthen the UCC rule on inspection.

In addition, almost every buyer would want to include a clause that prevents seller's terms from taking precedence over those of buyer. This can be done by simply stating on the order: *Acceptance of this order and shipment constitutes acceptance of its terms and conditions pursuant to UCC Section 2–207 (2)(a).* However, this clause would protect the buyer only when there is a clear conflict between the buyer's explicit terms and those of the seller. For example, if the buyer lists a price of $1 on the order without qualification and the seller's invoice and quotation both state that price shall be that in effect at time of delivery, then the clause makes the contract binding at the $1 price even if the seller has boosted its price to $2 (provided, of course, that the seller accepts the order).

However, the buyer may wish to be protected against instances where seller's explicit terms override those of the Uniform Commercial Code. This clause would work: *Implicit and explicit terms and conditions of the Uniform Commercial Code apply to this order with the sole exception of buyer's terms and conditions explicitly included herein.* In addition, the buyer would provide on the face of the order explicit instructions with respect to invoicing, delivery, and so on. These would then automatically become part of the contract.

Cases

CASE 5–1. SOUTHERN ELECTRONICS CORPORATION

Purchase order acknowledgments

Southern Electronics Corporation is an important prime contractor for the U.S. Air Force for missile guidance systems. All major purchases must be approved by the Air Force contracting officer, and periodic audits are made by the government's General Accounting Office to check conformance with procedures.

Most of the orders issued by Southern Electronics have contained no provision for price escalation. In almost every case, bidders have quoted fixed prices, and the business has been awarded to the low bidder. Because government regulations are quite strict, the company is careful about maintaining good records. Clerks even keep track of each purchase order acknowledgment. If the acknowledgment copy of the order is not returned within two weeks after the order is placed, the supplier gets a form letter requesting that he return it.

Once this procedure was set up, Carol Walters, the materials manager, and Clark Bedell, the purchasing agent, ceased to worry about acknowledgments. However, two incidents involving acknowledgments have recently been called to their attention:

1. An audit of the acknowledgment copy file shows that several suppliers have taken exception to the terms and conditions of the company's purchase orders when they have acknowledged them. Most notably, Apex Metals Corporation, one of the biggest companies in the world, insists on acknowledging Southern's orders with its own sales acknowledgment forms, which have terms and conditions quite different from those on Southern's purchase orders. The contracting officer

flatly refuses to accept Apex's terms. He particularly objects to Apex's clause: "Price subject to change without notice." He correctly points out that this condition, if accepted, would give Apex the right to charge almost any price it pleased when it actually delivered the order. Apex points out that it is against its policy to accept any restrictions on its pricing, or any terms but its own. It also points out that it has always been extremely conservative in pricing, and under no circumstances has it ever consciously sold its products at prices higher than those of its competitors. It says flatly that it must ask Southern Electronics to cancel its orders if it will not accept Apex's terms.

Unfortunately, Apex is the only supplier that can meet Southern's quality and delivery requirements. In addition, Apex's price is competitive, and no other producers in Apex's rather oligopolistic industry will offer better terms. Nevertheless, the contracting officer insists that Southern should not give Apex a blank check.

2. Another Southern supplier, Moon Screw Products Company, accepted Southern's fixed-price order without qualifications. Now Moon finds that its costs on the order are much higher than anticipated. The order calls for it to receive only $10,000, and Moon claims that its total costs are $60,000 and the small company is now having trouble meeting its payroll. The specifications on the order have been much more difficult to meet than Moon anticipated. Bedell checks Moon's story by getting bids from other suppliers with experience on items similar to those made by Moon and finds that he would be lucky to get the parts for $60,000 from an experienced supplier. Now Moon is threatened with bankruptcy if Southern tries to force delivery at the contract price. In addition, Southern won't get delivery of the parts when it needs them if Moon doesn't have money to meet its payroll.

Questions

1. What contract changes, if any, should Walters and Bedell recommend to the Air Force contracting officer on the Apex and Moon orders?
2. What, if anything, should Walters and Bedell have done before they placed their first orders with Apex and Moon?

CASE 5–2. ZERO CORPORATION (B)

The use of escalation clauses

Zero Corporation (see Case 2–1 for additional history and information about the company) has redesigned the fan it uses to cool its compressors. The fan was formerly an assembly consisting of several steel stampings screwed to a gray-iron casting. The new design is a one-piece aluminum die casting that costs substantially less.

The supplier, Broderick Zinc and Aluminum Corporation, suggested the new design and is willing to sell at a guaranteed unit price of 70 cents. However, Mr. Allen, the Broderick sales representative, suggests that this may not be the best possible deal for Zero. When it guarantees a price, Broderick must include some allowance to protect itself against fluctuations in raw materials prices. Currently, secondary aluminum alloy (No. 108) sells for 26 cents a pound. However, price changes of as much as 5 cents a pound during the course of a year are not at all uncommon. Since the casting weighs 0.9 pounds and Broderick must allow an additional 5 percent in calculating the weight of material used because of dross losses, the firm must obviously include some "fat" in any fixed-price quotation, to protect itself.

Allen says that his firm is willing to cut its price to 67 cents provided that Zero is willing to accept risks from price fluctuations in secondary aluminum. The 67-cent price is based on 26-cent 108 alloy, and Allen proposes that provision be made to adjust the price either upward or downward when the price of 108 alloy, as reported in the *American Metal Market*, changes. He suggests that the price be adjusted in exact multiples of 1 cent and that no adjustment be made unless the cost of aluminum used in the casting changes by at least that amount.

In addition, Broderick is willing to amortize the costs of molds used in making the die casting in the piece price. In other words, the $2,000 cost of the molds can be spread over the first order of 20,000 units with a 10-cent price increase. This arrangement permits Zero to pay for the tools as it makes savings from the use of the new lower cost design, and it need not make a big cash investment in tools. Both Zero and Broderick agree that since tools are being amortized, there should be a special cancellation clause in the contract that permits Zero to cancel only if it: (1) accepts responsibility for any parts that it authorized to be fabricated against the order, and (2) compensates the supplier for the balance of tool cost not yet amortized in the piece price at the time of cancellation.

Questions

1. Should Zero buy the die casting on the basis of a 70-cent fixed price or a 67-cent price subject to escalation due to changes in secondary aluminum prices? Justify your answer in terms of the price trend that has prevailed for 108 secondary aluminum alloy during the last year.

2. Suppose you are the Zero buyer negotiating this contract and you conclude that it is advantageous to accept the 67-cent price with escalation and also wish to amortize tooling the piece price. Draft the escalation and cancellation clauses that you would submit to your company's legal department for approval.

6

Forecasting for purchasing

The successful purchasing manager is a good (or lucky) forecaster. While most purchasing and materials managers would regard themselves as risk avoiders, they necessarily deal with chance and take risks more often than they care to admit. Here are some of the events that every purchasing manager would love to be able to forecast with precision:

1. Will a particular supplier complete an order on schedule and without quality failures?
2. Can a particular product be purchased at a price that the purchasing manager feels should be paid?
3. Should the purchasing manager be actively seeking or avoiding long-term commitments for particular products?
4. Should the purchasing manager be building inventory or operating from day-to-day stocks of particular purchased materials?
5. Will particular purchased materials continue to be available in ample quantities or should the purchasing manager be aggressively searching for alternate sources or substitute materials?
6. What is the secular trend of prices and costs for particular purchased materials and how does this relate to overall trends of prices and costs?

Purchasing management (as distinct from simply buying) is the art and science of coping with an uncertain future. Note that the uncertainty varies from particular questions about particular transactions to rather broad forecasts that reflect general economic trends. Some purchasing managers might well maintain that they don't really do any forecasting. After all, doesn't most purchasing simply boil down to filling a requisition that is passed on to the purchasing department by someone else in the organization who is a user or fabricator of purchased materials?

FORECASTING AVAILABILITY

Even when the purchasing manager plays a very passive role in the organization, some forecasting skill is required. Suppose, for example, she gets a purchase requisition dated January 2 calling for delivery on January 20. At least one implicit forecast has already been made, namely that the supplier will be able to deliver the item in less than three weeks. This may or may not be true. In every organization, purchases are almost routinely made which are not delivered at the desired time. In many cases, this reflects a poor forecast of lead-time usage.

Lead-time usage varies

Example. Suppose, for example, there were nine items in stores when the replenishment order was placed but there was a demand for ten before the new order was delivered. What caused the variation in lead-time usage? One or both of two possible reasons account for the failure: (1) demand during the expected lead time was greater than predicted or (2) the lead time itself varied. The former failure is internal to the organization; the latter is external. In Chapter 10, we will discuss in detail how to allow for random, unpredictable changes in lead-time usage. Note, however, that almost all major variations in supplier lead time are nonrandom. Supplier ability to respond to a new order is usually directly related to the business cycle or other nonrandom factors. When the cycle is near a peak, supplier lead times stretch out.

Impact of cycle. The purchasing manager who ignores these variations will be wrong most of the time. Suppose she assumes that the lead time is one month. If she happens to be buying at the bottom of the business cycle, the supplier may easily be able to deliver within two weeks. In this case, either the buyer is carrying inventory for two weeks longer than necessary or is taking some small element of extra risk in making a commitment before it is really necessary.

Ordering too soon is not usually as costly an error as ordering too late, however. At the peak of a business cycle, the expected supplier lead time of one month may stretch out to two months or even more. The supplier is swamped with orders and just cannot get them out in time. The buyer who is not alert to this will find that orders are just not being placed soon enough at the peak of the business cycle. Worse yet, by the time he adjusts to this and starts ordering early, the cycle will have turned. Supplier backlogs will have melted away and the buyer will be placing orders much too early.

Supplier lead time is a cyclical barometer that is not only carefully watched by purchasing managers but also by economists, including those who influence policy for the President and the Federal Reserve Board.

Buying policy barometer

NAPM survey. The best barometers of buying policy are developed from the monthly reports of the *Business Survey* of the National Association of Purchasing Management (NAPM). Each month the chairman of the NAPM Business Survey Committee sends a questionnaire like that in Figure 6–1 to about 200 purchasing managers. Membership on the committee is carefully balanced geographically and by industry so the collective response represents a reliable sample of the actions and outlook of all industrial purchasing managers.

Questions 5, 6, and 7 relate directly to supplier lead times. In question 4, note that committee members are asked to indicate their current buying policy for production materials, MRO supplies, and capital equipment. Under normal conditions, purchasing managers would probably be buying MRO supplies either on a hand-to-mouth basis or 30 days ahead. The typical lead time for production materials would probably be 30 or 60 days while that for capital equipment might be 90 days or 6 months. (Most routine capital equipment purchases are fairly readily available under ordinary circumstances although highly specialized equipment almost always has a lead time over six months.)

Each month, every conceivable buying policy is typically checked by at least a few members of the committee. However, the pattern of responses varies with the state of the business cycle. As business improves, purchasing managers buy more. At first, there is ample capacity and suppliers are able to respond promptly. However, as business continues to get better, capacity gradually becomes strained and lead times lengthen. This is reflected in the responses to NAPM's buying policy survey. The percent of respondents who report buying either hand-to-mouth or on about a 30-day basis declines while the number reporting commitments 60 days or more into the future increases.

Application. This phenomenon occurs with all categories of purchases but production materials are the most widely used as a cyclical barometer. As the boom begins to peak, there is usually a spectacular increase in the number of purchasing managers who are trying to buy 180 days or more ahead of needs in order to cope with shortages. This was demonstrated with particular clarity in the 1974–75 recession (even more than in subsequent cycles). Note in Figure 6–2, the sharp increase in the percent of purchasing managers trying to buy 180 days ahead of current needs. The economy reached reasonably full employment in December 1972, and from January 1973 until the fall of

FIGURE 6-1

1974, an increasing number of purchasing managers competed for what amounted to a fixed supply of material by ordering further and further ahead of actual need.

When purchasing managers are collectively extending their buying policy, the individual purchasing manager has no choice but to follow suit if he or she is to prevent stockouts. In addition, extended buying

FIGURE 6–4   Inventories and inventory investment

Source: U.S. Department of Commerce, *Business Conditions Digest.*

As the charts demonstrate, inventory change is the most volatile component of gross national product and excessive stocks are a major factor in every business recession.

that end product should also grow at 5 percent per year. This forecast would then be modified by technological changes, if any, that would influence demand for the material.

Work with suppliers. The purchaser of a highly specialized material would usually work closely with suppliers making sure that their capacity is expanding at a rate consistent with the overall forecast of demand. Obviously, if this is not done, the company's expansion would be limited by a shortage of key components or material. In certain industries, buyer and supplier expansions are closely coordinated. For example, an auto company that is planning a new aluminum foundry would almost always enter into a long-term contract for sufficient metal to keep that facility employed. This contract, in turn, might trigger an expansion in capacity by the basic metal producer.

Identify end use. Forecasting of demand is even more difficult when the buyer is one of many users of a particular material that has widespread application. For example, a publisher such as Time, Inc. may be one of the largest buyers of coated paper. But there are thousands of other buyers and coated paper has many applications besides "slick" magazines. What will total future demand be? The problem is further complicated by difficulty in identifying the available supply of particular commodities. Thus, it is fairly easy to estimate total present papermaking capacity and also what will be available in the next few years. The next step in the process is also not too difficult; namely, estimate supply of particular types of paper—in this case, coated stock. But beyond this, even a forecast of supply may become less precise. Obviously, Time, Inc. and other large publishers are not just concerned with overall supply of coated paper but with the particular types of that material which they use. If this were not difficult enough, they often cannot even identify every other user of the materials they buy let alone estimate what their future demand will be.

Basic commodity forecasts

The example above is fairly typical. It is usually not possible to estimate the demand for particular materials in methodical step-by-step "micro" fashion, adding up individual demands arrived at by individual and independent forecasts. Instead, so-called global forecasts are more likely to be used even though the technique is less than perfect.

Projection of past. A "global" forecast is partly a projection of past relationships adjusted by changes that the forecaster believes will take place. In most cases, the forecast will be related to the overall economy. Almost all materials and products have a life cycle that begins with rapid growth and ends with relative decline.

Plastics are a "growth" material. Each increase of 1 percent in industrial production may bring a 2 or 3 percent increase in demand for various plastic materials. At the other extreme, copper and steel are "mature" products; demand for these materials increases at a rate that is less than proportionate to growth of the overall economy. For example, in the ten-year period between 1966 and 1976, overall industrial production increased by more than 30 percent. During this period, steel production did not change at all and copper usage actually declined. In contrast, a 30 percent growth in industrial production was accompanied by more than a 100 percent increase in use of both polyvinyl chloride and polyethylene (the leading plastic materials) and a fivefold increase in polypropylene (the fastest growing of the major plastics).

All of the materials mentioned above are used in a wide variety of industries. In many cases, the manufacturers themselves are not able to identify every end application of their own products. But the figures above do suggest some significant relationships. If the past is a guide to the future, then an additional 30 percent increase in industrial production will produce little change in steel production but use of plastics will probably increase faster than industrial production.

Special factors.   Is the past a valid guide to the future? Unfortunately, not necessarily. Major errors may be made. But, as mentioned previously, projection of past trends is often the only technique that is practical. The purchasing manager may be forced to use it simply because nothing else works as well. In almost every case, conclusions reached through historical comparison must be adjusted to reflect special circumstances.

In the previous example, steel output failed to keep pace with industrial production partly because of a substantial growth in imports. Imports probably will not take a growing share of the domestic market in some future decade; in fact, their share may well decline. However, this is just one major factor affecting steel demand. The period from 1966 to 1976 was selected for this comparison partly because it is perhaps the last ten-year period when steel demand is not affected by mandatory regulations concerning automobile fuel consumption which, in turn, have produced automakers with enormous incentive to reduce product weight. It seems likely that this will reduce demand for steel markedly and increase demand for plastics.

The rational forecaster would have to make his or her own estimate of the effect of this major change on demand for both steel and plastics. It seems likely in the 1980s that demand for steel will continue to lag behind over-all economic growth while that for plastics will continue to increase more rapidly. If this conclusion is correct, the buyer of plastics would be disturbed about possible availability if suppliers did not have substantial expansion projects in the works. And some buyers may worry lest slack demand for steel and low profits might cause particular suppliers simply to fade away.

Input-output analysis. The technique described above is a crude form of input-output analysis that is probably adequate for most supply forecasts. However, actual input-output data may be useful in some purchase forecasting projects. An input-output table is a matrix that shows interrelationships among various industries. It would show, for example, the relationship between steel production and portland cement consumption. Thus, if one is to forecast portland cement demand, the input-output table would show the demand for cement in various industries including steel. The forecaster would then estimate output for the cement-consuming industries. Since the relationship of each of these industries to cement demand can be identified on the input-output table, a forecast for cement demand could then be developed.

Input-output tables are published periodically by the U.S. Department of Commerce. The data are historical and relationships do change over time. In addition, data are available only for major industries. For example, the input tables would show steel demand in various steel-using industries but would not provide insight into demand for particular highly specialized types of steel.

GENERAL ECONOMIC FORECASTS

Consensus predictions

Note that the forecasting techniques we have described so far in this chapter are linked to overall economic forecasts. The forecaster makes an assumption with respect to general economic conditions and then proceeds to predict what will happen to particular products or industries. Many real-life purchasing managers use general economic forecasts that they get from their corporate economists or simply read about on the financial pages of the local newspaper.

Methodology. The technique is casual. But for the small organization it is certainly practical and works reasonably well. For example, the purchasing manager of a machinery manufacturer may read that the consensus among economists is that there will be a modest recession in the coming year. She assumes that this forecast is as good as any. During the last recession that seemed to come closest to the consensus forecast, her company's sales dropped by 5 percent. This is about what top management expects in the year ahead, after taking various special conditions into account (which often tend to offset one another). She then proceeds with a broad plan of purchase that will lead to somewhat lower inventories by year-end and will also permit the company to conserve cash should business turn out to be markedly worse than expected.

In December and January, *Business Week, The Wall Street Journal,* and other business publications devote considerable editorial attention to the economic outlook as perceived by various "experts." The president presents every January an economic report prepared by the Council of Economic Advisers which describes in detail what is expected to happen and what the federal government intends to do about it. Forecasts by the "experts" as to the state of the general economy as well as employment, inflation, and production tend to be clustered tightly together. In effect, the experts study the same underlying data and reach pretty much the same conclusions.

Past becomes future.   The safest economic forecast is "more of the same." And economists are least likely to make major errors when they study the data and, in effect, simply project existing trends into the future. Unfortunately, they are most likely to make errors at critical points in the business cycle, especially at about the time a sharp recession begins. This is naturally the period when business executives would like their forecasts to be accurate. But they often are not—even the highly sophisticated forecasting expertise that is available to the president of the United States.

In at least one case, the president's advice was so bad that it was publicly embarrassing. In October 1974, President Gerald Ford formally requested Congress to enact higher taxes in order to restrict demand and fight inflation. The president had been advised by his economists to restrain what was perceived by the experts as a runaway boom. This conclusion was based on latest statistics gathered by the U.S. Department of Commerce, Department of Labor, and other sources. In general, these statistics were pretty good measures (with considerable margin for error but nevertheless the best data available) on what had actually been going on in the economy in July and August.

No one really knew in October what the economy was doing in October. In fact, a sharp recession had already begun. Both employment and production were declining. If Congress had acted swiftly in response to President Ford's request to boost taxes, the recession would have been dangerously aggravated. The economists began to identify the emerging recession in November and December. In January, President Ford was forced to make a rather embarrassing 180° turn in economic policy. He withdrew his request for tax *hikes* to curb inflation and asked for tax *cuts* to help cope with recession and possible excessive price deflation.

Poor data.   In most cases, errors in economic forecasting are not so obvious. They can be hidden by regular "reappraisals" wherein the forecast is gradually modified to fit new facts that emerge. The problem generally does not lie with the ability of economists to interpret facts. The problem lies with the data with which they work. The statistics simply are not as accurate as they appear to be and, for various reasons, are most likely to be erroneous at critical stages in the business cycle. In addition, there is always a considerable lag in time between actual events and availability of reliable statistical reports on what actually did happen.

Because of poor forecasts based on inadequate information, companies keep on adding to inventory for weeks or even months after the time has come when they should be cutting it. At the other end of the business cycle, they are often overly cautious at an upward turning point in the cycle. While purchasing managers hardly ever know as much about economics as the experts whose forecasts are published widely, they do enjoy privileged access to information that may not reach the experts until some months later. Thus, the purchasing manager not only needs better economic forecasts but is at least partly able to get them.

Major business barometers

Before discussing the information that is of special interest to the purchasing executive, let us look at some of the general business barometers that interest almost everyone in business and government. These measure what is being produced and how much, what is being saved and invested, and the prices that are being paid for goods, services, and money itself.

Production. Gross national product and national income are the broadest, most widely used measures of total output of goods and services. Estimates are made quarterly and are calculated in current dollars. GNP and national income (which is closely related) almost always go up in current dollars. Most of the gain usually represents higher prices, not an actual gain in output. For this reason, figures for "real" GNP are also published regularly. These are based on nominal GNP adjusted by an "implicit price deflator" to eliminate the distortion caused by inflation. Real GNP increases at an average annual rate of roughly 3 percent. The rate of improvement is very low and may even be negative during recession years. For short periods of recovery, the rate of annual gain may go as high as 10 percent.

GNP includes all kinds of spending and is not especially useful as a forecasting tool. The Federal Reserve Board industrial production index is a better barometer of what factories are currently producing. This index is based on physical output figures as much as possible and is therefore not supposed to be distorted by price change. The monthly index actually declines during recession years and rises during boom years. Unlike GNP, the index is available on a reasonably timely basis—about two and one-half weeks after the end of the month being reported for a preliminary estimate subject to later revision. Subindexes are also published for major industry groups. The index that is most widely published is seasonally adjusted to facilitate month-by-month comparison.

Factory employment statistics, which are gathered by the U.S. Department of Labor, tend to parallel the production index for obvious reasons. However, overall employment has increased more rapidly than factory employment because the nonmanufacturing parts of our economy have grown more rapidly. The nonmanufacturing sector is also more stable, a desirable feature that makes it less useful as a business forecasting barometer.

Production and employment are the broadest "coincident" indicators. That is, they measure where the economy is right now—or at least where it was at the time the data was collected. Under the Full Employment Act of 1946, the federal government is expected to take whatever steps are needed to assure full employment and, therefore, steadily rising output.

Prices.   The general price level tends to advance with production and employment but, unfortunately, does not necessarily decline. Every purchasing manager not only influences the general price level but is influenced by it. Our economy includes millions (or perhaps even billions) of different prices. To some extent, each is unique and reflects relative bargaining power of buyers and sellers. But prices are also determined by the value of money itself. The most precise measure of the purchasing power of the U.S. dollar is the implicit GNP price deflator. If the deflator this year is calculated at 5 percent, then one can say that money lost 5 percent of its value.

Purchasing managers are more likely to use more specialized price indexes to measure the purchase power of their companies' money. The Bureau of Labor Statistics (BLS) collects data and publishes monthly a wholesale price index of materials and products used in commerce and manufacturing. This broad index, in turn, has many components so it is possible to track overall price trends for every major industry and many individual product groups. Many purchasing managers also compile price indexes designed to measure what they pay for their own specialized purchases. These measure past price performance and are also helpful in projecting future price trends. Every purchasing manager should be the best qualified person in his or her organization to forecast future price trends which, in turn, influence company policies as well as profits.

Price for money.   Interest rates are a specialized form of price—that paid for the use of money. Purchasing managers are not directly concerned with borrowing on behalf of their companies. But they do indeed follow interest rates because the business cycle itself directly correlates with ups and downs in the interest rates that borrowers pay—especially short-term rates. The federal funds rate (the interest rate banks pay on overnight loans to one another) and the Treasury bill rate (interest paid by the U.S. Treasury on 13-week and 26-week borrowing) are widely used as general economic barometers. The federal funds rate is published after every business day; the latest Treasury bill rates are normally published on Tuesdays. Rising interest rates act as a brake on borrowing and will eventually slow the economy down. Declining rates indicate relatively more lenders than borrowers; they tend to encourage higher investment and production.

Investment. Inventory accumulation and capital investment are the main locomotives (along with government purchases of goods and services) that push the economy up hill and also, when the power is let up, permit it to slide down hill. The basic reason for this is that investment, and the payrolls it creates, stimulate demand for consumer goods and purchases but do not immediately do anything directly to satisfy that demand. For example, the bricklayer who works on a building gets paid and buys a T-bone steak. He makes a direct contribution to demand but does nothing to increase the supply of consumer items. In contrast, a farmer may grow wheat and use the proceeds to buy steak. The farmer's money simply moves in a circle. The demand for steak is offset by an increase in the supply of wheat so the net effect is neutral.

The economy is unstable primarily because of transactions whose effect is not neutral as with the farmer buying steak. Purchasing managers collectively are major (albeit involuntary) contributors to this instability in their collective inventory decisions. An addition to inventory temporarily creates a demand on the economy but adds nothing to supply. Inventory reduction has the opposite effect. The actions of an individual firm have no measurable impact but if thousands of businesses move in the same direction at about the same time as they often do, then the force is more than great enough to push the rest of the economy up and down with the inventory.

The purchasing manager not only must make inventory decisions but also is concerned with the collective course of inventory accumulation or liquidation—as is every other business executive. Economists have long known that changes in inventory level (particularly in manufacturing but also at wholesale and retail levels) are the single most important determinant of the business cycle. Timely, accurate inventory data would greatly improve economists' forecasting performance. Unfortunately, existing statistics are not timely nor are they accurate.

The Department of Commerce regularly publishes inventory data

FIGURE 6–5
Composite indexes

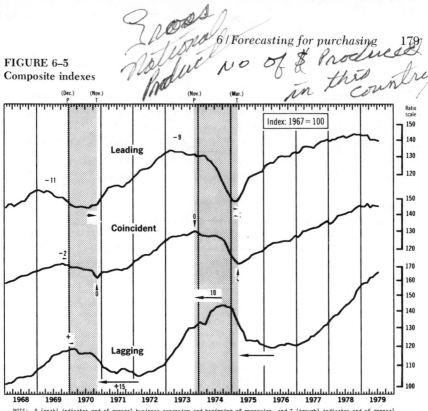

NOTE: P (peak) indicates end of general business expansion and beginning of recession, and T (trough) indicates end of general business recession and beginning of expansion; thus, shaded areas represent recessions. Numbers on the chart indicate length of leads (–) and lags (+) in months from business cycle turning dates.

Source: U.S. Department of Commerce, *Business Conditions Digest.*

This chart which shows several business cycles illustrates how the coincident indicators follow the leading indicators and are, in turn, followed by the lagging indicators.

declining. These barometers define where the economy was as the time that the data was gathered.

Lagging indicators. As the term implies, the lagging indicators run behind the general business cycle. Note that the index of lagging indicators kept on rising some months after the two recessions shown in the shaded areas actually began. Then it finally turned, began to decline, and kept on declining well into the subsequent period of subsequent recovery. The barometers included in this index are natural laggers.

Sometimes the lagging indicators give signals that are very useful in forecasting even though they are always supposed to be "behind." If a boom is beginning to falter, business executives may not begin ordering capital goods on a wide scale, preferring to work overtime or simply to let their customers wait. As a result, the lagging barometers will begin to slow down and flatten out even while the leading indicators are continuing to march on to new highs. This is a signal that says "caution" to economists. The boom may be petering out without the capital goods buying spree that is supposed to come at the end.

Leading indicators. While lagging and coincident indicators are useful to economists, it is the leading indicators that get the most attention. The U.S. Department of Commerce publishes statistics monthly on 62 of them in *Business Conditions Digest.* Twelve of these are used in compiling the composite index shown in Figure 6–5. Note in Table 6–1 that two of these—vendor performance and change in

TABLE 6–1
Key leading indicators used as components of composite index

Average workweek, production workers, manufacturing (hours).
Layoff rate, manufacturing (percent).
Vendor performance, companies reporting slower deliveries (percent).
Change in total liquid assets (percent).
Change in sensitive prices (WPI of crude materials excluding food, feeds) (percent).
Contracts and orders, plant and equipment (billions of 1972 dollars).
Net business formation index (1967 = 100).
Index of stock prices, 500 common stocks (1941–43 = 10).
Money balance (M1), (billions of 1972 dollars).
New orders, manufacture, consumer products and materials (billions of 1972 dollars).
Building permits (1967 = 100).
Change in inventories on hand and on order (annual rate, billions of 1972 dollars).

inventories on hand and on order—directly reflect the actions of purchasing managers and several others are readily related to the purchasing process.

As the term suggests and as Figure 6–5 shows, the leading indicators move ahead of the general business cycle. The composite index shown in Figure 6–5 clearly started turning down at least a few months in advance of the two recessions. Their "lead" is indicated on the chart: 11 months for the 1970 recession and 5 months for the 1973–75 recessions. The chart also indicates that the composite leading indicators bottomed out and began to edge back upward 8 months ahead of coincident indicators in the 1970 recession and one month ahead in the 1973–74 recession.

However, a look at the chart also suggests that the leading indicators do not make business forecasting a mechanistic process. The trend of the indicators, even though they allegedly "lead," becomes crystal clear only well after the fact. There is a lag of one month or more in gathering and publishing data. In addition, there can be prolonged periods in which the indicators may send out false signals.

Note, for example, that Figure 6–5 suggests that the leading indicators declined for at least three consecutive months during the second quarter of 1977. Looking back, we know that a recession was *not* developing at that time. But if a forecaster relied exclusively on these indicators in July 1977, a false recession forecast would have been inevitable. Similarly, when President Ford asked for higher taxes in 1974, the leading indicators had been wobbling around for months without any clear trend. The fact that they had given advance warning four or five months previously (as implied by Figure 6–4) only became obvious a year or so later.

NAPM BAROMETERS

Purchasing managers have readily available information that can make it easier to draw reliable conclusions from the government economic statistics such as the leading indicators. The *NAPM Business Survey* is available within days after the figures are compiled.

Application

Leading indicators. As indicated previously, question 5 of the survey, which relates to buying policy, is a leading economic indicator itself. Questions 1, 2, 3, and 4—which relate to production, new orders, prices, inventories, and employment—are useful primarily because they are more quickly able to identify accurately changes in trend than comparable government statistics. In each instance, purchasing managers are simply asked to report change in relation to the previous month: up, down, or the same. In theory, this should produce data that is not seasonally adjusted; in practice respondents apparently make a seasonal adjustment subconsciously reporting only what they perceive as "real" changes. For example, industrial production should almost always be higher in March than in February simply because March probably has three or four more working days (depending on holidays and leap years). But this is not "real" and research shows that it would probably be ignored by the NAPM respondents.

Relative change. Thus, survey results can be used as they are reported. However, the report for a particular month has meaning only if compared with previous months. Respondents to the survey typically check "better," "same," or "worse" for each business condition as it applies to their own company. Then the results are tabulated, giving equal weight to each respondent. For example, during a particular month, the chairman of Business Survey Committee may report that 42 percent of the responding companies reported more new orders received by their company than in the previous month, 22 percent reported the same, and 36 percent reported a lower level of orders.

Since 42 percent of the committee reports more orders, while only 36 percent reports fewer orders, we can probably assume that there was a moderate increase in total manufacturers' new orders during that month. And in an overwhelming majority of cases, this conclusion will be consistent with the Department of Commerce data that are subsequently published.

Measuring direction of change

This does not mean, however, that business is getting better—even if the survey results for production, prices, inventories, and employment are consistent with those for new orders. What counts is not so much the absolute results of the survey but the rate and direction of change. For example, suppose that last month 52 percent of the respondents reported an increase in new orders and 63 percent reported an increase the previous month. Even though new orders are apparently still increasing in an absolute sense, there is a relative decline. The rate of change in new orders is obviously negative. This may indicate a major change in the business cycle if it cannot be explained by seasonal fluctuation. The probability of a change increases sharply if the new trend persists.

Example. Suppose, for example, that the NAPM survey for three months shows the following:

Month	Better	Same	Worse	Consensus	Change
January	68%	12%	20%	+48%	
February	63	14	23	+40	− 8%
March	52	19	29	+23	−17

Note that in March the barometer is still strongly positive with 52 percent of respondents citing improvement and only 29 percent saying it is worse. However, the rate of change (the last column) is a likely harbinger of the future. The barometer's position is deteriorating at an accelerating rate.

This is exactly what happens to the NAPM production, inventory, and new order series just before a recession develops. The only time that the barometers will normally give a false signal is when some noncyclical event is distorting the data. For example, if General Motors Corporation were shut down by a strike during the hypothetical three-month period above, the NAPM barometers would behave as if a recession were developing. The reason, of course, is that General Motors is so big and has such an enormous impact on the economy that a strike would cause most of the NAPM barometers to falter.

Analysis of data

Moving average.   Both the NAPM series and the subsequent comparable government data tend to fluctuate erratically from month to
month. In most cases, the trend is not as clear-cut as the example
above. Some clues to the trend come from observation of the rate of
change of the barometer. It is also helpful, however, to plot three-
month moving averages. This was done in a research study[1] the author
made some years ago and NAPM and government data correlated remarkably well.

Production performance.   Figure 6–6 compares a three-month
moving average of the NAPM consensus forecast (i.e., the algebraic

FIGURE 6–6
Comparison of NAPM survey with changes in seasonally adjusted Federal Reserve
Board industrial production index (three-month moving average)

Source: Dean S. Ammer, *The NAPM Business Survey: Past Performances and Present Application in Forecasting* (New York: National Association of Purchasing Management, Inc., 1977), p.
2.14.8. Reprinted by permission.

The NAPM consensus forecast of industrial production closely parallels changes in the
Federal Reserve Board industrial production index. The major advantage of the NAPM
index is that it is available sooner and is not subject to later revision.

---

[1] The results of this research were published as part of the *Guide to Purchasing* that
the National Association of Purchasing Management distributes to its members: Chapter
2.14, *The NAPM Business Survey: Past Performance and Present Application in
Forecasting.*

184

sum of those reporting higher output less those reporting lower production) compared with a three-month moving average of the change in the seasonally adjusted Federal Reserve Board index of industrial production. Note how closely the zigs and zags of the two series coincide with the NAPM consensus being somewhat more volatile. While Figure 6–6 embraces just the six-year period between 1969 and 1975, other studies of the relationship between the NAPM survey and comparable government data yielded essentially the same correlations.

The NAPM consensus survey has always gone into a nose dive (as the chart shows for both 1969 and 1974) as recessions began and then climbed sharply just as the recession ended. Three successive monthly declines or increases in the three-month moving average are especially significant, especially if the move is consistent with the behavior of other barometers.

Employment. The NAPM consensus survey on employment is a more consistent performer than the production series, which is more likely to be distorted by strikes. As a business boom gets "tired," the three-month moving average begins to trace a persistent but irregular

FIGURE 6–7
Comparison of NAPM survey with changes in seasonally adjusted BLS employment in manufacturing (three-month moving average)

Source: Dean S. Ammer, *The NAPM Business Survey: Past Performance and Present Application in Forecasting* (New York: National Association of Purchasing Management, Inc., 1977), p. 2.14.11. Reprinted by permission.

Changes in factory employment as reported in the NAPM survey closely parallel data reported subsequently by the Bureau of Labor Statistics. However, the BLS data are subject to more erratic fluctuations on a month-to-month basis.

downward course as illustrated in Figure 6–7. Then shortly before a recession officially ends, it recovers sharply. It traces a pattern that parallels changes in manufacturing employment as reported by the Bureau of Labor Statistics but the latter series fluctuates more erratically, probably because of sampling error.

New orders.   While production and employment are not "leading" indicators, the NAPM series do lead the business cycle when their rate of change is close and when three-month moving averages are plotted. In contrast, new orders are a legitimate leading barometer (as is the NAPM inventory series mentioned earlier in this chapter). The NAPM new order series (see Figure 6–8) has consistently weakened on an

FIGURE 6–8
Comparison of NAPM survey with change in seasonally adjusted manufacturers new orders (three-month moving average)

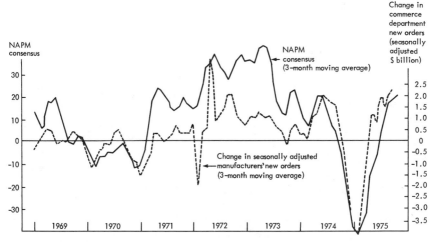

Source: Dean S. Ammer, *The NAPM Business Survey: Past Performance and Present Application in Forecasting* (New York: National Association of Purchasing Management, Inc., 1977), p. 2.14.15. Reprinted by permission.

Current new orders determine future production and employment so new orders are a critical leading indicator. Over previous business cycles, the NAPM new order survey has proved to be a more reliable, as well as more timely, barometer than the data of the U.S. Department of Commerce.

absolute basis well in advance of every post-World War II recession. It also rebounds promptly when recessions end although its "lead" is not as great as it is on the downside of the cycle.

Identifying recessions

One simple way to "test" for a recession is simply to take the algebraic sum of the percent of respondents reporting an increased volume of new orders less the percent reporting fewer orders. If the sum is negative (i.e., the number of respondents to the NAPM survey reporting fewer orders outnumbers those reporting more orders), a recession is a near certainty. In fact, as E. F. Andrews, long-time chairman of the NAPM Business Survey Committee points out, the probability of a cyclical swing is extremely high when the lines of his charts "cross" with a turnabout in the net consensus. Recovery comes when those reporting more new orders outnumber those reporting a reduction and a recession may be in the offing when the cutbacks exceed the increases.

The NAPM *Business Survey* report is usually released in the second week of each month with results for the preceding period. NAPM members receive as first class mail a *Report on Business* which includes the chairman's full report and charts. Nonmembers can usually read the substance of the report in *The Wall Street Journal, New York Times,* and other major newspapers.

FORECASTING PRICES

Purchasing and materials management executives track the business cycle because of its impact on both price and availability. Prices are obviously influenced by costs which, in turn, are related to a general rate of inflation that is closely tied to the overall business cycle. Prices are also influenced by demand, both real and psychological. This is also related to the business cycle.

Behavior of prices

While the general price level goes in but one direction—up—the rate of price inflation does fluctuate cyclically. Those of the various BLS wholesale price indexes are basically coincident barometers, mirroring the overall performance of the economy. The *NAPM Business Survey* price series can be constructed so that it behaves like a leading indicator on the downside but lags in recovery periods.

NAPM consensus. Figure 6–9 shows a three-month moving average of the NAPM price consensus (i.e., the percent reporting higher prices minus the percent reporting lower prices) plotted over the course of two business cycles. As can be seen, the consensus was always "positive" (i.e., prices were going up) except for a brief period in 1975. However, the consensus became less strongly inflationary some months before general business began to head downward in 1970 and 1974. During the subsequent recovery, however, the series quite logically lagged the cycle. In both cycles, prices did not begin to strengthen until after general business began to show measurable recovery. The price series was distorted by price controls during part of

FIGURE 6–9

Comparison of NAPM survey with seasonally adjusted BLS index of industrial materials price (3-month moving average)

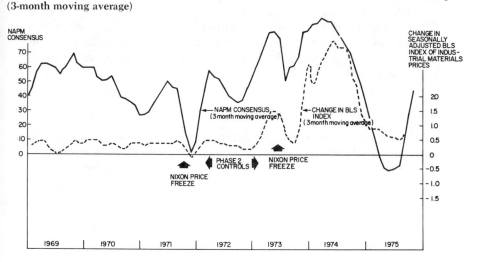

the period shown in Figure 6–9. Otherwise, the series can be expected to behave in this fashion during every business cycle, usually leading the BLS index of industrial materials prices by a few months.

Of course, the purchasing manager's interest in prices extends beyond overall trends to what will actually be paid for particular purchases. Individual prices are influenced by the general outlook but the forecaster must also take into account unique factors.

Characteristics. Those who take up purchasing as a career almost immediately learn and are sometimes surprised by these characteristics of supply and prices:

1. At some price, almost anything can be obtained. There is no such thing as a genuine "shortage"—over the long term at least. Even the scarcest materials are available in substantially increased quantities provided someone is willing to pay enough. During periods when demand temporarily pushes ahead of supply, the sophisticated buyer is perfectly willing to pay what is needed to get essential material.

2. Prices can go down even when costs of production are going up. This reduction need not come from increased efficiency. It may simply reflect a demand that is lagging supply. The purchasing manager's not-so-easy job is to relate demand and supply and estimate just what price is "fair" in that sellers will sell as much as they wish at that price and buyers will get what they want.

3. Some prices can be set without regard either to cost of production or demand. The product is unique, useful, and in high demand. In

this case, the buyer has no choice but to pay the price that is asked. Forecasting boils down to estimating in advance what the seller thinks the traffic will bear. Many monopoly-priced items tend to go up at about the same rate as overall inflation. This implies a cost-based pricing. In reality, the producer perceives that this will be regarded as "fair" by customers and does not want to incur their ill will.

Forecasting administered prices

In some cases, the producer has sufficient power to set a price almost independently of any market. In most cases, however, the producer must take into account the reactions of both competitors and customers. The purchasing manager who is trying to predict such prices will consider both cost of production and the supply-demand situation that exists in particular industries.

Example. Suppose, for example, the purchasing manager is trying to estimate the future price of gray-iron castings. He should consider the following five factors.

1. *Effect of general business conditions.* The predicted GNP will have a varied effect on the industries that use gray-iron casting. If GHP rises 3 percent, demand for gray-iron castings may not rise at all, or it may rise substantially more than 3 percent. The purchasing manager often can guess quite accurately what the overall effect of a change in GNP on demand for castings will be by studying what happened in previous years.

2. *Estimated changes in supply.* By using general business statistics and also drawing on the knowledge of the expansion plans of key suppliers in the industry, the purchasing manager can deduce how much additional capacity is planned, using techniques suggested in this chapter.

3. *Cost trends in the industry.* If contracts between foundries and the unions representing their workers are being renewed, the purchasing manager should estimate the cost of the settlement and its probable effect on the foundries' cost of production. He also should be familiar with the probable trend of the prices of key raw materials in gray-iron castings: pig iron, scrap iron, coke, and so on. And further, the purchasing manager should try to estimate what effect new equipment and various laborsaving devices will have on suppliers' costs when they are introduced.

4. *"Temper" of the market.* The purchasing manager and buyers should be in regular contact with all important suppliers. In this way they are always apprised of the state of the market. If producers are extremely confident, the near-term outlook is probably for firm prices. Sophisticated buyers know how to evaluate their suppliers' comments

on the market. They are sharp enough to spot market weakness when the optimists sound a little less optimistic and the pessimists moan a little louder than usual.

5. *Prices on new contracts.* If the purchasing manager has been successful in making new purchases at lower than expected prices, the market is obviously weakening. Similarly, if prices are rising slightly, the market is firmer. When current prices are changing, the purchasing manager can safely predict a change in total prices in the same direction, and rarely will be wrong. Price trends take time to reverse themselves. In addition, not all prices paid reflect the effects of new prices at the same time; prices usually are adjusted only when a new purchase is made and deliveries are made. For these reasons, purchase price indexes can be extremely useful tools for predicting short-term trends in prices.

Subjective evaluation. The purchasing manager's evaluation of the factors that influence the price of gray-iron castings is partly subjective—although it should be based on objective data as much as possible. The purchasing manager may wish to assign a percentage weighting of the importance of each factor in making the final estimate of the probable price change in castings. This may give the estimate an appearance of objectivity, but the final decision remains highly subjective and depends almost entirely on the materials manager's skill and experience.

In a large organization, the purchasing manager may want to back his or her judgment up with that of a "Delphi" panel of experts—particularly if an accurate forecast is critical to success. The basic idea is to give each member of the panel all information pertinent to the forecast. Panel members then make an individual forecast and add any new ideas that occur to them after they have read the composite contribution of the panel. It is possible to have several Delphi "rounds" in the hope that the panel will continue to gain insight from the collective contributions of other members of the panel to the forecast.[2]

Free market commodities

The Delphi approach can also be applied to materials whose prices are determined almost entirely by supply and demand. Unlike producers of administered-price items, commodity producers have almost no control over price. The producer of a gray-iron casting or an electric appliance sets a price for its product. This price reflects what competitors would charge for an equivalent product, but it is possible to have slight and sometimes even substantial differences. The producer

---

[2] The Delphi technique is applied to economic forecasting in Dean S. Ammer, "What Businessmen Expect from the 1970's," *Harvard Business Review,* January–February 1971, pp. 41–52.

does not have this option when price is set entirely by supply and demand. Theoretically, the producer of a free market commodity can produce and sell as much as it likes at the market price, but it can sell nothing should it try to charge slightly more than market.

Many free market commodities are agricultural in origin—wheat, crude rubber, corn, corn oil, soybeans, cotton, wool, and hides. Others are either the products of primary producers of various types or of scrap—scrap metals of all types, plywood, lead, tin, zinc, and various chemical and petroleum products.

Many of these products are traded on commodity exchanges, and the price on the exchange determines the price paid by every producer. In other cases, the material is not formally traded on an exchange but the price is widely publicized, moving up and down in response to changes in supply and demand. The general business outlook and cost of production ultimately affect demand and supply, but over a short term prices are determined entirely by sellers and buyers whose bids and asks determine prices on commodity exchanges.

Demand and supply. Demand for these commodities fluctuates considerably. When the business outlook is basically bullish, corporations buy not only for current production but also to add to inventories. When business executives are pessimistic about the future, they will use up their inventories and buy practically nothing, even for current production. Demand depends more on business sentiment and expectations than on actual business conditions.

While demand is subject to extremely wide swings, supply changes quite slowly. It takes time to bring additional facilities into production in response to high prices. And producers are reluctant to shut down marginal facilities until prices fall to ruinously low levels. The result of this supply-demand situation is highly unstable prices.

Purchasing managers who buy these volatile commodities can make or lose large sums of money for their companies. For example, an automobile manufacturer might use 2 million pounds of copper in its radiators per month. Suppose copper goes up 4 cents a pound. Costs rise $80,000 per month—but not for a while, at least, if the purchasing manager has anticipated the increase and increased inventories. On the other hand, if copper drops 4 cents, the purchasing manager can get maximum benefit from the decrease only if stocks were cut "to the bone" before the price dropped.

Available statistics. Industry statistics provide clues to future price changes. They are published in abbreviated form in the *Survey of Current Business* and in great detail in specialized journals. For most commodities, it is possible to get reasonably up-to-date figures on stocks-on-hand, current production, and sales. In theory, at least, a buildup of inventory tends to bring prices down, and reduction of inventory may be a harbinger of higher prices. In practice, most commodity prices have a habit of turning around before statistics become available. Thus, the buyer may learn only after the price change has occurred.

While commodity buyers carefully study all available statistics in order to make rational decisions, they can never be completely certain that a particular price trend will continue. The general rule, however, is that a current trend will prevail: if prices have been rising, they will probably continue to decline. But, of course, there is always a turning point—and this is what is most difficult to predict.

Slight changes in supply and demand often have a magnified effect on price. Demand and supply for most commodities is relatively inelastic over the short term. This means that, regardless of the price, buyers will keep buying and sellers will keep selling—over the short term, at least. When supply or demand get out of balance, the imbalance continues simply because neither buyer nor seller is inhibited very much by the price.

In fact, for a time at least, price change may induce behavior that continues the trend. For example, if copper rises by 2 cents per pound after a period of stable prices, buyers may well be tempted to build stocks in anticipation of further price increases. This extra demand pushes up prices even more, and the rising trend continues until eventually supply begins to get a little ahead of demand—either because production is increased or because every buyer has built up its own inventory as much as it desires or can afford.

Once the purchasing manager has developed a working forecast of the prices that will be paid in the coming year and the economic environment that is expected, he or she is then ready to develop a plan of purchase that is consistent with the company's short-term goals as well as its overall strategic plan. This planning process will be discussed in detail in the chapter that follows.

Case

CASE 6–1. NEW ENGLAND SHIPBUILDING CORPORATION

Forecasting purchase prices

New England Shipbuilding Corporation is one of the largest shipyards in the United States. It builds not only various types of warships and supporting craft for the U.S. Navy but also cargo ships for private ship lines. Like other American shipyards, the company would not exist were it not for Navy orders and heavy subsidies on merchant marine orders. While New England Shipbuilding and other major American shipbuilders believe they are at least as efficient as their foreign competitors—particularly the Japanese—their methods are not so superior that they can compete in world markets with foreign yards that pay wages lower than those prevailing in American yards. Consequently, despite government subsidies, the company is in an almost perpetual profit squeeze.

Its problems are compounded by the basic economics of shipbuilding. Individual ships require as much as three years to construct, and a shipbuilding firm may, at any given time, have no more than three or four ships under construction. Naturally, it does not know how much profit it realizes on any particular order until after the ship is completed. Any interim calculations represent no more than an educated guess. While the company does receive subsidies on its work, competition among American shipyards for available business is so keen that profit margins are extremely narrow both on Navy work and on merchant ship construction. In addition, shipbuilders have relatively little control over many of their costs. A shipbuilder is basically an assembler of steel and other components made by specialized suppliers and, in the case of New England Shipbuilding, purchased parts and materials account for more than 60 percent of the sales dollar.

Naturally, when a project stretches out over a period of two or three years, costs of purchased parts and materials can run way ahead of original estimates. In the past, the company has been able to protect itself against unanticipated fluctuations in material costs by incorporating price-redetermination or escalation clauses into its contracts. These clauses generally permit reasonable increases in both labor and material to be passed on to the customer. In recent years, however, customers have demanded more protection against unanticipated price changes, and competition has been so vigorous that the major shipyards have been forced to accede to their customers' requests.

The company is now bidding on a $30 million order. It hopes to get an edge on competitors if it can offer the customer a completely fixed price. The company estimates that work on the order will extend over a three-year period and that purchases of parts and materials for the order will amount to almost $20 million. Naturally, a wide range of purchased materials and parts will be required, although most of them will fall into three general categories: metals and metal products, electrical machinery, and nonelectrical machinery and equipment.

Walter Rogers, the materials manager, estimates that, roughly $8 million will be spent for electrical machinery and equipment of various types, $6 million for nonelectrical machinery, and the balance for various types of metal parts and products. He assumes that prices he pays for the products will advance roughly in line with the Bureau of Labor Statistics wholesale price indexes of metals and metal products, and machinery. He also notes that in the past prices of machinery have tended to advance about two thirds as rapidly as general wage rates. That is, if general wages advance by 10 percent during any particular year, the price of machinery would go up by roughly 7 percent. This is only an overall average, however. In practice, machinery is more likely to advance almost as much as wages when demand is strong, while in periods of weak demand machinery manufacturers and suppliers of other materials and parts usually absorb any contract increases they incur in wage rates.

A decrease in prices paid for purchased parts or materials seems highly unlikely. Rogers is certain that, at best, he will be able to hold the line with existing costs and prices over the three-year period in which deliveries of the parts and materials will be made. At worst, he fears that a full 15 percent escalation (which the company expects to get on this contract) would be required.

He has been ordered, however, not to pad his estimate of material costs by the maximum amount of escalation. That is, if it seems certain that prices will not increase by more than 15 percent in the next three years, Rogers cannot protect himself by increasing his estimate of purchased parts and materials from $20 million at present prices to $23 million at the price level that will prevail three years later. The company needs the new order badly and cannot afford to lose out to competitors. On the other hand, Rogers has also been warned not to underestimate material costs. In fact, George Warren, the president of the firm, told him, "I want you to estimate the lowest possible material cost on this job and then stick to your cost. We can't afford to pad our estimate on this job. We need it too badly. On the other hand, the profit margin will be so narrow that we can't afford to spend $20,500,000 for materials if our bid is based on material cost of $20 million. We're not in business for our health, either."

Rogers believes that delivery of materials will be spaced fairly evenly over a three-year period. This, of course, would blunt the effect of any continuing inflation of prices and cost, since the maximum inflation would be incurred only on material that is delivered toward the end of the contract, while no inflation over original prices is incurred on material that is purchased immediately. However, Rogers cannot afford to commit the company to buy and take delivery of the material before it is actually needed. The company does not have the cash to invest and will not have it until it gets progress payments from the customer. In addition, it is subject to cancellation clauses that would prevent the company from being reimbursed for materials that are purchased too far ahead of actual needs.

Question

Assume that New England Shipbuilding's costs of purchased parts and materials follow the pattern of the BLS wholesale price indexes for metals and metal products, nonelectrical machinery, and electrical machinery. Based on *present* economic conditions, what should New England Shipbuilding include in its estimate of material costs?

7

Materials management planning

Planning is a major part of every executive's job. In general, the higher the executive's rank, the greater the futurity of the planning. The chief executive officer should be almost exclusively occupied with long-term planning. Especially in a large organization, there is relatively little that can be done to influence the performance of the organization within the near future. The chief executive is normally concerned with such decisions as selection of key-operating executives, construction of new facilities, introduction of new product lines, major financing, and so on. The impact of these decisions is not usually felt for at least a year.

The day-to-day success of the company is in the hands of a chief operating executive. In large corporations, the chairperson of the board may be the chief executive officer, while the president is the chief operating officer. Regardless of the titles of the executives, however, every organization has two distinctly different types of management problem: strategic and long-range, concerned with the basic direction in which the organization is headed; and short-range, which focuses on day-to-day operating problems.

In most organizations, the materials manager can make significant contributions to the long-range planning process. Trends in purchase prices, for example, may be the single most important factor influencing a company's decision either to make something it is now buying, or vice versa. Like all other executives, the materials manager is also responsible for the professional development of subordinates. While this effort may have almost no impact on current operations, it is vital to the achievement of broad, long-range "strategic" plans.

STRATEGIC PLANNING

Definition and examples

Strategic planning is the process whereby managers seek to make optimum use of their organizations' resources. The principles that underlie the strategic planning process are easy to identify; their execution, however, is fraught with uncertainty. The idea behind strategic planning is to say, in effect, "here is what we have right now; there is where we think we should be going—taking into account where and when we start and how we are able to cope with the not always predictable external forces that are certain to influence our progress."

Purchasing participation. The materials manager and the purchasing director should obviously participate in the overall strategic planning process. Then they should make their own strategic plans consistent with the overall plan. The strategic plan must be realistic. A sow's ear cannot be turned into a silk purse—without applying a rather complex process, at least. The first step in the strategic planning process is probably to assess the relative promise of the areas of the business in which the organization is presently engaged.

In a perfect environment, the organization is already fully employed in fields that are very promising and in which it does very well. In this case, strategic planning boils down to full speed ahead, taking into account the organization's ability to marshall the human, physical, and financial resources it needs to achieve objectives and the external forces that are likely to influence its success. In most real-life organizations, the strategic planning process is more complex, involving careful assessment of the directions in which the organization should be heading.

Hypothetical case. As an example of how strategic planning might work, suppose that you are president of a company that manufactures automobile tires. The future course of your company's automobile tire business is obviously related to these variables:

1. *Future demand for new cars.* Every new car requires tires that will be made by your company or one of its competitors. There is almost nothing you can do to influence this demand. The best you can hope to do is to predict demand and then try to get a profitable share of the market.

2. *Replacement demand for tires.* This demand is fairly easy to predict at least a few years ahead. The cars that will require replacement tires have already been built. While demand for replacement obviously depends on utilization of existing automobiles, this is easier to predict than new car demand.

3. *Future costs and prices.* Every management can influence cost and prices but no management has complete control over them.

They are determined by competitors' actions, government regulations, union negotiations, technology, demand and supply of other products requiring similar materials or production resources, the overall state of the economy, and a host of other factors—including many that managements find it difficult to identify let alone cope with.

In many businesses, a large part of the strategic planning process would be concerned with what the organization could do to influence aggregate demand for its products. In the tire business, this part of the process would probably not be as important. Instead, competing manufacturers would be concerned primarily with what economic or technological strategies they could devise to favorably affect their share of the market.

The role of the purchasing director and materials manager in this early strategic planning process would be almost exclusively concerned with forecasting costs of purchased materials and their availability. In some cases, this would have a major effect on the strategic plan that might emerge. Soaring purchased materials costs and/or tight supply might cause a company either to back away from a particular business because of the threat of a squeeze on profit margins or it might identify an opportunity for integration backward into a supplier's business. In contrast, a forecast of ready availability and weak purchased materials prices would support an expansionist strategy.

A real-life tire company would probably come up with an aggregate demand forecast that would not be especially encouraging. It would presumably assume that basic demand for new cars and the tires that go on them would not grow much faster than the adult population. And technological improvement in the tires themselves would cause replacement demand to grow slowly.

Chances are that each competing tire company would come up with pretty much the same forecast of total demand. Their responses to the forecast might vary. In fact, quite different strategies could emerge. One company might attempt to boost its market share by spending heavily on more efficient plant, marketing, and improvements in product. Another company might take an opposite tack, deliberately letting its tiremaking facilities "run down" and spending every available nickel on diversification into business where basic demand is growing more rapidly than it is for tires and/or where profit margins are higher. The typical tire company would probably embark on a strategy that lies between these extremes. If the strategy is successful, it would lead the company to a higher return on its resources, after taking into account the risks that are involved.

The actual return that is earned by following a particular strategy would depend heavily on how successfully the purchasing department coped with its environment. Purchases constitute such a large percentage of the cost of the typical product that poor purchasing performance can make or break the most rationally conceived strategic plan. For this reason, the materials manager and purchasing director must devise their own strategic plans.

Critical factors

Strategic planning in materials management involves looking at the economic, social, and technology factors that affect the supply of critical materials and then determining (after taking risks into account) how the organization will cope with them. The details of the planning process obviously vary with the organization and the materials involved. However, almost every rational materials manager would seek answers to these questions:

1. *What social, political, or environmental factors may (will) affect supply?* This assessment is especially critical if the purchased material is imported and/or produced in a limited number of places. For example, phosphate is a cheap and basically plentiful raw material used primarily in making fertilizer. Most of the Western world's supplier comes from just two areas: central Florida and the northwest corner of Africa. While there are not normally any shortages of phosphate rock, all that would be needed to change the situation dramatically would be a cutoff in supplies from one of these two critical areas. In one instance, political instability poses the greatest potential danger to supply; in the other, it is conceivable that environmental regulations represent at least a latent threat.

A strategic purchase plan for phosphate rock would take both of these dangers into account. The plan would rationally try to assess the risk and compare it with the cost of hedging against it. In most real-life situations, it would probably not be economic to create a perfect hedge. Thus, the buyer of phosphate rock might try to protect supply with long-term contracts with Florida producers but would be sorely tempted to buy at least part of the organization's needs from Moroccan producers if prices were sufficiently attractive. In addition, a large inventory would allow some cushion against disruption in supply. But chances are that it would not pay to carry a stock so huge that near-perfect protection could be achieved. Thus, as with overall strategic planning, the measures that would be taken would rationally attempt to balance potential risks against costs.

2. *What economic factors would affect prices and supply?* Persistent general inflation can sometimes create distorted supply relationships—especially in capital intensive industries. To take an extreme example, suppose that a critical material (such as ammonia) is purchased from an industry that requires enormous investment in a physical plant but incurs almost no labor costs. At present, there is ample capacity and producers are earning reasonable profits on plants

that were built some years ago that would cost twice as much if they had to be replaced. Under ordinary circumstances, suppliers would respond to increases in demand by building additional capacity well in advance of actual need. In this instance, they might do nothing—or at least respond so slowly that there would be a prolonged period of shortage and sky-high prices. The reason for the delay in expansion is that extra output is so much more costly than before that producers would hold back until they were sure that prices would remain high enough to support the higher cost additions to capacity.

Demand from other purchasers would also affect both price and availability of key materials. The purchasing manager would obviously take into account demand from the buyer's direct competitors. In many instances, it would also be necessary to estimate demand from users of material in other industries and even in other countries.

While the buyer is most likely to worry about economic factors that would unfavorably affect price or availability, favorable influences should also be taken into account. For example, buyers of electronic components enjoyed a long period of stable or declining prices even during periods of general price inflation largely because they were able to buy from low-cost producers in Asia. For a long period, the best strategic purchase plan would have been to buy on short-term contracts taking advantage of increased competition.

3. *What technological factors will affect price or supply?* Prices sometimes plunge when a major technological breakthrough permits an item to be made more cheaply. In other instances, a change in technology in an industry having no relation to that of the buyer, may create an added demand for a particular material that will have an unfavorable impact on the buyer's price or availability.

BASIC OPERATING PLAN

The strategic plan is basically a longer term. It is concerned with gradually redeploying resources so that they will be used in the most effective possible function. The operating plan is a shorter term in perspective. It is concerned with what the organization will do right now—or in the next few years—using the resources that it already has. The materials manager plays a key role in the basic year-ahead operating plan.

Elements of plan

In every organization, the plan consists of two basic documents which basically estimate funds coming into the organization and funds being paid out. These are as follows:

1. *A forecast of revenues.* In a profit-making organization, this would be a conventional sales forecast. In a nonprofit organization, the equivalent would be a forecast of such revenue-producing activities as tax collections, tuitions, or hospital patient days.

2. *A budget.* This is a breakdown of expenses that are expected for some particular level of revenue. There is almost always a direct correlation between the revenue forecast and the budget, but it is rarely a one-to-one relationship. In most cases, a $1 change in income produces less than $1 of change in expenses.

At the same time that she is participating in the preparation of the company's overall operating plan, the materials manager prepares plans for her own activities. The materials management plan is interrelated with the organization's overall operating plan. It indicates what materials management must do if overall objectives are to be achieved, as well as contributions it can make to company success that are more or less unique. In making up the year-ahead plan, the materials manager not only must take into account the company's short-term goals but also indicate what, if anything, she hopes to contribute to longer term goals.

Typically, a materials manager might start to work on her plan three to six months before she submits it to top management for approval. In the course of the next three months, she may have to make several revisions in her plan to bring it in line with the plans of other activities of the business and to reflect changes in basic assumptions. After the plan is approved, there may be further changes. If the assumptions on which the plan is based change during the year, the materials manager would again revise her plan. Also, during the course of the year she would report progress in achieving objectives of the plan.

Achievement of objectives

The materials planning process always should be in terms of objectives. In his plan, the materials manager should indicate how he proposes to achieve each of his basic objectives. For example, suppose that his objectives are identical with those listed in Chapter 3. (Remember, however, that objectives vary from company to company and industry to industry; each materials manager must determine his own.) Some typical ways in which a materials manager might plan to achieve these objectives are discussed in the following paragraphs.

Low prices. Individual purchasing decisions obviously reflect price objectives. But the materials manager also should have an overall objective. Based on economic forecasts, knowledge of competitive conditions, and so on, the materials manager may wish to set an overall target for cost reduction—for example, 2 percent of total purchase volume, or $300,000 total savings.

High inventory turnover. To achieve this objective, the materials manager might institute programs to reduce the number of items carried in stock. He could also persuade vendors to carry special stocks available for immediate delivery, work to tighten lead times, and use similar techniques that will be discussed in later chapters of this book.

Low cost of acquisition and possession. This objective can be achieved with various programs to reduce the cost of inbound freight, using techniques that will be discussed in Chapter 16 on traffic management. It also can be achieved through improvements in the handling and storage of materials—materials handling equipment, better controls, and so on.

Continuity of supply. To a considerable extent, this objective is largely dependent on selection of suppliers and inventory policies, but it also can be achieved in part by improved liaison with other departments in the company that use materials. In this way changes in their needs can be rapidly communicated to suppliers.

Consistency of quality. If quality is a problem, this becomes one of the most important objectives. The materials manager may propose joint programs with the quality control department to educate suppliers concerning the company's quality standards. He may propose a program of statistical quality control and vendor certification. If the quality problem becomes serious enough, he may plan on introducing new suppliers who can meet specifications or propose a joint program with engineering to develop alternate designs whose specifications suppliers can meet better.

If quality is not a problem and vendors are likely to continue meeting specifications, the quality objective may require almost no planning by the materials manager. In fact, it is possible that he may go even further and propose that suppliers with lower quality standards be introduced if he feels the company is paying for quality it does not need.

Low payroll costs. The materials manager should plan on introducing or expanding use of laborsaving techniques, such as electronic data processing, in orter to keep clerical costs as low as possible. She also should review her organization at least once a year to determine changes in its structure that will permit jobs to be done by fewer personnel. She certainly should also try to prevent overtime expense by planning work ahead to even out work loads. hiring additional personnel if necessary, and improving organization and methods.

Favorable supplier relations. A program to improve supplier relations may include "supplier days" on which vendors are invited to tour company facilities, hear speeches, and so on. It also may include efforts to prevent favoritism in buying and to stimulate supplier interest in developing new products for the company. Improvements may even be made in parking, lobby facilities, and the like to make sales-persons' calls more pleasant.

Development of personnel. On-the-job training programs and night courses for high-potential personnel can help achieve this objective. So can plans for a more informal development of personnel. Ideally, the materials manager should include in his or her report evaluations of all key personnel and steps planned to improve their job skills. The plan should anticipate job openings that may come with expansion, retirement, and so on.

Good records. Each record and procedure should be subjected to "regular trials for life," and those that are unnecessary should be eliminated. Periodic studies also may indicate a need for new records or better record keeping.

Other objectives. The objectives that have been discussed so far are all basic ones. Most materials managers will have other objectives as well. These might include favorable reciprocal relations, better relations with other departments, improved liaison with engineering on new products and design changes, promotion of standardization, and better make-or-buy decisions. In each case, the materials manager should present the objective and indicate how he plans to achieve it. If other departments in the company are involved, this should be made clear in the plan. Naturally, these departments must concur with such a plan before it is put into action.

Ideally, the materials planning process should start at the bottom and work its way up. That is, the overall materials plan should represent a composite of the plans of the various individual departments that report to the materials manager. The planning process might begin with a meeting of the materials manager and his subordinates. At this stage, the group would agree on some very broad plan that seems to be consistent with top-management objectives. After agreeing on these very broad goals, each key subordinate would then make up an individual plan showing how he or she proposes to meet materials department objectives within the group. This plan would then be reviewed by the materials manager and other key subordinates. If it seems consistent with the overall plan, it would then be consolidated into a combined statement of objectives for the materials department which the materials manager would submit to top management for approval.

YEAR-AHEAD PRICE AND AVAILABILITY

While the purchasing manager and materials manager are concerned with all of their objectives, the most critical over the short term are getting what is needed at prices the organization can afford to pay. Thus, the year-ahead purchase plan logically begins with a forecast of price and availability. The purchasing manager and materials manager begin with a broad economic forecast following some of the principles outlined in Chapter 6. They would certainly study business statistics, review forecasts of professional economists, and make their own evaluation of market in their day-to-day contacts with suppliers.

Detailed forecasts

Specific predictions must be developed from broader forecasts. Using the techniques outlined in Chapter 6, a purchasing manager may conclude that the general rate of inflation will be about 6 percent. It would also be useful to be able to make the more specialized prediction that the BLS wholesale price index will go up 5 percent. But this is not enough.

The purchasing manager must also try to predict what will happen to prices paid for specific materials. Every organization uses a wide variety of materials and components. The breakdown shown in Table 7–1 is not untypical. It represents major types of purchases made by a

TABLE 7–1
Major purchased commodities for a manufacturer of business equipment and fixtures

    I. Production parts and materials
        A. Semifinished and raw materials
            1. Plastic molding compounds
            2. Zinc
            3. Sheet steel
            4. Gray-iron and castings
            5. Steel forgings
            6. Miscellaneous materials
        B. Component parts and assemblies
            1. Sheet steel stampings
            2. Ball and roller bearings
            3. Fractional horsepower electric motors
            4. Plated zinc die castings
            5. Miscellaneous components and assemblies
   II. Nonproduction materials
        A. Machine tools and equipment
        B. Maintenance, repair, and operating supplies
            1. Perishable tools
            2. Lubricants and cutting oils
            3. Other supplies
        C. Construction
  III. Transportation costs

manufacturer of business furniture and fixtures. Since purchases account for twice as big a share of product cost as labor for this manufacturer, it is essential that the purchasing director's forecast of price changes be reasonably accurate and reliable. Some purchasing managers deliberately pad their estimates. If they think that prices for a particular commodity group will advance by 4 percent, they estimate 5 percent. That way they always look good. Or at least that's what they think. They are kidding themselves. Their managements are rarely fooled by forecasts that are always "beaten." It is far better to present an honest forecast. If there is a need to hedge (as admittedly there often is), it can be done using the Bayesian probability techniques discussed later in this chapter. That is, the purchasing director does not say, "I predict steel prices will go up 5 percent next year." Instead, an honest forecast would state: "I believe that there is at least 50 percent probability that steel prices will go up 5 to 7 percent."

Timing of purchases

The purchasing manager will then devise a strategy that will optimize cost and risk. Most managers would strive to minimize unpleasant "surprises" where prices go up much more than expected and threaten profits. They recognize, of course, that price fluctuations introduce an element of risk into materials management that cannot be avoided. Realistic purchasing managers know that they may be wrong almost as often as they are right in forecasting. Nevertheless, they try to time their purchases to reflect predictions of future price and availability and use inventories as a hedge against uncertainty. Purchasing managers have always tried to make the timing process as precise as possible—using forecasts and all other information they can lay their hands on. But, as one purchasing manager pointed out, "There is no formula that will tell me when and how much to buy. The best I can do is to review all available information, try to interpret it as best I can, make my decision, and then hope I'm right. Regardless of how long you've been in the business, you're often wrong."

Poor forecasts. It is almost impossible for any buyer to be consistently "smarter" than the market. All buyers are constantly analyzing general business conditions and supply-demand relationships in particular commodities. So are thousands of speculators. As a result, changes in sentiment are almost immediately reflected in prices. Buyers tend to reach the same opinion regarding future prices at almost the same time. Consequently, their total buying—or lack of buying—tends to cause prices to readjust to the new conditions. Therefore, buying tends to be heavy when prices are high and light when prices are low. Obviously only a minority of buyers are in the market when they should be; i.e., when prices are low.

There is good reason for this situation. The purchasing manager's prime mission is to provide needed raw materials for operations. Unfortunately, she usually needs materials least when prices are low. Prices generally slump with overall business, and most materials managers must cut back purchases because of a drop in their company's sales. When prices are high, on the other hand, the purchasing manager often must buy regardless of whether or not she thinks the material can be bought more cheaply at a later date. The factory is running full blast and needs a steady flow of parts and materials.

Beating the system.   There is no single right formula applicable to timing of purchases in all situations. However, most successful purchasing managers follow the general procedures outlined below.

1. *Estimate materials needs.*   The usual approach is to try to make a rather firm estimate of materials consumption for at least several quarters, and possibly a year ahead. In addition, the materials manager tries to get a more tentative estimate of materials needs for a five-year or even a ten-year period. Both the long- and short-term estimates are revised at periodic intervals to bring them in line with the latest sales projections supplied by the company's market research department.

At all times, the purchasing manager's estimates should be based on the best available forecasts. During the period of the estimate, the purchasing manager will have to buy at least enough material to satisfy estimated use (less any reduction in inventories that might be desired). So purchases must always be timed to meet use requirements. In other words, the purchasing manager can buy "ahead" but cannot afford to buy "behind" actual requirements. Material must be available when it is scheduled to be used.

2. *Develop tentative plan of purchases.*   At this stage in planning, the purchasing manager ignores the effect of future price changes and the like on purchase timing. Requirements are broken down into economic lots and programmed for delivery, allowing sufficient lead time to prevent stockouts if suppliers fail to adhere to schedules.

3. *Watch for buying opportunities.*   Whenever prices look unusually favorable, the purchasing manager should consider buying in excess of requirements, working closely with financial executives. Most companies have limited funds available for forward buying, and the amount available can vary from month to month.

When a buying opportunity does appear, the purchasing manager is still faced with a timing problem. Should we buy ahead now, spending all the money available for forward buying. Or should we hold off? The Bayesian decision rule can sometimes be helpful. The procedure is identical with that described later in this chapter, except that the price change becomes a prior (or first) probability rather than a conditional (or secondary) probability, as it does in the example where a possible steel strike is followed by a possible price increase.

4. *Consider formulas.*   Purchasing managers also may get good results with various timing formulas. One such plan might work in the

following way: The purchasing manager expects the price of a material to average 30 cents a pound during the year. A buying plan is based on this assumption. If the price is 30 cents or more, buy only the absolute minimum of material needed for production. But for every 1-cent drop in price below 30 cents, use 10 percent of the forward-buying fund to accumulate inventory. Do this cumulatively. For example, if the price drops 1 cent, spend 10 percent of the fund; if it drops an additional cent (to 2 cents below the estimate average of 30 cents), use another 10 percent of the fund; and so on.

The advantage of this formula is that it encourages stock accumulation when prices are low and discourages it when they are high. However, the buyer is not protected against severe price drops, since the fund may be used before the bottom is reached. Nor will timing be advantageous should prices inch up progressively throughout the year. Formulas, when they are used, must be developed on a tailor-made basis to suit the needs of the manager applying them. They can never be used as substitutes for the judgment of a skilled and experienced buyer.

Reducing market risk

Unfortunately, it is almost impossible to be on the "right" side of the market at all times. The general rule is that the economic expectations of all users of and speculators in a particular commodity change at about the same time. As a result, everyone tends to accumulate or liquidate inventory at about the same time. Thus prices change quite rapidly after periods of stability, which makes it even more difficult to manage inventories profitably. The key to successful forward buying in commodities was described by one buyer as "knowing in advance what other buyers think will happen in the future; that is, it's knowing the future of the future." That is no easy task.

Many buyers try to neutralize the effects on profits of fluctuations in commodity prices. They do this in four ways: (1) averaging their purchases; (2) budgeted buying; (3) hedging in futures markets; and (4) last-in, first-out inventory accounting.

Averaging purchases. Averaging purchases is the simplest (but not always the most effective) method of coping with the price risks of volatile commodities. It involves keeping inventories as low as possible at all times and then buying on a hand-to-mouth basis for current production. With this approach, the average cost of the commodity used in production will be about the same as the average price for that commodity during the year.

The average-purchase technique permits a company to concentrate its efforts on making and selling a finished product without giving a

thought to commodity market fluctuations. It works well only when:
(1) the commodity is not too important in relation to overall product
cost; (2) increases in the cost of the commodity can be passed on
immediately to customers buying the end product; (3) the commodity
is not subject to particularly violent fluctuations; or (4) the commodity
is not produced abroad or under other circumstances where supply
lines are long and complex and likely to be disrupted by political
upheavals, labor trouble, and the like.

Budgeted buying.   If prices regularly fluctuate around some mean,
it is possible to beat the market with budgeted buying. The materials
manager budgets regular amounts to be spent for the material, regardless of its selling price. As a result, the company automatically buys
more when prices are low and less when they are high. For example, if
a purchasing manager spends $100,000 per year for a particular mate-
rial, the company would spend about $8,000 per month irrespective of
price. The limitations with this technique are obvious. If the price
goes up too much, the company will not be able to get enough material
to meet its needs. However, in modified form, at least, it is a technique
that minimizes the effect of day-to-day price fluctuations on overall
product cost.

Hedging in futures markets.   If a company must carry large inventories of a commodity for various reasons, it is always in danger of
suffering substantial losses when the commodity drops in price. This is
strictly a "paper loss" as long as the company is not forced to reduce
the selling prices of its products when the commodity drops in price.
In such cases, the "loss" is the additional profit that would have been
made if the company had postponed its purchase and got the commodity at lower prices, thereby making its profit margin bigger.

Suppose, for example, that copper in the "spot" market costs $1 per
pound. Your company has 1 million pounds in its inventory. This is
worth $1 million. But if copper prices fall, the company will be forced
to adjust its prices for an end product so the loss will be real. Many
real-life companies would simply take this risk. Over the longer term,
prices are more likely to go up than down and they might wind up
ahead.

Others would prefer to reduce risk. They can do this at a price as
long as the commodity is traded on an exchange. The company wish-
ing to avoid losses on a copper inventory worth $1 might, for example,
be able to sell on the commodity exchange a contract calling for future
delivery at a net price (after brokerage costs, and so on) of 99 cents per
pound. If copper goes up in price, it would lose on this contract but, of
course, this loss would be offset by an increase in the value of its actual
inventory. On the other hand, if copper goes down in price, the company can buy back this contract at a lower price and make a profit. If

copper drops to 80 cents per pound, the company makes a 19 cent per pound profit on its short sale (selling a contract at 99 cents and buying it back again at 80 cents) but this is offset by a loss on the inventory.

Last-in, first-out inventory accounting. Hedging is costly because of brokerage commissions and other costs. Consequently, it is not used ordinarily except when a company is subject to extraordinary market risks. In addition, with last-in, first-out accounting (Lifo), companies that can vary their selling prices with raw material costs need not worry too much about the effect of inventory losses on the profit and loss statement anyway.

Meeting company schedules

While high purchase prices do indeed adversely affect the company's income statement, they may be the lesser evil. Having no material available at all is even worse. The company may be forced to shut down completely. To a remarkable extent, most materials are always available to the buyer who wishes to pay the going price (and government controls don't make the purchase illegal). In fact, the buyer's only real concern is not lack of availability but simply how rapidly the supplier can respond to change. This responsiveness varies widely by commodity.

Unexpected changes. Naturally, the materials manager tries to predict his needs as precisely as possible so suppliers need not be asked to respond rapidly to an unexpected change in demand. However, every organization occasionally makes major errors in forecasts. A materials manager who is totally unprepared for a sharp *increase* in demand may scramble uncertainly trying to respond and then ultimately fail to get the additional material when it is needed. A sudden *decrease* in demand may be equally unfavorable; the materials manager then is deluged with a supply of material that cannot be cut off fast enough. Excess costs of storage and handling as well as scrap are inevitable.

The rational manager uses a formal or informal contingency plan as a guide to respond to a major shift in demand for each major commodity. Conceptually, it is sometimes useful to think of the demand estimate (which is usually derived from a sales forecast for the end product) as the mean of some distribution of estimates. For example, the materials manager whose major commodities are listed in Table 7–1 may estimate that demand for the company's office equipment will require 10,000 tons of cold-rolled sheet steel to be used in the company's manufacturing operation. While this is the best estimate he has, he knows full well the company probably won't need *exactly* 10,000 tons. Instead, this is the *mean* of the distribution of a number of possibilities. Under normal circumstances, however, the materials manager believes that demand will be for at least 9,000 tons and will not ordinarily exceed 11,000 tons.

Response. The materials manager then figures out how he will adjust to expected variations around his mean estimate. In most cases, this is easy; inventory provides the buffer. When usage runs somewhat ahead of normal, the company draws on inventory; when usage drops below expected levels it lets inventory build up until it has a chance to cut back on orders to suppliers.

Major shifts in usage pose a greater problem. In some cases, every solution is very expensive. Costs are held down, however, if the materials manager considers every possible alternative so he has time to make the best possible decision. Suppose, for example, that demand for the company's office equipment jumps unexpectedly by 25 percent. The materials manager who had been buying about 800 tons of steel per month now must have 1,000 tons per month. She first considers the normal lead time for the material—with steel, at least three months. Thus it would ordinarily take the steel mill three months to respond to the demand. During this three-month period, the materials manager could satisfy demand only if she had an extra 600 tons on hand for this contingency. The cost of this additional inventory would have to be weighed against other possible strategies, such as those suggested below.

1. *Do nothing.* The odds are against it, but the most profitable decision might be simply to let the company run out of steel and make customers for finished products wait their turn.

2. *Buy premium-priced steel.* Steel service centers carry large inventories of most of the popular types of steel for immediate delivery. Naturally, their prices are higher than those charged by the steel mills.

3. *Expedite delivery.* The materials manager may be able to persuade her regular supplier to respond more rapidly to an increase in demand. This is quite likely during a period of depressed general business conditions and all but impossible during a boom.

4. *Make special arrangements.* In some cases, the contingency plan may be based on some special arrangement. The supplier may agree to "guarantee" some extra reserve capacity to be available on short notice, or possibly the problem can be solved by carrying a stock of semifinished material that can be rushed into production if it is needed.

Delivery failures. Under ordinary circumstances, a contingency plan is needed only if there is an unexpected change in demand. Otherwise, normal inventories can serve as a buffer to even out expected fluctuations in supply or in usage. However, normal buffer stocks are never adequate to cope with a strike or a catastrophe such as a major fire. Natural disasters are usually all but impossible to allow for in contingency plans, but materials managers can and do protect their companies against the effects of strikes at supplier plants or strikes by common carriers. When making their plan, they take into account scheduled labor negotiations. If they feel that operations might be affected by a supplier strike, they try to prevent supply failures with some sort of contingency plan. Similarly, if a strike is expected at one of the company's own plants, the materials manager's plan might call for finished goods stocks to be built up in advance of the strike.

BAYESIAN ANALYSIS

Traditionally, materials planning has been carried out on an "all or nothing" basis. For example, suppose that a materials manager is concerned about coming union contract negotiations in the steel industry. Obviously, his plan of purchase should take into account a possible strike and, conceivably, a steel price increase following settlement of the strike. The traditional way to do this is to look at all the facts and then attempt to forecast precisely what will happen. For example, a materials manager might conclude that, as a result of contract negotiations, the steel industry will have a two- to three-week strike, followed by a 3 percent general increase in steel prices. He would then go ahead and plan his purchases accordingly—most likely building up a substantial inventory in advance of the strike deadline.

Decision under uncertainty

Of course, such a decision is not made with 100 percent probability. A well-informed materials manager can do a better job of predicting what will happen than an ordinary person, but he can easily be way off base. There may not be a steel strike at all, and prices may not increase. As a result, he may make a bad decision, spending thousands of dollars to build an inventory of steel that will not be needed. Bayesian analysis is a technique that permits a more realistic approach to decisions made under conditions of uncertainty. With the Bayesian approach, the materials manager does not have to suck in his breath and decide whether or not there is not going to be a strike—a situation that simply is not realistic. Instead he makes his decision reflect relative probabilities. That is, he admits he doesn't know what will happen but, after careful consideration of the facts, estimates the probability of various events occurring.

This approach also permits the relative value of each alternate decision to be taken into account. For example, the cost of running out of steel may be ten times greater than the cost of stockpiling it. Consequently, the materials manager might want to stockpile steel even if the odds are heavily against a strike. Theoretically, the materials manager might intuitively take this into account when making a decision. The Bayesian approach gives him a quantitative basis for weighing the relative values of alternate decisions, along with the probability of their occurrence.

Determination of probability.   The Bayesian approach requires that a probability be assigned to each possible outcome. The sum of these probabilities is, of course, equal to 100 percent. In planning ahead for a possible steel strike and steel price increase, the materials manager might want to take a number of probabilities into account in making a decision.

To keep the arithmetic simple, assume, however, that there are just two basic probabilities: no strike or a 90-day strike. Looking six months or more ahead to a union contract expiration date, no one can predict with certainty whether or not there will be a strike. So the best that can be done is what a bookie does on a horse race: make an expert study of the available facts and then estimate the odds.

The materials manager should take all factors into account. These would include the following.

1. *Past labor relations in the steel industry.*   If the steel industry almost always has had a strike every time the contract comes up for renewal, it becomes reasonable to expect a strike during the succeeding period.

2. *Attitudes of present union and company officials.*   Personalities sometimes play a major role in labor relations. A strike becomes much more likely if the union elects new officers who need to "prove" how effective they are in winning gains for the rank-and-file workers.

3. *General economic conditions.*   In general, the likelihood of a strike increases during periods of booming business and declines during periods when there is substantial unemployment. For example, in the past, steel strikes have always come off when the industry has had very little slack capacity and is hard pressed to meet orders. There has rarely been a strike during periods when there is plenty of slack capacity and the steel workers are suffering from underemployment.

Being objective, the materials manager who is on top of the job should be able to estimate the odds more reliably than many industry insiders who may become emotionally involved in the various issues. Suppose that the materials manager, after considering all of these factors, decides that the odds are 70 to 30 against a steel strike [$P(S) = 0.30$ and $P(NS) = 0.70$]. Theoretically, this means that if she took a random sample of all steel negotiations made under similar conditions, there would be no strike 70 times out of 100 and a 90-day strike the other 30 times.

Cost of protection.   If the cost of protecting against a strike were exactly equal to the losses suffered as a result of not having prepared for it, the decision should be obvious: do nothing. But, of course, the losses are most likely much greater than the cost of protection, so the issue is in doubt until the materials manager takes both probability and relative cost into account.

Suppose that protection against a 90-day strike requires an extra investment of $1 million in inventory to be on hand when the union contract expires. The inventory buildup might begin 90 days before the contract expiration date. If there were a strike, it would be worked off during the 90-day period after the strike begins. Average additional investment in inventory would be $500,000 during this six-month period.[1]

If the carrying cost of the inventory is 30 percent per year[2] or 15 percent for the six-month period that the company will be holding the inventory, extra carrying cost is 15 percent of $500,000, or $75,000. This must be compared with the losses that the company would incur if it were forced to shut down for 90 days because of the steel strike. Such losses are not easy to estimate. Some customers would undoubtedly wait until the company was able to resume deliveries of finished products, while other sales might be lost forever. In addition, the shutdown would undoubtedly hurt the company's market prospects—particularly if the company's competitors had stocked up on steel and were able to keep on delivering to customers without interruption.

Suppose that, after taking all of these factors into account, management estimates that a 90-day shutdown for lack of materials would cost $1 million. Then the Bayesian decision rule would be applied, taking both estimated probabilities and relative cost into account. The "expected value" of a shutdown is 30 percent of the $1 million cost of the shutdown, or a $300,000 loss. Similarly, the expected cost of protection against a strike that does not come off is equal to the $75,000 cost of carrying additional inventory, multiplied by the 70 percent probability that there will be no strike—or a $52,500 loss.

Thus the company stands to lose less if it is protected against a strike that does not happen. Therefore, it would protect itself against a strike even though the odds are 70 to 30 in favor of a peaceful settlement.

Conditional probability. In the example above, the Bayesian rule was applied to alternative possibilities of a single event. But, of course, in real life events are interrelated. One event may lead to others with

---

[1] The average investment is equal to half of the original investment. This is explained in Chapter 8 in detail; Figure 8–1 is of particular interest.

[2] Carrying cost would include rental or storage space, transportation of the inventory to and from the storage space, interest on money tied up in the inventory, and allowance for possible spoilage. The concept of carrying cost, or cost of possession, is explained in more detail in Chapter 10.

alternative possibilities. In Bayesian jargon, these secondary events are "conditional probabilities."

For example, the expiration of a union contract in the steel industry first gives rise to the probability of some increase in steel prices following either a peaceful settlement or a strike. Assume that there are just three possibilities: no price increase, a 2 percent price increase, or a 4 percent increase. Each of these probabilities exists, regardless of whether there is a strike. However, they take different values with different strike outcomes. If there is no strike, assume that there is a 50 percent probability that there will be no price increase $[P(0)|NS = 0.50]$, a 30 percent probability of a 2 percent increase $[P(0.02)|NS = 0.30]$, and a 20 percent probability of a 4 percent price increase $[P(0.04)|NS = 0.20]$[3].

On the other hand, if there is a strike, the steel industry will almost certainly be stuck with a much higher wage settlement, and the climate will be more favorable to a price increase. So the probability pattern shifts upward. With a strike, assume there is but a 20 percent probability of no price increase $[P(0)|S = 0.20]$, a 50 percent probability of a 2 percent price increase $[P(0.02)|S = 0.50]$, and a 30 percent probability of a 4 percent increase $[P(0.04)|S = 0.30]$.

The decision tree

There now are eight different probabilities to be considered. To prevent confusion, the materials manager may want to lay them out in a "decision tree" like that in Figure 7–1. The tree begins with the first set of probabilities, and each new set of conditional probabilities creates new sets of "branches."

The decision tree makes it easy to calculate the probability of various individual events. Conditional probabilities can be calculated by multiplying the probabilities indicated on each of the branches of the tree, beginning at the base in each case. For example, the probability that there will be a strike and a 2 percent price increase $[P(0.02|S)]$ on the decision tree is equal to the basic probability $[P(S) = 0.30]$ that there will be a strike multiplied by the conditional probability $[P(0.02)|S] = 0.50$ that there will be a 2 percent price increase following the strike. This probability is, therefore, 0.30 multiplied by 0.50, or 0.15.

Thus, there is a 15 percent probability that there will be both a strike and a 2 percent price increase. We will also want to calculate the probability that there will be a 2 percent price increase, strike or no

---

[3] To the statistician, these are conditional probabilities, and the notation | can be translated as "after." For example, $[P(0)|NS]$ can be read as the probability (P) of no price increase (0) after $(|)$ an agreement has been reached and there is to be no strike (NS).

FIGURE 7–1
Decision tree on steel

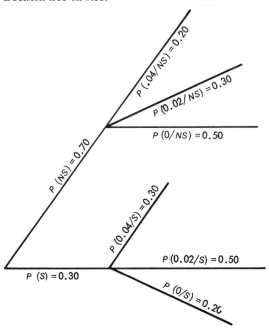

strike. This is equal to the probability that there will be a 2 percent price increase and a strike *plus* the probability that there will be a 2 percent price increase and no strike. The decision tree indicates that the latter probability is equal to $P(NS)$ multiplied by $P(0.02|NS)$ = 0.70×0.30, or 0.21. Thus there is a 21 percent probability that there will be a 2 percent increase, and no strike. Therefore, the probability that there will be a 2 percent price increase, strike or no strike, is equal to $0.21 + 0.15$, or 36 percent. Following this same approach, the probability that there will be no price increase, strike or no strike, is 41 percent (6 percent if there is a strike plus 35 percent if there is no strike). And there is a 23 percent probability that there will be a 4 percent price increase, strike or no strike (9 percent with a strike plus 14 percent without a strike).

Calculating expected value

It is now possible to estimate probable steel costs during the coming year, which amounts to $4 million per year at current prices. With a 2 percent price increase, these costs would rise to $4,080,000 (calculated by multiplying 1.02 by $4,000,000). With a 4 percent increase they would be $4,160,000. These costs are then weighed by their probabilities, as follows:

$$\$4,000,000 \times 41\% = \$1,640,000$$
$$\$4,080,000 \times 36\% = \$1,468,800$$
$$\$4,160,000 \times 23\% = \underline{\quad 956,800}$$

Expected value $4,065,600

Thus, there is an expected value that steel costs will increase by $65,600 per year or about 1.5 percent as the result of the coming labor negotiations in the industry. Note, however, that costs will *not* increase by precisely $65,600. There will still either be no increase in price at all, a 2 percent price increase that will cost $80,000 per year, or a 4 percent price increase that will cost $160,000. The $65,600 expected value merely indicates what average cost would be if a company were confronted with the same problem many, many times and outcomes occurred at random.

While the company will not be hit with an actual $65,600 increase in steel costs, regardless of what happens, this is the most realistic estimate to use in planning, since it takes all probabilities into account. If Bayesian analysis is applied to all other forecasts of purchase costs, total purchase costs would work out pretty much as planned because, of course, deviations from the expected values would occur at random and cancel each other out. If Bayesian analysis is not used, it would be necessary to forecast precisely what the steel price increase would be. Inevitably, major errors would be made simply because not even the best informed materials manager can do more than guess under such circumstances. There is tremendous uncertainty, and all a well-informed manager can hope to do is to suggest a range of probabilities.

Limitations

Not even the most well-informed person really knows what the probabilities are. While this is an obvious limitation to Bayesian analysis, it does not prevent it from being a useful technique. The fact is that all business decisions—including most of those made by materials managers—are made under conditions of uncertainty. If the materials manager knew exactly what was going to happen, he could presumably delegate his decision making to a computer and, in this case, there would not be much need for a materials manager.

The qualified materials manager should of course, be better able than anyone else in the company to come up with an estimate of the probability of a steel strike and the conditional probability of a price increase. In making an estimate, the materials manager would not only rely on gut "feel" for the situation but also get the opinions of the subordinates as well as suppliers and outside economists. However, the ultimate responsibility for decisions made to cope with uncertainty belongs to the materials manager alone (or to top management, if it makes the final decision).

PREPRODUCTION PLANNING

Purchase prices and availability are by no means the only uncertain elements in the planning process. Every project involves a series of steps, and the success and timing of each are often in doubt. Along with other key executives, materials managers are periodically involved in planning for some new activity. In a nonmanufacturing enterprise, this is usually the introduction of some new service or the construction and breaking in of some new facility. Typical nonmanufacturing projects which would involve the materials manager in planning are the opening of a new maintenance base for an airline, the construction of a new wing to a hospital, or the construction and initial operation of a new power-generating facility.

Basic process

In a manufacturing company, comparable activities would be the planning stages prior to production of some new product. If the new product is to be introduced on schedule, a long series of events also must take place on schedule. Naturally, some of these events involve the materials department.

Holding to schedule. Typically, the first event involving the new product occurs in the engineering department. Engineering makes up an elaborate schedule for completion of the design of the product and normally plans to release a steady flow of blueprints and other specifications to other departments in the company.

Each major activity in the company is responsible for holding to its own schedule. If one department slips behind schedule, it will almost inevitably put additional pressure on other departments to make up lost time. For example, if engineering is not able to complete the design of a particular component on schedule, then either purchasing or manufacturing will be under pressure to complete its share of the job. If the next department is not able to make up lost time, the whole program may fall behind schedule, and the company will ultimately suffer losses.

If the product is complex, the planning process can become extremely involved. To see how the process might work, however, consider a fairly simple product with just two components, subassembly A and subassembly B. These components are joined together to make a particular end product.

Before top management gives a final go-ahead on the product, each department reviews its role in detail and estimates the time required to complete each phase of its job. Usually, information from various activities concerned with the project is consolidated into a single master schedule. Each existing department is normally responsible for its phase of the schedule. However, the company may wish to create a special organization to handle the new project rather than delegate it on a functional basis to the various departments.

Organization by project. The company might create a "project team" that functions as a special division until a new product gets into production. Following the principles outlined in Chapter 4, this team would be responsible for all work up to the point where the product enters production and thereby becomes a regular activity of the company. Typically the project team includes representatives from all major departments concerned with the product. The team decisions are passed back to the appropriate departments, and the team members expedite within their own departments to make certain that schedules are adhered to.

For example, once purchase specifications are available, the materials representative on the product team might agree that he could get suppliers to deliver subassembly A in adequate quantities within 30 weeks and subassembly B within 20 weeks. These estimates, in turn, would be broken down for internal control into time estimates for each basic step in the materials cycle, starting with the process of getting quotations from the suppliers and ending when the supplier finally begins to deliver in production quantities. For purchased items, the materials cycle might consist of the following steps:

1. Get competitive bids.
2. Evaluate quotations and place orders.
3. Follow up on progress made by the supplier in tooling for production. If the supplier must purchase special tooling, this might also involve review of progress of the supplier's supplier.
4. Follow up to make certain that samples made from production tools are inspected and approved on schedule by the buyer's quality control department.
5. Make certain that production begins on schedule.

The materials department attempts to estimate realistic times for each of these steps. In some cases, the time allowance is more than adequate. Certain parts can be obtained almost overnight and could not possibly cause any problems. In such cases, however, the materials department does not make its own job too easy. It would not want to buy an item six months before it was needed just to make certain it was on hand, because this would tie up funds in inventory unnecessarily. It would hold off buying the item until just before it was actually needed, giving itself an adequate lead time.

In many cases, delivery of purchased parts and materials has to be closely coordinated with tooling programs in manufacturing. The materials management department is concerned not only with delivery of purchased parts but also with follow-up progress in purchasing any equipment that might be needed and in trying out and installing this equipment. Its preproduction control job is finished only after the initial pilot run of the new product has been completed.

Certain items would almost certainly be critical to the overall program. These are the ones for which the procurement or production cycle is longest. A delay in any of these critical items could cause the whole program to fall behind schedule. From experience, the project team knows which items might cause trouble, and progress on these items is followed up periodically to make certain that they are on schedule.

The Gantt chart

Procedures used in the follow-up process vary widely. Many of them, however, make use of one version or another of the Gantt chart (named for its inventor). The chart shown in Figure 7–2 is typical. Like

FIGURE 7–2
Gantt chart for new products program

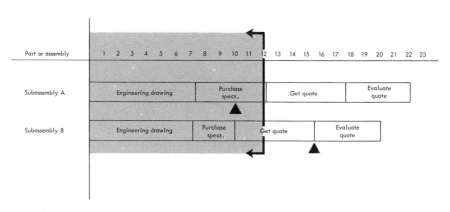

other Gantt charts, this one makes it easy to compare actual and scheduled progress on a particular project.

Scheduling basic jobs. The first step in developing the Gantt chart for a particular project is making up a schedule of the basic jobs required. For example, the chart in Figure 7–2 indicates that engineering drawings should be completed on subassembly A sometime in the 7th week, purchase specs should be ready in the 12th week, quotations should be received in the 17th week, and these quotations should be evaluated some time in the 22nd week.

The Gantt chart has a movable arrow or some other marking device to mark off the weeks as they roll by. In Figure 7–2, the shaded area indicates that the project is now in its 12th week. Actual progress on the project is also recorded on the chart, as indicated by the two small solid triangles underneath the schedule for each subassembly. One triangle indicates that, as of the 12th week, purchase specs on subassembly A are still being worked on in the engineering department and, in fact, they are only a little more than half complete. The arrow is therefore placed under the tenth week. This indicates that the work on subassembly A is now about two weeks behind schedule, and engineering is at the stage it should have reached by the tenth week.

In contrast, work on subassembly B is ahead of schedule. As of the 12th week, the purchasing department should have sent the specs out to suppliers for quotations but would not expect to get them back for another four weeks. However, the arrow indicates that all of the quotations are in, so this subassembly is four weeks ahead of schedule.

Unfortunately, the wrong item is ahead of schedule. The materials manager can glance at the chart and conclude that she can afford to be a little behind schedule on subassembly B, since the entire job on this item up to placement of the order only takes 20 weeks, while that for subassembly A should take 22 weeks. Consequently, the fact that subassembly B is ahead of schedule does her no good whatever. It just means there will be additional slack time that is not needed. However, subassembly A is critical. If it is two weeks behind schedule, the product that is assembled from A and B will be two weeks behind schedule. Consequently, the materials manager can tell at a glance that work must be speeded up on subassembly A, and she would undoubtedly request the engineering department to try to speed up its development of purchase specifications by working overtime or by some other means.

Basis for follow-up. A Gantt chart like that shown in Figure 7–2 can also be used by a project group for follow-up, since it includes all activities necessary for the project. The materials group would be likely to keep a detailed Gantt chart only for its phase of the operation, which in this case begins with the securing of quotations. Some follow-up might still be carried on to make certain that the engineering department is on schedule in delivering specs on subassembly B in the 10th week, as scheduled, and on subassembly A in the 12th week. But the materials department would not, of course, be responsible for following up on each detailed phase of the engineering job.

In the past, many companies kept Gantt charts on almost every component of a new product program. Only a few of the individual components were troublemakers, but it was difficult to determine in advance what they would be—and, in fact, hardly anyone tried. Sometimes, however, for various reasons, a component like subassembly B—which seemingly had plenty of slack time—would be held up and would become a bottleneck in the program.

The PERT technique

In the past 20 years, new techniques have been developed to spot potential bottlenecks in a program and to permit management to ignore the parts of a project that will not give any trouble. This relatively new technique is known as PERT,[4] or the critical path method. In every project, there are a number of activities going on simultaneously. In a really complicated project, such as development of a space vehicle, there may be literally tens of thousands of such activities. Most of these are not critical; that is, if they are delayed, the overall program will not be held up. However, in every project there is at least one bottleneck or "critical path" that will hold up the entire project if it gets behind schedule. This is the chain of events that requires the longest time to complete.

Simple network. Figure 7–3 shows a PERT network that could be constructed for subassembly A and subassembly B. The time indicated for the procurement cycle is identical with those in the Gantt chart in Figure 7–2, except that the PERT network assumes that no decision has yet been made as to whether this item should be purchased or made by an outside supplier. For this reason, there are four "paths" in the network. Two paths are for purchase of subassembly A and subassembly B and two cover manufacture of A and B. All four paths come together when manufactured costs and purchase quotations are evaluated for a make-or-buy decision. The network would, of course, extend on from this point, joining with other paths until the product or program is completed.

In constructing construct a PERT network such as that in Figure 7–3, you first write down each activity needed and note what other activity must be completed before this one can be started. You then make estimates of the time (in days or weeks) needed to do each job: an "optimistic" time, a, a "realistic" time m, and a "pessimistic" time b. You then calculate the expected time of the event, t_e, with the formula $t_e = a + 4m + b/6$.

---

[4] The initials stand for program evaluation review technique. PERT was originally developed by the Navy to control the Polaris missile program but is now widely used by all of the armed services, the National Aeronautics and Space Administration, and various defense and other aerospace firms. When the same technique is used in nondefense-related industries, such as construction, it is often called critical path method (CPM).

FIGURE 7–3
Typical **PERT** network

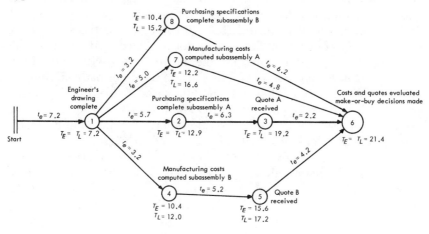

Computations for PERT Network

Preced- ing event	Event	a (opti- mistic)	m (real- istic)	b (pessi- mistic)	t_e	T_E	T_L	$T_L - T_E$
Start	1	1	4	26	7.2	7.2	7.2	0
1	2	2	5	12	5.7	12.9	12.9	0
1	4	1	3	6	3.2	10.4	12.0	1.6
1	7	2	4	12	5.0	12.2	16.6	4.4
1	8	1	3	6	3.2	10.4	15.2	4.8
2	3	4	6	10	6.3	19.2	19.2	0
3	6	1	2	4	2.2	21.4	21.4	0
4	5	3	5	8	5.2	15.6	17.2	1.6
5	6	1	4	8	4.2	19.8	21.4	1.6
7	6	1	5	8	4.8	17.0	21.4	4.4
8	6	4	6	9	6.2	16.6	21.4	4.8

The PERT network consists of a number of events (circles) joined by activities (arrows). Event times, T_E and T_L, are earliest and latest times event can be reached without upsetting overall schedule. Activity times, t_e are averages of three estimates of the time needed to complete each activity. Network in example is a simple one; complete networks can be built from networks similar to this.

This formula is an easy-to-calculate substitute for a normal distribution. Every estimate of time required to do a job can be looked upon as the mean of some distribution. The maximum and minimum times that are also estimated provide an approximation of three standard deviations variance around that mean. In theory, the mean estimate represents the best estimate of the time to do the job, and the actual time should fall between the minimum and maximum at least 99 percent of the time. The formula gives an approximation of the time that would be estimated were all possible times in the normal distribution "added up" by means of integral calculus.

After calculating expected times for each operation, you proceed to construct a PERT network similar to that in Figure 7–3. The critical path—the path that requires the longest time—includes events 1, 2, 3, and 6, and the total expected time, T_L, is equal to the sum of the expected times of each of these events, or 21.4 weeks. If events in this critical path get behind schedule, the entire project will be held up.

Noncritical to critical. There is slack in the other paths. Events on noncritical paths can fall behind schedule without affecting the overall project. Slack time for each noncritical path shows how far these noncritical paths can get behind schedule before they become critical.

For example, look at event 4 in the table in Figure 7–3. The expected time, t_e, of this event is 3.2 weeks, and the cumulative expected time, T_E, for the path up to event 4 is equal to the sum of the expected times of events 1 and 4, or 10.4 weeks. The path is not complete, however, until events 5 and 6 are completed. The expected times on this path for these remaining events are equal to 9.4 weeks (5.2 weeks to get from event 4 to event 5, and 4.2 weeks to get from 5 to 6). Since the total expected critical path time is 21.4 weeks, the project probably will not be held up as long as you can get up to event 4 in 12.0 weeks (21.4 weeks minus the 9.4 weeks expected time to get from 4 to 6). This becomes T_L, the latest that you can reach a point on a path without holding up the project. And, of course, T_L minus T_E is the slack, which is 1.6 weeks for the path up to event 4. If we are more than 1.6 weeks behind schedule, this path may then become critical.

Management normally limits its attention either to paths that are already critical or to those about to become critical. Typically, an entire PERT network is programmed into a computer. All transactions concerned with the network are then keypunched and entered into the computer. The computer then will calculate and recalculate critical paths, focusing management's efforts on events that are likely to delay the entire program.

PERT is particularly useful for extremely complex products, while a simple Gantt chart is usually adequate when there are no more than a dozen possible paths. Thus it is not surprising that PERT is used almost entirely in defense-related industries or construction, where the end product is made in relatively small quantities and is extremely complicated. Producers of conventional civilian products usually use a version of a Gantt chart, although they often rely on a computer to do the basic work of the chart.

PLANNING FOR PRODUCTION BUYING

The PERT process normally ends in manufacturing firms when the product is ready for production. The materials manager, purchasing manager, and manufacturing manager all play critical roles in making the production plan. Optimum purchase and manufacturing costs are almost always achieved when production is scheduled in a regular fashion—for example, 200 units per day. Labor and capital costs can be minimized both at the company's own plant and at those of its suppliers. Unfortunately, customers do not usually cooperate. Their buying patterns are often seasonal and also usually not easy to predict. As a result, most companies have to compromise between optimum manufacturing costs and marketing realities.

The hypothetical production plan in Table 7–2 represents such a compromise for a manufacturer of air conditioners, a product whose seasonal demand is obvious. In this case production is scheduled evenly at a rate of about 320 units per day. Inventory is built up during most of the year to be worked off in the spring months when almost all shipments to dealers are made. The plan shows not only production but also costs related to the plan: overtime during the critical spring months and carrying cost of inventory when production exceeds shipments.

Plan of purchase

One of the major factors determining the final production plan is the ability of manufacturing to respond to change in demand. The quicker the response, the lower the potential premium costs of overtime, layoffs, or inventory. This is also true of plans of purchase derived from the production plan. The materials manager must get purchased materials delivered before they are actually needed in production. The earlier the manager brings them in, the greater the inventory carrying cost. But this cost is at least partly offset by the benefit of having material on hand to meet unexpected increases in demand or potential future delays in supply. Procurement lead time is also determined by the stage of the manufacturing process at which the particular purchased item is used. The carton for an air conditioner that is completed on June 30 can be delivered from the carton supplier on June 29, if necessary. But a casting which must be machined before it is incorporated into a major component that is assembled into the finished product might have to be on hand sometime in May if there is to be no delay in the process.

Example of plan. Table 7–3 shows how a plan of purchase is developed for a gray-iron casting used in the air conditioner whose production plan is shown in Table 7–2. The production planner first checks the specifications to determine how many castings are used in each air conditioner. In this case, just one casting is actually used, but the company expects that about 5 percent of the castings purchased will be lost as scrap in the machining process or will simply disappear. Therefore, the company plans on buying 84,000 castings instead of just

TABLE 7–2
Production plan for 80,000 air conditioners

(1) Month	(2) Number of work days	(3) Production in units	(4) Beginning inventory	(5) Additions	(6) Shipments	(7) Ending inventory	(8) Interest at 0.5% per month	(9) Other excess costs	(10) Total extra costs
July	10*	3,200	—	$320,000	—	$ 320,000	$ 1,600	$ 320†	$ 1,920
August	22	7,040	$ 320,000	704,000	—	1,024,000	5,120	1,024	6,144
September	20	6,400	1,024,000	640,000	—	1,664,000	8,320	1,664	9,984
October	21	6,720	1,664,000	672,000	—	2,336,000	11,680	2,336	14,016
November	21	6,720	2,336,000	672,000	—	3,008,000	15,040	3,008	18,048
December	22	7,040	3,008,000	704,000	$ 500,000	3,212,000	16,060	3,212	19,272
January	20	9,600	3,212,000	960,000	1,500,000	2,672,000	13,360	20,672‡	34,032
February	20	9,600	2,672,000	960,000	2,000,000	1,632,000	8,160	19,632§	27,792
March	23	7,360	1,632,000	736,000	2,000,000	368,000	1,840	368	2,208
April	20‖	6,400	368,000	640,000	1,000,000	8,000	40	8	48
May	16#	5,120	8,000	512,000	500,000	20,000	100	20	120
June	15**	4,800	20,000	480,000	500,000	—	—	—	—
Totals	230	80,000			$8,000,000		$81,320	$52,264	$133,584

* Two-week vacation shutdown.
† Consisting of taxes and insurance of 10 cents per unit on inventory stored in plant's own warehouse.
‡ Equal to $18,000 overtime premium plus $2,672 storage cost.
§ Equal to $18,000 overtime premium plus $1,632 storage cost.
‖ Start on four-day week last two weeks of April.
Four-day week.
** Four-day week with three-day layoff at end of month.

TABLE 7-3
Plan of purchase for a gray-iron casting

| (1) | Actual production requirement | | | Suggested purchases | | | (8) |
| | (2) | (3) | (4) | (5) | (6) | (7) | Change in inventory |
Month	Quantity	Cost	Inventory	Quantity	Cost	Inventory	
May	6,720	$ 6,720	$ 6,720	8,000	$ 8,000	$ 8,000	$+ 1,280
June	7,392	7,392	14,112	16,000	16,000	24,000	+ 9,888
July	3,360	3,360	14,112	None	—	20,640	+ 6,528
August	7,056	7,056	13,776	8,000	8,000	21,248	+ 7,472
September	7,056	7,056	14,112	8,000	8,000	22,528	+ 8,416
October	7,392	7,392	14,448	16,000	16,000	31,472	+17,024
November	10,080	10,080	17,472	16,000	16,000	40,416	+22,944
December	10,080	10,080	20,160	12,000	12,000	45,024	+24,864
January	7,728	8,501*	18,581	—	—	34,944	+16,363
February	6,720	7,392	15,893	—	—	24,864	+ 8,971
March	5,376	5,914	13,306	—	—	17,136	+ 3,630
April	5,040	5,544	11,458	—	—	10,416	– 1,042
May	—	—	5,544	—	—	5,040	– 504
June	—	—	—	—	—	—	—
Total	84,000	$86,487	—	84,000	$84,000	—	—

* 10 percent price increase expected.

80,000 during the coming year. If losses seem to be running less than the 5 percent allowance, purchases can be cut back slightly toward the end of the year.

The plan of purchase, like the production plan, assumes that this particular model of air conditioner will not be produced after the fiscal year ends. If the company decides to continue the model, next year's plans can simply be joined on to this year's without difficulty.

The purchasing department predicts that the price of this casting will increase by 10 percent, from $1.00 to $1.10, about January 1. Therefore, as indicated in column 3 of Table 7–3, all castings purchased after December 31 are priced at $1.10 each rather than $1.00 each.

The purchasing department also believes there is some small chance of a strike at the foundry that supplies this casting. The foundry's labor agreement expires on December 31, and the purchasing department believes the foundry will reach an agreement with its union calling, of course, for higher wages. Since the market for gray-iron castings is already strong, this wage agreement will give the foundry the excuse it needs to boost prices. The purchase manager proposes that the company try to purchase its total requirements of 84,000 before January 1, with the supplier following a shipping schedule similar to that suggested in column 5 of Table 7–3. This schedule would offer advantages over the plan indicated in column 1, which is simply designed to have material on hand when it is needed. These advantages are:

1. The revised plan calls for shipment in full truckload quantities. The traffic department estimates that 8,000 of these castings would fit into the company's truck, which will be used to pick up the castings at the supplier's. The supplier can also conveniently manufacture in lots of 8,000, and his $1 price is based on shipments of at least 8,000. If the unadjusted plan indicated in column 2 were followed, the company truck would have to make several additional trips to the supplier's foundry during the year. In addition, the supplier might demand a price increase because he would be shipping in lots of fewer than 8,000 most of the time.

2. If the company purchases its full year's requirement of 84,000 castings before January, its purchase cost will be only $84,000 (as indicated in the total for column 6). If it buys according to the plan in column 1, costs for the year will be $86,487 because it will probably be necessary to purchase 24,864 castings at the higher price expected to go into effect on January 1. Thus the expected cash saving from the revised plan is $2,486 (24,864 castings × $0.10 per casting).

3. If the revised plan is followed, there is considerably less risk of delivery failure resulting from a strike. The materials manager might want to use Bayesian decision theory to estimate the expected value of

the loss from a strike occurring sometime between January 1 and April 30, if the plan suggested in column 1 is followed. Suppose, for example, she estimates the loss at $300,000. Even if the probability of a strike long enough to cripple the foundry's production schedules is only 5 percent, the expected loss would still be $15,000 (0.05 × $300,000).

4. Upward revisions in production are easier with the purchase plan in column 5. The company may discover later in the year that its sales estimate has been too conservative. If it has the bare minimum of castings on hand at the time it decides to boost its production schedule, it may have to wait several months before there are sufficient finished castings to permit an increase in the final assembly schedule. The supplier will not be able to respond immediately to the request for more production; chances are he will need at least a month's advance notice. In addition, there is roughly a two-month lead time with the company's own operations. Thus a total of three months may elapse before the decision to boost output can be reflected in increased shipments.

Suppose, for example, the company decides in July it would like to assemble an additional 2,000 air conditioners per month. In August (with good luck) the supplier may be able to ship 2,000 extra castings, and by October (with even more good luck) an extra 2,000 air conditioners will roll off the line.

In contrast, increased output would pose no problem for castings, at least, if the plan indicated in column 5 is followed. The castings would already be on hand. In addition, if the company wanted to increase its assembly schedule at the end of the year, there is a 95 percent chance (assuming no strike) that the castings could be ordered any time in January or February.

Faults of plan.   Unfortunately, every plan also has its costs. If the company followed its original plan, it could fairly easily cut back on purchases of castings any time up until March (assuming the vendor needs 30 days' notice of a cutback). With the revised plan, the company is firmly committed to purchase 84,000 castings by some time in November—months before it would probably come to realize that its sales forecast had been too optimistic.

In most real-life companies, the castings not needed could be stored and used in the following year. But inventory cannot be stored for free. Even if the company's sales forecast is perfect, inventory carrying cost will be higher if the schedule in column 5 is followed. Column 8 compares the inventory balance indicated by the plan in column 1 with that in column 5. For example, during the month of May, the first plan calls for an ending inventory of $6,720. This balance reflects planned receipts of 6,720 castings with no withdrawals from stock, since shipments are not scheduled to begin until July. In contrast, the plan in column 5 calls for purchase of 8,000 castings in May with no withdrawals. The difference of +$1,280 ($8,000 − $6,720) represents the extra inventory investment that is the major price paid for obtaining the advantages of the revised plan.

During the year, this revised plan increases purchased materials inventory by an average of $10,486.[5] Interest on this additional investment at 6 percent per year would amount to about $630. Total cost of carrying this inventory might amount to $2,500 or more, for reasons to be discussed in Chapter 10. However, the cash savings from the revised purchase plan are so much greater that there is little doubt that this is the better plan. Taking into account only the cash saving of $24,864 from buying the entire year's supply at the $1 price, the company should earn a return of about 237 percent ($24,864 ÷ $10,486 × 100) on its extra average investment of $10,486 in inventory. This return would be reduced by any additional cash storage costs that might be incurred, but these would be insignificant compared to the saving.[6]

Cost reduction. Each commodity purchase plan should also allow for the buyer's cost-reduction efforts. In a footnote to this plan, for example, the buyer should indicate what, if anything, he proposes to do to avoid paying the 10-cent price increase on the casting next year. His efforts to reduce costs would then become part of next year's plan. He might search for new gray-iron casting suppliers, or conceivably, he might propose that a die casting or sheet-metal stamping be substituted for the casting.

Cost reduction should be considered not only when making plans for individual commodity groups but also on a consolidated basis, with recommendations as to how to achieve definite goals by the application of specific cost-reduction techniques (discussed in later chapters).

However, lower costs are not the only objective of materials management. As we saw in Chapter 3, there are a number of primary and secondary objectives. These objectives are interrelated; success in achieving one may impair performance in achieving one or more of the others. The art of materials management is successful balancing of objectives into a coordinated plan and then achieving the goals of the plan.

Conflict of objectives is illustrated in the plan of purchase for gray-iron castings in Table 7–3. In this case, the objective of high inventory turnover is deliberately made secondary to achievement of the objectives of low prices and good delivery performance. Stocks are built up in anticipation of higher prices and possible shortages. In making her

---

[5] $$\frac{\$1,280 + 9,888 + 6,528 + 7,472 + 8,416 + 17,024 + 22,944 + 24,864 + 16,363 + 8,971 + 3,630 - 1,042 - 504}{12 \text{ months}} = \$10,486$$

[6] The principles behind these calculations are explained in Chapters 9 and 10.

purchase plan for each major commodity group, the materials manager is really balancing achievement of various objectives. When making the plan, she should consciously consider its effect on prices, inventory turnover, continuity of supply, relations with suppliers, quality, and low cost of acquisition and possession.

Key-parts control

The plan of purchase indicates exactly the inventory the materials manager plans to carry of each commodity. If the materials manager made a plan of purchase for every individual item, he could readily anticipate exactly what his inventory position would be during the period of the plan. All he would have to do is add up each plan of purchase to get a total. In practice, this is never done. It is not practical to make detailed plans of purchase for each item, and materials managers usually make plans only for major items; less important materials are ordered and stocked in accordance with the principles discussed in Chapters 9 and 10.

The plan of purchase may also be too general to be really useful in forecasting product costs. For example, a plan of purchase might be made (as it was in Table 7–3) for gray-iron castings used in all of a company's products. This plan would be extremely useful for inventory planning and allocating purchases of castings among suppliers, but it would not necessarily be useful for forecasting product cost, since the castings might be used in dozens of different products.

An obvious solution to this problem would be for the materials manager to make overall plans of purchase for major commodity groups and then break these plans down in detail into plans and forecasts for each product. In a typical materials department, however, this is an almost impossible job. It would be necessary to keep extremely accurate records and make rather elaborate calculations for literally thousands of different items. The cost would be high and errors frequent.

In practice, the "purchase plan" consists essentially of an overall estimate of requirements that is adjusted to take into account scrap, shipping quantities, and other factors. Normally these calculations are made by computer and do not take into account such "soft" factors as expected price changes or strikes.

80 percent buys 15 percent.   Price performance is more readily planned by keeping special price records of a sample of key items in each commodity group. Usually, 80 to 90 percent of the money is spent on only 10 to 15 percent of the items. If careful records are kept of these "big money" items, overall changes can be accurately estimated with a minimum of paperwork. This is the key-parts approach to cost control and forecasting.

Suppose a company finds that its key-parts sample (which may be 15 percent of all items) represents exactly 90 percent of total expenditures. If prices of the items in the sample increased exactly 1 percent, the value of *all* items increases 0.9 percent, even though there have been no changes at all in the prices of the nonsample items. In practice, of course, the nonsample items change in proportion to the sample items. A carefully selected sample not only includes expensive items but is also reasonably representative of the overall sample as to type of material, industry, method of fabrication, and so on.

The mechanics of preparing a key-parts index are not hard to understand. However, the job can be done easily only if the company already has the basic data on punched cards and can program its computer to do all the hack work. Otherwise the clerical effort is a major barrier in setting up such an index. It is necessary to compile a complete list of every item purchased and compute the value of the usage of each by multiplying unit price by usage. The high dollar-volume items are then culled from each commodity or product group so that the sample represents approximately 80 to 90 percent of the dollar volume.

Controlling product XYZ. Key-parts control is normally by product for production parts and materials because management needs product information for pricing and cost control purposes. Table 7–4 shows key-parts control for hypothetical product XYZ. It is a summary of groups of key parts for each commodity group. The sample's value

TABLE 7–4
Budgeted materials cost changes, product XYZ, 1980

Month	Beginning cost	Negotia- tion	Product change	Mate- rials cost	Supplier change	Other	Total change
January	$100.00	$(0.42)	$(0.22)	$0.14	$(0.05)		$(0.55)
February	99.45	(0.28)	0.60	0.75	(0.35)		0.72
March	100.17	(0.40)			(0.10)		(0.50)
April	99.67	(0.40)			(0.10)		(0.50)
May	99.17	(0.40)			(0.10)		(0.50)
June	98.67	(0.40)			(0.10)		(0.50)
July	98.17	(0.40)		1.05	(0.10)		0.55
August	98.72				(0.10)		(0.10)
September	98.62				(0.10)	3.10*	3.00
October	101.62				(0.10)		(0.10)
November	101.52				(0.10)		(0.10)
December	101.42				(0.10)		(0.10)
Total at end of year	$101.32	($2.70)	$ 0.38	$1.94	($1.40)	$3.10	$ 1.32

* Addition of new parts to sample formerly made in the shop and purchased from outside suppliers, effective September 1, 1980.

on January 1 is $100. The materials manager classifies the changes affecting price and projects them for the coming year.

The total price reduction of $2.70 for "negotiation" for the year is her estimate of savings that can be made. The total is based on individual forecasts of economic and competitive conditions for major commodity groups and on estimates of the probable success buyers will have in applying the cost-reduction techniques discussed in later chapters.

The predicted $0.38 cost increase due to "product change" is based on the materials manager's estimate of the cost of planned design changes. The $3.10 change classified as "other" arises from a make-or-buy decision. Both of these changes affect product mix. Since they are not economic, they will not be used to measure the success of the materials department in achieving its cost-reduction objectives.

An increase of $1.94 per unit is anticipated because of higher materials costs. This could include both increases in the cost of purchased raw materials and increases in prices of components as suppliers pass along higher raw material costs. In calculating the effect of increases in materials costs, the materials manager would estimate the amount of the increase per unit of raw material (using techniques that have already been discussed) and multiply by the amount of raw material in the product. For example, suppose that a 2 cents per pound increase in the price of copper were anticipated in January. If 7 pounds of copper were used in the product—either in shop-made or purchased components—the unit product costs would rise by 14 cents,[7] as indicated in Table 7–4.

The final major price change column in the materials plan is one that allows for "supplier change." It is an estimate of savings that will be made by bringing in new suppliers who charge lower prices than existing suppliers. It is based on both an evaluation of competitive conditions and an estimate of how successful buyers will be in performing one of the basic parts of their job.

Commodity price indexes

Key-parts systems work well in companies that produce a limited number of products in large volume. They are used, for example, by several leading automobile manufacturers.

They will not work well in companies that produce many products on a job-order basis. In such cases, individual products are manufac-

---

[7] In practice, this would rarely be literally correct. In many cases there is a lag of at least a month between the time a raw material increases in price and the time suppliers of parts fabricated from the material request a price adjustment. To allow for this, the materials manager would allow for two adjustments because of a change in materials costs: one for the material purchased directly, and a second, later adjustment for parts made of the material.

tured intermittently and it is seldom worthwhile to maintain key-parts control over every product. Management is interested primarily in the overall trend of costs; it needs information that will help it do a better job of estimating costs on new jobs that come in.

A commodity price index is best suited for this purpose. It is similar to key-parts control except for two basic differences: index numbers are used instead of actual dollar costs, and cost data are classified entirely by commodity instead of by product.

To see how such an index might be set up, consider the example of a hypothetical manufacturer of highly specialized, custom-made business machines that require the commodities listed in Table 7–1 above. Such a company might buy as many as 20,000 different items and make 100 different products, even though it employs no more than 1,000 persons. Almost every customer would require a product that was engineered specifically for his or her needs.

Selecting the sample. The mechanics of compiling the index are much like those used in developing key-parts control. Average monthly expenditures for each commodity are calculated from purchase records, and the more expensive items are selected for the sample. However, in developing the index, it is necessary to take particular pains to select a sample that is a truly representative cross section of the commodities purchased. Because the company makes so many different products in relatively small quantities, it is not true that 10 to 15 percent of the most expensive items account for 80 to 90 percent of the dollar volume of purchases. It may be necessary to work with a sample that comprises only 30 to 40 percent of total dollar volume.

The procedure used in calculating the base cost of the index sample is different from that used in key parts. Usage is not taken into account. Base cost is calculated simply by adding the unit prices of each item in the sample. This makes it vital to take relative usages into account when choosing the items represented in the sample.

For example, suppose the business machine manufacturer compiles an index of castings costs. If he uses an average of two small castings as miscellaneous components for every larger casting used for the machine base, then the sample should be divided 67 to 33 between the large and small castings.

Making the index. After the sample is selected, price changes are tabulated. The technique is similar to that used in Table 7–4. Imagine, in fact, that Product XYZ in Table 7–4 is an index of castings costs for the hypothetical business machine manufacturer. The beginning cost in January is $100. The unit price changes during January on the castings in the sample reduce total cost of the sample by $0.55—as in Table 7–4 to $99.45. But since this is an index, the index number of 99.45 is used instead of the dollar amount. This is because the total value of the sample has no significance; unlike a product index, it is merely the sum of current prices for a selected group of materials. It is easier to judge the effect of price changes with index numbers that automatically indicate the number of percentage points in change from the base period. Actual dollar figures rarely come to the convenient $100 figure of the example.

With a commodity index, it is is simple to estimate the effect of price changes on overall costs. For example, if a company were spending an average of $10,000 a month for castings, a drop in the castings price index from 100.00 to 99.45 would indicate a saving of $55 per month.

Commodity indexes ean be used for both production and nonproduction items. However, when they are used to measure changes in cost of a nonproduction group such as maintenance, repair, and operating supplies, the sample must be constructed with extra care, because a wide variety of items with erratic usage patterns falls into this category.

Composite indexes. Commodity indexes also can be used to build product indexes of composite products. If a company makes a wide variety of products on a job-order basis, it cannot afford to keep cost indexes for each product. It can, however, construct an index of a composite product; the company's various products are sufficiently similar so that cost changes of each follow similar patterns.

A composite index is made up of indexes for major commodities; it is weighted by the relative importance of each commodity in the typical end product. Table 7–5 shows the construction of such an index for

TABLE 7–5
Composite index of materials costs—machine tools

Component group	Percent weight	January		February		March	
		Index	Exten-sion	Index	Exten-sion	Index	Exten-sion
Electrical	35	100.00	35.00	102.00	35.70	101.00	35.35
Castings	20	100.00	20.00	90.00	18.00	90.00	18.00
Bearings	5	100.00	5.00	100.00	5.00	99.00	4.95
Hydarulic	15	100.00	15.00	96.00	14.40	97.00	14.55
Miscellaneous	25	100.00	25.00	100.00	25.00	94.00	23.50
Composite index			100.00		98.10		96.35

a hypothetical machine-tool manufacturer. Studies might show that the average purchased material cost for each machine tool is divided as indicated in the second column of the table: 35 percent for electrical, 20 percent for castings, and so forth. The monthly price index for each commodity group is then multiplied by its percentage weight (e.g., multiplying the electrical component index of 100.00 by its 35 percent weight gives an extension of 35.00), and the products are added to get the composite index.

Table 7–5 shows that material for a composite machine tool in January cost its precise base price of 100.00. In February and March, prices of components declined until the index reached 96.35, indicating an average 3.65 percent reduction in materials cost of machine tools.

Uses of indexes

Indexes and key-parts cost controls are expensive. They can take hundreds or even thousands of labor hours of work to set up, and even a relatively simple system can take 500 labor hours of work a year to maintain. Cost is undoubtedly one of the main reasons that indexes are not used more widely in materials management. Companies that do use them rarely abandon them; they are convinced that they are worth their cost. Indexes and key-parts controls permit more accurate forecasting of costs, stimulate superior materials performance, and help make the materials management job easier.

Provide accurate forecasts. An index or summary of key-parts cost is based on prices currently being paid for materials. But because of supplier and manufacturing lead times and inventories, there is always a considerable lag between the average order date for material and the date when the material is actually incorporated into an end product. In some industries, today's purchases appear in products six months hence; in few industries is this lead time less than two months. Indexes or key-parts systems permit material costs to be forecast with 99.99 percent accuracy during the lead time. When they are combined with the materials manager's price projections, it is possible to predict materials costs with considerable accuracy a year or more in advance.

The company controller can use projections of key-parts prices to plan the cash flow, to develop a projected profit and loss statement based on the sales estimate, and to develop data for pricing. Composite price indexes cannot be used so directly, but they are useful in forecasting cost trends. For example, if a composite index drops 3.65 percent (as in Table 7–5) and materials cost constitutes 50 percent of the sales dollar, management knows it can reduce average prices by 1.825 percent (i.e., 50 percent of 3.65 percent) in bidding for new business without narrowing its profit margin. It also can plan on spending 3.65 percent less for materials for the same physical output and can budget its cash accordingly.

Stimulate performance. Index and key-parts information provides a convenient yardstick for performance measurement. Comparison of actual key-parts prices with projected prices or with general price indexes indicates how well materials personnel have done their work and also stimulates improvement.

Simplify management. Materials management involves thousands or even millions of individual transactions each year. Materials managers can do their job effectively only if they avoid the distraction of numerous unimportant details and concentrate on significant problems. Price indexes help them function more effectively because they summarize the exact effect of thousands of materials transactions on cost and profits. They also make it easy to evaluate accurately the effect of future changes in materials prices on operating costs.

For example, suppose management becomes concerned about a possible price rise for a key raw material. With key parts or index data, it is an easy matter to calculate what product costs will be at various price levels for the raw material. It also is possible to calculate precisely when it pays to change to a substitute material or to initiate a program to redesign the product so that it no longer requires the material.

Indexes can also simplify inventory management. It is often practical to make a plan of purchase for each index item. When the materials manager adds up the projections in these plans, she knows exactly what 80 to 90 percent of the inventory investment will be months in advance. If she must change her plans because of faulty sales or price forecasts, she knows almost exactly how rapidly she can change with a minimum of detail work. For example, suppose a materials manager's current inventory of index items is equal to two months' production and she is already committed to a buildup to three months' stock. Because of a shortage of cash, management decides to cut back to one month's stock. The materials manager can do the job quickly and efficiently by concentrating her attention on the index items that comprise the biggest part of her costs.

Case

CASE 7–1. OWEN ELECTRIC COMPANY

Developing a plan of purchase for steel

"As if I didn't have enough trouble," Richard Owen, Jr., Owen Electric's purchasing manager, complained as he read *The Wall Street Journal*, "I've got to worry about the steel situation. David McDonald, president of the steel workers' union, has had things his own way just about every time steel negotiations come up. There was a strike in 1952, then another one in 1956, and I'll just bet there will be a strike in 1959."

Owen Electric is a small producer of electric motors. By close con-

trol of costs and good marketing, it has managed to compete successfully against such giants as General Electric and Westinghouse. Steel
is Owen Electric's second most important commodity after copper
and, in late 1958, the company's steel inventory situation is far from
favorable. In fact, sales have bounced back so fast from the 1957–58
recession that the company is operating almost on a hand-to-mouth
basis with steel as well as with copper.

Looking ahead, the company anticipates that it will require 50 tons
per month of steel through June 30; 35 tons per month until September 30; and 65 tons per month for the balance of the year 1959.
Owen has already ordered 170 tons of steel for first-quarter rolling
since, even if the company does not decide to build inventory in anticipation of a strike, he would like to get a little bit of cushion in its
inventory. If all goes according to plan, first-quarter purchases will
exceed usage by 20 tons, giving the company a little safety stock—
which it does not have in the fall of 1958. Adequate steel inventories
are particularly important because the company estimates that it
stands to lose irrevocably about $2,000 for every day that operations
are shut down for lack of material.

Owen, like most other purchasing agents he knows, believes that
there will almost certainly be a strike when the steel contract expires
July 1, 1959. Steel company sales representatives have been urging
their customers to buy ahead in anticipation of a strike, and lead times
for steel have already been lengthened. Owen doubts if he can even
get on any of his steel suppliers' first-quarter 1959 rolling schedule for
any tonnage over and above what he already has on order. However,
he can probably increase his purchases by as much as 100 percent
during the second quarter and get delivery before the union contract
expires on July 1.

The company does not have space available to store any extra steel
inventories over and above the 20-ton safety stock it hopes to accumulate during the first quarter. However, adequate storage space could
be rented for an average cost of $1.50 per ton per month, plus $2.00 per
ton to move the steel from the warehouse to the Owen Electric plant.
In addition, the company anticipates other modest looses as a result of
damage from extra handling, rust, and so forth, which might amount to
1 percent of the value of the steel stored. Purchases could be financed
with a 6.5 percent bank loan.

The last steel industry strike, in 1956, lasted about three weeks.
Unlike the Truman administration, which intervened in the 1952 steel
strike, the Eisenhower administration in power in 1956 and still in
power in 1959 believed in minimum interference in labor-
management disputes. The steel strike in 1956 lasted about three
weeks and resulted in what both steel producers and users regarded as
an inflationary wage settlement. This wage settlement helped trigger

an 8 percent increase in the BLS index for composite steel prices during the year 1956. Steel companies not only passed on their higher wage costs but also took advantage of an opportunity to pass on miscellaneous increases in various other costs and to attempt to restore what had been shrinking profit margins.

In late 1958, the steel companies are not only faced with higher wage costs but are also feeling the effects of much higher scrap prices. The Pittsburgh price of No. 1 heavy melting steel scrap has advanced about $10 per ton from its low of $35 earlier in the year. Steel companies are using a charge of as much as 50 percent scrap steel in their open-hearth furnaces.[8] During periods of peak demand, as much as half of this scrap must be purchased on the open market. The balance is generated within the mill as part of the steel-making process.

Owen Electric's weighted average price for various types and grades of steel used in 1958 is $148 per ton. Richard Owen estimates that even if there is no strike in 1959, there is a 50 percent probability that steel prices will increase by about 5 percent and a 40 percent probability that the increase will be limited to about 3 percent. He guesses that there is only a 10 percent probability of no price increase at all—even with no strike.

However, if there were a strike, Owen believes there is zero probability of no price increase and a 30 percent probability of an increase of as much as 7 percent. He guesses that the probability of a 5 percent increase would be about 40 percent and that there is a 30 percent probability of a 3 percent increase if there were a strike.

Owen believes that the odds strongly favor a strike, although, of course, he is not certain how long it would last. He sees four broad possibilities, however: a probability of 20 percent for no strike, a probability of about 40 percent for a three-week strike, a probability of 30 percent for a strike lasting three to six weeks, and only a 10 percent probability of one that would last six to eight weeks. Owen does not believe that a strike could possibly last more than eight weeks before either a settlement is reached voluntarily or President Eisenhower invokes the Taft-Hartley Act. Under the Taft-Hartley law, the president can order the strikers back to work for a period of 90 days if he feels that the strike is adversely affecting the economy. Owen guesses that if President Eisenhower invokes the act, there would be no second strike, and labor and management would almost certainly reach an agreement.

Questions

1. Recommend a plan of purchase and evaluate it with a Bayesian probability analysis.

---

[8] Present-day technology requires much less scrap.

2. With the benefit of hindsight, we now know that steel production was crippled for more than 100 days in the summer of 1959 until President Eisenhower finally invoked the Taft-Hartley Act, forcing the steel company employees to go back to work. However, the composite index of steel prices remained at $0.0698 per pound from November 1958 through 1960. Partly because of indirect government pressure but mostly because of falling demand and growing inroads from cheaper foreign steel, American steel producers were not able to raise their prices above the 1959 level for more than five years thereafter.

   a. How would your plan of purchase have worked during the 1959 strike?

   b. Could Owen have protected himself against a steel stockout, given the assumptions on which he based his decision?

8

Material requirements planning and production control basics

Material requirements planning (MRP) is a relatively new solution to an old problem: always having material on hand when needed without carrying excess inventory. MRP is the art and science of using a computer to collect and classify data and solve problems in production control and inventory management. With MRP, complex interrelationships can instantly be resolved. For example, suppose that item A is used in several dozen components of several dozen end products. The demand for these end products is changing constantly. How does this affect demand for item A? Before MRP, about all the average manufacturer could do was to carry a fat inventory of item A and just hope that it proved adequate. With MRP, each change in end product demand can be instantly reflected in inventory and production planning for each component, including those that are several stages away from the final production process.

MRP is not a fixed body of knowledge. Its horizons are continuing to expand as organizations become more adept at using computers to solve their problems. When the term began to be widely used in the late 1960s, material requirements planning pretty much boiled down to using a computer to perform operations that had previously been done by clerks. It also permitted use of time-tested techniques such as economic order quantities, application of probability theory to determine safety stocks, and statistical demand forecasting that were not really practical with manual methods.

In fact, the techniques discussed in Chapters 9 and 10 of this book (and others) have been available for years. They were not in wide use simply because the calculations needed to make them work were too time consuming and tedious. These techniques represented models that approximated real-life inventory systems. At first, MRP took them over with little change; now it has become more sophisticated and uses more complex models that come even closer to real life.

While MRP techniques are advancing steadily, basic goals have not changed. They include:

1. *Minimum protection against uncertainty.* Organizations build stockpiles of materials as protection against an uncertain future. They also often tend to require extra equipment and employees standing by to cope with events that may or may not occur. Efficient MRP cannot eliminate the unexpected (such as a strike at a supplier plant or a shipping delay) but it can rapidly transmit new information to the point in the system where it can be used immediately. This makes it possible for organizations to operate with less allowance for uncertainty. As a result, they wind up with less investment in inventory and facilities and with lower operating costs.

2. *Optimum balance between labor and capital inputs.* Almost all economic activity is carried on with some mix of labor and capital. To a remarkable extent, one factor of production is a substitute for another. In addition, one form of capital or labor may be a substitute for another. Examples make these abstractions easier to understand:

   a. A company estimates demand for a product at 1,000 units per year. Should it manufacture in lots of 100 or lots of 1,000? With the larger lot, it will have more of its capital tied up in inventory. On the other hand, both labor and equipment will probably be used more efficiently if the larger lot is produced.

   b. Every organization must invest substantial sums in stockpiles of materials. The magnitude of this investment is related, in part, to how frequently stocks are reviewed. To cite two extremes, an organization that physically reviews its inventory on an annual basis would require a substantially greater investment than one that made daily reviews. On the other hand, the reivew process itself is costly. MRP determines how frequently the physical review should be made which largely is a matter of evaluating optimum trade-off between labor and capital costs.

3. *Maximum utilization of labor and capital.* Every production process can be looked at a series of queues of materials waiting in line to be processed. The queues can be shortened by the addition of labor and/or capital inputs. Longer queues may permit the organization to get along with less labor or capital but only at the price of greater investment in the materials that are waiting in the queue and sacrifice of other objectives. MRP helps hold queues to the minimum that is needed for various capital, labor, and other constraints and also suggests optimal relationships.

In this and the next two chapters, we will be concerned with the overall MRP process. In the physical sense, MRP consists essentially of bits of data stored in a computer along with programs that are designed to manipulate the data in a way that provides management with information it needs to make decisions. Since this is not a book that is concerned with computer programming and operation, we will approach MRP less directly—in terms of its organization and the underlying techniques that are applied.

ORGANIZATION

Material requirements planning in manufacturing organizations is carried on by the production and inventory control department. Production control is simply the process of monitoring the performance of a group of workers or equipment and comparing the results of their efforts with a predetermined plan. The production controller's function is to see that the objectives of the plan are being met and that human and physical recources are being used as efficiently as possible.

Nonmanufacturing applications

The production control function is not limited to manufacturing. It is universal to all economic activity, although it cannot always be easily identified. The traffic department of an airline or railroad is engaged in production control when it decides to have equipment on hand in a particular city. The registrar of a university is engaged in production control when she determines that a particular classroom will be used for a particular course in materials management at a particular hour. The manager of a retail store is engaged in production control when she determines that eight salesclerks will be needed on Saturdays but only six on weekdays.

Production control is concerned with all of the resources needed to get a job done. Thus its scope extends beyond materials management as narrowly defined in Chapter 1. The production control manager is concerned with having not only the materials on hand to do the job but also the labor and equipment. The latter resources are often more important than the material and, of course, they are the direct responsibility of the operations manager responsible for getting the job done.

Materials management function

How, then, can one justify production control as a part of materials management rather than the operating management activity itself? There are basically four reasons.

1. *Of the three resources used in production, material is the only one that is external to the organization.* Over the short term, the

labor and equipment are already there. Production control is, in large, part, material requirements planning. It boils down to making sure that enough material is on hand so that workers and machines can be productively employed and customers will be satisfied.

2. *The skills required for materials management can readily be applied to production control problems involving labor and equipment.*

3. *Production control problems involving material, labor, and equipment are inevitably interrelated.* The basic production control problem is to bring all three resources together at the right time in the proper quantities. This is a single interrelated function; responsibility for it must be centralized in one group. To divide it between materials management and operations management is to invite chaos.

4. *The materials management organization is often considered part of operations management.* The author does not regard this as good practice in most cases, but it does have the advantage of resolving the problem of whether production control is part of materials management or operations management. When operations management embraces materials management, production control easily can be part of both, with no real conflict. In contrast, when production control is part of a materials management, production control easily can be part of both, with no real conflict. In contrast, when production control is part of a materials management department that is independent of manufacturing or operations management or organization, its decisions involving the scheduling of labor and equipment must nevertheless be consistent with manufacturing's objectives, just as the physical distribution part of materials management serves marketing's objectives. Otherwise there will be conflict.

The production control process is both easy and difficult to visualize. In small organizations it is carried on so inconspicuously that it does not seem to exist. In large organizations its existence is all too apparent, and the process becomes so complex that it is difficult to comprehend.

In the small organization, for example, production control and MRP consist primarily of a worker asking the boss which job to start on next and, from time to time, the boss checking up and asking the worker how he is coming along. This is more or less what happens in a very large organization, but here there may be tens of thousands of workers and thousands of bosses. In large organizations oral instructions are no longer adequate; in fact, there are so many activities going on simultaneously that it is difficult for any single person to grasp what is happening. The total report of whether or not everything is going according to plan can be found among tens or hundreds of millions of "bits" of information stored in computer memory, magnetic tape, punched card, or written records.

A MODEL PRODUCTION SYSTEM

The best way to grasp how production control and MRP work is to create a situation that is so easy to comprehend that no formal system is needed. Imagine that you are a small manufacturer with this equipment: two automatic lathes, one milling machine, and one drill press. Your finished products are custom made to customers' specifications. In some cases they require assembly operations incorporating purchased parts and parts machined on your screw machines.

Application of labor force and equipment plans

Following the principles outlined in Chapters 6 and 7, you do the best job you can of planning and forecasting. Your equipment plan consists of making do with what you have. Your labor force plan calls for 40 hours work per week by each of your four employees. Two of your employees are machinists who are able to operate with equal proficiency any of your machine tools. The other two are assemblers. In a pinch, the machinists could help the assemblers, but the assemblers have no training as machinists. The best an assembler could do would be to operate the drill press after one of the machinists set it up for him.

Calculate backlog. A simple production system can be based on calculation of backlogs of labor force and equipment (see Table 8–1).

TABLE 8–1
Calculation of total and active backlogs

Department	Weekly capacity (hours)	Orders on hand		Active backlog	
		Hours	*Weeks*	*Hours*	*Weeks*
Facilities and material					
Automatic lathes	80	800	10.0	32	0.40
Milling machine	40	220	5.5	8	0.20
Drill press	40	100	2.5	2	0.05
Assembly	80	1,200	15.0	200	2.5
Labor force					
Machinists	80	720	9.0	26	0.33
Assemblers	80	1,200	15.0	200	2.5

As orders flow in from customers, you estimate the time they will require in each department and then add these hours to the backlog. When an order is completed in a particular department, you deduct from your backlog. In your business, you keep separate backlogs concerned with the utilization of equipment and the utilization of labor force. Your goal is always to have enough of a backlog to keep your employees busy and also to utilize your equipment economically—especially your two automatic lathes, which are much costlier than your milling machine and drill lathe.

Adding an order to a backlog is a clerical operation. Table 8–1 indicates that you have in your files orders from customers calling for a total of 800 hours of lathe time, 220 hours of milling machine time, and so on. This does not mean that you are presently in a position to start all this work. Material must be on hand before work can begin. Therefore you must also keep track of an "active" backlog for each department.

Active backlog. In the lathe department, for example, you are presently ready to start jobs calling for 32 hours of machine time. Since your capacity in this department is 80 hours per week (two machines each working 40 hours), this 32-hour active backlog represents 32 ÷ 80, or 0.40 weeks (two days) of work for the automatic lathes. If you are the boss, this means that your employees can probably work on their own for the next two days without having to come to you for further instructions.

Most of your orders are started on one of the automatic lathes. The active backlog on subsequent operations depends at least partly on performance of equipment used in performing preceding operations. Thus, the active backlog for milling and drilling depends primarily on whether or not the parts currently being produced in the lathe department require subsequent milling and drilling. At present, there is only a 0.20 week (one-day) backlog for the milling machine and a 0.05 week (two-hour) backlog for the drill press. If one of the jobs presently on the screw machines does not require milling or drilling, it is likely that not only the drill press but also the milling machine will soon run out of work. While these machines have theoretical backlogs of 100 hours and 220 hours, respectively, the only orders that are at a stage where milling or drilling can actually be done amount to only one day's work for the milling machine and two hours' work for the drill press.

Goals. Your production plan assumes that your milling machine and drill press will not be fully utilized. You plan to employ just two machinists. If you anticipated continuous operation of the drill press and the milling machine, you would need three machinists. Under your present plan, you normally expect to employ one machinist virtually full time to operate the two automatic lathes. The second machinist would operate either the milling machine or the drill press. However, if there is a substantial active backlog for both milling and drilling, you may temporarily shut down the automatic lathes and assign one machinist to the drill press and the other to the milling machine.

Your major goal is to prevent active backlogs from temporarily shrinking to the point where one of your employees temporarily runs out of work and, in effect, gets paid for doing nothing. Your calculation of total and active labor force backlogs shows you how much work you presently have for your employees. For example, your two machinists have a weekly "capacity" without overtime of 80 hours per week. Since one machinist operates two automatic lathes, an 80-hour backlog of lathe time is equivalent to a 40-hour backlog of the lathe operator's time. Thus the total 800-hour backlog of time on the two lathes is equivalent to a 400-hour backlog for the machinists.

The drill press and milling machine each require one operator, so their 100-hour and 220-hour order backlogs represent an identical backlog of machinists' time. This, therefore, amounts to 220 hours + 100 hours = 320 hours. Adding the 320 hours to the 400 labor-hour backlog on the lathes gives a total machinists' backlog of 720 hours. This is equal to exactly nine weeks when the two machinists each work a 40-hour week. However, the present active backlog for the machinists amounts to only 26 hours or 0.33 weeks— equal to 2 hours on the drill press, 8 hours on the milling machine, and one half of the 32-hour active backlog on the two automatic lathes.

Preventing idle time. You would be quite concerned about an active backlog of only 0.33 weeks (or less than two days) for your machinists if the machinists were used only to operate production machines. You could temporarily prevent one of your machinists from running out of drilling or milling by quickly scheduling on the automatic lathes a job that requires a great deal of subsequent work on the drill press and milling machine. But your overall order position clearly implies that you have an imbalance between demand for automatic lathe work and for the subsequent machining operations. The lathe backlog represents 10 weeks' work for a machinist, while the combined milling machine and drill press backlog represents just eight (5.5 + 2.5) weeks' work. Assuming no change in your order mix, the day will come when your drill press and milling machine sit idle while the automatic lathes continue to operate.

Your solution to this problem is simply to transfer a machinist to assembly work. Fortunately, your active backlog in the assembly area is now two and one half weeks. You will probably transfer a machinist to assembly in the next day or so. This will cause the active backlog in assembly to shrink more rapidly. With three workers in the assembly area, your weekly capacity temporarily becomes 120 hours instead of 80 hours. You would immediately check to make certain that additional material was delivered to the assembly area so that its active backlog would continue to be adequate. This material would probably consist of in-process inventory coming from one of the three machining departments, as well as purchased parts you are not equipped to make.

Releases to purchasing and manufacturing

Proper timing of both purchases and manufacturing operations is vital to successful production control. As noted above, the production control process begins when an order from a customer is analyzed and requirements for both purchases and manufacturing operations are estimated. In the case of your small business, this boils down to estimates of machining and assembly times as well as calculations of specific purchase requirements. When an order is received, the estimated hours needed to fill it are added on to the backlogs of the various departments shown in Table 8–1.

Starting date. At this stage, no specific starting date has necessarily been determined for the order—even though the customer probably indicated when he wanted delivery and your salesperson made a specific delivery promise. For example, suppose it is June 1 and your salesperson accepted an order calling for 100 hours of automatic lathe work and 20 subsequent hours on the drill press, to be delivered by August 15. Backlog on the automatic lathe would automatically increase to 900 hours or 11½ weeks, after the 100 hours of new demand was added to the existing 800-hour backlog shown in Table 8–1. Similarly, the backlog on the drill press would increase to 120 hours, or three weeks.

At this time you would probably want to estimate when you will "release" this job for production. Under ordinary circumstances, your very latest release date would allow enough time for the order to be completed before August 15. Since you would probably run this order for 100 consecutive hours on just one lathe, this operation alone would take two and one half weeks. The 20-hour drilling operation will require another half week. The total cycle would therefore be at least three weeks if there were no delays. Thus you must release the job no later than July 25 if you are to meet the customer's requested delivery date.

Ordering material. Raw material for this order must also be on hand before July 25. You would undoubtedly get the raw material delivered at least a few weeks before the July 25 deadline. This would give you some safety margin should your supplier be late in delivering and would also permit you to start production well ahead of the required date if you found it convenient to do so. In this particular case, you would probably order the raw material on June 1 and get delivery on it in the next few weeks, if you did not already have it in stock. However, if the order were not to be released for many months, you would most likely hold up ordering raw material until a couple of months before you are ready to start production. There would be no point in committing yourself to material too long before you actually need it, and your customer would not allow you to buy too far ahead if he were held responsible for the material.

Your requisition to purchase material would be sent immediately to the purchasing department, which would then follow the procedures outlined in Chapters 12–14. This order and dozens of others would then figuratively—and perhaps literally—sit in a file cabinet pending further action. You might, in fact, have two separate files of orders— one covering orders for which materials are on hand and the other for orders where material is not on hand. In the latter file would be in- cluded some orders where material should have been delivered but has not been, for various reasons. From this you might well make up a "shortage" list indicating what materials were needed, checking at regular intervals with buyers in the purchasing department to see how suppliers were progressing in filling orders for materials not yet delivered.

Dispatching

When the raw material is on hand for an order, you can "release" that order for production and "dispatch" it from department to de- partment until it is completed. The minute an order is "dispatched" it becomes part of the active backlog of some department in manufactur- ing, until the order is finally completed. The process in your company is such that work on orders normally starts in the automatic lathe de- partment. Table 8–1 above shows an active backlog in this department of just 0.40 weeks (two days), even though total backlog is ten weeks.

Minimize inventory. This does not mean that there is sufficient purchased material on hand for just two days of production. Instead, it almost certainly reflects a deliberate policy of rationing the flow of new work to the shop. The production controller tries to release just enough new jobs to keep all departments operating according to plan. Nothing can be gained by releasing any more than this minimum, and in fact, manufacturing costs will probably be increased. In general, the greater the active backlog, the greater the investment in inventory. Also, efficiency usually declines when there is a large active backlog. This is partly psychological and partly physical, since extra handling operations are often required when a shop is jammed with excess in-process inventory.

First come, first served. Orders may be dispatched on a first-in, first-out basis. In this case, the order's initial release date can be esti- mated from the order backlog. For example, Table 8–1 shows a ten- week order backlog on the automatic lathes. If the first-in, first-out rule is followed in dispatching, the next order added to this backlog would not be released for ten weeks. Thus, if Table 8–1 reflects your backlog as of June, an order received on June 2 would not be started through the automatic lathe department until about August 15. While the order received on June 2 might be started later than all orders received on earlier dates, it would not necessarily be the last one finished. Each work station would have its own first-come, first-served queue. An early order requiring many operations might therefore take much longer to complete than a late order that passed through just one or two work stations.

The first-in, first-out rule of dispatching is easy to comprehend. It also prevents orders that would otherwise warrant a low priority from sitting around for weeks, or months, with possible deterioration of material. Otherwise the first-in, first-out system has no advantages and, in practice, is almost always superseded by other dispatching rules designed either to keep customers satisfied or simply to maximize the producer's profits.

Customer-oriented priorities. Pleasing customers is a legitimate materials management objective that can be reflected in dispatching procedures. A company may decide that it is "fair" to its customers if it releases orders in a sequence determined by the dates on which customers desire delivery. If all orders from all customers require essentially the same operations, customer-oriented priorities are easy to set: an order calling for delivery on August 15 is released before one calling for delivery on the 16th, and so on.

Under this dispatch rule, all orders will be ready for delivery ahead of schedule as long as the company's volume of orders is less than its capacity. On the other hand, if the company is trying to deliver more than it is capable of producing during any period, its performance will get progressively worse. The first order completed during the period may be on time, the second may be a day or two late, the third will be almost a week late, and so on.

Calculation of customer-oriented priorities requires more than a simple sorting of orders by customer's desired delivery date if different orders require different manufacturing processes. In this more typical case, an order requiring a lengthy process must be started before an order calling for just one or two operations. For example, an order requiring eight weeks of processing would get a tentative starting date of February 1 if the customer wanted delivery during the last week of March. On the other hand, an order with a delivery date of February 28 might get a tentative starting date of February 8 if three weeks' process time were estimated. Thus the latter order would be started after the former, even though it would be delivered sooner. It should be noted, however, that neither order would necessarily be started on these dates. If the shop had more business than it could handle, all orders would start late. If business were slack, the orders would be ahead of schedule.

Producer-oriented priorities.   All other factors being equal, most manufacturers try to please their customers. Unfortunately for the customers, all factors frequently are not equal—especially during periods of high demand. Other dispatching rules often take priority over those that are exclusively concerned with pleasing the customer. These rules, which can become quite complex, are concerned with minimizing costs and maximizing profits.

In the situation outlined in Table 8–1, your primary concern would probably be maintenance of a work load that will keep all four of your employees busy. Priority in dispatching might be given to jobs that require time on the milling machine and the drill press, so there will be work for both machinists. If jobs requiring milling and drilling simply dry up, you will probably try to give priority to jobs with lots of assembly work. With the milling machine and the drill press shut down, you need just one machinist on the automatic lathes. The second machinist would be transferred to the assembly department, increasing your labor force in that department by 50 percent. Your present active backlog of two and one half weeks' work for two assemblers would immediately become a 1.7-week active backlog with three assemblers. You would almost certainly run out of work for the assemblers if you did not immediately begin to release jobs for production that require a substantial amount of assembly time.

Chances are you would alternately follow just two dispatching rules with the model shown in Table 8–1. You would be concerned first with releasing types of work that make it possible to keep all four of your employees busy. Then you would probably follow a customer-oriented priority.

There are a variety of other dispatching priorities that you could follow. In larger organization, the computer could be programmed for any priority that management wants. In fact, it could move from priority to priority. Among the desirable priorities are:

1.   Shortest cycle or least work.   The goal here is to rush through all jobs that require relatively little work. These jobs require a minimum investment in in-process inventories and also can be delivered and invoiced quite rapidly.

2.   Longest cycle work.   Usually the most lucrative jobs in terms of total profit are those that require the most time. It also takes fewer of these jobs to load the shop with work, so they can mean less congestion, longer production runs, and greater profit.

3.   Fewest remaining operations.   If an order has been processed through most operations and is held up owing to some bottleneck operation, it might be given priority at this point simply to get rid of it (and to collect from the customer).

4.   Maximum delay rule.   If a job has been held up for some maximum period, it might be given priority both to please the customer and to prevent a particular job from floating around in the system for an indefinite period because no other priority can be applied.

Problems of rescheduling

In a very small shop, the production controller might apply various dispatching rules without really being conscious of them. She simply evaluates each order on its merits and determines its priority, taking all relevant factors into account. In a larger organization, specific rules are needed to guide the dispatcher. In the situation described in Table 8-1, the specific rules might be quite simple: dispatch orders in a sequence designed to meet completion dates desired by customers as long as this sequence permits all four employees to be employed productively. In a large shop, the dispatching rules would be much more complex and require considerable investment in computer "software." But, in every shop, small or large, circumstances would frequently require that exceptions be made in the dispatching rules. Either a customer's needs change, or the company finds it unable to follow its existing schedule. Here are some typical problems.

Change in customer demand. You might have an order that you did not plan to release for another month. But, unexpectedly, your customer asks you if you can deliver as soon as possible. If the customer is a good one, you will try to accommodate him if you can.

If purchased material needed for this customer's order is not already on hand, you will have to contact your supplier and ask her to speed up delivery. Then you will investigate to see what effect an earlier than expected release of this order will have on your own operations and on service to other customers. If business conditions are fairly slack, you may not have any problem. If other customers are also clamoring for early delivery of their orders, you may be able to please everyone only by working overtime—and you may pass this extra cost on to your customers.

Customer cutbacks may cause as many changes in your schedule as customer requests for speedy delivery. A cancellation of an order can be particularly inconvenient if it comes just as you are getting ready to release that order. You may not have purchased material on hand to permit you to start some succeeding order, and the cancellation may cause some of your equipment to be unexpectedly idled. In any case, the cancellation will force production control to scramble to revise the production plan.

Quality failure. Quality problems can occur at any stage of the process. When purchased material fails to meet specifications, production control attempts to find out when satisfactory material can be delivered and meanwhile must adjust schedules so that other orders can be filled using material that is already on hand. If quality failure occurs within the plant, the material that is ruined must be replaced. In addition, schedules might have to be readjusted to prevent a particular failure from affecting succeeding operations.

For example, suppose your shop is working on a particular order that requires an automatic lathe operation, milling, and subsequent assembly. Quality problems are encountered on the milling operation. This failure may touch off a whole chain of events in which production control must:

1. Determine when the problem will be solved by consulting with appropriate executives in the quality control, engineering, and manufacturing organizations.
2. Order additional raw material to replace products that were scrapped because of the quality failure.
3. Advise the company's marketing department of the effect of the quality failure on the schedule for completion of this order and any side effects it may have on other orders.
4. Revise dispatching sequences to reflect customer priorities indicated by the marketing department. This particular order can be completed in reasonable time only if it is now given priority over other orders. The quality failure will almost certainly cause at least one order to be late, and marketing would advise which customers it prefers to favor.

In addition, production control may have to change dispatching sequence in order to prevent internal operations from being dislocated. The order that is delayed at the milling machine was destined to move on to assembly. Unless another order is quickly dispatched, the assembly area may temporarily shut down, and excess costs will be incurred.

No material. A supplier may be late in delivering purchased parts and material. If the company itself is responsible for previous operations, excessive absenteeism or labor disputes may cause internal operations to get behind schedule. Equipment failures also can reduce effective capacity. Regardless of the cause, material that is not available will delay an order either at the start of the manufacturing cycle or at some work station in the plant. Production control must therefore go through a process similar to that required for a quality failure.

Short-interval scheduling

Shifts in demand, quality failures, or materials shortages can create such hopeless snarls in dispatching that routine procedures will not work, and the manager must step in to follow progress on an hour-by-hour basis. The technique used is called short-interval scheduling (SIS). The term is misleading because it implies that something is different about the scheduling. In reality, SIS is a method of *dispatch-*

ing; the schedule or sequence in which work is performed may not change at all. In many organizations, SIS becomes sort of a manual override on a computerized material requirements planning system. Something goes wrong that causes the assumptions on which the system is programmed to no longer be valid. In effect, the boss temporarily does not do what the computer says should be done but steps in and directs operations personally.

Close supervision. With conventional dispatching, the worker moves from job to job, much on her own, following a system of priorities that has been presented to her by management. With SIS, the priorities may not change but the manager personally dispatches each job, one at a time. He is then on the spot to inquire why a particular job is taking longer than anticipated and to correct immediately any conditions that inhibit optimum performance.

Workers will respond to SIS essentially because the boss is monitoring their performance almost hour by hour, and is also ready to help them with problems. SIS may also help workers overcome psychological handicaps. A huge backlog of work may be so frightening to basically conscientious employees that it causes them to slow down rather than to work faster. In extreme cases, the backlog may be so terrifying that the employee becomes almost completely unproductive, and no work whatever is done. When the manager applies SIS, productivity is restored because the worker emotionally must concern himself only with one job at a time, the one handed to him from the backlog by the supervisor. In many cases, SIS permits far more complex dispatching rules to be followed simply because the manager has the best grasp of the impact of any particular dispatching on all phases of the business. Thus, the manager can do something the employee cannot possibly do; she can vary the dispatching priority from job to job in order to fulfill current demands best.

Costly technique. The major disadvantage of SIS is the extra-close supervision entailed. There may also be more record keeping. Despite these disadvantages, SIS has broad applications not only in working off large backlogs in manufacturing operations but also in clerical operations. For example, the productivity of a typist may decline sharply if he is presented with a backlog that represents six months' work. In some cases, he may become so discouraged that output declines as a result of a subconscious decision. In other cases, the decision to make 6 months' work last for 12 months may be made quite consciously, since it is difficult for management to measure output over such a prolonged period in the absence of well-defined work standards. In either case, SIS may be the best answer. The work is passed out in small increments, and it is quite easy to monitor performance on each increment.

Expediting

When short-interval scheduling is used, there is no need for extensive expediting. The technique automatically limits the number of jobs in process, and it is relatively easy to locate each job and to measure its progress. However, with conventional dispatching, changes in production plans may be made so frequently that it is anyone's guess when a particular order will be completed. In fact, until computers became commonplace, it was not always an easy job even to *find* an order in process. Companies often employed expediters who were employed full time to physically track down in-process orders so they could report on progress to the company's sales department and to customers.

Basic problem. With conventional dispatching, an order is physically released to its first operation. The release "package" might include not only the raw material needed for the order but also specifications and operations sheets, which describe precisely what machines and tooling are to be used in completing the order. Each operation is then checked off as it is completed, and the partially fabricated material is moved to the next department, where it waits for a subsequent operation. Even in a medium-sized plant, each operating department might have dozens or even hundreds of different orders piled up in a not particularly orderly fashion. The supervisor in charge of the department eventually processes each order, following whatever dispatching rules he or she has been given.

Neither the supervisor nor anyone else in such a situation can accurately predict when a particular order will be completed. This would be difficult even with simple dispatching rules. For example, if the dispatch rule were simply "first come, first served," without exception, it would be easy to determine the relative priority of each order, but it would still be difficult to predict when the order would actually reach the head of the line. Process times on prior orders can vary substantially. In addition, a supervisor can never predict what the effective labor force or equipment inventory will be. The labor fluctuates each day because of absenteeism and turnover. Equipment also is subject to breakdowns. To make matters worse, probably no company has a single dispatching rule. With a complex dispatch rule, it is difficult to determine the relative priority of a particular order. In addition, company expediters may effectively be changing the dispatch rule on a daily or even hourly basis.

Role of the expediter. An expediter may track down a particular order by literally walking from department to department until he locates it physically. If it appears that the order will be delayed if it is simply left to the prevailing priorities, the expediter may ask the supervisor to give it special attention. This represents, of course, a new dispatching rule. What often happens is that the expedited order displaces some other order which then becomes the object of future expediting, and so on. Orders that receive no expediting keep being put aside in favor of expedited orders, and the expedited orders themselves may leapfrog ahead of one another as one expedited order yields priority to another expedited order, which, in turn, causes the first order to drop behind schedule and to be expedited again.

The computer has done much to eliminate overexpediting. Typically, a card is keypunched every time an operation is completed on an order. The computer can then print out summaries that show exactly where each order actually is at any particular time. The computer can also dispatch orders, following extremely complicated dispatching rules with ease. The computer's calculations can always be overridden, of course. Ideally, however, this is done only after taking into account not only a particular order that management wishes to speed up but also the effect that expediting will have on other orders in the system.

Key weakness

With the production control system discussed so far, the key weakness is that the manager never really knows when a particular order is going to be completed. She can predict when a particular order will be released relative to other orders, but the absolute release date depends on how much work is already in the system and how rapidly it is being completed.

Once the order enters the system, its completion date is determined by the dispatch rules that are applied as it moves from operation to operation. In the absence of expediting, the order either may be completed well ahead of the customer's desired date or it may be late. In many cases no one can predict when the order will emerge from the system.

For a company handling many small orders, this seemingly casual approach may be the most efficient system it can afford. Otherwise the cost of administering the order may be greater than the total value of the order. This may also be true of a company with a few very large orders—especially if the product is not complicated. In this case it is fairly easy to keep track of what is going on without a formal system. Organizations that fall between these extremes usually try to schedule output fairly precisely. They not only estimate in advance how much time each order will require at each work station but also try to predict precisely when this work will be done.

The MRP system is designed so that management can find out the exact status of every order—where it is in the system and whether or not it is behind the system. Based on the system of priorities that have been programmed, the system will automatically advance or hold back particular orders in order to achieve optimum results.

THE INVENTORY OBJECTIVE

The MRP system need not be very good provided the organization is willing to invest a good deal of money in purchased materials and in-process and finished goods inventories. The bigger the inventory, the easier it is for both marketing and manufacturing to do their jobs. If manufacturing has ample supplies of purchased materials and in-process stocks, its efficiency is limited only by the reliability of its equipment and the perseverance of its labor force. If there is a huge investment in finished goods stocks, marketing need not be concerned about its ability to satisfy customer demand or about the flexibility of manufacturing's response to changing markets.

The materials manager, in contrast, is very much concerned with inventory investment. Every company could spectacularly increase its profitability if it could hire a super materials manager who could magically whisk material from suppliers through manufacturing to customers so rapidly that the company could collect from its customers before it was forced to pay its employees and suppliers.

Need for inventory

Since organizations hire ordinary mortals as materials managers, they often find themselves saddled with a substantial permanent investment in inventories that is automatically generated by the materials management process. Even the extremely simple production model described in Table 8–1 generates as much as five different piles of inventory for each order. There is an investment in purchased material inventory before conversion to in-process inventory by the automatic lathe. Three different types of in-process inventory pile up ahead of the milling machine, drill press, and assembly area. Finally, there is an investment in finished goods stock up to the time the company's customer accepts delivery and pays the bill.

Successful material requirements planning keeps these investments as low as possible, with minimum adverse effects on manufacturing and marketing. When companies have too little inventory and run out of stock, manufacturing efficiency and customer relations are bound to be hurt. Stockouts of essential materials mean some interruption of production, which raises costs. They may also delay delivery of finished products to a customer. After a few such delays, even the most patient customer will start looking for a supplier who will give him better service.

Cost. The situation is almost as bad for the company that carries too much inventory. It may have material available when it is needed, but its costs will be so high that it will not make any profit on the business it gets by having material available. Inventories tie up a company's capital; they generate storage costs; and they deteriorate or become obsolete in storage. In all, as will be discussed in greater detail in Chapter 10, inventories may cost 25 percent or more per annum to carry; it can cost a company as much as $250,000 per year (and sometimes even more) to carry a $1 million inventory. Obviously, if through intelligent materials management the same company can get along with just $500,000 invested in inventory, the savings will be substantial.

Since a company with a $1 million inventory may have sales of no more than $8 million and profits of only $800,000, it does not take too much imagination to grasp how efficient inventory management can make a tremendous contribution to company profit objectives. Similarly, it is easy to guess what will happen to company profits if costs are raised 5 or 10 percent because of frequent delays in manufacturing due to lack of inventory, or what happens to both sales and profits if customers find they can get prompter service from a competitor who is able to have material on hand when it is needed.

Conflict. Thus, as in all the other phases of materials management, there is a conflict of objectives in inventory management. The objective of high inventory turnover conflicts with the objective of continuity of supply and other objectives (discussed in Chapter 3). Of all business assets, inventories are the least stable and most difficult to control. Unfortunately, both for their profits and for the economy as a whole, American corporations do a rather bad job of inventory management. Their inventories tend to be high when they should be low, and vice versa. Bad inventory planning has been one of the major causes of almost every business recession.

In the typical business cycle, inventory accumulation helps push business activities to a new high. Business then tapers off, but inventories continue to rise. Stocks become excessive. Businesses not only stop buying in excess of needs, but they buy substantially less than current consumption. This underbuying causes production to drop even more and so helps accelerate the downturn. Finally, equilibrium is reached at the bottom of the business cycle, and recovery begins. Usually the recovery catches business unprepared. Sales temporarily exceed production, and inventories drop further. When production catches up with and eventually exceeds sales, inventories start increasing, and the cycle begins all over again.

Nature of the problem

All businesses have difficulty managing their inventories. The major reason is inability to forecast accurately. When a materials manager adds to inventory, he is usually anticipating a need for the material. In many cases, the need comes later than anticipated, and sometimes it never materializes at all. The result is excessive inventory. Or, if demand comes sooner or is stronger than anticipated, the inventory is inadequate.

Slow movement.   The materials cycle is remarkably sluggish. Typically, more than a year may pass before a quantity of raw materials is transformed into a finished product. Theoretically, it would take less than a week to perform every operation necessary to transform various raw materials into a product like a television set. Chances are, however, that the iron ore, copper ore, bauxite, and other minerals used in making the TV set completed today were mined nearly a year before. The materials spent months either in various stockpiles or in transit between operations or plants. It may take only a few seconds to drill a hole in a small component on the TV set, but the material can lie on a factory floor for two days waiting to be scheduled on a machine that will perform this operation. Even completely automated processes have "pipelines" full of inventory awaiting processing.

Inventory functions

No business can operate without inventories. It needs them as a protection against uncertainty, for efficient processing of material, and to permit transit and handling.

Protection against uncertainty.   Because the materials cycle is long and complex, the materials manager must anticipate her needs at each stage. Inventories protect her against unforeseen failures in supply or increases in demand. Without inventories, a large plant would cease operations each time a motor on a machine tool failed. Even a flat tire on a supplier's delivery truck could interrupt production if it delayed a shipment of needed material. Inventories protect production against unanticipated delays.

Similarly, inventories also protect against sudden upsurges in demand. Even with the most advanced market research techniques, few manufacturers can estimate demand accurately—particularly for various individual models of their products. The room air-conditioner industry is an extreme example of this. Sales are greatly affected by both season and weather. During a hot, humid summer, sales may be 50 percent higher than during a cool summer. Air-conditioner manufacturers must not only guess how many appliances the public will want but which models it will prefer. And these decisions must be made in the fall and winter, months before the public is in a buying mood. If a company wants to sell as many air conditioners as the market will absorb, its only protection against a really hot summer—and soaring demands—is an extra-heavy inventory.

Efficient processing of material. Every purchase creates inventory. The investment is more or less permanent when the package size that is bought cannot be immediately used. Thus, a salt shaker is empty and you buy a pound of table salt, most of which will sit in a kitchen cabinet for months. Every organization is forced to carry inventory because package sizes of purchases do not match up exactly with needs.

In addition, unit costs normally are lowest when material is purchased, handled, and processed in large quantities, which in turn generates larger inventories. In addition, inventories act as a "cusion" between operations or processes. Production at various stages of a manufacturing cycle can never be synchronized perfectly; inventories take up the slack when one stage operates at a rate different from from that of the preceding or succeeding stage.

The components of any product are manufactured at widely varying rates of production. For example, it may be possible to make the fasteners used in a television set at the rate of 20,000 pieces per hour. TV assembly lines might operate at the rate of about 200 sets per hour. It would be completely impractical to synchronize fastener production with TV set assembly. In practice, fasteners are assembled onto the TV sets from an inventory strategically located near their point of use on the assembly line.

Transit and handling. Materials may be transported thousands of miles before they are incorporated into an end product. Jamaican bauxite may travel by ship to British Columbia to be made into aluminum ingot. From there it may be shipped to New Jersey to be rolled into aluminum sheet, which moves by rail to Detroit to be fabricated into a component for an automobile, which moves by truck to rail to an auto assembly plant, whence it is finally trucked to a dealer as part of a finished auto that eventually is sold to its ultimate user. All the time it is in transit, which may be a period of several months, this material is part of someone's inventory.

For the reasons given above, every manufacturer must carry a certain minimum inventory. In practice, almost every manufacturer carries an inventory that is substantially greater than the minimum. The manufacturer does so because:

1. The sales and manufacturing departments find it convenient to have stocks that are more than ample.
2. Prices of materials are expected to rise and therefore stocks up at lower prices.

3. Scheduling, production control, and inventory management are more difficult and costlier when stocks are kept at optimum level. The manufacturer may lack the skills necessary for such control or be unwilling to incur the control costs, so extra inventory is carried in order to prevent stockouts.

carry extra inventory to prevent stock out

Determining inventory levels

Inventory level is determined by just two decisions: when to buy and how much. The larger the quantity purchased, the greater the inventory. The earlier the decision to replenish stock, the greater the inventory. Thus inventory management boils down to "how much" and "when" decisions. It is cheaper to buy in larger quantities but this leads to bigger inventories. Similarly, the greater the quantity on hand when a decision is made to replenish, the smaller the risk of running out. But this reduced risk is paid for with higher inventory.

Order quantity. If usage is reasonably regular, each order creates an average inventory equal to one half the order quantity. Suppose a company has a choice of two policies, either to buy in lots of 100 or in lots of 500 units.

1. *Buy in lots of 100.* In this case, the inventory due to order quantity at the time an order is received is equal to exactly 100 units. If this inventory is not replenished until the lot of 100 units is completely used up, then the *average* inventory due to order quantity is equal to 100 units of beginning inventory plus 0 units of ending inventory divided by 2, or 50 units.

2. *Buy in lots of 500.* In this case, beginning inventory is 500 units and ending inventory is 0 units. The average inventory due to order quantity is therefore 500 plus 0 divided by 2 or 250 units.

A real-life storeroom would hold hundreds or thousands of different items whose inventory would fluctuate up and down like the examples above. For various reasons, order quantities would not be identical. However, aggregate inventory investment would (and should) be influenced by adjustments in order quantity. An increase in order quantity would boost inventory and a reduction would reduce it.

Order point. The preceding examples assume that inventory is replenished exactly when it runs out. In such cases, total inventory investment would be determined exclusively by order quantity. This is the ultimate in inventory management. Just as the stock of an item is used up, a new shipment arrives. This goal can almost be achieved in practice on noncritical items that are readily available from local suppliers. Thus, as an individual you may buy milk a quart at a time. When the container is empty, you go to a corner convenience store and replenish your stock.

Few real-life organizations can management even their inventory of noncritical items in such casual fashion. It's just too much work. It is much easier (and cheaper in operating costs but not in inventory investment) to anticipate needs. When an item is about to run out, you place an order which is delivered hours, days, or weeks before the stock from the previous order is actually used up.

Suppose, for example, you run out of milk and you go to the store and they're out too. After this experience, you may decide (provided you're an avid milk drinker) to keep one quart of milk in reserve at all times. Thus, when exactly one quart is left in your refrigerator, you go to the store and buy another quart. This gives you two quarts—one quart to be consumed immediately and the second as a reserve to be consumed later. This second quart becomes "working inventory" after you drink the first quart and a third quart that you buy then becomes the "reserve stock." However, if you are not able to replenish this reserve immediately, your inventory of milk would be completely used up.

Under normal conditions, however, your inventory of milk will vary between two quarts and one quart—the upper level is reached just after you buy an additional quart and the lower level just before you make the purchase. Average inventory is obviously one-and-one-half quarts—one pint of which is determined by your standard order quantity of one quart and one quart for reserve stock.

Safety stock.   Your reserve inventory is called *safety stock* in inventory management. It is determined by the inventory level at which you re-order, or your *order point.* Thus, in the example above, the order point is one quart and since no milk is consumed while you are at the store buying an additional quart, the safety stock is also one quart.

Figure 8–1 is a theoretical model that is consistent with your practice of going to the store to buy an additional quart of milk every time the milk on hand in the refrigerator is exactly one quart. As can be seen, inventory fluctuates between one unit and two units. Mathematically, average inventory is measured by the area under the curve. In this simple example, it is obviously 1½ units—1 unit because of the safety stock which is determined by our practice of replenishing when there is 1 unit on hand and ½ unit as a result of our quantity of 1 unit.

Lead-time usage.   In the model in Figure 8–1, there is no point whatever in carrying a safety stock. If we eliminate it, we would still always have milk to drink. It is not so easy to eliminate safety stock with real-life inventories—even those that consist of noncritical items which are no harder to obtain than a quart of milk. The basic reason for this is that replenishment orders for almost all real-life inventories must be placed days, weeks, or months before the stock on hand is actually used up. Administratively, it takes time to identify the need and to place the order. Even more important, the supplier must fill the order. This cannot always be done immediately even if the stock is

FIGURE 8-1
Inventory model

In this simple model, order quantity and safety stock are both equal to exactly one unit. If there were no variations in lead-time usage, inventory would fluctuate between a maximum of two units, reached just after a new shipment arrives, and one unit, a low point reached just before the new shipment comes in. The safety stock of one unit is available for use should (*a*) the supplier take longer than expected or (*b*) demand be greater than expected.

already in the supplier's warehouse. And months may pass if the item is made to order. Thus, replenishment of inventory requires that demand be forecast in advance of actual receipt of an order.

If the forecast is always perfect, we could develop a real-life model that looked like that in Figure 8-1. For example, suppose that we use one quart of milk per day and that we can always get a quart delivered if we call the dairy one day in advance. Thus, on Monday, we have two quarts in the refrigerator and we call the dairy and request delivery of one quart on Tuesday. By Tuesday, we have consumed one of the two quarts and our inventory is down to one quart, which is our safety stock. Delivery is made and inventory rebounds to two quarts. We call the dairy and order another quart for Wednesday and the cycle is repeated.

The safety stock of one quart serves two purposes. If we get extra thirsty, we can drink two quarts on a single day and not run out. Or if there is a severe blizzard or a strike by the milk truck drivers, we can get along for one day without a delivery and use up our safety stock.

Myths and lead-time realities. Thus, safety stock is needed because of two possible reasons for variation in lead-time usage: (1) usage during the lead time exceeds expectations or (2) the lead time itself is greater than expected because of supplier failure or other causes. It is important to note that the lead time itself is immaterial as long as the variations in lead-time usage can be predicted.

For example, suppose that an item has usage of one unit per week and a lead time of one year. Another item has a lead time of one week and also has usage of one item per week. Let's suppose that in both instances, we can be absolutely certain that usage will always be exactly one item per week, no more or less. In both cases, given perfect knowledge, we need no safety stock. Our inventory would then be equal to one half our order for each item, irrespective of the lead time.

Suppose we decide to order both items in lots of just one unit each. In one instance, we order on Monday for delivery the following Monday. In the second case, we order on the same Monday for delivery exactly 52 weeks later. If we follow this ordering pattern consistently, we will get two deliveries on each Monday—one ordered just 7 days before and the other ordered 52 weeks previously. In both instances our inventory on hand would vary between zero units just before the new order is delivered and one unit just after delivery is made. Thus, as long as lead-time usage is equally predictable, an item with a long supplier lead time requires a safety stock no larger than one with a short lead time. Safety stock is needed only because of *variations* in lead time and for no other reason.

Reasons for variations. Of course, the greater the lapse of time between placement of an order and delivery, the greater the probability that something unexpected will occur. Thus, an item that is directly imported from Taiwan or Japan requires a greater safety stock than one that comes from a supplier that is just across the street—even though foreign and domestic suppliers may intrinsically be equally reliable. More can go wrong when supply lines become extended. In fact, changing lead time is one of the most difficult problems of materials management. Suppose, for example, the normal lead time for an item is four weeks. If a buyer orders material on February 1, he can expect delivery on February 28. What happens if the lead time changes and the buyer is not aware of the change? If the lead time increases, the order that the buyer places on February 1 will not be delivered when it is needed on February 28. At best this will be an inconvenience; at worst it can cause an entire factory to shut down temporarily.

If lead time suddenly decreases, the effect is not quite so bad. Suppose the lead time shortens by 50 percent and the item that is due February 28 is actually delivered on February 14. In that case, the buyer's plant will be carrying substantially more inventory than is needed, for when lead time shortens, the need for inventory also is reduced.

Often the lead time changes unexpectedly. For example, a company may have originally ordered an item during a period of slack business when the lead time was two weeks. Business is booming the next time the item is ordered, but the stock clerk (or the computer) uses the same old lead time. The item actually arrives four weeks after the order is placed—two weeks after it was actually needed.

A stockout is a forceful reminder that lead time has lengthened. In contrast, a shorter lead time that causes excessive inventory investment may never be detected. If an item is first ordered during a period of general shortage, the lead time will be long. Then each time the item is reordered, the lead time allowance will be excessive, causing the company to carry inventory it does not really need.

JOB-LOT ORDERING

Companies that manufacture on a job-lot basis have the easiest job of inventory control. Each customer order is treated, in effect as a brand new product. The materials department reviews the bill of material for the customer's order and buys what is needed to do the job. If its timing is perfect on lead times, the company's raw material inventories are negligible. For example, if you used the production control system illustrated in Table 8–1, purchased material inventory would be converted by the automatic lathes into in-process stock almost immediately after it was delivered. If your scheduling were reasonably tight, in-process inventory would be moderate, and finished goods stocks would be disposed of by immediate shipment to customers.

The purest examples of job-lot ordering are found in the construction industry. When a construction firm wins a contract, its materials personnel must go to work immediately to get the material needed for the contract. There usually are no inventories to draw on, since construction firms almost always have suppliers deliver raw materials directly to the site. It would not be economic for a construction firm to carry an inventory of bricks, for example, since there would be too much handling expense in storing the inventory between jobs. It is much cheaper to buy the bricks needed for each contract and have the supplier deliver them to the site as needed.

Manufacturers of products that are largely made to customer specifications—machine tools, various types of equipment, special instruments, and so on—have problems similar to those of construction firms. Although they do all their work at the same location, each order is substantially different from its predecessors, and it is almost impossible to anticipate materials needs. Many firms do not even try; they simply calculate what material is needed for each order and then buy it.

Problems of control

With a system of job-lot ordering, each order must be scheduled separately. Different materials and components for the job are needed at different stages of construction or manufacture. The long lead-time items needed at earlier stages naturally get top priority. Materials personnel usually deliberately hold off buying short lead-time items until they have to. For example, they may know in January that an item with a lead time of three weeks will be needed in June, but they will make no commitment for the item until, perhaps, the last week in April, and even then they may request that the vendor hold up delivery until early June, although he actually might be able to deliver a few weeks ahead of schedule.

Purchased material on hand will not be released to start through the production process until in-process inventories of material are as low as possible. With perfect dispatching, each work station is about to run out of material just as a new order is moved in from preceding station.

Minimized losses. With good material control, materials are purchased and released for production only when needed for another reason: to minimize losses. The goals are to keep liabilities to a minimum should an order be canceled, reduce the cost of last-minute changes in specifications, and tie up a minimum of storage space for materials not needed immediately.

Problems arise when the lead time turns out to be different from the plan. Frequently an entire order can be held up because a supplier fails to deliver on schedule. Materials personnel try to spot lead-time problems as far in advance as possible. They also try to use all possible expediting methods (discussed in Chapter 17) to bring the lead time back to normal. Should a shortage develop, they immediately inform the manufacturing and sales departments so the job can be rescheduled. A typical form used for this purpose is shown in Figure 8–2.

Order quantity also can be a problem in job-order systems. Theoretically, the materials department simply can order the material specified in the bill of material for each job, and there are no problems. But what happens if usage is greater than anticipated because of miscalculations, spoilage in manufacturing, or shrinkage? Unless this is allowed for by ordering a little extra material, production may be plagued with work stoppages due to lack of material. It is no easy job to determine in advance how much extra material will be needed, and any material that is not used for the job may be wasted.

Solution by rules of thumb. Most companies try to solve problems of control with rules of thumb based on past experience. For example,

FIGURE 8-2

Courtesy Marion Power Shovel Co.

Lead times and delivery dates of purchased material are extremely important in a job-lot ordering system. The purchasing department of the Marion Power Shovel Co. uses this form to advise the production department of supplier shipping promises.

they may not overorder at all on materials with a unit cost of more than $100, but materials in the $50–100 range may warrant a 2 percent overorder and greater cushions would be allowed on even cheaper materials. It is pointless to be stingy with low-cost materials and, in fact, may not even be possible to do so. Suppliers often insist on selling in certain minimum quantities and may prefer not to be bothered at all with orders that amount to $5 or less. As a result, a company which needs 100 cotter pins for a particular job, at a cost of no more than $1 per thousand, may be forced to order many times more cotter pins than it actually needs.

Application of Bayesian rule

Occasionally the Bayesian decision rule (discussed in Chapter 7), can be helpful in determining the proper order quantity for a job lot. Suppose, for example, that a machine-tool manufacturer has an order to make a highly specialized piece of equipment for a customer. The equipment is designed for a very particular job, and there is little likelihood that there will ever be a repeat order for it. One of the components of the equipment is machined from a forging. In all, there are more than 150 machining operations on this particular component. Many of them are extremely precise. It is likely that at some stage of the long machining cycle someone will goof and cause the part to be scrapped. There may then be no choice but to start all over again with another forging.

Risk of scrap. The company actually needs only one good component for the equipment, but it intends to purchase several forgings and start them through the machining process simultaneously. Presumably most of the forgings will be scrapped at some stage of the machining process, but, if the company estimates its needs correctly, at least one forging will make it all the way through the process. The problem is to estimate how many forgings should be ordered and started through the process. If not enough forgings are ordered, the company may scrap one that is started and be forced to begin all over again. This would put the entire project months behind schedule. Conversely, it is wasteful to buy and machine more forgings than are actually needed; only one good one will ever be needed.

There is no quick and easy solution to a problem of this sort. Most companies would study the machining cycle carefully and then simply make the best possible estimate of their machining losses. They would then add some safety allowance, hold their breath, and go ahead, hoping that everything would work out. There is no way to avoid risk in making such decisions; this is what executives get paid for. The Bayesian decision rule, however, can help the materials manager and the manufacturing manager make a more rational decision, taking all risks into account.

Suppose the purchase price for the first forging made in the lot is $350, and each additional forging costs $200. Cash cost of machining the forgings is $500 each. To simplify calculations, assume that this cost is incurred even if the forging winds up being scrapped at some stage of the machining process.

The superintendent of the machine shop believes that the scrap rate is certain to be at least 50 percent and a minimum of two forgings must be started through the process. The superintendent believes there is a 60 percent probability that one of these castings will be good. He further guesses that there is a 90 percent probability of getting a single good part if 10 forgings are started through the machining process, and the probability of getting a single good part will increase to 99 percent if 30 forgings are started.

No one knows precisely how much will be lost if every forging is lost in the machining process. The general manager, however, believes that at least $25,000 will be lost if the company is not able to produce this component on schedule.

These probabilities and costs are no more than rough estimates based on previous experience. Many executives might take them into account almost subconsciously and then simply make a decision. In this case, for example, the manufacturing manager and the materials manager might arbitrarily agree that 12 forgings should be purchased and started through the machine process. This will prove to be the best of all decisions, of course, only if exactly 11 forgings are scrapped in the process. It will be a wasteful decision if only one or two forgings are scrapped, and it will be almost disastrous if all forgings are scrapped.

Three possible decisions. Bayesian analysis will not eliminate the uncertainty from such a decision, but it forms an orderly basis for rational review of the relative risks. There are three possible solutions to the problem outlined above:

1.   Buy and machine two forgings and accept a 40 percent risk that both forgings will be scrapped.

Purchase cost of two forgings	$ 550
Machining two forgings	1,000
40 percent probability of $25,000 loss	10,000
Total cost plus expected value	$11,550

2.   Buy and machine ten forgings and accept a 10 percent risk that all ten forgings will be scrapped.

Purchase cost of ten forgings	$2,150
Machining ten forgings	5,000
10 percent probability of $25,000 loss	2,500
Total cost plus expected value	$9,650

3.   Buy and machine 30 forgings and accept a 1 percent risk that all 30 forgings will be scrapped.

Purchase cost of 30 forgings	$ 6,150
Machining cost of 30 forgings	15,000
1 percent probability of $25,000 loss	250
Total cost plus expected value	$21,400

Since the cost of the risk is lowest with the second alternative, the company should buy a lot of ten forgings and accept a 10 percent risk that this will not be enough. This example is perhaps unrealistic in that only three probabilities are considered, in order to prevent calculations from becoming unduly cumbersome. A sophisticated material requirements planning system could take into account an entire spectrum of probabilities and provide an optimal risk-adjusted policy. Regardless of whether the approach is manual as illustrated here or computerized, it rarely pays to take actions that virtually eliminate the possibility of a stockout. The cost is simply too high. Purchasing a lot of ten forgings represents a hedge that is within the usual range of fluctuations that can reasonably be expected in this case. Purchasing a lot of 30, on the other hand, would protect against a most unusual situation. Under most circumstances, a company cannot afford to protect itself against something it expects to happen only very rarely. In every situation, of course, it is desirable to make every effort to consolidate requirements of different orders so that common items are ordered simultaneously.

Modified job-lot control

While construction contractors order almost everything on a contract-by-contract basis, manufacturers almost always draw on inventories for commonly used materials and job order only those that are unique to a particular order. This reduces the cost of job-lot ordering and eliminates some of its basic defects. Each customer order is regarded as a demand on a portion of a common pool of materials and components. While no materials and components are stocked until an order comes in to generate a demand, customer orders are not handled so independently that it is impossible to pool requirements and so reduce cost.

Figure 8–3 illustrates the production and inventory control record

FIGURE 8–3

Courtesy Diebold, Inc.

Inventory control card for the modified job-lot ordering system used by Diebold, Inc. Sales orders are posted as demand for material; purchase order or manufacturing work orders supply this demand.

used by a manufacturer of a widely diversified line of office equipment. The company manufactures more than 500 different products, and material control involves more than 15,000 different items.

The company cannot afford to manufacture so many different products to stock, nor is it economic to stock all the materials and components it uses. Thus job-lot material control is essential. Some of its disadvantages are eliminated by using as many common parts as possible in each product. Requirements for each individual item are combined by listing each item on a separate card so that purchases reflect the demand of each product in which the item is used.

As the company receives orders for its machines, a "demand" is generated that is posted to the record. For example, suppose the company received an order requiring 100 pieces of part No. 01-39424 (see Figure 8–3). On February 1, the record is posted to indicate that 100 pieces are reserved for sales order A 11190, with delivery required March 20.

The reservation is posted by an accounting machine that compares the requirement with existing inventories and previous reservations. Since this is the first entry, the machine shows a negative balance of 100 pieces available after it takes account of the new reservation. This generates a demand for the material. Since the lead time is 30 days[1] and the material is needed on March 20, the order must be placed by February 20. However, the material planner decides to place it immediately because the sprocket is supposed to carry an extra reservation of 150 pieces for unusual usage. So on February 6, purchase order J 8091 is issued for 1,000 pieces—the predetermined economic order quantity. The machine operator takes account of this order by posting the "on order" amount of 1,000 pieces and allocating 100 pieces of this amount to cover the reservation and 900 "available" for future reservations.

When the order is delivered on March 3, the records are posted to eliminate the 1,000 pieces on order and add 1,000 to the "balance in stores" column. On March 17, 100 pieces are drawn out of stores to be used for sales order A 11190, and the reservation that was made for this order on February 1 is canceled.

Electronic data processing is now routinely used to do the same job. Orders for finished products and their scheduled delivery dates are keypunched and transferred to the computer. Parts lists for each product are also either on magnetic tape or in the computer's "memory." The computer then automatically issues purchase orders and perform other operations in response to various other transactions that are fed into the computer as they occur.

---

[1] Shown in the upper right-hand corner of Figure 8–3.

ORDERING FOR INVENTORY

Even a modified job-order system has weaknesses. Material is not purchased until there is a definite need for it, so it often is not on hand for emergencies. There is no way to plan ahead and anticipate requirements so that large quantities of materials may be purchased at lower prices. Also, manufacturing costs are high, and customer service is slow. Because of these disadvantages, companies use job-order systems only when they are forced to do so because it is impossible to predict materials requirements for each order. Even companies that make thousands of semi-custom-made products avoid job-order material control whenever possible. All material that is common to a number of products is carried in stocks that are drawn on as needed.

"Perpetual" inventory control

Two-bin system. The oldest and simplest system of inventory control is the "two-bin system." One bin holds a reserve supply of material equal to the amount that will normally be consumed during the lead time, plus an extra amount for safety stock. The other holds the balance of the inventory. When stock in the second bin is used up, the order point is reached. A clerk requisitions a new supply of material and then draws on the reserve supply for his needs. When the order is delivered, the reserve supply is brought up to its former level, and the balance of the order is put into the other bin to be drawn on for immediate needs.

The two-bin system is simple to operate because there is no need for records. And, in most cases, there is no need even for two bins. The only requisite for successful operation of the system is that the order point of reserve stock be physically separated from the balance of the stock. This often can be done quite simply.

For example, suppose the item being controlled is pencils, for which usage averages four boxes a week and maximum lead time is one week. The reserve supply in a two-bin system might then be five boxes, including one box as safety stock for unexpected changes in usage or lead time. This supply need not be kept in a separate bin. It can be identified simply by putting a rubber band around it and then using up the other boxes in the inventory first. When the stock drops down to the point where it is necessary to use the boxes held by the rubber band, the order point has been reached.

The two-bin system is best suited for items of low value, fairly consistent usage, and short lead time. It is most commonly used for office supplies, and in smaller plants it also is used for maintenance, repair, and operating supplies. It rarely is suitable for production materials because it does not provide any record of stock on hand and is not sensitive to changes in demand or lead time.

Manually posted records. The two-bin system can be improved (but at the cost of additional record keeping) by keeping a "perpetual" record of additions to and withdrawals from stock. This is sometimes called a "max-min" system. It works exactly like the two-bin system except that a record is kept for each item and it is not necessary to segregate stock. Record cards similar to that shown in Figure 8–4 are used. All materials transactions are posted on these cards.

FIGURE 8–4

Material description											Location	Commodity number	
NONPRODUCTION MATERIAL RECORD													
Used for or by											Order Quan.	Unit of Meas	
MONTHLY USAGE													
Jan.	Feb.	March	April	May	June	July	Aug.	Sept.	Oct.	Nov.	Dec.	Min. Bal.	Order Time
Date	Reference	Quan. on order	Quantity received	Quan. disb.	Bal. in stock	Date	Reference		Quan. on order	Quan. received	Quan. disb.	Bal. in stock	

Typical nonproduction inventory control record card provides a perpetual inventory of the item. All receipts and additions to stock are posted; the balance is periodically verified with a physical count of stock on hand.

The stores clerk disburses material only when he gets a storage requisition. Data from requisitions is later posted to the record cards. Similarly, when an order point is reached, the clerk prepares a purchase requisition and posts the "on order" section of the record card. When material is received, the clerk posts the record card from her copy of the receiving report.

Each transaction can be substantiated by some document such as a receiving report, or requisition form. As a result, the clerk can be held responsible for any discrepancies between her records and actual inventories. Losses from pilferage or unauthorized use are minimized. In addition, the records always show the balance on hand and on order, so it is possible to calculate the value of the stock at any time. While the perpetual inventory system is much more expensive to operate than the two-bin system without records, its cost usually is more than justified for relatively valuable items subject to losses from pilferage.

While perpetual inventory systems are most commonly associated with items that are purchased, they are also used by many manufacturers to control finished goods inventories. Instead of ordering from an outside supplier when inventory drops to the reorder point, a work order is processed by production control for manufacture. In most cases, a dispatching and releasing process similar to that outlined earlier in this chapter is followed.

Application to EDP. Essentially the same clerical work described in the previous paragraphs can also be done with a computer. In fact, only the smallest organizations now use manual perpetual inventory systems. With a simple EDP system, receipts and disbursements are entered into the computer and it is then easy to get periodic printouts showing inventory on hand for each item. Applications of EDP to inventory management are described in more detail in later chapters.

Critical ratio

A computer can also readily be programmed to warn materials management when inventories are being run down at a greater than expected rate. This gives advance warning of future possible stockouts. As a result, materials managers can reduce the probability of disruption in supply while still carrying optimum inventory.

Suppose, for example, that a company sells annually 1,000 units of product X, which it makes in its own plant. As other company products, X is made in batches or job lots which are stored in the company warehouse until they are sold. Product X is manufactured in lots of 250, and production control estimates that a lead time of one month is needed to manufacture a new batch; thus a new batch requested by the physical distribution manager on June 1 should be delivered to the warehouse on July 1. Thus there should be at least a one-month supply, or about 83 units, of X in the warehouse when a new order is sent to manufacturing.

Lead-time problems. Everything will work perfectly so long as (1) lead-time demand is the expected 83 units, and (2) the manufacturing lead time is exactly one month, as predicted. In this ideal situation, the company will not have excess inventory, nor will it be unable to fill customer orders promptly. Real life is almost never so idyllic. There will tend to be either too little or too much of product X because:

1. *Sales may surge ahead during the lead-time period.* In this case, if manufacturing is not able to deliver a new lot of product X in *less* than one month, there will be a stockout.

2. *Sales of product X may lag behind expectations during the lead-time period.* In this case, the physical distribution manager will

receive a new lot of product X before she needs it. As a result, she will temporarily have more money tied up in inventory than she would like. She may also have trouble finding space for the additional material.

Worse yet, the distribution manager may discover that although she has too much product X, she has run out of product Y. Demand has been greater than expected for Y, and the reorder point for Y was reached shortly after that for X. Consequently, the badly needed lot of Y will be delivered after the unneeded lot of X. If manufacturing had known that Y was the critical item, it could have given it priority over X, and the company would have enjoyed both higher sales and lower inventory.

3. *The factory may be ahead of schedule.* In the worst of all cases, the factory may have just laid off employees whom it now must recall because of an unexpected surge of demand for X and other products. Its costs would have been much lower if it could have anticipated this demand and maintained a steady rate of operation. On other occasions, the shorter lead time does not result from the factory's need for orders but, for example, from greater availability of raw materials. The physical distribution manager should then cut back on lead time; otherwise, inventories will be too high.

4. *The factory may be behind schedule.* When this is the case, the effective lead time will be more than one month. Delivery of product X will be on time only if the physical distribution manager sets an order point that is greater than the previously predicted 83-unit minimum. Note, however, that the factory's total output cannot be increased simply by ordering sooner. If the factory's capacity is temporarily lagging behind demand, the physical distribution manager may be able to prevent stockouts by selective ordering of those items where a stockout is almost certain. The flow of orders to the factory would be reduced to what the factory could handle, and orders would be postponed on items not immediately needed. Inventories would then fill the gap between supply and demand.

Maintaining balance. For many companies, keeping the factory's output in balance with demand is one of the most difficult tasks in materials management. In the past, the job was almost impossibly difficult because there was no quick way for production control to compare current demand and inventory with production. Records simply could not be brought up to date fast enough. As a result, the factory was often producing products that really were not needed for current sales, and it learned too late about items in high demand.

The computer solves at least part of this problem. It permits overnight tabulation of production, orders, and inventories for every product, so production can be adjusted to demand much more rapidly than before. The computer also can easily perform calculations that show the rates at which inventories are being used. The key calculation is the "critical ratio" that shows the relationship between stock currently available and the minimum stock needed during the order lead time. With product X the critical ratio would reach 1.0 when the stock on hand (plus that already on order from the factory) dropped to the lead-time usage of 83 units.

The computer periodically recalculates critical ratios for every product. The new ratios reflect the latest orders from customers as well as new production. In a large company, literally hundreds of critical ratios may be calculated. Suppose there are just three products, with the following critical ratios:

Product	Ratio
X	1.0
Y	0.9
Z	1.5

In this simple example, there will probably be a stockout of product Y unless it is given priority in dispatching. Therefore, as long as Y is not competing with dozens of other products that also had critical ratios of less than 1.0, it will move toward the "head of the line" at each work station through which it is to be processed. Chances are that this would shorten the effective lead time enough to prevent a stockout.

Product X would also be released for production immediately, but it might not require expediting. The critical ratio of 1.5 for product Z indicates that it need not be run immediately. However, production control might choose to release it for production anyway, if it appears that the factory will need the work.

Using the critical ratio. In theory, production control tries to match the operating rate of the plant with expected demand, in accordance with the basic production plan. Over the short term, however, demand and supply will often get out of balance.

There will be periods when supply is temporarily ahead of demand. In that case, production control will release for production products whose critical ratios are greater than 1.0. This policy automatically builds up finished-goods inventories. For example, production control may find it must release for production all products whose critical ratio is 1.1 if it is to avoid layoffs and idle equipment. Total inventory investment theoretically could then increase by as much as 20 percent.[2]

---

[2] For example, suppose there is no allowance for safety stock ordinarily and the order quantity is 100 units. The average inventory would then be 50 units, as stock levels vary between a peak of 100 and a minimum of 0. Setting an order point that is 10 percent or 10 units higher generates a built-in safety stock of 10 units. Average inventory would then be 60 units—10 units from the built-in safety stock and 50 units from the order quantity. This is further explained in Chapters 9 and 10.

The higher inventory costs may be more than offset by the lower costs of stable production—or at least they should be if this policy is followed consistently.

There may also be periods when sales of finished goods exceed manufacturing capacity. Production control will then discover that it has more items with critical ratios of 1.0 or less than the plant can possibly handle. For example, it might discover that during a particular week it has on hand orders with critical ratios of 1.0 or less that call for 12,000 hours of labor and machine time. The plant, however, is capable of turning out only 10,000 hours of production. If the "pipeline" of in-process inventory is already at an optimum level, production control would be foolish to release more than 10,000 hours of work to the shop. The other 2,000 hours should be held over until the following week.

The critical ratio becomes the criterion that determines what work is to be released. All other factors being equal, work with the lowest critical ratio is released first. In a plant that is not able to keep up, the critical ratio of all work released for production will normally be less than 1.0. In a plant that is producing ahead of its sales, critical ratios will probably be greater than 1.0, but the items with lower relative critical ratios will still be released ahead of items with higher ratios,

The critical ratio of items entering the production process is a guide to future changes in basic capacity. If critical ratios are creeping up and the trend shows no sign of reversing, management must eventually cut its capacity by laying off employees and, ultimately, by getting rid of redundant equipment. If critical ratios are in a persistent declining trend, management will be forced to turn down sales (or to make customers wait) if it does not soon increase its effective capacity through overtime, hiring more employees, subcontracting, or other measures.

INVENTORY RECORDS

Critical ratios and other calculations in production and inventory control make it mandatory that a company identify parts of material with some sort of numerical system. Even small companies may carry thousands of different items in inventory. Obviously some system of classification is essential to prevent duplication of stock and to permit each item to be located readily. Almost every company assigns individual part numbers to its production parts and materials, and most companies also have some classification for nonproduction items.

Classification

The principles of classification are the same for all inventory items. In every case, the best approach is first to classify them into broad general categories and then progressively reclassify within each category. For example, one very broad category might be "tools"; a subcategory would be "machine-powered cutting tools," of which one type might be "milling machine cutters." The final classifications identify the specific classifications by size and type. For example, the specification number for a particular tool might be 18–26 444. The first digit might indicate that the item was a tool, the second that it was a machine-powered cutting tool, the next two that it was a milling machine cutter, and the last digits would identify the particular cutter.

Classification systems permit similar items to be stored in close proximity to one another, both for convenience and to facilitate joint ordering of similar items. Assignment of classification numbers also helps prevent duplication of inventories. Master lists indicate specifications of each item and the brands that meet specifications.

Chrysler's System. For example, the Chrysler Corporation assigns its specification No. NPUV 204 to an iron valve gate with outside screw and yoke, capable of withstanding pressures of 125 W.S.P. and 200 W.O.G. Chrysler does not have valves made to order; it uses standard types supplied by a number of manufacturers. Each supplier also has its own specification number. For example, the Chrysler NPUV 204 value is the equivalent of the 465½ valve supplied to Chrysler by Crane, the 1430 valve furnished by Lunkenheimer, the 651-A of Jenkins, and so on.

In the Chrysler storeroom, certain Jenkins, Lunkenheimer, or other valves may be located side by side under the same Chrysler specification number. If Chrysler did not use its own numbers, it could readily carry duplicate stores. For example, if a Lunkenheimer 1430 valve failed in service,, the stores clerk might think it necessary to buy another 1430 valve; he might not know that the Crane 465½ valve would do the same job, unless there was some classification system to group together like products of competing manufacturers.

Duplication and obsolescence. Even the best inventory systems are not perfect. Constant vigilance by materials personnel is necessary to prevent duplication and obsolescence of inventories. From time to time, engineers will specify new parts and materials when the job can be done with items already stocked, or requisitioners will insist on slightly different brands and automatically increase the number of items in stock. These problems are discussed in detail in later chapters.

Disposition of surplus

Duplication of inventory almost always leads to surplus. For this and other reasons, almost every company has surplus inventory that should be weeded out and disposed of. Materials management is responsible not only for identifying the surplus but also for getting rid of it. Methods for doing so are described in Chapter 13.

How surplus develops. If a company buys only what it needs, one might wonder why surplus stock is such a common problem. One reason is that even if an item can clearly be identified as surplus, there is a natural tendency to save it. Suppose, for example, that a company stocks extra ball bearings for a particular machine tool. From time to time, bearings wear out in the machine tool, so it pays to keep them in stock in order to minimize production shutdowns while the machine is being repaired.

Imagine that a particular bearing is used on just one machine and, finally, the machine itself is replaced. Suppose that there are two bearings in inventory at the time the machine is sold and that each of these originally cost $6. Thus the company has $12 worth of inventory it no longer needs.

What will happen to these bearings? With many inventory control systems, the answer is nothing. The bearings may just lie on the shelf for years and years. Ordinarily the only way such inventory can be disposed of is for a company to make periodic checks to determine whether there has been any "activity" for each item carried in inventory. The materials manager then sets rules—usually quite arbitrary—that material that has not been "active" for a period of perhaps a year is automatically disposed of.

A policy like this is quite easy to carry out in companies that use electronic data processing for inventory control. The computer can be programmed to automatically print out a list of inventory items on which there has been no activity for some predetermined period of time. These items are then investigated, and anything that is obsolete is sold for the best price the company can get.

Obviously it makes sense to get rid of items that you are sure you will never need. However, even though people may be aware of this intellectually, even in well-managed companies they may be emotionally inclined to save some items that will never be needed. This simply is not economic, even if an enormous loss must be taken on the item when it is disposed of. A $6 bearing that is no longer needed is worth nothing to the company, and it should be eliminated from inventory even if no more than 6 cents is realized from it. The loss that is taken on obsolete inventory can, of course, be charged off against income, and the company reduces its taxes. Equally important, inventory carrying cost is also reduced. For example, if the company's cash inventory carrying cost is 15 percent per year, then each $6 bearing costs 90 cents per year to carry in inventory.

It is hard enough for an organization to weed out inventory that actually may never be needed, but it is even more difficult to educate an organization into throwing out stuff that will eventually be needed but whose rate of usage is so low that it will take many years to use it up.

Weeding-out process. Suppose, for example, that a company has a regular usage of 100 units per month of some item and that it is economic to order this item in lots of 1,000. Everything goes along routinely as long as usage stays at 100 units per month. A new order is placed when inventory drops to some reorder point. Then a new shipment of 1,000 units arrives and the company has about a ten-month supply of that particular item.

Now, suppose the company loses one of the contracts that require this particular item. Usage drops to five pieces per month. At the time this happens, the company has 1,000 units in inventory, so it now has a 200-month inventory, enough to last about 17 years at the new rate of usage. With many inventory control systems, no changes would be made to account for this much slower rate of usage. The item would just stay in stock and gradually be used up over a period of 17 years, if usage continued at about five units per month.

This is extremely wasteful, however. The company will spend far more to carry the item in inventory for 17 years than it would to throw away the same item now and purchase it again in 16 years. Suppose, for example, that the company's cash carrying cost of inventory is a mere 10 percent per year (which, of course, is lower than it is for most companies). If the purchase price of the part is $10, the annual cash carrying cost would be 10 percent of $10, or $1 per year on each item. Even if interest is not compounded, total carrying cost would be $17 for each item by the end of 17 years. And if the carrying cost is compounded at 10 percent per year, total carrying cost would be more than $40. The fact is that it is impractical to carry an item in inventory more than seven years with a 10 percent carrying cost—even if it is necessary to give it away in order to get rid of it. A $1 per year carrying cost, compounded at 10 percent per year, has a value of $9.48 after seven years. In eight years, it reaches $11.44, which is more than the original cost of the item.

In this example, it would pay to save only a seven-year supply, or about 420 pieces, at the present rate of usage of 5 pieces per month. The other 580 pieces should be scrapped. If the item has a salvage value, inventory should be reduced even further. Of course, companies do not really know what their future usage of an item will be. All they really know is present usage. As a general rule of thumb, it rarely pays to carry more than a five-year inventory of anything, even if the item has negligible scrap value. In other words, a company holding more than a five-year supply at present rate of usage that knows of nothing that will increase this usage had best throw the stuff out. It pays to get rid of it. Many companies, in fact, apply even harsher rules, especially if they can convert the particular item into something that is useful or can obtain a substantial salvage value for it.

Unfortunately it often is not easy to detect this type of obsolescence. It can only be done by comparing present rates of usage with existing inventory. Without computerized inventory control, this can be an awkward, slow process. With a computer, it is possible to program so that current inventory can be compared with current rates of usage, and any excess stock can be weeded out. It is common practice with most MRP systems, for example, to program the computer to print out lists of items for which there has been no demand in the past 60 or 90 days.

Inventory accounting. All purchases and withdrawals from stock must be accounted for. In addition, company accounting departments issue periodic reports on inventories. The materials department uses these reports but usually is only indirectly concerned with their preparation. In most cases, the accounting department keeps separate records and gets copies of all documents concerned with materials transactions.

Accounting systems vary widely, and, since this is not a text on accounting, they will not be discussed here. However, essential to every system is some periodic review to make certain "theoretical" inventories indicated by stock records and the like correspond with actual inventories. This review usually is made by materials personnel (with assistance from other departments). Since it normally involves a physical count of all inventory items, it often is done during a vacation shutdown, to prevent disruption of operations. Discrepancies between actual inventories and theoretical balances shown on records are a reflection on the company's inventory control and the efficiency of its materials personnel. For this reason, many companies do not like to have physical inventories counted by the same person responsible for keeping the records of the stock. They prefer an independent check by an accountant.

It is also common to make periodic cycle counts to compare the actual inventory on hand of a selected group of items with the theoretical balances shown on a computer printout. Typically, the computer selects a half-dozen or more items each month at random. The stores clerk makes physical counts of balances on hand for these items and compares these with official records. A perfect score—with an exact match between balances actually on hand and those that are accounted for in the record-keeping system—indicates negligible losses through clerical errors, pilferage and other causes.

Cases

CASE 8-1. QUEENSTOWN CHEMICAL COMPANY

Developing an inventory reduction program

Queenstown Chemical Company is a leading producer of specialty chemicals. It makes thousands of different compounds for almost all of the major drug and fine chemical producers. Joanne Mead, Queenstown's director of purchases, is responsible for both raw material and finished goods inventories, in addition to directing the company's purchasing activities. At present, her biggest single problem is managing finished goods inventories, which in the last year have increased from $2 million to more than $10 million. Not only is the company running short of storage space, but its cash position is getting tight.

There is no easy solution to the problem. Queenstown's customers are aware that chemical shortages are a thing of the past, and they insist that the company stock their needs for immediate delivery. Where customers formerly carried 30 to 60 days' inventory to allow Queenstown plenty of lead time on new orders, they now insist on getting delivery in 10 days or less. If they do not get this rapid service, they can buy from Queenstown's competitors, who are willing to carry stock for their customers. Unfortunately, competition and overcapacity are facts of life in Queenstown's industry, and everyone believes it will be many years before producers can once again require customers to allow adequate lead time so they can schedule their production for each order and carry minimum finished goods inventories.

It occurs to Mead that she might try the same approach on her suppliers and get them to carry inventories for Queenstown. At present the company has $1 million invested in nonproduction inventories and $6 million in raw materials. Usage of nonproduction items is about $100,000 per month, and usage of raw material is about $2 million per month. Queenstown uses a perpetual inventory system. All materials transactions are posted to inventory records for each item, and clerks set order points based on past usage, lead-time estimates they get from purchasing, and their own experience. Whenever there is a shortage, they increase the safety stock. In general they are criticized for shortages, but, except for occasional campaigns to reduce inventories, management has rarely expressed concern over excess stocks.

Mead believes that inventories can be reduced substantially by requiring suppliers to carry inventories. "If we carry inventories for our customers, there is no reason why our suppliers shouldn't be willing to carry them for us," she declares at a meeting of the corporation's executive committee. She proposes that Queenstown make contracts with each of its major suppliers that call for them to maintain certain minimum stocks of materials available for immediate delivery. Queenstown will not pay for the material until it is delivered, but it will guarantee the supplier a market for it eventually.

For example, in its processes Queenstown uses a "9280" type of valve that must be replaced periodically. Usage of this valve varies widely from month to month but averages about 400 valves per year. Currently, Queenstown reorders when its inventory drops to 20 valves, and delivery takes about two weeks. Mead believes that the division could get along with just two valves if it had a deal with the valve distributor guaranteeing that 30 valves would always be on hand for overnight delivery. Since these valves cost $150 each, Mead's plan would reduce inventory investment by $2,700 on this item alone.

Mead's assistant, Robert Stark, disagrees with his boss's plan. He points out that it costs the supplier just as much to carry inventory as it does Queenstown. In addition, Mead's plan would require more frequent ordering, which raises costs for both buyer and seller. The result would be that overall costs would be higher than they are at present. He grants that Queenstown would probably be able to persuade its suppliers to stock without having to pay a premium. However, he feels that in the long run the division has to pay for every service it gets from its suppliers. As an alternate solution, he suggests that Queenstown discuss the problem with its suppliers and try to persuade them to offer lower prices because Queenstown is not requiring them to carry inventories. He admits, however, that this approach may not work too well on items that are price fixed.

Stark also suggests that Queenstown might be able to reduce inventories by trying to schedule its needs for maintenance items in advance. For example, the life of the "9280" valves can be accurately predicted. If the maintenance department were to schedule replacement far enough in advance, there would be no need to carry inventory. Orders could be placed for each job, and it would not be necessary to carry more than two or three valves in stock.

Question

How do you evaluate Mead's and Stark's proposals? Develop an inventory reduction program for Queenstown.

CASE 8–2. A.E.D. DIVISION

Predicting process losses

In September 1950, National Motors Corporation rceived a contract to tool a large government-owned facility in the Chicago area in order to become a second supplier of Hornet engines for the U.S. Air Force.

It proceeded immediately to establish a new Aircraft Engine Division (A.E.D.) to carry out the contract. The division was to tool for a capacity of 30 engines per day and received an initial production order for 1,000 engines. Price for the engines was to be negotiated. It was assumed that, after the plant became operative, the division's costs, because of automation, would be substantially below the then prevailing price for the Hornet engine of approximately $75,000. Before A.E.D. could commence production of acceptable engines, however, it had to produce two prototype engines which would be subject to extensive testing. These engines were to be assembled from parts made by A.E.D. and its suppliers. Until these engines were flight tested and approved, A.E.D. could not go into full-scale production.

In some cases it was acceptable to order semifinished components for the prototypes from existing suppliers of engine components. For example, A.E.D. intended eventually to develop a second supplier of crankshaft forgings. Naturally it would take some time before the new supplier could deliver acceptable material. Meanwhile, it was agreeable to the Air Force that A.E.D. buy crankshaft forgings from the existing supplier of forgings and run these forgings over its own machine tools in order to produce finished crankshafts for the two prototype engines that were needed to get approval to go into production.

The crankshaft was a particularly critical component. It required more than 70 machining operations, and many of these required considerable precision. Even the less critical operations could conceivably create problems, since all operations would be on brand new machines staffed with new employees.

The production control department did not know how long it would take to pass a forging through a complete machining cycle, but its guess was several months. One major problem was engineering changes. Production control wondered if it dared schedule long production runs on crankshafts because there was a steady stream of design changes, and some of these changes could not be incorporated at the company's leisure but had to be put in immediately. Nevertheless, it seemed that it would be all but impossible to have a machining cycle of much less than three months. That is, a forging which was begun on June 1st probably would not be completed until about September 1st.

One problem that production control faced immediately was the ordering of the crankshafts needed for the two prototype engines. From that time on, it was assumed that crankshaft forgings would be coming from a new supplier which the purchasing department was in the process of developing. It was absolutely essential, however, that production control get enough crankshaft forgings on hand from the existing supplier so that there would be at least two completed carnkshafts after all of the new machine tools were tried out. Production control was, of course, fully aware that some crankshaft forgings would be lost in the process, through either malfunctioning of the new equipment or—even more likely—errors made by inexperienced operators.

In the opinion of the production control manager, an allowance of about 5 percent for nonreworkable scrap on each operation would be adequate for the first production run. Since there were 70 operations, this implied to him that the scrap allowance should be 350 percent of the number of finished pieces actually desired. Since only two crankshafts were needed, his guess was that the company should start 12 forgings through the machining process. The production control manager knew full well that a big safety margin was necessary, since if the two forgings were not made on schedule, the program would be set back. For example, if all 12 forgings that he proposed to order were scrapped late in the machining cycle, the entire program might be set back at least six months before the division could get new forgings delivered from the supplier and start them through the machining cycle again.

On the other hand, it did not pay to buy too many forgings. First, the cost of each forging was $600 and, in addition, even the rough forgings were in danger of becoming obsolete because of engineering changes—especially if too many of them were carried in inventory. There was also a great advantage in having only a minimum number of forgings from the existing supplier, since the company wanted to get its new forging supplier approved and shipping forgings as soon as possible. Its price with the new supplier was based on the assumption that the supplier would get 100 percent of the business (although the other vendor, which would continue to supply the second prime contractor, was presumably available in the event of a strike). Thus, both A.E.D. and the other prime contractor would have the protection of two forging suppliers, while each of them paid only to tool a single supplier.

While the production control manager thought that an initial order for 12 forgings would be plenty, this was not a decision he made himself. He conferred with the division works manager and the general purchasing agent. These three executives, in turn, jointly recommended to the division general manager that 100 forgings be ordered at a price of $600 each.

When the senior buyer of forgings questioned the general purchasing agent about the large quantity of forgings being purchased for just two prototype engines, he was told the potential loss from failure to complete the two prototype engines was so great that A.E.D. could not afford to take any chances. "Bill Murray [the division general manager] told me that he would be willing to buy almost any number of forgings if this would guarantee him two good finished crankshafts on schedule," the general purchasing agent explained to his senior buyer.

The forgings were ordered in March 1951. Meanwhile, the company began receiving its initial shipments of machine tools and gradually began to lay out its crankshaft department. The first machining operations were performed on the 100 forgings in July 1951 and the company was confident that at least two forgings would be completed for installation for assembly by January 1952. Production of engines was scheduled to begin the following June, with output to be steadily increased up to 30 engines per day by late 1952. In the interim, the company had received several other production orders for variations of the same engine and was in the process of tooling for these variations and also making parts needed for prototype testing.

The crankshaft department was plagued with start-up problems throughout 1951. Deliveries of certain critical machines were behind schedule; tooling did not always function properly; and a steady stream of design changes helped create additional confusion. As a result, the lot of 100 forgings passed through the long machining cycle much more slowly than had been anticipated, and the scrap rate greatly exceeded the estimate of the production control manager. By March 1952, the division still had not completed a single crankshaft, and in May the last of the 100 forgings was scrapped. Additional forgings were purchased and the first acceptable crankshaft was completed in November 1952—roughly six months behind schedule.

Questions

1. Given no advance knowledge that scrap rates would exceed even the most pessimistic estimates, could A.E.D. have done anything to prevent its crankshaft machining problems from apparently holding up the entire program by about six months?

2. The A.E.D. case occurred in 1950. Certainly problems in manufacturing on the threshold of new technology have, if anything, become greater. However, companies like National Motors now enjoy the benefit computerized material requirements planning systems. How would MRP have helped A.E.D.? Could the problem still occur if A.E.D. had had a first-rate MRP system?

9

Order-point and periodic control systems

The inventory control systems discussed briefly in Chapter 8 involve fixed reorder points. An order is placed when inventory drops to some predetermined level. As has been pointed out, the inventory level is determined both by order quantity and order point. Inventory investment increases when order quantity and/or order points are raised and reduced when they are cut.

Conversely, the probability of running out of stock is reduced when the order point is raised. For example, if a clerk had reordered when inventory on hand or on order reached 20 units and experienced stockouts, the obvious reaction is to reorder when the balance reaches 30 units. This change in order point would provide an additional ten units of reserve stock.

Stockouts are also affected by order quantity. As order quantity increases, the interval between orders increases and there is less risk of running out of stock. This principle becomes obvious when one considers two extreme cases. Suppose that estimated usage is 52 units per year. If purchasing buys in lots of 100, there is almost 100 percent probability that there will be a stockout less than once a year. On the other hand, if the order quantity is one unit, stockouts are being risked once a week and there may be a high probability of more than one stockout per year.

Thus, all other factors being equal, the order point should be increased when order quantity is decreased and decreased when order quantity is increased. Safety stock, which is created when order point is raised above the amount that is expected to be used during the lead time, is needed only after order point is reached. The amount of safety stock required is related to the expected variation in lead time. Thus safety stock should be high when suppliers are unreliable and internal usage varies widely. It can be reduced sharply under conditions of stable demand and reliable suppliers.

A PROBLEM IN ORDER-POINT CONTROL

When demand can be predicted with reasonable accuracy and the value of the item is not too great, it is fairly easy to determine safety stock and order quantity. Commonsense rules can be applied.

Suppose, for example, that a company uses 20 typewriter ribbons per week and can get a 10 percent extra discount if it buys them in lots of one gross. Total lead time is only a week (or less, since the ribbons are available from a local office-supply distributor). What should be the order quantity, safety stock and order point?

Determining order quantity. The order quantity is easy to determine: It should be 144 ribbons in order to get the discount. By buying just a little more than seven weeks' supply with each order, costs are reduced 10 percent. This means that at the maximum the company is carrying three and a half weeks' more inventory than it would if it operated on a hand-to-mouth basis on typewriter ribbons. The 10 percent saving earned in three and a half weeks is equal to an annual return of more than 100 percent on the money invested in this inventory. In addition, it is more convenient and administrative costs are lower when the company buys in larger quantities.

What if there were no quantity discount, if the price for the typewriter ribbons were the same regardless of the quantity purchased? Chances are that most companies would still choose to buy in lots of roughly 144 ribbons if their usage were about 20 ribbons per week. With this order quantity and usage, average inventories of ribbon would be roughly four weeks' supply, including safety stock. Most managers would feel that it would not be worth the trouble and clerical expense to order such a minor item more often than six or seven times a year, even if this policy did result in carrying somewhat larger stocks of ribbons than absolutely necessary.

However, this attitude would be quite different if the ribbons were an extremely expensive material that accounted for a large percentage of total inventory investment. In such cases, materials managers are quite willing to order weekly or even daily in order to minimize their inventory investment. Most materials managers, as we shall discuss in detail later in this chapter, classify inventory items by dollar value of usage and then establish rules for determining order quantity. For example, a materials manager might not permit an order quantity greater than two weeks' usage for an item whose dollar value of usage is $10,000 per month, while he or she would require a minimum order quantity equal to 12 weeks' usage for an item whose dollar value of usage is only $10 per month.

Determining safety stock. The safety stock is determined by analyzing the past pattern of usage. Suppose that weekly usage during the past year has followed the pattern shown in Table 9–1. Suppose that the reorder point was set at 20 ribbons. Thus, when there are 20

TABLE 9–1
Usage of typewriter ribbons during a 52-week period

Number of ribbons used	Number of weeks with this usage
15 or fewer	6
16	3
17	4
18	6
19	7
20	12
21	5
22 to 30	8
30 to 40	0
More than 40	1

ribbons on hand, an order is placed for delivery one week later. In this case, as indicated in Table 9–1, the usage would have exceeded 20 ribbons during 14 periods—with usage of 21 ribbons during 5 periods, 22 to 30 ribbons during 8 periods and more than 40 ribbons during 1 period. Does this mean that we would have run out of typewriter ribbons 14 times during the year? It would if we bought just a week's supply. But we actually buy 144 ribbons, or more than seven weeks' usage. So it is only necessary to order between seven and eight times per year. Thus, at the very most, a stockout is risked no more than eight times per year with the usage pattern above; at any other time stocks are more than ample.

In actual practice, there would be considerably fewer than eight stockouts for an item with this usage pattern, an order quantity of 144 units, and no safety stock. The week when the previous order was almost used up would have coincided with the week when usage was greater than 20 units. Chances are (the probability can be calculated with precision, of course) that this would not happen more than two or three times per year.

With this pattern of usage and an order quantity of 144, a typical inventory planner would probably set the safety stock at 10 ribbons. The order point thus would be reached when stock dropped to 30 ribbons. With a safety stock of 10, there would be an occasional stockout (perhaps once every seven years) during the rare week when usage was greater than 30 ribbons and the order point would have been reached even if usage had been normal.

A good case could be made for setting a safety stock even lower than ten units, were the cost of the ribbons not so low that the saving from the reduced investment in safety stock probably would not offset the inconvenience of an occasional stockout. For example, a safety stock of five ribbons might bring one or two stockouts per year. This might cause slight inconvenience but certainly no serious problems, since typewriter ribbons are not that critical. They can be bought in a few hours on a rush basis. Chances are that the typists would not need fast service, anyway, since they often keep spare ribbons in their desks.

THE ABC SYSTEM

Materials managers rarely, if ever, worry much about stockouts of typewriter ribbons. This is not the case with many other items, particularly production parts and materials. In many cases a stockout of even a minor production part can be costly. For example, the bolts that hold the engines to the wings are just as important to an airframe manufacturer as the engines themselves; production is held up if either item is out of stock. But the engines may cost $100,000 each, while each bolt may be no more than a few dollars. A safety stock of eight bolts would cost only a few dollars a year to maintain, while a safety stock of eight engines would cost thousands. Obviously the investment in safety stock for the bolts is a much better value than investment for the engines, since it provides the same protection at a fraction of the cost.

Safety stocks almost always are a better value for low-cost items than they are for expensive ones. Modern inventory control systems take this into account by classifying items by value of usage. The high-value items have lower safety stocks because the cost of protection is so high. The low-value items carry much higher safety stocks.

10 percent of items, 70 percent of value. The basis of the "ABC" approach to inventory control, which provides maximum overall protection against stockouts for a given investment in safety stocks, assumes 10 percent of items and 70 percent of value of inventories for the most costly items. In every company, a big percentage of the investment in inventory is concentrated on relatively few high-value items. The first step in the ABC approach is to estimate average demand for each item in inventory and multiply this figure by unit cost to determine value of usage. For example, an item that costs $10 and has an annual usage of 1,000 units would have a usage value of $10,000, while an item that costs $100 with a usage of only 50 units per year would have a usage value of $5,000. Values of usage for each item are then listed in order of importance, with the greatest dollar-volume item topping the list.

The items are separated into three groups. The 10 percent that are most costly are A items; the next 20 percent are B items; and the balance are C items. In every case the A items will account for a heavy percentage of total expenditures and the C group will account for a surprisingly small percentage. The following relationship is typical:

Category	Percent of items	Percent of value
A	10	70
B	20	20
C	70	10

Although there are one seventh as many A items as C items, seven times as much is spent on A items as on C items. Thus the average expenditure of an A item is 49 times greater than the average expenditure for a C item. Investment in safety stock for the A item must be 49 times greater than for a C item in order to afford the same protection against stockouts (provided all other factors are equal).

Selective control. The ABC system permits selective inventory control. Safety stocks are kept low for the high-value items, which should be subject to extremely close control by materials personnel, anyway. The low-value items get less attention from materials personnel; stockouts are prevented by maintaining much higher safety stocks.

With ABC control, it is possible to risk fewer stockouts and reduce investment in inventories. This is proved by comparing ABC control with overall control. Inventories are divided into three classes: the expensive A items account for 10 percent of the total and roughly 70 percent of the value; the B items for 20 percent of the total and about 20 percent of the value; and the C items for 70 percent of the total and about 10 percent of the value.

Suppose, for example, that a company stocks 1,000 items in inventory and that its average investment is six weeks' usage, or $1 million, of which $200,000 is safety stock. Average order quantity is eight weeks' usage, and there is two weeks' safety stock. With this order quantity and safety stock, assume that the company experiences ten serious stockouts every year. These are distributed at random among the 1,000 items carried in inventory, and they are equally effective in disrupting production.

Now suppose that the company classifies its inventory by the ABC system. It breaks down as follows:

	Number of items	Average inventory investment	Investment in safety stock
A items	100	$ 700,000	$140,000
B items	200	200,000	40,000
C items	700	100,000	20,000
Total	1,000	$1,000,000	$200,000

The ten stockouts expected each year are distributed at random among all the 1,000 items. Thus, the chances of a stockout on an A item are the same as those for any B or C item. However, since C items comprise 70 percent of the total number of items in inventories, it is reasonable to expect that 70 percent of the potential stockouts will occur on these items, with just 20 percent on B items and 10 percent on A items. Thus, under normal circumstances, the following pattern can be expected: one stockout on the 100 A items; two on the 200 B items; and seven on the 700 C items.

Note the enormous difference in the prices paid for protection against stockouts. $700,000 is tied up in inventory, including $140,000 in safety stock, to hold the stockout rate to 1 percent per annum on A items. Seven times as many C items can be protected with a total safety stock investment only one seventh of that required on the A items. Thus the average investment in safety stock per A item is $1,400 ($140,000 ÷ 100 items) and only $28.57 ($20,000 ÷ 700) for each C item.

The same or better protection against stockouts can be provided at much lower cost by concentrating investment on the cheaper items, where protection can be bought more cheaply. For example, the company might decide to get along with no more than two weeks' average inventory of A items, of which only one half week is safety stock. The B items might not be changed at all, while safety stocks of C items would be doubled, leaving order quantities unchanged, as shown in the table below:

	Number of items	Average inventory investment	Investment in safety stock
A items	100	$233,333	$ 56,667
B items	200	200,000	40,000
C items	700	120,000	40,000
Total	1,000	$553,333	$136,667

Note that the company has succeeded in reducing inventory investment by $446,667—almost 50 percent. For reasons explored in detail in the next chapter, this could reduce operating costs by as much as $100,000 per year. Despite this spectacular cost reduction, protection against stockouts is actually increased. The stockout rate on C items was probably reduced by more than 50 percent when the safety stock was doubled, so no more than three stockouts of these items can be expected in the next five years, instead of seven. The rate on B items remains unchanged. The company is therefore ahead even if it triples its stockout rate on A items (three stockouts every five years, instead of just one), because of the sharp reductions in both order quantity and safety stock which cut average inventory by two thirds.

In practice, it probably is not necessary to suffer any increase in stockouts of A items. With the ABC approach the company has not only different inventory policies for the more expensive items but also different control procedures. Because there are so few A items, it may be economic to review their inventory status almost daily to spot deviations in demand and to maintain extremely close follow-up on suppliers to make certain they adhere to lead times. In other words, on costly items, tight control is substituted for the protection of inventory. This is economic, since it permits substantial reductions in inventory investment.

With the low-cost items, it is cheaper to carry inventory than to pay the salaries of the personnel needed for close control. It would take seven times as much effort to maintain tight control over the 700 C items as it would for the 100 A items, and it would be possible to reduce investment in C items by only one seventh as much as the reduction in the investment for A items. With the B items, a middle-of-the-road policy would probably be followed. There would be some control, but the company would also rely to a greater extent on inventories to protect against stockouts than it would with the A items.

DETERMINING LEVEL OF CONTROL

It should not be concluded that inventories are always essential to prevent disruption of production. In some cases a company using an order-point system can operate successfully with no inventory investment in many key parts and materials.

No finished goods. Suppose, for example, that a manufacturer of upholstered furniture offered hundreds of different types of furniture, each available in dozens of different fabrics. The product line would be so diverse and the product so bulky that it would be impossible to carry a finished goods inventory. Production of any particular piece of furniture would begin only after a firm order was received from a customer, but, of course, competitive pressures would force the company to ship as rapidly as possible after it got the order.

The problem is solved by carrying a diverse in-process inventory. While no upholstered furniture firm carries an inventory of finished furniture, all do carry stocks of finished components and fabrics that can rapidly be assembled into finished furniture. These stocks are drawn on as orders flow in. As long as the company's lead time for the finished product is greater than the lead time required for final assembly, the company can keep its delivery promises without an investment in a finished goods inventory.

This introduces an additional dimension to inventory management: level of control. If a product is complex, the materials manager must analyze it and determine the stage of fabrication that is critical. Usually, the inventory control process is automatic as long as stocks are in control at the critical level.

In a furniture factory, for example, this critical level might be the stocks of parts and other materials that are assembled directly into finished pieces of furniture. The company can respond reasonably rapidly to orders by drawing on parts inventories, which are maintained on an order-point basis. Production control would release materials for final assembly in accordance with some dispatching rule. In a furniture factory, dispatching priority would be strongly influenced by the desirability of shipping full cars of furniture to a single destination whenever possible. This dispatch rule might, for example, cause a North Carolina factory to delay shipment of furniture to a retailer in St. Louis until there were enough orders from this area to make up a full boxcar.

Applying the principle

This principle is better understood with a more complex example. A company makes product A, whose sales lead time is six weeks. Product A is assembled from subassemblies B and F and purchased component T. Subassembly B consists of manufactured components C, D, and E, which in turn are made from purchased parts and materials Y and Z. Similarly, subassembly F consists of manufactured components G and H and purchased component V. G and H in turn are made from purchased materials X and W.

Time-cycle chart. Each material, component, and assembly requires some lead time. If the materials manager starts with the lead time for final assembly of the product and then adds the lead times of the components, she can construct a time-cycle chart like that shown in Figure 9–1. The chart shows that, starting from scratch with no inventories at all, about 22 weeks' lead time would be needed before a finished product could be produced. The bottleneck item is material X, which must be fabricated into G, which in turn is assembled into F, which becomes part of A.

Obviously, the company must have inventories if it is going to offer delivery to customers in six weeks. It could carry protective stocks at every stage of manufacture, but there is an easier way which involves less control and usually will also reduce inventories. Stocks are maintained for only a few critical items; the others are purchased or manufactured only when there is a definite demand for them.

The concept is best explained graphically. Note that there is a horizontal line in Figure 9–1 at the six-week mark; this represents the sales

FIGURE 9–1
Time-cycle chart

The time-cycle chart makes it easy to determine which inventories require safety stock protection. For example, if sales lead time is six weeks, the parts C, D, E, G, and H require protection at manufacturing in-process level while purchased parts stocks are required of V and T. No other safety stocks are needed.

lead time. Only those items whose lead time intersects this six-week line need be started. These include components C, D, E, G, H, V, and T.

For example, suppose the materials manager decides from experience that a safety stock of 100 units each of C, D, E, G, H, V, and T will allow the company to take care of all foreseeable demand from customers. To simplify the arithmetic, assume that it is operating entirely on a job-lot basis; except for safety stock, it buys or fabricates exactly enough material to complete each order received from a customer.

Suppose a customer orders 20 units of product A. Components C, D, E, G, H, V, and T are drawn from stock. In order to deliver within six weeks, the chart shows that work must start on subassembly F within one week. If it suits convenience (and it may, since every factory manager likes to even out work loads in order to get more efficient operation), work on subassembly B can be held off for two weeks. Or, of course, work can be started immediately, to give the customer extra-prompt service.

Steps must also be taken to replenish safety stocks. Therefore materials and parts T, V, W, X, Y, and Z are ordered in sufficient quantities so that they ultimately can be manufactured into the key components for which safety stocks are carried.

Possible problems. The example above is greatly oversimplified. The assumption that identical safety stocks of the various key items could be carried is not correct. In actual practice, a much greater safety stock would be carried for part G, whose raw material X must be ordered 22 weeks ahead of final assembly, then for T, which requires a total lead time of only 10 weeks. If there were a 100-unit safety stock of T, a 220-unit safety stock of G would probably be needed to get the same protection against stockout, because of the difference in lead time.

In addition, it would not be possible to handle orders for much more than 100 units during any six-week period. Even if the later stages of the process could be accelerated, supply lines of purchased materials and semifabricated components would be emptied out.

Nor would the parts fabricating shop necessarily be operated strictly on a conventional "max-min" basis. Most likely would be a critical ratio approach, (described in Chapter 8), in which those parts where the critical ratio was lowest would be run. This would keep the fabricating shop operating on a fairly steady basis even if work at the later stages were intermittent and fluctuated with customer demand. Also, certain items would probably be purchased in excess of actual requirements, in order to reduce purchase costs.

It is not difficult to see how this selective control system can be applied to any of the inventory control systems described in this chapter and the previous chapter. It can also be used in conjunction with an

ABC system. The components and materials controlled selectively could be classified according to their value. Inventory levels would then be adjusted to afford varying degrees of protection in accordance with ABC rules.

STATISTICAL ANALYSIS OF DEMAND

Limitations of max-min systems

All of the inventory control systems discussed so far have been order-point, or max-min, systems. Control can be improved and inventory investment reduced through application of ABC systems, selective control, and other techniques, but these systems still have one fundamental weakness: They work well only when the lead time and the demand for material during the lead time can be predicted with reasonable accuracy. Unfortunately, usage and lead times of many items vary enormously. Many companies increase their production by 50 percent in an exceptionally prosperous year, and demand for individual products can change even more. What happens when demand suddenly surges upward on an item under a max-min system of inventory control?

Effect of demand change. Assume that an item normally has a usage of 1,000 units during its one-month lead-time period and that the previous year's usage pattern indicates a safety stock of 250 units to be more than adequate. If demand rises by 50 percent during the year and, as is often the case when business is increasing, lead times lengthen slightly, a whole series of stockouts is possible. The first stockout will come when usage during the lead time is 25 percent greater than normal. The inventory planner may consider usage abnormal and not increase safety stocks after this first stockout.

A second stockout will almost certainly touch off an analysis of the item's usage. Usually order point will be increased. Suppose that the item that used to have an average usage of 1,000 units a month has these usages for six months: 1,050, 1,100, 1,400, 1,250, 1,300, and 1,400. The planner notes that average usage during this six-month period was 1,250 units. He also notes that maximum usage was 1,400 units. He may increase the order point to 1,500 units, giving him a safety stock of about 250 units if lead-time usage continues to average 1,250 units.

If demand continues to rise, the inevitable result is another stockout. If the company is controlling thousands of different items with a simple max-min system, it will be plagued with stockouts. Eventually, however, order points and safety stocks are increased to the point where inventories are more than adequate to cope with peak demand. And, in fact, it is probable that they will be increased well beyond this point. In a period of rising demand, inventory planners are subject to almost daily harassment from production and sales executives because of shortages and stockouts. On the other hand, there will be few immediate complaints if they raise order points and safety stocks to the point where stockouts are highly unlikely, regardless of how much usage increases. Consequently planners now only boost order points to meet present demand but also allow for future growth of demand.

For example, an item that once had an order point of 1,250 units and a safety stock of 250 might wind up with an order point of 2,000 and a safety stock of 500, even though record consumption might not exceed 1,800 units. Eventually, planners would attempt to anticipate increased demand and build up stocks ahead of usage.

If this increase in demand were temporary, the results would be expensive. Suppose, for example, that on account of a business depression or some other cause the company's usage dropped well below its old norm of 1,000 units to 700 units a month. In such a case, its investment in inventories would initially be at least three times greater than necessary, and it would continue to be substantially excessive until max-min quantities were gradually adjusted back to the old levels.

Weaknesses of manual systems. Few organizations experience such stable demand for materials that they can rely on a manually controlled perpetual system such as we have described. In fact, these systems have three weaknesses that tend to make them almost unworkable:

1. Stock levels are actually set by clerks, since managers do not have the time to study inventory levels of individual items.
2. Reorder points and safety stocks often are not changed for years on end.
3. Delay in posting records makes them useless for control. Reorder of a critical item can be held up until the clerk gets around to posting the last withdrawal, indicating that the reorder point has been reached.

Need for MRP. The computer can make these systems workable. Happily, computers have become relatively so inexpensive that even small organizations can afford them. With computers, managers (not clerks) can determine overall inventory policy. Reorder points and safety stocks can readily be changed to reflect changed conditions. In a simple system, the computer will function simply as a tireless, superfast clerk. In more sophisticated MRP systems, the computer can anticipate changes in demand and usage and make appropriate adjustments in order points and safety stocks. Finally, the computer makes it possible to keep inventory records updated so that they can be used in day-to-day decision making.

Basic factors in forecasting

The computer also makes it practical to use numerous statistical techniques to forecast lead-time demand and to signal management that some change may have taken place. The easiest way to estimate lead time is simply to assume that what happened in the past will probably happen in the future. For example, suppose that an item was reordered when stock on hand was 100 units and that inventory had declined to 20 units by the time a new order was completed. Lead-time usage, therefore, is 80 units. This represents the most recent experience with the item; a computer can automatically reorder on the basis of previous lead time plus some safety stock allowance. Unfortunately, if this straightforward system is followed slavishly, the computer will be doing exactly what the clerks were doing—and, if anything, the smartest computer is even dumber than the dumbest clerk.

Demand for inventory is determined by four independent variables. It is probably pure luck if these variables cancel one another out and there has been no change in demand since the last time the item was ordered. The basic variables are secular, cyclical, seasonal, and random.

Secular change. Demand for every product is determined over the long term by one or more basic factors. For example, over the long term, the demand for housing is determined largely by new household formation—the number of single persons or couples who set up housekeeping for themselves each year. All other factors being equal (which they never are), builders would try to build enough new housing units each year to equal the number of new household formations and replace housing that is no longer usable.

Every item an organization may carry in its inventory is also subject to some secular influence, although, in many cases, it may be so insignificant that it can be ignored. In other cases it may be highly significant. For example, suppose that an auto parts distributor stocks mufflers that can be used only on 1979 Chevrolets. Demand will inevitably decline secularly from year to year as the number of 1979 Chevrolets on the road gradually delines. By the year 2000, the population of active 1979 Chevrolets would presumably be close to zero, and demand for this muffler would no longer exist.

Whenever secular change can be identified, a company would want to allow for it. For example, the auto parts distributor that estimates lead time usage for 1979 Chevrolet mufflers will be 1,000 mufflers on orders it places with suppliers in 1980 might reduce its estimate to 950 mufflers in 1982. And by 1990 the secular adjustment might amount to at least 500 mufflers, since by that time presumably about half of the 1979 Chevrolets will have been scrapped, and muffler demand will have been reduced accordingly.

The secular trend can usually be measured statistically. Actual data are plotted and the points are connected with a curve, using the least squares method. This method is explained in detail in almost every basic statistics text. However, much cruder techniques will normally work just as well in materials management. The materials manager is always concerned with *future* secular trends. While the past is often a valid guide to the future, it normally makes little difference whether the materials manager calculates precisely that the past secular growth rate, for example, was 2.21 percent per year or relies on the sloppier estimate of roughly 2 percent.

In many cases the past trend will have to be adjusted anyway to take into account the cumulative effect of past production and other changes. For example, the aluminum industry formerly enjoyed a secular growth trend of about 7 percent per year—substantially greater than the growth of either manufacturing activity or population. This growth was possible because aluminum was being continuously substituted for other materials, such as steel, wood, copper, glass, and zinc.

Of course, no industry can gain indefinitely at another's expense. In the case of aluminum, most of the substitutions of aluminum for competing materials (such as aluminum for steel or glass in beverage containers) have probably already been made. As a result, aluminum's secular growth rate has declined, and it would be misleading to base a forecast on a simple linear extrapolation of the old growth rate. As this is written, the current secular growth rate for aluminum is estimated at 4.5 to 5 percent, or only a little higher than the expected growth rate of overall industrial production.

If an error is made in forecasting secular change, its greatest impact will be on facilities rather than inventories. Companies that are overly optimistic on long-term growth trends find themselves saddled with capacity they will not need for years to come. Conversely, underestimates of the secular trend lead to loss of market position and opportunities for profit.

Cyclical variation. Unexpected changes in secular trends are so gradual that they rarely have any effect on short-term materials forecasting and planning. Errors in cyclical forecasting are far more likely to affect materials management. An unexpected shift in the business cycle works like a two-edged sword on materials management: it affects both the restocking lead time itself and also the lead-time usage. For example, suppose that under "normal" conditions an item has a lead time of one month and a lead-time usage of 100 units. The item is only ordered about once a year. Business begins to boom during a one-year period between orders, but order point continues to be based on the one-month lead time, with lead-time usage of 100 units. The item is reordered at the normal time but, owing to a huge backlog of orders, the lead time is now six weeks. In addition, the business boom begins to affect demand for the item itself. Demand is now 150 units per month instead of 100 per month. Thus, the anticipated lead-time usage of 100 is inadequate; 100 pieces are used up about three weeks after the new order is placed instead of one month. And, of course, the supplier is two weeks late, so the company is out of stock for a period of roughly three weeks.

During a recession, the two-edged sword works in reverse. Lead time usage is less than expected, and the lead time itself is shorter. For example, the order may be completed in three weeks instead of one month, as planned. In addition, usage is down to about 75 units per month. Thus, an extra 50 units are on hand when the new order is delivered. If this happens repeatedly, the company will find itself with far too much of its cash tied up in inventory.

Unfortunately, cyclical fluctuations in demand are far from uniform. They may lead, lag, or coincide with the general business cycle, as explained in Chapter 6. In addition, there may be an inverse relationship. For example, demand for new heavy trucks tends to fluctuate with the business cycle. Trucking companies add to their fleets when general business conditions are favorable. On the other hand, demand for spare parts for older trucks may have an inverse relationship with the business cycle; it flattens out and may even decline at the peak of a cycle. But parts demand may increase substantially when business is depressed as truck owners postpone purchases of new equipment and try to keep their older vehicles in operation through stepped-up spending on spare parts.

Seasonal demand. It is critical to distinguish cyclical changes in demand from seasonal ones. For example, suppose that a trucking company experiences a sharp drop in demand in the month of January. If this is a cyclical shift, the company should immediately cut back on plans for expansion. On the other hand, if extra-cold weather and heavy snowstorms are simply causing a greater than normal seasonal slump, the company should be ready for an upsurge in demand in the warmer months and may even want to lease additional equipment and hire extra employees.

Almost every product or service is subject to some seasonal variation. In most cases it is fairly easy to identify. For example, hospitals normally experience a drop in occupancy in the summer months and also during the period between Christmas and New Year's. Patients prefer to have elective surgery done during other periods, and so do their surgeons. Similarly, snow tires are almost never purchased in spring and early summer (in the Northern Hemisphere, at least), only bargain hunters buy Christmas tree ornaments in January, and so on.

In some cases, the seasonal variations are far more subtle. A government agency, for example, may discover that there is some seasonal variation in demand for office supplies, even though demand for that agency's services seems independent of seasonal variations. One reason for this is simply that the number of working days per week and per month is not consistent. Holidays may reduce a standard five-day week to three or four days; demand for supplies during that period will decline accordingly. Cold weather brings increased absenteeism and thereby reduces demand. Vacations have the same effect during July and August. If demand is measured monthly, there is automatically some seasonal variation simply because the months themselves do not have the same number of working days. February may have only 19 working days (assuming that Washington's Birthday is a holiday), while March may have as many as 23 working days in an organization that operates a regular five-day week.

Seasonal variations in demand can usually be predicted fairly precisely. However, continuous review is usually essential. Seasonal patterns gradually change. For example, there is now a sharp seasonal decline in overall industrial production in the month of July. This reflects the growing custom of shutting down factories for vacation. Fifty years ago, blue-collar workers did not get paid vacations, and the July seasonal slump was much more moderate.

The simplest (but not always most precise) way to estimate seasonal fluctuations is to assume that the pattern that prevailed in the past will prevail in the future. For most materials managers, this assumption may come sufficiently close to the truth so that more complex techniques of determining seasonality are not needed.

Suppose, for example, you want to measure seasonality of an item you have stocked for many years. You know of nothing that has happened (such as a tendency toward more vacation shutdowns in July) to change the seasonal pattern of demand, so you simply calculate the average monthly demand over a number of years. The results, which are shown in column 1 of Table 9–2, indicate an overall average demand of 1,353 units per year or 112.75 units per month. Averages for each month show a clear seasonal pattern. Peak demand occurs in spring and fall, and there are two marked periods of seasonal slump—in July and August and in January and February.

Seasonal variations like those shown in Table 9–2 must be taken into account if you are to interpret current sales trends correctly. For example, suppose that demand this year increases from 94 units in February to 110 units in March, a 17 percent increase. If you were ignorant of seasonal trends, you might regard this as a reason for celebration and be tempted to hire more workers and increase production. A glance at Table 9–2 shows how wrong you would be. Actually, the increase to 110 units is a *less than seasonal* increase, and your sales performance is weak rather than strong.

Seasonal adjustment (or "deseasonalizing") permits you to observe

TABLE 9–2
Calculation of seasonal variation in demand

		(1) Average demand	(2) Average demand for month	(3) Seasonal adjustment (percent)
January		110	0.976	+ 2.4
February		95	0.843	+15.7
March		115	1.020	− 2.0
April		118	1.047	− 4.7
May		120	1.064	− 6.4
June		125	1.109	−10.9
July		90	0.798	+20.2
August		100	0.887	+11.3
September		120	1.064	− 6.4
October		125	1.109	−10.9
November		120	1.064	− 6.4
December		115	1.020	− 2.0
	12	1,353		
Average all months		112.75		

nonseasonal influences more readily. You adjust for seasonal variation by dividing average monthly (or weekly) demand by average demand for that month. For example, Table 9–2 shows that average demand in January is 110, while average demand for all months of the year is 112.75 units. Dividing 110 by 112.75 gives a seasonal adjustment factor of 0.976. This means that owing to seasonal factors, demand during January is 97.6 percent of normal (column 2 in Table 9–2) and, therefore, a +2.4 percent seasonal adjustment (100.00 − 0.976) should be added to January data to make it comparable on a seasonally adjusted basis with data for other months.

Changes in seasonally adjusted data are assumed to be due to causes that are not seasonal. The change in demand in the example above from 94 units in February to 110 units in March represents an actual increase in demand of 16 units. But Table 9–2 shows that seasonal factors alone should increase demand by 20 units during this period. For almost all products, the rate of secular change is so slow that it would barely be discernible during a one-month period. Cyclical variation is a possibility. If the product were an important one, you would want to investigate to see if the drop in demand is being influenced by the business cycle. If that were the case, you would probably cut back on your next order.

Random fluctuations. It is quite possible, however, that the failure of demand to register a normal seasonal increase cannot be explained rationally. Such changes occur frequently at random. Some random fluctuations are related to seasonal factors, for example, sales of natural gas and fuel oil for heating, which reach a seasonal peak in January. But demand may be either lower or higher than expected, depending on the January weather in the northern part of the country. Similarly, a wet spring will flatten out the seasonal peak that is anticipated in fertilizer sales simply because mud prevents farmers from working their fields as early as they would like.

Weather is one of the few random fluctuations that can be identified and clearly related to a change in demand. Other random fluctuations are harder to identify. A major danger is that a change in demand will be looked upon as random—and therefore nonrecurring—when the cause is really secular, cyclical, or seasonal. For example, suppose an appliance manufacturer carefully identifies secular, cyclical, and seasonal factors and predicts a demand for 10,000 refrigerators during the month of March. He actually sells only 6,000 refrigerators. Is this deviation of 4,000 refrigerators from forecasted sales a random fluctuation, or can it be related to some cause? If it is random, then the company should simply ignore it and not cut back production.

With genuinely random variation (as in flipping a coin or throwing honest dice), periods when the company "loses" will be exactly offset by periods when it "wins." Thus a random decline in demand for refrigerators will be followed by a random increase in demand, and the best policy is simply to go on producing at the planned rate, which takes into account secular, cyclical, and seasonal changes in demand.

In an organization where human beings must make decisions, it is all too easy to write off the unpleasant and unexpected as chance happening. This may also be a sure route to the poorhouse. Conceivably, the unexpected shortfall of 4,000 refrigerators represents a cyclical fluctuation the company has not been perceptive enough to identify. Or some other nonrandom cause may be the villain; for example, a competitor may be cutting prices. In any case, if the cause is nonrandom, the company should do something.

Applying probability

A company can use statistical theory to help determine whether or not change is random and can therefore be ignored. First, it would try to adjust for any seasonal factors that might be influencing sales. Conceivably the sale of 6,000 refrigerators instead of 10,000, for example, may indicate a slower than expected seasonal pickup in sales following the winter lull. This might happen, for example, if the weather were exceptionally bad. It is also possible that sales of refrigerators may be influenced by an unusually early or late Easter. If seasonal factors have apparently had a negligible effect, the company might then compare the unfavorable variation of 4,000 refrigerators with expected random variations.

Based on its past experience and analysis of the market, the company might try to estimate the maximum random variation it can expect from its forecast after all explainable variations have been taken into account. Statistically, this estimate represents an estimate of three standard deviations, or 99.72 percent of all occurrences. If the company has sufficient data it may even be able to calculate precisely the standard deviation of fluctuations due to random causes with the following formula:

$$S_x = \sqrt{\frac{\Sigma(x - \bar{x})^2}{n - 1}}.$$

The company may get exactly the same answer using both of these approaches: its maximum expected fluctuation is 3,000 refrigerators and its calculated standard deviation is 1,000 refrigerators. In both cases, the company then estimates the standard deviation to be 1,000 and three standard deviations to be 3 × 1,000, or 3,000.

If this estimate is correct, the company would expect random fluctuations in monthly demand to be 3,000 refrigerators or less, 99.72 percent of the time. The odds thus overwhelmingly imply that a shortfall in demand of 4,000 refrigerators is at least partly nonrandom in character. Therefore, some action should be taken.

In fact, the company may infer that fluctuations well within the range of three standard deviations may be nonrandom. Elementary statistics tells us that almost two thirds of all random fluctuations should fall within a range of one standard deviation. For the refrigerator company, this would be 1,000 refrigerators more or less than the basic forecast. In this case, the odds are heavily against purely random variations that *consistently* fall outside a range of one standard deviation. For example, if demand seemingly lags behind the forecast by 2,000 units for several months running, the odds are that this is not a random fluctuation, but some unidentified nonrandom factor is at work.

Averaging and smoothing techniques

If the product is a major one such as a refrigerator, management would carefully study demand fluctuations on an individual basis. Variations due to nonrandom causes would be identified and appropriate decisions made. Random variations would be accommodated by allowing inventory levels to go up and down.

Minor items simply do not deserve that much management time. For better or worse, decisions must be made by clerks or computers. In some cases, it is easiest to assume that all fluctuations in lead-time usage are random and to protect against stockouts with adequate inventory. At the other extreme, it is possible to develop very complex statistical techniques where a computer takes into account secular, cyclical, and seasonal factors as well as random fluctuations in setting order points.

Most companies settle for a compromise between these two extremes. They periodically revise estimates of lead-time usage with techniques that partly, but not always entirely, take into account secular, cyclical, seasonal, and other variations.

The moving average. The simplest such technique employs moving averages. They permit usage figures to be brought up to date at regular intervals so that order quantities will reflect the latest changes in demand. For example, a company might use a four-week moving average to measure demand. Each week a new average demand is calculated, as follows:

Week no.	Usage	4-week average
1	10	
2	11	
3	12	
4	12	11
5	14	12
6	14	12.75
7	16	13.75

With the moving average, demand gradually changes to reflect current usage. Each week's demand is weighted equally.

The weight given current usage depends on the span of the moving average. For example, a four-week moving average is more sensitive to current demand than an eight-week average. On the other hand, an eight-week average is more likely to smooth out short-term random fluctuations that are not significant.

Moving averages always lag behind current usage. In addition, they present programming problems when used with electronic data processing equipment. For these reasons, many companies have adopted exponential smoothing techniques to measure demand.

Exponential smoothing. With exponential smoothing, current usage is weighted more heavily than past usage in forecasting demand. Exponential smoothing is easy to apply. One merely updates the previous demand or usage average by a fractional constant A. This formula is:

New average = Old average + A (Current demand − Old average).

For example, suppose that a demand of 80 units is forecast for the week and actual usage is 90 units. If a value of 0.1 is used for the constant A, the new average equals $80 + 0.1 (90 − 80) = 81$. If demand drops the following week to 71 units, the new average equals $81 + 0.1 (71 − 81) = 80$ units.

Note that the value of the constant A determines the effect of current demand on the new average. For example, a constant of 0.1 gives results close to those obtained with a 19-period moving average, while a constant of 0.5 is the equivalent of a 3-period moving average.

Change in trend. The exponential smoothing formula used above lags behind actual demand. To correct for lag due to trend, it is necessary first to measure the change in trend. Our formula is: Current trend = New average − old average. We can use exponential smoothing to measure the average trend just as we did for the demand itself:

New trend = A (Current trend) + $(1 - A)$ old trend.

Then,

$$\text{Expected demand} = \text{New average} + \frac{(1 - A)}{A} \text{ new trend.}$$

To see how the formulas are applied, assume that averages have been increasing by two units per period. In the current period, they have increased by just one unit (from 80 units to 81 units). The new trend is calculated by substituting:

New trend = A (current trend) + $(1 - A)$ old trend
$$= 0.1 \, (1) + (1 - 0.1) \, 2 = 1.9 \text{ units.}$$
Expected demand = New average + $(1 - A)/A$ (new trend)
$$= 81 + 0.9/0.1 \, (1.9) = 98.1 \text{ units.}$$

To use this forecast of demand to set an order point, it is necessary to first project the demand through the lead time. For example, if lead time is four weeks and the expected demand is 98.1 units, then the demand during the lead time will be 4×98.1 units, or 392 units. To take trend into account in the lead-time forecast, the following formula is used:

Lead-time expected demand
$$= \frac{\text{Lead time (lead time + 1) (new trend)}}{2} + \text{Expected demand}$$
$$= \frac{4 \times 5}{2} (1.9) + 98.1 = 117 \text{ units.}$$

The actual order point is equal to 117 units plus a safety stock that allows for uncertainties of demand (which may be calculated by applying the Poisson distribution discussed in Chapter 10).

Limitations. Exponential smoothing is not a perfect technique for forecasting demand. Like other statistical techniques, it is based on past demand and obviously cannot allow for new and unpredicted changes in demand. In addition, it may help increase inventories because, as was demonstrated in the example, small shifts in weekly demand can be magnified into substantial shifts in order points when trend is taken into account. Despite its weaknesses, however, exponential smoothing is an excellent technique, especially when used in conjunction with electronic data processing to control order points of thousands of low-value C items.

Lead-time change. Exponential smoothing is designed to adjust order points to changes in demand. But order points are affected also by supply. For example, suppose that usage of an item is 100 units per month. If vendor lead time is two months, then the order point must be set at 200 units plus safety stock. If vendor lead time increases to three months, the order point must be adjusted upward by 100 units.

Vendor lead times tend to fluctuate with the business cycle, usually leading it by a few months. Lack of planning becomes obvious when business is on the upswing. Materials managers are repeatedly plagued by stockouts as lead times lengthen. They react by increasing their order points. All too often, these order points are never cut back again when the lead times begin to shorten. At this stage of the cycle, there is no automatic mechanism that forces management to reset the order point.

A control for the order point can be built into an EDP system by having buyers check periodic printouts of vendor lead times. The materials manager can then easily set up controls to assure that order points are adjusted with the business cycle. Otherwise, inventory that creeps into the system because of shorter lead times may be difficult to weed out. There is no automatic forceful reminder of it, as there is when inventories are inadequate. Companies try to keep inventories from creeping up by insisting that suppliers adhere to delivery schedules. If the lead time allowed for an item is five weeks, they may insist that the supplier deliver during the fifth week even if she is quite capable of shipping within two weeks. This policy is not easy to police, however. For example, a company's receiving department cannot always be ordered to refuse all shipments that are more than one week early. The shipment is usually already delivered before the receiving clerk has a chance to check the "due date" on the purchase order. Also, many shipments arrive ahead of schedule at the request of the buyer, and it may be difficult for receiving clerks to distinguish between shipments that are supposed to be early and those that are not wanted.

PERIODIC ORDERING

If a company receives daily or weekly shipments of material, the controls used for order-point systems may break down completely. Inventories will be excessive and records may be misleading. The best solution to the problem may be periodic control or a hybrid system that combines periodic and order-point control.

Application

All the inventory systems discussed so far have been order-point systems, in which a certain quantity of material is ordered whenever stocks drop to the reorder point. Inventories are regulated by the period between orders; the order quantity is fixed. Periodic reordering is just the opposite: Inventories are regulated by the quantity ordered, and the period between orders is fixed. In other words, orders are placed at regular intervals for amounts needed to bring stocks up to the desired level.

Necessary conditions. Periodic reordering is commonly used when one or more of the following conditions prevails:

1. The item is ordered frequently and expenditures for it are sufficient to warrant tight control.
2. Inventory balances are determined only periodically, making an order-point system impractical.
3. Many items are ordered from the same supplier, and ordering jointly reduces prices, transportation, or paperwork.
4. Usage is discreet or irregular. For example, an item may be withdrawn from stock just one day in a month.
5. The item is purchased in large quantities and requires a substantial percentage of a supplier's capacity.
6. Either price does not vary with quantity purchased or quantity discounts are available even though an order is scheduled for partial shipments.

Periodic reordering is used almost always by companies that make a limited product line in large quantities. For example, it is widely used to control production parts inventories in the automobile and appliance industries. In these industries, where identical products are finished on assembly lines day after day, inventory management is regarded as the regulation of a flow of parts and materials. It is not thought of as a series of additions to and withdrawals from stock, as it is in job-lot systems or perpetual inventory systems used for nonproduction material.

An example. This flow concept is best illustrated by an example. Suppose an appliance manufacturer has scheduled 10,000 units of a particular model each month and requires a component that is unique to that model. The supplier quotes on the basis of 10,000 units per month but, usually, the purchase order itself does not authorize him to fabricate any parts or buy any raw material. This is authorized by releases from production control that amend the order. A system of releases with periodic ordering limits the buyer's liability for raw materials and finished stock should production be cut back. It also makes it easier to increase orders should requirements temporarily be greater than planned.

Table 9–3 shows the pattern of weekly usage, inventory, and releasing for the appliance manufacturer. In week no. 1, which is several months after the purchase order was placed, the supplier is authorized to ship 2,500 pieces. He had previously been authorized to fabricate two months' usage (20,000 pieces) and buy raw materials for five months' usage. In week no. 2, production control authorizes the supplier to make another shipment of 2,500 pieces, and the supplier has already given the buyer's traffic department the routing and car number for the first shipment, which is in transit.[1]

In week no. 3, the first shipment is received and a third shipment of 2,500 pieces is authorized. In week no. 4, production starts. A stock checker makes a count of stock on hand, and a usage of 3,000 pieces is indicated. Production control notes that usage has been greater than planned because of rescheduling. It warns the supplier but does not increase the weekly shipping authorization. In the following week usage jumps again, to 3,200 pieces, and the shipping release to the supplier is increased to 3,500 pieces in order to build up stocks that are now below normal.

Since it is the end of the month, the supplier's fabrication and material authorizations are reviewed. No changes in usage are predicted, so the supplier is authorized to buy material and fabricate an additional month's usage of 10,000 pieces. This increases cumulative fabrication authorizations to 30,000 pieces and material authorizations to 60,000, and the supplier continues to have a lead time of two months for fabrication and five months for materials.

During the sixth week, stocks remain unchanged and 2,500 units are received; thus usage is 2,500 units. The following week there is a wildcat strike at the plant, and the stock checker's report indicates that line stocks are up to 4,800 units and usage therefore is down to 500 units. Production control now cuts the supplier back to a shipment of 1,500 units.

Advantages and disadvantages

Note the similarity between the releasing procedure for periodic control and the dispatching system for job lots described in Chapter 8. In both cases, production control tries to keep material flowing to manufacturing at a rate that will keep every machine busy but will not cause excess stocks to be built up. The main difference is that with job-lot control, each order passing through the system calls for a different product; with periodic control, the product is identical.

---

[1] Companies that buy identical parts and materials for a number of plants sometimes reroute shipments in transit if shortages develop at a particular plant. Even companies with a single plant like to keep tabs on shipments in transit so they can ask the carrier to trace them if there are any delays.

TABLE 9–3
Material control with a periodic ordering system

Week No.	Weekly data					Cumulative data				
	On hand	In transit	Received	Apparent usage	Released	Fabrication authorized	Material authorized	Released	Received	Used
1	0	0	0	0	2,500	20,000	50,000	2,500	0	0
2	0	2,500	0	0	2,500	20,000	50,000	5,000	0	0
3	2,500	2,500	2,500	0	2,500	20,000	50,000	7,500	2,500	0
4	2,000	2,500	2,500	3,000	2,500	20,000	50,000	10,000	5,000	3,000
5	1,800	2,500	2,500	3,200	3,500	30,000	60,000	13,500	7,500	6,200
6	1,800	3,500	2,500	2,500	2,500	30,000	60,000	16,000	10,000	8,700
7	4,800	2,500	3,500	500	1,500	30,000	60,000	16,500	13,000	9,200

Note: With a periodic ordering system, stock levels are checked and orders placed at regular, predetermined intervals. In this example, suppliers fabricate approximately two months' usage of material and purchase raw material for an additional three months' usage. They then make weekly shipments of the exact amount of material needed.

Safety stocks. Despite the extremely close control it offers, periodic ordering does not eliminate the need for safety stocks. As with order-point systems, some protective stock is needed between the times material is ordered and delivered in order to allow for unanticipated delays in delivery or for extra usage. The process of determining safety stock is not unlike that for order-point systems. Investment in safety stocks can be reduced through application of ABC systems methods. The high-priced A items have the smallest safety stock. Protection against stockouts is achieved by reducing the period between orders. For example, stocks of A items might be checked for reorder twice weekly, B items every other week, and C items once a month.

Using the ABC approach with periodic ordering, automobile assembly plants make daily checks of stocks of high-priced materials such as engines, transmissions, and major body components, but check stock weekly or even monthly for minor items such as upholstery tacks. The principles of selective control can also be applied to periodic ordering. Suppose, for example, that the time-cycle chart in Figure 9–1 illustrated the lead-time cycle of an assembly controlled with periodic ordering. If the entire manufacturing process were so interrelated (through conveyor lines, automated equipment, and so on) that in-process inventories were automatically regulated, then it would be pointless to control anything but purchased parts and materials. In this case, there would be periodic control of all purchasing lead-time items only. Inventories of other items would always be exactly equal to the space they occupy on conveyor lines and in-process equipment, less any scrap that was generated.

Close control, high cost. Applications of periodic ordering are limited almost entirely to mass-production industries, where enormous quantities of a relatively limited number of items must be controlled. Periodic ordering permits such companies to operate with minimum inventories that often are only a fraction of what would be required with order-point control. Periodic ordering also has major disadvantages (which is why its applications are limited). It is expensive to operate, since it requires more clerical labor force than order-point systems do. Also, it usually is not practical unless usage is high or the item is extremely expensive. Otherwise it costs too much, because more frequent ordering can raise both unit shipping costs and prices of materials.

OTHER INVENTORY SYSTEMS

Periodic–order point combined

Many organizations which order relatively small quantities of a number of items from a common supplier can profitably use a combination order point–periodic system. For example, suppose that a hospital carries in inventory several hundred different items that it orders from a single medical-surgical supplies dealer. The supplier salesperson makes weekly calls. At that time, it is convenient to order whatever is low on stock and have it delivered the following week. In the pre-computer era, this was done simply by eyeballing the items on the shelves and ordering whichever item appeared to be running low.

With a computer, the approach is similar but more sophisticated. All transactions are entered into the computer. There are two ordering levels established in the program. The first is a conventional order point. When the computer says order point has been reached, an order must be placed the next time the salesperson calls or there is some risk of a stockout.

In addition the computer is programmed to alert the stores manager when some predetermined critical level is reached. This might be roughly one week's usage over and above the order point. It then becomes optional whether or not this item is ordered when the vendor makes the next call. If the item is low in value, it is convenient to do so and there is little extra inventory carrying cost incurred. With this combination system, the order quantity might vary somewhat. The stores manager would round up or down to the most convenient multiple that roughly equals the usage during the previous period.

Such combination systems work well mostly when investment in each inventory item is relatively low. Otherwise, the rounding up process plus the tendency to order at the critical point, rather than the order point, tends to raise inventory costs. But it does result in less ordering cost than would be incurred if each item was ordered only when it reached order point. Orders would then be triggered daily when there is no point in ordering except when the salesperson actually calls.

Top-management control

Regardless of the system used, periodic ordering or order point, top managers cannot hope to control the thousands of items in inventory on an individual basis. This is a job for clerks or computers. Management can only hope to control inventories on an overall basis. One of the best ways to do this is through standards used in conjunction with an overall materials plan.

For example, suppose the plan assumes that production and sales will be $1 million per month for the first three months of the year and then will increase steadily to a peak of $1.5 million in June. Obviously some inventory buildup is necessary to accommodate the sales increase. However, it is not necessary to increase inventories in proportion to the increase in output. Plants can operate with higher stock turnover ratios as production increases to near-capacity levels. What happens, in effect, is that materials move through the plant more rapidly when production increases. Thus, the need for in-process inventory may not increase as rapidly as output. Raw materials inventories may not change at all. The extra demand causes stocks to drop more rapidly to their reorder points. Outstanding purchase commitments would grow, but, if everything goes according to plan, actual stocks of purchased materials would not necessarily increase. In practice, however, they would probably tend to creep up, since stockouts would otherwise become more frequent simply because order points are reached more often.

With a 50 percent increase in sales, it might be possible to get along with as little as a 20 percent increase in inventories of purchased parts and raw materials. Inventories might increase, for example, from $500,000 in January to $600,000 by May 1. Then a drop in inventories to $400,000 might be projected through July. In other words, during the peak production period, management might anticipate cutting inventories if sales are expected to drop sharply when the peak is passed.

Once the plan is agreed upon, managers can maintain control by comparing the standards set in the plan with reports of actual performance. Since it normally takes a rather elaborate study to calculate precisely what inventories are, managers usually maintain control with weekly or daily reports of purchases, receivals, and output, which can provide approximate inventory balances. When these reports indicate deviation from standard, the materials manager investigates and takes necessary corrective action.

Should actual output vary substantially from the plan or should the sales forecast change, the materials manager must be ready to set new standards quickly. If the materials manager does not move fast, either there may be shortages or inventories will build up rapidly because of accumulated commitments. Suppose, for example, that sales and production in June are actually $1 million instead of $1.5 million. This automatically means an inventory buildup if there has been no advance warning, since it is impossible to cut back commitments too much within the procurement lead time. The materials manager must then devise a plan to get stocks back in balance. If sales are greater than expected in succeeding months, the problem is solved almost automatically. But if they are less than expected, new purchases may have to be cut back sharply for a number of months before a new equilibrium is reached.

When there are no unexpected changes in either demand or supplier lead times, the inventory management process can be made largely automatic. In many cases, optimum inventory levels can be calculated with a high degree of precision through the use of various analytical techniques. These techniques are discussed in detail in the next chapter.

Cases

CASE 9–1. A PROBLEM IN ORDER-POINT CONTROL

Suppose you work for a company that controls its inventories on a max-min basis, using perpetual inventory cards. Your company is introducing a new line of products that will result in greatly increased usage of a particular component. You analyze the sales forecast for this new product line and calculate that it will cause demand for the component to rise by about 800 units per month. Naturally, you decide to analyze the history of the component to determine what lead time and order quantities should be. You note the following data on the perpetual inventory card:

Date	Purchase requisition issued	Receipts	Disburse- ments	Balance on hand
1/2				922*
1/7			400	522
1/12	500			
1/29			400	122
2/10		500		622
2/15	500			
3/13		500		1,122
3/16			400	722
5/1	1,000		722	0
5/18		1,000		1,000
5/19			278	722
7/12	500		400	322
8/10		500		822
10/26			600	222
10/27	500			
11/18		500		722
12/12			200	522

* Balance carried forward.

It is expected that demand for the component will be more regular from the new product than it will be from other products, which will continue to vary erratically as it has in the past. The unit price f.o.b. buyer's plant is $1 in lots of 100 to 499 pieces, 95 cents in lots of 500 to 999 pieces, 92 cents in lots of 1,000 to 4,999 pieces, and 90 cents in lots of more than 5,000 pieces. Normal lead time is four weeks, but in emergencies you can get delivery in two to three weeks by doing a great deal of expediting.

Question

Calculate purchase quantities, safety stock, and order-point quantity, based on the data above.

CASE 9-2. BLUE MOTORS CORPORATION (A)

A problem in periodic ordering

Production and inventory control is not an easy job at Blue Motors, a large auto manufacturer. The company's investment in raw material and in-process inventories exceeds its investment in plant and equipment, and thus it is the company's biggest single asset. Control of production parts and materials inventories is particularly difficult at the company's automobile assembly plants, where the proper components to assemble hundreds of different trim and color combinations of the company's models must be on hand when needed. The company cannot afford to stop its assembly line because of a supply failure. On the other hand, storage space is limited. The company could not carry more than a few days' inventory of such bulky components as engines, radiators, and seat springs even if it were not the least bit concerned about tying up too much of its working capital in inventories.

The company tries to limit inventory investment with an ABC system. It carries less than a week's inventory of the bulky and expensive A items—engines, bodies, transmissions, and similar components. B items normally are limited to about two weeks' stock, and plants may carry as much as three months' stock of C items, although they try to hold it to 30 days' stock.

Blue Motors uses periodic ordering for all production parts and materials. Suppliers are authorized to purchase materials five months in advance and to fabricate two months in advance. Blue Motors stock checkers make periodic counts of material on hand. This information is compared with data on the number of parts that are on order and in transit. The total available supply is then compared with the demand indicated by the production schedule. Suppliers get new production releases each month that authorize them to fabricate and buy material for an additional month's requirements. The ordering and inventory control procedure used by Blue Motors is much like that shown in Table 9-3.

The stock checkers use different review periods for different types of item. Any item that is in critical supply is reviewed daily, regardless of its value. Most A items are reviewed daily, B items usually are reviewed twice a week, and C items always are reviewed at least once a month.

Until recently, all of Blue Motors's basic products have been assem-

bled in reasonably large quantities. The company's lowest volume item has been its convertible coupe, output of which has dropped to as low as two units per day at certain of the company's assembly plants. The company's newest product is what its advertising department calls a "customized" sports car. The new product is designed to compete with the sports cars turned out by various European manufacturers. Its price will be about $12,000. The company's marketing strategy is tailored to relatively few buyers who wish to own a high-quality automobile with unique design features. It already has widely advertised that production of the new car will be limited to 200 units per year in order to "protect the investment of its discriminating owners."

Current plans call for assembly of the car at the company's main plant in Detroit. Its production volume is so low that practically all of the components, few of which are interchangeable with the company's other cars, will be purchased. The company's own manufacturing plants prefer to concentrate on the more profitable, high-volume components of the company's other products.

Suppliers of major components have been reluctant to accept orders unless they are authorized to fabricate an entire year's requirements in one production run. Since production is limited to only 15 units per day during the period of peak demand, in spring, and will probably drop to 5 units during the slack season, the company's normal ordering procedures for ABC items may not be applicable. For example, a supplier might object to shipping small screws in lots of 50 or 100. Similarly, it would be costly to use a supplier truck to deliver only ten units of an A item like a radiator. On the other hand, the company wants to tie up as little of its valuable factory floor space as possible on the new program. Also, if an item cannot be delivered directly to the assembly line, where there is a limited amount of space, it must be stored in some other area of the plant, and a second handling will be necessary. This would raise costs, particularly for high-volume components.

Question

Recommend an ordering system for Blue Motors' new sports car. In making your recommendations, assume that a radiator is a typical A item, a door handle a typical B item, and a fastener a typical C item.

10

Analytical inventory
control techniques

Business executives have been making inventory decisions for years based on their instinct or "feel" for optimum cost. In general, their decision making has been pretty good. They know that large order quantities bring lower purchase prices but, at some point, the gain in purchase price (and in administrative costs when ordering less frequently) is more than offset by added cost of carrying inventory. They also know that there is some optimum order point and safety stock. By trial and error, they arrive at a level where stockout costs are minimal and so are inventory carrying costs.

Inventory management by intuition works—especially in smaller organizations. In fact, it is only recently that any other system has been economic for the small organization. All this has changed with the advent of low-cost electronic data processing. Now almost every organization can apply quantitative techniques of inventory management. In contrast, as recently as 20 years ago, not even a majority of large companies used some of the techniques described in this and other texts—even though the basic techniques themselves had been available for 50 years or more. In fact, a mere 10 percent of a sample of larger manufacturers in 1966 applied probability theory to safety stock determination, and even smaller percentages applied other quantitative techniques, such as those to be discussed in this chapter. In most cases, the reasons for not using them have not been valid ones: ignorance, resistance to change, and the like.

The turning point came in the late 1960s or early 1970s. At that time, the term material requirements planning (MRP) came into common usage. What it really meant was applying computer science techniques to that which every organization had been trying to do for years. In most real-life organizations, adoption of MRP meant using a

316

computer to apply techniques discussed here which had been around for years. MRP was "new" in that this had not been done before; it was "old" in that nothing novel was really being done. The computer simply did what a clerk was not fast enough to do.

Looking ahead

The techniques discussed in this chapter are basic to MRP even though they are not new. However, they do represent approximations which are no longer needed with computer technology. For example, ABC control assumes that an inventory neatly falls into three categories. The concept is extremely useful. In reality, however, every inventory is a continuous series. In theory, at least, each item can be treated individually, getting slightly less safety stock and relatively more personal control as it increases in value. Similar approximations are made in the formulas discussed in this chapter. With MRP, these approximations are not really necessary—although they are still convenient provided the inventory itself is not large enough to justify the more elaborate programming that must be used as the inventory model comes closer to reality. Relatively few men and women have been trained in modern material requirements planning techniques. Undoubtedly there will be wider adoption of these techniques when the supply of trained personnel comes anywhere near meeting the demand. However, there is no denying that some companies are thoroughly familiar with the techniques discussed in this chapter but still refrain from using some of them because they feel that their advantages are more than offset by their cost, as well as by other disadvantages. Nonprofit organizations have been inhibited not only by indifference and ignorance but also by the fact that rational materials management requires some assumption of a cost of capital. This is not too difficult for the profit-making organization but can be torturous for the organization that professes no interest in profit.

DETERMINING ORDER QUANTITY

As we have noted, the bigger the order quantity, the bigger the average inventory investment. A policy of buying in large quantities also has its virtues. Unit prices usually are lower. In addition, the larger the order quantity, the fewer the number of orders that must be processed and the fewer the shipments that need be handled. This reduces costs.

Consequently the materials manager is torn between a desire to keep inventories low by ordering in small quantities and a desire to reduce costs by buying large quantities. The cost of carrying inventories is called "cost of possession," and the cost of purchasing and processing the order is called "cost of acquisition." One of the most important goals in materials management is to strike the most economic balance between cost of possession and cost of acquisition in determining order quantities.

Cost of possession

Inventory costs at least 20 to 25 percent per year to carry. That is, each $1 million in inventory costs $200,000 to $250,000 per year to maintain. There are three major costs of possession: storage, obsolescence, and capital cost.

Storage cost. This is the most obvious inventory carrying cost. It includes rent for storage facilities, salaries of personnel and related storage expenses, taxes, and so on. Storage cost varies widely with the type of material stored, type of storage facilities used, and so on. Usually it is equal to at least 5 percent of the value of the material that is stored. Thus, if the inventory investment is $1 million, it almost always costs at least $50,000 per year to store it.

Storage cost varies widely. An inventory of sand has relatively little storage cost since all that is required is land on which to dump the sand. As long as the materials being stored are homogeneous, it is usually fairly easy to calculate storage cost, however. All one need do is to add up the annual costs associated with storage and divide by the average inventory investment.

The real-life calculation is usually more complicated than this. The problem is that most storage areas do not contain a homogeneous group of materials. For example, the general stores area of a hospital may contain both IV solutions and sutures (along with at least a thousand other items). The solutions are bulky relative to their value; the sutures take up very little space. In fact, $10,000 worth of sutures can probably be stored in an area that will hold no more than $200 worth of solutions. If overall storage costs amount to $30,000 per year on a $150,000 inventory or 20 percent per year, it is not correct to assume that the sutures cost $2,000 per year to store (20 percent of the $10,000 suture inventory) while $200 worth of solutions occupying the same space cost but $40 per year.

When materials are as different as solutions and sutures, storage cost cannot be allocated arbitrarily on the basis of value. Bulk and other factors must be taken into account. Otherwise, the materials manager will be led into carrying excessive inventories of the bulky item because he or she is making false assumptions about their true storage cost.

Obsolescence. When there are no inventories, there can be no obsolescence. But when many items are stored, it is inevitable that some of them will not be used, will shrink or disappear, or will spoil. Needs cannot be estimated with perfect accuracy, even with the most rigid inventory control systems. Well-managed companies ruthlessly weed out surplus inventory and dispose of it. The general rule is never to hold inventories for which there is no foreseeable need. In fact, companies sometimes dispose of materials even when there is a definite future need for them. If stocks are held long enough, the accumulated carrying charges will exceed their value.

Suppose, for example, that a company has $100 invested in a certain material for which there will be no use for at least two years. Carrying costs are 20 percent a year, or $40 for two years. It pays the company to sell the material immediately if it can find a buyer willing to pay $60 for it. In practice, many companies would be willing to sell the material for less than $60 because they prefer to have capital in case rather than in inventory, and also because there is always some uncertainty in predicting a need for material a year or more in advance.

Although some obsolescence is inevitable, it cannot be predicted (or it would be prevented simply by not investing in inventory). Therefore a part of the cost of possession is an allowance of "insurance premium" to cover losses from obsolescence. The charge naturally varies widely, but few companies can hold it to less than 1 percent of the value of the inventory per year.

Cost of capital. Inventories tie up a company's most versatile asset, cash. Every business has a limited amount of capital available to it from its owners and creditors. Each tries to use it as efficiently as possible to earn bigger profits. One barometer that shows how efficiently capital is being used is inventory turnover: the ratio of sales to inventory. A company can raise this ratio either by reducing inventories or by increasing sales without a corresponding increase in inventories. In either case, its earnings on investment are boosted.

Suppose, for example, that a company's sales are $1 million with total assets of $200,000—including $100,000 in inventories. If its profit margin on sales is 5 percent, profits of $50,000 provide a 25 percent return on assets. Inventory is turned over ten times a year ($1,000,000 ÷ $100,000). If the turnover rate can be doubled, the company's sales will be $2 million with the same assets. Profits increase to $100,000 and return on investment is 50 percent.

Capital never is so readily available that it can be invested in inventory at no cost. Were it not in inventory, it could always earn a return at least equal to the interest on government bonds. In many cases, it could get a much higher return.

The "opportunity cost" approach is one of the best ways to estimate the cost of the money tied up in inventory. It assumes that the capital costs whatever it would earn were it invested in the most advantageous alternatives. The minimum opportunity cost is the 6 to 10 percent return the capital would earn if it were invested in short-term securities or used to reduce the company's debt. The maximum can be much higher—even 50 percent or more, if the company is very pressed for cash and has many opportunities to employ capital profitability.

Opportunity cost varies widely not only from company to company but also from year to year (or even month to month) within a company. Because of this, a company's cost of possession can vary widely. In a company subject to wide swings in business, carrying costs can be extremely high at the peak of the business cycle, when there are many very profitable alternative investments available for the capital tied up in inventory. It also can be quite low in a business slump when a few investment opportunities are available. When a company's business is seasonal, its carrying costs (with the opportunity cost approach) also will vary seasonally, being very high at the peak of the season and low off-season.

Finally, opportunity cost is influenced by risk. It is not enough for a company to estimate that it could earn 20 percent on capital that is not invested in inventory. It must also make some assumption as to relative risk. This varies among different types of inventory. To cite one simple example, a store that sells high-fashion merchandise must assume a greater risk and consequent higher inventory carrying cost than one that carries staple items that are always in demand.

Inventory management, never an easy job, is almost impossible to perform perfectly when changes in the cost of possession are taken into account.

Cost of acquisition

Despite their desire to use capital efficiently and minimize storage cost and obsolescence, most companies deliberately carry inventories substantially bigger than they need be for protection against stockouts. They do this to reduce their cost of acquisition, since by ordering and buying large quantities they reduce both purchase cost and ordering cost.

Purchase cost. When a company buys in larger quantities, it usually pays lower unit prices. Suppliers will cut prices because their costs are lower when they get a single large order instead of several small ones. Not only are their administrative expenses reduced, but often they also can manufacture in larger lots and reduce unit costs. In addition, the buyer's bargaining power is increased by placing a large order, and it is easier to wangle concessions from suppliers. If the purchased material is fabricated in the company's own plant, costs may also be reduced if the shop gets jobs with long production runs.

Setup and ordering cost. Each lot that is manufactured may require a separate setup. Production equipment is shut down and a skilled mechanic makes necessary adjustments to ready the equipment for the next lot. There also are costs associated with each purchase—salaries and overhead in the purchasing department; expediting, receiving, and paying for the material; interplant and intraplant transportation; packaging, and so on.

Suppose, for example, a company decides to buy material in two separate lots rather than one big lot. It costs just as much to issue the purchase order for the smaller lot as for the bigger one. Therefore purchase order costs double, since two orders are required to buy two lots. There also is twice as much paperwork in the accounting, receiving, and inspection operations. Physically it will usually take more time to handle two smaller shipments than a single large one.[1] And, in most cases, a single big shipment can be packaged more economically and shipped for a lower tariff than two smaller shipments. Thus, the bigger the amount purchased, the lower the unit ordering cost.

Ordering cost is insignificant only with purchases of very high value. The cost of purchasing many small items may be substantially greater than the value of these items. For example, one large corporation made a study that revealed it cost its purchasing department $14.60 for each order it issued and it cost $3.86 to receive and inspect each shipment. High ordering costs make it desirable to carry rather large stocks of low-value items.

Setup costs in manufacturing vary even more widely than ordering costs. In some cases they are almost insignificant. For example, a furniture factory may be able to change the width or length of lumber that is being cut in a minute or two. In contrast, in an automobile factory it may require hundreds of labor-hours of skilled labor to install all of the dies needed to make roof panels.

EOQ formulas

Many formulas have been devised to weigh the variables of cost of acquisition, cost of possession, and usage in order to determine the most economic order quantity (EOQ). If usage does not vary much from week to week, the formulas are not too complex mathematically. When the usage pattern is complex, so are the formulas.

No quantity discount. The following formula can be used to determine EOQ when unit price is the same regardless of order quantity:

$$\text{EOQ} = \sqrt{\frac{2 \times (\text{annual usage in units}) \times (\text{order cost in \$/order})}{(\text{unit cost of material in \$/unit}) \times (\text{carrying cost in \%/yr.})}}.$$

Suppose, for example, annual usage of a material is 1,200 units and it costs $10 to handle an order for this material. The price is $1 per unit

---

[1] The difference varies with the bulk and weight of the shipments. It usually takes nearly twice as much time to handle two five-pound shipments as one ten-pound shipment. But it takes about twice as much time to unload a two-carload shipment as it does a one-carload shipment.

regardless of quantity purchased, and carrying cost of inventory is 24 percent per year. Then

$$\text{EOQ} = \sqrt{\frac{2 \times 1{,}200 \times \$10}{\$1 \times 0.24}} = 316 \text{ units.}$$

Quantity discount. If, as is frequently the case, the price does vary with the amount purchased, it is more difficult to calculate EOQ. A separate table for each carrying cost and order cost used is required. It consists of tabulations of total procurement cost (purchase cost plus ordering cost plus carrying cost) for a series of order quantities and annual usages.

Calculations to compile such a table are not difficult to make. For example, assume that a certain material has an annual usage of $1,200 and each purchase covers a three-month supply. With a $10 order cost and a 24 percent carrying cost, total annual procurement cost is $1,276 and consists of the following components.

Purchase cost......................................	$1,200
Order cost (4 orders @ $10/order)....................	40
Carrying cost (24% of $150)*	36
Total annual procurement cost.................	$1,276

* Note that even though $300 worth of material is ordered every three months, average inventory is $150, not $300. When the order is received at the beginning of the period, inventories rise by $300. Halfway through the period (after one and one half months), half of the order, or $150 worth, has presumably been consumed. At the end of the period, the entire order has been used. Average stock carried during the period therefore is $150, if usage has been reasonably regular.

When these calculations are made for various values of annual usage and order quantities, a table similar to that in Table 10–1 can be constructed and used to determine minimum annual procurement cost when purchase price varies with quantity purchased. For example, to find the $1,276 total annual procurement cost calculated above, first look at the "value of annual use" column in Table 10–1 and locate the row for $1,200. Then go across this row to the column for three months' order quantity, which indicates that the total procurement cost is $1,276 when annual use is $1,200 and purchase quantity is equal to three months' usage. This table is valid, of course, only when carrying cost is 24 percent and order cost is $10.

Using the table. An example illustrates how the table would be used in a real-life purchasing problem. Suppose a supplier has the following price schedule:

Order quantity	Unit price
1–499	$1.00
500–999	0.95
1,000 or more	0.925

TABLE 10–1
Comparative costs of various ordering policies

Value of annual use	Order quantity in months' supply						
	1	2	3	4	5	6	7
$ 100	221	162	143	134	129	126	124
102	223	164	145	136	131	128	126
104	225	166	147	138	133	130	128
106	227	168	149	140	135	132	131
108	229	170	151	142	137	134	133
1,050	1,181	1,131	1,122	1,122	1,127	1,133	1,141
1,060	1,191	1,141	1,132	1,132	1,137	1,144	1,151
1,070	1,201	1,151	1,142	1,143	1,148	1,154	1,162
1,080	1,211	1,162	1,152	1,153	1,158	1,165	1,173
1,090	1,221	1,172	1,163	1,164	1,169	1,175	1,183
1,100	1,231	1,182	1,173	1,174	1,179	1,186	1,194
1,110	1,241	1,192	1,183	1,184	1,190	1,197	1,205
1,120	1,251	1,202	1,194	1,195	1,200	1,207	1,216
1,130	1,261	1,213	1,204	1,205	1,211	1,218	1,226
1,140	1,271	1,223	1,214	1,216	1,221	1,228	1,237
1,150	1,282	1,233	1,225	1,226	1,232	1,239	1,248
1,160	1,292	1,243	1,235	1,236	1,242	1,250	1,258
1,170	1,302	1,253	1,245	1,247	1,253	1,260	1,269
1,180	1,312	1,264	1,255	1,257	1,263	1,271	1,280
1,190	1,322	1,274	1,266	1,268	1,274	1,281	1,290
1,200 ⋏........	1,332	1,284	1,276	1,278	1,284	1,292	1,301
1,210	1,342	1,294	1,286	1,288	1,295	1,303	1,312
1,220	1,352	1,304	1,297	1,299	1,305	1,313	1,323
1,230	1,362	1,315	1,307	1,309	1,316	1,324	1,333
1,240	1,372	1,325	1,317	1,320	1,326	1,334	1,344
19,750	20,068	20,205	20,383	20,570	20,762	20,955	21,150
19,800	20,118	20,256	20,434	20,622	20,814	21,008	21,203
19,850	20,169	20,307	20,486	20,674	20,867	21,061	21,257
19,900	20,219	20,358	20,537	20,726	20,919	21,114	21,310
19,950	20,270	20,409	20,589	20,778	20,972	21,167	21,364
20,000	20,320	20,460	20,640	20,830	21,024	21,220	21,417

Note: Table shows total annual cost for various values of annual use and various order quantities when carrying cost is 24 percent and ordering cost is $10. Total annual cost equals the sum of the value of annual use, the order cost, and the carrying cost.

If usage is 1,200 units per year, the value of the usage is $1,200 at the price of $1.00, $1,140 at the $0.95 price (i.e., 1,200 × $0.95), and $1,110 at the $0.925 price. The table indicates that minimum total procurement cost for a usage value of $1,200 per year is $1,276. This minimum is achieved with a three-month order quantity (i.e., 300 units per order).

With a usage value of $1,140, a company must order at least five months' supply (500 units) to get the $0.95 price. The table shows that total procurement cost is $1,221 with five months' supply and higher still if the company has bigger orders. Similarly, to get the $0.925 price and $1,110 annual usage, it must order ten months' supply at the minimum. In this case, a total annual procurement cost of $1,233 can be calculated readily. Obviously it pays the company to buy in lots of 500 at a unit price of $0.95.

Making EOQ fit the budget

So far, we have dealt only with the applications of EOQ formulas to individual items. They also can be useful tools for top-management control of overall inventory levels.

Suppose that you are a materials manager, and at a meeting of your company's executive committee it is agreed that inventories should be reduced by 10 percent. Your company is short of cash or the committee feels that sales and earnings will drop off sharply in coming months. If you were an old-style materials manager, you might have your staff review every item in stock to see where stocks could be reduced by ordering more frequently, or you might even make rather arbitrary cuts in safety stocks and order quantities.

EOQ formulas permit a more analytical approach. What, in effect, has management decided when it makes a decision to cut inventories? In the economist's jargon, its liquidity preference has increased. It has raised the interest rate on which it bases its investment decisions. This means that the inventory carrying cost in the EOQ formulas should be increased to reflect this higher "cost" for the use of the company's capital.

Suppose inventory is $1,200,000, including a $200,000 safety stock, and that the economic order quantity had been computed with a 16 percent carrying cost. Management wants a 10 percent (or $120,000) reduction in inventory investment without any change in safety stock. This means that the average inventory due to order quantity must be reduced from $1 million to $880,000. It is easy to determine the new carrying cost. From the formulas, we know that order quantity varies inversely with the square root of carrying cost (CC). We also know that average inventory exclusive of safety stock (AI) is determined by order quantity. Therefore,

$$\sqrt{\frac{CC_1}{CC_2}} = \frac{AI_2}{AI_1}.$$

Substituting,

$$\sqrt{\frac{16}{CC_2}} = \frac{\$880,000}{\$1,000,000},$$

and

$$CC_2 = 20.6\%.$$

The new inventory policy can be carried out by using a 20.6 percent carrying cost in calculating order quantities instead of a 16 percent cost. The new carrying cost should be used in calculating economic order quantity for all new stock items. There is no need to recalculate for items where EOQ was already figured with a carrying cost of 16 percent. As the calculations above demonstrate, the EOQ for the new carrying cost is 80 percent of that for the old. Companies that use electronic data processing systems to control inventories would simply program in the new 20.6 percent carrying cost, and the computer would automatically generate the appropriate order quantities.

EOQ for production parts

The economic order quantity for raw material is usually quite different from the economic lot size for fabrication of that material. Unless the purchasing and production control departments work very closely together, purchasing may buy in lot sizes that are not economic to manufacture. Suppose that the part with the EOQ that is calculated to be 316 units in the example used to explain the EOQ formula is a casting purchased for $1 that is then converted into a finished component, with an additional cash cost of $2. Cash cost of manufacture would include only direct labor and variable overhead. Other costs would not be included in the analysis, since they would be incurred independently of the lot size in which the part is manufactured.

Carrying cost is 24 percent per year, order cost $10 per order, and usage is 1,200 units per year. The purchasing department goes through the EOQ calculations illustrated and comes up with 316 units. Meanwhile, production control (which has its own computer) decides it will get scientific, too. Out-of-pocket machining cost of the part is $2, variable setup cost is $50, and, of course, annual usage and carrying cost are 1,200 units and 24 percent, respectively. Substituting into the economic lot size formula (which is the same as the EOQ formula except that machining cost is used instead of purchase cost and setup cost is substituted for order cost), production control discovers that:

$$\text{Economic lot size} = \sqrt{\frac{2 \times 1{,}200 \times \$50}{\$2 \times 0.24}} = 500 \text{ units}$$

An independent purchasing department would buy in lots of 316, while the shop would machine the purchased casting in lots of 500. Obviously, one or the other is wrong. What the company should do is consider the purchase and manufacture to be interrelated (which is exactly what the computer program would do). Order cost for the material and setup cost are considered as a single cost totaling $60. Purchasing and machining costs also are added together. Substituting in the formula arrives at:

$$EOQ = \sqrt{\frac{2 \times 1{,}200 \times \$60}{\$3 \times 0.24}} = 450 \text{ units.}$$

Thus, purchasing should buy in lots of 450—a compromise between the EOQ of 316 units and economic lot size of 500. This seeming conflict is fairly easy to resolve, especially in an organization in which both purchasing and production control report to a materials manager, who can reconcile any conflict of interest. However, EOQ formulas have weaknesses that are not so easy to resolve. As a result, few companies depend entirely on these formulas to determine order quantities, and some very successful firms do not use them at all.

Weaknesses of EOQ formulas

1. *Erratic usages.* The formulas we have used assume that usage of material is both predictable and evenly distributed. When this is not the case, the formulas are useless. Different, far more complex formulas can be developed for wide swings in usage, so long as those swings can be predicted. But if usage varies unpredictably, as it often does, no formula will work well.

2. *Faulty basic information.* EOQ calculations are only as accurate as the order cost and carrying cost information on which they are based. It is no easy job to calculate order or setup cost. In practice, order cost varies from commodity to commodity. Carrying cost, as we have seen, can vary with the company's opportunity cost for capital.

Both carrying cost and order cost calculations include elements of fixed and nonvariable costs that would be incurred over the short term regardless of the procurement actions taken. For example, included in a $10 order cost might be an allowance of 40 cents for the share of the purchasing agent's salary that would be allocated to that order. Theoretically, if the company can eliminate an order its costs should be 40 cents lower. But in practice, the purchasing agent's salary would not vary with the number of orders issued; she would be needed even if the company were to reduce its orders (by buying larger quantities) by 50 to 75 percent. Therefore, at least 40 cents (plus all other fixed costs) of the $10 order cost is incurred regardless of whether the order is actually placed or not.

Similarly, the true cash cost of an expensive setup may be negligible. Suppose there is sufficient slack time so that a machine shut down for setup would not be needed anyway. In addition, it is possible that there would be no work for the setup employee if he were not used for a particular job. However, the company would not dare lay him off because it needs him for other work on that same day. In this extreme case, the variable cost of a setup could be ignored.

Consideration of fixed and nonvariable costs can result in two different economic order quantities, one for short-term inventory management and another for long term. The former takes account only of cash out-of-pocket costs in calculating costs of possession and acquisition. The latter includes fixed and nonvariable costs. For example, a company's total cost of ordering may be $10 and total carrying cost may be 24 percent, but its cash out-of-pocket costs may be only $2 and 8 percent, respectively. Naturally, using out-of-pocket costs in the formulas gives answers that indicate economic order quantities different from those that result when total costs are used. Which answer is the right one? There is no general agreement on this. However, many cost accountants would say that total costs should be used when one is developing an overall, long-term inventory control program, while out-of-pocket costs give a more realistic EOQ when the formulas are being applied to individual purchases on a short-term or one-shot basis.

3. *Costly calculations.* It is no easy job to estimate cost of acquisition and cost of possession accurately. This requires hours of work by skilled cost accountants. Unfortunately, each major commodity group requires a different study, since the acquisition and possession costs of various commodities can vary widely. Actual calculation of EOQ can be time-consuming even when the simple formulas for steady usage (discussed earlier) are used. More elaborate formulas are even more expensive. In many cases, the cost of estimating cost of possession and acquisition and calculating EOQ exceeds the savings made by buying that quantity. Also, savings often are reduced because the company cannot buy the exact economic order quantity. If that quantity is 176 units, for example, it may have to buy the closest round lot—2 gross or 288 units, for example.

Applications for EOQ

Despite their weaknesses, economic order quantities can be applied to at least part of the purchases of almost every organization. They are particularly useful in companies equipped with electronic data processing equipment, which can eliminate much of the burden of calculation and also enables the use of more complex formulas.

EOQ formulas are particularly suitable for materials that have:

1. *Reasonably steady and predictable usage.* For example, a large insurance company with a stable work force and work load could profitably use EOQ formulas to buy supplies, but they would not be too useful in ordering materials for which demand is erratic.

2. *Relatively low cost.* A manufacturer might profitably use EOQ for thousands of different supply and maintenance items, which, in the aggregate, account for 10 to 15 percent of the purchases. But

the manufacturer would almost never use it for one or two key raw materials that might account for 50 percent of purchase volume. The high-volume items would get individual attention daily, and order quantities would reflect not only objective information (existing inventories, balances on order), but also subjective opinions on market sentiment, price expectations, and the like. Also, if a material is purchased in large quantities, it often is best controlled if regarded as a flow of material rather than as a series of separate order transactions. It thus becomes suitable for a periodic ordering system. The EOQ approach does not apply, since with periodic ordering the order quantity varies, while the review period between orders is kept constant.

3. Short lead time. EOQ formulas are best applied when there is little uncertainty about delivery promises. When lead time is long and delivery is less certain, the order quantity should be adjusted to reflect the materials manager's evaluation of the situation. For example, a company might wish to use EOQ formulas in ordering steel from a local warehouse that offers overnight delivery, but few companies would use them in ordering large quantities of steel directly from mills with a lead time of two to three months.

DETERMINING SAFETY STOCK

Average inventory levels are affected almost as much by safety stock as they are by order quantity. Safety stocks are necessary because it is not always possible to predict usages and lead times perfectly.

Table 10–2 shows a year's usage for a typical item. Total usage for the year was 468 units, or an average of 9 units per week. Actual weekly usage varied erratically from a low of 1 unit per week during the 8th week of the year to a peak of 14 units during the 44th week.

TABLE 10–2
Weekly demand for typical item

Week	Demand	Week	Demand	Week	Demand	Week	Demand
1	7	14	6	27	7	40	12
2	16	15	8	28	10	41	10
3	5	16	7	29	11	42	9
4	9	17	5	30	4	43	11
5	13	18	9	31	9	44	14
6	8	19	11	32	7	45	6
7	9	20	6	33	10	46	10
8	1	21	10	34	8	47	12
9	10	22	7	35	11	48	7
10	7	23	11	36	6	49	13
11	8	24	13	37	12	50	11
12	5	25	8	38	8	51	6
13	9	26	9	39	14	52	13

Lead time for this item is five weeks, so the order point would be 45 units (the average usage during the lead time) were there no safety stock. With a safety stock of 8 units, the order point would be 53 units. With this safety stock, as Figure 10–1 shows, there may have been one stockout during the year.

Applying probability theory

Probability of future stockouts with given safety stocks can be determined by analyzing usage history. The first step is to convert the

FIGURE 10–1
Inventory fluctuates in sawtooth pattern

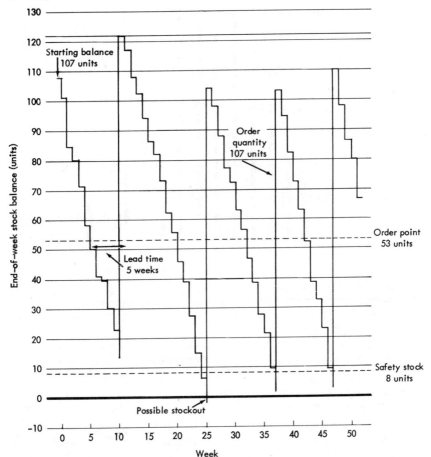

Inventory history of an item with the usage shown in Table 10–2, a lead time of five weeks, an order point of 53 units, and a safety stock of 8 units.

number of weeks' usage into percentages; that is, one week's usage is about 2 percent of a year's usage, two weeks' is about 4 percent, three weeks' is 6 percent, and so on. The next step is to make a chart in which one axis represents the demand in units and the other axis the percent of weeks in which there was this demand.

Figure 10–2 shows a chart for the data listed in Figure 10–1. Since one unit of usage occurred during a single week of the year, the chart

FIGURE 10–2
Lead-time demand follows Poisson distribution

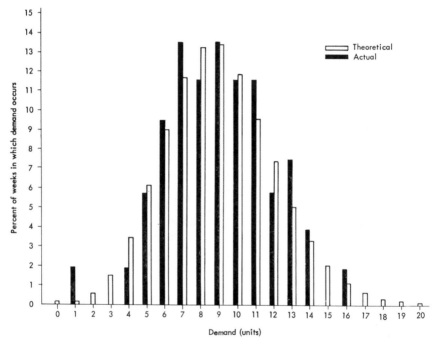

Comparison of actual distribution of demand for an item having the usage history illustrated in Table 10–2, with theoretical distribution based on Poisson distribution.

shows, for example, that weekly demand was one unit for 2 percent of the year (i.e., about 1 week out of 52); four units per week for another 2 percent of the year; and so on. When actual data is plotted in this fashion, as it is in Figure 10–2, the result is a chart that closely resembles a Poisson distribution, which is also shown in Figure 10–2. This makes it possible to calculate the probability of a stockout with considerable precision, since the characteristics of the Poisson curve are known.

Simplifying assumptions. Real-life inventory managers make other simplifying assumption to make their jobs even easier; they use the normal curve to approximate the Poisson distribution.[2] This assumption makes it possible to apply all the principles learned in an elementary statistics course.[3] Standard deviation can be calculated for each distribution and used to measure the dispersion of the occurrences.

We know, for example, that the distribution in Figure 10–2 has a mean value of 9 units per week or 45 units during the five-week lead time. Suppose, for convenience, that the standard deviation of this distribution is five units. Two standard deviations, therefore, are 10 units. We know from memory that when we move two standard deviations away from the mean of a normal curve we include approximately 95 percent of the area of the curve.[4] That is, 95 percent of all occurrences will have values that fall within two standard deviations of the mean value. Therefore, if the mean is 45 and two standard deviations are equal to 10 units, 95 percent of all occurrences will have values that are at least 35 units and no more than 55 units. The other 5 percent of the values that fall outside the limits of two standard deviations are either less than 35 or more than 55. Since the normal curve is symmetrical, usage is greater than 55 units 2.5 percent of the time and less than 35 units the other 2.5 percent. But, of course, a company would only be interested in periods when it is in danger of running out of stock. This happens only when average lead-time usage is greater than 45 units. Thus, with a safety stock equal to two standard deviations or ten units, it would be protected against stockouts 97.5 percent of the time.

As long as the lead-time usage pattern is almost normally distributed, the company can easily calculate the level of protection it would get with various safety stocks. For example, 15 units of safety stock would give the equivalent of three standard deviations of protection, limiting stockouts to less than 1 percent of all occurrences. Conversely, one standard deviation of protection would embrace only about 68 percent of the normal curve, and roughly 32 percent of the occurrences would fall outside these limits. However, only half of these occurrences would represent usages greater than the mean, so it would expect stockouts on about 16 percent (half of a 32 percent) of its reorders.

Thus, it is easy to see that as long as demand is normally distributed,

---

[2] In practice, the two look almost alike. The Poisson distribution resembles a normal curve whose distribution is skewed slightly to the right. Students should note, however, that a Poisson distribution is *not* a normal curve, and one can be a working approximation of the other only in very special cases.

[3] If you haven't taken such a course, the discussion that follows is guaranteed to be confusing. But you can still use the safety stock formula introduced in this chapter without difficulty.

[4] And, if you can't remember, every statistics text has an appendix that includes a table of area under the normal curve from which you can get this information.

the amount of safety stock needed depends entirely on the standard deviation of average usage and the number of standard deviations of protection desire. This gives rise to the formula:

$$\text{Safety stock} = K\sigma_x,$$

where K is the number of standard deviations and σ_x is the standard deviation. If K is equal to 2, for example, and the standard deviation is 5 units, then you would get 97.5 percent protection against stockouts with a safety stock equal to 10 units, as in the example.

This formula can be simplified even further by using the square root of the mean lead-time usage as a substitute for the standard deviation.[5] This eliminates the tedious calculation of the standard deviation with the formula

$$\sigma_x = \sqrt{\frac{\Sigma(X - \bar{X})^2}{N}}.$$

Our revised working formula becomes simply:

$$\text{Safety stock} = K \sqrt{\text{Average demand during lead time.}}$$

We then construct a table of K values like that in Table 10–3. The combination of "acceptable average number of years between stockouts" and "order quantity in months' supply" gives us the value of K that is appropriate to an ordering and stockout policy. For example, suppose that a company is willing to suffer one stockout every ten years and that order quantity is equal to a three-month supply. Thus, it orders four times per year or 40 times in ten years and is willing to risk one stockout. This is a stockout rate of 2.5 percent ($\frac{1}{40} \times 100$). The table indicates that the appropriate K value is 1.96. That is, if safety stock is equal to 1.96 standard deviations,[6] usage will exceed the mean value plus the safety stock only 2.5 percent of the time.

Using the normal curve. We can now practice on a sample problem. Assume that a company is willing to run out of stock every two years (why it wants to take any risk at all is explained a little later). The item in the example (Figure 10–1 and 10–2) has an order quantity of 107 units and an annual usage of 468 units. Thus orders are placed approximately four times per year, and during the two-year period in

---

[5] This approximation and the others we have made are possible only because mathematical conclusions are only as reliable as their least reliable component. In the case of safety stock computations, this is most likely our underlying estimates of lead time and usage during that lead time. In making them, we assume that what has happened in the past will necessarily occur in the future. But, of course, lead times and usage are affected by many nonrandom factors that we may not be able to identify. Consequently, short-cut computation methods are a lesser error and we need not worry about assming that something which roughly resembles a Poisson distribution is normal and that the square root of the mean is the standard deviation. As long as the empirical formula works better than anything else available, the mathematical niceties can be overlooked.

[6] Which we rounded off into two standard deviations in the previous example.

TABLE 10-3
K factors for determining safety stock

Acceptable average number of years between stockouts	*Order quantity in months' supply*											
	1	*2*	*3*	*4*	*5*	*6*	*7*	*8*	*9*	*10*	*11*	*12*
20	2.64	2.39	2.24	2.13	2.04	1.96	1.89	1.83	1.78	1.73	1.69	1.64
15	2.54	2.29	2.13	2.01	1.92	1.83	1.76	1.70	1.64	1.59	1.55	1.50
12	2.46	2.20	2.04	1.92	1.82	1.73	1.66	1.59	1.53	1.48	1.43	1.38
10	2.39	2.13	1.96	1.83	1.73	1.64	1.57	1.50	1.44	1.38	1.33	1.28
9	2.36	2.09	1.92	1.79	1.68	1.59	1.52	1.45	1.38	1.33	1.27	1.22
8	2.31	2.04	1.86	1.73	1.63	1.53	1.45	1.38	1.32	1.26	1.20	1.15
7	2.26	1.98	1.80	1.67	1.56	1.47	1.38	1.31	1.24	1.18	1.12	1.07
6	2.20	1.92	1.73	1.59	1.48	1.38	1.30	1.22	1.15	1.09	1.02	0.97
5	2.13	1.83	1.64	1.50	1.38	1.28	1.19	1.11	1.04	0.97	0.90	0.84
4	2.04	1.73	1.53	1.38	1.26	1.15	1.05	0.97	0.89	0.81	0.74	0.67
3	1.92	1.59	1.38	1.22	1.09	0.97	0.86	0.76	0.67	0.59	0.51	0.43
2	1.73	1.38	1.15	0.97	0.81	0.67	0.55	0.43	0.32	0.21	0.10	0
1	1.38	0.97	0.67	0.43	0.21	0	0	0	0	0	0	0

Note: *K* factors used to calculate the safety stock needed to provide various levels of protection against stockout for items whose usage pattern is similar to a normal curve.

which it expects one stockout it risks a stockout eight times, when inventories drop below order point during the order lead-time period. So it expects that one inventory cycle in eight (12.5 percent, or 0.125) will result in a stockout.

With this probability, $K = 1.15$. We find this in Table 10–3 by looking up the value for an order quantity of three months and an average of two years between stockouts. Since lead time is equal to 45 units of usage, we substitute in our formula

$$\text{Safety stock} = 1.15 \sqrt{45} = 8.$$

With a safety stock of 8 units, the order point becomes $45 + 8$, or 53 units.

Cost of a stockout. Whether or not eight units is really the correct safety stock depends on whether or not the company can afford to run out of stock once every two years. To find this out, we must determine the cost of the safety stock. If each unit is worth $100, then safety stock increases inventory by $800. If carrying cost is 24 percent, the safety stock costs 24 percent of $800, or $192 per year, to maintain. We could, by similar calculations, determine the protection against stockout and cost of other safety stocks. For example, we could reduce probability of stockouts to one in every 20 years with a safety stock of 15 units. This would cost $350 a year to maintain. Thus, for an extra cost of $158 per year, stockout frequency could be reduced from once every two years to once every 20 years.

Which is the right safety stock? The answer would be fairly easy if a company could calculate precisely the effect of a stockout. Suppose, for example, that a stockout cost $1,000. If there were a stockout once every two years, the annual stockout cost would then be $500; if frequency were cut to once every 20 years, it would be $50. In this case, an extra $158 of inventory carrying cost would reduce average annual stockout cost by $450, and it would clearly pay to carry the extra safety stock.

Correct decision. In real life, the decision is not so easy to make. It depends on both intangible and tangible factors. Each company must study the variables and calculate its own costs. If a stockout costs only a few hours of expediting time to persuade a supplier to shorten lead time by a few days, it obviously pays to keep safety stocks low. If, on the other hand, it means loss of business on an important contract, it may pay to carry very high safety stocks. Materials managers also should consider the profitability of the item and its effect on overall production and customer goodwill when they estimate their willingness to risk a stockout.

In general, managements tend to overprotect themselves against stockouts. All too often they are unwilling to accept the idea that if they want tight inventory control they must be willing to risk an occasional stockout. It takes a courageous materials manager to risk running out of stock when he knows it pays to take the risk. When the stockout does occur, the boss is all too likely to think only of the immediate loss and forget the enormous gains that come from low safety stocks and close control.

Application to ABC control

Probability theory can be applied to ABC systems of control. Representative A, B, and C items are selected. Then cost of various levels of protection can be calculated, using the formula for safety stock, the table of K factors in Table 10–3, the value of the item, and the carrying cost. Costs of each item can be averaged to get a representative cost of a certain level of protection for the inventory class. Each calculation is then plotted, and the final result is a chart resembling that in Figure 10–3, which is based on a carrying cost of 24 percent. Note that if management decides it is willing to risk a stockout once every five years on all items in inventory, it incurs the following costs:

	Investment in safety stocks	Carrying cost of safety stocks
A items	$ 620,000	$148,800
B items	450,000	108,000
C items	320,000	76,800
Total	$1,390,000	$333,600

With the ABC approach it is possible to get both greater overall protection against stockouts and lower carrying costs. For example, suppose that management is willing to accept the risk of a stockout once a year on A items, once every five years on B items, and once every ten years on C items. Using Figure 10–3, we see that the following costs will be incurred:

	Probable interval between stockouts (years)	Investment in safety stock	Carrying cost of safety stock
A items	1	$ 250,000	$ 60,000
B items	5	450,000	108,000
C items	10	390,000	93,600
Total		$1,090,000	$261,600

In this case, the ABC approach permits inventories to be reduced by $300,000 (from $1,390,000 to $1,090,000) and carrying costs are cut by $72,000 per year. Risk of stockout also is reduced. Protection on C items, which comprise 70 percent of the number of items in inventory, is doubled. Protection on B items is unchanged. Only the A items, comprising 10 percent of the total, are more vulnerable to stockout. Since these items get close control anyway—because they represent 70 percent of the inventory investment—their low safety stocks need not pose insurmountable problems.

FIGURE 10–3
ABC analysis of safety stock costs

Application of critical level

Probabilistic determination of safety stocks is quite practical with an inventory system that is completely manual. The inventory manager simply calculates order points using the "magic numbers" and formula shown in Table 10–3. The system will work well especially if the low-value "C" items get a fat safety stock and the "A" items are "eyeballed" by a stores clerk at regular intervals.

With EDP, it becomes practical to make the system more complicated. The first complication can be likened to a traffic light. A red-green system is pretty much what we have described so far. Before inventory reaches reorder point, the green light is on. We do nothing. When reorder point is reached, the red light flashes and we reorder. As long as lead-time usage falls within the maximum we have set with our order point, the reordering process is routine. In a real-life system, we would probably set fairly generous order points to take care of unanticipated delays or usage.

"Yellow" signal. Our system becomes more sophisticated but still practical for manual control if we introduce a third "signal" that, in effect, says "caution." This signal would flash at some predetermined level about the order point. Its meaning: inventory is close to reorder; if there seems to be some problem or if it is convenient, go ahead and reorder. Otherwise, do nothing.

For example, suppose that an item has estimated lead-time usage of 100 units. The standard deviation of the lead-time demand is assumed to be 10. We want 99+ percent protection against stockouts so we allow for a safety stock of 30 units and set our order point at 130 units. We might then set our intermediate critical point at 150 units. With manual control, the clerk would simply observe when the critical stage is reached, noting whether usage seemed to be running ahead of expectations or was just about what would be expected. If it were convenient to do so, the item might be reordered at this time—especially if it was low in value or other items from the same supplier were being reordered. Otherwise, the clerk would take no action. Use of an intermediate critical level would probably have some adverse effect on administrative costs. If order points were not cut slightly, it would also cause inventories to creep up since at least some items would be ordered before they actually reached reorder point. On the other hand, it should reduce stockouts and if order points are adjusted downward slightly to reflect the lower stockout risk, there need be no increase in inventory.

EDP application. Some EDP inventory control "packages" automatically report both critical level and reorder point. In this case, the actual decision making by materials management would be similar to that with the manual system described above. However, the computer is able to do even more. It can also compare the date at which the critical level is actually reached for a particular cycle with the normal date at which that level should be reached. If the difference lies outside the range expected with routine fluctuations in usage, the computer could then figuratively wave a red flag.

Suppose, for example, that the item with the lead-time usage of 100 units has an expected usage of 100 units per month and, of course, total lead time is therefore one month. Purchase quantity is 200 units and there were 100 units on hand when the last order was delivered. Thus, we start the cycle with 300 units on hand. We have set our critical level (arbitrarily) at 150 units. Therefore, this will be reached after 150 units are withdrawn. If usage is normal, this will take two weeks. In such cases, the computer may simply ignore the critical level although the materials manager may intervene if there are problems with the supplier involved.

Now let's suppose that critical level is reached just one week after the cycle begins. Usage is apparently moving ahead at the rate 600 units per month instead of 100 units per month. If this trend continues, there is certain to be a stockout. The computer would estimate the probability that this is a nonrandom variation in usage. It would do this by estimating the standard deviation of the average usage for a single week. Let's suppose that the calculated standard deviation is exactly equal to our shortcut calculation that estimates the standard deviation to be the square root of the average demand. If average weekly usage is 25 units, the standard deviation is therefore $\sqrt{25} = 5$. If we set three standard deviation limits, we would assume that weekly usage should "always" be at least 10 units $(25 - 3 \times 5)$ and no more than 40 units $(25 + 3 \times 5)$. An actual usage of 150 units falls way outside these confidence limits. Therefore, we assume that usage is being influenced by nonrandom factors.

The computer figuratively waves a red flag. If this is a high-value "A" item, we would first investigate to find out what is happening. If it is a low-value "C" item being controlled as part of a huge inventory, the computer might simply reorder all by itself without any intervention by the manager.

The computer could also readily be ordered to take the opposite course. Let's suppose that usage falls from the old average of 100 units to 50 units per month. A system of exponential smoothing (as discussed in Chapter 9) would eventually cut the order point back to reflect the new usage. The job can be done more promptly if the computer notes that inventories are running down at half the expected rate and advises the inventory manager of this seeming nonrandom behavior.

CONTROL OF PERIODIC ORDERING

Quantitative techniques for controlling periodic ordering systems are similar to those used in order-point systems. Both compare cost of acquisition with cost of possession. The major difference is that order-point systems are governed by order quantities, while periodic systems are governed by order review periods.

Comparison with order point

EOQ and safety stock. Table 10–4 shows monthly demand for a purchased inventory item over a two-year period. During this period,

TABLE 10–4
Monthly demand for typical purchase

Month	Demand	Month	Demand	Month	Demand
1	6	9	0	17	5
2	2	10	3	18	6
3	4	11	7	19	5
4	6	12	9	20	8
5	12	13	7	21	9
6	5	14	3	22	4
7	6	15	9	23	3
8	8	16	10	24	7

total demand was 144 units, and average monthly demand was 6 units. Assume that procurement lead time is one month, carrying cost is 24 percent per year, ordering cost is $10, and unit price is $20. With a conventional *order-point* system, the economic order quantity would be calculated as follows:

$$\text{EOQ} = \sqrt{\frac{2 \times 72 \text{ units per year} \times \$10 \text{ per order}}{\$20 \text{ per unit} \times 0.24 \text{ per year}}} = 17 \text{ units.}$$

With an order quantity of 17 units and a usage of 72 items per year, a company would issue 42 orders over a ten-year period. Now assume that it is willing to risk a stockout once every ten years. This is roughly one order in 40 or 2.5 percent of all occurrences, representing a limit of two standard deviations, giving a K value of 1.96. We already know that average monthly usage is six units and lead time is one month.

Therefore, we can use the formula,

$$\text{Safety stock} = K \sqrt{\text{Average lead-time demand.}}$$

Substituting:

$$\text{Safety stock} = 2.0 \sqrt{6} = 5 \text{ units.}$$

The order point would therefore be set at 11 units—the safety stock of 5 units plus the lead-time usage of 6 units. If the company orders in lots of 17, inventory would fluctuate between an average high of 22 units and an average low equal to the 5-unit safety stock.

Periodic system. What would happen if we applied periodic control to the same item? Lead time continues to be one month and, of course, carrying cost and ordering cost remain 24 percent and $10, respectively. With periodic control, order quantity will vary with usage. But we must determine the most economic review period and safety stock.

We will start with review period and temporarily ignore the safety stock problem. A company would need no safety stock, of course, if it knew in advance what lead-time usage would be. So we will temporarily assume perfect knowledge that demand will follow precisely the pattern indicated in Table 10–4. We will also arbitrarily set the review period at two months.

The company would start a month prior to month 1 and order 8 units, which is exactly what is needed in months 1 and 2. In month 2, it would then order 10 units, satisfying demand for months 3 and 4. If we assume it will continue to follow this pattern of ordering every other month and we plot the results, we get a chart like that in Figure 10–4. The dashed lines in the chart indicate the balance that is both on hand and on order at any given time, while the solid line shows the amount actually on hand. For example, the solid line indicates that at the beginning of month 2, there were two units in stock. The broken line indicates that an order for 10 units was placed, bringing the balance on hand and on order up to 12 units.

With the two-month review period, the company would naturally order six times per year. Since it costs $10 to issue each order, annual ordering cost would therefore be $60. If we were plotting annual cost for various review periods, this $60 cost for a two-month period would become point *A*, as in Figure 10–5.

Now we can calculate carrying cost. During the two-year period plotted in Figure 10–8, the company issues 12 orders for a total of 144 units. Therefore, average order quantity is 144 ÷ 12, or 12 units. Average inventory is equal to one half of the average order quantity and is therefore six units (which is precisely what it would be with a comparable order-point system). Since unit price is $20, the value of this average inventory is 6 × $20, or $120 Carrying cost is 24 percent of $120, or $28,80 per year. This is plotted as point *B* on Figure 10–5.

FIGURE 10–4
Model of periodic ordering system

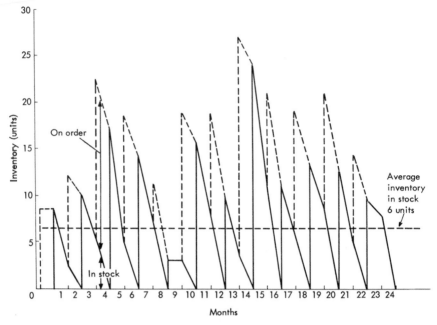

Inventory fluctuations of the item with the demand shown in Table 10–4, lead time of one month, and review period of two months. Solid line indicates inventory that is actually on hand, while broken line indicates total inventory on hand and on order. For example, at beginning of month 2, there are 2 pieces actually on hand and 12 pieces on hand and on order.

Optimum review period

Graphical analysis. Assume that we have gone through similar calculations for a number of other review periods and, in each case, plotted the appropriate annual ordering costs and carrying costs. We then wind up with two curves like the bottom two in Figure 10–5, which show ordering costs and inventory carrying costs for various review periods. The third curve in Figure 10–5 represents the sum of the other two curves. Thus, this curve represents total ordering costs and carrying cost for various review periods. It is plotted by simply adding together the appropriate ordering and carrying costs. For example, point *C* on the curve represents the sum of the $60 value of point *A* plus the $28.80 value of point *B*, giving a total annual cost of $88.80 with a review period of two months.

Review period formula. Inventory carrying costs steadily incrase as the review period is stretched out. Conversely, ordering costs steadily decline because fewer orders are issued as the review period in-

FIGURE 10–5
Graphic determination of EOQ

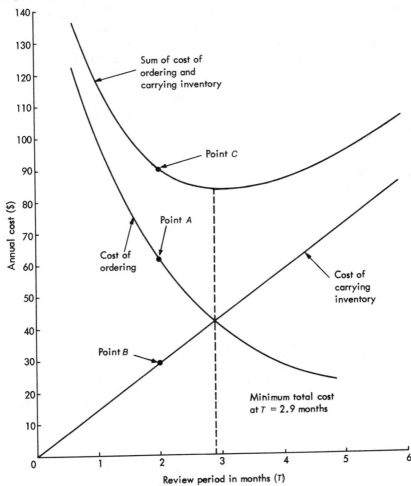

Optimum review period can be determined graphically by plotting total annual cost (purchase cost + ordering cost + carrying cost) for various review periods. It is just under three months for an item with annual usage of 72 units, unit price of $20, ordering cost of $10, and carrying cost of 24 percent.

creases. Total costs of ordering and carrying inventory first decline and then increase. Obviously, the ideal review period is that which occurs at the point of inflection of the curve. Visually, we can determine from Figure 10–5 that this is equal to about 2.8 months.

Of course, Figure 10–5 is valid only when unit price is $20 ordering cost is $10, carrying cost is 24 percent, and annual usage is 72 units. Other curves must be drawn to determine the optimum policy under other conditions. Fortunately for those who do not like to draw charts, the same problem can be solved mathematically, using differential calculus. The end product is a simple formula that makes it possible to calculate optimum review period for any ordering cost, annual usage, unit price, and carrying cost. Its only limitation is that, like the EOQ formula for order-point systems, usage must follow a reasonably regular pattern. The formula is:

$$T = \sqrt{\frac{288\ S}{ACI}},$$

where:

T = Review period (in months).
S = Variable cost of ordering (in dollars).
A = Annual usage (in units).
C = Unit cost (in dollars).
I = Annual carrying cost (as a decimal).

Using the data in the example, $S = \$10$, $I = 0.24$, $A = 72$, and $C = \$20$. Therefore $T = \sqrt{(288 \times 10)/(72 \times 20 \times 0.24)} = 2.9$ months, which is consistent with our graphic solution.

The optimum review period for an item can change. When sales are high, order quantities will be raised and average inventories will increase. If there is enough change, it may be necessary to reduce the review period between orders so as to have optimum costs. Similarly, the optimum review period is increased when sales fall. The point at which it pays to change can easily be calculated. If a company has two review periods, T_1 and T_2, the point of change comes when carrying cost and ordering cost for the two review periods are equal. Using our equations, this can be done as follows:

$$12\ S/T_1 + T_1\ ACI/24 = 12\ S/T_2 + T_2\ ACI/24.$$

Solving for AC, with the data in our example, we get:

$$AC = 288\ S/T_1 T_2 I.$$

Since $S = \$10$ and $I = 0.24$, then $AC = 12{,}000/T_1 T_2$. Again using the data in the example, $AC = \$6{,}000$ when $T_1 = 1$ and $T_2 = 2$; $\$2{,}000$ when $T_1 = 2$ and $T_2 = 3$; and so on. The result is the following table of optimum review periods for values of AC:

Value of annual use	Review period (months)
$6,001–up	1
2,001–6,000	2
1,001–2,000	3
601–1,000	4
401–600	5
Up to 400	6

Safety stocks

So far we have assumed that the company knows in advance what demand will be, so there has been no need for safety stocks. If demand is uncertain, however (as it almost always is in actual practice), it must protect against stockouts with safety stocks. In practice, most safety stocks used in periodic ordering systems are developed by trial and error. Fluctuations in lead-time usage are not genuinely random, and it may be incorrect to assume that usage follows a Poisson distribution, which, of course, is what we assumed when we developed the safety stock formula for order-point systems previously in this chapter. In many cases, however, these same basic assumptions can be made for a periodic-ordering system, and we can use a similar formula to determine safety stock. The major difference between the safety stock formula used for periodic systems is that the key variable is review period rather than order point or lead time. The formula for determining safety stock with a periodic ordering system is:

$$\text{Safety stock} = K \sqrt{\genfrac{}{}{0pt}{}{\text{Average usage during}}{\text{lead time} + \text{Review period}}}$$
$$\times \text{Average size of demand}.$$

Returning to the example illustrated in Table 10–4 and Figure 10–4, demand averages six units per month and lead time is one month. If the company uses a review period of three months, average

FIGURE 10–6
Periodic ordering with predictable pattern

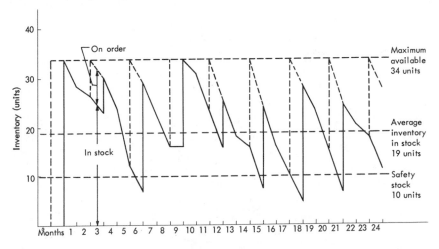

Inventory history of an item with usage history shown in Table 10–4, review period of three months, and order quantities equal to 34 units less whatever stock is already on hand when the order is placed.

344

demand during lead time plus review period is 24 units. From Table 10–3, we see that K is 1.96 if it wants to risk one stockout every ten years. Then, if all the demands are each one unit, we can substitute in our formula:

$$\text{Safety stock} = 1.96 \sqrt{24} \times 1 = 10 \text{ units.}$$

Order quantity then is equal to the safety stock of ten units plus the average demand during the lead time plus the review period of ten units *less* whatever units are available in stock at the time each order is being placed. Figure 10–6 shows how this system would have operated during the past two years, using a maximum of 34 (10 + 24) units.

Cases

CASE 10–1. EASTERN UNIVERSITY HOSPITAL

Ralph Galerneau, director of materials management of Eastern University Hospital, has a problem: despite considerable success in cutting inventories, his storage areas are so jammed that efficiency is being affected. The hospital is a 600-bed institution that is jammed into a plot of land in the older part of a large eastern city. The situation is certain to get even worse before it gets better. The hospital is in the midst of a major expansion program and, inevitably, purchases and withdrawals of supplies from inventory will increase and new items will probably have to be added to stocks.

The hospital will soon be opening a new $22 million day-care center that will draw its medical-surgical supplies from the same stores facilities that serve other buildings in the hospital complex. The main storeroom for medical-surgical supplies covers 4,620 square feet of floor space in the basement of one of the hospitals's older buildings. The materials management department has already made the aisles so narrow in this storage area that it is not only impossible to use modern materials handling equipment, but there is barely room for two persons to pass abreast of one another. Shelves extend from floor to ceiling and are usually jammed with material. It is necessary to rearrange material periodically simply to find space to store new shipments.

The materials management department also has available to it two other warehouse facilities which are not located on the hospital premises but are nearby. One of these facilities is rented for $354 per month and the other for $450. These facilities are used primarily for stationery and other supplies but are available for any overflow of medical-surgical supplies from the main storage area. However, not only is this extra storage space limited, but it is costly to transfer material from one storage area to another.

Total inventory of medical-surgical supplies is approximately $100,000 and considerable progress has been made in increasing inventory turnover to its current level of almost 15 times per year.

Galerneau is convinced that there is very little "fat" in this inventory. Physical counts are taken of each item every time it comes up for reorder and these are checked against the balances indicated by the computer. Furthermore, the computer selects 15 items at random once a month for an additional physical check. These periodic comparisons of actual physical balances with theoretical balances generally indicate there is relatively little room for further improvement.

The computer also produces a quarterly inventory aging report which indicates which items are slow moving and which are nonmoving. The latter are often sold back to the original supplier; otherwise, they are disposed of for the best price the purchasing department can obtain. Nonmoving items are no longer really a problem. The most recent report showed a balance of but $200.

Slow-moving items are inevitable because of both changing technology and changes in preferences of requisitioners. However, Galerneau doubts if any additional major improvements can be made in detecting such items and readjusting order points much more promptly than is already being done.

Physical congestion in the storage area is also reduced to an absolute minimum as a by-product of the materials management department's PAR delivery system. In order to reduce congestion in hospital corridors and elevators, supplies are delivered by materials management to the various nursing stations between 11 P.M. and 7 A.M. This not only speeds up the process, thereby cutting labor cost, but causes most withdrawals from stores to be made during periods of the day when stocks are not being replenished with new purchases from the hospital's suppliers.

While Galerneau would love to build a new facility with up-to-date materials-handling equipment, his plan is not without obstacles to be overcome in convincing the hospital administration and trustees that it absolutely must have one. The hospital's cash position is tight. Its borrowing power is also limited. If it did borrow, the interest rate would probably be at least 9 percent.

Land would be a problem even if the hospital were willing to construct a new stores building. The ideal facility would interconnect with other buildings in the hospital complex, and there simply is no convenient space available. Nor can additional land be purchased easily. The hospital premises are surrounded by old, privately owned buildings on small plots of land. Since the hospital is a private institution, it cannot acquire surrounding property by eminent domain. This makes it difficult, if not impossible, to acquire major plots of adjacent land rapidly, even at inflated prices.

Other hospitals have "solved" the problem of inadequate stores areas by leasing a central warehouse at some distance from the hospital. The cost of this space might be $3 per square foot per year. In addition, the hospital would have to invest in at least one truck whose operating cost, including drivers, might run as high as $15,000 per year.

Galerneau is presently pondering whether or not he should recommend some new stores facility to the hospital's administration and trustees. He has discovered that repairs, maintenance, and operation of the building in which the present storeroom is located run about $124,000 per year. This building has 55,000 square feet of floor space, of which 4,600 square feet in the basement are used to store medical-surgical supplies. No one really knows how much of the total expenses of $124,000 for the building should be allocated to materials management, although accountants tend to allocate such costs on the basis of square feet of space utilized. It should be noted, however, the basement space in a commercial building is always cheaper than space above ground.

The hospital calculates depreciation on its equipment to help determine which costs are reimbursable by Blue Cross–Blue Shield and other agencies but does not take depreciation into account on its older facilities. As a nonprofit organization, the hospital pays no taxes but does pay insurance premiums which, allocated to materials management, apparently amount to about $430 per year.

Obsolescence and shrinkage are reduced substantially as a result of the extremely close control that is maintained over inventories. No estimate has ever been made, but losses are probably less than 1 percent.

At present, both order points and purchase quantities are determined largely by judgment. The former is determined primarily by lead time and past usage and the latter by price breaks as well as by a desire to achieve maximum inventory turnover. Since the computer now makes it feasible to perform the needed calculations, Galerneau has been considering adoption of some sort of economic ordering procedure. He does not actually know the marginal costs of ordering and storing material, but the hospital's accounting system does provide average cost data. In addition to the overall costs of repairs and maintenance to the building in which it is located, the stores activity has an annual budget of $113,971, of which $105,551 is represented by salaries for 11 employees. The related receiving function, which occupies 1,675 square feet of loading dock and "break-out" area adjacent to the 4,600 square feet main stores area, has a total budget of $38,000, of which $34,000 is represented by salaries for four employees. However, only about 15 percent of the 38,000 receivals that are made each year are for medical-surgical stores. The others are either noninventory or go to other storage areas in the hospital complex.

The purchasing department has total annual direct costs of $75,233, of which $66,275 is payroll and, as with receiving, approximately 15 percent of all purchase orders issued are applicable to medical-surgical stores. Similarly, accounts payable, with six employees, has total annual direct costs of $45,000 and, of course, 15 percent of the orders it processes are applicable to items carried in medical-surgical stores.

Questions

1. Does Galerneau have sufficient information on carrying cost and ordering cost to use EOQ formulas?
2. Suppose that Galerneau's rough estimate of $500,000 for a new stores building turns out to be correct and that land adjacent to the hospital's other buildings becomes available. How would he go about justifying a request to the hospital's administrator and trustees for funds to construct the building?

CASE 10-2. OWEN ELECTRIC COMPANY (B)

Applying formulas to periodic ordering systems

Owen Electric Company (see Case 7–1) controls inventories of hardware used on its assembly line with periodic ordering. Weekly reports from stock checkers are sent to appropriate buyers, who post them to their records and periodically issue orders to bring stocks up to the required balance.

For example, the company uses about 10,000 pieces of a small screw machine part each month. On the 15th of each month, the buyer looks at the latest stock report and issues an order for a quantity sufficient to bring the inventory balance up to about 15,000 pieces when the order is delivered. Thus, if the stock checker's report indicates an inventory of 12,000 pieces and estimated usage during the 30-day lead time is 10,000 pieces, the buyer will place an order for 13,000 pieces. Should the next month's inventory rise or the usage forecast drop, he would adjust the order quantity accordingly. For example, he would order only 9,000 pieces with a 30-day usage projection for 8,000 pieces and a current stock of 14,000 pieces.

The unit price of the part purchased in quantities of 5,000 to 10,000 is $0.10. But the supplier is willing to cut the price to $0.095 if he gets orders that average 20,000 pieces. Owen Electric's controller estimates that it costs $10 to make each purchase, and the carrying cost of inventory is 24 percent.

Questions

1. Should Owen Electric take advantage of the supplier's offer?
2. What is the company's most economic order period if the supplier's price does not vary with order quantity?

11

Sourcing: Make, buy, or lease

Theoretically, a company has a choice of three basic decisions in deciding how to produce a new product. It can:

1. Purchase the product complete from a contract manufacturer.
2. Purchase some components and materials and manufacture and assemble the balance in its own plant.
3. Manufacture the product completely, starting with the extraction of basic raw materials.

In practice, almost no companies can seriously consider the third alternative. Even relatively simple products require an amazing diversity of materials in various stages of fabrication. The largest, most highly integrated companies rely on outside suppliers for at least some components and materials.[1] And some companies choose the first alternative and obtain a new product completely from an outside supplier. They usually do this either because they are a merchandising or engineering organization with no manufacturing facilities or because the product is not suited to their facilities. Sears, Roebuck's purchases of its own brands of appliances are a good example of the former; a business machine maker's purchase and resale to customers of special forms to use in its machines is an example of the latter.

---

[1] For example, the U.S. Steel Corporation spends about 40 percent of its sales dollar for outside purchases, even though it has completely integrated steel-making facilities and also mines its iron ore, coal, and limestone. Ford Motor Company makes all major parts of its automobiles and much of the raw materials used in making them, including steel, glass, and so on. Yet Ford spends more than half of its sales dollar on outside suppliers—about twice as much as it spends on wages and salaries.

348

The general rule, however, is that an organization will make some things and buy others. This applies even to service organizations. Large hospitals, for example, often operate their own print shops and laundries but are purchasers of food, drugs, and numerous other items. But service organizations and manufacturers sometimes generate their own electric power. They may even carry on service or manufacturing activities having nothing to do with their basic business, either because they happen to have the raw material or because the activity simply was not being performed by anyone else.

For manufacturers, make-or-buy decisions must constantly be made. No manufacturer makes all of his own raw materials, so it is largely a matter of deciding at which stage of fabrication a component should be purchased. The company may buy a component complete from an outside supplier, buy it semifinished, or buy the raw material.

MAKE-OR-BUY CRITERIA

Companies usually prefer to do their own fabricating. They buy only raw materials or semifinished parts in cases where the following is true of the finished component:

1. Can be made more cheaply by the company than by outside suppliers, or might require the company to rely on a limited number of vendors for its supply.
2. Is vital to the company's product and requires extremely close quality control.
3. Is readily manufactured with the company's existing facilities and is similar to other items with which the company has had considerable manufacturing experience.
4. Requires extensive investment in facilities that are not already available at supplier plants.
5. Has a demand that is both relatively large and stable.

Companies will usually buy a finished component from an outside supplier when:

1. They do not already have facilities to make it, and there are more profitable opportunities for investing company capital.
2. Existing facilities can be used more economically to make other components.
3. The skills of company personnel are not readily adapted to the making of the component.
4. Patents or other legal barriers prevent the company from making the component.
5. Demand for the component is either temporary or seasonal.

6. The supplier can utilize economically specialized equipment to make the product by grouping orders from several customers, and demand is not so great that any individual customer could economically utilize this equipment.

Other factors. Some companies, by tradition, prefer to make almost every component of their products. Others prefer to buy as much as possible from outside suppliers. In general, an aggressive company in an industry that is expanding very rapidly with many technological changes (e.g., electronics) will prefer to buy many of its components from outside suppliers. In such industries, the company has many opportunities to employ its capital profitably through horizontal diversification—expanding its line of finished products.

A company in a stable or declining industry, on the other hand, has fewer attractive opportunities to invest its capital in expanding sales of its end products. It will be attracted, almost by default, to integration—making a bigger share of its sales dollar in its own manufacturing plants—in order to boost profits.

For example, the major auto companies have steadily increased the percentage of product that they make in their own plants. In most cases, they have been tempted to make the items that yield high profits to suppliers. Both Ford Motor Company and Chrysler Corporation have built plants to manufacture automobile glass, but it is no coincidence that neither has shown any signs of building textile mills to make upholstery cloth for cars. Efficient glass producers earn about a 20 percent return on their investment, while in the highly competitive textile industry even efficient producers consider themselves fortunate if they average a 10 percent return.

A company may be effectively prevented from making an item by its own labor relations policies. If it is extremely generous with wages and fringe benefits for its employees, there will be some industries where it simply is not competitive even if its methods are better than those of potential competitors. For this reason, if no other, a high-wage employer like IBM or Eastman Kodak could probably never earn even modest profits in the low-wage textile industry. And it is far cheaper for the highly unionized auto companies to buy certain items from nonunion suppliers than to attempt to make the same items themselves.

Cost comparison. When a company decides to make an item that it has been buying, it always eliminates the supplier's sales expenses and usually eliminates some freight costs. If its production costs are identical to those of the supplier, the company also gains the supplier's profit and usually at least part of the fixed overhead expenses incurred by the supplier.

Suppose a supplier had the following unit cost on a component:

Direct material	$0.20	
Direct labor	0.10	
Variable overhead	0.12	
Direct cost		$0.42
Fixed overhead	$0.08	
Manufacturing cost		0.50
Sales expense	$0.02	
Administrative expense	0.01	
Total cost		0.53
Profit	$0.06	
Supplier's price		0.59
Inbound freight	$0.01	
Buyer's cost		$0.60

If a company were to make this item rather than buy it, it could conceivably reduce its costs from 60 cents per unit to 42 cents. This might be true if the company has idle equipment that could be used to make the part and if its only additional overhead expenses would be covered by the 12 cents allowance for variable overhead in the unit-cost estimate. Even if the company had to invest in additional facilities and incur normal fixed overhead, its cost would presumably be only 50 cents per unit if it could use the facilities as economically as the supplier.

Savings sometimes illusory. Companies often are confronted with opportunities to make rather than buy that yield theoretical savings comparable to these. In some cases they try to take advantage of them. But they often continue to buy the item even though they may be capable of making it. In most cases it is not to their advantage to make the item for a number of reasons, including:

1. The company's direct costs may be substantially higher than the direct costs of the supplier. The supplier presumably is one of the most efficient producers of the item and has achieved his existing costs only after management and labor have acquired considerable experience. And even if the buyer can produce as efficiently as the supplier, his saving will be reduced by start-up cost. No company can immediately produce a new item at peak efficiency; costs on initial production runs are always well above standard.

2. A company has less flexibility with "make" items. It can easily change suppliers if it wishes to redesign the item so that it makes use of different materials. This can be expensive if the company has invested in equipment to make the item. Similarly, the company can exploit changes in market conditions on "buy" items and take advantage of lower prices offered by suppliers eager for new business.

3. Savings in overhead often are illusory. Fixed overhead rarely rises immediately after a company starts using idle facilities to make a part it has previously purchased, but eventually it creeps up. When

business expands to capacity operations, fixed overhead increases and must be absorbed by each component that is produced. Similarly, if business slumps, fixed overhead is underabsorbed, and unit cost rises. For example, the eight-cent allowance for fixed overhead in the preceding cost breakdown is valid only for a given volume. If business dropped 50 percent, the allowance would have to be doubled, to 16 cents. If the part were purchased, an outside supplier would also have difficulty absorbing fixed overhead when volume declines. But it would not dare try to recoup the added unit costs by increasing prices. In fact, competition might become so intense during a slump that price cutting would be required.

4. There may be better profit opportunities in other areas. Each "make" part requires some investment in facilities, inventories, and top-management time. Even though this investment is profitable, the company may be able to earn even bigger profits by using its resources to expand the business it knows best—its end-product line.

Buy instead of make. Often companies decide to buy items that they have been making. In some cases they even dispose of plant and equipment used to make the item. Such decisions are almost always economic if the supplier's price is lower than the company's direct cash cost of making the part. Sometimes they are worthwhile even if the company has been making substantial profits on the item, for it may be able to use its resources still more profitably on other items.

Similarly, when a company's facilities are temporarily taxed beyond capacity, it may decide to buy part of its needs from an outside supplier. For example, a company with a captive foundry may temporarily buy part of its castings from outside suppliers when business is exceptionally good. Even if the prices of the purchased castings are higher than the company's own costs, the company may not wish to increase its investment in foundry facilities when the need for them may be temporary. When business drops off, the company can return to making all its own castings and need no longer rely on an outside supplier.

Companies that follow this practice may incur the resentment of suppliers who get orders from them when business is good and they need them least and then lose the orders when business is bad and they need them most. Suppliers may not cooperate when the company wants to subcontract again. In fact, a supplier's long-term business strategy would take into account how "permanent" are its positions with particular customers. Those that are strictly "fair-weather friends" would be treated as marginal during periods of booming business. The most successful "rationing" device during such periods is to charge higher prices to the customers that are probably not going to stick with you anyway and try to build lasting relationships with the customers who will be around when there is a recession. Ethical purchasing managers never try to convince suppliers that business is permanent when they know it will move back into the shop as soon as capacity is available to handle it.

Split items. A company may simultaneously make and buy certain materials and components. For example, Ford Motor Company makes part of the steel for its cars in its own steel mills and buys the balance from independent steel producers such as National Steel Corporation. When a company does this, it enjoys most of the advantages of making without losing the advantages of buying. Its profits from making the item can be calculated precisely because there is an exact market price from the outside supplier. The company is protected, at least partly, against strikes at the supplier's plant or other supply failures. It enjoys the benefits of both its own and the supplier's improvements in technology. In addition, when a company has its own facilities to make an item, a supplier may hesitate to increase prices because the costs of production can be precisely estimated and the captive plant stands ready to take a bigger share of the business if it becomes profitable to do so.

A company often can reduce its average costs by buying part of its requirements and making the balance. The captive facility then can operate near capacity almost regardless of business conditions. When business is good, the supplier may make 50 percent and the captive plant 50 percent. When business is bad, the captive plant's production remains steady despite the decline in demand, and its share may increase to 80 percent or 90 percent, while the outside supplier feels the brunt of the business decline. His share drops to 10 or 20 percent of the business, and the actual output drops by an even greater amount. Needless to say, suppliers are not happy when they are asked to bear more than their share of a business slump, and sometimes they demand a contract providing that the percentage split be fixed regardless of general business conditions.

CONTROLLING CAPTIVE ITEMS

When a company makes and buys the same item, it knows precisely how competitive its manufacturing operations are. Ideally, every company would like the cost of each of its operations to be as low as those of the most efficient outside producer. The materials manager can render the company a real service by devoting a substantial amount of effort to locating shop items whose costs are higher than those of leading suppliers.

Stimulate improvement. When captive manufacturing operations are not subjected to outside competition with frequent make-or-buy decisions, they may become complacent and inefficient. Their methods many not be up to date; they may be lagging in productivity, and their costs may be much higher than those of efficient outside producers. When this happens, the company's overall competitive strength can dwindle.

Suppose, for example, that one company making finished electric refrigerators were to attempt to make all of its components from basic raw materials, while a competitor elected to manufacture parts only when it could do so at substantially lower cost than it could obtain from outside suppliers. If the captive manufacturing operations of the integrated company had costs that were higher than the market prices paid for parts by its competitor, then its total product costs would be correspondingly higher. Its profits would be less despite its greater investment in facilities that would be needed to make all components.

All well-managed companies try to keep their manufacturing facilities up to date. They also try to keep costs under control with budgets and the like. If the component itself is not sold directly to a customer but is incorporated into one of the company's products, however, it never faces the acid test of market competition. The materials manager can help manufacturing simulate such competition by periodically reviewing various items made in captive operations to make certain that their production costs do not exceed market prices.

Decentralize buying.   Big companies go even further. They have decentralized organization structures in which one division may sell all of its output to one or more of the company's other divisions. For example, Ford Motor Company's Engine & Foundry Division sells its auto engines to the Ford Division, which is responsible for assembling cars and trucks.

In such a decentralized structure, the buying division (which is the unit responsible for the end product) treats the manufacturing division as much as possible as an outside supplier in order to simulate conditions in a competitive market. In some cases it can do this rather directly. For example, if the supplying division makes a product that the using division is also buying from an outside supplier, the market price is known. Similarly, if the manufacturing division makes something for which there is a published market price (steel or crude oil) it is not difficult to set a realistic market price.

Simulate competition.   A problem arises when the captive operation makes a product that is unique and for which quotations are not readily available from outside suppliers. For example, the Fisher Body Division of General Motors makes body stampings that are shared by all GM cars. No outside supplier is equipped to make these bodies in the quantities required by General Motors, nor would it ever seriously consider buying any major part of its body stamping needs from an outside supplier because of its enormous investment in Fisher Body's facilities. Under such circumstances, the best the purchasing manager can do is to simulate market conditions for the captive operation. She can vigorously negotiate with the captive plant to get it to price its output at a level she feels would be competitive if alternate suppliers were available. In negotiating, she uses all of the cost analysis techniques that will be discussed in succeeding chapters.

Some purchasing managers spend a great deal of time on intracompany purchases from manufacturing plants. Why do they go to the trouble? After all, if a buying division persuades a supply division of the same company to reduce its prices by $1, the two divisions are just trading dollars. The buying division's profits go up $1 because of the lower price; the supplying division's profits decline $1. The net effect on overall company profit is nil.

Realistic profits.   One reason big companies go to such trouble is that they feel their manufacturing divisions will be more efficient in the long run if they are subject to as much competitive pressure as the materials manager can exert. Another equally important reason is that a company can calculate realistic profits for an operation only if its output is priced at market levels. If a plant whose prices are competitive does not earn adequate profits, either its management is at fault or it is in the wrong business. With realistic profit figures, a company can measure its managers' performance and also can direct new investments into areas that yield maximum profits.

Suppose, for example, that a television manufacturer makes his own cabinets. Each television set costs $135 to make, and the company sells them to distributors for $150. Therefore the company makes $15 profit on each TV set, or 10 percent on sales.

If the company's cost of making each cabinet is $13.50, how much profit is the company earning by making its own cabinets? An amateur accountant might say that since the company is earning a 10 percent profit on each set it must automatically be earning 10 percent on each major component. But the fact is that it would be impossible to say whether the company's cabinets operation is profitable or not, since the company sells no cabinets. Possibly the company is producing a cabinet worth $30 for a cost of only $13.50. In that case, it should expand its cabinet line to supply outside companies and go out of the TV set business itself. Or, as is more likely, the cabinet that costs $13.50 may be available from a specialist producer for $14. In that case, the cabinets, with a return of less than 4 percent on sales, are eating into the company's profit margin. If the company can dispose of its cabinet plant and invest the proceeds in a more profitable part of the business, it can boost its overall profit margin.

Opportunity cost.   The materials manager is the natural link between a company's own manufacturing operations and competitive operations of outside suppliers. Ideally, he should be constantly prodding manufacturing to make items he is currently buying, if these items are potentially profitable. At the same time he should be working to take items out of manufacturing that do not belong there.

The materials manager's basic yardstick for make-or-buy analysis is the company's own opportunity cost of capital. This, of course, represents the return that the company should be able to earn on new investments. For example, a company that consistently earns a 15 percent return on its net assets probably has an opportunity cost of capital of about 15 percent.

The higher the opportunity cost, the more limited the company's ability to make things instead of buying them. For example, a highly profitable company with an opportunity cost of 30 percent or more would find it profitable to buy almost every component of its end product. The reason, of course, is that it is impossible to earn this sort of return in most businesses, and the company's own suppliers would have to settle for lower returns. Conversely, a company in a declining industry with declining opportunity costs and huge cash flow might be a lot less fussy and settle for a lot less.

LEASING

Companies with very high opportunity costs of capital often prefer to lease many of their assets. For example, a company that earns 20 percent on its own capital might prefer to lease a fleet of cars for its salespeople rather than buy them. The leasing firm might be willing to settle for a 10 percent return on capital. Consequently, even if the company could buy, sell, and maintain cars as efficiently as the leasing firm, its opportunity cost of capital would be so much higher that it would prefer to delegate the job to the leasing firm.

Almost any product can be leased. Transportation equipment of all types is especially popular because credit risk is greatly reduced on a product that can easily be taken away from the lessee and is readily marketable. However, many types of specialized machinery and equipment are leased as well as buildings.

Advantages. Companies that lease do so both to avoid the responsibility of ownership and to make capital available for other purposes. They prefer to lease certain highly specialized types of equipment because they need not worry about its maintenance or possible obsolescence; all they need do is operate the equipment, with none of the responsibilities of owning it. In addition, a company gets some tax advantage by leasing. Rent can always be charged entirely as an operating expense and thus is completely deductible from taxable income. On the other hand, if a company owns equipment, it must capitalize its cost. Depreciation charges deductible as operating expense must be spaced over the life of the equipment.

In some cases the lessor may be willing to pay for the lessee's tax privileges. Capital-intensive industries like airlines frequently generate more investment tax credit and accelerated depreciation than they can profitably use in reducing their own tax liability. One solution is to sell new equipment to third-party lessors who can make better use of the investment tax credits. The airline then leases back the equipment and enjoys the advantage of a financing scheme that does not increase the amount of debt on its own balance sheet.

Except when there is an extraordinary tax break, the lessee must pay for these advantages. The rent that is paid not only includes an adequate amount to cover probable maintenance, depreciation, taxes, and other expenses but also a healthy profit for the lessor. Typically, a lessor might allow for a 10 percent return on the investment in calculating the rent. The return would be higher yet on equipment on short-term lease that is subject to high obsolescence, and it would be lower on buildings with very long-term leases.

Why then do some insurance companies and banks prefer to lease electronic data processing equipment when they are eager to make an investment with a guaranteed return of 10 to 11 percent? Such institutions may not want to own this equipment. Maintenance is much too costly and too highly specialized for them. When equipment is leased, the supplier must fix it if it breaks down. In addition, EDP equipment is subject to rapid obsolescence. The lessee can almost always change over to the newest model with greater ease and less cost than the owner of obsolescent equipment. Companies also lease simply to get capital to use for other purposes. They may sell their own facilities and then lease them back again. Until a few years ago, leasing was also a type of loan that was not shown on the balance sheet. As a result, investors were sometimes deceived into believing that the company was in stronger financial condition than it actually was. New accounting rules now require that leases be capitalized, eliminating this advantage.

In the past, companies could also reduce financing costs substantially through sale and leaseback from municipalities in which their facilities were located. In order to encourage the company to build its plant and provide employment, a city would become legal owner of the plant, financing it with tax-free municipal bonds issued on the strength of the company's long-term lease of the facilities. This permitted the company to get financing for perhaps 4 or 5 percent instead of the much higher interest rate that would be charged if the financing were carried out through conventional channels. This tax loophole is currently available only for pollution-control projects.

Decisions to make, buy, or lease affect both manufacturing and materials activities. They should not be made without the approval of both the manufacturing manager and the materials manager. Other departments also help shape make-or-buy decisions, which are among the most basic decisions in the management of a business. Once the decision is made to buy, however, the materials manager and his or her buyers become the dominant factors in selecting the supplier. The next three chapters discuss the buying process in detail.

Case _____

CASE 11–1. MIRACLE TOY CORPORATION

Make-or-buy decision on corrugated cartons

The Miracle Toy Corporation is one of the largest manufacturers in its field. It has been consistently profitable since it was founded by Hubert Mack in 1936. The Mack family still owns more than 60 percent of the company's stock. For this reason, dividend policy has been extremely conservative. A dividend payout averaging no more than 33 percent of earnings has been more than adequate for the family's needs. The company has been able to finance all of its growth internally, and it currently has the most up-to-date facilities in the industry.

Despite heavy expenditures for plant and equipment, the cash flow from earnings and depreciation has been so great that the company's financial position is very strong (see balance sheet in Exhibit 1). In fact, Helen Carlson, the company's treasurer, is becoming concerned lest the U.S. Internal Revenue Service charge that the company has been accumulating cash it does not really need by holding back on dividends to wealthy stockholders, who are subject to extremely high surtax rates on their personal income. Carlson feels that it is in the best interests of the company to have available a healthy reserve in cash or marketable securities to protect the company during a business downturn and also for any profitable investments the company might wish to make.

Robert Axelrod, manager of the company's manufacturing engineering department, thinks he may have a solution to the excess cash problem. He proposes that the company invest in a small plant to produce cartons.

The company currently spends about $800,000 per year for various types and sizes of cartons. At present, it buys them from three suppliers. Two of these suppliers are divisions of much larger corporations. One, however, is much smaller and depends on Miracle Toy for about 25 percent of its business. Prices for cartons fluctuate somewhat. When there is excess capacity, they drop; when capacity is tight, they inch upward. Current prices reflect a recovery from a previous price-cutting period.

Axelrod believes that the company can profitably invest in a plant capable of turning out all but $50,000 of its current annual carton

EXHIBIT 1

MIRACLE TOY CORPORATION
Summary of condensed financial statements

Assets			*Liabilities*	
Cash	$3,922,000		Current liabilities	$ 3,364,200
U.S. government			Common stock and	
bonds	3,265,000		surplus	15,846,000
Accounts and notes			Total	$19,210,200
receivable	1,910,000			
Inventories	2,050,000			
Current				
assets		$11,147,000		
Plant and				
equipment	$9,881,900			
Less:				
Depreciation	2,000,700			
		$ 7,881,200		
Land		182,000		
Total		$19,210,200		

MIRACLE TOY CORPORATION
Income Statement
For Year Ended June 30

	1974	1975	1976	1977	1978
Sales	$18,902,000	$18,786,000	$21,942,000	$23,942,000	$24,020,000
Net profit before tax	2,020,000	1,682,000	2,689,000	2,532,000	2,910,000

needs. (The plant would not produce the small number of cartons that require special lithographing). At the start, Miracle Toy would be able to take less than half of the plant's production for its own use in packaging toys; the balance (about $1 million worth of cartons) would be sold to outside customers. As Miracle Toy's business grew, it could rely on the carton plant for its increased needs and cut back on sales to outsiders.

Total investment in facilities would be approximately $1,100,000. This estimate does not include any allowance for land, which the company already owns and which probably is worth $50,000 to $75,000. Nor does it include any allowance for start-up costs—the unusually high operating costs that are almost always incurred when a plant starts producing. Axelrod estimates that these costs will be at least $50,000.

Axelrod estimates that the plant would earn a 10 percent profit on sales to outside customers and would also save the company about $90,000 in boxboard costs (see Exhibit 2). He believes that sale of the extra capacity would be no problem, since most of the company's

EXHIBIT 2

Estimate of costs and revenues on proposed carton plant at standard volume

		Sales to
Sales to outside customers		$1,000,000
Reduction in purchases of cartons from outside suppliers		750,000
		$1,750,000
Cost of purchased paperboard	$710,000	
Inks, plates, and other factory supplies	165,000	
Wages and salaries	495,000	
Depreciation, taxes, and other expenses	190,000	
		1,560,000
Profit from carton operations		$ 190,000

suppliers purchase cartons. He points out that suppliers should be willing to buy Miracle Toy cartons provided that they were competitive in price and quality. In fact, Miracle Toy is already indirectly buying a substantial number of cartons in addition to those it buys directly to package its end products, since many of Miracle Toy's suppliers use cartons to package the company's purchases.

Question

Suppose you were the materials manager of the Miracle Toy Corporation. How would you react to Axelrod's proposal? State your position and make a detailed analysis of his proposal.

12

Finding qualified suppliers

The buying process is deceptively simple. Competing suppliers submit bids. If each offers acceptable delivery, quality, and service, a purchase order is issued to the lowest bidder. This is the clerical framework. Within it operates a buying process that requires both extensive knowledge and remarkably keen judgment.

Good buyers never ask a supplier to quote unless they have some knowledge of its qualifications. In fact, they would prefer to solicit quotations only from suppliers with perfect records for quality, service, and delivery. If they could do this all the time, their jobs would be much easier. All they would need to do is request quotations from three or four such suppliers and then award the business to the low bidder.

Unfortunately, real-life suppliers are not so perfect. Most buyers are not completely satisfied with the quality, service, and delivery of even their best and most reliable suppliers. In addition, they must spend a great deal of time looking for new suppliers capable of taking care of their changing needs. No company can stand still. It must continuously be developing new products and processes, which in turn require new suppliers. No supplier can afford to stand still, either. Each is looking for new customers, and each must be investigated carefully by the buyer before being trusted with an order.

BUYING ERRORS ARE COSTLY

The costs of mistakes in buying are always substantial; sometimes they are staggering. If buyers pay suppliers higher prices than are justified, a company's profits and competitive position may be undermined. As was pointed out in Chapter 1, in the average company a 2 percent change in total materials cost brings a 10 percent change in profits.

If a buyer buys materials of unsatisfactory quality or a vendor fails to deliver, the costs may be enormous. Imagine what would happen if an auto company purchased parts for a critical component like a steering gear or brakes that failed completely after a year's service in the field. Hundreds of thousands of cars would be defective. The company's reputation would certainly suffer. In addition, it would incur losses from lawsuits and from the enormous expense of replacing the defective part in thousands of cars.

Quality failure can be a nightmare when it is not detected until long after the product is in use. It can even be costly when it is spotted immediately by sharp-eyed inspectors. A shipment of material that does not meet minimum quality specifications is the equivalent of no shipment at all. Worse yet, it may mean continued delivery failure until the supplier can correct the defect.

If a supplier fails to deliver an item and the buyer's inventories are exhausted, the costs of the production stoppage that results can be huge. Customers are dissatisfied; sales and profits are lost that can never be recouped. In addition, the direct cost is substantial. A plant employing about 300 persons has fixed costs of at least several thousand dollars per day, which are incurred whether the plant is operating or not.

If a buyer fails to achieve the fourth buying objective, service, in dealings with suppliers, the consequences are not nearly so spectacular as with a major quality or delivery failure. In some cases, however, they can be even more significant economically. Outstanding suppliers sometimes provide their customers with products and ideas that can have tremendous impact on sales and profits for years to come.

CHANNELS OF DISTRIBUTION

Industrial buyers commonly buy materials both directly from producers and through various local distributors. In general, they buy production materials used in fairly large quantities directly from the manufacturer, in order to get lowest possible prices. Nonproduction materials and supplies normally come from local mill supply houses or distributors, who buy from the manufacturers in large quantities and then resell to their customers in smaller quantities.

As a general rule, buyers prefer to deal directly with the manufacturer whenever possible. There are no middlemen making extra profits on each purchase, and communication is easier when the buyer has technical problems to discuss with the manufacturer. However, distributors do have a legitimate economic role. When the buyer requires their services, the higher prices they may charge are more than justified. In fact, when quantities are relatively small, they are usually the most economic form of distribution.

Buying direct

When a company uses reasonably large quantities of production parts and materials, it almost always pays to buy directly from the manufacturer. Suppliers of standard and semistandard items—steel, chemicals, ball bearings, paper, and so on—sometimes require a minimum factory order on direct purchases.[1] All large users, however, buy directly from the factory or mill. Suppliers of parts that are custom made to the buyer's blueprints and specifications almost always sell direct, even if quantities are small.

Full-time sales staff. Supplier sales representatives are the liaison between their customers and the home office and factory. The salespersons of practically all large and many small companies are full-time employees. They usually are paid a straight salary plus some bonus based on performance and company profits. They may also receive a commission based on sales volume, which may or may not supplement a regular salary.

It is probably to the buyer's advantage to deal with representatives who are paid a straight salary, since they might be more interested in providing outstanding service to their customers, even at the expense of immediate gains in sales volume. However, there is not much a buyer can do to control the way in which a supplier pays its sales staff. Nor, in most cases, can he or she even find out the method; most suppliers are extremely reluctant to discuss such an intimate detail of their business with customers.

Manufacturers' representatives. Many smaller firms sell through manufacturers' representatives. They pay a flat commission on sales volume, which ranges from 1 percent or less on extremely high-volume items to more than 10 percent on equipment and parts purchased in very small quantities. Typically, each manufacturers' representative serves several noncompeting firms in an area. In most cases, they sell products to the same customers, so the representative often can service several accounts on a single sales call.

While some buyers complain that the commissions earned by manufacturers' representatives are too high, this method of selling is probably the most economical one for the firms that use it. The company need not maintain sales offices in areas where they would not be economical. Its sales costs are not rigid but vary directly with sales volume.

On the other hand, a manufacturers' representative usually cannot

---

[1] For example, mills demand a minimum order of 10,000 pounds for most types of sheet steel. Users who want smaller quantities must buy from a steel warehouse firm that specializes in buying mill quantities and then reselling in smaller quantities to users in its area. Warehouse prices usually are at least 25 percent higher than mill prices. Warehouses earn this premium by offering prompt delivery of small quantities and other services.

give any one company all of her time, nor can she be expected to know as much about the company's products as a full-time sales representative. As a result, critics say that neither buyer nor seller gets the best service through a manufacturers' representative when problems arise. In fact, as pointed out in Chapter 5, buyers should be wary of manufacturers' reps who attempt to do much more than run errands. They are not empowered to enter into contracts on behalf of the firms they represent and, in practice, can do little more than make very minor decisions. On the other hand, some, but by no means all, full-time sales representatives are thoroughly familiar with the details of their product and are able to make many decisions without consulting the home office.

Buying from distributors

A distributor is a dealer who handles a wide range of products for a number of manufacturers in an area. A distributor may have an exclusive franchise for a manufacturer's products and not handle competing brands. In other cases, each distributor in an area would handle all major brands. Distributors usually buy materials in fairly large quantities, store them, and then resell in small quantities to customers in their area. About 23 percent of the typical distributor's sales are drop shipments, in which the material is shipped directly from the factory to the user. In such cases, the distributor still takes title to the goods, even though he or she does not handle them physically. But in this case this function is really no different from that of a manufacturers' representative.

Even on drop shipments, however, the manufacturer invoices the distributor, who reinvoices the user of the material. The distributor's profit comes from the difference between the price at which the goods are sold and the price at which they are bought. Unlike the manufacturers' representative, the distributor receives no commission and, except where it is prohibited by so-called fair trade laws, is perfectly free to resell at any price she chooses.

Distributor markups vary with the quantity and type of material sold. Average gross margin of the distributor is 20 to 25 percent of sales. To earn this margin, the distributor anticipates the needs of the customers in buying, stores the material until there is a demand for it (an average period of about three months), and then delivers it to the user.

Role of the sales rep

The modern sales representative is not necessarily a bubbling extrovert, but almost always does have a reasonably pleasant personality.

The fact is that many sales reps get business simply because customers enjoy doing business with them. If all other factors are equal, why shouldn't a buyer deal with someone he likes and trusts? Personality factors are just as important in buyer-seller relations as they are in other phases of business.

While every buyer is certainly influenced to some extent by the personalities of the sales reps who call, she also has more objective reasons for preferring some sales reps to others. A good sales rep knows not only his company's products but also something about his customer's problems. He is around when the buyer needs him but does not make unnecessary calls that waste time for both of them. When the salesperson is competent, there are few problems regarding quality and delivery. The salesman will follow up on most of them himself and thus save the buyer considerable trouble.

Firms with able sales representatives always get more business. And they deserve it, for they offer superior service to their customers. Able sales reps naturally seek out prospective customers; many a company learns about a supplier only because one of his sales reps happened to call. The professional buyer doesn't always play such a passive role, however. She spends a substantial amount of time actively looking for new suppliers who can serve her needs better.

FINDING A SUPPLIER

Buyers most commonly find suppliers for an item either by drawing on their experience with comparable items or by inviting quotations from the same suppliers who made the item on a previous order. Every buyer must often locate new suppliers, however. She wants to stimulate competition on items she regularly buys, and she must also buy new items that present suppliers are not equipped to handle. Buyers usually locate new vendors by checking purchasing directories and catalog and vendor files or through personal contacts with supplier sales reps or other buyers.   *question 4.*

Directories. There are numerous directories that list potential suppliers both alphabetically and by type of product sold. Probably the most widely used directory is the buyer's local telephone book. In the yellow pages are listed all local suppliers for various merchandise.

Purchasing directories, such as *Thomas' Register of American Manufacturers, Conover-Mast Purchasing Directory,* and *MacRae's Blue Book,* are widely used by industrial buyers. Each is carefully edited to include only those products that are useful to the industrial buyer, and each lists upwards of a quarter of a million supply sources, both alphabetically and by product. A buyer can quickly locate almost every domestic supplier of an item simply by turning to the product classification in the directory in which he is interested.

Many states publish directories of all industries within their boundaries. Every buyer should have the directory of the home state if there is one. It can be an extremely useful supplement to the general purchasing directory, which might not list all suppliers or commodities in which he might be interested. Trade associations also issue purchasing directories for specialized commodities. The *Rubber Red Book* is typical of these; it specializes in very detailed listings and product classifications for rubber products manufacturers and so is an invaluable reference for a buyer of such products. Every buying department should be equipped with all available specialized commodity directories in its fields of interest.

Catalog files and vendor lists. The typical purchasing department is bombarded with thousands of pieces of direct-mail sales literature every year. Although they discard at least 90 percent of this mail, most purchasing executives carefully review and save any catalogs that might be useful. A big purchasing department may have several thousand different supplier catalogs in its files.

Some purchasing departments try to boost the usefulness of their catalog files by carefully classifying their contents both by supplier name and by-product. For example, they may store the catalogs on shelves or in file cabinets alphabetically by supplier name and then keep a separate card file by type of commodity. Some companies have even developed numerical file cards on which they imitate the Dewey decimal system used in libraries, assigning a code number to each commodity group.

The purchasing department of an office equipment manufacturer uses these basic groupings:

1000—Bearings and bushings
2000—Electrical equipment and supplies
3000—Factory equipment
4000—Gears
5000—Mill supplies
6000—Office supplies and equipment
7000—Steel, brass, aluminum, etc.
8000—Taps and drills
9000—Miscellaneous

The third digit in the identifying number indicates the type of material, and the fourth digit classifies it further. For example, in category 7000, 7010 identifies a general steel product, while 7011 is for steel wire, 7012 for steel bars, and so on. Specific catalogs are then identified in numerical sequence, with a decimal point after the commodity number. For example, the number 7011.01 might refer to a U.S. Steel catalog of steel wire, which is the first of several wire catalogs on file. 7011.02 might be Republic Steel's wire products catalog, and so on.

Buyers specializing in high-volume production parts and materials rarely rely on catalogs, since everything they buy is custom made to company specifications. But they would probably use some sort of vendor list. The simplest of these would be a file of 3 × 5 cards arranged alphabetically by supplier name. On each card would be the supplier's address, telephone number, names of officers and sales representatives, and an indication of the type of work the supplier is equipped to handle. The buyer then can review this list whenever a new item must be bought to see if anyone on it is interested in quoting.

Personal contacts. Buyers talk to sales representatives of potential vendors even when they have no immediate need for the products they sell. When a need does arise, they can refer to the sales rep's calling card or "leave behind" sales literature to see if the company should be considered.

Buyers often get tips on potential suppliers for offbeat items by asking other buyers for assistance. Many of them use their membership in the National Association of Purchasing Management or some other purchasing organization as a vehicle for becoming acquainted with purchasing personnel in other companies who can be useful sources of information. They also carefully read many trade publications regularly. When they see an add by a company that might be a potential supplier, they tear it out and file it for future reference.

Similarly, buyers get information about potential new suppliers through regular attendance at trade shows where suppliers have booths and display their products. Some companies take even more direct measures to stimulate sales calls from promising new suppliers. They have displays of their products in their lobbies, so that suppliers will know precisely what they buy. Some companies have even set up (during a defense program, when they had to get many new suppliers in a hurry) exhibits of the items they buy in public halls and invited all potential suppliers to come and look at them.

INVESTIGATION OF SUPPLIERS

No buyer should place orders with a supplier about whom she knows nothing. At best, there is danger of substandard performance in price, quality, delivery, or service. At worst, there is danger of fraud. Almost every buyer occasionally is approached by a sharp operator trying to pass off shoddy merchandise at exorbitant prices, and sometimes the swindler is successful.

Caveat emptor. In a typical racket, a pencil salesman calls and claims that his company has printed the name of the buyer's company on several thousand pencils because of confusion with another customer who has a similar name. If the name of the buyer's company is Universal Screw Machine Corp., for example, the salesman might claim that his firm has accidentally printed this name on pencils ordered by the Universal Screw Products Corp. The salesman appears to be upset over the error and offers the buyer distress prices if she will take the pencils off his hands. The salesman is lying, of course. The company's name is printed on the pencils only after it orders them. And the buyer doesn't get a distress price at all; she pays a high price for the poorest quality of pencils available.

In another, similar racket the salesperson claims to be representing a firm that is financially hard pressed. If the buyer will pay cash, she promises extra concessions. What happens is that the buyer winds up with low-quality merchandise worth about half of what he paid. Since it is not economic to sue and the transaction usually is perfectly legal anyway, the buyer is bilked.

Unscrupulous firms will also bypass the purchasing department and try to obligate the company indirectly into dealing with them by performing services directly for the company's department managers. This "back door selling" can be prevented by simply requiring all outsiders to register with the purchasing department. Other rackets will disappear only if every buyer investigates each supplier before placing an order. But everyone likes to get something for nothing, and if the racketeers can convince the buyer that he must move fast, he might forego investigation in his eagerness to exploit what appears to be an opportunity for a bargain. The fact remains that every supplier should be investigated, even those whose morals and ethics are above reproach.

Unfortunately for the buyer, a completely honorable supplier can also cause losses to the buyer's company, for he may be incompetent, a poor manager, and unable to keep promises made in good faith. For this reason, many buyers avoid asking a supplier even to quote on business until they have learned something about her facilities, personnel, financial resources, and reputation.

Facilities

Suppliers often are remarkably eager to get orders they are not equipped to handle. From the supplier's point of view, the best way to expand a business is to get the orders first and then worry about buying the needed equipment. The buyer has a somewhat different point of view. He almost always buys best when he deals with suppliers who already have the equipment and skills needed. Costs usually are lower and quality is higher when the supplier performs almost every operation on the product or service himself.

Equipment lists. The buyer should listen carefully to the sales agent's description of the supplier's facilities. If he is buying parts made to his specifications directly from a small manufacturer, he should ask for a list of machine tools and equipment. He then can accurately determine if the supplier is actually equipped to do the job. The buyer also can get useful descriptions of a supplier's facilities from a Dun & Bradstreet report (see Figure 12–1) or from *Moody's Industrials* or some other financial reference.

If the supplier is located nearby, the buyer should always arrange to

FIGURE 12–1
Dun & Bradstreet, Inc. business information report

```
Dun & Bradstreet, Inc.          BUSINESS INFORMATION REPORT
Please note whether name, business and street address
correspond with your inquiry


SIC        D-U-N-S              © DUN & BRADSTREET, INC.      STARTED      RATING
34 69      04-426-3226          CD 13 APR 21 19--     1957        DD1
           ARNOLD METAL PRODUCTS CO   METAL STAMPINGS

           53 S MAIN ST
           DAWSON MICH   49666                        SUMMARY
             TEL 215 999-0000
                                                      PAYMENTS  DISC
             SAMUEL B. ARNOLD )                       SALES     $177,250
             GEORGE T. ARNOLD ) PARTNERS              WORTH     $42,961
                                                      EMPLOYS   10
                                                      RECORD    CLEAR

                                                      CONDITION STRONG
                                                      TREND     UP

PAYMENTS     HC      OWE   P DUE TERMS    APR 19--     SOLD
             3000    1500    1 10 30  Disc             Over 3 yrs
             2500    1000    1 10 30  Disc             Over 3 yrs
             2000     500    2 20 30  Disc             Old Account

FINANCE      On Apr 21 19-- S. B. Arnold, Partner, submitted the following statement
             dated Dec 31 19--
             Cash            $    4,870    Accts Pay         $    6,121
             Accts Rec           15,472    Notes Pay (Curr)       2,400
             Mdse                14,619    Accruals               3,583
                             -----------                     -----------
             Current             34,961    Current                12,104
             Fixt & Equip ($4,183)  22,840  Notes Pay (Def)       5,000
             CSV of Life Ins      2,264    NET WORTH             42,961
                             -----------                     -----------
             Total Assets        60,065    Total                 60,065
             Annual sales $177,250; gross profit $47,821; net income $8,204.  Fire
             insurance mdse $15,000; fixt $20,000.  Annual rent $3,000.
             Signed Apr 21 19-- ARNOLD METAL PRODUCTS CO by Samuel B. Arnold, Partner.
                             -----0-----
             New equipment purchased last Sep was financed by bank loan.  Monthly
             payments on loan are $200.
             Arnold reported sales for the three months ended Mar 31 were up 10%
             compared to the same period last year.  Increase was attributed by
             management to additional capacity provided by new equipment.
             Profit is being made and retained resulting in an increase in net worth.
             Current debt is light in relation to worth.  Inventory turnover is rapid.

BANKING      Balances average high four figures.  Loans granted to low five figures,
             secured by equipment, now owing high four figures.  Relations satisfactory.

HISTORY      Style registered Feb 1 1965 by partners.  S. ARNOLD, born 1918, married.
             1939 graduate of Lehigh University.  1939-50 employed by Industrial Machine
             Corporation, Detroit, and 1950-56 production manager with Aerial Motors Inc.,
             Detroit.  Started this business in 1957.  G. ARNOLD, born 1940, single, son
             of Samuel.  Graduated in 1963, Dawson Institute of Technology.  Served U.S.
             Air Force 1963-1964.  Admitted to partnership Feb 1965.

OPERATION    Manufactures perforated metal stampings for industrial concerns.  Sells
             on Net 30 day terms.  Has twelve accounts.  Territory greater Detroit area.
             Employs ten including partners.  LOCATION: Rents 5,000 square feet in one
             story cinder block building in normal condition.  Located in central business
             section of main street.  Premises neat.
             4-21 (803 77) PRA
```

Although they are most often used to check a customer's credit, Dun & Bradstreet reports are also good sources of information about potential suppliers' facilities and finances.

see his facilities. If the contract is sufficiently important, the buyer should visit the supplier's plant even if it is hundreds of miles away. And he may wish to bring along product, process, or quality control engineers from his own company to assist in evaluating the supplier's facilities.

A buyer's tour of a distributor's facilities can be more superficial than one of a supplier's manufacturing plant. The distributor should certainly be adequately stocked. Equally important to the buyer are the distributor's employees. If their morale is high, if they seem alert and intelligent, the buyer has a reasonably good chance of getting prompt service with a minimum of errors. The distributor's housekeeping also may be significant. The buyer usually has good reason to expect sloppy service from sloppy-looking facilities.

Plant visits. A manufacturing plant usually is much more complex than a distribution facility and takes much more skill to evaluate. Every buyer who has ever been conducted through a supplier plant has heard the sales rep boast of its modern facilities and equipment. If the buyer is an expert in the supplier's industry, it will not take long to see if the sales rep's praise is justified.

If the buyer is not thoroughly familiar with the industry, he or she can still get clues as to the quality of the facilities by seeking answers to these questions:

1. Is the equipment up to date? If the equipment looks new and modern (and doesn't just have a fresh coat of paint on it), the buyer usually can assume that it is reasonably efficient and in good condition. In some cases, she might bluntly ask the supplier when the equipment was purchased. If the buyer notices a number of machines shut down for repairs, she may conclude that the equipment is older than it looks.

2. Is there effective material control? If the supplier has in-process inventory piled haphazardly throughout the plant, his production scheduling may be defective, or equipment breakdowns may be creating production bottlenecks.

3. Are working conditions good? The buyer is more likely to get the quality and output she wants from a plant that is well lighted and well ventilated and that has guards on machines to prevent accidents.

4. Are facilities well maintained? If a supplier skimps on maintenance in obvious areas, he may also skimp in the less obvious ones that cause shutdowns.

5. What are the supplier's fire-protection facilities? If the plant has its own water tower and sprinkler, fires will cause less damage and will be less likely to hold up work on the buyer's orders.

6. Is the work pace fast but unhurried? A well-operated plant doesn't have idle workers in one area and harried workers in another.

7. Does the supplier have the equipment to handle the buyer's order? The buyer should ask to see the equipment that is to be used on her orders. The buyer should ask about the approximate capacity of each machine, to make certain that her needs can be accommodated. She may also wish to make note of each machine's model number and specifications so that she can review the supplier's facilities with experts at her own plant.
8. Does the supplier have efficient receiving and shipping facilities? The buyer should note particularly whether the supplier can ship his order by the most economical type of carrier. If the buyer's traffic manager would prefer shipment by rail, for example, the supplier cannot ship at low cost unless he has its own siding.
9. Is the supplier currently making products similar to those in which the buyer is interested? If the buyer's order will be different from the supplier's usual line, there might be problems. If it is similar, the buyer can get a good idea of how her order will be handled by watching work on similar orders.

Many companies require buyers to make out detailed reports each time they visit a supplier plant. These reports are filed and can be referred to by other buyers interested in doing business with that supplier. However, a company should not use one report as a guide indefinitely. Follow-up visits are essential to keep up to date on changes the supplier may have made. A series of reports can then be analyzed for trend. A company naturally is more willing to place business with a supplier that is progressively improving than with one that is standing still or even slipping behind.

Personnel

Although buyers should do their best to evaluate a supplier's facilities objectively, this is sometimes difficult and occasionally almost impossible. Some facilities simply do not lend themselves to the type of superficial appraisal a buyer can give on a plant tour. For example, both efficient and inefficient chemical plants look like a maze of pipes and storage tanks to the casual observer. Supplier managements may also superficially appear to be homogeneous, but they are not. It is the buyer's job to distinguish between really competent managements and the also-rans.

Regardless of their products and processes, all companies depend heavily on the caliber of their managers; a good supplier always has good managers. The buyer is particularly qualified to evaluate the supplier's materials manager. He should insist on meeting her, as well as other company executives. He may also, if the contract is an important one, arrange for these executives to meet their counterparts in his own company. If each of the supplier's department heads knows his job thoroughly, the buyer has less to worry about when he places the order.

If the contract is a major one, the buyer should not confine his study of the supplier's personnel to the top managers. He should meet lower level supervisors as well. The supplier's key employees should be backed up by bright, alert subordinates who are being trained to take over in the future.

The supplier's labor relations also should interest the buyer. Do the workers appear contented and reasonably interested in their jobs? Or are they sullen and obviously doing work they hate simply because they must eat? In the latter case, the buyer should not be too surprised if he sometimes gets substandard workmanship on his orders. The buyer should bluntly ask the supplier to show him records on strikes and work stoppages. If they have been frequent, the buyer can expect both an environment leading to poor quality and frequent failures to meet delivery promises.

Financial resources

Why should a company be interested in the financial strength of its suppliers? It need not rely on their credit, nor is it making an investment in them. The answer is that the best suppliers are financially strong and are making healthy profits.

Advantages of strong suppliers. In general, it is sound to prefer an extremely profitable vendor to a less profitable one—all other factors being equal. The company with big profits is in a much better position to reduce prices (if it can be persuaded to do so). Its methods and management usually are superior. It also is more likely to be a better source of new products and techniques than its more marginal competitors.

Certainly no buyer wants to give important purchase orders to a weak supplier and then have it suddenly go bankrupt. Also, a supplier who is making adequate profits and is strong financially can take temporary losses if it underbids or has trouble with an order. The buyer need not worry about such a supplier's coming back after it has accepted an order and demanding extra payments to complete it, financial advances, and so on.

If the supplier is large and publicly owned, the buyer should ask a sales representative for a copy of the latest annual report to stockholders. Such reports often contain interesting descriptions of company operations as well as basic financial data. If the company does not widely distribute its financial reports to stockholders, the buyer has other sources of financial information. She often can get balance sheet and income data and similar basic information from the latest edition of *Moody's Industrials*. Or, if the supplier is too small to be listed in

Moody's, the buyer can get a Dun & Bradstreet report. The D & B report will usually include a financial statement. In addition, it will indicate the company's credit standing with its suppliers and the overall credit rating assigned it by Dun & Bradstreet.

Financial analysis. The buyer, or better yet, a financial analyst on the materials manager's staff, should periodically review the latest balance sheet and income statement of each major supplier. If the balance sheet shows that the supplier's business is deteriorating, the buyer should investigate and may want to change suppliers before the company's financial condition becomes critical.

The buyer should also be particularly interested in the trend of the company's profits. If profit margins are widening, she may have a legitimate basis for asking the supplier to reduce prices. And certainly she should complain vigorously if such a supplier should increase prices. If the profit margin is narrowing, it may mean that the supplier is gradually becoming less efficient and less competitive. Or it could mean that the prices are too low and the buyer can expect pressure for price increases.

No buyer or materials manager is expected to be an expert financial analyst. However, he should be sufficiently familiar with balance sheets and income statements to make intelligent comparisons of competing suppliers and to spot individual strengths and weaknesses.

The financial statements of a hypothetical supplier are illustrated in Figure 12–2. How would a financial analyst go about reviewing them? One of the best approaches is to calculate various financial ratios for the supplier and compare them with ratios for competing suppliers.[2] *Question 6* The following ratios are particularly significant:

1. *The current ratio.* This is the ratio of current assets to current liabilities. It indicates the ability of the company to pay its immediate obligations. In the ABC Company (Figure 12–2), this ratio is 2.5 ($500,000/$200,000). Most analysts agree that it should be at least 2.5 and when it gets below 1.0 the company usually is on the brink of default on its obligations. The ratio of cash plus accounts receivable to current liabilities ($100,000 + $200,000/$200,000 = 1.5 for ABC Company) is an even better measure of liquidity. Inventories cannot be quickly converted into cash, so they are excluded from current assets. If a manufacturing company is in good financial condition, this "quick" ratio or "acid test" should be at least 1.5.

2. *Profit ratios.* Profitability can be measured by earnings both as a percent of sales and as a percent of net worth. The ABC Company's aftertax earnings are 5 percent of sales and just over 14 percent

---

[2] Each year, Dun & Bradstreet publishes 14 important financial ratios for 72 different industries. The title of the publication changes from year to year. Business executives can get complimentary copies by writing to Dun & Bradstreet, 99 Church Street, New York, N.Y. 10008.

FIGURE 12-2

ABC COMPANY
Condensed financial statement

Assets			Liabilities		
Cash	$100,000		Accounts payable ..	$ 50,000	
Accounts receivable ...	200,000		Wages payable	50,000	
Inventories	200,000		Accrued taxes	100,000	
Current Assets		$ 500,000	Current Liabilities		$ 200,000
Land		$ 50,000	Long-term debt		100,000
Plant and			Common stock	$100,000	
equipment $500,000			Capital surplus	100,000	
Less: De-			Earned surplus	500,000	
preciation 100,000					700,000
		$400,000	Total Current		
Fixed assets		$ 450,000	Liabilities		$1,000,000
Good will, etc.		50,000			
Total Current Assets		$1,000,000			

ABC COMPANY
Income Statement

Net sales		$2,000,000
Less:		
Purchases	$1,000,000	
Payrolls	500,000	
Other expenses	200,000	
Operating costs	$1,700,000	
Less: Sales and administrative expense ..	100,000	
Total costs		1,800,000
Operating profit		200,000
Less: Taxes		100,000
Net Profit		$ 100,000

($100,000/$700,000) of net worth. Average earnings on sales and net worth vary from industry to industry and also from year to year. Large companies tend to be more profitable than small firms. ABC's relative profitability can best be measured by comparing it with sales and earnings statistics published by the Securities and Exchange Commission and the Federal Trade Commission in the *Quarterly Financial Report for Manufacturing Corporations*. The *Report* (which is available from the U.S. Government Printing Office on a subscription basis) would probably show ABC to be relatively more profitable than other firms of comparable size, and it might even be above the average of its industry.

4—*Debt ratios.* A company that is heavily in debt will have difficulty raising money to invest in improvements. Two ratios measure the extent of a company's indebtedness. The ratio of funded debt to net working capital should rarely exceed 1.0. In the case of the ABC Company, it is 0.33 ($100,000/$300,000). The ratio of current debt to tangible net worth should normally be under 0.75, ABC's is about 0.28 ($200,000/$700,000).

Inventory turnover. Dividing net sales by inventories indicates how rapidly the company is turning over its inventories. This is a barometer of the company's materials management skill. ABC's ratio of 10.0 is probably above average, although the only good way to determine whether the ratio is high or low is to compare it with that of other companies in ABC's industry.

The ratios given above are danger signals. A buyer can successfully deal with a supplier who is financially marginal for years, but he or she should not do so blindly. Whenever any of the key financial ratios of a supplier are substandard, the buyer should investigate. She may directly ask the supplier to describe his problems, or she may request that her own company's controller make a more detailed analysis of the supplier's financial statements.

Financial limitations. Regardless of how strong a supplier is financially and how able he is in every other respect, few buyers care to concentrate too great a percentage of their purchase volume on a single supplier. Nor do they care to have the supplier become dependent on them for too great a share of the overall business. When they place too much business with a single supplier, buyers not only limit competition but they unnecessarily restrict their freedom of action in changing suppliers. No buyer need worry too much about taking a small order away from one supplier and giving it to a competitor. But only a cold-blooded ogre would cancel orders on short notice when they are almost the sole source of the supplier's income and hundreds of workers (sometimes entire communities) depend on the orders for their livelihood.

Suppliers who have staked too much on a single corporation have lived to regret it, too. For example, at one time the Murray Corporation of America depended on Ford Motor Company for as much as 30 to 40 percent of its sales. Then Ford decided to make almost all of its own auto body stampings. Murray was hit with a sharp drop in business from which it has never recovered fully. Chrysler Corporation had an even closer relationship with Briggs Manufacturing Company, which depended on it for practically all of its automobile business. When Chrysler decided to make its own automobile bodies, Briggs's only solution was to go out of the auto body business completely and sell its facilities to Chrysler.

There are no hard and fast rules as to how much business can be safely concentrated on a single supplier, but few companies want to use more than 10 percent of a supplier's capacity unless there is some special reason for doing so. When companies break this rule, there is usually some special angle. An obvious one is nepotism. A parent who controls one corporation may set up a son or daughter in another firm as a supplier. This practice is usually frowned upon—although it does not necessarily work against the best interests of the purchaser.

Other companies may become wed to some particular supplier for even more legitimate reasons. A company may become interested in the work that a particular supplier is doing and then place a majority of its business with that supplier after it acquires a financial interest. This is often the cheapest way for a large corporation to acquire the technological know-how of some specialized supplier.

Reputation

If a potential supplier has a bad reputation, one should clearly avoid doing business with him. Credit reports often provide clues to a supplier's reputation. They describe the backgrounds of the principals and also mention any outstanding litigation. The buyer should also ask a new supplier for a list of his major customers and vendors. Chances are that she may be acquainted with at least a few of the exectives of these firms who can give her an unprejudiced view of the potential supplier's reputation. If the buyer belongs to a group like the National Association of Purchasing Management, she may get tips on suppliers' reputations from her fellow members.

When she investigates a supplier's reputation, the buyer will be interested not only in conformance to ethical standards but also in experience others have had with the supplier in regard to meeting quality standards and keeping delivery promises.

DEVELOPING NEW SUPPLIERS

Ideally, a supplier should have the equipment, know-how, and financial capacity needed for each order he accepts. In real life this often is not the case. Buyers may deliberately give business to inexperienced suppliers. Sometimes they have no choice, but, usually they have good reason for deliberately gambling on a new supplier.

New products. A buyer looking for a supplier of something that has never been made before must obviously select an inexperienced supplier. Sometimes, of course, the buyer is taking little risk. The latest design of automobile bumper guard may look entirely different from last year's model, but last year's suppliers can probably handle it without great difficulty. The products that give the buyer problems are those that are completely different from anything that has been made before. For example, the first buyer who had to find a source for a space capsule nose cone really had a problem. The product was extremely difficult to make, and there was no producer with experience.

Competition. Buyers go to great pains to develop new and untried suppliers even when there is nothing new or revolutionary about the product and there are several qualified producers. Their usual reason is to stimulate competition in the field. When there are few producers of an item, competition can be less than vigorous. At worst there may even be collusion among producers on bidding. This results in higher prices for the buyer and occasionally also sloppy service and poor quality.

Sometimes a buyer may wish to develop a new supplier even when existing vendors are doing an excellent job. Demand for the purchased product may be growing so fast that additional capacity is needed. Or the buyer may wish to develop a vendor in a geographic area that cannot easily be served by existing suppliers. For example, when an American company builds a facility abroad, it will not want to import key purchases for its American suppliers but will immediately attempt to develop local vendors.

The development process. Regardless of the motive, most good buyers are always in the process of developing at least one or two new suppliers. They cannot always use conventional techniques to locate them, particularly if they are considering introducing a supplier to work that is not presently in his line. Sometimes they develop new sources by suggesting that certain dependable suppliers broaden their product lines. Often they play a more passive role; the supplier suggests to the buyer that he be considered for an order not presently in his line. The more aggressive buyers may even go out and actively solicit bids from potential suppliers with management and equipment that they believe could be adapted to a particular item.

The most important criterion by far in selecting suppliers that are to be developed on new products in management. If the supplier's management is good enough, some buyers are willing to ignore almost all other criteria. In fact, when they want the new supplier badly enough, they will go to great lengths to help it. They may lend it money, equipment, and skilled personnel and be extremely generous in pricing orders until the new supplier gains experience.

In most cases, of course, buyers are not quite so eager to develop a new supplier. But in order to induce a well-managed firm to enter a particular line, they may be willing to place long-term contracts to make it worthwhile for the supplier to invest in plant and equipment needed to enter the new field.

Buyers usually like to start a new supplier with a small part of their total needs. Then, if the supplier has difficulties, they can still fall back on more experienced suppliers for the majority of their requirements. They naturally prefer to negotiate prices from the new supplier that are lower than those charged by established producers. In many cases they are successful in this, particularly when the supplier is being introduced because the buyer considers prices charged by existing producers excessive. Buyers may be forced to discard accepted criteria in supplier selection when they are developing a new source, but they do this only when there is no other choice.

BUYING ABROAD

The ground rules may be quite different when the buyer brings in a foreign supplier. Buying abroad is a post–World War II phenomenon as far as the typical industrial purchasing agent is concerned. Of course, Americans purchased billions of dollars worth of imports prior to the 1950s, when foreign purchasing became commonplace among American industrial purchasing agents. But (to oversimplify a little), at that time American imports fell into two broad categories: raw materials and various other items that were not available in the United States, and specialized finished goods that foreign firms had developed. Nickel and crude rubber are examples of the former category; Scotch whiskey and French perfume are examples of the latter.

Why imports have grown

Prior to World War II, industrial purchasing agents were limited almost entirely to American suppliers for almost everything they bought (except the specialized raw materials not available in the United States). It is only since the late 1950s that many foreign firms have effectively penetrated U.S. industrial markets. This phenomenon was triggered by many developments. Most important of these were a general easing of trade restrictions in the United States, rapid economic development in Western Europe and Japan, development of the international corporation, and more rapid communication.

Trade barriers. The United States was a high-tariff nation from the 19th century until the 1940s. Tariffs were originally raised to permit infant industries to compete with more efficient firms in England and elsewhere in Europe. For example, when the iron and steel industry began in America, it was much less efficient than the British and German industries. High tariffs permitted American steel firms to charge higher prices, giving them the profits they needed to prosper and grow. By the late 19th century, this "infant industry" argument could no longer be used to justify high tariffs. The United States had become the world's greatest industrial power. Despite high wages, its manufactured products were among the lowest cost in the world.

But high tariffs continued to protect most of our industries. In fact, the overall tariff schedule reached an all-time high when the Smoot-Hawley Tariff was enacted in 1930. This raised the average duty to 52.8 percent of the average value of imports. In addition, of course, duties on many individual items were so high that there were no imports at all.

U.S. tariff policy changed during the Roosevelt administration in the 1930s, and tariffs have been cut substantially since that time. As a result, tariffs now usually offered only a modest barrier to imports of most products. Consequently, there are countless products where an efficient foreign producer can compete for American business. As a result, American purchasing agents buy millions of tons of foreign steel and are also relying on overseas suppliers for countless other items, including ball bearings, office equipment, machine tools, electrical components, and so on.

Economic development overseas.   Contrary to public opinion, lowering of tariff barriers usually does not bring a flood of imports from "cheap labor" countries. In fact, nations with the lowest wages in the world generally could not compete in American markets even if there were no tariffs or shipping costs. Factories in low-income areas of Latin America, India, and the other desperately poor areas of the world are almost always so inefficient that their costs are high despite pitifully low wages. To compete with American firms, the industrial purchasing agent looks almost entirely to the high-wage nations of Western Europe and Japan. These nations have wages and standards of living that are comparable to those of the United States.

Manufacturers in Western Europe and Japan compete primarily in the same way American firms compete, namely, by being more efficient than their rivals. The Japanese steel industry, for example, offsets its competitive disadvantage of being forced to import most raw materials by locating its mills near harbors and making more intensive use of the efficient oxygen steel-making process than American firms do.

The purchasing agent who buys abroad is not an exploiter of coolie labor but is simply broadening the supply base. If there are ten qualified producers of a particular product in the United States, there may well be another ten producers in the rest of the world. Some of these foreign firms will be among the most efficient; others still will not measure up to the standards set by American firms.

The international corporation.   Many big firms buy and sell to themselves across international borders. A subsidiary of a firm in one nation may specialize in products that it markets to subsidiaries in other nations. The economies of the United States and Western Europe are becoming more and more dependent on the activities of giant multinational corporations whose plants are increasingly being built almost without regard to national borders and whose managements are multinational. Purchasing agents in these firms, more than any other, look upon the world as their potential source of supply.

Perhaps 90 percent of the international firms are American based. The United States still represents their biggest market, but usually overseas operations have more growth potential. Among the biggest American internationals are firms such as General Motors, Ford, Exxon

(Esso), Emhart, International Telephone & Telegraph Corporation, John Deere, International Business Machines, and Singer. Among the foreign-based internationals are the Shell Oil Group (British and Dutch), Swedish Ball Bearing, Phillips Lamp (Dutch), Ciba Pharmaceuticals (Swiss), Massey Ferguson (Canadian), and Unilever (Dutch and British).

Buyers within the international corporation almost automatically look beyond national borders when searching for new suppliers. A few of the internationals have purchasing representatives in almost every major capital. For example, Ford Motor Company not only buys in England and in Germany, where it operates huge plants, but also in Japan. And a Ford purchasing representative in Germany or England is not necessarily concerned only with purchases for use within these countries. He or she may be searching for a supplier for a Ford plant in some other country.

Jets and telephones. Industrial purchasing is basically a communication process. While in the office, the industrial purchasing agent is usually either in a meeting with suppliers or other executives in the firm or is talking on the telephone. The purchasing agent also may spend as much as 25 percent of his or her time outside the office visiting existing or potential suppliers. The jet plane now brings the New York City–based purchasing agent as close to London as he used to be to St. Louis in the prop-plane era. And purchasing agents in the big international firms routinely make overseas telephone calls. As a result, American purchasing agents can now keep in close touch with overseas suppliers and can, therefore, rely on them to do jobs that could have been delegated only to domestic firms a few decades ago. As a result, national boundaries become less significant each year.

Problems in buying abroad

Development of the Common Market and other free-trade areas has, of course, been a tremendous stimulus to the growth of international buying. There are no tariffs at all within the Common Market, so a buyer in Germany need not be the least inhibited about placing orders in Belgium or France, for example. Barriers between trading blocs are also crumbling, so international buying will undoubtedly continue to grow. But there is no denying that, all other factors being equal it is still easier to deal with the supplier who is just down the street.

Communication. Language is often the biggest barrier to successful foreign purchasing. Industrial purchasing is a highly technical process. It is essential that buyer and seller be genuinely fluent in the same language. Unfortunately, the American purchasing agent sometimes has difficulty communicating even with the British. The language is the same but the precise vocabulary is sometimes sufficiently different to pose problems in communication between firms that have never done business with each other. The problem is worse, of course, in dealing with firms on the Continent and, in dealing with the Japanese, the American can normally just speak English and hopes to be understood. The communication problem is made more difficult by cultural differences among the various nations. As a result, there is always a danger of slight misunderstandings in international buying, even between firms that have been doing business with each other for years.

Legal and financial. Purchase law is different in each country. Consequently, buyer and seller must exercise much greater care in negotiating contracts, because each is working from a different legal framework. Trade terms must also be carefully defined. Most purchases from American suppliers are made either f.o.b. on some common carrier at the supplier's plant or the price includes delivery to the buyer's plant. Foreign buying usually involves water freight and greater variety of terms and conditions is naturally available. The International Chamber of Commerce publishes a directory of trade terms which many buyers find helpful. The easiest way to buy foreign goods is to insist on a contract payable in U.S. dollars on a c.i.f. (cost-insurance-freight) basis. In this case, the merchandise is the property of the exporter until it safely reaches a dock in the importer's country.

Financing of foreign purchases is, of course, complicated by the fact that two currencies are involved which are probably changing in value relative to each other. The risk of change in value must be borne by someone and it may be reflected in the seller's prices even when the quotation is in U.S. dollars. Some buyers and sellers try to hedge this risk by buying or selling currency futures. Others take a neutral position and simply mail the supplier a purchase order, expecting a bill when shipment is made. When the seller and buyer have not done much business, bills of exchange must be used where, in effect, the seller is guaranteed payment ex dock or on some other basis.

Fortunately, these initial difficulties can usually be worked out, and many American firms use precisely the same procedures in buying from foreigners as they use with domestic firms. The purchase order calls for payment in U.S. dollars, the supplier ships the material and invoices, and the invoice is paid by simply mailing the supplier a check.

However, basic commodities such as tin are often purchased with the seller's currency, while parts and materials made to the buyer's specification may be purchased with buyer's or seller's currency. When firms have not had much previous dealing with one another, more elaborate terms of payment must be used which assure the seller of payment on delivery of merchandise. The details can easily be worked out with banks that specialize in foreign trade—but the process is more time-consuming than domestic purchasing.

Quality standards. The industrial buyer likes to get precisely the quality needed. Poor-quality products will perform unsatisfactorily; premium-quality products will be wasteful if the extra quality is not needed. In dealing with American suppliers, the purchasing agent has thousands of standards to guide her. She can tell a supplier, for example, that she wants a "Class 3" fit on a particular item, and there are engineering standards to guide both buyer and seller as to precisely what a Class 3 fit is. The European version of a Class 3 fit may not be the same as the American. The problem is complicated by the fact that most other nations today use the metric system of measurement and, of course, all of their engineering standards are metric. The foreign manufacturer who wants American business must be prepared to meet American engineering standards, but his lack of familiarity with these standards may cause quality problems. In the last few years, more and more manufacturers have converted to the metric system. In time the metric system will be the standard of measurement around the world.

Sometimes American buyers compensate for this simply by setting slightly higher quality standards when buying from foreigners. Of course, this is wasteful if they get more quality than they really need. In fact, some American buyers have complained that European suppliers are inclined to be too fussy and wish they could speed things up a little and cut costs.

When American purchasing agents start buying abroad they also discover that they require quality characteristics that have never been spelled out in formal specifications. These rump specifications were developed over time as buyer and seller got to know each other's needs and abilities. The foreign supplier will not necessarily have this background, and there will be quality problems until buyer and seller get used to each other. Unfortunately, the physical distance that separates buyer and seller makes even simple quality problems difficult to work out. This difficulty is being resolved in part by increased use of the overseas telephone and travel, but there is no doubt that it is still a barrier to foreign purchasing.

Lead times and inventories. While many purchasing agents travel around the world by jet plane, the products they buy abroad usually move by slow boat. As a result, lead times are almost always much longer when buying abroad. If an item has a three-month lead time in the United States, it may be necessary to allow six months when buying it abroad. Greater protective stocks are needed to protect against unexpected fluctuations in supply and demand of the material being bought. Even if the foreign supplier is as reliable as the American competition, international shipping schedules are an added variable, particularly in winter months when gales often sweep the North Atlantic shipping lanes. The United States and the United Kingdom in particular are also vulnerable to periodic strikes by dockworkers and various other maritime unions. These can cut off supplies for months on end.

Thus, there may be a greater real cost in buying overseas which can only be offset if the price charged by the foreign firm is a little lower than that charged by its domestic competitor. In some cases, however, the buyer can have cake and eat it too. The foreign supplier may offer both a lower price and speedier delivery. This happy situation is most likely to occur when the U.S. economy is at the peak of the boom, while foreign economies have at least a little slack capacity. In addition, some foreign suppliers—most notably the Japanese—are so eager to export that they will offer better deliveries for overseas customers than they provide in their own home market.

Purchasing agents experienced in foreign buying usually protect themselves with adequate inventories even when the foreigner quotes speedier delivery. The foreigner may be as prone as an American counterpart to be overoptimistic on delivery. In addition, the buyer is not as well informed on foreign economic conditions as he or she is on the domestic situation. The buyer is much more likely to be caught unprepared by unexpected developments. So he wisely protects himself with greater safety stock.

The foreigner—except perhaps the British or Canadian supplier—has one built-in advantage over American competitors: relative freedom from strikes. Factories in the other advanced nations of the world are at least as heavily unionized as those in the United States, but labor and management in foreign firms recognize that they will lose export markets if deliveries are held up because of strikes, so agreements are usually reached amicably. The Japanese workers often "strike" by working so hard that their supervisors are embarrassed and lose face. This type of "strike" is effective in the Japanese culture and, of course, it does not cause export orders to be held up. The northern European worker does not worry about embarrassing the boss by working too hard but arbitration almost always prevents labor-management disputes from erupting into work stoppages—except in Great Britain and Canada, where strikes occur about as frequently as in the United States.

What to buy

There is no doubt, however, that additional competition is beneficial to both the American suppliers and their foreign competitors. Unfortunately, in some cases, the domestic producer may enjoy a natural monopoly even if it is less efficient than the foreigner. It is rarely, if ever, economic to import bulky, relatively cheap commodities that are plentiful in the United States. For example, the United States may not be the world's lowest cost producer of cement, but it costs so much to ship that only a few areas of the United States could afford to use the imported cement even if the foreign producer all but gave it away.

Breaking domestic monopolies. In contrast, products with a very high value per unit of weight and volume are naturals for foreign buying. Sometimes this may be the only way to break what is effectively a domestic monopoly. For example, the United States is probably the world's lowest cost producer of heavy electrical equipment. Yet, in the 1950s, the Tennessee Valley Authority and various privately owned public utilities found that foreign producers provided the only real source of price competition. It later was proved that the domestic firms had illegally conspired to fix prices.

Foreign producers may also be the only real source of price competition, even when there is apparently no violation of the antitrust laws but the market is dominated by a limited number of producers who avoid price competition. There is little price competition among American steel producers, for example. Each firm knows that if it cuts prices, rival firms will meet its price. The end result is a price war in which all producers earn lower profits than before. Consequently, American steel prices have not tended to respond to changes in competitive market condition. Foreign steel producers have been more flexible; they know they have to cut prices in order to make inroads into the American market. This upset the price equilibrium that prevailed among domestic producers, and there is now more price competition in the steel industry than at any other time in the 20th century.

Competition is sometimes even limited on an international basis. Competition may be limited to producers in a single nation while all other producers are dedicated to stable prices. The ball bearing industry is a good example. The Swedish firm SKF operates plants in the United States and in Western Europe. It has competitors, but ball bearing buyers in the United States have discovered that there is only modest price competition between SKF and major American firms such as the New Departure Division of General Motors Corporation. Much of the needed price competition has come in recent years from Japanese firms such as Toyo Bearing which are eager to establish themselves in the American market.

U.S. competitive strengths. Bearings are, of course, almost an ideal product to consider for foreign buying. They are high in value relative to their weight and bulk. Their material content is relatively low and their labor content relatively high. In general, raw material costs in other industrialized nations are at least as high as they are in the United States. More often than not, they are higher. In fact, the United States is an exporter of many industrial raw materials, so American manufacturers enjoy costs as low as any in the world. An American steel mill, for example, might pay $50 per ton for metallurgical coal delivered from a mine in West Virginia. A German mill would pay $80 or more per ton for the same coal shipped across the Atlantic. Similarly, American steel mills would pay $80 to $90 per ton for steel scrap, while the delivered cost to a Japanese mill of that same American scrap might be $120. Both American and foreign steel mills rely heavily on ores imported from various nonindustrial nations such as Brazil and India. Delivered costs of the ore are roughly comparable.

Costs of plant and equipment are also often roughly comparable in the United States and in other foreign nations. If it costs $20 million to build an ammonia plant in the United States, it probably will cost roughly the same amount to build a similar facility in Germany or Great Britain. In some cases, the foreign construction cost may be higher—particularly if the plant represents technology that is imported from the United States.

The American producer also may enjoy lower investment per unit of output because of economies of scale. If it requires a $1 million investment to produce 1,000 units per year of a particular product, an investment of only $1,800,000 may be needed to produce 2,000 units of the product. The American market is almost as big as that of all of the other free industrial nations of the world combined, so American producers are more likely to be able to afford huge plants that require minimum capital investment per unit of output.

Financing costs of the foreign plant are almost always higher. The American manufacturer can usually borrow at lower interest rates than foreign competitors. The U.S. firms also can raise money fairly easily by selling stock. In contrast, financial markets in every European country except Great Britain are relatively undeveloped. In Germany, for example, almost all financing is done by a few big banks, and business executives find it difficult to sell their securities direct to the public.

Lower capital costs and sometimes lower construction costs per unit of output give American producers an enormous competitive advantage in capital-intensive industries. American producers of such products as industrial chemicals, steel, cement, petroleum, synthetic fibers, paper, and other products requiring a high capital investment per worker usually enjoy the lowest production costs in the world. If their prices are higher than foreign producers, it is the result of inferior technology or competitive conditions.

Foreign strengths. The foreign firm can penetrate American markets only when it is smarter than its American competitors or when it can take full advantage of lower wage rates. The highest wage foreign firms must almost always be smarter to compete successfully in the American market. For example, the Swedish firms Atlas Copco, Saab, and A. G. Volvo enjoy substantial sales in the United States, not because their costs are particularly low (Swedish wage costs are higher than American levels) but because of product acceptance. Similarly, Scotch whiskey enjoys a big market in the United States even though it can be produced no more cheaply than American whiskey.

However, when an American firm shops abroad for something it can easily get in the United States, it is most likely to be successful with products having a high labor requirement, relatively low material cost, and limited capital investment per unit of output. The foreign producer's only real advantage in such cases is a lower wage level. Typically, all of the other costs are at least as high as those of the American competitors. In addition, part of the foreigner's wage advantage is fictitious. One cannot assume that foreign labor costs are half as much as American costs just because the wage rate may be but one half as high. The real advantage is probably closer to 25 or 30 percent and may even be less than this. Foreign workers usually enjoy more holidays and other benefits than American workers. Also, the work pace in foreign shops is often slower than that in the United States.

In addition, the foreign producer does not always have a competitive advantage even on products with high labor input. Machine tools are a good example. Their labor requirement is very high; raw material cost per unit of product is relatively low; and plant and equipment investment per dollar of product sales is moderate. Thus, machine tools would seem to be an ideal product for a foreign producer. In some cases they are. European and Japanese manufacturers make many excellent machine tools and equipment which they successfully export to the United States. But, on balance, the United States exports more machine tools than it imports. We are very low-cost producers of heavy specialized machine tools, large stamping presses, and various other capital goods. American and foreign producers both use unautomated methods to produce such products. Higher American wage rates are not, therefore, offset by a high degree of automation. The American advantage is derived from the enormous scale of the home market. Consequently, American producers can design and build their products in larger lots than foreigners. An American firm may be able to spread fixed costs of designing and building a particular machine over perhaps 100 units, while the market of the foreign firm may be limited to perhaps 10 or 20 units. This gives the American firm a tremendous competitive edge over its foreign competitors which the foreigner can overcome only if he is successful in developing a superior design. Some foreign firms have become dominant in their fields for this reason, even though their home market is extremely limited. For example, the Swiss firm of Brown Boveri is a world leader in electric melting furnaces even though the Swiss market probably takes only a small part of its output. Similarly, the Swedish firm, Atlas Copco, is a world leader in construction tools.

Relations with foreign vendors

Locating suppliers.   The process of locating foreign suppliers is essentially the same as that for finding the domestic variety. In many cases, the buyer's role is quite passive. Sales agents representing the foreign firms will call on him and solicit his business. The buyer then proceeds to investigate the supplier in the usual way. If the contract warrants it, the buyer would insist on seeing the seller's plant abroad.

In fact, many companies now aggressively seek out foreign suppliers and send their buyers abroad to establish contact with potential suppliers. Leads on potential suppliers can come from foreign purchasing directories, word-of-mouth recommendations from fellow American purchasing agents, customs brokers, and the foreign nation's commercial attaché or chamber of commerce. Various major industrial shows also can provide leads. Among the best known are the Hanover Trade Fair in Germany and the Tool Show in Milan, Italy. Both shows are international in scope. Those who find it inconvenient to attend can request catalogs that list major exhibitors and the products they are displaying. The giant Japanese trading companies—Mitsui, Mitsubishi, Sumitomo, and Itoh—can also provide leads. They maintain offices in major American cities and can provide a variety of services.

Negotiation.   The bigger foreign firms are used to doing business with Americans and can be expected to behave much as American firms. National personality does affect supplier relations, however. The Japanese, in particular, are famous for being indirect. American buyers, who are interested in getting right down to business, sometimes complain of what they have called the "snow job" they get when they visit Japanese firms. From the moment they land at Tokyo airport they are feted by their eager Japanese hosts. The food and entertainment are enjoyable but, for the American not used to this, the Japanese seem to take a long time to get down to business. Of course, the American buyer must adapt to foreign business customs. In Japan, in particular, business is mixed with a great deal of wining and dining—so the buyer might just as well be prepared to proceed with actual business somewhat more slowly than he or she would in the United States.

Negotiations, particularly with the Japanese, must be quite indirect. Typically, a foreigner visiting a Japanese supplier would be invited to a room where tea is served and hot towels are offered for the hands and face. Several hours might be spent in courteous light conversation before the subject at hand is approached. The buyer's hosts are ultra hospitable. In fact, while American buyers usually grow to become genuinely fond of their Japanese suppliers, they often return from visits to Japan in a state of complete exhaustion from the continuous hospitality of their hosts.

Business relations with Communist countries also pose special problems. Dealings are with a government agency rather than a private firm, which tends to slow the process of negotiation. As long as political relations between the United States and a particular country are going along rather smoothly, the industrial purchasing manager will be welcomed. All of the Communist nations would like to increase their imports from the capitalist West but are limited by lack of foreign exchange. The purchasing agent may be able to do the exporting branch of the company a real service if she can find something to buy on a reciprocal basis from the Communist country. In some cases, out and out barter trade is essential.

Ethical problems. Each culture develops its own code of ethics. Practices that may be perfectly acceptable in one culture are not in another. Business ethics among the economically advanced nations of the world are usually similar, but problems sometimes arise. When they do, the buyer must use the best judgment. In extreme cases, it may be wise to explain American practices to the foreigner. In others, it is best to go along with local practice. For example, it is not at all uncommon for business executives to exchange gifts in Japan and Europe. The American buyer who visits Japan, in particular, should have a gift for each of his hosts which he can present at the time of his departure. The practice is also not uncommon in Europe.

While social customs may be substantially different in dealing with foreign suppliers, the analytical buying techniques discussed in future chapters are known and practiced in the other advanced nations of the world. So after they become acquainted with foreign suppliers, American buyers can treat them pretty much as they would their American competitors.

Cases _____

CASE 12–1. LAWRENCE PLASTICS COMPANY

Dealing with dishonest suppliers

The Lawrence Plastics Company is a medium-sized molder of both injection-molded and compression-molded plastics. It makes various toys for a department store chain, knobs for several manufacturers of television sets, and miscellaneous parts for a number of other manufacturers. The company employs 250 persons and its stock is owned entirely by the Lawrence family and certain key executives. The company's founder, George H. Lawrence, serves as president and chairman of the board, and his son, Walter G. Lawrence, is vice president and general sales manager. Other members of the company's top-management group include a treasurer, a superintendent, a chief engineer, and a purchasing agent.

Alberta Harrison, the purchasing agent, has complete responsibility not only for the company's buying but also for inventory control of both raw materials and supplies. To a limited extent, she is also the company's traffic specialist and handles most contacts with carriers. In addition, Harrison is responsible for receiving and shipping, and the supervisors of these departments report to her.

While she has a secretary who assists her on routine purchases, Harrison herself conducts all interviews with suppliers. This takes about one third of her time, but Harrison is convinced that it is worth all of that—and more. The company has a firm rule that no commitments can be made for purchased materials and services by anyone outside the purchasing department. Operating personnel are permitted to talk to suppliers, but they are expected to make it completely clear that purchases can be authorized only by the purchasing department.

Harrison feels that this rule is workable only if she makes a genuine effort to investigate each supplier thoroughly to see if he has anything at all to offer that will help operating personnel do a better job. If the supplier has something to offer that might be worthwhile, Harrison then asks the appropriate operating executive for his opinion. For example, one supplier recently offered a new type of floor-cleaning compound that he claimed was superior. Harrison permitted the supplier to give his presentation to the maintenance supervisor, who thought the new product warranted a trial. Harrison got a sample for the supervisor to test. The supervisor reported that he liked the new compound, so now Harrison buys it.

Two weeks ago, Harrison had a caller by whom she was not impressed. His name was Harold LaPorte, and his card indicated that he was president of the LaPorte Tool Company. LaPorte mentioned that he was a good friend of Howard Lawrence, the brother of the president of Lawrence Plastics. He said that Howard Lawrence (who operates a business in a city 500 miles away) had suggested that he call on Lawrence Plastics because he was certain they would be interested in LaPorte's service. La Porte claimed he had developed a "metallic revitalization process" that could make old worn tools and dies as good as new. While he refused to discuss the details of his process (he had to keep it secret until he worked out the details of the patent application), he implied that it involved plating or coating the worn tool with some special hard alloy. He supported his presentation with testimonial letters from several satisfied customers in the city where Howard Lawrence's business is located. He said he hoped that Lawrence Plastics would become another satisfied customer so it would recommend LaPorte to other companies in the area.

In order to get Lawrence to try the service, LaPorte proposed that he be given a trial order for demonstration purposes. No fee was mentioned, but Harrison assumed that the first order would be at nominal cost. Nonetheless Harrison was cool to LaPorte's proposal. She had never heard of any of LaPorte's customers, was automatically biased against secret processes, and also reacted unfavorably to LaPorte's personality. She said she would think over LaPorte's proposal, discuss it with other Lawrence executives, and get in touch with him in a few weeks. As soon as LaPorte had left, Harrison requested a credit report on the LaPorte Tool Company.

A few days later, Harrison received the credit report. It was not favorable. Harold LaPorte had operated under two other names at various times in his career. He had been arrested and convicted in 1938 for nonsupport of a child. In 1943 he was arrested, but not convicted, on a charge of violating the regulations of the Office of Price Administration in dealings in scrap metals. In 1949 he was involved in a suit that charged him with selling used cars under misleading circumstances. The report indicated that LaPorte was in the "metal business" but credit investigators could find no record of any facilities or bank accounts and recommended that no credit be granted to LaPorte. The report thus confirmed Harrison's suspicions. She dropped LaPorte from consideration as a supplier under any circumstances and made a mental note to mention LaPorte at the next meeting of her local purchasing agents' association so that other companies in the area might not be hoodwinked by his sales pitch.

A week later, Harrison received an invoice calling for Lawrence Plastics to pay LaPorte $185 for reworking an extrusion mold. The controller had passed it on to Harrison because he had no record of any purchase order being issued for the mold to be reworked. Harrison investigated and discovered that LaPorte had managed to impress the supervisor of the tool room with his presentation. The supervisor had given the mold to LaPorte so that LaPorte's "engineers could study the mold to see how they could apply the LaPorte process to it."

Harrison now called LaPorte and asked him why he had sent Lawrence an invoice for $185 for just "studying" the mold. LaPorte replied that the bill covered engineering time in developing an application of the process. He said that the process could be applied should Harrison authorize it, and that there would be an additional charge of $185. Harrison replied that she had investigated LaPorte's record and did not want to have any dealings with him, and she asked him to return the mold (which it would cost Lawrence about $2,500 to replace). LaPorte refused to do so until his invoice for engineering time was honored.

Questions

1. What action should Harrison take?
2. What, if anything, could she have done to prevent this problem from arising in the first place?

CASE 12–2. MUSKEGON FURNITURE COMPANY

Investigating a new supplier

Muskegon Furniture is a medium-sized manufacturer of wooden office furniture. It buys its lumber and most of its hardware. Its manufacturing facilities are devoted primarily to finishing wooden parts and assembling finished products. One of its high-volume purchase parts is a metal drawer pull used in its most popular line. This part, along with all other metal hardware parts, is handled by Barbara Schwartz, one of the company's buyers. Schwartz has purchased the part from the Akron Stamping and Hardware Corporation for a number of years. Akron has never changed its price of 40 cents for the part despite several increases in labor and material costs. Apparently, increased volume (from about 50,000 units a year at the beginning to about 250,000 currently) and various improvements in manufacturing techniques have offset rising costs.

While Schwartz is completely satisfied with Akron's quality and service, she feels that it is about time she got competitive quotations on the drawer pull. So she solicits bids from several of Akron's regular competitors. In addition, she invites Americon Industries to quote. Until a few weeks ago, Schwartz had never heard of Americon. At that time, Americon's president, a Mr. Sloan, called on Schwartz and asked for the opportunity to bid on a job. He showed Schwartz a list of his equipment and also indicated that he was already making a number of small parts for several well-known customers.

Schwartz reviews Americon's sales literature and is impressed enough to mail Sloan blueprints of the drawer pull and to ask him to quote. However, she warns Sloan that he won't necessarily get the job even if he is low bidder, since price is not the only factor that determines Muskegon's buying decisions.

Americon's bid, based on tooling for 250,000 units per year, is 30 cents. It is the only bid Schwartz gets that is below Akron's price of 40 cents. Schwartz checks Americon's bid carefully. While it is obvious that Americon is figuring costs closely and will have to work hard to make a fair profit, Schwartz becomes convinced that the bid is a legitimate one that Americon can live up to. She checks with two of Americon's current customers, whose purchasing agents she knows through her membership in a local purchasing agents' association, and finds that they are thoroughly satisfied with Americon's quality and service.

Schwartz visits Americon's plant and discovers that, while it is a little smaller than she anticipated, it is equipped to make the drawer pull. However, the company has only one press capable of forming the part. As long as there is no breakdown, this press is quite capable of handling all of Muskegon's needs, although Americon might have some difficulty in meeting schedules if Muskegon's requirements increased substantially.

Schwartz then gets a copy of Americon's most recent financial statement. The balance sheet shows total assets of $630,000, including $24,000 in cash, $60,000 in accounts receivable, $225,000 in inventories, and the balance in plant and equipment. Current liabilities are $205,000, there is a mortgage of $195,000, and the balance represents the owners' equity. Last year's sales were $600,000, and profits after taxes were $38,000.

Question

Prepare a report analyzing the pros and cons of buying drawer pulls from Americon and recommend a buying decision.

13

The basic buying process

The first step in the buying process is defining what is to be bought. Seemingly identical suppliers often offer different "bundles" of goods and services. The buyer must determine which particular "bundle" best meets objectives. Some suppliers of production parts and materials offer substantial engineering assistance to their customers; others simply make the item to specification. There is often even wider variation among vendors of supplier-designed products. As indicated in Chapter 15, there are often major differences in quality among competing supplier-designed products.

The job of selecting the supplier may be difficult even when buying from distributors selling identical manufacturer-designed products. Suppose distributor A offers a 20 percent discount from manufacturer's list while distributor B offers a 25 percent discount? The product is supposedly available off-the-shelf for immediate delivery. Does this mean that the buyer automatically buys from distributor B? Usually it does, but not necessarily. In terms of total cost, the buyer may be ahead buying from distributor A even though invoice price will be higher.

In fact, price is just one of four objectives in the buying process. The others are continuity of supply, consistency of quality, and favorable supplier relations. The preceding chapter dealt with the selection of potential suppliers, or, more specifically, with the evaluation of a company's ability to supply. This chapter will discuss the process of selecting among a number of qualified potential suppliers.

QUALITY IS PARAMOUNT

Of the four basic buying objectives, quality may well be the most important. If the buyer does not get the quality of material needed, he

393

or she gets nothing of any worth. Price, delivery, and favorable supplier relations become unimportant.

Quality is also the least understood buying objective. The price, delivery, and service objectives are fairly obvious. The quality objective seems obvious—but it is not. For example, professional buyers are always interested in paying the lowest prices for material and getting the delivery and service they need, but they do not necessarily seek the highest possible quality. On the contrary, they usually are interested in getting the minimum quality necessary for the material to perform its function satisfactorily. For example, for most applications silver is a higher quality metal than copper. It is easier to draw and has superior electrical conductivity. Yet silver is almost never used to make electrical wire, despite the fact that it is the best metal for this purpose. The reason, of course, is price. Silver is 40 to 50 times more expensive than copper, which does an adequate job.

Quality and price. Quality is usually linked with price. A $12,000 Cadillac automobile is of better quality than a $5,000 Chevrolet. Which car is the better value depends on its function. If the car is to be used for company errands, the Chevrolet is undoubtedly the car to buy. It will serve the function somewhat better than the Cadillac because it is shorter and easier to maneuver. It will last almost as long, be cheaper to operate and maintain, and costs half as much. But if the car is to be used to impress company customers, the Cadillac will probably serve the function more than twice as well as the Chevrolet.

Note that quality is related to function. In one sense, the Chevrolet is actually a higher quality car than the Cadillac. Similarly, a $12 pair of blue jeans can be of higher quality than a $75 pair of fine woolen slacks, if they are to be used as work clothes.

Sales representatives try to convince their prospects that the products are superior in quality to those of competitors. In fact, if a buyer tells a sales rep the price is too high, the standard rejoinder is that the quality is high, too. In such cases, the buyer and the sales rep both may be right. Then it is up to the buyer to determine if the sales agent's company is offering the quality he really needs.

Setting quality criteria. Quality determination is only partly the buyer's responsibility. Also vitally interested are the departments concerned with using and specifying the purchased material. Ideally, the users and specifiers should set objective quality standards for each purchased item. Then the buyer need not be concerned about the quality so long as the supplier meets those standards. Unfortunately, for many items this cannot be done in practice. Often it is impossible or impractical to establish standards sufficiently detailed so that the buyer would be assured of satisfactory quality if the supplier met them. Sometimes, the users and specifiers do not really know what standards should be set. They want the "best available at a reasonable price." In some cases each supplier's product is different and performance is the user's only really dependable guide to quality.

Thus quality criteria vary from product to product. No company can use the same criteria to measure the quality of every item it buys. And, regardless of the criteria used, quality is always a problem. Specifications can rarely be so precise that an unscrupulous supplier cannot find a way to beat them. "It's amazing," one contracting officer for the U.S. Army once said, "how ingenious contractors are in spotting loopholes in specifications." One supplier almost succeeded in selling back to the army canned sweet potatoes that had been sold as surplus because they were spoiled.

What makes quality?

Ethical suppliers do not try to pass off shoddy goods. But they can and do ship substandard merchandise. It is the buyer's job to define the quality that is needed as precisely as possible and then to make sure that the supplier meets the specification. How this is done depends in large part on what is being purchased. If the vendor is furnishing a component or material used in the buyer's end product, then quality needs will be defined with very precise engineering specifications. If the item being purchased is designed by the supplier, other criteria must be applied. Usually, these relate to the performance of the product rather than its intrinsic physical characteristics. (See Figure 13–1.)

Restrictive specifications. To prevent misunderstandings, specifications should be as clear and explicit as possible. They should be written so as to encourage a maximum number of suppliers to bid.

FIGURE 13–1

Sometimes the user's opinion is the buyer's best guide to quality. One purchasing department sends this form to users of material whenever it makes changes in suppliers or specifications.

Preclusive specifications that restrict the number of bidders to a few are a problem in almost every company. They allow for a minimum of competition, and buyers find it impossible to do a first-rate job.

Purchasing personnel can never relent in their efforts to prevent specifications from becoming restrictive. Working against them are almost all of their regular suppliers and many specifiers and users of material in their own company. Every supplier dreams of customer specifications tailored to its products or processes. No longer would it have to fight for business against a number of competitors. Instead, it automatically gets an order whenever a need arises.

SECURING QUOTATIONS

When the buyer has reviewed specifications to make certain that they are as unrestrictive as possible, he is ready to solicit quotations from potential suppliers. With new items, buyers try to get at least three competitive quotations (provided the item is not proprietary). For major purchases, six to eight quotations are not uncommon, and, when the buyer has difficulty in finding a supplier, he may issue as many as 100 quotation requests.

While buyers should not hesitate to permit any qualified supplier to bid, they obviously cannot permit every possible supplier to quote for every projected purchase. They simply do not have the time or the clerical help to prepare that many quotation requests. Many buyers methodically rotate their lists of potential suppliers in requesting quotations. If a supplier is high bidder on several quotations, his name is temporarily dropped from the list. Suppliers who already have a substantial amount of the buying company's business may also be dropped temporarily if the buyer wants to avoid taking too great a percentage of their capacity.

Buyers often are too generous with quotation requests. It is pointless, for example, to go to the trouble of formally requesting a quotation from a supplier who consistently refuses to sell at prices different from those shown in his catalog or published price lists.[1] Nor should a buyer ever request a quotation from a supplier with whom she has no intention of doing business. Quotations are expensive to prepare, and it is unethical to ask suppliers to prepare them when they will not get an order regardless of what price they quote. In general, price should be the only unknown about the supplier at the time the quotation is requested. The buyer should already have investigated the supplier's potential quality, delivery, and service capabilities, although some-

---

[1] The buyer should not automatically assume, however, that a supplier will not offer concessions on published prices if requested to do so by the buyer or if required to do so by competitive forces.

times it is not worthwhile to make a really intensive investigation until the supplier has submitted a favorable quotation.

Exceptions to quotations

The quotation request should include complete specifications for the material, the quantities required, and a tentative delivery schedule. In addition, most purchasing departments indicate a deadline for submission of quotations; some, including almost all government buying offices, refuse to consider late bids. Some companies also print their purchase terms and conditions on their quotation requests.

If suppliers return quotations with all the information requested and take no exception to any terms or conditions, the buyer is ready to analyze her quotes and select the supplier. However, this is frequently not the case. More often suppliers propose changes in specifications, delivery schedules, and purchase terms, and they also may make errors.

Exceptions to specifications. On production parts, suppliers frequently take exception to specifications. They usually suggest minor changes that will permit them to make the part more economically. Occasionally, they may even propose a complete redesign. Most companies try to encourage such suggestions, since they frequently reduce the cost of the item. Some companies even go so far as to include a statement in their quotation request that suggestions are welcomed. For example, Ford Motor Company quotation requests include this statement:

> We will welcome suggestions regarding design changes that you believe will facilitate the tooling or fabrication of the part or both. However, all such changes must have the approval of our Engineering Department and arrangements must be made to incorporate such changes on our blueprints because our purchase orders will specify delivery as per our blueprint.

As the Ford statement indicates, the purchasing department must submit all proposed changes to the engineering department for approval. Most large companies have routine procedures to handle such changes and use quotation request forms similar to that in Figure 2–3 in Chapter 2. The buyer can do nothing with the supplier's quotation until engineering approves or rejects the proposed change. If the change is approved, she usually will get new quotations from other bidders.

Changes in schedule. If suppliers cannot deliver material when it is needed, they are automatically disqualified. But sometimes suppliers propose delivery changes that are not so clear-cut. The delivery date requested by the buyer may be unrealistic, and the supplier simply must be given more time to fill the order. In this case, the buyer may have to propose a change in schedule to the various managers in the company who are concerned.

Occasionally a supplier may make what amounts to a counter-proposal on delivery terms. For example, the buyer may have requested a quotation for 10,000 units of an item with delivery in ten monthly shipments. Suppose a supplier suggests either a single shipment of 10,000 pieces or two shipments of 5,000 pieces each. Obviously that supplier's bid is not comparable to bids that agree to the original plan.

The buyer should request the supplier to requote on the same delivery basis as originally requested. Then he should compare the two bids from the same supplier. If the supplier offers a lower price for different delivery terms, the buyer should analyze them to see if they are really advantageous. Suppose the supplier quotes a price of $1.00 per unit if it can ship in a lot of 10,000 pieces and a price of $1.10 if it must schedule its shipments over a period of ten months at the rate of 1,000 units per month. In effect, the supplier is offering to reduce the total cost of the purchase by $1,000 ($0.10 × 10,000) if the buyer will accept the entire order in a single shipment. For this saving the buyer must carry for ten months an average $5,000 inventory instead of a $500 inventory. The buyer can readily determine if this is worthwhile by applying the principles discussed in the chapters on inventory management. If the savings exceed the additional carrying cost (less the saving in procurement cost by processing a single shipment instead of ten separate ones) and possible obsolescence, then the offer to purchase the larger quantity is attractive. The buyer should then go back to the other suppliers who quoted and ask them to requote on the same basis.

Purchase terms. The buyer should study each supplier's quotation to make certain that all offer comparable terms and conditions. For example, one supplier may quote a firm price, another may insist on some provision for escalation for labor and material costs, and a third may insist on "price in effect at time of delivery." Obviously these quotations are not comparable, even if all three suppliers quote identical prices.

The buyer should try to persuade suppliers to revise their bids and accept the terms and conditions she wants. On pricing terms, for example, most buyers prefer fixed-price contracts for short lead-time items, although they will accept escalation on long lead-time contracts in order to prevent suppliers from inflating their bids to allow for possible higher costs.

If the bidder flatly refuses to quote within the terms and conditions desired, the buyer has two choices. She may disqualify the bid, or she may accept it while making allowance for the disadvantageous terms.

In the latter case, the buyer may put a price tag on the supplier's terms. Suppose, for example, that a supplier's current price is $1 and his terms are "price in effect at time of delivery." The buyer may have to inflate this bid to $1.02 or $1.03 when comparing it to the quotations of suppliers who are willing to guarantee fixed prices.

Errors. The buyer should review each quotation carefully to make certain the supplier has made no mistakes in preparing it. He should make sure that the supplier's quotation covers the exact requirements described in the quotation request. If it does not, he should return it to the supplier and ask her to requote. The buyer should be particularly wary of bids that are unusually high or low. If a dependable low-cost supplier submits a bid that is substantially higher than those of her competitors, the buyer should return it and have the supplier check it for errors. The buyer should be equally cautious about exceptionally low bids. Only the most inexperienced and naïve buyers will quietly accept a bid of 10 cents for an item that is worth at least $1. This is not only unethical—it is uneconomic. The supplier eventually will detect the error and will either request a price increase or, if she feels she has been treated unfairly, refuse to do business with the buyer's company.

If a supplier rechecks a bid and insists that no errors have been made, the buyer should still be cautious if he is convinced that the bid is unrealistic. If the bidder is not too familiar with the buyer's requirements, the buyer may simply disqualify the bid. But if the bidder is an experienced, reliable supplier, the buyer may wish to review the bid in detail with him to make certain there are no errors. He also may arrange to have the specifications explained to the supplier by product or quality control engineers.

Total cost versus price

Bids from competing suppliers may not be comparable even after allowance has been made for errors and exceptions to specifications. Essentially three elements of cost are involved in almost every purchase: the actual price charged by the supplier, the cost of getting the material from the seller to the buyer, and the cost of holding the material until it is actually needed by the buyer. The first two cost elements are essentially covered if the seller quotes a price that is f.o.b. buyer's plant. The third element is always present (except on items that used on receipt) and varies with the supplier.

Simple example. Suppose that supplier A always delivers on the exact date that is requested by the buyer. In contrast, the delivery performance of supplier B is erratic. Sometimes B is on time; sometimes the wrong item is shipped; and other times B is late. Clearly A is a better supplier than B. Therefore, should not the buyer deal only with A? The obvious answer is: not necessarily. If B charges prices that are well below those charged by A, it may be the most economic source of supply.

In many instances, buyers protect themselves against erratic supplier performance simply by carrying a more than adequate inventory. If the buyer is doing business with A, an order is placed when there is one week's inventory on hand; if the supplier is B, a prudent buyer reorders when the inventory reaches a one-month supply. Thus, the cost of doing business with supplier B includes an extra and permanent investment in protective inventory over and above the prices charged by the supplier. Similarly, a poor supplier almost always creates extra costs for the buyer in paperwork, telephone calls, and so on.

Clearly, A is the supplier to select if A and B charge exactly the same price. But what if the prices charged by B are markedly lower? Remember purchasing is an economic process. The object of the game is to gain maximum value while still achieving objectives. At some lower price, it may pay to do business with a poor supplier. The buyer can make a rational decision only if bids from competing suppliers are adjusted to make them truly comparable. In the case of A and B, this might be giving the poor supplier a 5 percent handicap for the extra expense generated for the buyer's organization. Thus, A and B are regarded as offering equally attractive quotations if A quotes $1.05 and B quotes $1.00. In many cases, the buyer's judgment as to the poor supplier's handicap is arbitrary since some of the losses from poor service are hard to quantify. But even an arbitrary judgment is better than none. Otherwise, the buyer will either treat A and B as equal—which they are not—or will simply refuse to do business with B, a decision that is irrational if the terms offered by B are sufficiently attractive.

Consignment. In other instances, competing suppliers may have comparable performance but do not offer like "packages" of product and service. Supplier A agrees to set aside a particular stock in order to meet a buyer's unexpected needs. While Supplier B has a good record in meeting changing demands, its customers must take their chances. Clearly supplier A is offering more "product" than B and if price is identical, the buyer should choose A. Vendors—particularly distributors as distinct from manufacturers—often try to differentiate themselves from their rivals with various forms of such nonprice competition. Usually they involve some form of protection with inventory against the buyer's unexpected demands.

The ultimate form of protection (and perhaps the most useful one) is consignment, where the seller allots an inventory to its customer who takes title to the goods only when they are used. This eliminates the need for the buyer to tie up capital in inventory but, of course, increases the seller's inventory. As a result, a price that is at least 1 percent, and possibly as much as 5 percent, higher may be justified when goods are available on consignment. Thus, the buyer may be willing to pay from $1.01 to $1.05 for an item on consignment that might be worth no more than $1.00 with a conventional purchase. The exact differential depends on cost of capital and inventory turnover. For example, if inventory of the particular purchase turns over 6 times per year and capital cost is assumed to be 24 percent, then the privilege of consignment is worth 4 percent (two months' interest at 24 percent per year.)

Consignment usually requires a somewhat larger inventory than the buyer would normally have. One reason for this is that the vendor that offers it is probably not local (or it would provide support with its own on-site inventory). It is often a device that permits an out-of-town distributor to compete with local firms and, in some cases, the buyer enjoys the benefits of the consignment without paying its real cost in the form of a higher purchase price.

Analysis of quotations

Bids from competing suppliers must be restated on a comparable basis if the purchase decision is to be made objectively. Price is the common denominator. The value of special services consignment must be assessed in terms of their worth to the buyer and added onto the basic price. Suppliers that do not offer special terms may be asked if they wish to do so; similarly, suppliers that do offer them may be asked to requote on a conventional basis. The buyer seeks sufficient information so that bids from competing suppliers can be tabulated on a work sheet (see Figure 13–2) and analyzed on a comparable basis. If competing suppliers offer identical "packages," this comparison is easy to make. The supplier that quotes $1.01 is clearly offering a better deal than the vendor that quotes $1.02.

What to consider. For most real-life major purchases, comparison is not that easy. A number of factors would have to be considered including:

1. Net unit prices proposed for various purchase quantities.
2. Terms of payment.
3. Setup costs and minimum charges, if any.
4. Cost of any special tools to be purchased by buyer for supplier's use.
5. Unit shipping cost if the item is sold on a basis other than f.o.b. buyer's plant.
6. Other charges, if any, offset by the economic value to the buyer of any special benefits offered by the supplier.
7. Possible arbitrary allowances for premium costs that may be incurred in buying from a marginal supplier.

FIGURE 13–2

			QUOTATION CHART						

Part Name_____ Part No._____

Specification_____ Model_____

Group

INQUIRY			QUOTATION						
DATE	SOURCE	QUANTITY	DATE REFERENCE	QUANTITY	PRICE	TOOL COST	DELIVERY	F.O.B.	TERMS

PART NO._____

Courtesy Chrysler Corporation

Chrysler Corporation uses this form to compare quotations from competing suppliers of production parts. Chrysler buyers keep separate quotation records for each part.

In some cases, the buyer can select the lowest cost supplier with no more than a glance at the recap sheet. If the low bidder is satisfactory in all other respects, it gets the order. However, many buying decisions, particularly important ones, cannot be made so easily. Quotations must be recalculated to make them comparable, quotations may not be for identical items, or all bids may be too high.

Bids comparable economically. Quotations from suppliers frequently cannot be compared until the buyer adjusts them to make them comparable. For example, suppose a buyer compares two bids for a part weighing one pound, having a usage of 10,000 units per year, and requiring an investment in special tools. Shipment is to be made in lots of 1,000 pieces.

Supplier A quotes a unit price of $1 f.o.b. buyer's plant with a $2,500 charge for special tools and a special setup charge of $10 for each 1,000-piece lot. The payment terms are 2/10, net 30. Supplier B quotes a unit price of 95 cents f.o.b. shipping point with a $3,500 tool charge and no setup charges. The payment terms are net 30 days, and the LTL freight rate from supplier's plant to the buyer's plant for 1,000-pound shipments is 70 cents per cwt.

It is not immediately obvious which of the two bids is the lower. The buyer must tabulate them for comparison. The buyer would immediately make the following adjustments in the quotations:

	Supplier A	Supplier B
Unit price quoted	$1.00	$0.95
Unit freight cost paid by buyer (1 lb. × $0.007/lb.)	—	0.007
Unit cost of setup charge for 1,000-piece lots	0.01	—
Adjusted unit price	$1.01	$0.957
Tool cost	$2,500	$3,500
Payment terms	2/10, net 30	net 30

The table above shows that the adjusted unit price of supplier B is $0.053 lower but tool charge is $1,000 higher. Therefore, B must ship 18,867 pieces ($1,000/0.053) before the lower unit price more than offsets the higher tool charge. This would take almost 22 months with a usage of 10,000 pieces per year.

In practice, the buyer would want to be reasonably certain that the part will stay in production for at least two years before she would give the order to supplier B. There are two reasons for the buyer to make the break-even point between A and B more than 22 months' usage:

1. The higher tooling cost for supplier B requires an immediate cash outlay. Cash in hand is always worth more than cash derived from savings made in the future. The cash itself is worth some interest during the period. In addition, if the buyer's calculations are incorrect and the part becomes obsolete immediately, there is less loss.

2. Supplier A offers a 2 percent discount if bills are paid within ten days; supplier B does not. If the buyer's accounting department pays bills within ten days as a matter of routine, A's discount is a clear saving of $200 per year and the piece-cost saving by buying from B is reduced from $612 per year to $412 per year. The 2 percent discount is a definite "plus" for A, even if the buyer's accounting department ordinarily takes 30 days to pay bills. The 2 percent discount is earned, in effect, if the bill is paid 20 days earlier; this is equal to an annual interest rate of 36 percent. There are few solvent companies that are so strapped for cash that they can afford to overlook such a profitable short-term investment opportunity. In fact, for most purchases any difference in payment terms between suppliers can be considered a direct difference in price.

If the buyer knows precisely how many pieces he will buy over the life of the tooling, he can compare quotations with precision. If the part in the example were to have a life of precisely two years (or a total usage of 20,000 pieces), then the buyer could make the following comparison between suppliers A and B.

	Supplier A	Supplier B
Total piece cost (20,000 pieces at adjusted prices)	$20,200	$19,140
Tool cost	2,500	3,500
Total cost	$22,700	$22,640
Savings buying from supplier B		$ 60
Discount earned on payment terms	$ 454	—
Net advantage buying from supplier A (including payment terms)	$ 394	

The bids above are so close that it is a toss-up whether the buyer would give the order to supplier A or B. However, there is no doubt that A offers a slightly better deal when payment terms are considered. The buyer, however, would not necessarily give A the order after making this comparison. It is possible that supplier B can negotiate a better deal with the tool shop that quoted $3,500, as compared with the $2,500 tooling quote from supplier A.

NEGOTIATION WITH BIDDERS

While it is unethical to disclose competitors' bids, some negotiation with the low bidder is normal. In fact, there is no guarantee that the low bidder will get the contract. The low bid will be rejected if the buyer believes it is unrealistic and reflects lack of familiarity with specifications. The buyer may also feel that all bids are high, including the lowest one. In this case, there are two alternatives: to ask everyone to requote or to negotiate directly with the low bidder or the firm to which the buyer would like to award the contract. Such favoritism need not indicate collusion. A buyer may feel it is advantageous to give preference to a certain supplier for a number of legitimate reasons, including reciprocity, proximity of the supplier's plant, a history of favorable relations with a particular supplier, or the belief that a particular supplier will, in the long run, be the lowest cost producer and the greatest contributor to the buyer's cost-reduction program, new product efforts, and so on.

Possibly minor changes in specifications can be made that will reduce costs. Sometimes the supplier will permit the buyer to compare the details of the cost estimate with the buyer's own estimate. When this is done, differences often can be resolved. For example, a supplier may have included a certain manufacturing or inspection operation not considered necessary by the buyer. The buyer's quality control or product engineers can be called on to clarify specifications and ascertain if the operation is really needed.

Reducing quotations

Persistence needed.   The buyer doesn't necessarily give up even if the lower bidder flatly refuses to reduce her quotation. If he still is convinced that the supplier's price is too high after he has unsuccessfully attempted to negotiate a price reduction, the buyer may take one of several courses of action:

1. *Solicit bids from new, untried suppliers.*   When he does not have time to do this because of delivery pressures, the buyer may be forced to accept the existing supplier's bid, but he should then go to work to locate new suppliers. He may wish to warn his existing supplier that he is looking for a new source. This will put some pressure on the supplier to reduce her costs.

2. *Suggest that the item be made in the plant rather than bought from an outside supplier.*   The threat of an adverse make-or-buy decision may put pressure on the supplier to reduce his costs and prices. For example, in Chapter 11, it was brought out that automobile companies invested in glassmaking facilities primarily because they were not satisfied with prices charged by their suppliers for windshield glass. The case of the Mohawk Aluminum & Chemical Corporation in Chapter 16 is a good example of how this technique can be applied to transportation charges. Mohawk uses a threat to build dock facilities to handle barge shipments as a lever to negotiate a substantial reduction in rail freight rates for alumina.

3. *Propose that a high-priced component be "designed out" of the product.*   For example, high and wildly fluctuating prices of copper have encouraged users of that metal to search for substitutes. Similarly, aluminum and plastics have been widely substituted for steel.

Buyer's concessions.   The measures above are fairly drastic. The buyer need not go to such trouble until he is certain that he really has negotiated the best possible price with supplier. He should continue negotiations until all possibilities for reducing prices have been exhausted. In many cases, the supplier will be willing to cut prices if the buyer in turn makes certain concessions. The buyer can offer:

1. *A long-term contract for the item.*   With such a contract, the supplier may feel secure enough to invest in additional specialized equipment that will reduce costs. It may also be persuaded to regard the contract as "bread and butter" business that will pay its overhead and permit it to make profits on its standard line. The mail-order houses buy in this way. They offer long-term contracts provided that the supplier will quote rock-bottom prices.

2. *Changes in specifications or design that permit the item to be adapted to the supplier's manufacturing processes.*   In many cases, minor changes bring substantial savings. Both buyers and engineers

should be alert to such changes; in many cases the value analysis techniques discussed in the following chapter help stimulate suggestions for change.

3. Additional business on similar items to permit grouping of shipments and production runs in order to cut costs. This technique can be applied to any material or service. For example, a buyer may be able to get price concessions if she offers to buy all office supplies from a single vendor. The same approach may work with production parts and materials (although here the buyer may not want to become too dependent on a single supplier). Even if the buyer gets no price concession, order grouping will almost always reduce both administrative and freight costs. Fewer shipments weigh more, and lower rates are charged per pound; they also cut administrative costs for both buyer and seller. This idea has become so popular in recent years that it is sometimes considered a basic buying concept. It is described as *systems contracting* and is described in detail in Chapter 18.

4. Contracyclical buying. Some industries are seasonal or cyclical. Suppliers in these industries will make major price concessions during their slack season. A good example of this is the electrical equipment industry. Although the demand for electric power increases each year and is relatively unaffected by the business cycle, equipment demand is quite unstable. Utilities tend to be either in a rush for equipment or not the least bit interested in it. As a result, the equipment manufacturers either are operating at full capacity with an enormous order backlog or their plants are almost idle because of lack of business. In return for price concessions, the purchasing department of the Tennessee Valley Authority tries to do much of its buying during the slack season. Other utilities have not been so farsighted—or they have hesitated to tie up their money in equipment until there is a definite need for it.

Some purchasing departments deliberately negotiate long-term contracts during the industry's slack season. Suppliers in such industries know that depressed business during this period is normal. Theoretically, they should have no more reason to offer a price concession on a long-term contract when business is temporarily slow than at any other time of the year. But suppliers are human. An almost empty factory has a psychological effect on a business executive even though he knows the condition is temporary. He is most likely to be inclined to cut prices than he would be during the busy season—even though delivery dates on the orders are identical.

One purchasing agent in a small Midwestern city claims that she cut costs by nearly 5 percent by negotiating all of her contracts for mill supplies during the month of August. Her suppliers are in a one-industry area, and during August the industry is almost completely idle. The purchasing agent solicits quotations for the following year during August. Although suppliers are fully aware that they will be delivering against the purchase order throughout the year, the purchasing agent claims that psychologically they feel less secure during this slack month and will quote slightly lower prices.

Fixed-price items

If the purchased material is industry priced, the buyer usually is wasting time if she tries to negotiate a price reduction, particularly if the company is not a significant user of the item. In such cases the supplier often is selling the identical item to many customers, and in some cases other sellers also are selling the identical item. It is both illegal (according to the Robinson-Patman Act) and unethical for a supplier to discriminate among customers. If a supplier cuts the price for one customer, he must cut it for all customers. This makes price cuts extremely expensive and very difficult to negotiate. In some cases, if the item is legally price fixed by fair-trade laws, it even may be illegal for the seller to reduce the price under any conditions.

Even such rigid pricing leaves the buyer plenty of room to negotiate lower prices. He often has the opportunity to:

1. *Become a "unique" user.* Sometimes it is possible to become a "unique" user of a material with changes in specifications. When this is the case, buyer and seller can negotiate any price they please. Then, if the supplier reduces her price, she need not reduce prices of similar items sold to other customers. This is one of the reasons large mail-order houses use private brands. For example, the Whirlpool Corporation makes refrigerators and home-laundry equipment both under its own brand name and under Sears, Roebuck's Kenmore brand. Whirlpool presumably charges Sears less for equipment carrying the Kenmore brand name than it charges its own wholesalers for almost identical merchandise carrying the Whirlpool name. Were Sears to attempt to get similar prices on the Whirlpool brand, it would almost certainly run afoul of the Robinson-Patman Act (see Chapter 5).

When a company succeeds in becoming a unique user of an item that would otherwise be price fixed, the resulting price structure is sometimes weird. Auto companies, for example, pay less for exhaust tail pipes than they would have to pay for the steel tubing from which the tail pipes are made. The tail pipes are designed to fit each model of car, and their prices are negotiated by the auto company and its suppliers. The tubing from which the pipe is made is a standard commodity, sold at identical fixed prices by all producers. Tubing prices cannot be reduced through negotiaton but tail pipe prices can. As a result, auto companies use their buying power to get low prices from tail pipe fabricators, whose costs are low because they have their own tubing mills to convert steel strip into the tubing that is made into finished tail pipes.

2. *Negotiate payment terms.* Although the price of a material may be fixed, individual sellers of the material often have different payment terms. For example, mill supply houses have been known to offer thinly disguised reductions on price-fixed items by offering unusually generous payment terms. The standard discount for paying an invoice within ten days is either 1 or 2 percent, but some buyers get trade discounts as high as 7 percent from distributors. Obviously this is a concealed price cut, not just a concession to get the buyer to pay the bill promptly. A price reduction of 7 percent for paying a bill in 10 days instead of 30 is the equivalent of paying interest at the rate of approximately 150 percent per annum. Needless to say, few distributors are so hard pressed for cash that they will pay such an interest rate; most can borrow from a bank at 12 percent per annum or less.

3. *Use concealed discounts.* When a company buys both price-fixed and nonprice-fixed items from the same supplier (as is often the case in buying from mill supply distributors), it is not difficult to negotiate discounts on the price-fixed items. The buyer simply lists both price-fixed and nonprice-fixed items on the purchase order. By previous agreement he deducts his negotiated discount on the price-fixed items from the prices of the nonprice-fixed items.

4. *Use vendor inventory.* As we saw in Chapters 9 and 10, inventories are expensive to maintain. If a buyer can get a supplier to carry part of her inventories for her, she is getting the equivalent of a reduction in purchase price. For example, a buyer may negotiate an agreement whereby the vendor guarantees that a 60- to 90-day stock will be maintained exclusively for the buyer's requirements. The buyer then can operate on a hand-to-mouth basis with no fear of stockouts. She buys small quantities from the vendor, who periodically replenishes her stock when it drops to some predetermined level. As noted previously, so-called stockless purchasing is often part of an overall "systems contract" in which a buyer makes an agreement to purchase all items of a particular type from a single supplier.

5. *Obtain quantity discounts.* Sometimes a buyer can persuade a supplier to give her a quantity discount even though she is not actually buying the quantities required for such a concession. For example, suppose a supplier's price schedule provides for an extra 10 percent discount on purchases of more than 1,000 units. If the buyer uses only 100 units per month, he certainly would not want to buy a ten-month supply to earn the discount. But he might be able to persuade the supplier to give him the discount anyway. His gimmick: a purchase order for 1,000 units that does not call for immediate delivery but permits the buyer to draw on material as he needs it. Then the

buyer can get 100 units each month as he requires and still get the discount for buying the larger quantity.

Companies with several plants often can persuade suppliers to consider companywide volume when calculating quantity discounts, even though each plant may order its needs separately. For example, products such as light bulbs are often sold on a "national accounts" basis. If a company with several plants bought light bulbs on a hit-or-miss basis, it might get hardly any discount from the list price. But if it combines the buying power of all its plants and buys directly from the manufacturer on a national accounts basis, it may get a discount of 30 percent or more. Centralized purchasing of this sort also permits a company to exercise more effectively its reciprocal power to persuade suppliers to become customers.

6. *Adjust packaging and shipping.* There is almost no limit to the number of ways an imaginative buyer can find to reduce costs—even when the prices of the items she buys are theoretically fixed. Various packaging and shipping arrangements offer numerous possibilities. The simple act of buying "f.o.b. our plant" instead of "f.o.b. shipping point" can in itself bring substantial savings. Packaging and palletizing arrangements also can cut costs. For example, one company has persuaded its vendors to ship in cartons that it can reuse for shipments to its own customers.

7. *Get extra services.* Sometimes a supplier can be persuaded to render extra services. If these have economic value to the buyer, they are obviously worth negotiating. If scrap generated by the buyer's process has no market value, the supplier is doing the buyer a service by hauling it away. (But the buyer had better be absolutely certain she cannot make a profit on the scrap by selling it herself.) Similarly, suppliers may train buyer's personnel in the use of his equipment or material.

Among smaller hospitals, suppliers sometimes take over much of the materials management function. They periodically check buyer's stocks and automatically replenish them if they feel they are too low. In most cases, the supplier is overly generous in keeping the hospital well stocked with his product but chances are that inventories would be no lower if the hospital tried to manage them, especially in hospitals that are too small to be able to justify employment of a full-time, well-trained materials manager.

NEGOTIATING TECHNIQUES

While no supplier can be persuaded to do something that is not perceived to be in its best interest, a buyer who is good at negotiation can still wind up with a better deal than one who is unskilled and simply antagonizes suppliers.

Definition

Negotiation is a trading process. Buyer and seller assess each other's needs. The object of the game is to get more from the other party than is given up in return. In a fruitful negotiation both buyer and seller "win" because each has identified something that it wants from the other party that has greater value than what is being given up in exchange.

For example, suppose that a vendor cuts prices 10 percent if the buyer agrees to a contract covering an entire year's requirements. Seemingly this is a "victory" for the buyer who makes a 10 percent saving. But it is also a "victory" for the supplier who is guaranteed what amounts to a monopoly position with that customer for a 1-year period. Both parties enter voluntarily into this agreement because they believe they are better off with the agreement than they would be without it. Thus, negotiation is not a process by which anyone is persuaded to do something that is inconsistent with objectives. It is simply a process by which each party searches for ways in which "trade" will benefit both parties.

Unfortunately, the word "negotiation" carries many connotations that are not consistent with modern buying practices. To some, negotiation means the haggling that might take place in a public market in the Eastern Hemisphere. Buyer and seller carry on an animated conversation, exchanging either insults or compliments. The buyer starts negotiation by offering a price well below that which he knows he ultimately must pay. The seller's demands are equally outrageous; her first offer may be two or three times what the merchandise is actually worth. After some time spent in haggling, buyer and seller finally agree on a price that is close to what each could have predicted before negotiation was begun.

Some buyers use a rather crude version of this basic approach to negotiation. They are never satisfied with any quotation, regardless of how low it is. Some of the more obnoxious buyers try to browbeat suppliers into submitting lower quotations. Their negotiating techniques are pretty much limited to pounding on the table and demanding concessions. Such buyers are quite rightly called chiselers by their suppliers. In most cases, the price reductions they negotiate are illusory. Suppliers who know them for what they are simply quote higher than normal and then make "concessions" when the buyer figuratively—and, occasionally, literally—pounds on the table and demands them.

Basic rules

Successful buyers have a more sophisticated approach to negotiation. They know that they can negotiate nothing but what suppliers are willing to concede. So they concentrate on creating an environment conducive to voluntary concessions by suppliers. Some of the principles applied by successful negotiators include:

1. *Put yourself in the supplier's shoes.* One of the most basic principles of successful selling is to think in terms of the customer's requirements. When a buyer is trying to wangle concessions from a supplier, the shoe is on the other foot: he is trying to sell the supplier. So he should think in terms of the supplier's objectives, not his own. For example, he might say to the supplier: "If you offer me a price concession, I will try to work you in as a supplier of some new products that we currently have in the development stages." He would *not* say: "If you cut prices, you will help me meet my quota on cost reduction." If you were the seller, which approach would appeal to you—the one where the buyer in effect says, "Let me help you," or where he says, "Help me"?

2. *Let the supplier do most of the talking.* The vice president in charge of purchases of a large electrical equipment manufacturer once said: "Supplier sales reps can't stand silence. They'll talk just to fill the vacuum, and in the process they often talk themselves into making just the concessions you want." This is the exact opposite of the approach used by "old-school" buyers who try to browbeat suppliers into making concessions, and it is infinitely more effective. After all, sales representatives are professional persuaders. They consider overcoming customer resistance to be the greatest test of their skill. If a buyer challenges the price or quality of their product, they're ready with counterarguments. But what if the buyer says almost nothing? In this atmosphere, the sales rep is at a disadvantage and may well end up making concessions that she never intended to make at the outset.

The deadpan approach has another basic advantage. The supplier may begin to believe that the buyer's position is much stronger than it actually is. The ethical buyer never lies. But he doesn't spill everything he knows. It would be unethical, for example, to tell the supplier that you can buy the item at a lower price if this just isn't true. But if the supplier begins to believe this herself because of the buyer's silence, that is the supplier's problem.

3. *Let the supplier save face.* The buyer should at all costs avoid a showdown. She never wants to force the supplier into a position where she says, "Here are my terms—take them or leave them." Once the supplier does this, he must lose face if he makes further concessions. Similarly, a buyer should never imply, directly or indirectly, that cost breakdowns or similar data submitted by a supplier are false or misleading. Such breakdowns always justify the supplier's position. When the buyer analyzes them and finds they are incorrect, she should point out the "errors" or "misinterpretations" in them. But under no circumstances should she imply that the data were created solely for use as a sales tool by the supplier.

4. *Satisfy the supplier's needs.* Most suppliers have two outstanding characteristics. They genuinely like selling, and they feel somewhat insecure. Smart buyers cater to these characteristics. They give the supplier a chance to sell them. Thus a good buyer provides a test for the supplier's skills that is both stimulating and satisfying. The buyer should also remember that many of his suppliers are in businesses that are subject to violent ups and downs. Suppliers inevitably are attracted to buyers who make them feel secure and who do not unnecessarily increase their insecurity so long as their terms are competitive. They often will offer better terms to such buyers simply because their emotional needs are partly fulfilled.

5. *Talk to the proper person.* Some buyers make the mistake of trying to negotiate with the wrong person in the supplier's organization. When they do, they are simply wasting their time. For example, most supplier sales representatives have limited powers to negotiate purchase terms and conditions. Sometimes they have no authority at all. Most suppliers give their sales reps a little leeway. For example, they may be instructed to quote a price of $100 for an item, which they can cut to $95 without consulting the home office if they are forced to do so in negotiation. In such a case, the buyer should try to estimate in advance approximately what concessions the supplier is willing to make. If she is satisfied with these concessions, she can conclude negotiations shortly with the sales rep. If she is not satisfied, she should negotiate with higher level officials in the supplier organization. If the purchase is an extremely important one for both buyer and seller, the top management of both companies may become involved before negotiations are concluded. Minor purchases, on the other hand, rarely involve much negotiation. If the desired agreement cannot be reached with the supplier sales representative, the buyer will either accept the supplier's terms or start looking for another supplier.

6. *Sell the supplier.* Intelligent suppliers try to get business from companies that are going places. They very wisely recognize that their own growth is linked to that of their customers. The buyer should try to convince the supplier that the buyer's firm is worth doing business with over the longer term, even if this involves temporary sacrifices on the part of the supplier. This approach obviously has its limitations. It can be used with considerable success for a buyer who works for IBM or Polaroid but it is a moot point how effective it would be were it applied by a purchasing agent of a bankrupt railroad.

7. *Take up one point at a time.* A series of little concessions will add up to a big concession. Each little concession is relatively painless, but taken together they may be more than the supplier can swallow. It can safely be assumed that the supplier can figure out what is going on in this process. But it is just possible that he will wind up conceding slightly more than he originally intended if the process represents a series of little nibbles instead of one big bite.

8. *Don't rush the process.* Of course, only major purchases are worth the trouble of prolonged negotiation. But if it is worth the effort, give yourself sufficient time to be effective. The seller should never get the idea that you are eager to wrap up negotiations so that you can proceed to more important business. On the contrary, you should try to make the supplier eager to conclude negotiations by giving you at least part of what you request.

A top supplier executive may be eager to complete negotiations simply because he must move on to the next customer. One very successful hospital group purchasing director takes advantage of this. Her major contracts are almost always negotiated with a top supplier executive who flies in to see her with the object of buttoning up the deal after a single day's session. She quite deliberately goes through the process to the end, winding up with the remark, "it looks pretty good to me but I am not sure what my superiors will think. They are very concerned with the way costs have been going up and I know they want me to do a little better than what you have proposed." In some cases, the supplier executive (obviously in a hurry) will offer an additional concession. At this point, the director of purchases concludes that she is "almost certain" the deal will be binding—and it is.

9. *Be honest and impersonal.* The director of purchases was telling the truth, of course. Her superiors do indeed want to pay lower prices and they will be happier if she gets a better deal. Even if there were no ethical problems, a good purchasing manager never lies to a supplier. To be successful as a negotiator, one must have credibility. Also, the negotiation process should be carried on in an impersonal fashion. Never deal in personalities.

The negotiating session

Major purchases of equipment or parts almost always require formal negotiating sessions. Usually they are held in the purchasing manager's office. The vendor generally will send a top sales official to assist the local sales representative. He may also send his controller, chief engineer, or manufacturing superintendent if the discussion involves their specialties. The purchasing executives also may draw on other departments for technical assistance, especially on quality control and engineering.

Advance planning. The participants in a negotiating session accomplish more if the session is planned in advance, with an agenda indicating what is to be discussed. Purchasing should be prepared to discuss price and delivery terms. Engineering and quality control experts may be called upon to discuss the proposed purchase in terms of their specialties. Shrewd purchasing executives never go into a negotiating session unprepared. They try to anticipate what the supplier will propose so they can be ready with a counterproposal.

Some go so far as to conduct prenegotiating sessions in which all the participants except the supplier's representatives meet to plan the real session. Good planning pays off. In some cases, the supplier can be caught off guard, and the result is a greater concession than she had originally intended to grant. In every case, good planning reduces the probability that some important area for negotiation will be neglected.

Negotiating sessions take varying amounts of time. Two hours may be adequate for many rather important purchases. Sometimes a full day or longer must be allowed, particularly if there are a great many engineering details to review. In any event, the atmosphere should be calm and unhurried. Some purchasing executives even believe in spending the first few minutes of the session in discussing completely irrelevant subjects—such as who won yesterday's ball game—in order to create the proper atmosphere.

Every effort should be made to prevent the participants from becoming the least bit emotional. When there is sharp disagreement, the chair should make note of it and pass on to the next topic on the agenda. Perhaps the disagreement can be resolved at another session, or one party may concede to the other rather than see negotiations broken off. When every point has been covered, the chairperson should summarize all points of agreement—and disagreement—and conclude the meeting. Many materials executives follow up such meetings with a written summary of the minutes in order to prevent any possible misunderstanding. A letter would then be sent to the supplier which outlined the areas where agreement was reached and also made counterproposals to resolve questions on which agreement has not as yet been reached.

Prenegotiation. The formal negotiation session is a simple straightforward approach to the problem of reaching agreement with the supplier on prices and other contract terms. Many Americans and almost all foreigners prefer a less direct approach in which business and social activity are intermixed.

For example, buyer and seller may enjoy 18 holes of golf together without discussing business problems at all. Then in the locker room each may gently sound the other out on the basic problem. Neither party presents anything that could be construed as a formal offer or counteroffer at this time. Each simply listens sympathetically as the other discusses problems and objectives. No attempt is made to conclude an agreement.

The basic purpose of the locker-room session is for buyer and seller to understand each other's attitudes and problems. Each can then tailor his or her formal proposal to fit more closely the needs of the other. The buyer-seller golf game (or hunting and fishing expeditions, or similar jaunts) may be regarded as fun by the casual observer. And it is. But when he gets closer to the process, he realizes that its major purpose is still business—and the sales rep on the golf course may be working just as hard as the person who is beating the bushes for customers in more obvious ways. While it may be inefficient and wasteful, the prenegotiation session that is conducted on the golf course is often the most efficient way that buyer and seller can reconcile differences and concentrate on common objectives. There is no way that a buyer can force a supplier to do what he wants—or vice versa. Informal contact is often an ideal way to achieve a meeting of the minds so that each can understand the other's goals and do what can be done to achieve a compromise that is consistent with the objectives of both parties.

ORDER PLACEMENT AND DELIVERY

Single versus multiple sources

The negotiation process winds up with the placement of one or more orders. At some stage in the process, a basic decision must be made: Should the purchase be a single or multiple source? In most real-life purchases, the business is awarded to a single supplier whose price is the lowest among those bidding—or it becomes the lowest when adjusted to account for other factors affecting the buyer's direct costs. But this is not always the case. If a supplier quoting a higher price offers better quality, delivery, or service, it may get the order. Reciprocity and other factors also influence the selection of suppliers. In general, however, the buyer is on the defensive if the low bidder does not get the job. Many companies require buyers to enter detailed explanations in their records when this is the case, and some buyers prefer to make an explanation even when it is not required in order to protect themselves against charges of collusion.

Companies may have as many as four or five suppliers for a given item simultaneously. But, in most cases, buyers rely on a single supplier for all of their requirements of a particular item. If the item does not become obsolete, they will solicit bids from other suppliers from time to time to make sure that their supplier is still competitive. In addition, they make use of learning-curve analysis and other techniques to make certain that their supplier is passing on the benefits of productivity improvements by reducing prices periodically.

Advantages of a single source.   By buying all requirements of a particular item from a single source, buyers can gain several advantages:

- They make maximum use of their buying power. They concentrate all requirements for a certain item on a single supplier and thereby get the largest possible quantity discount.

2. There is less administrative work for the buyer's entire organization, since purchase orders, receiving reports, inspection reports, checks, and so on are issued to only one supplier per item.

3. Suppliers often offer special price concessions if they can make 100 percent of the requirements of a given item, since they then can set up their production in the most economic manner and invest in more efficient tooling.

4. Less investment in special tooling is usually needed. One supplier generally needs only one set of tools; with two suppliers each needs a set.

5. Suppliers have more incentive to aid in methods improvement. If a supplier is the sole source for an item, he is more likely to regard himself as a partner in the company's product, particularly if he is manufacturing the item under a long-term contract. As a result, he will be more likely to devote part of his research and development efforts to improvements.

Advantages of multiple sources. Despite these advantages, many companies do their utmost to avoid relying on a single source for all but the most unimportant items. They try to have at least two suppliers for each item, and sometimes they have three or four, for one or more of the following reasons:

1. With several sources, there is less risk of interruption of supply due to quality problems, strikes, fires, and so on. If one supplier fails, the other(s) can take up the slack.

2. With two or more suppliers for one item, a healthy competitive spirit can develop in which each vies to improve methods and reduce costs in order to get a greater share of the business. With a single source, the supplier may become so well versed in making the item that she gets a virtual monopoly of its manufacture and, sometimes, no competitor brought in at a later date can meet her prices.

3. Many items either require little or no tooling or are used in such large quantities that duplicate tooling is necessary anyway. In these cases, there is no cost premium for tooling a second source.

4. The unit price of the item is no higher with two or more sources than it would be if all requirements were concentrated on a single source.

5. The buyer has found a new supplier with low prices whom she would like to introduce to the item but whom she is not yet familiar enough with to trust with 100 percent of the business.

6. There is simply no valid reason *not* to buy from multiple suppliers. Because of the nature of the items being bought, all suppliers offer pretty much the same quality, price, and service. For the con-

sumer, this principle might be applied to the purchase of a local newspaper at any of a number of newstands or drugstores that one passes on the way to work.

Placing the order

When the buyer concludes negotiations and finally settles on a supplier, he places the order. He may simply mail a purchase order with the agreed-on terms and conditions to the supplier. Or, if he wants the supplier to start on the order immediately, he may telephone or wire her that she has been awarded the contract. The purchase order then is sent in a few days.

The buyer's job ends with the placement of the order only on minor, short lead-time items for which there is no immediate need. In such cases, the supplier ships when she receives the order and the transaction is complete. No buyer, however, would dare place an important order for parts, material, or equipment and then forget about it. He always would make some sort of routine follow-up even if there were no problems.

Acknowledgment of orders. Routine follow-up may start with acknowledgment of the order. A copy of the purchase order is kept in a separate file of unacknowledged open orders until an acknowledgment is received. If the supplier does not acknowledge within a week after he should have received the order, a buyer or expediter either phones or sends him a written reminder.

Some companies persistently follow up for acknowledgments of orders until they finally get them from suppliers. They know that in most cases the supplier is legally committed to the terms and conditions of the order only after he has formally acknowledged or actually filled the order. Also, when there is no follow-up for acknowledgments, there theoretically could be serious problems if the order should have been mislaid or lost in the mail. The company might suddenly discover a few days before the material was needed for production that the supplier had no record of the order. The result would certainly be a critical shortage, and possibly even a shutdown.

Nevertheless, many companies do not bother to follow up except when they are required to do so by government regulations, as on defense contracts. They maintain that such follow-up is expensive and never is worth the trouble or the expense it causes. The rare order that goes astray need not cause any trouble, either. In most cases, the vendor would have already been notified of the order by telephone or letter of commitment, and he would inquire if he did not receive a formal purchase order. In other cases, companies would discover that an order had gone astray through routine follow-up or when a supplier sales representative called to discuss his business prospects.

The company that insists on acknowledgment of its purchase orders may sometimes get information it does not want—namely, that the supplier takes exception to its purchase order terms and conditions. One way (not necessarily a good one) to circumvent this problem is simply to refuse an acknowledgement. For example, one company uses this clause as a substitute for an acknowledgment copy of the order:

> Delivery is a major condition of this order. If for any reason you cannot meet the terms of this purchase order you must reply within 72 hours indicating any deviations. The absence of a reply will constitute an acceptance of this order and an agreement to meet the terms and conditions as specified above and on the reverse side hereof.

It is a moot point whether this clause would actually be enforceable. That is, if a supplier simply did nothing, the buyer might not be able to hold it to the terms and conditions of its purchase order. But the clause does open the problem up, and a supplier who was acting in good faith would not deliberately ignore it.

Routine progress follow-up. Regardless of whether or not they worry about acknowledgments of purchase orders, most purchasing departments do make routine checks on suppliers' progress on orders. The frequency of follow-up depends on the importance and urgency of the item. Minor items may get no follow-up as long as inventories are ample. Most of the more important items get at least one progress check, which is most often made a week or two before the promised delivery date.

The procedure for handling such a check need not be complicated. One of the more popular procedures involves keeping copies of the purchase orders in file folders marked with the date for which follow-up is scheduled. Each morning (or once a week), a secretary gives the buyer the file folder of orders to be checked that day.

Often the follow-up process is entirely automatic and the buyer does not get into the act at all if there are not problems. A clerk sends a postcard requesting progress information on each order a week or ten days before shipment is promised. The buyer is consulted only if the vendor advises that he cannot meet his original delivery promise. When delivery is not made on the scheduled date, the buyer may request information using a form similar to Figure 13–3. If she needed the item badly, however, she would telephone the supplier for information.

More complex follow-up systems are used for major production parts and equipment. The buyer estimates what progress the supplier should have made on the order at various dates if he is to complete it on schedule. For example, he might check progress on an order for a production part when completion of tooling is scheduled, when tools

FIGURE 13-3

PURCHASING DEPT.

NORTH ADAMS, MASS.

MARSHALL STREET

SPRAGUE ELECTRIC COMPANY

FIRST CLASS PERMIT NO. 458   NORTH ADAMS, MASS.

B U S I N E S S   R E P L Y   M A I L

No
Postage Stamp
Necessary
If Mailed in the
United States

Postage
Will Be Paid
by
Addressee

Gentlemen:

Our records indicate that your shipping promise on purchase order(s) referenced on the attached card has not been maintained. This has seriously jeopardized our production schedule.

Please confirm your intention to ship by a wire or phone call to the buyer who issued the order.

If shipment has been made, please furnish complete routing information by returning this card so that material can be traced.

Thank you.

                    PURCHASING DEPT.
                    SPRAGUE ELECTRIC COMPANY

Courtesy Sprague Electric Co.

Many companies use double postcards for routine follow-up at various stages. The card above is used when the supplier has not kept his delivery promise. The supplier then returns the second card to the buyer with the shipping promise noted on it.

are to be tried out, and when initial production is scheduled. If everything is going according to plan on each of these and other critical dates, he is reasonably certain that actual production shipments will be made on schedule.

In the typical purchasing department, more than 99 percent of all orders can be handled with little or no follow-up. Routine progress checks are insurance against failure, but they are not necessary except in a few cases. This is fortunate, since the less than 1 percent of all orders that are problems manage to take an enormous percentage of

420

the materials executive's time. Dealing with these orders is discussed in the next chapter.

SALE OF SCRAP AND SURPLUS

The buying process does not necessarily end when satisfactory material is received on schedule. The buyer also must sell surplus and scrap materials that are inevitably generated when material is used or becomes obsolete. This is one of the incidental but by no means unimportant jobs of the materials department.

Selling scrap and surplus is a function of the materials department in most companies because the sales department concentrates its efforts on marketing end products. The materials department is much more familiar with potential buyers of scrap and salvage materials; in fact, it may sell much of its process scrap back to its raw materials suppliers.

Even medium-sized companies may realize hundreds of thousands of dollars a year through scrap and surplus sales. Three basic types of material are sold: process scrap; miscellaneous scrap and salvage material; and surplus material and equipment.

Process scrap. There are few production processes that waste no raw material. Only rarely does all raw material wind up in the finished product; usually some becomes process scrap. For example, in the machining of metal, about half of the raw material may end up in the finished product; the rest will be process scrap, chips, and turnings. This scrap metal has a value ranging from about $90 per ton for steel chips to 80 cents or more per pound for copper and costlier metals. Since even small metalworking plants frequently use tons of metal each month, process scrap sales are an important source of revenue for them.

Miscellaneous scrap and salvage. Every plant must dispose of tons of material each year because it is usable neither in finished products nor as process scrap. Cartons, pallets, and boxes are among the most important miscellaneous items. In most areas there is a ready market for scrap paper and lumber for plants that do not find ways to reuse such materials themselves.

Surplus material and equipment. As we have seen (in Chapter 8), no company should carry inventories it does not need. Surplus materials should be sold as soon as it becomes reasonably certain that there is no immediate need for them. Obsolete equipment should also be sold as soon as no immediate use can be foreseen for it.

Scrap segregation. Scrap and surplus have value to a buyer only if they can be used. For this reason, companies are almost as careful in handling them as they are in handling newly purchased materials. It is particularly important to keep scrap segregated. In some cases, a scrap material will have no value at all if it is mixed in with other materials. In every case it will have more value if it is reasonably clean and free from impurities. Many companies use a color-code system for scrap collection and segregation. For example, red barrels at strategic locations in the plant might be used only for aluminum turnings, while yellow barrels would be used only for stainless steel.

Processing.   As with any other product, top prices on scrap sales go only to those who deliver top-quality materials. Many companies invest in processing equipment both to facilitate handling of scrap and to improve its quality. For example, they may buy equipment to dry out and clean metal turnings that are soaked with oil. They may bale both metal and paper scrap to get a higher price and to make them easier to handle. They may even wind up with equipment to reprocess the scrap into usable end products. For example, several large corporations have invested in plants to convert their scrap paper into corrugated paper for new cartons.

Sale.   Scrap is normally sold by asking a number of scrap brokers or dealers to bid (see Figure 13–4) on either a specific quantity or a year's needs of some commodity. Some companies sell to all comers on a cash basis; others will deal only with reputable brokers and dealers with established credit. In either case, the high bidder always gets the material. Published market prices are available for many scrap materials, and it is common practice to use these prices as the basis for long-term contracts on scrap sales. Variations in the quality of scrap sometimes forbid this, however. Regardless of the pricing technique used, the seller always can get a somewhat better price if she exercises her ingenuity. A buyer who is selling scrap looks for buyers with the same thoroughness with which he recruits suppliers when he is buying material.

This is particularly true for specialized scrap and salvage materials for which no real market exists. In some cases, dealers will not buy such material because they do not know where they can sell it. In others, dealers may identify a market and reward their own initiative by offering the seller a price well below what they can sell it for. In such cases the buyer is much better off if she can eliminate the middleman and negotiate a deal directly with the user of the scrap material. For example, Aeroquip Corporation of Jackson, Michigan, increased its return on surplus oleum spirits 500 percent by locating a small local buyer with a specialized use for the material.

Disputes over quality are prevented by permitting each interested bidder to inspect the material physically in advance. If the material is standardized, this is not necessary; well-defined specifications are available on which buyer and seller can agree in advance. For exam-

422

FIGURE 13–4
Invitation to bid for scrap materials

Courtesy Marquardt Aircraft Co.

The form used to solicit bids on scrap and surplus material that a company has for sale is not much different from the form used to solicit bids for material it wishes to buy.

ple, the National Association of Secondary Material Industries publishes specifications on cotton rags, paper, and nonferrous scrap materials, while the Institute of Scrap Iron and Steel, publishes specifications for iron and steel scrap. In such cases it is usually fairly easy to determine whether or not the material meets desired specifications. Occasionally disputes arise over weights—often because the weight has changed in transit between buyer and seller owing to material drying out on being exposed to the hot sun, and so on. Companies prevent such disputes by insisting that the weight shown on their scales determine the buyer's payment or by using some local public scale where the weighmaster's certificate is the basis for payment.

Cases

CASE 13-1. GREAT LAKES SUPPLY COMPANY

Selecting the right supplier

Although Great Lakes Auto Supply Company does some manufacturing, it is primarily a distributor. It buys auto parts from independent manufacturers and resells them to thousands of service stations and repair shops. The parts that Great Lakes buys are almost identical with those distributed by the service departments of the auto manufacturers themselves. Great Lakes is successful because it is willing to undersell the original equipment manufacturers on service parts. For example, the manufacturer purchases mufflers at a unit price of $4.64 for one of the nation's most popular brands of car. It resells them to its dealers for $13.60, and they in turn sell them to the ultimate consumer for $21.00 plus a charge for installation labor. Great Lakes buys almost the same muffler from one of its suppliers for $5.56 (it buys in smaller quantities than the original equipment manufacturer and so must pay a higher price). It resells the muffler for $7.50 and the gas station charges the ultimate consumer $15.00 plus installation labor.

The auto manufacturers and their franchised dealers refer to Great Lakes and its suppliers as "gyp" manufacturers. They point out that the gyps do no engineering but simply copy the parts of the auto manufacturers. They claim that the gyps produce parts of inferior quality. Consumers, attracted by the lower prices charged by the gyps, obviously do not accept the auto companies' charges. Yet the charge that the gyps copy their designs is certainly true.

For example, Walter Norris, Great Lakes' vice president in charge of purchases, recently secured quotations on replacement floor mats for 1973 Blue Motors sedans. Suppliers got no specifications; instead, they were asked to quote on the basis of "original equipment qualities." Norris got the following bids for 10,000 mats:

Supplier	Price	F.o.b.	Tools	Terms
Western Rubber Products	$6.64	Shipping point	$ 90	2/10, net 30
Alexander Corporation	6.50	Great Lakes plant	220	Net 20th prox.
Roberts Rubber Company	6.88	Great Lakes plant	130	1/10, net 30
Wartly Rubber, Inc.	5.68	Shipping point	100	Net 30 days

The mat used as original equipment on Blue Motors cars weighs 9.2 pounds, and Norris assumes that the suppliers will give him a mat of the same weight. Norris understands from one of his suppliers that Blue Motors pays an average of $5.50 for the mat. Since Blue Motors uses an average of 2,000 mats per day from each of its suppliers, Norris is not the least bit surprised that none of his bids is that low. In fact, he suspects that Blue Motor's price may be even lower than this.

Norris has made an analysis in which he compares the Blue Motors mat with mats he has purchased for various other auto models. He concludes that a fair price for the Blue Motors mat is probably between $6.20 and $6.50. He passes this on to Western and Roberts and asks them if they would be interested in requoting. Both suppliers reply that their costs have gone up since they quoted last and Norris's estimate of a fair price for the mat is out of date. Western and Roberts are currently supplying other mats to Great Lakes. Alexander and Wartly make mats for other auto part distributors but have never been Great Lakes suppliers. Norris has some doubts as to whether or not Wartly can supply the desired quality, although Wartly has had considerable experience in producing mats for the "gyp" trade.

Questions

1. Which supplier should Norris choose? Support your recommendations with an analysis, making assumptions where necessary.
2. What special studies might be called for in this case?

CASE 13–2. ADAMS EQUIPMENT CORPORATION

Sale of scrap iron

Adams Equipment Corporation is a manufacturer of pumps and similar equipment. Its products are made primarily from gray-iron castings, and approximately two carloads of gray-iron chips are generated in the Adams plant each day.

Eastern States Scrap Metal has been buying Adams's scrap and salvage products on a regular basis since the Adams company was founded more than 30 years ago. Joseph Adams, the founder of Adams Equipment, and Morris Levine, the founder and president of Eastern States Scrap Metal, have had a long-standing history of successful business relationships that date back to the years when both men managed rather small businesses. Now Adams Equipment employs more than 1,000 persons in its factory, while Eastern States is one of the largest scrap metal brokers and dealers in the United States.

Although Joseph Adams was originally responsible for developing the relationship with Eastern States, the actual administration of the contract with Eastern States is part of the overall responsibility of Roberta Hallowell, the materials manager of Adams Equipment. This has hardly been one of Hallowell's more pressing chores. The scrap contract more or less handles itself. Employees of Eastern States have complete access to the Adams plant and remove scrap iron as it is generated and load it into gondola cars in the Adams railroad siding. The cars then eventually are picked up at the Adams siding and shipped either to another scrap broker or to a foundry which deals directly with Eastern States. Eastern States forwards a check each month to Adams and a statement that indicates the total amount of scrap sold and the price per ton that Eastern States is paying.

Eastern States naturally has substantial expenses in removing the scrap from the Adams plant and, consequently, the price it pays Adams for the scrap is less than the market price. Hallowell, in studying the situation, notes that the price Eastern pays Adams is apparently about $6 per ton less than the posted price for the large metropolitan area in which the Adams plant is located. But, of course, Eastern States has several workers permanently employed at the Adams plant and has also made investments in materials handling equipment, trucks, and other items.

Hallowell is by no means convinced that Eastern States is giving Adams anything but a fair price. Relations between Eastern States executives and Adams executives have always been amicable.

Eastern States not only has been a model firm with which to deal but, in addition, has rendered services to Adams that have not necessarily been profitable for them. For example, Eastern States has been willing to purchase other types of salvage and scrap materials from Adams even when there has not been a big enough market for such material to be worth the trouble. If Adams wanted to get rid of some scrap paper products—which often have negligible scrap value— Eastern States has been willing to take it off Adams's hands and, apparently, pass on the entire proceeds of the sale to Adams (if the material has any value at all). In other cases, Eastern States has handled small amounts of miscellaneous scrap material where the value has not really been worth the trouble. For example, Adams occasionally scraps equipment that has no salvage value other than as scrap metal. Eastern States, although it really is not set up for such small-scale business, has been willing to pick up such material and to give Adams a fair price for it.

Eastern States is in a highly competitive business. From time to time other scrap firms have solicited the Adams account but, apparently, have had nothing to offer that Adams is not already getting from Eastern States. These firms were willing to pay market price but, of course, if they performed the extra services that Eastern States performs, they would charge for them. Hallowell has not personally had any contact with any of Eastern States's potential competitors as she has only been on her existing job for about two years. She has gathered, however, that there has not been too much solicitation of business by rival scrap firms in recent years because apparently they have come to recognize that Eastern States is "in" at Adams.

Hallowell wonders if it might not be a bad idea for Eastern States to get some competition, but she has no valid reason to question the quality of Eastern States service or the price it pays.

Questions

1. What are the advantages and disadvantages of a long-standing relationship such as that between Adams and Eastern States?
2. Is this relationship necessarily in the best interests of both firms? Explain.

14

Buying for production

[handwritten: most purchasing organizations will break it into two groups]

Purchasing is a specialized skill in itself. But it also can be categorized into subspecialities. The most clear-cut division of purchasing skills comes about by dividing purchases into two categories: buying for production and subsequent resale as part of some larger, more complex product; and nonproduction supplies, equipment, and services purchased for the exclusive use of the buying organization.

All organizations engage in nonproduction buying. Buying for production is limited to manufacturing firms. Production parts and materials are usually exclusive products manufactured to buyer's specifications. Because manufacturers often spend enormous amounts of money on them (over $30 billion per year in the case of the General Motors Corporation), the most successful purchasing executives typically devote almost all of their time to problems associated with buying for production. In some cases, the product purchased for production is not much different from that purchased for nonproduction. For example, Chevrolet buys glass from Libbey-Owens-Ford that is custom-shaped to be fitted directly onto its cars as they are assembled. Like every other large organization, it also buys glass for repair and replacement in its factories and offices. However, it may spend $100 million per year on glass for production and perhaps no more than a few hundred thousand dollars on glass for repairs and maintenance. The latter glass is probably identical to that purchased by Ford for the same purpose. In the former case, however, a Chevrolet windshield would not fit a Ford car and is a unique product.

CHARACTERISTICS

Buying for production has these three important economic characteristics that make it a subject worthy of separate discussion:

1. *Quotations from competing suppliers reflect identical specifications.* Normally, the buyer's organization designs the component that is to be purchased and each supplier is asked to quote on identical specifications. When there is more than one supplier, it is all but impossible to distinguish one vendor's product from another (except that buyers sometimes deliberately require that an identifying mark be made on the component in case there are quality problems later on).

Obviously, competition can be quite keen when each competing supplier is quoting on the same specifications. In contrast, suppliers of nonproduction supplies and equipment are able often to differentiate their products. While competing products do essentially the same job, they are made to different specifications and it can be claimed that one product is of higher quality than another. This complicates the buying processes and tends to reduce price competition.

2. *Prices paid for custom-designed production components are unique.* They reflect seller's costs, competitive pressures, and buyer's ability or willingness to pay. In contrast, sellers of nonproduction materials and equipment are not only influenced by negotiation with particular customers but also by the effect of these negotiations on prices charged other customers—now or at some time in the future. The Robinson-Patman Act makes it illegal for suppliers to discriminate in price among like classes of purchasers for like items. Also, of course, it is usually not good marketing practice to sell an identical item to one customer for $10 and then turn around and sell it to someone else for $15.

For the reasons mentioned above, suppliers of nonproduction supplies and equipment usually have fairly consistent price schedules. A canny buyer may do better than one who is asleep (especially when going through a distributor) but there are limitations. In contrast, when the part is made to the buyer's specification, the deal is unique. In the final analysis, it is determined solely by what buyer and seller will accept.

3. *Production parts and materials are usually (but not always) used in much larger quantities than nonproduction items.* This applies both to the custom-designed variety (such as the bumper or steering wheel used on a particular model of Chevrolet car) and also to parts and materials used on a variety of competing products (such as tires or steel of various specifications that are used simultaneously on competing brands of automobiles). These larger volume purchases warrant use of specialized purchasing techniques that would not be economic with many purchases of supplies.

THE PRICING PROCESS

While every buyer would maintain that production components are purchased in competitive markets, this is hardly ever competition in the "pure" sense. In a truly competitive market, no individual buyer or seller can influence price. In contrast, when buying production parts, each individual buyer and seller negotiates a unique price. Thus, the price that Chevrolet pays Libbey-Owens-Ford for the molded windshields used in its current models is determined exclusively by Libbey-Owens Ford and Chevrolet. It is competitive in the sense that if it were any higher Chevrolet might well either make its own windshields or buy them from some other supplier. If it were any lower, in contrast, Libbey-Owens Ford would simply refuse to produce the windshields, telling Chevrolet to take its business elsewhere. This is what economists call an "administered" price, determined by a process of "imperfect" competition. When there is relatively little competition among producers, the administered price usually is high enough to yield handsome profits. When there are many producers and competition is keen, profits shrink even though an individual producer theoretically is free to charge any price he or she pleases.

Administered prices are quite different from prices determined by pure competition. Pure competition prevails only when there are a large number of buyers and sellers and the product is homogeneous. One seller's product is as good as that of any other seller, and no single buyer or seller can influence prices. Everyone must do business at the prevailing market price, which is determined by the collective action of all buyers and sellers.

Buyer's economic role

When reasonably pure competition prevails, as it does for most materials traded on commodity exchanges, materials management is primarily concerned with price forecasting and timing of purchases. When imperfect competition prevails, as it does for 99 percent of the items that a typical company buys, the scope of the materials management job is far broader. It is intimately concerned with the pricing process and product quality.

In most cases the supplier does not have the last word on prices. Able buyers can exert tremendous leverage if they understand how prices are set and do not hesitate to use their skills. In doing so, they are doing a service not only to their own company but also to the supplier and to the economy as a whole.

When competition is imperfect and prices are not regulated impersonally by market forces, some other regulatory force is needed. In a totalitarian economy, the force is exerted arbitrarily by government officials. In a free economy, it is exerted by negotiation between buyer and seller. Every time a buyer challenges a vendor's bid, she forces the vendor to recheck costs and review ways in which productivity can be increased. She becomes a substitute for the impersonal competitive market forces that determine the prices of materials traded on commodity markets. In this role, buyers are collectively a tremendous force in the overall economy. When they award business to the efficient, low-cost producers and force the high-cost producers either to mend their ways or to go out of business, they help make the overall economy wealthier and more productive.

Suppliers also benefit when buyers challenge their prices, although few suppliers are aware of the benefit and even fewer would admit it. Pressure from buyers stimulates improvements and prevents complacency. Although sloppy purchasing will certainly permit a supplier to boost profits temporarily, the day of reckoning comes eventually. Only the supplier who is efficient can hope to earn high profits indefinitely.

Administered prices

Pricing can be a real problem with imperfect competition. The supplier cannot simply sell at some market price, because there is no market. Nor, in most cases, can the supplier set a price that will yield the highest possible return. Instead, he must grope for a price that is high enough to be profitable but not so high that a buyer will turn to a competitor's product.

In many cases, the supplier's estimate of what the "right" price should be is not much better than the buyer's estimate. Few suppliers will admit this, of course. But the reasons are obvious in the light of the supplier's pricing process on items where imperfect competition prevails and prices must be administered. In such cases, prices are determined by each producer on the basis of:

1. Probable demand at various prices.
2. Selling prices of similar products by competitors.
3. Profit objectives.
4. Cost of production at various levels of output.

Establishing an administered price is as much an art as it is a science. Each of the four factors above must be considered in making the final pricing decision. The desired profits often are not achieved because of changes in demand, lower prices of competitors, or the cost of production.

Effect of demand. When a supplier gets an inquiry from a buyer, he knows what the immediate demand is. He may not know what the ultimate demand from that buyer will be. In most cases, the buyer does not know either; she can only guess what her company's future prospects are. But she should pass on to the supplier any information on future demand that is not confidential in order to help negotiate the most realistic price.

The buyer also should try to determine what demand, if any, buyers in other companies will have for the supplier's products. He will not necessarily get accurate information from the supplier; he may have to base his estimate on his own general knowledge of the market. In general, the stronger the demand for the supplier's products and services, the higher the price the supplier can seek. It is the buyer's job to undermine this demand by finding numerous alternate supply sources that are eager, able, and available.

Competitors' selling prices. Every company's sales department tries to keep up to date on the selling prices of competitors. With some products this is easy. Published prices are readily available, and producers actually sell at the published prices. For other products the job is more difficult. In fact, in many cases neither buyer nor seller is fully informed about the selling prices of all possible competitors. The buyer often is better informed than the seller, since she can always solicit bids from a number of suppliers. But many suppliers are better informed than some buyers give them credit for. Only a foolish (and unethical) buyer will deliberately mislead suppliers as to their competitors' selling prices. But a buyer need not go out of her way to tip off a supplier when the competitors are raising their prices.

However, it may not do any harm to "leak" news of price cutting. The supplier who cuts prices on a selective basis would prefer that competitors not know what he is doing, since they will usually match or even try to beat his prices. From the buyer's point of view, competition is increased if each seller is well informed on the pricing strategy of competitors—provided there is no collusion among suppliers. If such price competition is concealed, it is possible that a company competing with the buyer's firm may be gaining a price advantage in purchasing. In most cases, sellers are extremely well informed on competitors' strategies, and the buyer can tell them nothing they do not already know. In fact, it is usually the buyer who can learn from the seller, rather than vice versa.

Profit objectives. Well-managed companies almost always set specific targets for profits in relation to both sales and net worth. For example, a company might seek to earn 15 percent before taxes on sales and 25 percent on net worth or invested capital. One of the easiest ways to achieve this objective is to set selling prices high enough so that they virtually guarantee success. Almost every supplier will do this if demand, competitors' selling prices, and customer acceptance of his prices permit it. No smart buyer objects if a supplier achieves his profit objectives, but she prefers to have it done through lower costs and increased efficiency rather than through high prices.

Cost of production. No supplier is eager to sell below his total costs, and any supplier would be extremely foolish to sell for less than his cash out-of-pocket cost. Cost of production is the single most important factor in price determination, since it sets the minimum level below which prices drop only on rare occasions. The supplier's pricing theoretically rests firmly on his estimates of cost of production. To this cost estimate he adds a profit that reflects his profit objectives, moderated by his estimate of competitors' selling prices and demand.

For example, if a supplier calculates that unit costs will total $1.00 for an item and his profit objective is a 20 percent return on sales, his bid would be $1.25. Up to this point, the estimate may well be made by a junior employee in the cost-estimating department or even by a computer. But before the bid is submitted to the customer, a top executive—the sales manager, general manager, or president—will usually study it. The price may then be modified to reflect overall demand and competitors' selling prices. Usually the senior executive will reduce the bid. Strong competition or a weak market prevent the desired profit markup from being added in full to the estimated cost. When business is booming, the senior executive may raise the bid and shoot for a higher than standard profit. No executive ever was fired for making too much profit for the company.

SUPPLIERS' COST ESTIMATES

The vendor pricing process is much less exact than we have implied so far. The supplier does not work with a rigid estimate of costs to which she adds a profit that is flexible and determined by market conditions. Instead, her whole cost estimate is quite flexible. The reason for this is that costs can never be calculated exactly until after they have actually been incurred. And sometimes they can never really be determined. One major problem is that of joint costs chargeable to several products. For example, if a mining company recovers several minerals from the same ore, how does it allocate the cost of digging the ore to the finished minerals? Or how does a company allocate the salary of its chief executive to its various products? By the amount of time he spends on each product, by sales volume, by gross profit on each product, or by some other means? Regardless of the method used, the allocation is arbitrary, as any student of cost accounting knows.

A supplier's price quotation is, of necessity, based on estimated future costs that she thinks will be incurred if she gets the business. Such estimates are no more than educated guesses, regardless of the proficiency of the estimators. This is true regardless of the cost-estimating system used. Most systems break cost into four major components: direct material cost, direct labor cost, manufacturing overhead, and administrative expenses. Each component is estimated separately.

Direct material cost

The easiest component to estimate is usually direct material cost. Direct material includes any purchased part or material that is used directly in the product. Some cost accountants even consider paint, packaging, and plating materials direct material, although there is no universal agreement on this. Cost accountants do not regard materials consumed in the production process (such as cutting oils) as direct material. All maintenance, repair, and operating supplies are considered indirect material and are part of the manufacturing overhead, since they are not incorporated directly into the product.

Usually the cost estimator determines the cost of direct material simply by asking the purchasing department for the price. He then calculates usage and multiplies by the unit price. It is not necessarily an easy job to estimate materials usage. The estimate of the stainless steel molding shown in Table 14–1 is a case in point. The estimator must be able to calculate the initial blank size of stainless steel needed from the blueprint of the finished molding. Once he knows the blank size, the job is not too difficult. He calculates the weight and then multiplies by the price per pound to get the cost. Sometimes estimates

TABLE 14–1
Cost estimate, automobile door molding

Material cost:
  SAE 51430 stainless steel
  $0.018'' \times 1.6125'' \times 21.16'' = 0.1735$ lbs.
  0.1735 lbs. $\times$ \$0.8912/lb \$0.1546
  Packaging material 0.0084
Labor cost:

Equipment	Operation	Minutes	Labor rate per minute	Cost
Roll form	Load coil, form, sweep & cut-off	0.031	\$0.070	\$0.0022
Light press (2 stage die)	Open flang, notch, trim end to shape	0.082	0.066	.0054
Light press	Form end, close flange	0.082	0.066	.0054
Light press (2 stage die)	Open flange, notch	0.066	0.066	.0044
Light press (2 stage die)	Form, end turn down flange	0.066	0.066	.0044
Automatic polish	Load & unload–3 at a time, 2 men	0.044	0.076	.0033
Hand polish	Polish formed ends	0.082	0.076	.0063
Packaging	Package	0.055	0.064	.0035

Total labor cost \$0 0348
Manufacturing overhead 0.0698

Total manufacturing cost \$0.2673
Commercial and administrative expense 0.0133

Total cost \$0.2810
Profit 0.0420

Price .... \$0.3230 of material cost are wrong because the unit price changes. The most common error, however, is a bad estimate of usage. Either the estimator's calculations are incorrect, or he fails to make the proper allowance for process scrap and shrinkage.

Direct labor cost

Errors are made even more frequently in estimating labor costs. Direct labor includes all work performed directly on the product—assembly, machine operations, and so on. It does not include work that is indirectly performed on it—inspection, materials handling, maintenance, supervision, and so on. The estimator first decides what operations are needed and estimates the time required to perform each of them. He then calculates the cost by multiplying the time by the wages that must be paid. For example, suppose a worker who is paid $4.20 per hour can consistently produce at the rate of 120 units per hour. The worker's time costs $0.07 per minute ($4.20 per hour divided by 60 minutes per hour), and each operation takes 0.5 minutes (60 divided by 120). Therefore the direct labor cost per operation is $0.035 (0.5 times $0.07). Similar calculations are illustrated in Table 14–1.

Errors rarely are made in estimating wages, since the estimator knows what the average wages are for each job skill. Actual labor costs differ from estimates mostly because of variations in the time required to perform various operations. In calculating the time, the estimator must be able to visualize an operation and, in effect, make a mental time study. To the actual standard, the estimator then adds an allowance (usually about 10 percent) for delays, rest periods, and other inefficiencies. Even if the estimator makes no errors, the estimate will be unrealistic if the workers fail to perform up to standard.

Overhead

Manufacturing overhead and sales and administrative expenses both are overhead. One is overhead associated with the factory—MRO supplies, indirect labor, depreciation, and so on. The other is overhead associated with the office—clerical and executive salaries, office supplies and rent, and the like. A cost estimator has little difficulty in estimating overhead. For example, note how easy it is to calculate the overhead in the estimate in Table 14–1. The estimator assumes that manufacturing overhead is 200 percent of direct labor and that administrative overhead is 5 percent of total manufacturing cost.

These calculations are deceptively simple. Allocation of overhead is essentially arbitrary and usually has little relation to the direct cost of making the product. The reason for this is the nature of overhead, which includes all costs other than direct labor and direct material costs. Overhead must be charged in some way to the product in order to be recouped. In calculating overhead, accountants try to include all miscellaneous costs directly associated with the product or its manufacturing operations, but in many cases this is not feasible. Important expenses—building depreciation and maintenance, part of the payroll, and expenditures for various supplies—cannot be traced directly to any one product or operation. Allocation must be made on some arbitrary basis, usually as a percentage of the direct labor cost or total cost.

Types of overhead. There are three types of manufacturing overhead: fixed, nonvariable, and variable.

Fixed overhead means exactly what the term implies. It includes costs that are incurred regardless of how much the plant produces. Real estate taxes, certain insurance premiums, depreciation on buildings and some equipment, salaries of certain personnel (like security guards), and so on, all cost the same regardless of whether the plant is operating at 100 percent capacity or at only 10 percent.

Nonvariable overhead is not quite so rigid as fixed overhead. It will vary slightly with changes in production volume but will not vary in direct proportion to such changes. For example, when a plant is producing near capacity, there might be a need for two receiving department supervisors, one on the first shift and one on the second. When the plant is operating at 75 percent capacity, these supervisors are still needed, and nonvariable overhead remains unchanged. But when operations are cut back to 40 percent capacity, it is possible to get along with a single receiving department supervisor, and the "nonvariable" overhead varies.

Sales and administrative expense (i.e., the cost of operating the "front office") usually behaves very much as nonvariable manufacturing overhead. It is relatively unresponsive to small changes in sales or production volume, but when there are major changes in sales it will increase or decrease.

Variable overhead is similar to direct labor and direct material costs in that it varies in direct proportion to production volume. If production volume doubles, variable overhead also doubles. Examples of variable overhead include the cost of most public utility services, perishable tools, various operating supplies, and depreciation that is calculated on the basis of machine-hours.

Changes in fixed costs. Variable overhead can usually be related to product cost reasonably accurately. It is fixed and nonvariable overhead that create problems in pricing. Product and equipment mix can affect overhead and product costs even though a particular product continues to be made in exactly the same way as before. For example, suppose that products X and Y are made in the same department. Total fixed and nonvariable overhead costs are $100,000 per year and, since direct labor in the department amounts to about $50,000 per year, the overhead is recovered by a 200 percent charge to direct labor.

The company then buys a new machine that will be used only on product Y. Depreciation and other nonvariable costs associated with this machine amount to $10,000 per year. This automatically raises the overhead rate by 20 percent to a new level of 220 percent of direct labor. This change causes the reported costs of *both* products to increase even though the new machine is used exclusively on just one product! If the company were producing both products on a cost-plus basis, it might be able to collect higher prices for both—provided the customer's auditor did not complain.

Cost-volume relationship

Misleading information. Companies often get misleading information from their accounting systems even when they are not trying to hoodwink customers. No company can predict precisely what its future production volume will be, yet volume is a major factor in determining overhead absorption and product cost. Table 14–2 shows why

TABLE 14–2
Costs, profits, and prices at two production levels

	100,000 units production		110,000 units production	
	Total cost	*Unit cost*	*Total cost*	*Unit cost*
Direct material	$ 15,000	$0.15	$ 16,500	$0.15
Direct labor	20,000	0.20	22,000	0.20
Fixed overhead	25,000	0.25	25,000	0.225
Nonvariable overhead	10,000	0.10	10,500	0.096
Variable overhead	15,000	0.15	16,500	0.15
Sales and administrative expense	5,000	0.05	5,250	0.048
Total operating cost	$ 90,000	$0.90	$ 95,750	$0.869
Profit....................	10,000	0.10	14,250	0.131
Sales (selling price)	$100,000	$1.00	$110,000	$1.00
Profit (as percent of sales) ...	10.0%		13.0%	

Note: This table shows the effect of an increase in production volume on unit cost. When volume goes up, fixed overhead is overabsorbed and unit costs decline, opening opportunities for buyers to negotiate price reductions.

this is true. One column shows costs for a hypothetical manufacturer whose production volume is 100,000 units of an item that it sells for $1.00. At this volume, its unit profit is 10 cents. A total profit of $10,000 or 10 percent on sales permits it to achieve desired return on investment.

Now suppose that this manufacturer is able to boost its sales by 10 percent, to 110,000 units. Note that its costs do not go up proportionately. They increase by only $5,750—from $90,000 to $95,750. In other words, the additional 10,000 units produced cost only 57½ cents each ($5,750/10,000). If the manufacturer can maintain its selling price of $1 each for the extra volume, it can boost its profits 42½ percent (from $10,000 to $14,250) with only a 10 percent increase in sales. The reason for this, of course, is that fixed and nonvariable costs do not increase proportionately as output expands. These costs are what accountants call "overabsorbed"—i.e., already paid for by being allocated over a lower level of output.

Of course, if the company could plan on a production of 110,000 units it could cut prices and still achieve its profit objective. If we assume that a $10,000 profit provides an adequate return on investment, then a unit profit of just over 9 cents would be required if production were 110,000 units. With costs of $0.869 at this level of output (see Table 14–2) the price could be cut from $1.00 to about $0.96.

The break-even chart. If a series of cost-volume relationships is calculated and plotted, the result is a break-even chart. Figure 14–1 illustrates such a chart for the data in Table 14–2. The break-even chart is invaluable for pricing decisions. With it, the supplier can determine the precise effect of any change in volume on costs and profits. The supplier also can use the break-even chart to predict costs and profits from the sales forecast.

The break-even chart graphically illustrates the effect of relatively small changes in volume on costs and profits. It proves that there is nothing sacred about a supplier's cost estimate regardless of how ably it is made. Unit costs of a given product are affected not only by the proficiency with which the product is made but also by the supplier's overall efficiency and by the amount of business he succeeds in getting from other customers. Thus no buyer need feel restrained from asking a supplier to reduce a bid.

Despite the buyer's best efforts, suppliers usually succeed in avoiding price cuts when costs decline because of an overall increase in sales. During these periods, demand is strong and markets are tight. The result is sharply higher profits. On the other hand, when sales drop off during business downturn, suppliers will study their break-even charts. They may decide that it pays to sell below full cost if necessary in order to keep plants operating at levels sufficient to absorb overhead costs.

Using the chart. Suppose a supplier with a break-even chart like that in Figure 14–1 is operating at 50 percent capacity. He is producing 50,000 units and his price is $1 per unit. A mail-order house offers him a contract to produce 20,000 units for 70 cents. Can the supplier afford to take the order? He looks at his break-even chart. With present

438

FIGURE 14-1
Break-even chart

The break-even chart is an excellent guide for profit planning and forecasting of costs. It shows what costs will be at any level of production.

volume, he is losing $13,000. With the additional order, his revenues rise by $14,000, but the break-even chart shows that the costs only rise by $11,000, from $63,000 to $74,000. Obviously it pays the supplier to take the order (provided that other customers do not insist on price cuts) even though the business is not theoretically "profitable."

USING COST DATA

The cost-volume principle is particularly applicable when a supplier enters a foreign market. It maintains a high price in the home market and then sells surplus production for whatever the traffic will bear in a foreign market. Naturally, this type of competition is not welcomed in the market that is being invaded, and it is not permitted under the rules of the General Agreement on Trade and Tariffs (GATT). Nevertheless, it is clear that American purchasing managers have sometimes saved substantial amounts of money for their company by buying from foreign producers at prices lower than those charged either by American producers or by foreign producers in their own home markets.

A buyer need not understand supplier pricing to buy from a foreign producer who quotes a lower price. This knowledge has other applications, however. Fortunately, in some cases the supplier may be quite willing to give the buyer access to his cost estimates and records. The buyer definitely has the right to examine the supplier's cost if there is provision for her to do so in the purchase contract. For example, price redetermination and cost plus fixed-fee contracts always include some provision for an audit of costs. If there is no provision, however, the supplier has every right to keep his costs to himself. In many cases, this is no handicap to the skilled purchase analyst or buyer. She can accurately estimate the costs anyway. When it is difficult to estimate the absolute level of the supplier's costs, the buyer can still apply the cost-volume principle and accurately estimate the effect of a change in volume on the supplier's cost.

Applying the cost-volume principle

Every supplier's cost curve resembles that in Figure 14–1. Costs are always lowest and profit margins greatest when the plant is operating near maximum capacity. Suppliers always have extra incentive to build sales volume when their plants are operating below their optimum. As we have noted, they not only stand to make their standard profit on this business but will also gain increased overhead absorption. The cost-volume relationship can be profitably applied to make-or-buy decisions. It should also be taken into account when volume rises either because business is good or because a buyer groups orders of like items to make them more attractive to a supplier.

Make or buy.   It sometimes pays to make an item even though it can be bought more cheaply from an outside supplier. When it makes an item a plant is able to absorb part of its fixed overhead. This is true only when the plant is operating at a fraction of its normal capacity. When it is operating at capacity, on the other hand, it sometimes is economical to buy items from an outside supplier even though they theoretically can be made at lower cost in the buyer's plant. The reason for this is that costs can soar over standard when a plant is operated beyond its normal capacity. Expansion may not always be a solution, since additional capacity increases the fixed and nonvariable costs that must be absorbed.

Grouping orders. Many buyers get spectacular cost reductions by offering suppliers a "package" of business for all requirements of a group of similar items. Both buyer and seller benefit, since it is possible to process like items in large quantities at lower costs. Production is greater and unit overhead is lower. As is obvious from the figures in Table 14–2, a supplier making 100,000 units of an item often is willing to offer price concessions if she can get a customer to take an extra 10,000 units. The costs justify a price reduction and the profits will be greater if the supplier offers a price cut less than the actual reduction in costs.

Exploiting sales gains. When business is good, companies buy more from their suppliers. Since the extra volume helps reduce costs, smart buyers do not hesitate to ask their suppliers to pass on the benefits by cutting prices. If suppliers know that no one else will sell the item at lower prices, they usually will refuse to cut prices. (Needless to say, they are usually less than candid about the real reason they decline to reduce prices; generally they insist that costs have gone up.) Even when costs have gone up, the buyer's efforts may not have been in vain. In some cases he can persuade the supplier to absorb increases in wages and materials costs that are almost inevitable when business is good.

Basis for negotiation. Suppose, for example, that a purchase agreement is negotiated for a particular item at a time when volume is 1,000 units per month. The buyer estimates cost of manufacture as follows:

Material	$0.50
Direct labor	0.15
Overhead	0.30
Sales and administrative expense	0.05
Profit	0.10
Price	$1.10

Business conditions improve and volume gradually increases to 1,200 pieces per month. Meanwhile material prices advance by 3 percent and wages go up 5 percent. The supplier would like to boost his price. The buyer counters by requesting a price reduction. She agrees that a 5 percent increase in material costs should boost the price by about $0.025. She also admits that a 3 percent wage boost would boost the supplier's direct labor costs by almost $0.005 and that when this boost is applied to indirect labor and salaries, the total applicable increase in the wage bill could be the equivalent of as much as $0.01 per unit.

Thus, if the supplier seeks an increase of about $0.015, it is justified by higher costs. However, the buyer points out that this is more than offset by reductions in cost. Perhaps half of the supplier's overhead may be fixed or nonvariable. Once this overhead is absorbed, the supplier need only allow a 15-cent overhead charge in his price, instead of 30 cents. Thus if the supplier could afford to sell the first 1,000 units per month for $1.10, he should be able to sell 200 additional units for 15 cents less, or 95 cents. His average price should therefore be $1.075 per unit (1,000 × $1.10 + 200 × $0.95/1,200) when volume is 1,200 units per unit. This price gives the supplier the same unit profit of 10 cents that he enjoyed before. And it gives him a higher total profit—$120 per month when volume is 1,200 units, compared with $100 when volume was only 1,000 units. Thus, the supplier is ahead when he cuts prices, as long as volume increases.

The supplier and the buyer might finally agree on a price of $1.09—deducting $0.025 for increased volume and allowing $0.015 for higher basic costs.

Amortization. Supplier costs may also be reduced when special set-ups, tooling, start-up costs, or equipment associated with a new order are amortized. Suppose, for example, a supplier must spend $1,000 to rearrange her plant when she accepts a particular order. She does not dare propose that the customer pay for this as a separate charge, since her quotation, almost by definition, indicates she is fully able and ready to handle this order. But the rearrangement cost is real. If the supplier simply lumps it in with overhead, the cost will be spread over a number of jobs, implying, incorrectly, that costs on these other jobs have increased. Instead the supplier amortizes the special cost over the life of the initial contract. If this is for 10,000 pieces, the amortization of $1,000 would then amount to 10 cents a unit. If the supplier gets a second order, her profit will increase by 10 cents a unit, since the $1,000 extraordinary will have been fully recouped.

Smart buyers study the supplier's operation and try to identify such nonrecurring costs so they can get the benefit of lower prices after all special costs have been fully organized. Suppliers do not necessarily cut prices without a struggle. But the buyer still has a few more aces up his sleeve, if he needs them. He may want to make a fresh study of the overall cost of making the item or he may wish to apply the learning curve.

Buyer cost estimates

A buyer should be able to estimate the direct material cost of a purchased part as accurately as the supplier's estimator can. He can readily calculate the amount of material that will be used, and he usually knows the price of the raw material. The buyer should also be able to estimate the approximate labor cost. He is familiar with the supplier's equipment and processes, and he should be able to estimate how fast they will operate. He easily can find out what wage rates are in the supplier's area from employers' associations or from his own industrial relations department. The buyer normally can get burden rates for various types of manufacturing operation from his own company's cost department.

Thus, the buyer has all the raw material to make a reasonably good cost estimate. And, in fact, many skilled buyers can estimate costs with at least 95 percent accuracy. Some of them follow the same procedure as the accountant, estimating labor, material, and overhead separately. Others do just as well by comparing the new item with similar items and by drawing on their past experience.

The buyer's estimate becomes a useful target price. If the buyer calculates that the price of an item should be $1.00, then he will certainly think twice before he accepts a bid of either $0.50 or $2.00. In both cases he should ask the supplier to double-check his quotation for errors. He may, provided the supplier is willing, compare his cost estimate with that of the supplier.

While many buyers can prepare reasonably accurate cost estimates, they are not professionals. Some large companies have expert cost estimators working on purchased parts. Their estimates are used to budget costs, negotiate purchase prices, and measure the performance of purchasing personnel. Table 14–3 illustrates an estimate of an automobile-engine air cleaner that was used for this purpose. The estimator believes that a price of $2.54 would provide the supplier

TABLE 14–3
Purchased part price objective (14″ air cleaner and silencer assembly, dry type, 8 cyl.)

Objective price	$ 2.5400
Current price	2.6500
Current price (over) under objective	$(0.11)

Comments:

Material cost of make parts—steel	$0.6343
Purchase cost of element assembly, including freight	0.4850
Purchase parts cost, including paint and carton	0.2415
Labor cost at $0.0346/min	0.2488
Burden cost	0.5476
Total manufacturing cost—painted and packaged	$2.1572
Product development engineering at 3% of manufacturing cost	0.0647
Adjusted manufacturing cost	$2.2219
Administrative and commercial at 5%	0.1111
Total cost with administrative and commercial	$2.3330
Profit on element assembly at 5% of total cost	0.0262
Profit on remainder of assembly at 10% of total cost	0.1808
Estimated selling price—painted and packaged	$2.5400

Source: Ford Motor Co.

with an adequate 10 percent profit on the air cleaner. The actual price is $2.65.

The 11-cent difference between the estimator's target price and the actual price is a target for the buyer in negotiation. The buyer can ask the supplier why he cannot produce the cleaner for $2.54. This may result in a detailed comparison of the buyer's estimate with the supplier's estimate. If the buyer's estimator is competent, the supplier may be hard put to justify the 11-cent price difference.

Detailed buyer cost estimates normally are used only for major items that are made by highly specialized suppliers. Since they are expensive to prepare, it is pointless to do so unless expenditures for the item are substantial. It also is pointless to make them if the normal process of soliciting competitive bids brings prices down to the level of the estimates. However, for many components there is not that much competition. Some are so complicated that only a few suppliers can produce them. Others, like the automotive air cleaner in Table 14–3, are not complicated, but one or two suppliers have become so adept at making them that their costs are much lower than those of any other potential producer. Their know-how gives these suppliers an advantage that effectively eliminates most potential competitors. In this case, the buyer's cost estimate is a substitute for a more competitive market.

The learning curve

Every supplier selling a custom-made product is to some extent a monopolist. Competition is restricted because: (1) The supplier has unique experience with the item that makes production costs inherently lower than those of an inexperienced producer. (2) It is both costly and troublesome for the buyer to change suppliers. Often new tooling must be made. Quality and delivery problems develop. Sheer inertia makes it easier to continue doing business with the existing supplier.

If the purchased part or assembly is extremely complicated and order quantities are small, it will not do the buyer much good to negotiate strictly on the basis of cost of production. The supplier's skills will increase so much with experience that past costs are not a good guide to future costs unless the supplier's experience is taken into account. The solution in such cases is the "learning curve" approach, which is widely used, especially in industries such as aerospace and electronics where order quantities are quite small, parts are extremely complex, and labor input per unit is very high.

Basic calculations. The principle behind the learning curve is quite simple: each job is performed more efficiently as it is repeated. While this relationship between efficiency and experience has always been obvious, it was not until World War II that any attempt was made to quantify it. At that time, studies showed that labor hours per unit of product in the airframe industry declined by about 20 percent whenever the production count was doubled. This is an 80 percent learning curve. It means that if the first unit of a product takes 100 hours of labor, the second unit will take 80 hours, the fourth unit 64 hours, the eighth unit 51.2 hours, and so on.

The cost of any lot with any learning curve can be calculated with the formula:

$$\log Y_i = \log Y_1 - b \log i$$

where:

i = Production count beginning with first unit or lot.
Y_1 = Direct labor hours (or dollars of direct labor cost) required to produce the first lot.
Y_i = Direct labor hours (or dollars) required to produce i^{th} lot.
b = Slope of the learning curve calculated from the formula:
2^b = Learning curve rate.

For example, for an 80 percent curve, $2^b = 0.80$, and therefore $b = 0.322$.

Now apply the formula to a case where the curve is 80 percent and the ith unit in which you are interested is the eighth unit or lot. $Y_1 = 100$ hours. You want to calculate the hours required to produce the eighth unit or lot. Therefore, $i = 8$. Substituting into the formula:

$$\log Y_8 = \log(100) - (0.322)(\log 8)$$
$$\log Y_8 = 2.000 - (0.322) \times (0.903) = 1.709$$

therefore,

$$Y_8 = 51.2 \text{ hours.}$$

To get this answer, you must be proficient in the use of log tables. But it is easy to verify the formula when the production count is 8. The correct answer is equal to 80 percent of 80 percent of 80 percent, or 51.2 percent of the original cost, because production is doubled three times.

Plotting the results. Calculations with the formula are slow and tedious. It is much easier to use a chart. Learning curves can be calculated for various levels of operating efficiency on log-log paper. For example, Figure 14-2 shows an 80 percent learning curve used by North American Rockwell Corp. The vertical scale indicates the vendor's direct labor costs and the horizontal scale shows units of output. The curve slopes downward because as the vendor gains experience he is able to make the product with fewer labor hours.

FIGURE 14–2
Learning curve

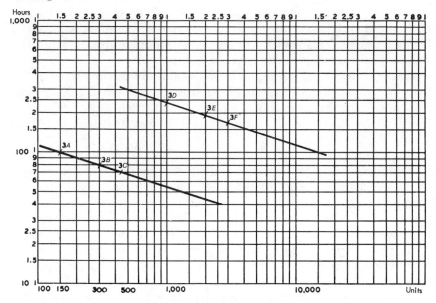

The learning curve is based on the principle that the number of labor hours needed to produce an item declines as the supplier gains experience. This 80 percent learning curve is used by North American Rockwell Corp.

Applications.   The learning curve is an excellent negotiating tool. Two typical applications are given below.

Problem No. 1.   150 pieces of a special machined forging were purchased from company A for $100 each. You now want 300 more pieces to be made and shipped in two lots of 150 pieces each. How much should you pay?

Plot point 3A (see Figure 14–2) at $100 (or 100 hours if you were measuring your learning curve in hours rather than dollars) and 150 units. Plot point 3B for double this total quantity, 300 units, and 80 percent of the price of $80. These two points establish the 80 percent slope.

Cost goes down etc. —

The principle behind the learning curve is that costs decline in an arithmetic progression as quantity increases in a geometric progression. In this case, the cost of the second lot is 80 percent that of the first lot and the cost of the *fourth* (and not the third) lot is 80 percent of the cost of the second lot. The cost of the third lot cannot be calculated so readily. It is an easy matter to pick it off the chart, however, at point 3C where the curve intersects the cumulative production count of 450 which would be reached when the third lot is completed. The chart indicates that the cost is $71.

You may wish to price the second and third lots separately at $80 and $71, respectively. Or you may wish to negotiate a combined price, equal to the average of the $80 price and the $71 price, or $75.50. Note, however, that if the supplier is going to make the ship the second order in one lot of 300, this learning curve does not apply; instead, you use a different rule which will be covered later.

Problem No. 2. This example shows the most typical use of the learning curve. Suppose you made an initial purchase of 1,000 pieces of a welded forging assembly at a price of $300 each. Now 2,000 additional pieces are needed, to be shipped in two lots of 1,000. What should the price be?

Analysis of supplier's costs shows the following: $10,000 was spent for tooling that was amortized over the first order and will not contribute to the costs of the additional order. Raw materials costs were $65 per piece on the first order, but, due to the general price increase, they will go up to $70 on the subsequent order. Plating and heat treating costs totaled $5 per unit and are not subject to the learning curve. X-ray cost $2 per piece on the first order. They are believed to be subject to the curve, and the supplier intends to negotiate a lower price.

The supplier has just granted a 10 percent wage increase to his production workers and is going to be forced to go on a 48-hour week because of the increased work load. Direct labor amounted to $100 per part on the first lot. The supplier made no profit on the original order and feels he is entitled to a 10 percent price increase in order to earn a fair profit.

The computation is as follows:

Original price		$300.00 ea.
Less tooling, $10,000, for 1,000 pieces equals $10 ea.		10.00
		$290.00
Less items not subject to curve:		
Material	$65.00 ea.	
Plating and heat treating	5.00	
	$70.00	70.00
Balance of costs subject to learning curve		$220.00
Plus:		
10% wage increase	$10.00	
Overtime cost	8.80	
	$18.80	18.80
Adjusted costs (including X ray) subject to learning curve		$238.80

In Figure 14–2, plot point *3D* at 1,000 units and $238.80. Then plot point *3E* at double the quantity and 80 percent of the price ($191) to establish the 80 percent curve. Point *3F* then shows that the cost of the third lot of 1,000 pieces is $167.

If you wish to get a single price on a lot of 2,000 pieces, to be shipped in lots of 1,000, you would average these two costs of $167 and $191, giving you an average cost of $179 subject to the learning curve. Total costs would then break down as follows:

Costs subject to learning	$179.00
Raw material ($65 previously subcontracted and $5 increased cost)	70.00
Plating and heat treating (previously subcontracted)	5.00
Net price before profit	$254.00
10 percent profit on sales	28.22
Adjusted price for new order	$282.22

Limitations.   The example above probably is not realistic, however. The supplier might well make and ship a lot of 2,000 rather than ship in lots of 1,000. In fact, one major problem in using the learning curve is change in purchase quantity. Only rarely is the second order for the same quantity as the first order. In some cases, the change in quantity is more significant to pricing than the supplier's experience. A company can determine the effect of change in quantity and experience on various types of item only by studying cost changes on a number of items. North American Rockwell's materials department made such a study. It believes that an 80 percent learning curve with various changes in purchase quantity results in the following relationships:

Percent increase in quantity (new order divided by old orders)	*Percent of old price that should be paid for new order*
10	67
50	63
100	60
150	57
200	55
500	47
1,000	41
1,500	37

The learning curve has other limitations. The most obvious one is that buyer and supplier often will not agree on which learning curve should be applied. The differences in price that result from using various learning curves can be enormous. With a 90 percent curve, prices on succeeding orders would run 100, 90, 81, 72 and so forth. With a 70 percent curve, the decline would be much steeper: 100, 70, 49, 35, and so forth. Such disagreements can best be resolved by comparison of the cost experiences of a number of companies making similar products. But, obviously, the learning curve serves as a basis of negotiation; it is not so precise that the buyer can present the supplier with his learning curve analysis on a basis of take it or lose the business.

The learning curve should be used carefully. It cannot be applied to standard items on which a supplier has already reached optimum efficiency. Nor can it be applied to a cost estimate. If there are errors in the estimated price for the first order, the errors will not be magically eliminated by applying the learning curve to determine the price for the second order. Nor can one curve be applied universally to all items. The 80 percent curve works for certain types of aircraft parts; it will not work for everything. Each company must devise its own learning curves after making a study of the effect of production experience on the costs of various items. Skillfully used, the learning curve can thus be a useful tool to assure that the buyer continues to get fair value on components and parts purchases long after the original order has been placed.

VALUE ANALYSIS

In a broad sense, the learning curve is one of the tools of value analysis. To put it mildly, the semantics of management are not exact. While individual writers may define their terms quite precisely, their definitions are not universally accepted either by many practitioners or by writers (some of whom try to be "original" simply by inventing new words to describe old ideas).

Definition

Value analysis is a term that was regarded as semantic double-talk when it was first introduced more than 30 years ago. In the broader sense, value analysis is almost any organized technique that can be applied to cost reduction. It is often used interchangeably with the term value engineering. While its meaning is still not precise, value analysis is associated primarily with purchased components while value engineering is as likely to be associated with entire products. Both are disciplined techniques designed to squeeze waste out of products without impairing their utility. The basic ideas of value analysis and value engineering can be applied to nonproduction supplies and services but their major applications are directed toward components and end products with a heavy emphasis on both purchasing and engineering.

The term was invented by L. D. Miles of the General Electric Company in 1946. Essentially the same activity that Miles instituted at General Electric in 1946 had been carried out in the Armed Forces in World War II by various officers who, in turn, persuaded the Ford Motor Company to give it a try under the name purchase analysis at about that the same time Miles was introducing the concept at General Electric.

There are almost as many specific definitions of value analysis as there are value analysts. But few would quarrel with this general definition:

> Value analysis is the study of the relationship of design, function, and cost of any product, material or service with the object of reducing its cost through modification of design or material specification, manufacture by a more efficient process, change in source of supply (external or internal), or possible elimination or incorporation into a related item.

The objective of value analysis is to get more value from an item in terms of function. As the examples in Figure 14–3 graphically show,

FIGURE 14–3
Examples of value analysis

This push button was made as a screw machine part. Research among suppliers turned up one that could cold head the part from aluminum wire. Cost of the item dropped from 19 to 2 cents.

Readily available zinc die-cast nuts were successfully substituted for acorn brass nuts turned out on screw machines. Use of a standard reduced cost from $12.24/M to $5.76/M.

This machined clamp bar cost 32 cents. The design was changed so that the item could be made from a stamping with two nuts resistance welded on. New cost: 8 cents, plus $350 for tools.

A rolled thread specialist studied this steel J-bolt and suggested the words "cut thread" be removed from the drawing. The part is bought now for 1.5 cents as against 11.7 cents—an $80,000 saving.

Courtesy General Electric Co.

the value analyst seeks to perform a function at lower cost. The function of the J-bolt in Figure 14–3, for example, is performed equally well whether the threads are rolled or cut. But there is an enormous difference in cost between the two processes; switching from cut threads to rolled threads reduces cost by nearly 90 percent.

Organizing for value analysis

While every firm can benefit from value analysis, only the bigger companies can afford full-time value analysts. At present, no more than a few hundred companies have them; some of these, however, are fairly small companies. For example, a toy manufacturer has a value analyst in its purchasing department even though it spends only $6 million a year for purchased parts and materials.

According to experienced practitioners, a full-time analyst should be able to save more than eight times his or her salary even in a small company. Even so, only very large companies in the process industries tend to have full-time analysts. One reason is that opportunities for savings are limited to nonproduction materials. There are no production parts in the process industries, and it is difficult to save through value analysis on basic raw materials.

The staff function. Anyone can apply value analysis principles: buyers, manufacturing engineers, design engineers, and others. However, some special training is necessary before an individual becomes proficient at value analysis, and it is best carried on by someone who is free from the distractions of other duties. For these reasons, value analysis is normally organized as a separate staff activity, except in small firms that cannot afford to hire a full-time analyst. Typically, the chief analyst reports directly to the director of purchases or the materials manager. The value analysts usually work on value analysis projects of their own and also coordinate value analysis activities of other materials personnel.

The typical value analyst has several projects of his own to work on at all times. He periodically reports his progress on existing projects and also suggests new projects. In addition, he might instruct other materials personnel in value analysis techniques and assist in getting their ideas approved by all the departments involved.

When a value analysis project is completed, a written report usually is submitted to all interested parties. Figure 14–4 shows a typical value analysis report. The Celanese Corporation saved $1,490.25 by changing its specification for cresylic acid. Before the change was approved, it was analyzed by the Celanese laboratory, and the accounting department audited the savings estimate to make certain it was realistic.

Value analysis committees. The committee approach to value analysis is particularly well suited to the small company that cannot afford a full-time analyst. The typical value analysis committee includes members from the purchasing, production, product engineering, manufacturing engineering, and cost departments. It might meet once or twice a month. Specific projects—for example, a commodity group such as steel stampings or specific products—are selected for

FIGURE 14–4
Value analysis report

```
COMPLETED COST REDUCTION PROJECT
PURCHASING DEPT.      GEN-1479 (4-58)
COMMODITY
     Cresylic Acid (meta para feed)
TYPE OF REDUCTION  PROJECT STARTED  PROJECT COMPLETED  LOCATION                    PROJECT NUMBER
 ☒A      ☐B       Nov., 19—        March, 19—        Point Pleasant Plant            12
DESCRIPTION OF COST REDUCTION
```

By special arrangement with Productol Company samples of certain mixtures
were obtained and evaluated in the plant laboratory. It was found that
certain blends would result in a feed equal to that which normally would
be priced to us at $1.15 per gal. and that components would be priced so
that a savings would be realized. Therefore, 26,000 gals. was purchased
for blending and it is hoped this can be repeated once each quarter in the
future.

```
20,392 gals.  Grade 25A (MP) @ $1.15/gal less freight equalization  $20,163.73
 5,961 gals.  Grade 2876 (special xyl) @ $0.90/gal less freight
                                                  equalization        4,413.28
26,353 gals.  Blend equal to Grade 25 (MP) delivered for             $24,577.01
Normal cost @ $1.15/gal. less $4,238.69 (freight equalization)
                                        would have been               26,067.26

                                        One time saving             $ 1,490.25
```

No extra handling occurred since materials could be mixed either in feed
or product tanks.

```
                              AMOUNT OF SAVINGS
ONE TIME SAVINGS                     RECURRING SAVINGS
                   ANNUAL VOLUME       : UNIT SAVING    : ESTIMATED ANNUAL SAVINGS
$1,490.25                              :                : $6,000.00
                                OFFSETTING COSTS
CAPITAL            EXPENSE            INVENTORY LOSS     TOTAL OFFSETTING COSTS
$                  $                 $                  $ None
DEPARTMENT AFFECTED      OTHER PARTICIPATING DEPARTMENTS
                                        Plant Manager.
 Production        Laboratory, Central Purchasing, Operations Control (NYO),

AUDITED BY:        Accounting                      JBL          QEA.
                            DEPARTMENT                        INDIVIDUAL

SUBMITTED BY:      H. O. Thombs, Mgr.   Operations Service Dept.   4/22/—
                   INDIVIDUAL             TITLE                    DATE
```

Courtesy Celanese Corp. of America

Many companies have standard forms for reporting value analysis projects. This report
of the Celanese Corporation of America is typical.

analysis at each meeting. Each member of the group studies the project in advance of the meeting. The combined and varied skills of the
group frequently lead to ideas that cut costs.

The committee form of organization works well in value analysis. It
helps generate ideas that no individual member of the group could
probably come up with on his own. However, after the committee
meets, someone must see that these ideas are thoroughly investigated

452

and, if possible, applied. If a company has full-time value analysts, they can handle the necessary follow-through. Otherwise, the chairman of the committee must administer the program to make certain that the committee's recommendations are acted on.

Value analysis projects often take months to bring to a successful conclusion. In some cases, almost every major department in the company must approve suggestions before they are incorporated. As a result, committee members cannot simply meet, dream up new ideas, and then go back to their regular jobs and forget all about value analysis until the next meeting. Someone must follow through ideas if anything is to be accomplished.

Value analysis techniques

Tests for value. One of the simplest—and sometimes one of the most effective—value analysis techniques was developed by General Electric Company. Each part being analyzed is subjected to "Ten Tests for Value." The value analyst asks herself these questions as she studies the part:

1. Does its use contribute value?
2. Is its cost proportionate to its usefulness?
3. Does it need all of its features?
4. Is there anything better for the intended use?
5. Can a usable part be made by a lower cost method?
6. Can a standard product be found that will be usable?
7. Is it made on proper tooling, considering the quantities used?
8. Do material, reasonable labor, overhead, and profit total its cost?
9. Will another dependable supplier provide it for less?
10. Is anyone buying it for less?

If a part "flunks" any of these tests, the analyst makes a more detailed investigation. For example, the high-cost design of each part in Figure 14–3 would flunk one or more value tests. The push button fails tests 2, 4, 5, and 9, and the acorn nut fails tests 2, 5, and 6. What tests would the clamp bar and J-bolt fail?

As the tests for value imply, the value analyst believes in creative skepticism. She is never satisfied that any item has the ideal design and is being produced at the ideal cost. An item that may pass all the tests for value today may fail one of them tomorrow as lower cost processes and designs are discovered. The value analyst must keep abreast of all new developments. She must also be versed in cost estimating in order to evaluate the effect of new developments on the cost of the items she analyzes.

Comparative analysis. Sometimes the analyst can get more leads on potential savings by making comparative analyses of similar items rather than by applying tests of value individually to each item. For example, the analyst might review all of the die castings the company buys. Simple comparison might give the analyst some clues. Castings should get progressively more expensive as their weight increases, special features such as inserts are added, usage decreases, and so on. Whenever there is an inconsistency, the analyst investigates.

Some analysts plot the weight of like parts against their cost per pound. As indicated in Figure 14–5, the price per pound should progressively decrease as weight increases. Parts that do not follow the curve (for example, part 7 in Figure 14–5) are not necessarily poor values, since they may have special features that justify a cost pre-

FIGURE 14–5

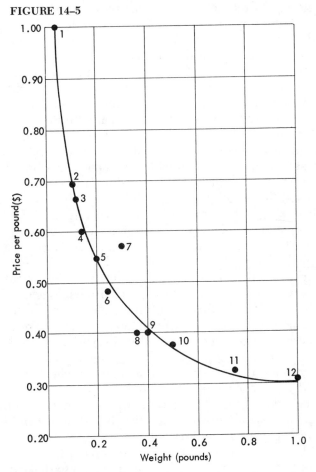

Weight analysis is a widely used value analysis technique for comparing like items. As weight increases, cost per pound should decrease. Parts that do not follow the pattern (such as No. 7 above) are analyzed in more detail.

454

mium. But they should be investigated, and in many cases they are good prospects for a detailed individual analysis.

Even if the cost curve fails to locate any good prospects for value analysis, it still may be useful. The curve can be used to make quick cost estimates of new items. Suppose that a new part weighs 0.8 pound and is similar to the parts in Figure 14–5. A glance at the chart shows that this part should cost about 31 cents per pound, so the unit price must be about 25 cents (0.8 lb × $0.31 per lb.).

Cost of each property. Another basic technique of value analysis is to determine the cost of each property of the item. For example, if the purpose of the item is to cover something, its cost per square foot might be calculated and compared with the cost per square foot of other materials. If the item does some other job, it might be analyzed in terms of the properties needed. For example, light bulbs can be analyzed on the basis of their cost per watt-hour of life, electrical capacitators on the basis of their capacitance, and so on.

A variation of this approach is to evaluate an item on the basis of its cost per function. This approach would work well with the machined clamp bar in Figure 14–3. This bar performs the function of holding two bolts or studs. The cost of this function with the old design is 32 cents. This cost is high, since ordinarily nuts will hold studs or bolts for a cost of only a penny or two each. This approach would naturally lead the analyst to look for a way in which nuts could perform the function at lower cost. The result is the 8-cent design that uses two standard nuts fastened to a small plate.

Brainstorming. The advertising industry originated brainstorming as a technique to stimulate creative thinking of advertising copy. It is a group activity in which four to ten persons participate. Each participant applies imagination to a single problem and is encouraged to propose any idea that comes to mind no matter how ridiculous it may seem. Every idea is duly noted by the chairperson; none is criticized during the meeting lest this inhibit the creative power of the participants. The hope is that one idea, even though it may be ridiculous, will touch off other suggestions, which ultimately will lead to a genuinely original and workable solution to the problem.

Brainstorming is as useful in value analysis where ideas often are inhibited by preconceived notions and prejudices. The value analyst gets used to being told, "Why change, we've been doing it this way for 20 years," "It just won't work," and the like. Results can be achieved only if the analyst can remove all preconceived ideas about how a product should be made and concentrates on the function of the item. Brainstorming can provide an ideal environment to shake out old prejudices and look at a problem in a new light. If some of the ideas proposed are a little wild, they can readily be discarded in the evaluation stage following the brainstorming session. Most sessions last no more than a couple of hours (the participants generally are exhausted by then). Usually dozens of ideas are generated, and only one good one is needed to solve the problem in question.

Buyer-supplier seminars.   Even small companies often have thousands of suppliers, and each supplier usually knows far more about his specialty than any of his customers do. One of the most profitable value analysis techniques is to draw on this pool of supplier know-how for cost-reduction ideas. Buyers try to do this in their day-to-day contacts with suppliers. Some companies go further: They organize supplier seminars to which they invite top executives from all the companies with which they deal.

The seminars are usually held at the buyer's plant or at a nearby hotel. They almost always feature a luncheon or dinner at which company executives introduce new products, outline corporate objectives, and discuss future plans and their effect on suppliers. But the real purpose of the meeting is to permit suppliers to tour the company's facilities and study its products in detail.

Some companies make up special product displays in which they have every detail part of their product spread out on a table or attached to a display board. Suggestions for improvement are solicited from suppliers, even for items that the supplier does not manufacture. The results can be amazing. For example, the Whirlpool Corporation held a supplier seminar at its home laundry plant in St. Joseph, Michigan. Suppliers made more than 300 suggestions for improvements. About a dozen of these were acceptable, and they resulted in unit savings of more than 90 cents on every combination washer-dryer made by the company.

Some companies that have held successful supplier seminars try to stimulate supplier suggestions on a continuing basis. They do this with permanent product displays in which they show all of the major components of their product. One of the "Big Three" auto companies goes even further: Its product display room has components of not only its own cars but competitors' products as well.

Selling value analysis

Value analysis is a staff activity. The value analyst can accomplish nothing without the help and cooperation of those with whom she must work—buyers, engineers, suppliers, and others. A considerable part of her time must be spent in arousing enthusiasm for cost reduction and value analysis in everyone she contacts.

To suppliers.   Seminars do a lot to stimulate supplier interest in value analysis, but some companies do even more. For example, many have published booklets in which they explain their problems to suppliers. Other go in for gimmicks like that used by Aerosol Tech-

FIGURE 14–6

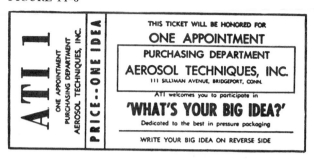

Aerosol Techniques, Inc., uses this simulated theater ticket to stimulate supplier cost-reduction ideas. "Tickets" were mailed to all suppliers and also were available in the reception room of the company offices. They have space on the back for the supplier to note his ideas.

niques, Inc., shown in Figure 14–6. International Minerals & Chemicals Corporation puts to good use a blackboard in the room where suppliers wait to see the company's buyers. On the board is lettered a "Dear Supplier" message. One such message read: "What have you contributed to IMC's Purchasing for Profit Program this year? Be prepared to give a definite written answer by July 1."

Many companies have had considerable success with vendor value awards (see Figure 14–7). If a supplier has been consistently helpful with cost reduction, he or she gets a certificate in recognition of achievement. Suppliers receive the certificates gladly both because they like to know that their efforts are appreciated and because they can use the certificates as a selling tool. What better advertising is there than the written testimony of satisfied customers?

Suppliers are catching on to the fact that value analysis can be a tool they can use to boost sales and profits. Their sales message in effect becomes, "Buy from me because I can help you save with value analysis." Suppliers whose products are suitable offer value analysis service to their customers. Figure 14–8 shows typical promotional material used by a supplier to promote a value-oriented approach to customer problems.

A few firms go even further. One foundry in the South invited its customers to a three-day value analysis seminar at which they had one of the top analysts as a guest lecturer. The foundry made no attempt to sell customers on its products. In fact, they even charged tuition to the customers to attend the seminar. "We benefit even though there was no sales pitch," the foundry's president explained "because if our customers learn about value when they're visiting us, they will associate us with the concept and we're bound to benefit eventually."

The Defense Department now includes value analysis clauses in

FIGURE 14–7
Vendor value award

An Award of

VENDOR VALUE

conferred upon

ABC Supply Company

In recognition of consistently helpful service and cooperation
in the field of cost reduction.

The Purchasing Department of

John Manufacturing Company

makes this award in conformance with the principles appearing below.

"The Vendor's Know-How is the Buyer's Greatest Asset".

Jan. 2, 19—

Date

Richard Roe

Purchasing Agent

The tests of a

VENDOR'S VALUE

1. He knows precisely how the customer uses his product.
2. He makes every effort to help the customer with standardization.
3. He tries to help customers cut costs by eliminating unnecessary features in his products.
4. He knows all his own capabilities and how they can help the customer.
5. He stays informed on—and tries to top—features of competitive products.
6. He tries to simplify his products before he's forced into it by the customer.
7. He stays informed on new processes and materials, and discusses them with the customer.
8. He tries to package his products in the cheapest and most efficient way.
9. He promotes the idea of blanket orders and other devices to help the customer cut costs.
10. He tries to give each customer the best possible price on his product.

Copyright 1957, Purchasing Magazine

Some companies present vendor value awards to suppliers who have made outstanding contributions to their value analysis programs. Suppliers like the awards because they can use them as a selling tool with new prospects.

458

FIGURE 14-8
Value analysis promotional material

TI MATERIALS SYSTEM **APPLICATION** REPORT
M4-2

TEMPERED TOP-LAY

APPLICATION:

Contact blade assembly with contacts over and under.

ORIGINAL DESIGN:

Fabricate spring blade and then stake rivet and washer to it.

Disadvantages: Mass of rivet head is limited by shank diameter, thus restricting current capacity of assembly; staking operation often breaks web; difficulty of achieving symmetry by double heading, especially with less ductile materials like silver cadmium oxide.

TI DESIGN:

Bond contact segments to top and bottom of blade material and then fabricate by conventional tooling.

Advantages: Greater design freedom since contact mass is not restricted; reduced costs inherent in "over and under" design; higher quality because the bonding process continuously monitors bond strength.

DESIGN NOTES:

1. Tri-layer contacts (copper core as heat sink, for example) reduce need of precious metal to fill contact gap.

2. When design requires segment thickness less than $\frac{1}{3}$ the width, consider use of clad profile-shaped wire rather than strip.

3. The TI bonding process yields a composite with segment stock parallel to grain of base material. Where this is objectionable, 45 degree blanking or use of base metal without grain orientation is recommended.

TEMPERED TOP-LAY

...featuring continuous bonding of two contact segments to thin-gauge material without compromise in temper.

OLD METHOD

NEW METHOD

ORIGINAL DESIGN
Rivet and washer staked to pre-fabricated blade.

TI DESIGN
"Over and under" contact segments bonded to base material prior to fabrication.

METALS & CONTROLS INC.
34 FOREST ST. · ATTLEBORO, MASS.
A CORPORATE DIVISION OF
TEXAS INSTRUMENTS
INCORPORATED

HCG B5460-2 8-64
Printed in U.S.A.

Typical example of value analysis promotional material developed by suppliers who offer a marketing approach oriented to value analysis to their customers.

many of its contracts. These give contractors tangible incentive to cut costs. Expenses of the value analysis program are allowable as costs, and the supplier is permitted to add to her profit part of the savings made with successful value analysis programs.

Within the company. The value analyst must not only sell value analysis to others in the company; he must also sell himself. Almost all of the value analyst's proposals will mean stepping on someone's toes. His forte is change, and this means, in effect, proving that what is being done now is not too good. If the value analyst does not tread carefully, his ideas will inevitably be taken as implied criticism of those responsible for the older, higher cost approach.

Value analysts sell themselves and their ideas with talks and presentations in which they explain value analysis concepts to others in the organization. Value news bulletins are another means of doing this. Their objective is to stimulate enthusiasm for value analysis. They review the cost-reduction progress that has been made to date and also single out individuals who have made outstanding contributions to value analysis. Full-time analysts usually try to give all the credit for successful projects to others. That way they get better cooperation on future projects.

Standardization

Value analysis projects are usually designed to reduce the cost of a particular item by changing it in some way. In most cases, this involves a lower cost material or process or eliminating some feature that is not needed. Occasionally, it can involve a change to a *higher cost* process or material. Note that the sixth of the General Electric's "Ten Tests for Value" is: can a standard part be used? When production quantities are relatively small, it is sometimes cheaper to use a standard item even if it is intrinsically more expensive. For example, if a manufacturer had a product that required an electric motor that was standard in every respect except that only 0.95 horsepower was needed, it would probably pay simply to buy a slightly larger standard 1.0 horsepower motor.

However, if production quantities are large, the special is economic. Note that the mechanical parts on your automobile are not really standard. Each is custom-designed. The basic reason for this is cost. The engineer studies the function that the component is to perform and designs a product that exactly fills the need. There may also be some economic advantage in buying a "special."

Everyone tends to pay almost the same price when buying standard products in comparable quantities. The seller is reluctant to offer concessions to one customer for fear that it will be necessary to pass these on to all customers. In contrast, the price paid for a custom-designed product is determined strictly by buyer and seller. For this reason, the auto companies pay less for items like tail pipes made from steel tubing that is formed to their unique specifications than they would have to pay for the standard steel pipe unformed, where essentially the same price is paid by all customers.

While standardization has its limitations in application to high-volume purchased components, it is still a major part of every overall value analysis program. The typical manufacturer of assembled products must buy or make thousands of components. The mix is so complex that it is inevitable that there will be some duplication or overlap. Careful review can often identify parts which can simply be eliminated, they usually can be replaced by a similar component which performs the same function. Since standardization is even more applicable to lower volume applications including nonproduction purchases, it will be discussed in greater detail in the next chapter.

NEGOTIATING PRICE INCREASES

Production versus nonproduction

In some cases, standardization and value analysis programs are spurred by rising prices. Inflation affects all purchases. But there is a significant difference between how production buyers and nonproduction buyers cope with it. The nonproduction buyer has two basic remedies: to incorporate some escalation clause into the basic contract (provided it is not a simple fixed price deal) or to buy from someone else. These remedies also apply to production purchases.

But the production buyer has other problems as well as opportunities. The product that is purchased is unique and the price that is negotiated is exclusive to one buyer and one seller. In addition, neither buyer nor seller can often easily terminate the relationship that exists between them. In many cases, the supplier has invested substantial sums in plant and equipment to serve a particular customer's needs. The buyer also is often locked in. Either no other supplier can meet company needs on short notice or there is simply no one else available who can do the job economically.

In many cases, because of the impact of the learning curve, the item has become effectively proprietary. The supplier has had so much "practice" in making it that no one else is really competitive. Yet there must be negotiation of price changes if the supplier is to earn an adequate profit but not a return so high that it is inconsistent with the basic spirit of the long-standing relationship between buyer and supplier.

Bargaining power

In most real-life negotiations of price changes on production parts, neither buyer nor seller is all powerful. But ability to change price does reflect relative bargaining power and this can change. Sometimes suppliers cannot only pass on higher costs but also give themselves a "bonus" in the form of higher profit margins. In other instances, suppliers must simply absorb increases in costs and work extra hard to boost productivity in order to avoid narrowing profit margins.

When demand is strong, no purchasing manager can expect consistently to avoid compensating suppliers for increases in cost. But often she can prevent suppliers from getting price increases in excess of cost increases. Suppose a purchasing manager gets a letter from a supplier saying that "effective immediately, the prices of our products are hereby increased 5 percent." What does she do? Her course of action depends on the nature of the commodity. If it is one that is standard and sold to a number of users, she has much less flexibility and bargaining power than if the commodity is made to order for the materials manager's company.

For example, if there is an industrywide price adjustment on a standard commodity like copper, it would be a waste of time for an individual buyer to try to persuade the Kennecott Copper Corporation that this increase should not be applied to him. The best he can do is to look for a lower cost supplier or for a substitute material. The buyer is not so restricted on items made to his company's specifications, where the price is determined by negotiation between buyer and seller. When a supplier increases the price of these items, he must give the buyer a good reason for doing so. The usual reason is "higher costs," and few would deny that both labor and raw materials costs progressively creep higher and higher year after year.

Justifying the increase

No buyers worth their salt will accept a price increase on a purchased component with the simple explanation of "higher costs." They will insist on substantiation from the supplier that costs really have risen. Sometimes the supplier will furnish a breakdown of her costs (and, in fact, such a breakdown may be provided for in the purchase order terms and conditions). In any case she should be willing to furnish some quantitative evidence.

If the price increase is caused by higher labor costs, the supplier normally will tell the buyer what her average increase is in cents per hour. She also should be willing to indicate either the number of standard hours of direct and indirect labor used in making each part or the total old and new labor cost in dollars per unit. If the price increase is caused by higher materials costs, the supplier should be willing to disclose the materials costs, materials specifications, and the precise materials usage per unit.

Needless to say, the documentation offered by a supplier will always "prove" that his price increase is completely valid. This does not mean that the buyer should accept the "proof," however. The fact is that many suppliers have never attempted to calculate closely the unit costs of the items they produce. When overall costs rise, they simply add enough to the price of each item to achieve their profit objective. Often the individual price increases represent the sales manager's best estimate of "what the traffic will bear." Some parts are increased by less than the amount of the cost increase because the supplier feels his competitive position on these items is weak; others are increased by much more. Thus the buyer should never be reluctant to ask for substantiation (or feel that she is challenging the supplier's integrity by doing so).

Cost analysis

Since the "evidence" submitted will always "prove" the increase justified, how does the buyer determine whether or not he should accept it? The skilled buyer can determine with amazing accuracy precisely how much a supplier's costs have increased if he is given a little data to work with. Suppose, for example, that a supplier wishes to increase the unit price of a part by 5 percent, from $1.00 to $1.05, on account of higher labor and materials costs. The supplier submits the following cost breakdown to prove that the increase is justified by higher cost of production:

	Old cost	New cost
Materials cost: 0.5 lbs. brass bar stock at $0.62/lb.	$0.31	at $0.66/lb. = $0.33
Labor cost	0.20	0.21
Overhead (at 200%)	0.40	0.42
Total cost	$0.91	$0.96
Profit	0.09	0.09
Price	$1.00	$1.05

Before the buyer even bothers analyzing the supplier's cost breakdown, she should ask herself these questions:

1. Is the supplier's proposed new price still competitive with that of other qualified producers?
2. Do purchase order terms and conditions permit price escalation?
3. Are other producers in the supplier's industry also confronted with these higher costs, and are they succeeding in passing them on to their customers?
4. Has the supplier passed on, in the form of price reductions, the benefits of increased productivity or other changes that have cut his costs?

If the answer to any of these questions is no, then the buyer has a basis for negotiation with the supplier other than cost of production. In such a case, she might possibly be able to convince the supplier that he should forego his price increase without making any analysis of cost.

But assume that the buyer must analyze costs. She does this most easily by analyzing each basic component: material, labor, overhead, and profit.

Material.   This is the easiest component to analyze. Most raw material costs are readily available, and it does not take too much study to verify the weight of material used by the supplier. In the example cited, which is a part made of brass bar stock, the buyer would check the supplier's old and new costs per pound against price lists available from the major brass mills. These price lists would include also the weight of each diameter bar per linear foot. Thus it sould be simple to verify the supplier's estimate of unit weight.

When the buyer is reviewing a price increase charged to higher materials costs, he should be sure to check also for a change in the value of scrap material. Usually when the price of the finished raw material goes up, so does the price of scrap. If the material has a relatively high value, the value of process scrap can become significant. This is true particularly if the design of the part generates a great deal of scrap. For example, some finished brass screw machine parts weigh only about half as much as the bar stock from which they are machined. Since brass is a relatively expensive metal, this scrap is valuable. If its price goes up, the price the buyer pays for the finished part should be reduced.

In some cases, the buyer may wish to determine the market in which the supplier is buying his raw material. In the United States, there is sometimes a significant difference between the price quoted by domestic producers and that charged for material of foreign origin. There is almost always a major price difference between different modes of distribution—e.g., purchasing direct from a mill rather than from a distributor. The buyer should insist that purchase be based on using the lowest cost material available—even though this may not be identical with that used by the supplier. The supplier may bitterly resist the buyer's attempt to "interfere," but this is nevertheless a reasonable subject for negotiation.

Labor.   In the example given, the supplier indicated that its direct labor cost per unit had increased by 5 percent, from $0.20 to $0.21. The buyer should ask the supplier what the wage increase is in cents per hour and also what the new average wage is. Naturally, these figures should indicate a 5 percent increase. The buyer should then compare the supplier's wage figures with overall wage averages issued by the Bureau of Labor Statistics for the supplier's industry and area. In addition, the buyer can often get excellent wage statistics from the local Chamber of Commerce or manufacturers' association. In most cases, the buyer will not have to get such data at first hand; her own industrial relations department often has excellent statistics on average wages and is also familiar with the pattern of wage increases. Needless to say, the supplier's indicated wages and wage increases should not be too far out of line with industry and area averages. If they are, the buyer has a point for negotiation.

Overhead. As all students of cost accounting soon learn, all labor is not "direct" labor. Wages paid to employees who are not directly concerned with making the product are an "indirect" labor expense and are charged to various overhead (or burden) accounts. Indirect labor in most manufacturing companies is by no means an insignificant expense. Typically it amounts to between 60 and 75 percent of direct labor costs. In highly automated plants, of course, the ratio is much higher. In fact, in a completely automated plant (i.e., with no production workers), the ratio of indirect labor to direct labor costs would be infinite. In such a case, the cost accounting convention of separating direct labor cost from overhead would be meaningless, since there would be no direct labor costs and buyers would concern themselves only with changes in direct materials and overhead costs.

In any event, overhead consists of many costs in addition to indirect labor. Therefore, in no case does a 5 percent increase in wages automatically increase a supplier's overhead costs by exactly 5 percent (from $0.40 to $0.42) as it does in the example given above. The buyer thus has a negotiating point even if the 5 percent wage increase is completely justified.

Frequently buyers and suppliers will disagree about the total labor cost content of a given part. The supplier's estimate of the cost of direct and indirect labor as a percentage of selling price usually will be higher than the buyer's. Smart buyers try to accumulate as much comparative data as possible. They try to get estimates from their own cost department of what relative costs should be on the type of work the supplier is performing. They also build up files of comparative data from competing suppliers. Buyers should always remember, however, that cost data they get from suppliers are nearly always confidential. They should never show such data to a competing supplier without the express permission of the supplier from whom they obtained the information. Nor should they attempt to play off one supplier against another by implying they have data that they actually do not have. Experienced buyers can follow these rules of the game and still be able to estimate a supplier's cost structure with considerable accuracy.

Profit. The example given shows that the supplier theoretically is not increasing the unit profit of 9 cents with the price increase. This may mean that the supplier feels his competitive position is such that he cannot hope to boost profits when he raises prices. Or—and far more likely—it means that the supplier has made up a cost breakdown especially designed to please the buyer and convince her that higher prices do not mean higher profits.

One of the major objectives in setting administered prices is an adequate return on investment. Many companies try to achieve this objective by setting as a target a given percentage of profit on sales. Naturally, when costs and prices go up, profits go up proportionately. Most suppliers follow this accounting convention. Therefore a buyer can assume, regardless of what the supplier's cost breakdown shows, that a request for a price increase includes a request for added profit. If competitive conditions warrant it, the buyer should not be outraged at such a request. And in fact she should hesitate to use her buying power (if she has enough) to push down the price of an item so far that there is no profit in it for the supplier. However, the buyer who feels her suppliers are "entitled to a profit" is naïve. It is not the buyer's job to help the suppliers make profits. On the contrary, the buyer's role is to serve as a countervailing force that limits supplier profits. If the buyer is really effective, she may occasionally eliminate the inefficient and unprofitable supplier from her ranks. She will be looked upon as a villain by that supplier but to the overall economy and to the company, she will just be doing her job. No buyer can prevent the most efficient producer from being very profitable indeed. And, of course, in a free society, neither buyer nor seller is forced to accept the other's terms. The agreement is voluntary and must therefore be mutually advantageous.

Need for pressure. In the example given, cost analysis has opened up several areas for negotiation of the supplier's price increase. The buyer could ask for a credit against the increase in materials cost because the scrap being generated also had a higher value, or claim that the supplier's wage increase was being applied to the entire overhead even though indirect labor was probably less than half of total overhead.

The supplier, of course, can always flatly refuse to reduce the amount of the price increase. Or, as is far more likely, he can attempt to work up new figures to "prove" that the increase is really justified and that only the original "justification" was in error. Sometimes the supplier will cheerfully reduce the amount of the increase. In this case, it is quite possible that he has anticipated the buyer's attempts at price reduction and has deliberately padded estimates so that he will end up with what he actually wants after he has made substantial concessions in negotiation with the buyer.

Error in supplier pricing

So far we have discussed only price increases that result from higher wages or raw material costs. These are the most common price increases. But buyers sometimes encounter suppliers who accept an order at a certain price and then find they cannot meet this price. There has been no change in basic wages and materials costs. The supplier's problem is that either more material or more direct labor hours is being used than had been anticipated.

Unless the purchase order terms permit price redetermination (see Chapter 5), the buyer should normally treat such requests unsympathetically. No supplier can be right all the time, and the best supplier will sometimes be too optimistic when making the cost estimate on which the quotation is based. But this will be offset by the jobs on which the supplier's profits are higher than expected. If a buyer permits suppliers to charge higher prices every time they bid too low on a job, his competitive bidding process will become a farce. Suppose, for example, that a supplier bid $100 on a job and the next lowest bid was $105. If the supplier later requests a higher price, the buyer might well have been better off if he had given the order to the competitor who bid $105.

"Buying" the business. Suppliers themselves are familiar with the buyer's dilemma. It is a time-honored strategy to "buy" business by deliberately quoting low prices. Suppose that XYZ Company has been doing business with ABC Company for years. ABC's prices are reasonable and its quality and delivery are excellent. As ABC's competitor, you would like to get a slice of XYZ's business. You are as good as ABC but no better. How do you go about getting your foot in the XYZ door? One common strategy is to undercut ABC's price, selling below cost if necessary. Then, after you are in, you will try to recoup your losses over time from more profitable XYZ business.

This strategy occasionally backfires badly. A new supplier underestimates the difficulty of a particular job and costs begin to run away from him. While the buyer's reaction may be unsympathetic in such cases, her bargaining position may also be weak when a supplier exerts strong pressure for a price increase. Suppose, for example, that the buyer places an order with a supplier in June for delivery in December. If manufacturing lead time is six months, what does the buyer do if in November the supplier refuses to ship unless he is awarded a general price increase? In practice, the buyer probably would settle with the supplier. If she wanted to, she could refuse to adjust the contract and attempt to enforce it with legal action. However, this is rarely done by industrial buyers, whose supplier relations seldom deteriorate to the point where even a threat of legal action is necessary.

Honest error. A far more common problem in industrial purchasing is the supplier who comes to the buyer and says: "We bid too low on this job. We just didn't anticipate the difficulties we've had. Costs have been so high that we cannot continue to produce on the job unless we get some sort of price relief." The buyer investigates and discovers that costs have indeed been so high and the job has actually been more difficult than either he or any of the suppliers who quoted on the job probably could anticipate.

' Even then the buyer may insist that the supplier deliver at the purchase order price. Buyers for government agencies have no other choice. If their purchase order does not specifically call for price redetermination or excalation, they can do nothing. Industrial buyers usually can be more flexible. If they feel that specifications were misleading or that the supplier might be useful on future contracts, they may renegotiate the price even though they are not required to do so.

In fact, buyers have discovered during periods of shortage that a fixed-price contract does not guarantee that material will actually be delivered. If economic conditions change substantially after a contract is negotiated, then the buyer may have no choice but to agree to revise the contract even if this is not required. As one buyer said, "if the deal becomes highly unprofitable for a supplier, you can sue until hell freezes over but you simply won't get what you want when you want it unless you make it profitable for the supplier."

Cases

CASE 14–1.   CONSOLIDATED ELECTRIC COMPANY*

A problem in value analysis

Consolidated Electric Company has designed a system to measure impurities of gases. It anticipates that this system will have wide application among natural gas pipeline and distribution plants, chemical producers, and others. The system picks up a sample of gas (see Exhibit 1) that is sucked into a chamber where its composition is measured. The sample is then discarded and the process is repeated. During the moment when one sample is being measured, the rotary valve is closed. This causes the gas to force the relief flipper valve up (see Exhibit 1), providing an alternate and continuous path of flow. As the rotary valve opens for a new sample, the spring closes the flapper and shuts off the alternate path.

Roberts Company, one of Consolidated's regular suppliers of special valves, has designed a relief valve, model No. 3360100, for the system. Stated simply, the function of the relief valve is to provide a continuous flow. Its function is illustrated schematically in Exhibit 2, and engineering details are shown in Consolidated's drawing No. 7436359 (see Exhibit 3).

The valve has an aluminum body (see illustrations in Exhibits 4 and 5) and male and female half sections. It is assembled with mating threads that are made airtight by means of a Neoprene rubber "O" ring. The female body has a male AN (i.e., made to Army-Navy stan-

---

* This case study is based on an actual value analysis problem encountered by the General Electric Company.

468

EXHIBIT 1

dards) air-line fitting, while the male body has two threaded holes for accepting AN fittings and two for stud mounting. The female body has two decals, one indicating the direction of flow and the other identifying the supplier. The flapper has a molded Teflon surface that seats on a knife-edge diameter to provide a closed-valve position. It is held in

EXHIBIT 2

EXHIBIT 3

VALVE, VACUUM
RELIEF

GENERAL ⊕ ELECTRIC

B | 7436359

REVISIONS

SYM	DESCRIPTION	DATE	APPROVAL
A			
B	TO REVISE LOCATION OF 1.828 DIM.		
C	D ADDED NOTE TO LMEE ENGR.		

NOTES:
1. WITH A VACUUM OF 15 INCHES OF MERCURY APPLIED AT THE EXHAUST PORT, THE VACUUM AT THE INLET PORT MUST BE MANUALLY ADJUSTABLE BETWEEN THE LIMITS OF 1 INCH OF MERCURY AND 12 INCHES OF MERCURY.
2. TEMPERATURE: -55°C TO +71°C OPERATING -62°C TO +85°C NON-OPERATING
3. VIBRATION: 10 TO 55 CPS, .060 INCHES DOUBLE AMPLITUDE 90 MINUTES IN EACH OF THREE ORTHOGONAL PLANES.
4. SALT SPRAY: 50 HOURS
5. HUMIDITY: 10 DAYS AT 95-100% REL. HUMIDITY
6. SHOCK: 18 IMPACT SHOCKS OF 15G, CONSISTING OF 3 SHOCKS IN OPPOSITE DIRECTIONS ALONG EACH OF 3 MUTUALLY PERPENDICULAR AXES, EACH SHOCK IMPULSE HAVING A TIME DURATION OF 11 ±1 MILLI-SECONDS
7. MATERIALS & WORKMANSHIP TO BE IN ACCORDANCE WITH REQUIREMENTS OF MIL-E-5400
8. WEIGHT - THE WEIGHT OF THE VALVE MUST NOT EXCEED 6 OUNCES.

MATERIAL MUST MEET G.E.
INCOMING INSPECTION & TEST.
SAMPLE PER MIL-STD-105A
TEST NONE

PURCHASE ORDER FROM CORNELIUS
CO. MINNEAPOLIS, MINN. OR ANOTHER
APPROVED VENDOR
SPECIFICATION CONTROL DRAWING
THE ITEM(S) SHALL BE CONSTRUCTED TO
MEET THE REQUIREMENTS LISTED HEREON.

EXHIBIT 4

EXHIBIT 5

place and can be adjusted with a spring, stud, and locking nut. The assembly contains ten individual parts.

Roberts Company has quoted a unit price of $73.20 for an order of 546 pieces.

Questions

1. Does Roberts's quote represent good value?
2. How might costs be reduced through value analysis?

CASE 14–2. BLUE MOTORS CORPORATION (B)

Negotiating a supplier price increase

Blue Motors spends about $10 million a year on "chrome" moldings used to decorate the sides of its various automobile models. The moldings are made from a relatively low-cost type of stainless steel. There are three basic steps in the process. First the stainless steel is run through a series of rollers to form the desired cross section. Then the rolled molding is cut to length, and notches and holes are pierced in a press operation. Finally, the completed moldings are inspected for scratches, polished if necessary, and packaged for shipment. Most suppliers perform the two basic operations—rolling and forming—on a single machine. Occasionally, supplementary press operations are required. Inspection and buffing out of scratches are always necessary.

All together, Blue Motors buys about 40 different moldings, but it uses only two different cross sections. Most of the differences between parts come at the press stage rather than at the rolling stage. For example, a four-door car might have four different moldings running along each side—on the front fender, the front door, the rear door, and the rear quarter panel. The moldings are almost identical (in fact, to the casual observer they would blend together to look like a single molding running the length of the car); the only differences are in length, holes, and the forming of the ends.

Blue Motors buys its moldings from three suppliers: Detroit Molding Corporation, Galway Corporation, and Stainless Forming Company. In addition, there are two other suppliers of moldings to the auto industry, Great Lakes Molding Company and Albertson Corporation. Blue Motors has done business with Great Lakes and Albertson in the past. But it prefers to limit itself to three suppliers, and these two firms were not competitive when the last buy was made.

The technology of the stainless steel molding industry is far from complex. The equipment is standard throughout the industry, and relatively little know-how is required to operate it. There is just one big problem: making a profit at the prices the auto companies are willing to pay. Although there are only five producers, competition among them is so keen that four of them have been forced to move their plants from the Detroit and Cleveland areas to the South, where wages are much lower. The lowest cost producer in the industry is the Galway Corporation, which has always been located in South Carolina.

Blue Motors broke the market for stainless steel moldings when it brought Galway in as a supplier. Galway's original prices were nearly 20 percent lower than those charged by the northern companies. Galway had no difficulty in increasing its share of Blue Motors' business to 33 percent of total requirements, and it later got substantial contracts from Blue Motors' competitors. The northern companies could not compete. They tried to get their employees to take wage cuts and boost their productivity. They were unsuccessful on both counts. To stay in business, they moved their plants South to get a more placid and lower cost labor supply.

Galway's competitors took heavy losses at first. But gradually they were able to get their new nonunion plants operating efficiently and apparently were making modest profits charging prices that were about 5 percent higher than those of Galway. Janet Barnes, purchasing manager of Blue Motors, has just concluded negotiations for moldings for the new models with Galway's competitors. She tried to get them to cut prices by 5 percent but they pointed out that their costs had gone up by 20 percent since the earlier contracts were negotiated. After considerable negotiation, it was agreed to hold the line on prices.

As a result, Galway continued to sell moldings at average prices that were 5 percent below its competitors when the new model year began in the fall. Then in December, Barnes received a letter from Galway requesting a 10 percent general price increase. The letter said that the reason for the increase was higher costs of labor and materials. Barnes wrote Joseph Galway and asked him to substantiate the increase, since she knew of no increase in wage and materials costs since the contracts had been negotiated three months earlier.

The following week Galway arrived at Barnes's office in Detroit accompanied by his Detroit sales representative, controller, and general sales manager. Galway had work sheets on which he had broken down what he claimed were the actual manufacturing costs of each molding, based on the most recent production run. Typical is the breakdown of part CF-101172, the right rear quarter panel molding for Blue Motors' Stardust sedan:

0.16 lb. of stainless steel at $0.92	$0.1472
Labor	0.1600
Overhead	0.4900
Total manufacturing cost	$0.7972
Sales and administrative expense	0.0797
Total cost.................................	$0.8769
Loss	(0.0269)
Price	$0.8500

Barnes was ready to talk to Galway. Her purchase analyst, Roberta Spade, had prepared detailed cost estimates of the moldings. Her breakdown of part CF-101172 was as follows:

0.15 lb. of stainless steel at $0.92	$0.1380
Labor—1.51 minutes at $0.9	0.1365
Burden at 250%	0.3413
Total manufacturing cost	$0.6158
Sales and administrative expense	0.0300
Total cost	$0.6458
Profit	0.0720
	$0.7178
Estimated price	$0.7180

After exchanging pleasantries, Barnes said to Galway, "I'm glad you're up in Detroit to discuss molding prices again. We have made a detailed cost analysis, and frankly we think there's still plenty of room for price reduction."

Galway replied, "That isn't what my records show. I know we're the lowest cost producer in the business—and you know it, too—and we just can't make out at these prices. Here are my records to prove it."

Galway's controller then produced detailed records of actual direct labor and overhead costs for Spade and Barnes to examine. Spade immediately asked if she might study the records for a few days. Galway refused. He said that his costs were actually nobody's business but his own, and he didn't intend to let these detailed records out of his sight. Spade then made a superficial examination of the records in the presence of the others. She concluded that the records supported Galway's statement that he was losing money on Blue Motors' molding orders.

Spade and Barnes now pointed out that their orders were not issued on a cost-plus basis. They said their estimates showed that an efficient producer should be able to cut prices and still make money on Blue Motors' orders. Galway asked them if they could support their claim. Spade then showed Galway her own detailed estimates.

"That estimate looks mighty fine on paper," Galway declared, "but you've never had any experience running a molding factory."

Spade replied that she had spent some time in almost every molding plant in the country, including Galway's own, and that these figures were based on efficient operation of modern equipment not unlike that she had seen in the Galway plant.

The group then proceeded to compare estimates. The difference of 0.01 lb. in stainless steel usage was readily resolved. It turned out that Galway's costs were based on a size he had purchased some months before to protect himself against a steel strike. He agreed that his materials cost would drop to the $0.1380 shown in Spade's estimate as soon as he started using stainless strip of exactly the right size.

The difference in labor cost between Galway's and Spade's estimates was all but resolved. Spade agreed that she had neglected to include all of the hand-polishing operations that Galway insisted were necessary to meet Blue Motors' inspection standards. But she claimed that total labor cost, including the polishing costs, should not exceed $0.15. Galway finally agreed that $0.15 was a good target, provided that Barnes would get Blue Motors's quality control manager to visit the Galway plant and agree to accept parts with the polishing labor possible with a $0.15 direct labor allowance.

Galway and Spade found it impossible to reconcile their differences on overhead and administrative expense. Spade claimed that these costs depended heavily on volume of production and that Blue Motors could not be held responsible for Galway's underabsorbence of overhead. Spade suggested that the reason that Galway's overhead was high was because his sales volume was off from the previous year. Galway had lost part of the business it had previously enjoyed from one of Blue Motors' competitors. Overall auto sales were off from the year before and auto manufacturers were using less molding on each car because of the increased popularity of smaller cars, which had less "chrome" decoration.

Galway declared that the breakdown showed his actual costs, and that he knew full well he was the most efficient producer in the industry. He told Barnes that no "young punk" (meaning Spade) was going to tell him what his costs should be and how his business should be run. He said he expected an answer from Barnes when she returned to Detroit the following week.

Barnes knew that if she awarded any increase to Galway her other molding suppliers would undoubtedly hear of it and also ask for price adjustments. Negotiation with the others would be particularly difficult if Barnes were forced to give Galway a price increase that eliminated the differential between Galway and his competitors.

Question

How should Barnes and Spade plan negotiations with Galway and the other molding suppliers?

CASE 14–3. NUCLEONICS CORPORATION

Use of the learning curve in negotiation

Nucleonics Corporation of America is the prime contractor for the U.S. Air Force's Greyhound missile. The company has relied heavily on subcontractors in the development and manufacture of the missile, and about 65 percent of the sales dollar is for purchased components. In the early stages of the missile's development, when Nucleonics had an Air Force research and development contract, the company did a great deal of contracting on a cost- plus-fixed-fee basis. These contracts were converted to price redetermination as soon as suppliers knew enough about specifications to quote reasonably realistic prices.

Now many suppliers have had sufficient experience to be willing to quote on a fixed-price basis, and the materials manager, Mr. Swinbourne, buys a number of small components at fixed prices. However, he prefers to continue to buy the more complex items on a basis that permits prices to be redetermined periodically by either party. He believes these items are so specialized and his suppliers now have so much experience with them that no competitor could successfully produce them at lower cost. As a result, if suppliers were awarded fixed-price contracts after competitive bidding, they could easily charge prices high enough to earn rather exorbitant profits.

This is true even of some relatively simple parts. For example, Boston Electronics makes a special resistor used in the missile's guidance system. Tolerances on this resistor are extremely tight, and at first the company had a fantastically high scrap rate. At least 100 resistors were rejected for every one accepted. The company accepted its first order for 2,000 resistors at $6 each, with price redetermination. After it completed half of this order, the company submitted the following cost breakdown and requested a new price:

Material	$0.92
Labor	1.22
Manufacturing overhead	9.24
Total manufacturing cost	$11.38
Sales and administrative expenses	0.56
Total cost	$11.94

Nucleonics' materials manager was particularly shocked by Boston's enormous overhead charge. Boston's sales manager explained that these charges included the cost of scrap that had been run. After substantial negotiation, Nucleonics finally agreed to pay Boston $11.94 for the second batch of 1,000 resistors provided that Boston would stick to a price of $6.00 for the first batch. Boston agreed, since it believed it had found a way to reduce its scrap substantially.

While Boston was completing this order, Nucleonics got an extension of its prime contract from the Air Force. It placed an order with Boston for an additional 4,000 resistors. The order was priced at $6 with a redetermination clause. Calculating that Boston should be gaining additional experience and should be reducing costs, Nucleonics' materials manager decided to invoke the redetermination clause and reopen price negotiations on the second order.

In accordance with the provisions of the clause, Boston submits the following unit cost breakdown for the final lot of 1,000 pieces made on the initial production order:

Material	$0.87
Labor	1.05
Manufacturing overhead	2.25
Total manufacturing cost	$4.17
Sales and administrative expenses	0.21
Total cost	$4.38

Boston suggests that since the second order will be manufactured in lots of 2,000, it can afford to reduce its price to $4.85 and still make a 10 percent profit on sales. It regrets that it cannot make any further price reduction because its suppliers are increasing prices and so materials costs will rise by 2 cents per resistor. In addition, Boston recently negotiated a new two-year contract with its union that called for wage increases of 30 cents per hour. Boston's current average wage is $5.30 per hour.

Questions

1. Should Nucleonics accept Boston's offer of a $4.85 price?
2. What price would be reasonable based on Boston's current costs, its projected increases in cost, and the experience it has gained, based on an 80 percent learning curve?

15

Buying supplier-designed products

In the previous chapter, we discussed some of the major problems that concern the buyer of high-volume production components. This form of purchasing is carried on by manufacturing companies to the tune of hundreds of billions of dollars annually. But most purchase *transactions* even by large manufacturing companies involve goods and services that are designed by their suppliers and offered for sale to all customers. In addition, almost all purchases by nonmanufacturing organizations are concerned with supplier-designed products.

CHARACTERISTICS *question*

The supplier-designed product has these characteristics that differentiate it from the high-volume production component:

(1.) *Quality is likely to be determined by performance of the product rather than the ability of the supplier to meet the buyer's engineering specifications.* The buyer of the supplier-designed item may not know how the product is made; he or she measures quality in terms of what the product will do. In contrast, the supplier of the high-volume production item may not always know very much about how its product actually functions as part of some larger assembly. This is perfectly ok as long as the supplier simply manufactures to the buyer's specifications.

(2.) *One supplier-designed product may be genuinely superior to that of another supplier.* In contrast, buyer-designed products purchased from competing suppliers are identical as long as suppliers are conforming to buyer specifications. Thus, Ford may use interchangeably in its cars a particular component that is being purchased simultaneously from three or four suppliers. In contrast, the Ford truck is a

476

supplier-designed product that is quite different from the Chevrolet and Doge trucks with which it competes. Price becomes just one of the factors that determine whose brand is going to be purchased.

3. Users of supplier-designed products play a much bigger role in the purchasing process than is normally the case with buyer-designed products. When a company is buying to its own unique specifications, a competent purchasing manager will get quotations from several competing vendors. As long as each supplier has a record of good performance in meeting specifications and delivering on time, the decision on who gets the business may be made entirely in the purchasing department. In contrast, the user of materials often has strong brand preferences on supplier-designed items. These always affect the purchase decision. For example, the surgeon may request that the hospital purchasing manager buy Ethicon brand sutures. The basic buying decision is then made before the hospital solicits bids from suppliers.

4. Supplier-designed items are likely to be sold through distributors or dealers; buyer-designed items are usually bought directly from the manufacturer. There are many exceptions to this generalization. Some manufacturers of supplier-designed items—especially those that are very expensive and require a great deal of engineering and other technical expertise—sell directly to their customers. In general, however, the supplier-designed item is sold to individual customers in relatively small quantities and intermediate levels of distribution between manufacturer and customer are needed.

5. There are often two prices involved in purchases of supplier-designed purchases. The first price is not directly negotiated by the ultimate buyer; it is the price at which the manufacturer sells to the distributor. This price is always "administered." It is based on the manufacturer's costs but is also strongly influenced by what the manufacturer thinks the traffic will bear and how much competitors charge for comparable products. Only rarely can it be influenced by an individual buyer of the end product. However, customers collectively influence manufacturers' selling prices to their distributors. Prices will be firm and may creep up when the product is in strong demand. If the customers stay away in droves, the manufacturer may make a direct price cut or offer some special allowance to dealers in order to encourage them either to cut their prices or to spend more on selling.

The second price in the transaction is that at which the dealer sells to the purchaser. It is negotiable and subject to all of the usual rules of competition. In fact, the retail price may be quite competitive even when the product is manufactured in a market that is largely monopolistic. For example, price competition among the big auto manufacturers is conspicuously absent at the manufacturer level. Each manufacturer simply sets a price at which it will sell to dealers and then spends substantial sums on promotion to convince the general public that the product is worth the price that has been set.

The dealer's actual selling price, in contrast, is determined competitively among many dealers selling identical products. Even on products that are far more specialized than automobiles, there is often considerable competition at the dealer level. For example, while the prices set by manufacturers of hospital medical-surgical supplies and drugs are largely monopolistic, there is considerable competition among dealers, each of whom handles each major manufacturer's lines.

Most organizations buy two distinct groups of supplier-designed products: supplies and equipment. Supplies are almost always purchased from various distributors and dealers; equipment is more likely to be purchased directly from manufacturers, both because of its cost and its technical complexity.

SUPPLIES

Manufacturing organizations ordinarily spend most of their purchase dollars on production parts and materials but most of their orders are issued for various supplies, usually of relatively small value. These include factory supplies (called MRO for maintenance, repair, and operating supplies) such as tools, lubricants, light bulbs, as well as all of the supplies used by the plant's maintenance personnel. They also include office supplies of all types. Nonmanufacturing organizations naturally also purchase a wide variety of office supplies as well as various specialized items. For example, the typical general hospital spends as much as 25 percent of its revenue dollar on purchases of various medical-surgical supplies, drugs, dietary supplies, and other items.

Price

The same purchasing objectives that apply to production components apply to supplies. But the emphasis may be different. Price is still important but it sometimes takes a back seat to other objectives. For example, a supplier's ability and willingness to carry a full inventory is much more important in supplies purchases than it is in buying for production.

Limited bargaining power The strategy and basic economics of achieving the price objective in buying supplier-designed products is essentially the same. But the execution and the details are quite different. The buyer usually negotiates with a distributor rather than a manufacturer. This sharply limits bargaining power. If the manufacturer's price is simply too high, the buyer's only recourse is to search for a lower cost brand that will perform satisfactorily.

Direct negotiations can usually be carried on only with the distributor who does not normally have discretionary power over more than roughly 30 cents of the supplies sales dollar. The other 70 cents of the $1 price that is paid by the supplies buyer represents what the distributor pays the manufacturer. This is usually an administered price schedule that is available to all of the manufacturer's distributors. It is not totally right, of course. Prices are adjusted up and down by manufacturers who sell through distributors to reflect changes in market share and competitive conditions.

Rebates. Manufacturers sometimes offer either temporary or permanent rebates to their distributors when they are seeking to increase or simply to maintain their market share. These rebates are a thinly concealed form of price cutting. The manufacturer who uses them hopes either to give a distributor more incentive to sell its particular brand or to permit it to offer wider discounts from list price to customers. Under ideal circumstances (which probably never occur in practice), competing manufacturers will not realize that there has been effective price cutting until after they have lost a substantial share of their market to the firm that offers rebates to distributors.

Needless to say, the distributor that is getting a special rebate does not necessarily pass this information on to its customers. Those who are "happy" with the prices they are paying won't benefit from the rebate at all. The hard bargaining purchasing manager often can only deduce that there is some sort of rebate when she negotiates a price with a distributor that seemingly cannot possibly be profitable.

This also occurs with retail purchases. The various promotions run by supermarkets are good examples. Similarly, the auto manufacturers almost always pass on a rebate of several hundred dollars per vehicle to their dealers either on models that are not selling well or near the end of the model year when buyers would otherwise be prone to wait for next year's cars to appear on the market. The dealer uses the rebate either to pass on to price-conscious customers as an extra discount or to offer a larger trade-in allowance.

Negotiation with distributors. The principles of negotiating with distributors are essentially the same as those for dealing with manufacturers, which were discussed in detail in the previous chapters. In both cases, negotiation is a trading process in which both buyer and seller "win" by gaining more than they are required to give up. The details are different, however. As mentioned previously, the supplies buyer is obviously seeking a lower price but the seller's willingness to carry buyer's inventory may also be an important economic advantage.

What then does the buyer have to offer the seller? Essentially the

480

same benefits as in production buying but with somewhat different emphasis. These include:

1. More business. The rational buyer of supplies tries to maximize buying power by having suppliers bid on all requirements for a particular "family" of items for an extended period. For example, a buyer may make a list of electrical supplies purchases over the past year and then ask competing distributors to bid on furnishing all estimated requirements over the coming year. This contract is far more attractive to a distributor than a chance to quote on just a few hundred feet of electrical cable. Inevitably there will be more competition. Ideally, the buyer would get fixed-price quotations on a long "laundry list" of items. In practice, this is usually not practical and the quotation for the "systems contract" likely consists of a series of discounts from manufacturers' list prices.

2. Lower costs. The distributor is subject to the same cost-volume relationship as the manufacturer (as discussed in the previous chapter.) However, the impact on profits is probably greater for the typical distributor. The distributor pays out perhaps 70 cents to the manufacturer, incurs costs of roughly 25 cents in selling and physical distribution costs, and earns a profit of 5 cents—or less. Much of the 25 cents represents fixed or nonvariable costs of operating the business—salaries, rent, taxes, and so on. As a result, the *marginal* profit from extra business may be three or four times the *average* profit. This gives the distributor strong incentive to shade prices either to get extra business or to avoid losing business to a competitor.

There are also real economies when a customer buys a greater share of its needs from a particular distributor. The cost of delivering supplies is essentially the same for each delivery, almost irrespective of the quantity delivered. Suppose, for example, that a distributor estimates that it costs $10 to deliver a shipment to a particular customer. If there is $100 worth of merchandise for that customer, delivery costs amount to 10 percent of sales. However, if there is $500 worth, they only amount to 2 percent of sales.

The same economies can be made in sales costs (provided the salesperson does not work on straight commission). If the customer and distributor make a deal to cover all requirements for a year, the salesperson need not call on that customer quite so frequently. The time that is saved can be devoted (hopefully) to get extra business from other customers. In addition, the costs of making a particular sales call on a larger customer are spread over a higher volume of business.

Suppose, for example, that a sales call costs $50. If this yields a $200 order, sales costs amount to 25 percent of sales. But if the same call yields a $1,000 order, they amount to but 5 percent of sales. Obviously, a shrewd purchasing manager will demand that part of these savings in sales and distribution costs be shared with the buying organization in the form of lower prices (or its equivalent in supplier inventory protection).

In some cases, remarkable savings can be achieved by spreading sales and distribution costs over a broader base. For example, printed forms and office supplies have traditionally been marketed on an order-by-order basis. The salesperson makes her rounds from customer to customer, sometimes calling as often as weekly. Each order is relatively small so selling costs are high as a percent of total sales.

As a result, savings of as much as 25 percent on price plus a variety of fringe benefits including supplier inventory protection can be achieved with systems contracts on printed supplies. A single supplier bids on an organization's entire requirements for printed forms and office supplies. It is usually able to cut prices substantially simply because there is no need to pay a salesperson for weekly calls.

No loss of business. So-called personal selling is rampant in the marketing of supplier-designed products and services. Distributors get business simply because the person who makes the buying decision likes the salesperson. Note that this is as good a reason as any to buy an identical product from one distributor instead of another as long as price and related economic benefits are not important.

Since distributors do not want to compete on the basis of price if they can help it, they often stress "service" which, in turn, often translates simply into buying from someone you like. In certain instances, there is tangible reason for this prejudice: graft. In fact, obscure manufacturers and distributors have been known to run advertisements suggesting that a customer be his own salesman; i.e., collect a sales "commission" by selling something to himself when acting as a buyer for a company.

Top management can protect the organization against personal selling first by delegating all buying to a professional purchasing office. The next step, which is more directly concerned with this chapter, is to make certain that the purchasing department regularly solicits competitive bids from distributors. To a great extent, a distributor will charge competitive prices simply because it fears loss of business.

Unfortunately, it is not necessarily economic for most organizations to get competitive bids on many, if not most, supplies purchases. The basic problem is that the cost of getting the bids is often greater than the value of the purchase. On repetitive supplies purchases such as printed forms or office supplies, this difficulty can be circumvented with competitive bidding on "systems" contracts. The supplier, in effect, bids on what amount to several hundred individual purchases that will take place over a period of perhaps a year. *Doesn't pay to bid*

On other purchases, this is not practical. Every organization makes large numbers of relatively low-value purchases of various supplies which are necessarily unique in character. In some cases, the price objective simply must be sacrificed for convenience. For example, if a company car breaks down several hundred miles from the home office, it is rarely economic to get competitive bids on repairing it. The friendly local garage will simply charge what it feels the traffic will bear.

On other purchases, the buying organization can try to operate like the Internal Revenue Service does in selecting tax returns for audit. It can get competitive bids often enough so that the supplier is never quite sure whether or not they are being obtained on a particular purchase. All studies show that almost every distributor will charge slightly lower prices on many items if there is a fear that the customer is getting quotations from someone else. This hint of potential competition can be fairly subtle. For example, suppose a buyer calls a supplier and simply says, "send me over two of your Ajax No. 3000 valves and bill against purchase order 13205." If the supplier does not have any standing order with this customer, it is fairly obvious that price is not too important. Competitive bids are not being solicited; the supplier gets the order without even having to quote a price.

The supplier is less certain when a buyer calls and asks if the supplier has the valves and what is the price. After finding the price, the buyer does not place the order immediately. She can either say, "I will call you back" or "you may be getting a purchase order from me in a few days." Suppliers don't like this type of buyer but they will often offer slightly lower prices when they deduce that other suppliers may be bidding on the same order. Needless to say, the buyer may frequently just note the price and simply issue the order without further ado much as the IRS presumably accepts our tax returns without examining them. But we are afraid to be too imaginative in filling out our tax returns lest we be the ones who are called upon to justify them. Suppliers also fear uncertainty.

Quality

Once a price is agreed upon, it is well defined. There is little or no ambiguity. In contrast, quality is hard to measure, especially on supplier-designed purchases. Every organization buys numerous supplies in small quantities. With the exception of large-scale purchasers such as the federal government, buyers do not have the technological resources to measure the quality of these purchases objectively. A factory buys lubricating oil for its machinery; a hospital buys disposable syringes; a bank buys forms. The quality of each of these groups of products can be measured with appropriate engineering tests. But none of these buyers is able to make these measurements and its volume of purchases does not justify acquiring the skills that are needed.

Evaluation.   How then does the factory determine whether Shell's lubricating oil is better or worse than that sold by Texaco? The answer is that all too often the buyer hasn't the vaguest idea. In some cases, it is possible to find out through independent testing services. In most instances, the buyer simply does not know. Naturally each supplier can "prove" that its product is better. But such information is automatically suspect for obvious reasons.

The best that the buyer can do is to ask users of the material to perform an evaluation. This is carried in terms of the functions that the product fulfills for the buyer—not necessarily those for which it was designed. The evaluation process is a form of value analysis. The buyer asks the users what functions the particular product performs for them and also to indicate the relative importance of these particular functions.

Example.   To see how this system of user evaluation works, let's apply it to a product that almost everyone wears at least once (at birth): the plastic identification bracelet that is attached to every patient's wrist upon admission to a hospital. There are about a half-dozen competing brands of I.D. bracelets. Hospitals pay as little as 3 cents for the cheaper brands and 15 cents or more for the leading brand. While all brands look pretty much the same to the hospital patient, most nurses believe that there are significant differences in quality and urge hospital purchasing managers to favor particular brands. Since the competing brands are not identical, how can the buyer relate price to quality?

Let's first imagine that there are two competing brands: X and Y. The steps followed in the analysis that follows apply to these imaginary brands but are applicable to all supplier-designed products.[1]

1. Identify the useful characteristics of the product. Obviously, the using department should be in full agreement on this list of characteristics. In the case of I.D. bracelets, assume that useful characteristics include: (1) legibility for the duration of any patient's stay in the hospital; (2) ease of attachment to the patient's body; (3) ease of removal at time of discharge from hospital; (4) comfort and freedom from skin allergies caused by the I.D. device; (5) difficulty of removal during patient's stay in the hospital; and (6) compatibility with the hospital's overall recordkeeping and identification system.

2. Determine the relative importance of each key characteristic. . . . Some characteristics are more important than others. In addition, minimum standards must be set for each. For example, it . . . must be reasonably easy to remove an I.D. bracelet. (If not, a tattoo would be the perfect identification technique.) Thus, a failure on a key characteristic should rule out a product that would otherwise be superior.

---

[1] This example was originally published in the June 1978 of *Hospital Purchasing Management* and is reproduced here with the express permission of the Hospital Purchasing Institute Inc., its parent and publisher.

The total ratings for relative importance should add up to 100. When this is done, the perfect product will wind up with a rating of 100. The job of assessing relative importance is not an easy one. It should be done by a panel, and the final ratings will reflect either a consensus or simply a numerical averaging of the "votes." Some of the decisions will be tough. Those that appear in Table 15–1 are arbitrary and should . . . be treated simply as a demonstration of the calculations that are involved.

TABLE 15–1
How purchasing and nursing might evaluate two competing I.D. bands

		Brand X		Brand Y	
Characteristic	Relative importance	User rating	Extension	User rating	Extension
Legibility	25%	90	22.50	95	23.75
Attachability	10	100	10.00	95	9.50
Ease of removal	5	100	5.00	100	5.00
Comfort	20	70	14.00	80	16.00
"Stays on"	25	100	25.00	100	25.00
Compatibility with system	15	80	12.00	100	15.00
	100%		88.50		94.25

3. **Each product should be evaluated for each characteristic.** This evaluation might represent a numerical averaging of the opinions of a panel or it might represent a consensus that is hammered out in a committee meeting. Each individual evaluation would range from 0 to 100. A score of 0 on any vital characteristic would obviously cause the product to be unacceptable.

4. **Scores for each product should be calculated and related to price.** Calculation of a composite score is not difficult and is illustrated in Table 15–1. The score for each characteristic is multiplied by the weight given that characteristic, and these weighted scores are then added up. The higher the score, the more closely the product comes to meeting user needs. When the highest-scoring product has the most attractive price, the purchase decision is obvious.

Let's suppose, as often happens, that the brand with the higher quality evaluation commands a higher price. What should the hospital buy? Suppose that brand X with a score of 88.50 sells for 10 cents and brand Y, with a score of 94.25, costs 15 cents. Which purchase offers the better value?

To find out, the purchasing manager would sit down with the top nurses in her institution and try to determine subjectively whether the more desirable characteristics of product Y are worth the price premium. Another approach would be for the users simply to state whether or not the cheaper product is acceptable. If it is, the buying decision is obvious. If it is not, the purchasing manager would ask them to justify their decision as rationally as possible. If the analysis seemed reasonable, she would then simply file this as proof that purchase was made rationally.

question 7

Standardization

Suppose that some nurses like the cheaper I.D. bracelet and others strongly prefer the more costly one. One decision that the hospital purchasing manager should probably *not* make is to buy both brands. The costs of carrying inventory loom relatively larger with supplies purchases than with production components. For example, suppose Chevrolet discovered that it had to use a 1-inch bolt for some applications but that it could eliminate a 7/8-inch bolt by substituting the longer 1-inch bolt. It would not pay to do this if the bolts were used on Chevrolet cars. The saving from eliminating the inventory of 7/8-inch bolts would be offset many times over by the premium price paid for the millions of 1-inch bolts that would be substituted.

However, this substitution or its equivalent might be economic if Chevrolet used the bolts in its maintenance department. Even relatively small organizations may be forced to carry thousands of different supply items in stock and it can always eliminate some of them economically with a standardization program. In fact, if it does not have such a program, it will find that each year the number of items that it stocks will increase. Items are added but nothing is taken away.

Typical program. For example, Figure 15–1 shows what happened as a result of a standardization program at Bryant Electric Company, Bridgeport, Connecticut. The company reviewed 1,447 items carried in stock and found it could eliminate 794 of them. Unit costs were reduced because fewer items were bought in larger quantities; carrying costs were reduced because of a net reduction in inventories. Total savings are estimated at $102,000 in the two years since the program was started.

Bryant's experience with standardization is not unique. For example, before it set standards, one large Cleveland auto parts manufacturer stocked several hundred different types of oil and other lubricants in its plants. Each production supervisor requistioned the precise type of oil he thought would best serve his needs. A standardization study showed that less than 50 different types of oil were needed to do every possible lubrication job in the company's factories. As a result, the company uses 80 percent fewer types of lubricant than before. Inventories are lower, and prices have also been reduced because the company can buy each type of lubricant in larger quantities.

Definition of standard. The examples cited above are dramatic, but they illustrate why standardization is important in industry. Stan-

486

FIGURE 15–1
Bryant Electric Company standardization program

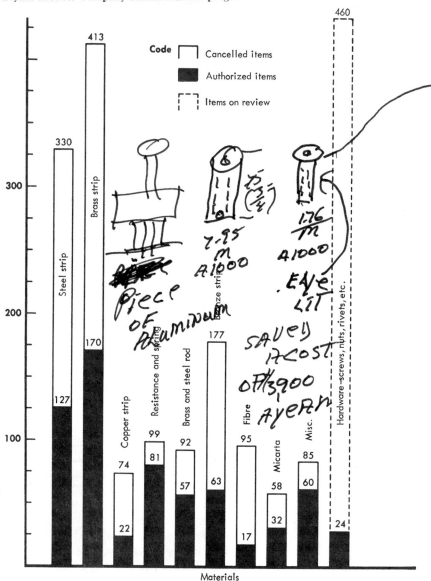

Courtesy Bryant Electric Co.

The standardization program of Bryant Electric Company was an outstanding success. In two years the number of items stocked was reduced by more than 50 percent, and savings totaled $102,000.

dardization is essential to a modern mass-production economy. Almost
every major industry has standards to classify its products. *question*

A standard is defined as "that which has been established as a
model to which an object or an action may be compared."[2] The purpose
of a standard is to provide a criterion for judgment. Companies are
concerned with standards both for the products they design and for the
materials designed by their suppliers. In the former case, the company
may create its own standards or work to the standards of an industry.
For example, when an office-furniture firm designs a drawer pull, it
may work within industry standards for strength, shape, durability,
and so on. But the final design is unique—although it may become one
of the company's own standards for drawer pulls. The materials the
company buys usually are in accord with the supplier's industry standards. For example, the engineer may specify that the drawer pull be
made of steel specified in an American Iron & Steel Institute standard.

Companywide standards.   Although industry standards help prevent unnecessary variation in specifications, the needs of our economy
are so great that each industry usually offers many more standard
products than any single consumer can possibly use. In addition, many
industries try to sell by brand name rather than by industry standards.
For this reason, many companies establish their own standards, not
only for products they design for themselves but also for products
designed by their suppliers. For example, Chrysler Corporation has set
its own standards for the carbide tool inserts it buys (see Figure 15–2)
by specifying the exact dimensions and grades it requires. If Chrysler
did not go to the trouble of doing this, it would soon find itself using far
more different types of carbide insert than it does at present.

When there are no written standards each user of material has carte
blanche to specify what he or she needs. For example, note that
Chrysler has five different types of square carbide insert. No. SQ–122
has a ⅜-inch square cross section with 0.2156-inch clearance and
¹/₃₂-inch corner radius. The comparable dimensions for the next size,
SQ–163, are ½ inch, 0.386 inch, and ³/₆₄ inch, respectively. If one size
is too small, the next size is used. But what would happen if there were
no standards? Each user would calculate the dimensions that most
closely suited her needs. Eventually Chrysler would wind up buying
and stocking several dozen different sizes of insert with dimensions
intermediate between those of SQ–122 and SQ–163.

The experiences of Bryant Electric, the auto parts company, and
numerous other companies prove that there is a natural tendency for
companies to stock more and more different items to do the same job.
Each user likes to get the item that is *exactly* what she wants and will
not settle for the nearest standard item if she can help it. As a result,

---

[2] *Industrial Standardization—Company Programs and Practices,* Studies in Business Policy No. 85 (New York: National Industrial Conference Board, 1957), p. 7.

FIGURE 15–2

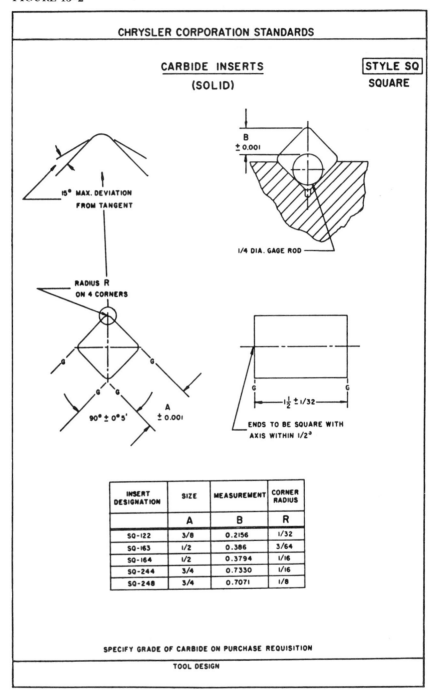

CHRYSLER CORPORATION STANDARDS

CARBIDE INSERTS
(SOLID)

STYLE SQ
SQUARE

INSERT DESIGNATION	SIZE	MEASUREMENT	CORNER RADIUS
	A	B	R
SQ-122	3/8	0.2156	1/32
SQ-163	1/2	0.386	3/64
SQ-164	1/2	0.3794	1/16
SQ-244	3/4	0.7330	1/16
SQ-248	3/4	0.7071	1/8

SPECIFY GRADE OF CARBIDE ON PURCHASE REQUISITION

TOOL DESIGN

Courtesy Chrysler Corp.

A company can limit the number of items it stocks by developing its own specifications. For example, this standard indicates that Chrysler Corporation uses only five sizes of square carbide insert.

standardization is a continuing process. Periodic reviews of every item are essential to root out the items that are no longer needed.

How to standardize

Bryant Electric's standardization program is fairly typical. Decisions were made by a committee that included representatives from every major department. The chairperson was the company's standards engineer. The first step in the program was to list all inventory items in detail on large (14″ × 24″) accounting sheets. (Figure 15–3

FIGURE 15–3

	BRYANT MATERIAL STANDARDIZATION PROGRAM							
Material Description Thk Width Length PDS	Ann. Act.	Part No.	Dwg. No.	Part Desc.	Cat. No.	Dwg. No.	Material Substitution Thk Width Length PDS	Remarks
016x5/32xC Brass 2676-6	570	E27214 E27844	14514C 15207C	Bracket Bracket	FS40 FS40	14526A 14540C	016x5/32 Brass 2676-6	Bracket width 5/32 required
016x255xC Brass 2676-6	100	E21236 E21237	9922C 9921B	Contact Contact	20 20	9920L 9920L	016x1/4 Brass 2676-6	1/4 width o.k.
016x255xC Brass 2676-10	360	E29438 E29439 E29440 E20654 E21287 E21679 E24024	15914D 15913D 8030C 8979C 10015B 10213C 8979C	Brush Brush Contact Contact Brush Contact Contact	207 204 200 4013 5128 310 15	8051L 8014L 15455L B01076 10012A 14141A Cat. card	016x1/4 Brass 2676-10	Ex. Hd. Temper required
016x255xC Brass 2676-4	48	E28254	15600C	Strap	5269	15599A	016x1/4 Brass 2676-6	1/2 hd. o.k.
016x255xC Brass 2676-11	924	E20126	8943C	Brush	706	6294B	016x1/4 Brass 2676-10	-10 o.k. per 6/10 lab rpt.
016x7/16xC Brass 2676-8	10	E2737	3125A	Washer	392	4957B	Slit from 1" wide 2676-5	1/4 hd. o.k.
016x13/32xC Brass 2676-10	2376	E2757 E4238 E13064 E16123 E18213 E22163	7671C 6340C 7671C 6180C 6180C 10459C	Contact Contact Contact Contact Contact Contact	70 4229 4190 421 421 337660	1800A 4299A Cat. card 10783B 10783B 4299A	016x13/32 Brass 2676-10	Ex. hd. Temper Required
016x15/16xC Brass 2676-3	500	E17718	7152C	Housing	746	SK521	016x15/16 Steel 7300-5	Steel o.k.

Courtesy Bryant Electric Co.

The first step in a standardization program is to list all items stocked. Bryant Electric Company did this for the brass strip listed above and changed much of the 0.255-inch-wide material to a standard 0.25-inch width.

shows a part of Bryant's listing of various types of brass strip.) Listed initially for each item was a description of the material, its usage, and how it was used. (Potential substitutes for the material were listed later.) The committee then reviewed the list to make certain that there were detailed buying specifications for each item, and possible substitutions were proposed.

Economic substitution. Even if a substitute is technically feasible, it is not necessarily economic to use it. The economics of standardization are not complex. All one need do is compare cost of acquisition and carrying cost before the substitution was made with costs after it was made. For example, suppose an item costs $0.10 and 500 units per year are used. Its substitute, which is also stocked, costs $0.105. Assume that ordering cost is $10 and carrying cost is 24 percent. If the higher cost item is substituted, purchase cost is increased by $5 per year (500 units × $0.005). But, assuming that the item formerly was purchased once a year, ordering cost is cut by $10 and carrying cost by $6 (24 percent of $25).

Items not needed. A similar approach can be used for obsolescent items. An item is worth eliminating directly if the carrying cost which probably will be incurred before it is used exceeds the purchase cost less the scrap or salvage value. Many well-managed companies consider an item obsolescent if it has not been used for the past 12 months and there is no immediate need for it. If they can sell the item back to the supplier or to another company that needs it, they do so, even if they must take a 50 percent loss to make the sale.

Standardization programs are designed primarily to root out unneeded inventories, but they also can bring direct savings on material. Most companies must stock thousands of repair parts for their equipment. Standardization programs can locate duplicate inventories—cases, for example, where a spare fan belt or ball bearing stocked for one manufacturer's machine is identical with a spare part for a different manufacturer's machine. Stocks of such components can be combined by tracing each component back to the standards of the original manufacturer. Once the buyer knows who made the component, he is foolish to pay a premium price for it to the equipment manufacturer. He can buy at much lower cost directly from the original manufacturer's distributor.

The Tennessee Valley Authority made substantial savings in buying spare parts by doing just this. For example, it used to buy replacement V-belts for certain pulverizing equipment from the equipment manufacturer (who, in turn, had purchased them from a V-belt supplier). The price of the special steel-cable V-belts was $12.08 each from the equipment manufacturer. It was reduced to $5.67 by buying directly from the V-belt manufacturer. The TVA and numerous private companies have made comparable savings on other items. Most manufacturers can make enormous profits (markups of 400 to 500 percent are not uncommon) on their service parts business. Smart buyers often can circumvent the equipment manufacturer and buy at lower prices directly from the supplier.

CAPITAL EQUIPMENT PURCHASES

The typical materials manager is both buyer and user of equipment. As a user of items such as fork trucks and electric typewriters, the materials manager would be the final authority on whether or not a particular brand of equipment met the needs for which it was purchased. As a buyer, the materials manager (or more likely, the purchasing manager) would actually make the purchase.

Since most such purchases involve highly specialized equipment, some organizations permit the actual users of the item or their representatives (such as the master mechanic in a factory) to function as de facto purchasing managers. The master mechanic, director of manufacturing engineering, or the equivalent in nonmanufacturing organizations, are technical experts. They know what is needed and they understand how the equipment works. Thus, it seemingly makes sense for them to make the buying decisions. Yet well-managed organizations insist that such purchases be channeled through their purchasing departments. Why?

Even if the user knows exactly what is needed, the purchase is almost always more complicated than simply telling the supplier to ship model 100. A purchasing professional who deals with such problems daily is more likely to be able to anticipate problems than a particular department manager who is just an occasional buyer. Questions that the purchasing manager will ask include the following:

1. What will happen if the supplier does not deliver the equipment on schedule? Lack of needed equipment could easily disrupt operations. The purchasing manager may well try to negotiate some sort of penalty clause in the contract if delivery is delayed for any reason.

2. What will happen if the equipment does not perform according to expectations? Again, some sort of contract clause may be negotiated with the supplier. In some cases, the price that is actually paid for the equipment will be related to performance. In other cases, the buyer will try to define as clearly as possible the seller's obligation should the equipment not perform satisfactorily. In many cases this will involve drawn-out discussions with the supplier who often would prefer simply to ship the machine and then forget about it.

A survey by *Purchasing* magazine showed that purchasing managers commonly negotiated numerous clauses in buying equipment that were performance related.[2] These dealt with installation requirements (cited by 88 percent of respondents), operator training (75 percent), operator safety (72 percent), maintenance (38 percent), and energy consumption (29 percent). In order to get what is bargained for, the most important factor is previous experience with the firm (cited by 89 percent of respondents.) Nevertheless, 75 percent assure that performance meets expectations by withholding part of the purchase price until users are satisfied. It is also common practice to visit other cus-

---

[2] "Capital Equipment Buying: One Strike and You're Out," *Purchasing*, March 8, 1978, pp. 59–63.

tomers of the supplier in order to see the equipment in operation and to insist on predelivery tests of the equipment.

3. *Who is liable if the equipment becomes a safety hazard itself or turns out products that are safety hazards?* Buyer and seller may well have different points of view and some agreement must be negotiated. Otherwise, the manufacturer's liability will be limited to that prescribed by the Uniform Commercial Code.

4. *How much should the equipment cost?* If delivery can be made fairly soon after the order is placed, this problem is fairly easy to resolve. The buyer simply issues a fixed-price purchase order. If the design and manufacture of the facility or equipment stretches out over a period of years, some sort of price escalation clause will be needed since neither buyer nor seller will wish to commit themselves to a particular level of wage and material costs.

Role of purchasing

Economic versus technical. Thus, while the purchasing manager almost never determines the brand and model of equipment that is being ordered, purchasing's role is by no means that of a "rubber stamp." In well-managed organizations, there is a division of responsibility on equipment purchases. The using department has technical responsibility and purchasing manager is responsible for all economic factors relating to the transaction.

A competent purchasing manager may also play an indirect role in the selection of the particular brand and model. This is done by making certain that the technical experts review products offered by all competing manufacturers. In effect, the purchasing manager works to prevent the user from being "sold" by a fast-talking sales representative before all alternatives have been considered.

It is conceivable that an organization's technical experts will become so enamored of particular mechanical or electronic features of new equipment that they will partly lose sight of the reasons for making the purchase. Both the purchasing manager and the controller are likely not to forget the real reason for the purchase. In fact, there are only two reasons why any organization buys equipment: to continue to operate or to improve cash flow.

Least-cost decision. Companies invest in things such as parking lots and pollution control devices not because these investments directly contribute to profits but simply because they have to. If they did not make such investments, they would eventually be forced to discontinue operation.

In this case, the object of the game is to spend as little as possible to achieve the "survival objective." It may not always be easy to select a "least cost" decision. There is always uncertainty on how new equipment will perform. In addition, there may be some trade-off between capital and labor. One alternative may require a large labor input and relatively low-capital investment while another may minimize labor cost but only at the expense of a larger investment. The correct alternative can be selected by treating each as if the decision were being made to improve profits and boost cash flow. The alternative requiring high labor input is treated as the "defender" in the analysis (using techniques discussed in subsequent paragraphs) and the capital investment becomes the "challenger."

Only investments where there is no alternative require little or no analysis. The others can all be treated as efforts to maximize profits either by cutting costs or increasing revenues. The purchasing manager would hardly ever make the basic analysis but should be familiar with it since purchasing is part of the team that must make the final decision.

Criteria. Capital investment must earn a return and all techniques for analyzing alternative investments assume that the goal is maximum return on capital. There is no foolproof way to make the proper decision. All capital investment involves some forecast of the future. There are always uncertainties about both the economic and physical life of the equipment, the demand for its output, and related future operating costs. In general, the greater the risk, the higher the return that should be promised before the investment is made. Shorter term investments (i.e., where the equipment is assumed to have a relatively short life or the payoff is very rapid) are usually less risky than longer term ones and, consequently, a lower return may be acceptable.

MAPI formula   *Question 6*

While it is sometimes scoffed at as being "unsophisticated," the first-year return formula of the Machinery and Allied Products Institute (MAPI) remains one of the most popular techniques for analyzing capital equipment purchases. The application of one of MAPI's formula by the Norton Company, a leading manufacturer of abrasives, is illustrated in Figure 15–4.

Norton is considering the purchase of a new handling system for abrasive grain. Norton estimates that the new equipment will reduce labor and other costs by $96,000 a year. On the other hand, the older equipment has operating advantages amounting to $14,500 a year because of lower taxes, less power consumption, and less maintenance. Net operating advantage of the new equipment thus is $81,500 ($96,000 − $14,500). To this must be added the capital cost (prorated over 15 years) and interest of $2,500 to cover needed improvements on the old equipment. These capital charges plus the $81,500 adverse operating cost of the old machine total $85,670, compared

FIGURE 15–4

		Sheet 1 of 3 Sheets

1926 $MAPi$

NORTON COMPANY
EQUIPMENT REPLACEMENT ANALYSIS

Est. No. ..7831..
Date ..4/20/-..

Line No.		PRESENT			PROPOSED
1	Description ..Present Grain Handling System.. in Plant #2		Description Pl. #2 Portable Grain Tanks, Bldg. Add.; TBS & Magnorite System		
2	Salvage value	$ 0	Cost installed		$ 689,200
3	Age	40 yrs.	Service life		* 31 yrs.
4	Equipment Number		Est'd. salvage value		$ 0
5	Department	Pr. Whl.-Abr.#2	Salvage ratio		0 %

ADVERSE MINIMUMS

6	Operating inferiority (line 29)	$ 81,500	Total cost installed	$ 689,200
7	Loss salvage value - next year	0	Chart %	31½ %
8	Interest - salvage value	0	Interest %	10 %
9	Proration - capital addition 25,000	* 1,670	Total %	
10	Interest - capital addition @ 10%	2,500		
11	ADVERSE MINIMUM $ 85,670 (A)		ADVERSE MINIMUM $ 93,000 (B)
12	GAIN FROM REPLACEMENT (next year) (A - B)	$ - 7,300	

OPERATING ADVANTAGE (next year)

			PRESENT	PROPOSED
	Income Advantages			
13	X Superiority of product		$	$
14	Increased output			
15	X Other			
	Cost Advantages			
16	Direct labor }			* 75,000
17	Indirect labor }			
18	Fringe benefit cost (20 %)			15,000
19	Maintenance		* 6,000	
20	Supplies Cap Replacement			1,000
21	Tools			
22	Spoilage Reduction in Rejections due to streaks			5,000
23	Down time			
24	X Floor space			
25	Power		500	
26	Property taxes and insurance		* 8,100	
27	X Other			
	(8½ year payback period DCF return on investment 11½%)*			
28			$ 14,500 (C)	$ 96,000 (D)
29	Net Operating Advantage (D - C)		$ 81,500 (to line 6)	

Remarks: This analysis has been computed without appraisal of intangible benefits checked above, and discussed in detail on attached sheet. Acceptance of this proposal is tantamount to evaluating all these benefits at a minimum of $7,300 per year. This is considered satisfactory.

Recommendation: Approval recommended

Signed ..C.U.T.
Date ..4/20/-..

Approved ....
Date ....

Norton Company uses an analysis technique developed by the Machinery & Allied Products Institute to determine whether or not it pays to replace capital equipment.

with an annual charge of $93,000 for interest and depreciation on the new equipment. Thus costs are theoretically $7,300 higher if Norton buys the new equipment. Norton decides to buy it anyway because it feels the intangible benefit of improved product quality with the new equipment is worth $7,300.

Note that Norton's profits will actually increase when it buys the new machine. Included in the "cost" is an allowance of 10 percent for interest. If we assume that Norton buys the equipment with idle cash, its profits increase because the 10 percent interest charge was included in the cost calculation.

Note also that if Norton were willing to accept a 5 percent return on capital, the interest cost of the new equipment would drop to $34,460. The "adverse minimum" on the new equipment would be $58,540 per year, and on the old equipment (giving effect to an interest rate reduction on the $25,000 investment in improvements) it would be $84,420. Thus the company would theoretically save $25,880 per year by investing in the new equipment instead of incurring a $7,300 cost increase to improve quality.

The MAPI formulas are very useful in comparing the relative desirability of investing in various types of equipment. The interest rate can be varied to reflect the company's availability of capital and willingness to invest in a not too certain future.

Other approaches

The MAPI method is probably the most widely used approach to capital equipment analysis. It is easy to use and leads its users to the correct investment decision most of the time. However, the method has its weaknesses. All versions of the MAPI method involve comparison of a first-year return with the amount of the investment. But, of course, a company does not buy new plant and equipment just for the first-year return; the return is spread out over a number of years. In effect, a company gives up cash today for new equipment in order to get a series of cash returns that are spread out over the life of the equipment. The problem is to relate the value of future payments to present costs.

Proponents of the MAPI method claim that its alleged weakness in considering only first-year results is unimportant. The future is so uncertain, they argue, that it is hard enough to estimate what will happen in the first year, let alone in succeeding years. Also, they point out that highly subjective factors such as higher quality are major determinants of investment decisions, and there is no point in being more precise numerically if the heart of the decision is really qualitative. Nevertheless, the MAPI method has lost popularity gradually as the controllers' offices of more companies have become staffed with business school graduates trained in the application of more complex methods.

Payback period. One simple calculation is almost always made, regardless of what other methods are used. Payback period is calculated by relating the cost of the equipment to the profit it earns and then estimating the number of years it takes for the equipment to pay for itself. The basic objective is to purchase the equipment with the fastest payback period. Suppose, for example, that a company can eliminate an employee whom it pays $10,000 per year by buying a machine that costs $20,000. If there were no income tax, the machine would pay for itself in two years. The corporate income tax and various tax credits make calculations more complicated.

To keep things from getting too complicated, assume that the machine has a ten-year life and is depreciated on a straight-line basis with a depreciation charge of $2,000 per year. In addition, assume that there is a corporate income tax rate of exactly 50 percent.

To figure the payback period, first deduct $2,000 for depreciation from the $10,000 return. This leaves a $8,000 gross profit from the machine. Half of this profit is taxable, so after corporate income tax there is a net profit of $4,000. The cash flow is equal to the $4,000 net profit plus the $2,000 depreciation, or $6,000. Therefore, the machine should pay for itself in about three and one-third years.

Discounting future payments. Many companies use a more sophisticated approach: discounted cash flow. They assume that a minimum return must be made on their capital, and an investment is not made if this standard is not met. For example, a company may assume that it must earn a 20 percent return after tax on new investment in plant and equipment. It then discounts the value of future cash flows to the present at this rate.

Table 15–2 shows the present value of $1 earned during various periods in the future at various interest rates. It assumes that earnings are spread evenly during the year (and not periodic such as when a bank credits interest to a savings account). Thus, the table indicates

TABLE 15–2
Present value of future payment of $1, discounted at various rates*

Year	6%	9%	12%	15%	18%	20%	22%
1	$0.971	$0.956	$0.942	$0.929	$0.915	$0.909	$0.901
2	0.914	0.874	0.836	0.799	0.764	0.751	0.731
3	0.861	0.799	0.741	0.688	0.639	0.621	0.593
4	0.811	0.730	0.657	0.592	0.533	0.513	0.482
5	0.764	0.667	0.583	0.510	0.446	0.424	0.391
6	0.719	0.610	0.517	0.439	0.372	0.350	0.317
7	0.677	0.557	0.459	0.378	0.311	0.290	0.258
8	0.638	0.509	0.407	0.325	0.260	0.239	0.209
9	0.601	0.466	0.361	0.280	0.217	0.198	0.170
10	0.566	0.425	0.320	0.241	0.181	0.164	0.138

* Calculations assume that return from the investment is continuous throughout the year. For example, a payment of $1 for an entire year would be continuous if you receive roughly 0.3 cent per day starting January 1 and continuing until December 31. This is, of course, a closer approximation to actual operating conditions that discounts based on the return being received at the end of a period (as would be true of deposits in a savings bank, for example).

that $1.00 of earnings spread out evenly over a period of the next year has a present value of $0.971 provided the discount rate is 6 percent.

In the case of the Norton Company, the assumed rate of return (as indicated on line 27 of the form shown in Figure 15–4) is 11.5 percent. Let's round this off to 12 percent to make it fit our table. (The actual capital rate that a company would select would be a management decision based on its estimated opportunity cost of capital or the minimum return that it believes it should earn on an investment with a particular risk.)

As can be seen from the table, a dollar earned over the next year has a present value of $0.942 when discounted at 12 percent. Suppose our company is considering an investment that yields a cash flow of $6,000 per year over a period of ten years (as in the example used to show how payback period is calculated). We would make a discounted cash flow analysis by first adding up the discounted values of $1 for the cash flow expected over the life of the machine at our minimum expected return. In this case, the life of the equipment is ten years and the minimum rate of return is 12 percent. Adding up the values shown in Table 15–2: 0.942 + 0.836 + 0.741 + 0.657 + 0.583 + 0.517 + 0.459 + 0.407 + 0.361 + 0.320 = 5.823.

This means that a payment of $1 per year spread out over a period of ten years has a present value of $5.82 when discounted at 12 percent. Since cash flow is actually $6,000 per year, the present value of the total cash flow is $5.82 times $6,000 or $34,920. Because the actual investment is only $20,000, our investment criterion is clearly being met if we buy the equipment. In fact, this investment would be acceptable even if our criterion was as high as 22 percent. However, whether or not the investment is actually made would also depend on a qualitative assessment of the risks involved and other available alternatives.

Application. The three basic techniques of evaluating profit-making investments are associated almost exclusively with the profit-making sectors of our economy. This is unfortunate. Investments in the nonprofit sectors, both private and government, also tie up capital and can be presumed to earn a return. In some cases, it is not easy to estimate this return. For example, how much "profit" (i.e., avoidance of fire losses) does a fire truck earn? Despite the obvious difficulty, progressive nonprofit organizations are applying "profit" criteria to investments in both equipment and inventory.

Even the most profit-conscious organizations buy capital equipment that yields no direct return at all. For example, investment in pollution control equipment in the process industries not only does not earn a direct profit but actually earns a negative return by increasing operating costs. The formulas discussed in the preceding paragraphs can still be made to "work," however. One simply (and correctly) assumes the return on such investments to be infinite. If a company does not invest in pollution control equipment required by law, it will earn no return at all because it cannot legally operate.

The buying process

In this case, the "infinite" return can be increased (impossible for the mathematician but practical for the business executive!) by doing a better job of buying the equipment. Capital purchases can be classified into three categories: (1) those that are completely proprietary; (2) those where there are similar products differentiated by performance and brand; and (3) those where the product is essentially homogeneous.

If the equipment is completely proprietary, the buying organization would simply prepare an analysis of the return that should be earned using the techniques described earlier in this chapter. Top management would then evaluate all subjective factors and make a decision.

If there are several types or brands of equipment, it is possible that a profit analysis would be prepared for each alternative. In addition, the company's engineers and executives might go through a complicated version of the value analysis process illustrated in Table 15–1. The purchasing manager would then proceed to work out the business details of the transaction; economic effectiveness would be related to the degree to which the equipment is proprietary. If it is completely so, price is usually pretty much a matter of take-it-or-leave-it—although sometimes a company can use the risk involved in trying new equipment as a lever in obtaining concessions.

If one brand of equipment is largely substitutable for another, the purchasing manager can often win direct or indirect concessions. In fact, many equipment purchases are quite competitive—as illustrated by the example in Figure 15–5. In this case, the purchasing manager obtained quotations on a new electrolytic cell on which competing suppliers presumably quoted to buyer's specifications. Note the variation in prices. This is fairly typical and is proof of the value of competitive bidding. This example also shows why the low bidder does not necessarily get the contract. In this case, the award is made to the second lowest bidder.

The electrolytic cell in the example is really a form of construction contract. As the construction becomes less specialized, competition tends to become keener. An experienced purchasing manager can save a great deal with competitive bidding. After the contract is awarded, purchasing and the appropriate engineering group within the buying organization would then work together to assure timely and satisfactory completion of the contract.

FIGURE 15–5

November 5, 19___

MEMO TO: Chief Engineer
     cc: Plant Manager
       Project Engineer
       Plant Purchasing Agent
       Asst. Director of Purchasing

FROM: Purchasing Engineer

SUBJECT: QUOTATION ANALYSIS–ELECTROLYTIC CELL–LITHIUM
       HYDRIDE EXPANSION

     The following are the vendors and prices quoted for a fabricated steel electrolytic cell for the Lithium Hydride expansion:

VENDOR	*DELIVERY*	*F.O.B. POINT*	*TOTAL PRICE*
A_____ Welding Co.	3 Weeks	Exton, Pa.	$ 835.00*
F_____ Welding Shop	1 Week	Exton, Pa.	864.00
N_____ Steel Co.	6–8 weeks	Nazareth, Pa.	1,127.00
B & M Co.	3 weeks	Phila., Pa.	1,780.00
A. J. S & Co.	3 weeks	Exton, Pa.	840.00
P–P Co.	4 weeks	Exton, Pa.	1,235.00

     When A___, the low bidder, was contacted and advised of the special requirements as to soundness of weld, they advised that this would require a different method of welding and the cost increase would be approximately $100.00. We had also asked if they could bend two of the corners, instead of welding them, thereby eliminating about 25% of possible trouble area in the wetted section and they advised that they did not have the equipment to bend that heavy plate. A. J. S, being the next lowest bidder, were asked the same question and they advised that they had anticipated the importance of these welds and had provided for it in their original quotation of $840.00 and they also advised that they could bend two of the corners, thereby reducing the welding, with no change in price.

     On the basis of price, delivery and quality workmanship, were commended that this cell be fabricated by A. J. S & Company. S has advised that they will put a code welder on this job and make every effort to produce the very best welding possible.

W. H. Snell

Quotations on capital equipment must be carefully analyzed. Not only are prices and terms different for various suppliers, but so are the products themselves, since each supplier quotes on its own design.

Cases

CASE 15–1: ST. LOUIS OFFICE FURNITURE COMPANY

A problem in user brand preference

The St. Louis Office Furniture Company is a medium-sized company that specializes in steel desks and filing cabinets. It buys steel from several mills, forms it in its press shops, welds it into desks and cabinets and then finishes and paints the completed products. The finishing operation is necessary because the metal is rough where it has been welded and worked in presses and must be sanded down to a smooth finish before painting. This is an extremely dirty and disagreeable job. Workers run abrasive wheels against the semifinished cabinets until they are smooth. Not only is this physically hard to do and requires some skill, but the job is extremely unpleasant. The wheels are noisy, the abrasive grit fills the air and settles into the workers' clothes, and the workers are invariably hot and uncomfortable. They must wear masks to prevent their lungs from being contaminated with dust, and the friction of the abrasive generates heat, which is almost unbearable in the hot summer months.

Because their job is so unpleasant, the metal finishers are extremely well paid. They average about $1 per hour more than the average worker at St. Louis Furniture. Despite the high pay, good metal finishers are scarce, and they tend to be extremely independent. Absences and tardiness are far more frequent than among other workers. The scarcity of metal finishers and their high pay gives management a double incentive to do everything it can to raise their productivity. The company's materials manager, Edwina Kellogg, has been working for the past few months with Reynolds Abrasive, a major supplier, on a new abrasive that will cut at least 25 percent faster and last 10 percent longer than the abrasive currently used. Although the new product is much more expensive than the current one, if it works it will raise the productivity of the metal finishers by enough so that the cost premium will be offset many times over.

Kellogg naturally has kept the plant superintendent and others informed of her work on the abrasive. When she gets the first test shipment, she and the superintendent will arrange for a test on Sunday, when the plant is shut down. The supervisor of the metal finishing line and one of the company's time study engineers participate in the tests. The supervisor, a former metal finisher himself, uses the abrasive on a few cabinets, while the time-study engineer makes observations. The time studies confirm the supplier's claim: the abrasive is 25 percent faster. The supervisor, however, says he doesn't like the new abrasive. He says it just doesn't feel right, although he does not dispute the time study's indication that it is faster. He says he is sure the employees won't like the new abrasive. The others are reluctant to see such a big saving evaporate simply because the abrasive doesn't "feel right." They decide that the best thing to do is to change the brand of abrasive quietly and see how the workers react. Then, after the workers get used to the feel of the new product, they can make new time studies and raise the standard.

The workers arrive on Monday morning and almost immediately notice the change in abrasive. They ask the supervisor what is going on and are told that the company has decided to purchase a higher quality abrasive that will work faster. No mention is made of any future changes in work standards. The employees grumble that the new abrasive isn't as good as the old. After giving the new product a few minutes' trial, they accuse the company of trying to slip in a cheaper new product that requires them to work harder. They flatly refuse to work until they are given the old abrasive again. The supervisor gives them the old abrasive to keep production going and advises Kellogg that she had better keep on buying the old product because the workers will not accept any changes.

Questions

1. Should Kellogg follow the supervisor's advice?
2. What can be done to get the employees to adopt the new product and accept a new time study?
3. Did Kellogg handle this problem correctly from the beginning? What mistakes did she make?

CASE 15–2. STANFORD SHIRT COMPANY

Purchase of capital equipment

Stanford Shirt Company has a national reputation as a manufacturer of high-quality shirts. For 40 years the company has catered to the executive who likes the very finest ready-made shirts. Until recently, Stanford's cheapest shirt retailed for $15. While the company has earned an enviable reputation for quality, its growth has been limited by its pricing policies. Most people are not willing to pay premium prices for shirts. Finally, the company decided to enter the medium-priced shirt field and created its Stanfast line. The brand name chosen was designed to be similar to the Stanford brand name in the hope of trading on the company's reputation but sufficiently different to prevent the two lines from being confused.

The Stanfast line is designed to retail for $9. Part of the savings comes from narrowing the dealer's profit margin from nearly 50 percent to the 30 percent that is more common on lower priced shirts. The

Stanfast shirts also are made of cheaper cloth and buttons. In the manufacturing operations, the company is able to make only minor savings through the elimination of a few sewing operations. It is difficult to make greater savings because both shirts must be sewed together in approximately the same way.

As a result, the company's profits on the new line have been disappointing. The company's profit plan calls for a 20 percent return after taxes on investment in all new projects. The new line of shirts definitely is not earning its fair share of the desired return on investment and, in fact, unit profits are currently less than 5 cents per shirt, and everyone in the organization is searching for ways to widen the profit margin without hurting quality.

The purchasing director, Frank Adams, believes he may have the answer. Currently, all of the company's shirts are ironed by hand. Finished shirts are conveyed in hampers to women workers, who pick them out of the hamper, iron them, and then fold and pack them in boxes. The women work on piece rate, and the company's total labor cost per shirt for these operations is 22 cents. The company controller estimates that the variable overhead applicable to this operation is about 12 cents.

Laundries have been using semiautomatic shirt ironing machines for years. The freshly laundered shirts are folded over a series of forms, and it is possible to iron and pack a shirt with about 1.2 minutes of direct labor. Ironing machines have never been used much by shirt manufacturers, however. Newly manufactured shirts are much harder to iron, and the laundry equipment will not remove all of the wrinkles. In addition, shirt manufacturers are convinced that their products will sell better if they are ironed perfectly. So far, laundry equipment manufacturers have failed to devise a machine that can approach the quality achieved by a skilled woman equipped with a hand iron and ironing board.

Alma Laundry Machine Corporation thinks it has made a breakthrough. Its M–9 shirt-ironing machine will turn out 60 shirts per hour that are almost wrinkle-free. Adams arranges to ship a gross of newly manufactured Stanfast shirts to the Alma plant and himself watches the machine iron them. Accompanying him on the trip is Stanford's quality control manager, Joanne Connally. The two managers agree that while the M–9 doesn't do a good enough job for the Stanford line, it should be adequate for the Stanfast line.

On checking with the personnel department, Adams discovers that an operator for the machine would probably have to be paid $4.80 per hour. In addition, fringe benefits (which would become part of variable overhead) amount to $1.20 per hour.

Alma insists that its estimated production rate of 60 shirts per hour includes more than adequate allowances for downtime, delays, rest periods, and so on. The supplier also claims that maintenance expenses on the machine will average less than $1,000 per year, and that it probably has a useful life of at least ten years on three-shift operation. All other variable overhead expenses in connection with the machine total about $0.002 per shirt ironed. The machine costs $40,000 installed, and Stanford can easily make use of at least one machine working two shifts, five days per week. Adam doubts that the scrap value of the hand equipment that the machine would replace is more than $200.

Question

Should Stanford buy the machine? Support your conclusions with (1) a MAPI investment analysis, (2) a calculation of cash payback period, and (3) a discounted cash flow analysis. Assume corporate income tax rate of exactly 50 percent and straight-line depreciation.

16

Buying transportation services and physical distribution

Question 1

Physical distribution is concerned with getting goods from seller to buyer. In the process, goods are moved and they are also stored. Most of the money is spent moving them. American manufacturers spend over $100 billion per year transporting goods from mines and quarries to various fabricating locations and finally to ultimate consumers. They are served by a huge private transportation industry consisting of trucks, railroads, pipelines, barges, and aircraft. In addition, almost every manufacturer is in the transportation business itself. In most cases, this participation is limited to a few trucks that make deliveries to customers and also occasionally pick up purchases. In some instances, however, the manufacturer's transportation enterprise is a big business in itself and may include hundreds of vehicles of various types.

For reasons that will be explained later in this chapter, the do-it-yourself movement is growing in transportation. However, every organization relies on common carriers—organizations that carry freight over defined route structures for all shippers. The truck is the most popular common carrier and is especially suitable for hauling goods that are packaged in containers of various styles. Railroads also haul millions of tons of packaged goods of various sorts as well as many items shipped unpackaged. Ships and barges are efficient, low-cost methods of transporting material. Barges usually offer cheaper rates than railroads or trucks for bulk commodities and, of course, ships are the only alternative to air transport when oceans must be crossed. Air is the fastest mode of transport and is occasionally (but not usually) the cheapest.

Transportation is a purchased service and is bought like any other service on the basis of quality and price. The main difference is that transportation is partly or wholly regulated by various government agencies. Intercontinental tariffs are set often by cartels that are sanctioned tacitly or overtly by concerned governments. The U.S. Constitution gives the federal government the power to regulate interstate commerce and this power has been exercised since the 19th century through the Interstate Commerce Commission and other federal agencies. Finally, individual states universally regulate commerce within their own borders and carriers are also subject to a variety of not-always-consistent regulations by other levels of government.

THE TRAFFIC DEPARTMENT

Were it not for the unique character of its regulation, transportation services would probably be just another purchasing function in most organizations. However, complex regulations make transportation purchasing sufficiently different from conventional purchasing activities so that in larger companies it is usually not carried on in the purchasing department but in a separate traffic department.

Traffic management is a big job in most industries. In the typical manufacturing company, transportation services are the third greatest expenditure; only purchased materials and labor are more important. Producers of bulky, low-cost materials may spend as much as one fourth of their sales dollar on transportation, and even those who produce items of very high value may directly or indirectly pay out 5 or 10 percent of their sales dollar for transportation services.

Most larger companies have a separate traffic or physical distribution department. The traffic manager is a major executive; in some cases he or she reports directly to the president of the company. Even when the traffic manager does not, he may be only one echelon lower in the organization, reporting to the materials manager, purchasing manager, or marketing manager. Growing recognition of the importance of the physical distribution function (see Chapter 1) is not only upgrading traffic but bringing it closer to related materials activities.

Basic responsibilities   *question 2*

The traffic department is responsible for problems related to the purchase of transportation services, including the selection of mode of transport and of carrier, negotiation of rates, tracing and expediting of shipments, filing and negotiation of claims for lost or damaged shipments, and audit of freight bills. In addition, as the company's experts on transportation, traffic personnel are involved in many special studies designed to minimize transportation costs or to advise management

506

about the effect that various decisions (such as plant location or product distribution) would have on transportation cost.

Traffic is intimately involved in materials management and physical distribution even in companies where there are no organizational ties linking traffic with other materials management activities. The choice of a carrier automatically influences inventory levels. Fast, highly reliable modes of transportation permit less inventory than is required for slower, more erratic modes. The traffic function is also intimately related to problems of warehouse and plant location. In simple cases, the location must be easily accessible to low-cost transportation; in more complex cases, inventory investment, transportation cost, and other variables combine to determine optimum location.

The typical traffic department also has a number of miscellaneous functions, including the handling of all passenger reservations for employers traveling on company business and the moving of household effects of employees transferred from one company plant to another. Sometimes the traffic manager also is responsible for the operation of all company-owned vehicles; even if she is not, she should always be consulted prior to their purchase.

Traffic also is concerned with packaging material. The heavier the package, the higher the freight costs to ship the product. On the other hand, lightweight packaging is more liable to damage in shipment. For this reason, many tariffs are based on shipments being made in certain types of packaging.

Traffic usually is concerned with both inbound and outbound shipments of materials and finished products. Many traffic departments become intimately involved with charter carriers or company-owned trucks. Normally, however, most of their dealings are with various common carriers, including railroads, trucks, pipelines, and water carriers.

Picking the carrier   *Question 3*

Railroads are by far the most important common carriers in terms of tonnage handled (about half the total). Trucks are second in tonnage but lead in dollar volume. Pipelines handle almost as much tonnage as trucks but get only a small fraction of their revenue. The reason for the discrepancies between shares of tonnage and revenue of the various carriers is obvious: the rate per ton-mile for all commodities is not the same. A trucker who hauls a ton of household goods for one mile may get 100 times as much as a pipeline gets for moving a ton of crude oil the same distance.

Know

A company should buy transportation services just as it buys any other commodity—on the bases of quality, price, and service. It should try to direct its business to carriers that provide prompt delivery with a minimum of lost or damaged shipments, cooperate readily in tracing and rerouting shipments, make a minimum of errors in invoicing, and so on. These are sound criteria for selecting among like types of carrier, which charge identical rates when they are subject to regulation (See Figure 16–1.)

The transportation buyer must also select among various types of transportation service. The two basic criteria are price and service. Carriers that give fast service charge relatively higher tariffs and those charging the lowest rate usually provide the slowest service. Shipment over water is the cheapest and usually the slowest way to ship any commodity—particularly in specialized bulk carriers that transport oil, coal, grain, and like commodities. Pipeline is the lowest cost overland mode of shipment—so cheap that even coal can be pulverized and mixed into slurry and then pumped through special pipelines. Most materials cannot be transported in ships or pipelines, however, and shippers must choose among a variety of higher cost, but usually faster, carriers.

Rail freight: Although the relative importance of railroads has declined substantially since World War II, they still are the most important carriers. Rail freight rates in carload lots are always lower than air freight, parcel post, or rates charged by freight forwarders. For many commodities they are cheaper than truck rates, and sometimes they are competitive with barge and ship rates. They rarely are cheaper than pipeline rates.

With the exception of materials that can be pumped through a pipeline, rail shipment—particularly in trainload quantities with oversized boxcars—is usually the cheapest possible mode of overland shipment. However, shippers of manufactured goods rarely are able to generate enough traffic to move their goods in trainload quantities; their lowest cost mode of shipment is often in full carload lots for shipments between points equipped with railroad sidings. When a company does not have a siding, it must transfer its shipment from the railroad boxcar to a truck. This creates extra transport and handling expenses which usually make it more economic to ship 100 percent by truck or may even force a company to relocate near a siding if its costs are to remain competitive.

Truck freight. Almost every factory is equipped with a dock to receive truck shipments; in fact, truck lines are the most important common carrier for most manufactured goods. Truck rates often are as low as those charged by railroads for finished manufactured products, and service usually is faster. Trucks are especially competitive on shorter hauls. They may offer overnight service between cities that are only a few hundred miles apart. Both interstate truck and rail rates are regulated by the Interstate Commerce Commission, which tries to set rates that permit fair competition between the two carriers. Trucks

FIGURE 16–1
Transportation method on comparison chart

Transporta- tion media	Description	Application	Can be traced
Carload and truckload	Full rail car or trailer	Where quantity is sufficient to warrant (differs with product)	Yes
Truck	Motor truck	For all shipments over 50 pounds not requiring emergency air service	Yes
Freight forwarder	Truck pickup for assembly into carloads, includes truck delivery at destination	For all shipments over 50 pounds not requiring emergency air service. Forwarder usually on long haul	Yes
Air freight	No. 1. Regular passenger airlines which also handle air freight up to a limited size and weight	Rush shipments over 20 pounds. Usually as fast as Air Express	Yes
	No. 2. Cargo air carriers handling freight only	Rush shipments over 20 pounds Usually as fast as Air Express.	Yes
Air express	Complete pickup and delivery service using all commercial airlines on shipments of limited size and weight	Extreme emergency only!	Very difficult
Air freight forwarder	Brokerage service using all commercial airlines and surface transportation when necessary	Extreme emergency only!	Yes
United Parcel Service	UPS picks up and delivers	Preferred method for small nonrush shipments	Yes
Parcel post	4th class regular mail	Up to 20 pounds when transit time is not important. 40 pounds up to 150 miles	No
	Express mail	Very small rush shipments!	No

This chart is a guide to the relative merits of various types of transportation service. In recent years, the United Parcel Service has become a low-cost, reliable substitute for parcel post and Railway Express.

have substantially increased their share of traffic at the expense of the railroads since the 1950s, but recently the railroads have been holding their own despite fierce competition from competing carriers.

Shipment by air. Air cargo shipments have increased at a fantastic rate as technology has worked to reduce real costs. Since the end of World War II physical volume of air freight has increased at least 100 times, although total tonnage is still a small fraction of that carried by

Can be expedited	Cost comparison	Remarks
Yes (in advance)	Cheapest method	Total charges depend upon minimum weight required, routing used, and many other factors. *Contact Traffic Department* for best method
Yes (in advance)	Economical method of shipping over 50 pounds	Recommended truck routings when singleline service is available
Yes (in advance)	Economical method of shipping over 50 pounds	Superior to motor truck service in many specific cases. Should never be used on shipments over 10,000 pounds without consulting traffic department
(Yes in advance)	2½ to 3 times more costly than truck or freight forwarder. Cheaper than Railway Express in many cases. (Check with traffic departments)	In rare cases may be delayed to give priority to mail or Air Express
Yes (in advance)	2½ to 3 times more costly than truck or freight forwarder. Cheaper than Railway Express in many cases. (Check with traffic department)	Good service between major cities
Difficult	3 to 4 times more costly than Air freight generally	We have no choice of airlines used or routings chosen by express company. Air freight service is comparable in most cases. (*Contact traffic department*)
Yes (in advance)	Usually more costly than Air Express (except over 100 pounds) *Always more costly than air freight*	Cost is prohibitive except in cases when a few hours' transit time differential is vital. (*Contact traffic department*)
No	Comparable in cost to parcel post but greatly superior service	Preferred method for small shipments. Occasionally disrupted by strikes
No	No longer cheap	Generally not advisable except on very small packages on which delivery is not urgent
No	Overnight service at reasonable cost	Generally not advisable except on very small packages on which delivery is urgent

rail and truck. The only factor that has tempered growth is the fact that air tariffs are still two to ten times higher than those charged by railroads and truck lines.

If rates are so high, how have air shipments managed to grow so fast? Obviously because for some shipments, speed is the only important factor and the shipment must be made in the fastest possible manner, almost regardless of the cost. There are at least two other reasons for the rapid growth of air shipments. First, air tariffs are not as high as they appear. In most cases, it is possible to use much lighter containers when shipping by air, and sometimes no packaging at all is needed. Thus the total weight paid for when shipping by air is often less than it would be if shipment were made by surface transportation. This reduces the premium paid for air shipment. For certain extremely fragile shipments that would require especially heavy packaging if shipped by surface freight, it may actually be cheaper to ship by air. Air shipments also permit buyers to carry lower inventories. If they can get overnight shipment, they need not carry an item in inventory. For this reason, air shipment is quite commonly used for repair parts for machinery.

The cheapest type of air shipment is air freight. The shipper delivers the goods to the local airport and they are handled by a regularly scheduled passenger airline or air cargo carrier. For a substantial premium (usually about 200 to 300 percent), the shipper can get faster, more complete service with air express or by using an air freight forwarder. The tariff for such shipments includes pickup and delivery by truck and routing over the best available commercial air routes.

The U.S. Postal Service serves as forwarder on Express Mail, which guarantees overnight delivery between designated post offices. The service is economic on light shipments where the need is urgent but the shipper must deliver the package to a designated post office.

Barge and pipeline. Shippers of bulky, relatively inexpensive raw materials try to ship by water or pipeline whenever possible in order to keep transportation costs at a minimum. In fact, chemical, aluminum, steel, and power plants often are intentionally located at deep-water ports or on inland waterways in order to reduce the cost of inbound raw materials. Water shipment is slow, but the rates always are low. Also, when railroads or trucks are faced with competition from water carriers, they are more prone to offer rate reductions.

Only fluids can be shipped through pipelines, and pipeline shipment often is more expensive than water shipment. However, the pipeline is the most economic vehicle for shipping natural gas, oil products, and anything else that can be made into a fluid to inland points.

Piggyback and fishyback. Sometimes the most efficient way to ship is by using two carriers—truck trailer and either railroad or ship. "Piggyback" shipments are made by loading truck trailers aboard railroad flatcars for shipments between cities. The trailer is delivered from the shipper's plant to the flatcar by truck, which also moves it to the customer's plant. "Fishyback" shipments are made by loading the truck trailers on a barge or ship. After the water shipment, the trailers can be towed by truck to their final destination.

Most intercontinental ocean freight moves in standardized containers that are smaller than a truck trailer. These containers are loaded onto trucks, carried to dockside, put into ships, and then removed from the ships and carried by truck to their final destination. Containerization is now almost universal for shipment of smaller manufactured items.

Piggyback and fishyback shipments combine many of the advantages of shipping by rail, barge, or ship with those of shipping by truck, including the following: *Question 4*

X   *Reduced handling expense.* Material need be handled only when it is loaded into the truck trailer and when it is unloaded at the final destination.

Lower rates. Shipment between points not on rail sidings often is cheaper by piggyback than by motor freight, since the long intercity haul can be made by rail. With fishyback, it is possible to eliminate extra handling and packaging for export by loading the truck trailer directly onto the ship.

Faster service. Since they minimize handling and enable shipments to be routed by the best service available, piggyback and fishyback usually permit quicker deliveries than the conventional approaches to surface transportation.

Reduced pilferage. Containers and trailers are sealed when they are shipped and not opened until they reach their final destination. This greatly reduces losses from pilferage when merchandise is handled while it is still in transit.

Almost anything shipped in sufficient quantity to fill a standardized container and not so large that it will not fit into a trailer is now shipped that way. Poor rail service in the eastern United States has probably prevented piggyback from expanding further at the expense of truckload traffic.

Small shipments

Every common carrier has minimum rates that are charged regardless of how small a shipment is. Railroads and trucks always charge for 100 pounds even when a shipment weighs much less. In addition, they charge premiums for LCL (less than carload) and LTL (less than truckload) shipments. Table 16–1 shows rates for various shipments of iron and steel articles between two Ohio cities. Note that rates are much higher for small shipments. For example, it costs 91 cents per cwt. to ship 2,000 pounds but only 12 cents per cwt. when the shipment weighs more than 26,290 pounds.

If the shipment is small enough, it does not pay to ship by truck or rail. Shipments of 100 pounds or less can usually be shipped at much lower cost either by parcel post or United Parcel Service. When the package is small and fast service is desired, intercity bus service is a somewhat higher cost alternative. Commercial freight forwarders are a possibility for somewhat heavier shipments. They consolidate small

TABLE 16-1
Typical routings and rates—iron and steel articles

Weight (lbs.)	Rate (per cwt.)	Carrier
0–2,160	$0.91	Allmen Transfer Co.
2,160–5,450	0.51	Allmen Transfer Co.
5,451–11,200	0.26½	Allmen Transfer Co.
		Lake Erie Cartage Co.
		Kaplan Trucking
11,201–26,290	0.17½	Allmen Transfer Co.
		Modern Motor Express
		Kaplan Trucking
26,291 and over	0.12	Lake Erie Cartage Co.
		Kaplan Trucking
		Glenn Cartage
40,000 and over	0.13	Erie R.R.
80,000 and over	0.12	B & O R.R.
		Penn Central R.R.

Source: Purchasing manual, B. F. Goodrich Co.

shipments from a number of customers into carload and truckload quantities.

Nonprofit shippers' associations also help cut costs of small shipments. Shippers—usually smaller businesses and manufacturers in a particular area—band together for the purpose of consolidating shipments and negotiating with common carriers. They usually hire a traffic expert as director of their association. As long as the group is nonprofit, it is exempt from ICC regulation. Otherwise, its basic function is not much unlike that of the freight forwarder, except that the shippers get all of the benefits when they have their own association.

Routing, delays, and damage

Once the carrier is selected, the traffic manager's job would seem to be complete—but it rarely is. The carrier does not necessarily carry out its part of the bargain. Trucking companies do not always have trucks immediately available and, if they are busy, do not maintain their promised schedules. With railroads, the problem may start when boxcars are requested. Plenty of them are usually available in periods of depressed business, but during boom periods there is often a shortage. The shipper frequently has no recourse but to wait his turn, although he can ask the Interstate Commerce Commission for help. The ICC has the power to allocate cars to various railroads (and even can, for example, order a railroad to supply some of its cars to a competing road that is hard pressed). But, of course, the ICC cannot create cars out of thin air—so shipments are delayed during periods of car shortage.

Routing. The traffic manager's problems do not end when the shipment is loaded on the railroad boxcar or truck. The shipment must be routed. Rail and truck lines crisscross the United States in a huge grid. There may be a half-dozen or more ways to get from one point to another. Each route will involve several competing carriers. If the originating carrier is permitted to select the routing, the shipment will usually be carried over that carrier's lines for the greatest distance possible. This is often not in the shipper's interest since that carrier's franchise does not necessarily run in a straight line between the points that the shipper wishes to connect.

If the originating carrier has to connect with another carrier, its choice will be influenced by how much reciprocal business it gets from that carrier. Again, this may not be in the shipper's best interest. For this and other reasons, traffic managers normally direct the originating carrier to route their shipments in a way that they select. In most cases, responsibility rests with the firm that is purchasing the material rather than the supplier. The routing becomes a standard part of the purchase order, and the supplier's traffic department follows its customer's instructions.

Tracing. The supplier's traffic department may trace shipments for its customers. Typically, the buyer follows up with the supplier's sales department to determine why a particular shipment has not yet been received. The sales department may then discover that the item has been shipped. It might give the appropriate bill of lading or waybill number to the buyer so the traffic department could trace the shipment, or it might do the tracing for the customer.

In big companies, dozens of traffic clerks spend almost all of their working lives on the telephone tracing shipments. The procedure is fairly simple. Given the waybill or bill of lading number (i.e., the shipper's receipt for the shipment), the carrier's clerk can determine precisely what boxcar or truck the shipment is on. The clerk then traces the car or truck and reports back to the shipper when it is due at its destination.

Big shippers often find it convenient to reroute full truck or carloads. For example, at any given time an auto producer might have hundreds of boxcars en route from its major manufacturing plants in Michigan to assembly plants scattered throughout the country. If shortages develop at a particular assembly plant, a boxcar can be rerouted in transit to that plant. This practice cuts lead time substantially and permits the firm to get along with a lower inventory investment.

Damage claims. Even if cars are not rerouted, goods are shuffled back and forth a great deal while they are in transit. Not surprisingly, there is a good deal of damage. Common carriers are forced to pay out hundreds of millions of dollars per year in damage claims to shippers. Even if the shipper is reimbursed in full, damaged shipments cause

FIGURE 16-2

The Mason & Dixon Lines, Inc.

STANDARD FORM FOR PRESENTATION OF LOSS AND DAMAGE CLAIM

	(Claimant's Number)

Brown Toy Company _____ 115 King Street, Kingsport, Tennessee
(Name of firm by whom claim is presented) _____ (Address of claimant)

The Mason & Dixon Lines, Inc. _____ November 17, —
(Name of Carrier) _____ (Date)

Knoxville, Tennessee _____ (Carrier's Number)
(Address)

This claim for $ __ $3.00 __ is made against the carrier named above by __ Brown Toy Company
(Amount of claim) _____ (Name of claimant)

for __ Damage __ in connection with the following described shipments:
(Loss or damage)

Description of shipment____ Toys, iron and rubber

Name and address of consignor (shipper)__ John Jones Manufacturing Company

Shipped from____ Knoxville, Tennessee ____, To__
(City, town or station) _____ (City, town or station)

Final Destination__ Kingsport, Tennessee __ Routed via
(City, town or station)

Bill of Lading issued by__ shipper ____Co.; Date of Bill of Lading __ November 17, —

Paid Freight Bill (Pro) Number.____ 3-1875 __; Expense Bill Serial No.__

Name and address of consignee (Whom shipped to)__ Brown Toy Company, 115 King Street, Kingsport,

If Shipment reconsigned enroute, state particulars:_____ Tenn.

DETAILED STATEMENT SHOWING HOW AMOUNT CLAIMED IS DETERMINED
(Number and description of articles, nature and extent of loss or damage, invoice price of articles, amount of claim, etc.)

2 - Sleepy-time Dogs (Rubber) - Damaged	@ 1.50 each	3.00

	Total Amount Claimed	$3.00

THE FOLLOWING DOCUMENTS ARE SUBMITTED IN SUPPORT OF CLAIM.
(X) 1. Original bill of lading, if not previously surrendered to carrier.
(X) 2. Original paid freight ("expense") bill.
(X) 3. Original invoice or certified copy.
    4. Other particulars obtainable in proof of loss or damage claimed.

Remarks_____

The foregoing statement of facts is hereby certified to as correct. Brown Toy Company
_____ Per:
Write any further remarks on back hereof: _____ (Signature of claimant)

Courtesy The Mason & Dixon Lines, Inc.

To speed claim processing, motor carriers request that claimants use standard forms like that above. Railroads have a similar form. Claims should be backed by a copy of the bill of lading, the original paid freight bill, and a copy of the invoice for the material to prove that the claim does not exceed the value of the loss.

production delays, and the processing of claims is a huge burden on the typical firm's traffic department.

Not all claims are the carrier's fault. In fact, the carriers maintain that most claims occur as a result of inadequate packaging. One problem is that frugal shippers keep using the same cartons over and over again. Carriers maintain that most corrugated cartons are designed for one-shot use and should then be discarded.

The exact cause of damage is not clear-cut in many cases. The shipment would certainly not have been damaged if it had been handled with sufficient care. But it might also be true that there need not have been any damage had the merchandise been packed more carefully in costlier containers. Traffic departments spend a great deal of time investigating damaged shipments and making claims against carriers. They also work with their own company's packaging engineers and others on ways to reduce damages. Shippers are becoming increasingly conscious of the simple truth that they are losers on damaged shipments even if they are reimbursed in full by carriers.

The procedure for claiming damages is fairly straightforward. The shipper presents the carrier with a claim similar to that shown in Figure 16–2 along with the bill of lading, the paid freight bill, and a copy of the supplier's invoice or other evidence that establishes the value of the damaged merchandise. The claimant may include photographs of the damage both to help verify the claim and to serve as a basis for the development of ways to prevent future damage. Naturally, carriers must include an allowance for damage claims in their tariffs, and it is to everyone's interest to help minimize such claims.

TARIFFS OF COMMON CARRIERS

Like other prices, the tariffs charged by common carriers are influenced by supply, demand, and cost of production. They also are influenced by peculiar variables of their own. Unlike most other sellers of goods and services, common carriers are not free to set their own rates, nor can they operate wherever and whenever they please. Each carrier must have a franchise to operate at all, and, as a condition of the franchise, almost every phase of the carrier's business is subject to regulation. In fact, carriers are not even free to cease operations without getting approval from one or more regulatory agencies. *Now*

The Interstate Commerce Commission is the most important regulatory agency for interstate railroads, motor carriers, and barge line operators. The Federal Power Commission regulates pipelines. Intrastate shipments are regulated by various states agencies.

Economics of rate structures

Regulatory agencies try to set rates that are fair to shippers and at the same time permit carriers to earn an adequate return on their investment. This is not an easy job. It is almost impossible to determine the cost of handling a particular type of shipment. In addition, regulatory agencies are subject to considerable noneconomic pressures.

Cost determination. Each carrier ships thousands of different items between thousands of different terminals. A big railroad, for example, is available to carry any type of shipment from any terminal on its own or another railroad's line to any other station. It would be a difficult enough job to determine the cost of an individual shipment if all costs were direct. Unfortunately, most costs do not vary directly either with the type of shipment or with the distance it is carried. They are fixed, or nonvariable.

For example, railroads must spend prodigious sums on maintenance of their roadbed. Most such expenditures are necessary regardless of whether the road handles one train a minute or one train a year. How then does one calculate the wear and tear on the road from an LCL shipment of shirts from the factory in Troy, New York, to a department store in Memphis, Tennessee? The shipment may move over several railroads, and chances are that several alternate routes are available. The expenses of each road involved will be almost exactly the same whether or not the shirts are shipped.

It is impossible for a carrier to determine the real cost of any single shipment or even any group of shipments. About the best it can do is determine the average cost per ton-mile for all shipments by dividing total costs shipped by total ton-miles. It also can calculate the average cost per shipment by dividing total costs by total number of shipments. Special studies also can yield valuable information concerning the relative costs of handling various types of shipment. But when it comes to determining what the costs and rates should be for transporting a particular commodity such as shirts from one point to another, arbitrary assumptions must be made.

Almost any rate can be justified, depending on the assumptions that are made. Competition can sometimes be used as a basis for rate setting, but competing modes of transport often find themselves in the same boat. None of them can assign costs so well that rates make much sense. Competiton does work in some respects, however. Carriers "discover" that costs are lower when competing modes of transport are available. Costs often are high and service is poor on routes where a carrier enjoys a monopoly.

Pressures on rates. Tariffs are influenced by both political and economic forces. Since a company in a given community can compete more effectively if it has favorable freight rates, regulatory bodies often are pressed by local communities and industries to set low rates. In fact, much of the original pressure for regulation of carriers came from farmers and small business executives who believed that the railroads were getting too big a share of their output by charging high tariffs to ship their goods to market.

Even today, rates are almost always lower when carriers have competition. For example, on coast-to-coast shipments, railroads are conscious of competition from ships using the Panama Canal. This sometimes makes the coast-to-coast rate lower than rates charged for shipping identical commodities to inland points. Competition from barge traffic on the Mississippi and Ohio rivers keeps rail rates low in those areas. Railroads in the Great Lakes area have been forced to reduce some rates because of competition from ships using the St. Lawrence Seaway.

Even if a carrier has little effective competition, it cannot afford to charge too high a tariff. It it does, the traffic may simply disappear. A rock quarry, for example, will go out of business if it cannot negotiate a competitive freight rate. The major cost of the rock delivered to the user is freight. The lower the freight rate, the greater the distance from the quarry that the rock can be shipped and still remain competitive with rock from other quarries.

In some cases, the traffic is created only if the rate is sufficiently attractive to make it possible for the shipper to earn a profit. For example, the Kaiser Steel Corporation once found itself with excess capacity for sheet steel coils used in auto production. General Motors was willing to buy this steel for use in its midwestern plants. The only problem was that Kaiser could not afford to ship the steel across the continent from its mill in California. In order to get this lucrative business, rail carriers agreed with Kaiser on a special low tariff based on 50-car-unit-trains. The railroads would probably go broke if they charged this rate to every shipper but as a special inducement to get business they would not otherwise obtain, it was profitable.

What traffic will bear.   In general, most tariffs are based on "whatever the traffic will bear." If the product has an extremely high value per pound, freight cost is relatively unimportant to the shipper. For example, a freight cost of $5 would have an almost insignificant effect on the cost of a very fine chair designed to sell for $400, but it would be quite significant for a chair intended to sell for $40. Whenever possible, carriers try to distinguish between inexpensive and expensive products in order to charge what the traffic will bear. Usually only part of the premium paid to ship the higher cost commodity is justified by the greater cost of damage claims and other costs that characterize the more expensive item.

To add to the confusion, the rate is not necessarily identical in both directions. For example, the lowest rate at which one could ship a truckload of "printed matter" from Boston to Philadelphia was 87 cents per cwt. But one could ship a truckload of the same printed matter from Philadelphia to Boston for only 72 cents per cwt. The rates should be identical. Why do they differ by more than 20 percent? The most likely explanation is that shippers of printed matter from Philadelphia to Boston were more successful in negotiating with carriers and arguing the validity of a lower rate before the Interstate Commerce Commission than shippers in the opposite direction were. Or possibly there is more southbound traffic, so that trucks sometimes must travel partly loaded or empty northward from Philadelphia to Boston. The northbound traffic will not take as high a tariff as the southbound traffic, so the carriers established a differential designed to encourage more northbound shipments.

Similarly, it has traditionally been cheaper to ship something from Europe or Japan to the United States than vice versa. For example, iron or steel pipe once cost $38.25 per ton to ship from New York to Germany but only $20.75 to ship from Germany to New York. Similarly, it cost $0.00664 per ton-mile to ship automobiles from New York to Rio de Janeiro but only $0.00222 to ship from London to Rio. American manufacturers have complained bitterly that this discrimination in ocean freight rates puts them at a competitive disadvantage with foreign manufacturers. The conference of shipping lines that sets the rates justifies them on the basis that cargo space that is outbound from the United States is relatively more scarce than inbound space. This, of course, is a roundabout way of saying that rates are set for what the traffic will bear.

The density of the product also is important in determining tariffs. A carload of lightweight, bulky material costs almost as much to transport as a carload of very heavy materials. The carrier naturally must charge a higher rate per hundredweight for the low-density material in order to recoup the costs. For example, the *National Motor Freight Classification*[1] indicated the following rates per hundredweight on LTL (less than truckload) shipments from Washington, D.C., to Atlanta, Georgia:

Density (per cu. ft.)	Rate (per cwt.)
Less than 6 pounds	$7.31
6–12 pounds	3.79
More than 12 pounds	3.26

Class and commodity rates

So complex are rate structures that it is even possible to pay two different rates for identical shipments with identical origins and destinations. For example, the tariff for shipping a carload of steel from Baltimore to San Francisco was either $3.98 per cwt. or $2.43 per cwt. The higher was the "class" rate, the lower was the "commodity" rate.

Carriers have class rates for almost everything. As the term implies, the rates are created by dividing goods into classes (or classifications)

---

[1] The *National Motor Freight Classification*, published by the American Trucking Association, 1424 16th Street, N.W., Washington, D.C., provides up-to-date information on truck rates. Its counterpart for rail rates is the *Uniform Freight Classification*, available from the Tariff Publishing Office, 202 Union Station, Chicago, Illinois. Since tariffs change quite frequently due to economic and competitive conditions, the real-life traffic manager must subscribe to these services to keep up to date. Because of these frequent changes, the examples of freight rates quoted in this text are for comparative purposes only. The odds favor their being out of date before the printer's ink is dry on this page.

and setting rates for each class. An occasional shipper of a commodity will check first to see if there is a commodity rate for the shipment he wishes to make. If there is not, he will always find a class rate.

A frequent shipper of a commodity between two points is foolish to pay a class rate. When no commodity rate is available, she negotiates one with the carrier. The proposed rate is reviewed by the ICC and hearings are held. At these hearings, the shipper's competitors may object if they feel the proposed rate is too low and gives her an "unfair" competitive advantage. Competing carriers also may protest if they feel the rate is too low and will cause them to lose traffic. The final commodity rate[2] usually represents a compromise among the conflicting interests of the shipper, her carrier (or carriers), competitors of the shipper, and competing carriers. However, in every case the commodity rate is lower than the class rate, so it is well worth a big shipper's ⟵ *know* trouble to obtain commodity rates for all key commodities she handles.

COST-REDUCTION OPPORTUNITIES

Because rate structures are so complex, there are many opportunities for traffic experts to make tremendous savings in buying transportation. They often can save their companies millions of dollars by finding "loopholes" that permit shipments to be made at lower tariffs and also by spotting errors that carriers make in computing charges. For example, North American Aviation Division of North American Rockwell Corp. was able to reduce its $2,929,400 annual freight bill by $597,344 in a traffic cost-reduction program. More than $180,000 of the savings came from overpayments detected in audits of freight bills that had already been paid. The balance came from more economical shipping methods. More than $143,000 was saved by making increased use of pool car shipments. Savings of more than $230,000 came from consolidation of service from air cargo carriers, use of company-owned trucks returning empty from deliveries, special fixtures in freight cars, and so on.

Auditing freight bills

Of the savings made by the North American Aviation traffic department, the most surprising may well be the huge sum recouped by auditing freight bills to detect overcharges. It might appear that North American had been extremely inefficient to accept such overcharges in the first place or that its carriers were either inefficient or dishonest. Neither is true.

---

[2] Note that there is a separate rate for each commodity and each point of origin and destination. Thus, a traffic department in large corporation may be working with hundreds of thousands of rates.

520

Every well-managed company audits its freight bills and makes enormous savings as a result. The rate structure is so complex that errors are inevitable. Moreover, when two different rates apply to the same commodity (and there is always the problem of classifying the shipment), who is to blame the carrier if it charges the higher of the two rates? Many such mistakes are the shipper's fault. The carrier's rate clerk never sees the shipment and must rely on the shipper's description of the material. If the description is incomplete, he naturally applies the higher rate. The lower the class number, the lower the rate. In other words, a Class 77½ rating carries a lower tariff than a Class 100 rating. Class ratings vary substantially with the completeness of the shipping order description. For example:

If you ship:	And describe them as:	They will be rated:	They should be rated:
Cotton work shirts	Cotton shirts	Class 100	Class 77½
Crude sulfate of soda	Chemicals	Class 100	Class 50
Wooden forks or spoons	Woodenware	Class 100	Class 50
Portable phonographs	Phonographs	Class 125	Class 110
Solid toy blocks	Toy blocks	Class 85	Class 70
Cotter pins, iron or steel	Hardware	Class 70	Class 50

Even after freight bills have been audited once, it is still possible for a skilled auditor to detect errors. For this reason, almost every big corporation sends bills that its own auditors have checked to an independent auditing firm for a second review. Such firms find it profitable to check clients' bills for a commission of 30 to 60 percent on the errors they detect. They will also provide complete traffic management service for smaller companies.

Not every freight bill is incorrect, of course. In fact, more than 99 percent usually are not challenged. Monsanto Chemical's experience is not untypical. It limits its audit to invoices that exceed $100; at that it must check about 600 of them a day. About 20 of these are "pickups," that is, bills picked up for further investigation because of some discrepancy. On about half of the pickups there is a discrepancy between the rate charged by the carrier and the rate Monsanto feels should be paid. The balance of the pickups result from errors in computation. Monsanto's experience in auditing freight invoices is typical of most large companies with first-rate traffic departments.

Charter truck

Switching from common carriers to private chartered truck has been a surefire cost-reduction technique for many traffic departments. For example, Montgomery Ward cut its transportation costs by $2,500,000 a year with a company-operated fleet of 280 trucks. Big savings result mainly because charter rates are not regulated. A company can carry the "cream" of its traffic in its own trucks and ship the balance by common carrier. It saves enormous amounts in this way because common carriers charge rates much higher than their true cost for some shipments in order to offset losses on other shipments. For example, almost all common carriers lose money on LTL and LCL shipments, whereas carload and truckload rates for most finished manufactured goods are extremely profitable, especially when shipment is between two points on the carrier's main line.

Interstate Commerce Commission regulations may prohibit common carriers from cutting rates in order to hang on to business they might lose to captive carriers. Only common carriers of agricultural products are exempt from ICC regulation, although this rule has been modified in recent years. In some cases, manufacturers make use of farm trucks to haul merchandise one way—and the trucks presumably haul produce the rest of the time. Care must be taken to avoid violation of ICC regulations, however.

It is perfectly legal for a company to use a chartered truck to deliver goods and then return empty to the plant, and many companies believe that this seemingly uneconomical mode of transport is much cheaper than common carrier. Naturally, traffic managers try to route their trucks so that they expend a maximum amount of time traveling with payloads. One way to do this is to use the trucks to pick up materials from suppliers after they have made deliveries to customers in the same area. One New York–based manufacturer of steel laboratory furniture uses a charter truck to make weekly deliveries to customers in the Milwaukee and Chicago area. The truck returns with steel purchased from Chicago mills. In this particular case, the company's choice of steel suppliers is influenced by the fact that many of its customers are in the Chicago area. Were the company to buy its steel from mills nearer New York—in Bethlehem, Pennsylvania, or Sparrows Point, Maryland, for example—it would have to ship by common carrier, since it does not have many customers in these areas.[3]

Individual firms can also cooperate with one another in order to make more efficient use of charter trucks. For example, a manufacturer in New York might have have heavy outbound traffic to Chicago, while a Chicago manufacturer might have heavy shipping to New York. If the two can cooperate in some fashion, they can get more efficient utilization of their charter trucks. They have to be careful to avoid acting as a common carrier, but in many cases such cooperation is possible and does not violate ICC regulations.

---

[3] Close cooperation between purchasing and traffic is essential to take advantage of deals like these. This is obviously much easier to effect when the two functions are grouped together in a unified materials organization similar to those discussed in Chapter 4.

Many companies claim they would prefer charter trucks even if they made no direct cost savings with them. With their own trucks they are able to work on tighter schedules and enjoy lower cost packaging and materials handling. The trucks may even be used as a promotion device with the firm's brand name prominently displayed on them.

Tighter scheduling. When a shipper controls his own fleet, he can more easily regulate relative priorities of various shipments. Sometimes he also can offer prompter service to customers or reduce his in-transit inventories. For example, the Admiral Corporation reduced its average time to ship TV sets from several plants near Chicago to its New York distributor from 50 to 30 hours when it started using chartered trucks.

Packaging and materials handling. It often is practical to equip chartered or company trucks with special racks or other materials handling devices to cut packaging and materials handling costs. Comparable savings often can be made by leasing specially equipped railroad cars from common carriers. Even when special racks will not eliminate packaging, it still is possible to cut packaging costs by using company trucks. Since carriers are responsible for damage to goods in transit, they naturally insist that shipments be securely packaged. In some cases, it is possible to ship in lighter, cheaper containers with little increase in damage. For example, the Douglas Furniture Company cut packaging costs $25,000 per year because it was able to use 150-pound test cartons in its own trucks instead of the 200-pound test cartons required by common carriers. In addition, it cut its damage losses 80 percent because merchandise was handled more gently in company-operated trucks.

Goodwill and convenience. A company-owned truck with the company name and trademark emblazoned on its side is a rolling advertisement. In addition, customers are more likely to be impressed when delivery is made by company truck instead of by common carrier. There is good reason for this. A company often can give better service with its own trucks, and it is almost always more convenient to dispatch a company-owned vehicle than to call on a common carrier.

Despite their advantages, however, there is no doubt that charter trucks would not be used so widely today were it not for the rate structure and antiquated regulations governing common carriers. Few manufacturers or distributors can operate truck lines as efficiently as common carriers, and most would not want to do so were it not so advantageous.

Other cost-reduction techniques

Sometimes a company can get common carriers to reduce rates simply by threatening to charter its own trucks. The process is an involved one, because the carrier cannot cut rates unless it has approval to do so from the ICC or some other regulatory body. The carrier's competitors will often resist its request for rate reduction. Competitors of the shipper benefiting from the reduction also may protest.

Classification change. An easier route to rate reduction sometimes lies in creating a brand new rate classification for the item. The shipper must convince the carrier and the regulatory body that her product is unique and should get a lower rate because it either costs less to ship or is worth less than other products in the same rate class. For example, the *National Motor Freight Classification* shows the following classifications for a simple item like a garment hanger:

Hangers, garment, aluminum, aluminum alloy, magnesium
   metal, or magnesium metal alloy, NOI, in boxes .... Class 100
Hangers, garment, plastic, or plastic and metal combined,
   in boxes .... Class 100
Hangers, garment, NOI, in barrels, boxes, or crates .... Class 100
Hangers, skirt or trouser, cast aluminum, in boxes...................... Class 85
Hangers, garment, wire, or wire and paper combined, in barrels,
   boxes, or crates .... Class 70
Hangers, garment, wood, or wood and wire combined, in barrels,
   boxes, or crates .... Class 70
Hangers, garment, pulpboard, printed or not printed, in barrels,
   boxes, or crates .... Class 55

The lower the class number, the lower the tariff that will apply. Thus the cheapest hanger to ship is one that is "garment, pulpboard, printed or not printed, in barrels, boxes, or crates." The most expensive is the first one listed. If a company should develop a new type of garment hanger—one of molded fiberglass, for example—how does it determine what rate class should apply? Of course, it always can ship the product as "hangers," but then the carrier would apply the highest tariff. Or it could describe the item in terms of the rate class that best fitted it. Fiberglass hangers presumably would be considered "hangers, garment, plastic, or plastic and metal combined in boxes." In this case they would be shipped as Class 100.

If there were any legitimate basis for doing so, the traffic manager would try to get the fiberglass hangers assigned to a lower class than the plastic hangers. She might claim, for example, that fiberglass hangers had a higher density, were of lower value, or less subject to damage than ordinary plastic hangers, and therefore they were entitled to a lower rate class. In this particular case, she probably would not be successful since fiberglass would probably be considered a superior form of plastic.

Needless to say, shipper should be extremely careful in describing shipments. To earn a lower rate, the shipment not only must fit the specifications of that rate but must be described as such.

Reducing demurrage charges. Railroads allow 24 to 48 hours to unload a boxcar. If the car is held beyond this free time, they make a penalty charge called "demurrage." This charge has been increased several times in recent years because railroads complained that approved demurrage rates did not permit an adequate return on their investment in boxcars. However, the charge has apparently not increased enough to make it profitable for railroads to invest in boxcars, and idle cars remain a problem for the railroads. From the shipper's point of view, the boxcar is a reasonably cheap storage area even if demurrage charges must be paid. However, shippers naturally try to keep demurrage charges low, and the traffic department makes periodic studies to analyze charges and recommend changes in procedure that will reduce them.

In many cases, materials managers can reduce demurrage charges substantially by carefully scheduling shipments so that unloading facilities are never overtaxed. Periodic studies show whether or not cars are being handled in the most economical fashion. They must take account not only of demurrage charges but also of unloading the storage costs. Sometimes it pays to incur extra demurrage charges; for example, it may be cheaper to pay demurrage than to have an unloading crew work overtime at premium rates. Also, many companies prefer to pay demurrage during peak production periods rather than to invest in the additional storage space that would be required to eliminate it. Partly as a result of this practice, the average boxcar moves loaded in trains only about 23 days per year and moves empty for 14 days. The rest of time the car sits idle on various sidings.

Specific projects

Every traffic department always has at least one or two special cost-reduction studies under way. Particularly promising for cost reduction are changes in packaging specifications, various pool car arrangements, and various facilities studies.

Packaging. Although it may not be directly responsible for package design, the traffic department should be concerned with packaging specifications. It can analyze damage claims, and, if there is almost no damage because of poor packaging, perhaps a less expensive package can be used. If damage claims are high, more costly packaging might be worthwhile. Needless to say, traffic engineers prefer to select the lightest possible package. A shipper must pay freight not only for the product but also for the package that holds it. In some cases, costs may be reduced by selecting a container that weighs less even though it may cost slightly more.

Pool cars. Shippers try to avoid paying high LCL and LTL rates whenever possible. One way to do this is to pool a number of small shipments headed in the same direction. For example, many Eastern manufacturers load orders for a number of West Coast customers in a single car. Thus a manufacturer may load orders for distributors located in a number of California cities in a boxcar with a San Francisco destination. When the car arrives, the orders are separated and carried by company-owned truck or by some other conveyance to their separate destinations.

Pool cars also can be used for purchased materials. In this case the company pools all shipments from suppliers in a given area. For example, an auto company with a Los Angeles assembly plant might arrange for pool cars to leave at regular intervals from all cities in which it has a number of parts suppliers. Suppliers then deliver to the loading point, where a carloading firm pools their shipments. Such arrangements may save hundreds of thousands of dollars. Needless to say, purchasing and traffic must work together closely when there are pool car arrangements. In many cases, choice of a supplier will be influenced by proximity to a pool carloading point.

Facilities studies. Traffic considerations also are important in determining the location of any new facilities. Using linear programming and other operations research techniques, the physical distribution or traffic manager can determine the relative transportation costs to and from various proposed locations.

Cases

CASE 16–1. EACKER TELEVISION AND RADIO CORPORATION

Creating a traffic department

Eacker Television and Radio Corporation of Chicago, Illinois, has always specialized in high-quality, semi-custom-made electronic equipment. The company was founded in 1946, and its first major product consisted of a radio-phonograph combination designed to retail for $900. In 1949 the company produced its first television set. It did not attempt to compete with the big mass producers of TV sets; its design emphasized quality and retailed for about $475. Practically all sales went to six distributors in New York, Atlanta, St. Louis, Chicago, Dallas, and San Francisco. In 1964 the company broadened its line and introduced color television. Again the emphasis was on quality, nor price.

The color TV line was an immediate success, and the company began to grow. By 1966 there were 500 employees, compared to fewer than 100 just ten years earlier. Don Eacker, the company's founder and president, felt that the company had now grown to the point where it could profit from an integrated materials activity. He promoted his purchasing agent, Roberta Strong, to materials manager and made her responsible for inventory control, shipping and receiving, and traffic, as well as purchasing.

Strong in turn hired Robert Alexander as a traffic expert. She explained to Alexander when she hired him that she herself knew very little about traffic management but was certain that substantial savings could be made, since the company was currently spending nearly $550,000 per year on transportation services.

Prior to the creation of the independent materials department, traffic had been something of a stepchild in the Eacker organization. The sales department was responsible for all outbound shipments. Practically all shipments were made by the Great Lakes Trucking Company, a leading Midwestern trucking firm. If the shipment was directed to a destination outside of Great Lakes's territory, the Great Lakes traffic manager routed it through other trucking firms.

Inbound shipments were the responsibility of the purchasing department. As Strong puts it: "I buy from suppliers within a 300-mile radius of Chicago and require all vendors to quote f.o.b. our plant. This makes it easier to compare bids of competing suppliers and makes the vendor responsible for delivery to our plant on the date we request it. It also gives the vendor an incentive to combine shipments in one geographical area and thus keep his costs down."

While Strong is convinced that this approach may have been the most economic one while the Eacker Company was small, she is open to any suggestions that Alexander may have for improvement.

Questions

1. Prepare a program of traffic management for Eacker Television and Radio Corporation.
2. What should Alexander's duties and responsibilities as traffic manager be?
3. Suggest specific areas of investigation to reduce the company's transportation costs.

CASE 16–2. MOHAWK ALUMINUM AND CHEMICAL CORPORATION

Freight rate negotiation

Mohawk Aluminum and Chemical Corporation ships bauxite from its mines in the Carribean to a tidewater plant in Louisiana, where it converts the bauxite into alumina. Currently, it is shipping 400,000 tons of alumina per year to a reduction plant on the Ohio River, where the alumina is converted into aluminum. The Ohio River facility is strategically located for several reasons. First, it is reasonably close to most of the major aluminum fabricators in the East and Midwest. Second, it can get favorable rates from huge steam power plants located close to the West Virginia coalfields. Third, it can get alumina by both barge and rail.

Currently, Mohawk gets all of its alumina by rail. The current rate is $6.10 per ton. Mohawk's traffic manager, Herbert Reynolds, has been working hard to get the railroads to reduce this rate. He warns the carriers that they must be competitive with barges if they are going to continue to haul Mohawk's alumina. He says that he believes he could get water carriers to transport alumina for as little as $5 per ton and suggests that the railroads try to meet this rate.

The railroads point out that it is not fair to compare their rates with those charged by barge companies. Their service is faster. In addition, Mohawk cannot handle barge transportation until it invests in terminal facilities. Reynolds is fully aware of this, of course, and has already gotten an estimate on the cost of constructing such facilities. Mohawk's investment would have to be at least $4 million.

Reynolds believes that his position would be strengthened for negotiation with the railroads if he actually had river terminal facilities to handle barge shipments. But, on the other hand, $4 million is a lot of money to spend for bargaining power. His guess is that the railroads have an out-of-pocket cost of $4.00 to $4.50 per ton for hauling alumina. If they had to, he is quite certain that they would be willing to cut rates to as little as $4.75 per ton in order to hold the traffic. He believes that the best barge rate he could negotiate would be between $5.00 and $5.25 per ton—after having invested $4 million in terminal facilities.

Recently, Reynolds called in top railroad officials and bluntly informed them that Mohawk would go ahead with construction of barge terminal facilities if it were not possible to get a more favorable rate on alumina. He pointed out that the traffic currently was worth more than $2,400,000 to the railroads, and in the future it would be worth a lot more, since demand for aluminum was steadily increasing. He said he preferred the faster rail service to barge, but in most cases Mohawk is in no hurry to get material, since it carries large inventories of alumina at its Ohio River plant.

Questions

1. What is the highest rate Reynolds can afford to accept from the railroads before he seriously proposes construction of terminal facilities to his company's finance committee?
2. Has Reynolds exhausted every possibility for rate negotiation other than actually going ahead with building terminal facilities?

CASE 16–3. CONTINENTAL COPPER & STEEL INDUSTRIES

Negotiation of a reduction in freight rates

Donald S. Helm, director of traffic, Continental Copper & Steel Industries, Inc., keeps a detailed record of distribution costs as percentages of gross sales by area. He analyzed shipments of insulated copper and wire cable moving from his company's Hatfield Wire & Cable Division plants in the New York area to Kansas City, Missouri, Omaha, Nebraska, and Minneapolis. He determined that the transportation costs involved were excessive when compared to those on similar shipments to other areas.

The rates were as follows:

> To Kansas City: $2.15 per cwt. with a 24,000-lb. minimum; $1.90 per cwt. with a 30,000-lb. minimum; $1.82 per cwt. with a 34,000-lb. minimum.
>
> To Omaha: $1.96 per cwt. with a 30,000-lb. minimum.
>
> To Minneapolis: $1.83 per cwt. with a 30,000-lb. minimum; $1.75 per cwt. with a 34,000-lb. minimum.

Helm realized that the motor carrier industry had worked with truck manufacturers to develop bigger semitrailers and more powerful tractors capable of pulling heavier loads. He also knew many states had gradually liberalized highway restrictions of motor vehicle sizes and weights. He reasoned that motor carriers could transport 40,000-pound payloads from New York to the destination points of the shipments involved.

Helm concluded that if he could offer the motor carriers larger shipments, which would increase their revenue per truck-mile, they might be willing to reciprocate with lower rates.

To determine whether or not Hatfield Wire and Cable could take advantage of bigger shipping quantities, Helm checked with his sales manager, who assured him that customers in the area he was studying would purchase in 40,000-pound truckload volumes. He also checked warehouse inventory costs to determine if an increase in inventory was worthwhile.

Helm's next job was to find a carrier who would work with him to develop and propose lower freight rates based on a higher minimum weight. The proposal would have to be made before the Standing Rate Committee of the Eastern Central Motor Carriers Association, the tariff publishing agency for the motor carriers serving the area in which the shipments moved.

Helm knew that technically he could appear before the ECMCA and propose the rates himself. But as a practical matter he also knew that a rate sponsored by a carrier member has a better chance of being approved. The carrier has to meet several requirements. First, he must be sympathetic to the proposal. Then he must be authorized to serve the points involved. The carrier's equipment must be able to handle the heavier shipments contemplated. Service in general has to be good. Finally, the carrier must have a low claims ratio (the ratio of the number of lost or damaged shipments to the number of claim-free shipments). Helm considered a low claims ratio important because cable can be damaged easily if it is not handled carefully.

All Helm's qualifications were met by Interstate System, operating out of Grand Rapids, Michigan. Helm and his assistant traffic manager, Florence Machette, worked closely with John P. Ryan, director of sales for Interstate, and on May 20, 1964, Helm submitted his proposal to Interstate's traffic department.

The proposal for the New York to Minneapolis rates included the following data (similar information was submitted for the other two destinations):

> Full description of the commodity as it was described in the existing tariffs: Cable, electric, brass, bronze or copper, NOI. Wire, brass, bronze, or copper, covered, insulated or plain.
>
> Origin and destination point: New York to Minneapolis.
>
> Mileage between the two points: 1,232.
>
> Number of tariff containing the class rates: 25-E.
>
> Existing first-class rate: $5.45.
>
> Proposed rate: $1.65.
>
> Percentage relationship between the proposed rate and the first-class rate: 30.3%.
>
> Proposed minimum weight: 40,000 lbs.
>
> Carrier truck-mile earnings the proposed rate would produce: 53.6 cents.
>
> Present rates, their percentage relationships to the first-class rate, minimum weights, and current truck-mile earnings: $1.83; 33.6%; 30,000 lbs.; 44.6 cents. $1.75; 32.1%; 34,000 lbs; 48.3 cents.
>
> Present rates and minimum weights via rail piggyback service ($1.83, 30,000 lbs.; $1.75, 34,000 lbs.).
>
> Present rates and minimum weights via regular rail service ($1.55, 30,000 lbs., with $1.24 per cwt. applying on any excess over 30,000 lbs.).

In each case, the truck-mile earnings via Helm's proposed rates were higher than earnings via the rates then in effect: 53.6 cents on 40,000-pound minimum, compared with $1.75 per cwt. for the lowest 30,000-pound minimum shipments and 48.3 cents on 34,000-pound minimum shipments.

In effect, Helm was proposing a rate of $1.65 per cwt. with a 40,000-pound, minimum, compared with $1.75 per cwt. for the lowest existing rate, which was based on a volume minimum weight of 34,000 pounds.

Meanwhile, Interstate's sales director, Ryan, was asked by his traffic department to fill out a detailed questionnaire on the proposed change. (See Exhibit 1.) This gave the traffic department additional data it needed to determine whether or not to support the rate proposal.

In reviewing the proposal, Interstate considered such factors as the amount of tonnage moving annually from the account, whether the new rates would discriminate against any shippers or geographic areas, the annual tonnage involved in the particular movement,

EXHIBIT 1

**STANDARD
DOCKET PROPOSAL FORM**
(Submit in duplicate)

Do not use this space

Dkt. No.

NAME OF TARIFF PUBLISHING AGENCY WITH WHICH PROPOSAL IS FILED:

Proponent's File No.

Date

PROPOSAL ORIGINATED BY: (Company)

Check one: Motor Carrier / Consignor / Consignee

(Official)
(Address)
(Street) (City) (Zone) (State)

1. PROPOSED COMMODITY DESCRIPTION AND PACKING, or RULE OR REGULATION: (Show the exact commodity description to be employed using classification description where possible. If a change in rule or regulation is involved, quote the entire rule or regulation as it is desired, or state the desired change and clearly identify it in connection with the present rule or regulation with item and tariff where published.)

REMINDER - DOES INVOLVED COMMODITY DESCRIPTION CONFORM TO N.M.F.C. DESCRIPTION IN FURTHERANCE OF E.C.M.C.A CONTINUING TARIFF IMPROVEMENT PROGRAM?

2. N. M. F. CLASSIFICATION REFERENCE OF ARTICLES SHOWN IN PARAGRAPH 1: Item _____ N.M.F.C. No. ___
Supp. _____ , Ratings: LTL _____ , TL or Vol. _____ , Min. Wt. _____ lbs.

3. BASIC DETAIL: (GIVE FULL TARIFF AUTHORITY FOR ALL PRESENT AND COMPETITIVE RATES SHOWN BELOW.)

TERRITORY				PROPOSED BASIS					PRESENT BASIS			
FROM	TO	MILES	First Class Rate	* Rate or Rating	% of First Class	Min. Weight	Truck Mile Earnings	MOTOR		RAIL or OTHER	
(Unless otherwise indicated)								Rate or Rating	Min. Weight	Rate or Rating	Min. Weight

* Is proposed rate subject to increase under Conversion Table, Master Tariff, etc? Yes ☐ No ☐

TARIFF AUTHORITY	Item No.	Tariff No.	MF. I.C.C. No.†	Issued By
MOTOR Rate				
MOTOR Rating				
RAIL or OTHER Rate				
RAIL or OTHER Rating				

† If tariff is filed under I.C.C. No. or I.C.C.F.F. No., so state.

Docket proposal form calls for information on movement, including present and proposed rates, and detailed statement of justification for rate change. ECMCA officials say inadequate information is a primary reason why proposals are rejected. Forms are available from ECMCA and other carrier tariff bureaus.

whether the volume warranted a deviation in the established rate structure, the existence of a precedent for the new rates, and the competitive necessity for the new rates.

Interstate submitted the proposal to the Standing Rate Committee of the Eastern Central Motor Carriers Association. The proposal was assigned Docket No. SR-18192 and the hearing date was set three weeks later.

To notify all members and interested shippers of the hearing ECMCA published the proposal, along with 35 other new rate proposals, in its weekly docket bulletin mailed to all subscribers. This publication alerts interested shippers and carriers to pending rate proposals. They can support or object to the proposals by appearing in person, by mail, or, in the case of ECMCA, by telephone. Speakerphone facilities permit full discussion between any interested party and the entire Standing Rate Committee at one time via one phone call.

Here is the proposal as it was published in the Docket Bulletin:

SR-18192 Amend ECMCA Tariffs 22-K and 27-C as follows:

(TARIFF 22-K)—Add rates from New York, N.Y., to Kansas City, Mo., 171 cents and Omaha, Neb., 179 cents, min. wt, 40,000 lbs. to apply on Cable, electric, copper steel amored lead covered or armored lead covered, NOI; Wire, brass, bronze or copper, insulated or plain or copper clad steel, covered, insulated or plain.

(TARIFF 27-C)—Add a rate of 165 cents at 40M from New York, N.Y., to Minneapolis, Minn., to apply on Cable, electric, brass, bronze or copper, NOI; Wire, brass, bronze or copper, covered, insulated or plain.

The Standing Rate Committee, composed of three members of the ECMCA staff, heard testimony in support of the proposal from Interstate System and from Continental Copper & Steel Industries, Inc. It also heard testimony from other motor carriers and shippers opposing the new rates.

The Standing Rate Committee then issued its report rejecting the proposed rates. The committee stated that there appeared to be no competitive necessity for the setting of new rates.

At this point, the carrier had three choices: appeal the Standing Rate Committee's decision to the General Rate Committee, composed of approximately 30 members; accept the decision; or take "independent action" and have the rate published to apply via its line, with other carriers free to have the rate published for their account also.

In this case, Interstate decided to take independent action and had the rates published for its account. They became effective and 1964 (New York to Minneapolis) and November 13, 1964 (New York) other carriers became party to the rates, meaning that they too agreed to charge the new rates.

Helm estimates that the publication of these three rates is saving his company between $6,000 and $7,000 annually. During the year, Helm was able to negotiate 20 freight-rate adjustments which trim the company's transportation bill by an estimated $50,000–$60,000 annually.

"Good traffic management," says Helm, "is good business. We hear a lot of talk to the effect that nothing can be done about the trend toward higher freight rates. That's just not true.

"Freight rates can be negotiated just as the price of any other service or product can be negotiated. If you can show carriers how they can increase their earnings through greater revenue per trip, as we did in this case, or through reduced operating expense, or that the present rates are discriminatory or unjust or unreasonable, the carriers will listen to you.

"But be reasonable," continues Helm. "Remember, they're in business to make money, just as you are. Be frank with the carriers. Give them all the facts they need to help you, and when they do succeed in lowering your freight rates, be appreciative."

Questions

1. How does negotiation of a freight rate differ from negotiation of price paid for a conventional purchase?
2. Why would Interstate be willing to cut its tariff in order to please Hatfield, since Hatfield would have to ship its products in any case, even if it were forced to continue to pay a higher tariff?
3. Is the new tariff fair to smaller producers of insulated copper wire who do not have enough volume to ship in 40,000-pound lots?
4. What would you guess the Rate Committee meant when it said there was no competitive necessity for the lower rate? Why did Interstate go ahead and cut the rate anyway?

17

Problems in supplier relations

One of the basic objectives of materials management is favorable relations with outside suppliers. This is not too difficult to achieve when:

1. Suppliers perform outstandingly well on quality and delivery after they accept orders at competitive prices.
2. A strictly businesslike buyer-seller relationship prevails.

Unfortunately, suppliers do fail to keep delivery promises and do not always meet quality standards. Sometimes they are responsible for the failure; sometimes others are responsible. Buyer-seller relations also are subject to numerous pressures. Some of these pressures reflect the character of the buyers and sellers themselves; others are exerted by outside influences.

PRICE

In theory, price should never be a "problem" after the supplier accepts an order. In practice, it is often a major difficulty. On highly technical purchases, it is often not possible to define the price precisely. As often happens on purchase of complex military equipment, the supplier discovers that costs are much higher than anticipated and seeks a higher price. The buyer is left wondering if the correct purchase decision was made. For example, suppose supplier A quotes $200 million on a military contract and supplier B quotes $250 million. All other factors being equal, supplier A should get the contract. But after the award, suppose that supplier A is half way through and discovers that costs will be $300 million.

The textbook answer in this problem is that supplier A must simply incur a loss of $100 million on this contract if it was accepted at a fixed price. In real life, this is not practical. In most cases, there have been a sufficient number of changes in specifications so that supplier A could not be held to its fixed price. But even if it could, this would not necessarily be in the buyer's interest. The basic problem is that the supplier is well along on a contract for equipment that is badly needed. The buyer may be able to get a court to order the supplier to perform. But, at best, this results in long delays while litigation progresses. At worst, the buyer simply loses the work that has been done to date because the supplier is forced into bankruptcy as costs exceed revenues on a major order.

While the most widely publicized cases of a low bidder not being able to meet its obligations occur on military contracts, they are not at all uncommon on strictly civilian purchases. It is actually in a supplier's selfish interest deliberately to bid low enough on a new contract to be assured of getting the order. It may then acquire enough expertise on follow-on orders so that it can later boost prices without fear of competition. Or it can simply go to its customer halfway through a job and demand a price increase. The buyer may be forced to concede this even though it is not allowable under the terms of the contract.

Obviously, the buyer should not award business to a supplier suspected of deliberately bidding below cost in order to gain an effective monopoly position. But every buyer (and every supplier) makes honest errors in judgment. As a result, price is often a very real problem in buyer-supplier relations. However, it is not as common as problems in quality or delivery.

DELIVERY FAILURE

The most basic supplier failure is failure to deliver. There are many reasons why a supplier might not deliver on schedule. These include manufacturing difficulties, shortages of raw materials, labor trouble, transportation tie-ups, and just plain bad management.

More often than not, a supplier delivery failure creates no real problem. The material is not needed immediately, or an alternate supply is readily available. Sometimes the user of the material can work out his own solution to the problem and need not even ask the buyer for help. In other cases, the user of the material raises a lot of smoke, but the buyer later discovers that there is no fire. The buyer should not rush to head off a shortage due to a delivery failure until she investigates and is absolutely certain that a shortage will exist if action is not taken. She may also discover that the cost of eliminating the shortage is greater than the loss that results from it. It is pointless, for example, to incur substantial cost air shipping material when production control can make minor revisions in schedule that postpone the need for the material.

The shortage plan

The buyer's skill is tested only when a supplier fails to deliver material that is needed immediately. The buyer must find out the cause of the failure promptly and then develop a plan to cope with it. If she moves fast, she may be able to avoid a costly shutdown resulting from lack of material.

As soon as she learns that a supplier may fail to deliver, the buyer should get the following information:

1. When and how much the supplier can deliver.
2. Current inventories and probable requirements. (Possibly stocks are more than adequate and there is no need for the supplier to ship in the near future anyway.)
3. Cause of the delivery failure.
4. Availability of alternate sources of supply.

From this data, the buyer must develop a plan to cope with the shortage. Whenever possible, she tries to prevent production from being disrupted. But the buyer always should be realistic. If the shortage is so serious that some curtailment of output is inevitable, she should allow for this in the plan. A shutdown that is planned in advance is almost always less costly than one that comes as a complete surprise.

In some cases the buyer may be able to use imagination and find some way to prevent a production shutdown even when the situation seems almost hopeless. Suppose, for example, that a key supplier of production parts is shut down because of a strike. The buyer advises all concerned departments with a strike report. (Figure 17–1). He tries to estimate how long the strike will last; checks current stocks, both on hand and in transit; and considers ways to cope with the shortage. Perhaps it can be licked by immediately starting a second supplier on the item or by making the item in the buyer's plant. Perhaps, although not very likely, surplus stocks can be purchased from some other user. Perhaps defective or used items can be reworked to make them acceptable or a substitute can be found. Perhaps extra stock can be "discovered" by shortening supply lines. For example, if a part goes into a subassembly that in turn is assembled into something else, the shortage might not be so serious as it first appears. All the in-process stock can be used before assembly of the end product is delayed.

Field expediting. Sometimes delivery failure is only partial. A supplier cannot produce desired quantities because of manufacturing

FIGURE 17-1

FORD DIVISION FORD MOTOR COMPANY		STRIKE REPORT			DATE	
VENDOR'S NAME		VENDOR'S ADDRESS		AFFECTED PLANT		
NATURE OF ACTUAL OR INDICATED INTERRUPTION OF SUPPLY						
NAME OF LOCAL	NO.	UNION AFFILIATION OF LOCAL	LOCAL PRESIDENT'S NAME	NO. PERSONNEL INVOLVED	TIME & DATE OF STRIKE	
PART NO. AND DESCRIPTION		VEHICLE MODELS AFFECTED		SUPPLY CONDITION		
STATUS OF BUYING DEPT. ACTION						
				PURCHASING AGENT OR DEPT. MANAGER		

Courtesy Ford Motor Co.

When a strike stops production at a supplier plant, the buyer should immediately advise all departments concerned with a strike report and develop a plan to cope with the materials shortage that the strike probably will cause.

problems. Or, in many cases, the supplier is not responsible for the delivery failure. Demand for material has increased, and the supplier is called on to exceed original delivery promises.

In such cases, if the shortage is critical, a buyer or expediter may spend all his waking hours in the supplier's plant until the shortage is licked. Many suppliers privately regard their customers' expediters as a first-class nuisance. In their opinion, they accomplish nothing; if anything, they get in the way at a time when the supplier has enough problems. However, suppliers seldom dare protest openly against the use of expediters, since their customers can retort that the expediters would not be needed if the supplier had delivered the materials promptly.

Why do companies use expediters even when they are fairly certain that the supplier is doing everything he can to cope with the shortage? There are at least four reasons:

1. *The presence of the expediter may stimulate supplier personnel to greater efforts.* If a customer is interested enough in getting

prompt delivery to dispatch a field expediter to the supplier's plant, supplier personnel will be more impressed with the need for delivery.

2. *The expediter can make certain that the supplier is actually doing everything possible to overcome the shortage.* If a supplier has half a dozen customers pressing him for delivery, some customers are going to be served more promptly than others. An expediter ensures that her company is getting high priority.

3. *The expediter can keep the buyer up to date with reliable, firsthand information on current delivery status.* Daily telephone reports can keep the buyer posted as to whether the shortage is going to get worse or become less critical.

4. *The expediter can sometimes assist the supplier.* If the supplier can be helped with changes in specifications or quality control procedures, the expediter can relay this information to the home office. Sometimes the supplier needs technical help or raw material. The expediter can arrange for the loan of the company's personnel and get the buyer to help in obtaining raw materials. The supplier may be willing to work his plant overtime only if the buyer is willing to pay the extra costs that will be incurred. A field expediter can evaluate the need for overtime and secure approval for the cost from the home office.

Anticipating shortages

Many delivery problems can be anticipated before an order is placed. They are the result of a supplier's having accepted more business than it is able to handle. You can understand why this would come about only if you put yourself in the other person's shoes. Suppose that you were a supplier and that, to the best of your knowledge, your backlog of work would prevent you from accepting any new business for deliveries prior to next July. One of your customers sends you an order demanding June delivery. Would you accept the order?

Inflated order books. If you were extremely conscientious, you might accept the order on a conditional basis, pointing out to the customer that you are now booked into July and that it might be difficult for you to deliver in June. However, most real-life suppliers are not so squeamish. They might well simply accept the order and hope for the best. There is good reason for their attitude:

1. *Their own order backlog is not firm.* It is quite possible that there will be some cancellations, making the June deadline easy to meet.

2. *They need the business.* You do not get business by turning orders down and, you want to be able to satisfy all of your customers' needs.

3. *Customers may be padding their own delivery needs.* If a buyer wants an item in June, this may mean that he actually needs the item in July and he is just giving himself a safety margin. Naturally suppliers catch on to this game and start playing it too. The buyer is padding his delivery promise, and the supplier starts to play the opposite game and pad hers. On the average, everything works out all right. For all of these reasons, the supplier may be able to meet a delivery promise that is theoretically impossible to meet. However, every now and then something will go wrong, and she will fall way behind.

Cyclical effect: NAPM index. During periods of depressed business, suppliers can usually easily fill the delivery promises they make. They have enough slack capacity so that the roof must almost fall in before they fall behind. During periods when business is booming, the opposite is true. The supplier's own scheduling is so tight that a single heavy snowstorm can create a production scheduling nightmare. In addition, the supplier may be at the mercy of his own suppliers.

Thus, when the buyer places an order, she should make some mental adjustment as to possible risk of delivery failure due to business being just too good. Her best overall barometer is probably the Vendor Performance Index of the National Bureau of Economic Research. This index, which is compiled monthly in cooperation with the National Association of Purchasing Management, is published on an unadjusted basis in the NAPM *Bulletin* and later in various government economic publications, including *Business Conditions Digest*. The index indicates the percent of purchasing agents reporting slower deliveries. During recessions, it is typically in the 25 percent range. That is, only 25 percent of the respondents report slower deliveries. In such cases, one can generally assume that suppliers will be able to meet their delivery promises unless there are unforeseen difficulties.

In contrast, at the peak of the business cycle, the index goes to 75 percent or more. This means that almost every purchasing agent is having trouble holding suppliers to their delivery promises. During such periods, the buyer had best accept supplier promises with some degree of reservation. It also is not a bad idea for her to pad her own requirements; that is, if she really needs the item in July, she should ask for it in June. When she does this, she is adding to the general confusion of lead times and delivery promises that prevails during boom periods. But if everyone else plays the game the same way and tacitly assumes that she does too, does she have any choice?

It is usually easy to determine when the buyer should be stretching out her own lead times if the underlying cause of tighter policy is general prosperity. It is much more difficult to determine in advance that particular suppliers may be in a bind even though general business conditions show plenty of slack. It is not always in the supplier's best interest to give his customers accurate information about his order backlog, and this is something that is not easy to estimate without access to supplier records. In some cases, conclusions must be based entirely on industry data gathered by the Department of Commerce and industry trade associations.

Overoptimism. Sometimes suppliers fall behind on deliveries simply because they are overoptimistic. The buyer can sometimes prevent this by reviewing the equipment the supplier has available to use on a particular order and then determining what safety allowance, if any, the supplier has allowed for. This is a particularly useful technique if the order involves some particularly complex piece of machinery. For example, suppose a supplier has one piece of equipment that the buyer's order will be tying up an average of 80 hours per week. This need create no problem as long as everything goes according to plan. But, of course, a minor breakdown of the equipment can immediately trigger a delivery failure.

It is, of course, almost impossible to prevent suppliers from becoming too ambitious or overoptimistic, and in many cases the buyer simply does not have enough information to know just how extended the supplier is. The problem is made more difficult by the fact that during periods when delivery failures occur, almost every supplier in an industry may be short of capacity. As a result, the buyer has little or no choice but to place orders with a supplier who is already hard pressed to keep up. In some cases, her only effective insurance is to avoid putting all her eggs in one basket and to buy the same item from several suppliers. However, one supplier's failure may still cripple the buyer. This is particularly true if a supplier suddenly starts to have quality problems. If one supplier has difficulty, chances are that the others may find themselves in the same boat. The quality problem may not shut down every supplier, but it will most likely prevent other suppliers from stepping up output enough to take up the slack of the supplier who falls behind.

QUALITY FAILURE

In many industries, the greatest single cause of delivery failure is quality failure. Quality problems begin with a complaint by either the user or the quality control department that a purchased item is of substandard quality. In the case of items purchased by brand or on the basis of performance specifications, the user may complain that the item does not perform as it should. In such cases, the buyer contacts the supplier and advises her of the problem.

All purchases should be inspected and approved on receipt. Under the Uniform Commercial Code, this should be done within a few weeks after the shipment is received if the supplier is to be held responsible. The purchase must be suitable for the use intended. In most organizations the inspection process is necessarily superficial for most purchases. The specialized technical resources needed to make a careful review of quality simply are not available. As a result, the inspection process may simply consist of opening a few cartons and verifying that they contain the products called for on the purchase order. With equipment, the buyer operates it to make certain that it performs in accordance with the terms of the order.

The rejection process is more complicated on purchased parts and materials that are made to the buyer's own technical specifications. The buyer must have an inspection procedure to verify that the shipment meets these specifications. On many complex purchases, the inspection procedure itself is defined in the purchase contract since the acceptability of the shipment is determined largely by the procedure that is used to determine whether or not it is ok.

For example, suppose that a company is buying a part for which its engineers insist that one dimension be 2.000 inches with a tolerance of plus or minus 0.005 inch. This theoretically would mean that the company will reject all parts where the dimension does not measure between 1.995 and 2.005 inches. In practice, it would not reject every part not meeting this requirement. Regardless of the inspection method used, the company always tacitly agrees to accept some parts that lie outside its specifications. The reason is that no inspection is 100 percent foolproof. For example, if an inspector carefully measures each piece to make sure its dimension is between 1.995 and 2.005 inches, we still cannot be 100 percent confident that every defective piece will be culled out. In fact, so-called 100 percent inspection (where every piece is inspected) is often no more than 85 percent efficient. That is, if there are 100 defective pieces in a lot, only about 85 of them will be detected by the inspector. The others will be passed through to the final product.

Basic inspection problems

Quality control engineers are realistic about the probability of inferior quality being accepted. They design quality control procedures that will keep rejects within reasonably acceptable limits. As was discussed in Chapter 13, they recognize that a supplier's quality can never be any better than the process and devise inspection methods that will reliably indicate whether or not the process is in control.

Variables and attributes. There are two distinct ways to inspect a product: by variables and by attributes. With inspection by variables, the characteristic is actually measured; inspection by attributes simply separates the good pieces from the bad pieces. Inspection by variables is more useful for controlling the process, while inspection by attributes may be quite adequate for the buyer who must decide whether or not to accept a shipment from a supplier.

A go, no-go gauge is commonly used to inspect hole diameters by attributes. The hole meets specifications if the go end of the gauge goes into the hole and the no-go is too large to do so. For a 2.000-inch hole with a tolerance of plus or minus 0.005 inch, the go end of the gauge might be 1.9945 inches in diameter. With an allowance of 0.0005 inch for clearance, the gauge enters any hole that is at least 1.995 inches in diameter. Therefore, when the go gauge goes, one can be certain that the hole meets the requirements for the minimum diameter of 0.995 inch. Similarly, the no-go gauge might be 2.0045 inches in diameter. Allowing for 0.0005-inch clearance, it will not enter any hole smaller than the maximum diameter of 2.005 inches.

Inspection by attributes is fast and relatively cheap. In many cases it is the only inspection technique that is available. There is no way to inspect by variables when the quality being measured involves human taste or smell. Color also is often measured by the inspector's eye rather than instruments so inspection must be by attributes. For example, inspectors of dyed cloth or printed labels make visual comparisons with standard color samples. The two colors either "match" or they do not.

One can be more precise when gauges are available to measure a specific physical quality. For example, an inside micrometer or dial indicator will measure the precise diameter of a hole. It might indicate that a particular hole is 2.004 inches in diameter. The inspector knows not only whether or not the hole meets specifications but also how close it comes to the desired mean diameter. This additional information is invaluable in controlling the process. If holes gradually start getting bigger, the process can quickly be corrected (perhaps by sharpening the drill) before it drifts out of control.

Acceptable quality level (AQL). In theory, the supplier need not be concerned with customers' inspection methods. All he need do is meet specifications and he has done his job. In practice, however, inspection methods are often all-important to both buyer and seller and must be well defined. If an item is critical enough so that quality becomes a problem, then agreement on inspection methods is essential. The standard is often more lax than would be indicated by literal interpretation of the specifications.

For example, if the specification calls for a hole to be 2.000 inches with a tolerance of plus or minus 0.005 inch, the uninitiated might assume that all holes must fall between 1.995 and 2.005 inches. This may not be true, however. In some cases, the tolerance was put on the blueprint by a draftsman who was simply following empirical rules. It appears to be fairly easy to hold this tolerance, so that is what the draftsman specifies. The engineer may not care at all what tolerance this particular dimension is held to as long as the hole is made with a standard half-inch drill. When a particular specification causes quality problems, the buyer should immediately make certain that the specification is really vital to the functioning of the product.

In most cases, the decision is almost entirely economic. In general, the tighter the quality standards, the higher the cost. Offsetting this higher unit material cost, entirely or partly, is a reduction in the cost of inspecting and using material made to tighter specifications. Material that barely meets the buyer's standard can often fall below standard. In this case, careful inspection and control in succeeding operations is essential. If the material is much, much better than minimum, this costly control is not needed.

Actual quality. The real quality may be different from the indicated standard even if the engineer actually believes the specification is essential to the product. The real quality standard is not known until the supplier also knows how the buyer will measure how this standard is being met and how much allowance she will make for deviations from it.

Most real-life quality limits fall between two extremes. At one extreme, the most quality-conscious buyer would tell the supplier he would reject an entire shipment if a single piece falls outside his desired quality limits of 2.000 inches plus or minus 0.005 inch. If the buyer were really fussy, he might inspect every piece by attributes with an inspection machine that automatically rejects any part that falls outside the desired limits. A single rejection would cause the entire shipment to be rejected. The reasoning behind this blanket rejection is logical. The buyer is requiring the supplier to select a process where all output falls within required specifications and a single defect then becomes excellent evidence that the supplier's process is out of control.

Few buyers would want to pay for such perfection—and they probably would not get it even if they were willing. A supplier who stands to have an entire shipment refused if there is a single reject would not dare to use the process that is really suitable for the item. She would have to use the next best process—if one were available. The reason for this is that the ideal process may be only 99.9 percent perfect even if it is always in control. Thus there would be at least one defective piece in almost every shipment. If the buyer inspected every piece, he would probably find the defective piece and would then reject the entire shipment.

Random fluctuations will always produce an imperfect piece occasionally. The odds against this can be narrowed even further by selecting even better and more expensive processes. But, unfortunately, there is no foolproof method to assure that standards will always be met. In addition, the supplier will not necessarily adjust her process if a single reject is detected. She would simply reinspect the lot and then resell it to the same customer. Experience would prove that the rigid quality requirements still would not prevent an occasional reject from sneaking through—particularly if the reject did not trigger a change in the basic process.

At the other extreme, the buyer who is not worried about quality would simply make certain that the item was made by the desired process. He would be satisfied with whatever the process would produce as long as it was functioning—in control or out of control.

These two extremes represent rather wide differences in cost even if the same process is involved. In the first case, the supplier would have to exercise great care in manufacture and would also be forced to subject production to elaborate quality control procedures. In extreme cases, the supplier might spend a great deal more on inspection than on production. In the second case, the seller need not spend anything on quality control.

Supplier quality problems

The quality control manager, not the purchasing manager, is responsible for monitoring quality of supplier shipments. The inspection techniques that are used represent an evaluation of engineers' specifications. The engineers who write the specifications would like to have 100 percent of the vendor's shipments fall within tolerances even though they know that this will never be the case. In fact, some companies refuse to disclose to suppliers precisely what their acceptable quality level is because they are afraid that by doing so they will encourage them to reduce standards to the minimum needed to pass inspection. As a result, many inexperienced vendors may find shipments rejected simply because they underestimated the buyer's quality standards.

In such cases both buyer and seller lose. When there is no mutual trust on quality standards, the buyer does not get something for nothing. On the contrary, the experienced seller will soon learn how to beat the system. There are enough quality problems even if buyer and seller have an excellent relationship. Otherwise, there will be constant problems even if specifications are seemingly consistent.

Conflicting standards. For example, if a supplier manufactured and inspected his product so that 95 percent of the pieces were within tolerances and the buyer's inspectors worked to a sampling plan that required 99 percent reliability, practically all of the supplier's shipments would be rejected. A supplier might get occasional rejections even if his quality standards were identical to those of the buyer. For example, while the supplier might check a small sample and find it within tolerances, the buyer might check an entirely different sample from the same shipment and find it exceeded acceptable tolerances. In practice, many suppliers find they must manufacture to quality standards slightly higher than those required by their customers in order to eliminate occasional rejections of this sort and also to provide themselves with a little leeway on quality before it becomes a problem.

This can also cause conflict to develop between the materials department and quality control. In many cases, quality control's interpretations of specifications are not consistent with what materials managers regard as good purchasing practice. The buyer likes to pay for precisely the quality she needs—no more, no less. It is obviously wasteful for suppliers to manufacture a higher quality standard than is really indicated by the specification. Theoretically, there should never be a conflict where specifications are clearly spelled out. However, in most real-life cases, specifications are simply not all that well defined. In the aerospace and electronics industries in particular they are almost never as tight as would normally be dictated by good purchasing practice. Suppliers are often working with newly developed technology, and the problems have not been ironed out.

This may be true even of items that suppliers have been making for years. For example, it is quite difficult for automotive engineers to specify precisely how smooth a "chrome-plated" part such as a bumper guard should be. The process of making the bumper guard automatically generates a number of scratches which must be buffed out at considerable cost. The buyer naturally wants to pay for the minimum amount of buffing that will do the job. Inevitably, cases arise where after the supplier gets the order, he complains that his quotation was based on less buffing than is presently being required by quality control. As a result, the supplier's shipments are not accepted. The buyer is in a quandary. She cannot help but ask herself whether or not the supplier is just using this as an alibi to get a higher price for the item after he gets the order. Or, for all the buyer knows, quality control has quietly restructured its own ground rules. Inspection of "appearance" items on automobiles involves a great deal of latitude. Each inspector is supposed to look at the item and determine whether or not it is suitable in appearance to go on a finished automobile. Unfortunately, it is the last scratches that are the most difficult and most costly to get rid of. Whenever a new supplier is introduced, there is almost always a lot of disagreement that must be resolved before the supplier knows what is really required on the item.

Quality certification

When buyer and seller agree on quality levels, it is sometimes possible to eliminate a great deal of extra inspection with quality certification. A supplier whose quality control procedures meet the buyer's standards then simply ships the material, which gets little or no incoming inspection by the buyer.

With this approach, the buyer specifies in considerable detail precisely what tolerances must be maintained, the AQL for each dimension, and the inspection and sampling procedures to be used. The supplier then certifies that it meets these requirements on each shipment. The buyer need only make occasional spot checks of shipments to make certain that the supplier is not getting lax.

With quality certification, much duplicate inspection is avoided, since for most shipments the buyer's receiving inspection can be quite superficial. This can reduce costs substantially, especially for precision parts with many dimensions that must be held within close tolerances. Certification also has boosted quality for most companies that have tried it. Supplier responsibility is clearly specified, and most suppliers take pride in having their quality level certified by their customers.

Companies with quality certification programs are careful, however, to limit their use to suppliers of proved reliability. They rarely have so much faith in a new supplier that they will accept shipments without a thorough inspection. If the volume of business with the supplier is substantial, the buying company may station one of its inspectors at the supplier's plant to monitor the process. This is more likely to assure high quality than inspecting after material is received, since it helps assure that the supplier's process is in control. The obvious disadvantage is the cost of maintaining an inspector in the field. This tends to limit the practice to military and aerospace products where quality problems are particularly acute. Most other organizations settle either for a quality certification program or conventional receiving inspection.

Buyer's quality role. When a shipment is found defective, the buyer first investigates to make sure that the supplier is really responsible for the defects. He may discover that the rejection was due to changes in specifications, inspection procedures, and so on, that were not incorporated into the purchase agreement. If this is the case, the supplier is not responsible for the rejection.

In most cases, however, the rejection is either wholly or partly the supplier's responsibility. The usual procedure is for the buyer to review the inspection report and pass it on to the supplier. If the supplier agrees that the shipment should be rejected and accepts responsibility for the defects, she will indicate how she wishes to dispose of the shipment. (This is often covered by a standing agreement.) The supplier may want to have the shipment returned to her, scrapped, or salvaged by the buyer. If it is scrapped or salvaged, there must, of course, be agreement concerning scrap credits to the supplier (if the buyer sells it to a scrap dealer) or on charges to the supplier for the buyer's salvage work. Should the supplier deny responsibility for the rejection, the buyer must thoroughly investigate and try to reach an amicable agreement with the supplier that still protects her own company's interests.

Regardless of who is responsible for the quality problem, the buyer should do everything he can to prevent recurrence. He should make certain that the supplier is taking all possible measures to boost quality. If the supplier persists in shipping merchandise that does not pass inspection, the buyer may have to switch suppliers.

Poor quality creates the worst possible type of delivery failure. Unlike other supply failures, there is no advance warning before the material is actually received. Nor is the problem necessarily solved if the supplier succeeds in making a shipment to replace the rejected one, for that shipment may also be rejected. Fortunately for many a buyer of precision parts, quality control departments often relax standards and accept shipments with minor defects when there will be a critical shortage if they are rejected. But this does not by any means take the pressure off the buyer to get suppliers who can consistently meet quality standards.

Zero defects. Quality has a natural tendency to get sloppy. In fact, experience shows that it automatically deteriorates if buyer and seller become the least bit complacent. The zero defects program is designed to fight complacency. Its theme is that nothing less than zero defects is good enough. Zero defects programs were originally developed to boost quality of components used on missiles and spacecraft, but the idea has spread to other industries. The concept of zero defects is simply that quality depends on the motivation of the people who make the product. If you tell these people that you are willing to accept 4 or 5 percent defects, you will probably get just that and maybe a lot more. Instead, you set your goal at zero defects and try to motivate everyone in the organization to work toward this target.

The materials manager and his buyers are catalysts in zero defects programs. They are administered by the quality control department (which is usually part of the manufacturing organization) and applied to both purchased and manufactured items. The materials department is responsible for getting the message through to the company's suppliers, and it works with quality control in arranging seminars and other programs designed to make supplier personnel conscious of the need for zero defects. The end result may not literally be zero defects but at least a higher quality level than prevailed before the zero defects program was begun.

PROBLEMS IN VENDOR SELECTION

Even if a buyer succeeds in getting suppliers who offer outstanding quality, delivery, and service at rock-bottom prices, his selection of sources will not satisfy everyone in the company. In fact, in many cases there are strong forces pushing business toward suppliers who do not necessarily measure up to these basic but tough economic criteria. The environment in which a buyer and the company operate also influences selection of suppliers. Relations with customers, top executives within a company, and the community in which the company operates may dictate selection of suppliers on other than strictly economic terms.

Reciprocity

When a company makes a point of buying from its customers, it is practicing reciprocity. For example, an oil company may buy its pipe only from those steel companies that use its industrial lubricants. Or a chemical company may sell one raw material to another chemical company and buy a second material from that company.

Such reciprocity (or "trade relations," as it is often called) is more widespread in American industry than many business executives care to admit. Purchasing executives often consciously favor their company's customers when selecting suppliers. One purchasing executive for a chemical company (who prefers to remain anonymous) was able to increase his company's sales by $3,516,000 in a single year by calling on his 50 largest suppliers and asking them to become better customers of his company if they wished to continue as important suppliers. On his travels, the purchasing agent was armed with statistics indicating precisely how much his company sold to each supplier and how much it purchased from him.

Many company sales reps travel from customer to customer equipped with similar statistics. Usually it is considered fair and ethical to deal reciprocally on a proportionate basis—as long as quantities purchased are reasonably great. For example, if a chemical company bought 10 percent of its bags from a paper company, it might reasonably expect to get 10 percent of the paper company's chemical purchases (provided, of course, that the chemical company made the chemicals needed for making paper).

Economics of reciprocity.   Proponents of reciprocity maintain that it is simply an application of the Golden Rule: "Do unto your customers as you would have them do unto you." Actually, reciprocity is a vicious practice that saps the efficiency of the economy. When firms can sell on some basis other than the price, quality, and delivery of their product, their efforts are unavoidably misdirected. There is bound to be some waste.

In some cases, the waste is obvious. For example, if all firms could secure business only on the basis of the price and quality of their products, the efficient, low-cost firms would get the business and the marginal producers would disappear. When reciprocity permits an inefficient firm to stay in business and prevents the efficient producer from getting the business it deserves, the real costs to the overall economy are slightly higher and aggregate productivity is reduced. This happens every time a purchasing agent accepts slightly higher prices or slightly inferior quality from a supplier because of reciprocity considerations.

It also happens—although much less obviously—when reciprocity is the basis for selecting among suppliers who offer identical prices and almost identical quality, service, and delivery. Even in the tightest oligopoly there is usually a faint flicker of competition. Reciprocity reduces constructive competition even further. The result inevitably is slightly higher costs and less efficiency, which cannot be detected because low-cost producers make little or no effort to undercut their less efficient collaborators in the oligopoly.

Effect on firm. Few economists would deny that reciprocity reduces the efficiency and productivity of the economy as a whole. But economists do not necessarily make good business executives. The business executive's job is to manage the individual firm, not the economy as a whole. And the plain fact is that reciprocity need not hurt an individual company. On the contrary, reciprocity is so widespread that many firms' sales and profits would be reduced substantially if they did not practice it.

Suppose a company has a choice of buying materials from two competing suppliers who charge identical prices. One supplier is a customer; the other is not. Should the company offend a good customer by buying from its competitor? The only excuse for doing so would be if it could make the competing supplier a customer, too. So the only "right" decision from the viewpoint of the business executive is one that is based on reciprocity.

The situation is only a little different when the customer and would-be supplier offers to sell goods that are either slightly more expensive or inferior in quality to those of other suppliers. In such cases, the company is paying a definite price for reciprocity. Whether or not it accepts the deal depends on whether or not the premium is worth the benefit that is gained. Most companies refuse to pay higher prices to suppliers who are also customers. They usually find it more profitable to buy from the more efficient suppliers and bluntly demand that these suppliers reciprocate by becoming customers. Sometimes, of course, this is not possible. For various reasons the more efficient supplier may not be able to use the company's products. In that case the price premium paid to hold a customer by making him a supplier should be regarded as an indirect price reduction on the products sold to that supplier.

Reciprocity is a significant problem only in industries selling goods to other industries. Few consumer-goods manufacturers can push reciprocity on their suppliers, nor would it be worth the trouble to do so.

For example, not only would the R. J. Reynolds Tobacco Company have a hard time trying to force all employees of its suppliers to smoke Camels or Winstons, but the effect on sales would be negligible if it did succeed in doing so. Not so with a company that both makes and buys products of industrial consumers. For example, a typical chemical company's major purchases are chemical raw materials, and as much as 50 percent of its sales go to other chemical companies. Every major chemical company is both customer and supplier to a number of other major chemical companies. Under the circumstances, reciprocity is inevitable.

Legal basis. Until about 1970, many large companies were organized formally for reciprocity. They had trade relations departments that usually functioned as adjuncts of the marketing department but occasionally were tacked on to the purchasing department. These were stamped out as a result of action by the Justice Department which threatened suit under the antitrust laws. Reciprocity, like sin, still exists. But it has largely gone underground. While it is probably perfectly legal—especially when practiced by smaller firms—its image is basically unfavorable. Both buyers and sellers often have pangs of conscience when they engage in it. Our "free enterprise ethic" dictates that products should be bought and sold on their own merits. It somehow seems dishonorable to favor a supplier simply because he is an existing or potential customer. Yet, as we have already pointed out, reciprocity may be a useful policy for an individual firm.

Back-door selling

When a salesperson deliberately bypasses the purchasing department and makes a sales call on personnel in the department using product, he is engaging in "back-door" selling. Most companies frown on back-door selling. Many companies go so far as to require supplier sales reps to get written permission from the purchasing department before they may call on engineering or manufacturing personnel. (A salesperson's interview permit is shown in Figure 17–2.)

Discouraging back-door selling. Companies try to prevent suppliers from making sale calls on operating personnel for at least four reasons:

1. *To increase efficiency.* They simply do not want salespeople to waste the time of operating personnel. The company's purchasing personnel get paid to interview supplier sales reps; operating personnel are supposed to concern themselves with their own operations.

2. *To control purchase commitments.* If personnel outside of purchasing have dealings with suppliers, they may innocently commit the company to purchases that have not been properly authorized.

550

Expenditures can be closely controlled only if the authority to commit the company is limited.

3. *To maintain competition.* If a supplier persuades the user of a material that his product is the only one that will do the job, the purchasing department may be handicapped in its efforts to reduce costs. If it is forced to buy one brand exclusively, it cannot get bids from competing suppliers. Sometimes a supplier can gain a tremendous advantage by working with the user of the material even if he does not succeed in getting preclusive specifications tailored to his products. He can become more familiar with the operating problems in the buyer's plant and can more easily locate applications for his products. This, of course, is to the buyer's advantage, but not if it is done at the cost of freezing out all of the supplier's competitors.

4. *To maintain security.* Many companies, even those not engaged in defense work with security regulations, do not like to have outsiders strolling around almost at will in their plants and offices. They do not want their new product plans and other advance efforts to become widely known. Since supplier sales reps usually call on the company's competitors as well and often are not averse to gossip, better security is maintained by restricting them to the purchasing department except under special circumstances.

FIGURE 17-2

```
                                              COPY

              SALESPERSON'S INTERVIEW PERMIT


    Issued to_____ Date_____

    Company_____ Time_____

    Permission is hereby given to the above Salesperson to interview

    Mr./Ms._____ at_____
    with the understanding that s/he will not initiate contact with
    any other person or department unless authorized by the under-
    signed; No purchase commitment or change in an existing order
    is to be made unless authorized by the Purchasing Dept.; All
    proposals for Materials or Services must be submitted to the
    attention of the Purchasing Dept.

                         PURCHASING DEPARTMENT

                         By_____

    THIS PERMIT GOOD ONLY ON DATE ISSUED AND MUST BE
    RETURNED TO THE PURCHASING DEPT. BY THE SALESPERSON
    ON DEPARTURE, BEARING THE SIGNATURE OF THE PERSON
    INTERVIEWED.

              Interviewed by_____
```

This interview permit is designed to regulate back-door selling. The purchasing department uses it to control supplier sales calls on operating personnel.

Need for calls.   Despite the efforts to discourage them, most sales people make as many calls on operating personnel as they do on purchasing personnel. Many salespeople get more business by calling on the engineers who specify material and the factory superintendents who use it than they do from the purchasing personnel who theoretically buy it. If engineers or superintendents can be sold on a supplier's brand, sometimes the salesperson's job is done. The brand is specified on the requisition, and the buyer buys it. Most companies permit their buyers to ignore a brand name on a requisition so they can get quotations from manufacturers of competing brands. But some buyers will go to great lengths to avoid offending the requisitioner, and most buyers will try to give some consideration to the requisitioner's preferences.

Thus back-door selling is effective. In fact, from the marketer's point of view, it is absolutely essential for any product that is not sold on the basis of detailed specifications. For most specialized equipment purchases as well as countless other items, the user of the item is the real buyer. In many organizations, top management interferes with the buying process for totally nonrational reasons. For example, a marketing vice president may be personally very interested in cars, so she interferes with the purchasing department in the purchase of company-owned sales rep's automobiles. Friendship between top managers and suppliers also influence the procurement process.

While no form of back-door selling is good practice, few would deny that there is a real need for contact between suppliers and operating personnel. Materials managers and buyers cannot be experts on every product. In most cases, they cannot hope to know as much about the details of the product as the engineer who specifies it or the manufacturing supervisor who uses it. This is particularly true when the product is designed partly or wholly by the supplier. In such cases some exchange of information between supplier and user is essential and should be encouraged.

The question is—when does an innocent exchange of information become back-door selling? This varies with the product and the personnel involved. Well-managed materials departments are careful to devise procedures that prevent unauthorized purchases from being made and brand preferences from creeping into specifications. However, rules and regulations will do only half the job. The other half can be done only when there is goodwill between the materials department and the departments it serves. Good purchasing executives do their best to cultivate good interdepartmental relations. Some even go so far as to hold seminars for operating personnel in which they explain their objectives and why it is to the company's best interest to have purchases made by professional buyers rather than by persons who use or specify the material purchased.

Personal purchases

Many purchasing departments use one hand trying to avoid being bypassed through back-door selling while with the other they try to be bypassed on personal purchases. It is safe to say that personal purchases are a problem in every company. Should the company use its buying power to purchase things for employees at a discount, or shouldn't it? In general, companies have one of three policies on personal purchases:

1. *They explicitly forbid them.* In this case, a buyer may ignore the rules for his personal friends by informally lining them up with suppliers who, he knows, are willing to sell at a discount. But this would have to be a clandestine procedure and would occur only occasionally.

2. *They permit suggesting sources of supply.* Most companies permit buyers to suggest sources of supply to company personnel if they have the time and desire to do so. In such cases, the buyer will often make a deal with a supplier whereby employees of the company can get a discount if they are sent by the buyer.

3. *They encourage personal purchases.* Some companies will cooperate on personal purchases to the extent of issuing company purchase orders for the material and then reinvoicing the employee. With this approach, the employee can buy at the same price as the company. Most companies restrict issuing of purchase orders for personal purchases to top executives. Some are less strict, and a few firms even operate company stores. For example, oil companies operating in remote areas of the Middle East are almost forced to assist employees with personal purchases through operating company stores that sell at relatively low prices.

Policies on personal purchases vary not only from company to company but with rank within a company. Generally, top executives and purchasing personnel themselves make far more extensive use of the company's buying power on personal purchases than others in the organization.

A lenient policy on personal purchases helps boost employee morale. It also can increase employees' effective purchasing power, particularly in areas where there are no "discount houses" and there is little price competition among retailers. On the other hand, personal purchases are expensive for a company. Valuable purchasing department time is wasted on trivial purchases. Vendor goodwill can be endangered by nuisance purchases for employees. If the company uses its purchase orders to make them, personal purchases can take accounting department time, and there also is the problem of collecting an invoice rendered to an employee. Community relations also can become a problem. Local merchants resent a company that uses its buying power to help employees purchase at a discount from out-of-town suppliers.

Local purchases

If all other factors are equal, it is to the buyer's advantage to buy from a local supplier. She usually can get prompter service, and her lead time will be shorter. In addition, it makes for good community relations when a company spends its money locally whenever possible. This is particularly true of a franchised monopoly such as a public utility, which must maintain the goodwill of the community and is also trying to stimulate business in its service area.

Municipal and state purchasing agents usually encounter strong pressure to buy within the boundaries they serve. The money they spend comes from taxes collected within the state or city, so it is reasonable that they should make some effort to spend it on businesses in the same area. However, public purchasing agents should not subsidize local industry with tax money if they can buy more cheaply elsewhere—unless they are forced to do so by statute. Federal government agencies, for example, at one time could lawfully buy from a foreign supplier only if the delivered price was more than 25 percent below that of the lowest cost domestic supplier. This "buy American" act resulted in millions of dollars of hidden subsidies to higher cost domestic producers.

Boards of hospitals and other nonprofit institutions also sometimes exert pressure on purchasing departments of the institutions they control not only to buy locally—but to favor a board member. In many cases, they get away with it even though they are clearly using their influence to feather their own nests at the expense of the public at large. If done quietly, no one is the wiser—and the purchasing manager often does not dare complain at the risk of losing her job.

ETHICS

Ethics is perhaps the only problem in purchasing and materials management that receives widespread publicity. A big-city newspaper can count on at least three or four big stories a year concerning purchasing ethics. A top federal government official accepts entertainment from a major defense contractor; a city purchasing official favors a supplier who is a close personal friend; the president of a large corporation is part owner of a firm that is a major supplier. These are typical stories that make the front page periodically.

On the average, professional buyers and materials managers probably have higher moral standards than most of their fellow citizens. But they also are subjected to more temptations. Buyers spend millions of dollars of their employers' money each year. As a result, they wield tremendous economic power and are the objects of considerable attention from suppliers. They are in an excellent position to be dishonest if they want to be. Buyers can bluntly demand kickbacks and other favors from suppliers. Sometimes they can almost make themselves millionaires before they are caught. For this reason, materials managers are careful to select buyers with strong character and high moral standards, as well as to devise procedures and controls to prevent them from giving in to temptation. Partly because of this practice, many of the scandals that have been exposed did not involve materials personnel but improper relations between operating executives and suppliers. One case that received widespread publicity involved William C. Newberg, president of the Chrysler Corporation, and Chrysler suppliers in which Newberg was a silent partner.

Gifts and entertainment

Even though they may be completely honest, buyers and top-management executives will often receive many wholly unsolicited favors from suppliers. These range from an occasional lunch or entertainment at a convention to Christmas gifts, theater or football tickets, and other favors.

Recipients include not only buyers and materials managers but everyone else who is someone's customer. In many cases, marketing managers regard the practice as a waste of money, but they often continue out of force of habit, if for no other reason. Even if a company spends substantial sums on gifts and entertainment of customers, the cost in relation to sales is trivial. For example, a supplier may give an $8 bottle of whiskey to a customer from whom it received $100,000 worth of business during the year.

Tax deduction. Business gifts are normally deductible as business expense by the supplier. This is defended on the basis that the purpose of the gift is to influence the customer, and it is, therefore, part of the customer's marketing effort. A gift given purely for the sake of giving would not be a legitimate business expense. Thus, "friendship" in the purest sense has nothing to do with the average business gift.

Considering this simple fact, what then should the buyer's attitude be if a supplier or potential supplier offers him a gift or other favor? Under no circumstances should he accept anything from a supplier if it will tend to obligate him directly or indirectly to favor that supplier. There is no general agreement on what a buyer can ethically accept from a supplier. Some believe the buyer should refuse anything except gifts of nominal value used for advertising and sales promotion purposes. Most managements have a somewhat more lenient attitude.

No gifts. A few companies and almost all government agencies have written policies forbidding any employee to accept any favors from suppliers. When a buyer receives an unsolicited gift, she is expected to return it with a letter advising the supplier of the no-gift policy. The top procurement official often goes further and warns the supplier that he will lose business if he continues to send unsolicited gifts. When a company receives gifts that are perishable and cannot be returned (food, flowers, and so on), it may donate them to some charitable institution. The only gifts that are acceptable are advertising novelties such as ballpoint pens with the supplier's name on them, calendars, and the like, which are often passed out at conventions and trade shows by the exhibitors.

Gifts of nominal value only. In the course of normal business relations, certain amenities are both accepted and customary. Buyers and sellers often conduct business over cocktails and lunch or on the golf course at the local country club. In such cases, either may pick up the check. Many completely honorable buyers and sellers remember each other with a gift at Christmas. In many cases, their frequent business dealings have led to friendships that endure even after they are no longer active in business. They naturally would resent any implication that such gifts were unethical. However, there is no doubt that there have been some misguided applications of the Christmas spirit in the business world.

Ethical behavior

A buyer can be completely honest, resolutely refusing all favors from suppliers, and still be guilty of unethical behavior. In fact, it is extremely difficult for a buyer with the best of intentions to be wholly ethical at all times. To do so she must always be completely equitable and honest in her dealings with all suppliers. This is not easy in an atmosphere in which each supplier is vying for the buyer's favor. The buyer is bound to be attracted to the personalities of some supplier sales reps and repelled by others. Theoretically, this should not influence buying decisions. But since buyers are human beings, they are bound to be influenced by the personalities of the people with whom they deal. The best buyers can subordinate their personal feelings with respect to suppliers and make fairly objective buying decisions that bring maximum benefit to their company, even if this involves awarding business to suppliers whom they personally dislike and not awarding it to individuals they like.

Although a buyer is expected to work hard to negotiate the best possible purchase for the company, he should never stoop to unethical techniques for achieving this goal. If he does, he will eventually develop a reputation for underhanded dealing, and suppliers will no longer trust him. Among the practices in which no ethical buyer indulges are:

1. *Permitting a favored supplier to examine the quotations of competitors.* All quotations submitted to a buyer are confidential and should not be shown to any outsider. Nor should a buyer disclose to competitors any information he might have about a supplier's costs, processes, new products, or the like, unless he has the supplier's explicit permission to do so.

2. *Giving a favored supplier a chance to "reconsider" a bid or special information that is not given to all suppliers.* All suppliers should get the same treatment from the buyer. The only exception to this rule is when the purchasing department discriminates in order to achieve some legitimate corporate objective. For example, if a supplier has an effective monopoly, the buyer may bend over backwards in order to develop an efficient competitor.

3. *Giving the supplier misleading information to get him to reduce prices.* The buyer with scruples never asks a supplier to meet a lower bid that exists only in the buyer's imagination. Nor does he give the supplier fictitious information regarding planned production schedules, and so forth, so that the supplier will be encouraged to grant bigger discounts or other benefits.

4. *Using company buying power to force suppliers to sell at prices well below cost.* This is not only unethical but uneconomic, since only a reasonably prosperous supplier can be useful for future contracts. The buyer need not be carried away with compassion for the supplier, however. Every supplier has a right to go broke if it wants to. The buyer can prevent cases of undue supplier dependence by avoiding excessive commitment to a supplier who could be badly hurt if the buyer withheld business.

5. *Asking suppliers for quotations when they have no chance of getting the business.* It often is convenient for a buyer to use quotations from an outside supplier to check up on an established supplier or to compare with shop costs. The quote is used only to negotiate a price reduction from the established supplier or stimulate a cost-reduction drive in the buyer's manufacturing plant. The supplier who quotes has absolutely no chance of getting the business regardless of the quotation. Since quotations are expensive to prepare, the buyer who requests them under false pretenses is, in effect, guilty of stealing from the supplier.

6. *Having a financial interest in any firm that is a supplier.* In such cases there is an obvious conflict of interest. Most companies do permit buyers to own stock in suppliers that are so large or diversified that the buyer's actions would have no significant effect on

sales or profits. For example, few would object if a buyer of utility services owned a few shares of American Telephone & Telegraph. AT&T is so big that no buyer could significantly affect its profits; it also is a monopoly in its service areas, so the buyer would not have an alternate source of supply, anyway.

Few business executives would deny that industrial purchasing ethics today are higher than they have ever been. Scandals make news because they are relatively rare. One reason for this is the work of the National Association of Purchasing Management in boosting the stature and recognition of purchasing. The NAPM's code of good practice, to which its members subscribe, is illustrated in Figure 17–3.

FIGURE 17–3

Principles and Standards of Purchasing Practice

1. To consider, first, the interest of his company in all transactions and to carry out and believe in its established policies.
2. To be receptive to competent counsel from his colleagues and to be guided by such counsel without impairing the dignity and responsibility of his office.
3. To buy without prejudice, seeking to obtain the maximum ultimate value for each dollar of expenditure.
4. To strive consistently for knowledge of the materials and processes of manufacture and to establish practical methods for the conduct of his office.
5. To subscribe and work for honesty and truth in buying and selling and to denounce all forms and manifestations of commercial bribery.
6. To accord a prompt and courteous reception, so far as conditions will permit, to all who call upon a legitimate business mission.
7. To respect his obligations and to require that obligations to him and to his concern be respected, consistent with good business practice.
8. To avoid sharp practice.
9. To counsel and assist fellow purchasing agents in the performance of their duties, whenever occasion permits.
10. To cooperate with all organizations and individuals engaged in activities designed to enhance the development and standing of purchasing.

This code of ethics was developed by the National Association of Purchasing Management to guide the conduct of its 20,000 members.

PROMOTING SUPPLIER GOODWILL

Supplier relations are a problem even when both buyer and seller have the highest possible ethical standards. A supplier who does not get business may sometimes wonder if the buyer isn't unjustly favoring some "pet" supplier.

Buyers try to promote supplier goodwill as much as possible. Salesreps never are left waiting in the lobby for more than a few minutes without some explanation. If a buyer is busy, she will usually try to

558

FIGURE 17–4

CONTENTS

Courtesy General Electric Co.

Many companies have "welcome" booklets in which they describe their purchasing policies, organization, and products to suppliers. Shown here is the table of contents of *Selling to General Electric.*

arrange for the salesperson to see another buyer, if he wishes to do so. If the salesperson is from out of town, buyers often will make a prearranged appointment to make certain they are not busy when she calls.

Buyers always will listen sympathetically to the salesperson's presentation, even though they may not have any foreseeable need for the product. Seasoned buyers also have mastered the art of ending an interview. If they are busy and the salesperson has nothing new to present, they know how to rise, thank the salesrep for calling, and conclude the interview in a tactful way. They want the salesrep to like them and to like the company, and they do their best to make the visit a pleasant experience.

Large companies even publish purchasing directories to help their suppliers. In them they list the major commodities they buy and a breakdown of their purchasing organization, so that the visiting sales rep can readily locate the buyer specializing in his product line. They also try to explain company purchasing policies and procedures so that there will be no misunderstandings. Figure 17–4 illustrates the contents page of the booklet, *Selling to General Electric*, which was prepared to help the 45,000 firms that sell to that company.

Many companies go still further to bolster supplier relations. They arrange hotel and transportation reservations for visiting salesreps. Most firms permit purchasing personnel to buy lunches for suppliers and extend other courtesies. A few firms even remember suppliers with a Christmas gift of nominal value.

The Ford Motor Company even has a supplier "board of appeal" in its corporate purchasing office. Any vendor who feels that a Ford buyer was unfair can carry a complaint to this group which will then investigate and make certain that Ford policies toward suppliers are carried out in a fair and consistent fashion.

Why do they go to the trouble? Suppliers not only can use a company's products but they also may become some of the company's biggest boosters if they are sold on the company as a customer. Equally important, suppliers can be an important source of cost-reduction ideas.

Cases

CASE 17–1. COLONIAL LAUNDRY EQUIPMENT COMPANY

Coping with supplier labor trouble

Production will shut down at the Colonial Laundry Equipment Company's main plant in Louisville, Kentucky, unless the company's purchasing director, Kenneth Caldwell, can achieve "the impossible." Colonial makes coin-operated washing machines for use in apartment buildings and stores. The transmission housing in its product is made from a gray-iron casting that the company buys from the Allied Foundry Company.

Allied has now been shut down by a strike. Its union, the United Foundry Workers, is demanding a wage increase of 50 cents per hour for its members. Allied insists that it cannot afford any increase at all and cites its shrinking profit margins and the price cutting currently prevalent in the industry as evidence. Caldwell believes that the strike may be a long one, not only because the company and union are so far apart on a wage settlement but also because Allied's labor relations have never been too placid. The UFW local at Allied is unusually beligerent, according to Allied's management. In addition, Caldwell suspects that the company's labor relations policies have been a little heavy-handed.

Allied has suffered from a series of one-day walkouts over the past year. In addition, its quality has suffered; apparently some of its workers no longer take any pride in their work. For these reasons, Colonial's inventories of castings are somewhat lower than they would be otherwise. Although Caldwell was aware of the fact that the company's union contract expired on June 30 and that a strike was likely on July 1, he was unable to accumulate more than one week's inventory of castings. He had hoped to get at least three weeks ahead, which would take up all available storage space at the Colonial plant.

Because Allied had definitely been slipping on both quality and delivery, Colonial had already solicited bids from other foundries, as follows:

Supplier	Price	Cost of patterns	Delivery promise after receipt of order (weekly)
Consolidated Gray Iron	$2.65	$1,950	8
Archer Foundry	3.10	1,800	6
Young Industries	2.40	2,200	6

Colonial is currently paying Allied $2.20 per casting. Allied's price and its competitors' bids all are based on shipment of approximately 4,000 castings per month in lots of 1,000, and each supplier would be willing to quote the same price for a volume as low as 2,000 castings per month. Caldwell has hesitated to switch sources previously because he was unable to find a supplier who could meet Allied's price. He hoped that Allied would straighten out its problems without a price increase. Now he doubts that Allied will be able to hold to the $2.20 price, since the settlement of its strike will be too costly to permit it to do so. Caldwell expects a price increase of at least 10 cents after Allied settles with the union.

Of course, Caldwell has no idea when the settlement will be made, but he doubts that Allied's workers will still be on strike in six weeks, when he can get his first castings from Archer or Young if he places an order with them now. This is not Caldwell's only alternative, however. The patterns that Allied uses were paid for by Colonial. If Caldwell can get them from the Allied plant, he can cut the lead time needed to start up a new source by at least several weeks.

None of the other foundries can give Caldwell a firm promise as to when it can start production with Allied's patterns, since none of them has ever seen the patterns. It might be possible to use them without any rework at all, or it might be necessary to make substantial changes. Nor can the other vendors be held to the prices they have quoted if they use Allied's patterns. Their quotations are based on patterns of their own design. But Caldwell doubts that there would be more than a small price increase were Archer, Young, or Consolidated to use Allied's patterns.

However, Caldwell does have another problem, even if he can get the patterns out and they can be used. If Archer, Young, or Consolidated work hard to deliver castings as promptly as possible during Allied's strike, they naturally expect some reward in the form of future business. They believe it would be unfair to extend themselves to help Colonial in an emergency and then promptly lose the business once Allied settled its strike. On the other hand, Allied has been supplying Colonial for several years, and except for occasional difficulties resulting from its poor labor relations, it has been a dependable, low-cost supplier. Also, it is possible that Allied's competitors may likewise be faced with labor problems and higher costs in the next six months when their union contracts expire.

Questions

1. What course of action do you recommend that Caldwell follow to cope with the shortage of castings?
2. What should he do after Allied's strike has been settled?
3. What, if anything, could he have done to prevent these difficulties from arising?

CASE 17–2. JOHNSON INSTRUMENT COMPANY

Gifts and entertainment from suppliers

Johnson Instrument Company manufactures a line of precision instruments that have both civilian and military applications. Because of its defense business, the company is especially careful to keep its relations with suppliers "as clean as a hound's tooth." It takes great pains to get competitive bids on every order. When a contract is not placed with the low bidder, an explanation is written into the purchase record so that government contract auditors will know there has been no collusion.

Naturally, the company has a firm policy prohibiting any of its employees to accept gifts or gratuities from suppliers. The only exceptions to this rule are business lunches and advertising novelties of nominal value. Johnson Instrument does not even like to have its suppliers pay for all lunches. Its materials executives have expense accounts and are expected to pick up their fair share of the checks.

Alice Browning is one of the company's buyers. She handles a wide variety of maintenance, repair, and operating supplies, including all of the lumber used by the plant. One of the major suppliers is the Warren Lumber Company, a well-known local firm with a deserved reputation for integrity and dependability. Browning is a dedicated baseball fan, and Ned Warren, the young sales manager of Warren Lumber, knows it. Warren is also familiar with Johnson's policy on gifts and has never offered Browning any gift of more than nominal value at Christmas.

Two days before the World Series, Browning receives two box seat tickets for a weekend game, with this note:

> DEAR ALICE:
> I intended to use these myself. Unfortunately, I had forgotten that my brother and sister-in-law are coming to stay with us for the weekend. They're not interested in baseball, and at this late date I don't think I could get tickets for them anyway. So it looks as if I'm going to miss the game. I know how crazy you are about baseball. Why don't you use them?
>
> > Cordially,
> > NED

Needless to say, Browning would very much like to go to the game. But there is no doubt that the tickets are of more than nominal value. The list price is $10 each, and they're actually worth more, since scalpers are selling them for as much as $20. Not only would it be against the company's policy for her to accept the tickets, but Browning is honest enough to admit to herself that while Warren may have sent her the tickets as a gesture of friendship, he will undoubtedly regard them as a legitimate deduction for "sales expense" and not as a personal gift.

On the other hand, Browning is equally certain that the gift is not going to influence her buying decisions in any way. Warren is her lowest cost lumber supplier (in fact, he is the only major lumber supplier in the area), and Browning will not buy any more lumber than what the plant requires, regardless of how much she likes Warren. In addition, Browning can say with complete objectivity that she wouldn't think of jeopardizing her reputation or integrity for the sake of $20 worth of baseball tickets. If she returns the tickets to Warren, she is saying in effect, "This $20 gift will corrupt me." Also she is, by implication, insulting Warren, since she is then tacitly accusing Warren of trying to bribe her when, in fact, Warren might have no such intention. So, in returning the tickets, Browning might well jeopardize what has been an excellent business relationship between Warren and herself.

Questions

1. What should Browning do?
2. If Warren should offer to let Browning and/or other employees of Johnson's purchasing department make personal purchases of lumber and other supplies at the same wholesale prices paid by the company, would it be ethical for Browning to accept this offer? Should Browning attempt to solicit such a discount for personal purchases?

CASE 17–3. HARRISON MACHINERY CORPORATION

Conflict between reciprocity and "fair trade"

Harrison Machinery Corporation is a leading producer of equipment used in the construction industry. Much of the company's output is sold to contractors in the United States and abroad, but a substantial share is also sold to various manufacturers in the United States who use the equipment in their own maintenance and construction departments. Harrison has an integrated materials department. It is headed by a corporate materials manager, Jean Hyde. Hyde directs a small staff at corporate headquarters and is also functionally responsible for materials management at the company's 13 decentralized plants. Each plant has its own purchasing agent or materials manager who reports to the plant or division manager.

Most purchases are made at the plant level, and Hyde is responsible only for broad policies and procedures. However, a substantial part of the corporation's purchasing is done at the corporate office. In general, most items that are sold on a "national account" basis are at least negotiated at corporate headquarters; on other items, Hyde's staff may actually issue purchase orders. To be handled by the corporate materials staff, an item must meet one of the following criteria:

1. More than one Harrison plant uses the item, and central purchasing can get a lower price by combining the requirements of several plants. For this reason and no other, the central staff at Harrison

corporate headquarters buys various production parts that are common to a number of Harrison products.

2. The item is "customer sensitive." Corporate purchasing buys all products used in significant amounts which are manufactured by Harrison customers. The corporate purchasing staff works closely with the corporate marketing staff on reciprocal arrangements. For example, Harrison's steel purchases are awarded on the basis of reciprocal purchases of Harrison's products by the various steel companies. From time to time, Hyde has deviated from this policy. As she says, "I won't buy from a company just because it buys Harrison products. Every supplier, including suppliers who are already customers, has to earn our business and give us the quality, price, and delivery we want and need." Buy Hyde admits that since steel prices are identical and that all of the major firms offer comparable quality and delivery, she winds up buying steel pretty much on a reciprocal basis.

On occasion, Hyde has purchased foreign steel at prices 5 to 10 percent below those offered by American firms and so far has had no complaints from American suppliers. One reason for this, Hyde is the first to admit, is that they just haven't known about it. None of her American suppliers is so well informed as to Harrison's precise needs that Hyde does not have some flexibility. The foreign steel purchases were made during a period when both the steel industry and its customers were girding themselves for an industrywide steel strike. So Hyde would have had a good excuse for buying the foreign steel had one of the steel suppliers heard about it.

Some of the commodities that Hyde's staff buys meet both criteria for central office purchase: it is not only the cheapest way to buy them but also a practical way for the company to earn "reciprocal credit" among its customers. Fluorescent light bulbs are a good example. Harrison spends about $90,000 per year on fluorescent light bulbs used in its various factories and offices. This business is split among three major light bulb producers, all of whom are Harrison customers. Traditionally, the division of business has been in direct proportion to the importance of the light bulb manufacturer as a Harrison customer. The division is based on the previous year's reciprocal sales. For example, Harrison is now buying about half of its bulbs from one of the three firms and the balance of the business is shared almost equally by the other two firms.

Harrison's sales records show that the three light bulb manufacturers purchase about $800,000 worth of Harrison products each year. Consolidated Electric accounts for 50 percent of this, while the other two manufacturers each purchase about $200,000 worth of Harrison products. Consequently, Harrison has traditionally divided its bulb purchases on a 50–25–25 basis, with Consolidated getting the lion's share. Harrison need not have divided its purchases so precisely. None

of the three bulb manufacturers knew exactly what its relative importance was as a Harrison customer. As long as each got a reasonable
share of the Harrison business, there probably would not have been
any complaints. But Harrison had no incentive to do anything other
than give its customer its fair share of reciprocal business. All three
manufacturers offer excellent quality and service and charge identical
prices.

By buying directly from the "national sales office" of each of the
three firms, Harrison is able to get the maximum discount. This discount brings Harrison's prices down to a level that is only about 10
percent higher than that which the light bulb manufacturers charge
their own distributors.

Harrison formerly bought bulbs from local distributors. However,
several years ago, the bulb manufacturers set up national accounts
sales offices that catered especially to the needs of large corporations
like Harrison that operated plants all over the country. These industrial users were often more important as customers than many distributors and they had long been pressing the bulb manufacturers for
more favorable prices. Moreover, the large users do not need many of
the services offered by the distributor, and the bulb manufacturers can
enjoy bigger profits if they bypass their distributors on such sales.
Sales to national accounts also give the bulb manufacturers valuable
statistics so that they may know if they are getting their share of reciprocal sales from their suppliers.

The distributor in Harrison's area felt the loss of business keenly
when Harrison switched over to buying directly from the light bulb
manufacturers. Six months ago, this distributor presented one of Harrison's buyers with an attractive proposition which Hyde finally approved. The distributor agreed to sell light bulbs to Harrison at a price
that was only 5 percent above the distributor's cost and 5 percent
below the price charged Harrison by the bulb manufacturers. The
distributor pledged Harrison to confidence, however. His agreement
with the manufacturer requires him to sell light bulbs according to a
price schedule that is set by the manufacturer. The schedule allows
the distributor approximately 25 percent over cost for most accounts.
The distributor can do business with Harrison for much less because of
Harrison's enormous volume. Also, this represents marginal business
to him and any profit he makes is "gravy." Both Harrison and the light
bulb distributor benefit from the new arrangement and, of course,
Harrison is continuing to use its customers' products even though it is
not buying them directly.

However, Consolidated Electric, the biggest light bulb manufacturer, recently asked Hyde why she was no longer buying its light
bulbs. The national accounts sales manager of Consolidated politely
pointed out that Consolidated was continuing to buy Harrison's prod-

ucts and he could see no reason why Harrison should not reciprocate. He asked Hyde if she had any reason to consider Consolidated's service or quality to be inferior to that of its competitors. As he put it, "I don't think you should buy our products just because we buy your products. However, as long as our price, quality and service are as good as our competitors, I think you should definitely consider us when you are buying fluorescent light bulbs. Yet, our records show that you have not bought a single bulb from us for six months now. What is wrong? If our service or quality has fallen down we want to hear about it. On the other hand, if it hasn't, I think you owe us some explanation."

Question

What are the issues in this case? How can Hyde best resolve them?

18

Control of
administrative costs

A company with 2,000 employees may have 100 persons working in its various materials management activities: purchasing, production control, traffic, and so on. More than 85 percent of these jobs are predominantly clerical even in the majority of organizations where most of the clerical drudgery has seemingly been taken over by the computer. A fantastic number of labor hours are devoted to filling out thousands of different forms, keeping records, and the like. One company with about 5,000 employees found that its materials personnel filled out more than one million pieces of paper a year. The computer is taking over much of the processing of this paperwork, but everything that goes into the computer is usually written on a piece of paper and is then keypunched. So while the computer speeds analysis of business data, it may in effect mean more paperwork.

PAPERWORK IS COSTLY

All surveys show that paperwork in materials management is increasing much faster than general business activities. The costs of this paperwork are obviously substantial. It probably costs at least 25 cents to fill out each purchase requisition, request for quotation, purchase order, receiving report, inspection report, and accounts payable voucher, and 15 cents for posting each inventory record and keypunching each tabulating card. Even a small company will issue thousands of purchase requisitions per year. Since each requisition may generate a need for one or more quotation requests, purchase orders, and so on, clerical costs can easily mushroom.

Accountants sometimes divide a materials department's total operating costs by the output of some key document, such as a purchase order. Such comparisons have limited usefulness as barometers of operating efficiency, but they can dramatically illustrate the high cost of paperwork. For example, the writer once estimated that it cost the purchasing department of Ford Division of Ford Motor Company $58 to issue each of its purchase orders. The full cost of carrying an inventory of medical-surgical supplies in a large hospital for one year is often equal to the value of the inventory itself. Most of the carrying cost is represented by salaries paid to clerks and other stores personnel whose job is mostly record keeping.

Need for paperwork. Is all this paperwork necessary? Much of it is. The materials management process inherently involves a lot of detail. A company with only a few hundred employees will have thousands of different items that must be controlled in some fashion, while a big corporation may have hundreds of thousands of items to control. Records must be kept for each item. If a company is to do a first-rate job of materials management, it must have systems designed to bring any deviation from routine to the attention of the materials manager immediately.

It behooves each materials manager to get the information he or she needs for making decisions with a minimum of paperwork and clerical work force. In so doing, he helps achieve one of his primary objectives: to manage materials with minimum operating cost. This in itself is adequate motivation for a program to eliminate clerical effort through improved forms and procedures and mechanization. But managers should be interested in reducing the enormous amount of clerical effort required in materials management even if they were able to persuade clerks to work without pay.

Effect on materials. The bigger the clerical work force, the more complex the materials organization structure inevitably becomes. Each supervisor has a limited span of control. As the work force grows, more supervisors are required; inevitably more levels of organization are needed. The organization becomes progressively more complex. Top materials managers are forced to devote an increasing amount of their time to managing people rather than managing materials. This reduces their efficiency.

In a large, complex organization, procedures for transmitting information to make decisions become cumbersome and time-consuming. All other factors being equal, a small organization can always move faster than a big one. In materials management, speedy transmission of information permits faster materials cycles with lower inventories and less obsolescence.

When clerks are eliminated through improvements in procedures or through mechanization, it is not just the simple organization structure that permits faster flow of information. The new methods can speed data transmission directly, since they are inherently faster. For example, if a company computes its inventory balance by manually totaling and extending the balances on thousands of record cards, the job will probably take a week or two, regardless of how many clerks are assigned to it. On the other hand, if inventory records are kept on computer tape, it is easy to get daily inventory reports.

Reduction of errors.   Not only do people require far more management effort than machines do, but they also are more prone to make mistakes. If a clerk is posting hundreds of inventory records each day, it is inevitable that he will occasionally make an error. Most such errors can be detected by having the work double-checked by another person. But management can be certain that on rare occasions an error will go through undetected, regardless of how many different persons try to spot it. A clerk will enter "100" as an inventory balance when he should enter "10," or a form will be mislaid and he will simply overlook an item entirely. If the error is not detected, the item will not be available when it should be, and a costly shutdown may result.

Companies will have problems of this sort as long as they have employees, but they can reduce the chances for error by reducing the number of times basic data must be transcribed by human beings and by giving as much of the job as possible to machines. No machine can actually think, but it can perform repetitive operations without fatigue and with built-in controls that detect any errors that might occur.

CLERICAL QUALITY CONTROL

Clerical errors are a perpetual source of nightmares for materials managers. There are thousands of opportunities for such errors to be made every day. And many of them can be serious—a purchase order is directed to the wrong vendor, a shipment is routed to a destination where it is not needed, and incorrect amount of material is ordered, and so on. Procedures in materials departments are very carefully designed to minimize errors, but a few inevitably sneak through the best designed system. All that the materials manager can do is devise the best system she can afford and then be certain that it operates the way it should.

Design of the system.   Materials managers do not always like to admit it, but every paperwork system represents a compromise among conflicting objectives. The simple fact is that the manager can spend only so much to prevent errors, and it is never economic to have a system that is so foolproof that all probability of error is eliminated. In the ideal system, the marginal cost of preventing errors is roughly equal to the losses suffered from errors.

Suppose, for example, that a company presently suffers from one serious clerical error in the purchasing department each month. It guesses that it suffers from perhaps a hundred or more other minor errors. Many of these are never detected, since they create no problems. The materials manager is convinced that he or she has the best possible procedures for error prevention that he can afford with present budget. The employees are conscientious and motivated and, in general, are doing a satisfactory job.

The materials manager believes that the only way to reduce errors is by hiring an extra clerk to proofread key forms. If this is done, the number of important errors will decline by about 50 percent. Instead of 12 serious errors per year, there will be just 6. Should the materials manager add the extra error checker to the payroll? To decide, balance the cost of the extra employee against the benefit. If the checker's salary and fringe benefits add up to $9,000 per year, then errors must be worth $5,000 each to the materials manager to justify the extra employee to eliminate them. They may not be worth this much; if so, in theory, the materials manager should not hire the extra checker. In practice, it might be done anyway. Errors are visible and very embarassing. There are noneconomic reasons why the materials manager would try to eliminate them. In any event, an extra clerk soon gets built into the budget structure and is readily accepted.

Monitoring the process. When the materials manager is convinced that she has the best system she can afford, she should still look for better ways to do the job. But the day-to-day job is largely control—making certain that the system operates the way it should. Quality control principles can be applied to such systems just as if they were tangible products. In both cases, the concept is based on the principle that a process will fluctuate at random within some predetermined case when it is "in control." When it moves out of this range, it is "out of control" and should be corrected.

The process is monitored with a control chart on which sample data are periodically plotted. In industrial quality control, an inspector periodically checks a group of parts and plots the results. In paperwork quality control, the procedure is essentially the same: a sample of paperwork is inspected periodically, and the results are tabulated and plotted.

As in statistical quality control, the process will fluctuate at random in a range that is three standard deviations around the mean. The mean is found experimentally. Suppose that, over a long period of time, as a materials manager you make random checks of your paper flow, comparing actual error with possible errors. You discover that three and one-half errors are made in every 100 occurrences and are satisfied that this is normal behavior of the process. You recognize, however, that the error percentage will fluctuate at random around this mean.

You know from your study of statistics that 99.72 percent of all occurrences will fall within three standard deviations of a normal distribution. You expect to control your process by periodically inspecting a sample of paperwork where there are 100 opportunities to make an error. You expect on the average to find three and one-half errors in the sample. You calculate your expected standard deviation with the formula

$$s = \sqrt{\frac{P(1 - P)}{n}},$$

where P = the percent defective and n = number of observations.

$$s = \sqrt{\frac{0.035(1 - 0.035)}{100}} = 0.0184.$$

If one standard deviation is 0.0184, then three standard deviations is equal to about 0.55. Therefore, the upper control limit of the process becomes 0.09—the mean defective of 0.035 plus three standard deviations, or 0.055. Thus, 100 samples drawn from your process can contain as many as nine defectives. However, the probability that the process is going out of control increases as you drift away from the expected mean. This shows up clearly on the control chart shown in Figure 18–1. The first sample drawn from the process has 7.5 percent defectives. This warns management that while the process may not yet be out of control, it could be headed in that direction. Observation 2

FIGURE 18–1

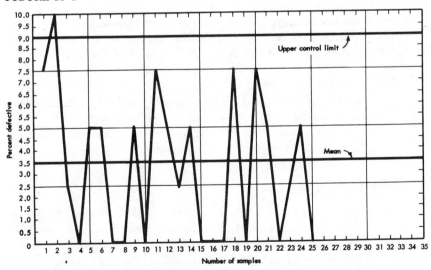

Control limits can be established for statistical quality control of paperwork just as they can be used to monitor manufacturing processes. In this example, an average of three and one-half errors is expected in each sample. When the paperwork process is "in control," errors will fluctuate at random between a maximum of nine errors per sample and a minimum of no errors. If more than nine errors are made in a sample, something has gone wrong, and management should investigate.

confirms this suspicion; the defective rate is 10 percent and beyond the upper control limit. Something is obviously wrong; management would investigate and take corrective measures. Observation 3 indicates that the process is back in control again. Observation 4 indicates no defectives whatever. This is the effective lower control limit. When the process goes down to this limit, management might also investigate—not to find out what went wrong but to find out what has changed. Sometimes improvements sneak into the process undetected. They may disappear spontaneously unless management discovers them and incorporates them into operating procedures. Statistical quality control not only is a device to detect processing faults but also can detect changes that help improve the process. When the process breaks through the lower control limit, the odds heavily favor some favorable change having occurred that should be investigated. The behavior of the process as plotted in Figure 18–1 implies that the true mean of the process is now lower than the original estimate of 3.5 percent. Note that a majority of observations fall below 3.5 percent.

PROCEDURES TO CUT COSTS

In bigger organizations, the materials manager may have an administrative assistant (sometimes even an entire staff department) whose job is largely devoted to improving forms and procedures. Periodically, each form and report used should "stand trial for its life." If its existence cannot be justified, it should be eliminated. Even in the best managed departments, such "trials" occasionally uncover paperwork that can be eliminated. Conditions change but if there is no control the obsolete forms and procedures will continue anyway unless someone does something about them. Periodic reviews are valuable even if they do not reveal any paperwork that can be eliminated. They can alert management to savings in clerical time, which can result from such improvements as special ordering procedures, combining of forms, and changes in forms design.

Special ordering procedures

Transactions in purchasing departments vary widely. Consecutively numbered purchase orders may be issued for a $20,000 machine tool, a $10 charge to fix a flat tire on a company truck, and a contract to purchase $100,000 worth of production parts. Different types of orders warrant different treatment if they are to get the control they deserve without excessive paperwork. This can be done with blanket orders, "stockless" purchasing, cash pickup orders, and similar procedures.

Blanket orders. Items that are used regularly often require a dozen or more purchases a year. Each time inventory drops to the reorder point, the stores department issues a requisition that touches off a complete purchase transaction. A company can cut paperwork, of course, by ordering less often and in larger quantities, but this is an expensive solution to the problem. Increased inventory carrying cost may more than offset the savings in paperwork. Blanket orders offer a better solution. The buyer issues an order good for a year's requirements to be shipped "as released." Then, whenever stock of material runs low, the buyer simply telephones the supplier and asks him to ship against the outstanding blanket order.

Blanket orders help save on repeat items in four ways:

1. *They usually reduce paperwork.* A single blanket order is substituted for many individual orders. There is some saving in paperwork even when the buyer sends written release forms (as is customary on important purchases) to the supplier each time she wants a shipment. In this case the buyer still is relieved of the need to get quotations for each transaction. And, in most cases, the releasing procedure is less complex than the ordering procedure.

2. *They save the time of skilled buyers.* Once a blanket order is placed, the job of ordering can be transferred from a skilled (and highly paid) buyer to a clerk (or even to a machine, if the company has electronic data processing equipment). The clerk simply writes out a release against the blanket order and mails it to the supplier.

In some cases, it is convenient for the user of the material to do his own ordering—especially in cases where the user is in charge of the inventory. For example, a hospital materials manager may establish a blanket order for drugs, but the inventory is under the direct control of the hospital pharmacist who then has authority to issue releases against the blanket order.

3. *They facilitate price negotiation.* Suppliers often will quote lower prices when they are bidding for a year's requirements rather than for a single order. Multiplant companies can go even further; they can combine requirements for all plants on a single blanket order in order to maximize their buying power.

4. *They permit closer inventory control.* Blanket orders help companies operate with shorter lead times and lower inventories. If they can get an order for a year's requirements, suppliers often can be persuaded to stock the material so it is available for immediate delivery. This permits the buyer to operate hand to mouth, with almost no safety stock.

"Stockless" purchasing. This term is misleading but the practice is still worthwhile. With "stockless" purchasing, there is still inventory but the supplier carries it rather than the purchaser. A naïve purchaser may think this is the same as getting something for nothing. It isn't. The cost of carrying inventory is very real and someone has to carry it. If a supplier carries extra stock to protect a customer because the

customer depends on this inventory, then the customer must obviously indirectly pay the supplier for carrying the inventory. There is no free lunch.

Or is there a free lunch? A stockless purchasing agreement (also sometimes called a *systems contract*) is a special type of blanket order that does eliminate some steps in the materials management process and reduce costs for both buyer and seller. Here are some of its ramifications:

1. *The supplier may deliver directly to individual users in the buyer's organization, bypassing the buyer's storeroom.* From the buyer's point of view, an intermediate level of inventory is eliminated. As long as this is not offset by an increase in the separate inventories that are maintained (both formally and informally) in the user areas, there is indeed a net reduction in the buyer's inventory investment, which is how the term "stockless" purchasing came into being. However, the supplier must do an extra-careful job which often requires additional inventory if user needs are to be served promptly without the buffer stock that the buyer would otherwise carry in a general stores area.

2. *The materials management department is no longer a "middleman" on routine transactions.* The major saving comes from this reduction of administrative costs. The purchasing department negotiates the stockless purchasing agreement or systems contract like any conventional blanket order. It winds up with an agreement that it will buy all of the organization's requirements for a particular group of related items (e.g., office supplies) from a particular supplier at a well-defined schedule of prices for some period of time. Once this agreement is made, the using departments are allowed to do their own "buying." When they need something that falls within their agreement, they simply order directly from the supplier and material is delivered to them. The supplier typically submits a consolidated bill to the buyer's organization monthly. This is reviewed in accounts payable and compared with the prices specified on the agreement and receiving reports to make certain that everything is in order. The major saving comes from eliminating most of the intermediate transactions involving purchasing and other materials management activities.

Stockless purchasing and systems contracts provide the advantages of centralized purchasing (with professional negotiation of a basic agreement covering the organization's total needs) without incurring the disadvantage of excessive paperwork on relatively minor transactions. The technique should be limited to relatively minor supply purchases that are made as the need arises. Office supplies and similar items are good candidates. Stockless purchasing should not be used for major purchases.

Cash pickup orders. While stockless purchasing contracts are ideal for low-value purchases for which there is continuing demand, they cannot be universally applied to all small orders. Every organization makes hundreds and even thousands of small purchases that simply cannot be anticipated in advance. It may not be practical to negotiate systems contracts to cover them. Yet if these low-value purchases are handled in conventional fashion, the cost of making the purchase will often exceed the value of the item that is being bought. Few organizations can process the paperwork necessary for a complete purchase transaction for much less than $10. And a typical supplier probably loses money on every conventional order it receives with a value of $10 or less. Small orders are bad news for both buyer and seller. Yet, of necessity, a substantial percentage of the orders issued (50 percent in many smaller companies and 25 percent in big corporations) are for $50 or less. Even though such orders may comprise less than 5 percent of total expenditures, they can consume a disproportionate share of the total administrative and clerical expenses.

With conventional purchasing procedures, an order for a $5 item will get the same administrative treatment as a major order. Special procedures help bypass costly administrative controls on small orders. One of the simplest is merely to authorize a supplier to ship and bill on the basis of a telephone order. The only records of the transaction are the requisition and the receiving report. No purchase order is issued; the purchase is cleared by matching the requisition, the receiving report, and the supplier's invoice.

Another short cut eliminates the invoicing process; the buyer pays cash for the order. Typical is the small-order procedure used by Argus Cameras, Inc., for local purchases (see Figure 18–2). The purchase requisition doubles as a purchase order. When the buyer gets it, he or she telephones the order to the supplier, fills in the supplier's name and price on the requisition, and makes out a check to pay for the order. When the supplier delivers, the check and one copy of the purchase order requisition are ready for pickup at Argus's receiving dock.

"Blank check" orders. Other companies go one step further. In effect, they give the supplier a blank check for purchases that may amount to as much as $1,000. Typically, the buyer's data processing system automatically generates a purchase order when inventory of a particular item reaches the reorder point. A purchase order form is automatically printed out. Into it is incorporated a bank draft made out in the supplier's favor. When the supplier delivers the item, it fills in the bank draft for the amount due and then deposits the draft in its own bank on the date called for on the payment instructions that are enclosed with the purchase order. The bank draft is usually limited to $500–$1,000 in order to limit the buyer's potential liability. Technically, it is a "draft" rather than a "check." If the seller does not deliver material satisfactory to the buyer, the draft may be rejected by the buyer. Otherwise, the draft works just like a blank check. Neither

FIGURE 18–2
Small order purchase requisition form

| ACCOUNT NO | | A/P | REQ. NO. **6502** | WRITTEN BY | DELIVER TO | STD. COST | V/R |

DATE

MISCELLANEOUS PURCHASE REQUISITION

1. PREPARE ONLY FOR NON–PRODUCTIVE PURCHASES.
2. FILL IN ALL NECESSARY INFORMATION IN WHITE AREAS OF THE REQUISITION.
3. REMOVE YOUR FOLLOW–UP COPY AND FORWARD TO PURCHASING DEPARTMENT.

PURCHASE ORDER ☐
LOCAL ORDER ☐

No. ▨▨▨▨▨

THIS NUMBER MUST APPEAR ON INVOICE AND PACKING SLIP

DATE OF ORDER

SHIP TO
ARGUS CAMERAS
ANN ARBOR, MICHIGAN

VENDOR ADDRESS

DIRECTOR OF PURCHASING

BUYER

FOR MICHIGAN SALES AND/OR USE TAX THIS ORDER IS: TAXABLE ☐ NON–TAXABLE ☐

THIS ORDER IS CONFIRMING: RECEIPT ☐ WIRE ☐ PHONE ☐ SALESMAN ☐ _____ ☐

| TERMS | F.O.B. | SHIP VIA | DELIVERY: |

QUANTITY	UNITS	DESCRIPTION	PRICE

REQUIRED DELIVERY BY: DEPARTMENTAL AUTHORIZATION   DATE IN PURCHASING

SPECIAL INSTRUCTIONS AND/OR SUGGESTED VENDOR:

PURCHASING FOLLOW-UP

REQ. NO.	AMOUNT
GROSS AMOUNT	
CASH DISCOUNT (3704)	
EXCISE TAX	
SALES TAX	
TOTAL AMOUNT THIS ORDER	

DATE

argus cameras
Division of Sylvania Electric Products Inc.
Ann Arbor, Michigan
CAMERAS AND OPTICAL INSTRUMENTS

74–100
764

No. 13229

PAY TO THE ORDER OF _____

NOT VALID IN EXCESS OF $100.00

PAY EXACTLY _____ DOLLARS _____ CENTS $ _____   AMOUNT

ANN ARBOR BANK
ANN ARBOR, MICH.

00 - 301014 - 3

AUTHORIZED SIGNATURE
PURCHASE ACCOUNT

This Argus Cameras purchase requisition doubles as purchase order on small orders. The buyer phones the order, and the supplier gets a copy and payment upon delivery.

buyer nor supplier need bother processing an invoice for the material. Some companies have succeeded in reducing the number of purchase invoices they process by as much as 75 to 80 percent using this "blank check" system. In addition, they have sometimes succeeded in persuading suppliers to give them an extra discount on their purchases. Suppliers are willing to do this both because of the saving in paperwork for them but, even more importantly, because they get paid immediately with cash orders and do not have to wait 30 days or even more for their money.

Despite their advantages, many managers view special small-order procedures with mixed enthusiasm. They like to eliminate paperwork, but they are afraid that small orders will encourage unnecessary expenditures, discourage grouping of orders that might reduce costs even more, or stimulate a lax environment where there will be repeated last-minute "emergencies" calling for small orders. Companies that do have small-order procedures maintain extremely close control over them for these and other reasons.

Combining forms

Certain data are repeated again and again in materials transactions. Part numbers and names appear on almost every form used in every department in a company. Supplier names appear on buy records and quotation requests and are repeated on numerous other forms, including purchase orders, receiving reports, inspection reports, inventory records, and so on. Order quantities and prices similarly are repeated again and again.

Each time information is transcribed, not only is clerical cost incurred but a costly error is risked. Thus it pays to combine forms to make use of common information whenever possible. This can be done both by making one form do several jobs and by preparing different forms with a single, simultaneous operation. The traveling requisition is a good example of the former; combination purchase order, receiving-report forms and various duplicating techniques are good examples of the latter.

The traveling requisition. With conventional procedures, a separate requisition is filled out to authorize each purchase of an item. This means that common date, such as item number, description of the item, and so on, will be copied over and over again in requisitioning frequently used items. The traveling requisition is larger than the conventional requisition form and also is made of heavier paper. A permanent traveling requisition is kept for each item on stock (see Figure 18–3). On it is space for common data and also for data specifically describing a particular purchase.

When stock drops to the reorder point the stores clerk pulls out the traveling requisition from the file and sends it to the buyer. After the

578

FIGURE 18–3

Traveling requisition form

54612	Impeller Assembly, part no. 625	ORDER POINT	1
	Type 316 Elc Stainless Steel	E.O.Q.	2
	22" diameter, 3 vane, right hand	PURCHASE UNIT	ea
		ISSUE UNIT	ea

BY REQUISITIONER			BY PURCHASER						
REQUIRED		CHARGE NO.	P. O. NO.	V E N	PRICE	TERMS	F.O.B.	#	VENDOR
DATE	QTY.								
								1	City Supply Co.
6/4/—	2	160401	9-16/20	1	320 ºº	2/10/30	St. Louis	2	ABC Dist.
10/7/—	2	160401	9-19760	4	318 ºº	2/10/30	Baltimore	3	J. Doe & Co.
3/4/—	2	160401	9-13240	3	300 ºº	net	Bartow	4	State Mfg. Co.
								5	
								6	
								7	
								8	
							LOCATION		3R4-5
							EQUIPMENT		
							For Type 2,		
							Model B, Pump		

In a typical traveling requisition form, the requisitioner fills in data on the left of the card, and the purchaser acts on this data and returns the form to the requisitioner, who files it until stocks drop again to the reorder point.

purchase is made, the buyer or clerk posts the order data to the requisition, which travels back to the stores clerk. He notes that the purchase has been made and then refiles it until it is needed for the next purchase. Since the traveling requisition form provides a complete purchase history, some buyers also use it as a purchase record. Other buyers, particularly of commodities with high dollar volume, prefer to keep separate purchase records. They wish to keep a more detailed record than is possible on the traveling requisition, and they often are afraid that stores personnel or others will reveal competitive price data to favored suppliers.

Occasionally, traveling requisitions also double as inventory records. It is not difficult to include space for stores receipts and withdrawals on the form. Most companies prefer to post to a separate stores record, however. Then, if the traveling requisition is lost, there is still a basic record of the item in the stockroom.

Other combination forms. With electric typewriters, which can make about ten reasonably clear carbon copies, it is possible to combine physically many forms that use common data. Most common is the purchase order–receiving report, which consists of an 8″ × 10″ copy "snap-out" type of form with one-time carbon paper inserted. The first four or five copies of the form are a conventional purchase-order set. The last copies become the receiving report. Since most of the basic purchase-order data is also needed for the receiving report, this combination of forms can save a considerable amount of typing. It does not completely eliminate the need for separate receiving reports, however. Many orders are not completed in a single shipment, and, of course, a separate receiving report is needed for each shipment.

In similar fashion, many companies have a combined receiving report and inspection report or inspection report-move ticket. The combination can also be achieved with duplicating equipment. For example, a purchase order set might include a duplicate master, which in turn is used with a second master to run off copies of receiving reports and other documents.

Forms design

The materials department usually does not design its own forms. Larger companies have separate "office services" or "procedures" departments (usually as a staff activity reporting to the controller) staffed with forms and procedures experts who serve the entire company. Smaller companies usually rely on their forms suppliers to assist them in design.

The materials department should naturally make use of any help it can get in designing forms. However, the materials manager should never forget that she—not the manager of the procedures group—is ultimately responsible for every phase of administering her department, including its forms and procedures. Therefore the materials manager should be familiar with the general principles of forms design, since she is responsible for and should approve every form her department uses.

Principles. A good form transmits needed information at minimum cost. The forms designer should observe six principles:

1. *Keep design as simple as possible.* The more complex the form, the more difficult (and costly) will be its use. Procedures and forms should be as foolproof as possible.

2. *Allow adequate space.* Forms that are tight on space are inefficient. If data is filled in by typewriter, there should be space between lines equal to typewriter double spacing. If the form is filled in with pencil (and this may be preferable because it eliminates the need to type a "finished" copy from a rough, handwritten copy), there should be enough space for rather large handwriting and rather lengthy descriptions.

3. *Keep copies to a minimum.* Naturally everyone vitally concerned with a transaction should get a copy of the form, but copies never should go to persons or departments with only occasional interest in the transactions. Instead, if anything, such persons should have

forms directed through them—that is, they receive the executed form, look at it, and then pass it on to someone who actually uses the information it contains.

4. *"Try each form for its life" at least once a year.* Forms and procedures frequently become obsolete, but sometimes they live on simply because no one periodically reviews their application to make certain that there still is good reason for their existence.

5. *Reduce handwritten data to an absolute minimum.* Use multiple-choice answers on a form when there are a limited number of alternatives; then all the clerk need do is check the appropriate one. If the information required should change, do not be afraid to scrap existing forms and change the design to accommodate the new data. The cost of the paper and printing is negligible compared to the cost of the time of those who fill out the forms.

6. *Keep data in sequence.* Information on a form should be listed in the sequence in which it naturally comes to the person filling in the form. If a form moves from department to department, the first department using the form should fill in the top part of the form, with succeeding departments filling in information in sequence.

Design criteria. Typewritten forms should be laid out to minimize carriage returns, positioning, and spacing required to type in the data. Each of these has a price in keystrokes:

Carriage return	5 keystrokes
Horizontal space	1 keystroke
Tabular stop	5 keystrokes
Hand positioning	12½ keystrokes
Vertical space	2½ keystrokes

The materials manager can evaluate the forms designs he approves simply by adding the number of keystrokes. The fewer the keystrokes, the lower the clerical cost. If one form requires 1,200 keystrokes and another form doing a similar job requires only 600, the materials manager may well consider requesting that the first form be redesigned, since it costs about twice as much to fill out as the second one does.

ELECTRONIC DATA PROCESSING

The techniques discussed so far help reduce paperwork. But, to be realistic, their impact on the overall materials job is minor. Even if they are applied intensively, 80 or 90 percent of the work of materials management will continue to be clerical. Mechanization is more promising: It permits machines to be substituted for people.

Every materials department is mechanized to some extent. It has duplicating equipment, copying machines, dictating machines, electric desk calculators, electric typewriters, and so on. At this stage of mechanization, machines do various jobs, but data continues to flow in conventional fashion on conventional forms and records.

Integrated data processing is more advanced. Data moves from operation to operation in a form that permits each machine to operate automatically from the instructions it receives in some "common language." The vehicle of the common language is either punched cards or tape.

Punched card systems

The older systems involve punched cards and the cards are still widely used even though information is now more likely to be entered into a computer directly. In fact, punched card systems predate the computer and some companies still use these noncomputerized systems for automatic typing of purchase orders and similar clerical chores. With a punched card system, every transaction that has any effect on inventory is keypunched on the cards. In some cases, this is done automatically when a form is typed; special typewriters are available that can be set to keypunch certain data after it has been typed. In most cases, a keypunch operator must record the data onto the cards in a separate operation.

Punched cards also can be used to automate purchasing operations. Typical is a system used by the Sprague Electric Company, in which the purchase requisition is a punched card (see Figure 18–4). The buyer fills in the variable data—purchase order number, purchase quantity, vendor's promised delivery date, and so on—in pencil, and a keypunch operator punches this information on a new "buy" card.

FIGURE 18–4

Courtesy Sprague Electric Co.

Sprague Electric Company uses punched cards as purchase requisitions. Buyers fill in purchasing data, which is then punched on another "buy" card.

582

This buy card, along with a deck of cards for the vendor's name and address (see Figure 18–5) is fed into a machine that automatically prints a purchase order (see Figure 18–6).

The cards used to print the purchase order are saved until the supplier delivers. They then can be combined with another punched card and used to print a receiving report. They also can be used to print reports on open orders. For example, Sprague Electric makes runoffs of all open orders the week before they are due (see Figure 18–7). It also makes separate runoffs of orders where delivery is behind schedule, and uses the same punched cards to print out expediting notices that are mailed to suppliers.

Punched cards have many other uses in materials management. If a card is punched for each materials transaction, it is possible to use the cards to print almost any form used in materials management. In addition, the cards can be combined and recombined to produce a wide variety of reports. Cards for each withdrawal, receival, rejection, and

FIGURE 18–5

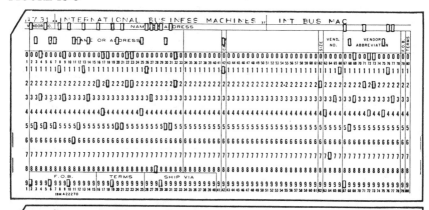

Punched cards hold a limited amount of data. Four cards (above and on facing page) are needed to print a typical supplier's name and address.

purchase can be combined to run off a complete inventory report. The report can be made according to supplier, product, part number, or in almost any other way desired.

Application of computers

Punched-card data processing systems predate the electronic data processing computer. Now the two are almost synonymous. Companies that use punched-card equipment almost always analyze this data in a computer. In fact, the punched card itself is gradually becoming obsolete. Data is increasingly being entered into computers by other, less mechanical means. Even when cards are correctly punched, errors can be made because the process is mechanical and the cards themselves can bend or become damaged. In addition, the entry process is limited by the speed with which the cards can be processed—which is at a snail's pace as compared with the computer's ability to absorb information.

FIGURE 18–5 (*continued*)

Courtesy Sprague Electric Co.

584

FIGURE 18–6

When the punched buy card and the vendor deck are fed into the proper tabulating equipment, a purchase order like the one shown here is printed automatically.

Electronic data processing has revolutionized materials management. It is taking over control of the entire clerical phase of materials management and is giving managers tools to manage materials as they've never been managed before. The computer can analyze, in minutes, data that would take a small army of clerks weeks to process. As a result, the materials manager can get data for making decisions much faster than before; she also can get more data than would be possible with manual or mechanical techniques.

Materials management by computer normally starts with a magnetic tape that is, in effect, a list of the items to be controlled, and a program that tells the computer what to do with this basic list and the variable data fed into it. The program is an attempt to simulate a clerk's reaction to data; it permits the computer to regulate itself and make basic operating decisions. This ability to "think," plus its fantastic operating speed, are what make a computer and electronic data processing different from punched-card mechanical processing.

The basic magnetic tape consists of more than a simple parts list. Included are not only such basic data as each part number, part name,

FIGURE 18–7

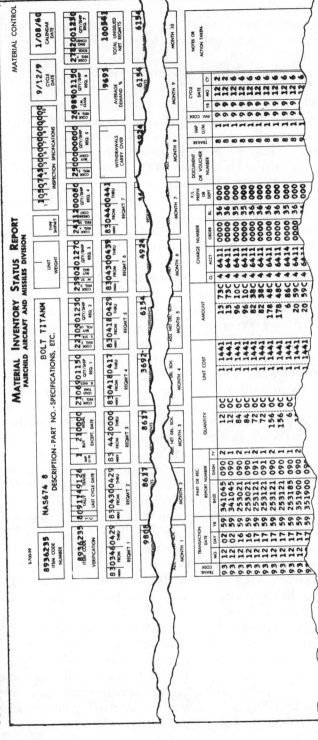

Punched buy cards can be used also to print various reports. Sprague Electric Company, for example, prints a weekly report of all open orders due the following week.

and product usage, but also such materials management information as safety stock, unit weight, lead time, inventory balance, and inspection requirements.

When a program is devised and desired basic information is on tape, variable information is fed into the system. Every transaction affecting the status of the items controlled is fed into the computer for compilation and analysis. Included would be all receivals and withdrawals of stock, placement of purchase orders, and usage schedules. The usual procedure is to describe each transaction on punched cards, usually punched by a keypunch operator. This is virtually the only manual operation required with EDP and sometimes even it can be eliminatd. The data can be entered with a "mark-sense" pencil that permits the cards to be punched automatically. Or, in some cases, information can be transmitted directly to the computer as it is generated.

The information on the cards may be read directly into the computer. Usually, however, it is transferred to magnetic tape which, in turn, is fed into the computer. This additional operation is needed to keep the costly computer working at peak efficiency. It is physically impossible to feed data from punched cards into the computer at a rate much faster than 2,000 characters per second. This is wasteful, since computers are capable of handling an input of 1 million characters per second or more, and magnetic tape feeds in data at the rate of about 50,000 characters per second.

Periodically, usually once or twice a week, the magnetic tape listing transactions is fed into the computer and compared with the permanent data already in the program. The computer compares the two sets of data and makes necessary calculations. Its conclusions appear on reports made on a high-speed printer to which it is linked.

Basic job. A well-designed EDP system will handle all routine materials management transactions. It will:

1. *Provide up-to-date reports.* Current inventories of each item can be calculated and printed in detail. In addition, almost any type of inventory summary can readily be compiled for analysis. The computer can also be programmed to compile estimates of future inventories based on projected schedules of purchase and usage.

2. *Complete materials transaction records.* Not only the inventory balances but a complete record of each transaction for each item can be compiled and printed automatically.

3. *Compute economic order quantities and usages.* The computer can automatically analyze previous usage of an item and revise anticipated usages in accordance with some formula. It then can recompute economic order quantity. If there is a need for them, the computer can be programmed to use mathematically complex ordering formulas for which a clerk would have neither understanding nor the time to make the necessary calculations.

4. *Make routine materials decisions.* The computer can review the lead time and planned usage of each item. When inventory drops to the reorder point, it can be programmed to print automatically a purchase requisition calling for a new buy. If there is no need to get competitive bids, the computer can be programmed to print a purchase order instead of a requisition.

The computer would not necessarily take action whenever it receives a requisition or when inventory drops to a reorder point. It might be programmed to wait until there was further demand for an item. For example, suppose the computer received a requisition for an item on June 1 that was required on September 1 and lead time was four weeks. The computer would hold off ordering that item until late in July and, in the meanwhile, would go ahead and accumulate other orders for that item, grouping them together into a single big order. Thus, the computer can automatically be programmed to search for the biggest possible quantity discount.

Computers can also be made delivery conscious. For example, when a predetermined lead time has elapsed or when inventories drop to some dangerously low level, the computer can be programmed to print automatically a notice calling for expediting. The supplier's promised delivery date also can be fed into the computer, and another expediting notice is generated if the material is not received before this time. If an item needs expediting for several consecutive buys—or if delivery is consistently early—the computer can analyze the purchase history and calculate a new time.

5. *Provide up-to-date cost data.* The computer can easily be programmed to multiply purchase quantities and inventory balances by unit prices. This gives the controller current reports on inventory investment and also an accurate estimate of future cash needs to pay for deliveries against open purchase orders.

The computer can also be programmed to make a special report on all items where there is a price change; this naturally would facilitate the materials manager's control over purchase prices. It would also be easy to print from data already in the computer special reports showing expenditures by supplier. This information would be useful both for reciprocity and for various reports that prime contractors must make for the armed services on relations with small business, and so on.

Direct communication. In some organizations, a supplier's computer and a buyer's computer "talk" to one another directly over telephone wires. A need for material is identified in the buyer's computer. The computer "knows" that this material is bought from a particular supplier so it simply transmits an order to that supplier's computer which then proceeds to issue the necessary instructions for the order to be filled. When the order is complete, the seller's computer "tells" the buyer's computer that delivery will be made and proceeds to invoice—in effecting, informing the computer directly how much is due on the order. The buyer's computer verifies this and, after the actual delivery of the material has been made and the computer advised, payment is made automatically. In some cases, the actual transfer of funds may be made without actually writing a check on the bank account; in most instances, the computer simply writes a check when payment is due.

Problems with electronic data processing

Although they have revolutioned business procedures, computers are not a completely unmixed blessing. They are expensive. Big firms often have several million dollars invested in a single computer center, in addition to paying substantial sums in monthly rental for the computer itself. The smaller firm can get along with a smaller computer or may even simply rent time on someone else's machine.

The cost of developing a program and transferring data from manual records to the computer can also be enormous. Between 20,000 and 50,000 labor-hours may be needed to translate the basic data for an inventory of 6,000 items into "machine language." Many companies that have adopted EDP systems control 20,000 or more items with them. Needless to say, their investment in EDP start-up cost is even greater.

Because of these high costs, only a few giant corporations could conceivably afford to use a computer exclusively for materials management. The normal practice is to share the computer among all the major departments of the business. Usually the biggest user is finance—for payroll, general accounting, and cost accounting. The marketing and engineering departments are also big users of computers.

When a computer is used reasonably close to its effective capacity, it will normally effect savings in clerical costs that offset high operating costs. In some companies, materials management employment has been reduced by 50 percent or more after the introduction of the computer. In most cases, however, reduction in employment has been more modest. In fact, it is a moot point whether or not the computer has actually reduced materials management operating costs. Instead, its real benefits are represented by tighter control. If the personnel relations problems that are inevitable when the computer requires large-scale reclassification and transfers of employees is taken into account, its impact on materials management operations (as distinct from overall performance) may be negative on balance.

There are also problems in programming the computer. Even the most routine clerical job has dozens of minor problems that require decisions. Each problem must be anticipated in programming the computer. A few of them are bound to be overlooked. For example, suppose a company has programmed a computer to generate a buy notice if safety stock drops to a given level. Regardless of the reason the stock drops, the computer faithfully follows instructions and generates the buy notices. This can create problems if other controls are not programmed into the computer as well.

Suppose, for example, there are engineering or quality control problems with a given product. Management wants to let stocks run down until the problem is solved. With manual inventory control, the clerks would simply ignore the declining stock balances on the items affected and would write no requisitions until they were told the problem was solved. With automatic control, the computer would flood the buying department with dozens or even hundreds of useless buy notices. If they are not properly regulated, automatic systems can generate so much unnecessary paperwork that their usefulness is substantially reduced.

Every company that has attempted to set up an EDP system for materials management has encountered expensive and troublesome "bugs" that must be ironed out before the system works well. However, practically all of them agree that the results are worth the effort and cost.

A typical application

Fairchild Industries Corporation uses a computer and related equipment for materials management. Basic scheduling data and parts lists are stored on magnetic drums in the memory part of the computer. Every material transaction—schedule changes, purchase orders, receivals, and so on—is recorded on punched cards (see Figure 18–8). Information is then transferred to magnetic tape so it can be fed to the computer at a faster rate.

Nine times per month the tape is fed into the computer, along with a predetermined program (i.e., set of instructions that tell the computer what to do). The computer automatically performs the calculations that the program directs. Results of these calculations are printed on individual material inventory status reports for each item controlled. Figure 18–9 shows transactions for a typical active item.

Reports for action. In addition to status reports for each of 21,000 active items in controls, the computer simultaneously prints orders calling for specific action on items that need it. When stocks of an item drop to the point where they equal probable usage during the lead time plus the safety stock, the computer calculates the economic order

590

FIGURE 18-8

Fairchild Industries Corporation keypunches every materials transaction on 21,000 components onto cards like this one. The data are then transferred to magnetic tape.

quantity and prints a buy notice. Similarly, if stock on hand or on order exceeds foreseeable demand, it prints a cancellation notice. The computer also prints three different types of expediting notice:

1. When there is a variance between the planned delivery schedule and the supplier's actual schedule.
2. When inventory drops to one half the safety stock.
3. When there is not enough stock for current operations.

If some purchasing action is not taken, the computer is programmed to find out why. If an order is not placed after the computer issues a buy notice, the computer asks why when the follow-up time programmed into it has expired. For example, the computer might print a buy notice on March 1 requesting that a purchase order for material be placed by March 15. If the order is not placed and recorded on the magnetic tape, the computer may print a notice asking why the order was not placed when the tape is run through it on March 15. If engineering has issued a "hold" on the item requesting that all new commitments for an item be delayed because of possible design changes, the computer is programmed to take this into account and refrain from printing new buy notices until the part is taken off the "hold" list.

Quantities calculated by the computer include predetermined contingency factors. Lead times are always up to date, since the buyer must indicate a new lead time when he places the order and this information is passed on to the computer. Order points also are regularly brought up to date. The computer is programmed to forecast demand and calculate order points, using the exponential smoothing techniques discussed in Chapter 9.

FIGURE 18–9

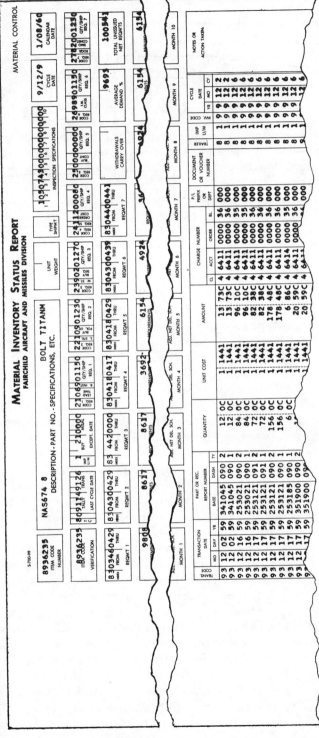

Fairchild Industries Corporation runs a magnetic tape of all materials transactions through its computer nine times per month. Every transaction for each item is automatically printed on a Material Inventory Status Report.

Fairchild's gains. Electronic data processing has helped Fairchild do a better materials management job at lower cost. Before EDP, the company had 26 persons in its material control department and 41 persons in its procurement department. After the introduction of EDP, there were only 38 persons in a new combined purchasing and material control department. The heavy personnel cut came in material control activities, where the computer took over about 90 percent of the clerical work. In addition to cutting administrative overhead (most of which is offset by the share of the computer's rental that is chargeable to materials management), Fairchild has enjoyed these benefits through EDP:

1. *Fewer delays in manufacturing due to late deliveries, and less expediting expense.* With the computer there are fewer cases where material is ordered late and delivery must be rushed to meet schedules.

2. *Lower average inventories.* The computer issues a buy notice only when needed. Long lead-time items are bought before short lead-time items; material is scheduled for delivery only when it is actually required. This reduces average inventories. Stockouts from excessively low inventories are prevented because the computer maintains a much closer surveillance of inventory position than was possible before. The computer makes a complete review of all inventory items nine times a month and recomputes safety stocks and order points to take account of changes in usage.

3. *Lower average costs of material.* Economic order quantities are programmed into the computer. Buy notices are accumulated until they are absolutely needed because of lead time. As a result, there are fewer buys in larger quantities, and purchasing can get lower prices.

4. *Better planning of cash flow.* Reports of open purchase commitments (the computer is informed whenever a purchase order is issued) permit the controller to project cash needs with precision. Funds not needed can either be invested in short-term securities or used to reduce loans.

5. *Improved cost control.* Product costs can be tabulated from data on the computer. Changes in costs can be picked up accurately and rapidly. Formerly the controller got monthly product cost tabulations two weeks late; now she gets weekly reports with only five days' delay. Major cost changes get special attention. Any price change greater than 10 percent for an order of more than $25 is picked up by the computer and reported separately for review and analysis.

6. *Faster purchasing.* Formerly, contract extensions had to be added manually to each material control card before new requirements could be figured. This was a slow, tedious job. Now the change in end product requirements is put into the computer and all of the detail work is done automatically. Purchasing knows the effect of a

contract change almost in a matter of hours. Similarly, when a contract is cut back, purchasing can move faster on cancellations.

Fairchild's price. All these benefits were not gained without sacrifice. Besides the recurring expense of operating the computer, Fairchild had to make a one-time investment of roughly 5,000 hours of labor, including 1,800 hours at overtime rates, to translate its materials records into a form that could be handled by the computer. Even with the best programming that can be devised, the computer cannot do what the lowliest clerk can: think. If some data must be handled in a slightly different fashion, a clerk will automatically make allowances. With a computer the problem must be anticipated, or there will be trouble.

For example, with conventional programming the computer will not issue a buy notice until the lead time requires it. This is desirable in most cases, of course—but not always. If a certain item is in short supply, a buyer may wish to order as soon as there is a requirement, even if this is months before he would be required to do so by the lead time. A clerk could work from a special list of all such items. A computer can only follow the instructions in its program. Fairchild overcame this particular problem by programming the computer to handle certain items as "buy instant." The computer is programmed so that it generates a buy notice for such items as soon as there are requirements.

Other problems have not been solved that easily. One that took a great deal of time to overcome was minimum buys. Suppose the computer calculates that 12 cotter pins are needed and generates a buy notice to that effect. If the buyer's vendor requires a minimum order of $5, the actual purchase quantity might be 1,000 cotter pins.

When the purchase order data are fed into the computer, the trouble begins. The computer compares a requirement of 12 pieces with a potential inventory of 1,000 pieces and proceeds to take steps to prevent excessive inventories from accumulating by printing a purchase order cancellation notice for 988 pieces. This wasted paperwork can be corrected by another special addition to the program that tells the computer to handle minimum order parts in a special way.

The computer will not solve the problem of usage variation, either. It can compute procurement lead times and safety stock by almost any mathematical technique. But if usage varies erratically, eventually the computer will make a mistake: either safety stock will be inadequate and there will actually be a stockout before a new shipment arrives, or the safety stock will be so big that inventories will be excessive. Clerks also have trouble with erratic demand fluctuations, but sometimes they manage to do a better job of controlling them than a computer can.

For this and other reasons, almost every organization continues to control some items manually and will almost always override its computer under certain circumstances. The computer is a fast clerk and it is accurate. But its "judgment" is only as good as that of the people who run it. Despite this limitation, the computer has become a major materials management tool—especially in material requirements and inventory control but also in other phases of materials management.

Cases

CASE 18–1.   CAROLINA PAPER COMPANY

Improving records and administrative controls

The Catawassa mill of the Carolina Paper Company was built in 1910 to take advantage of the ample supplies of timber in the area as well as the almost unlimited water supply available from the Catawassa River. Since 1945, the mill has more than trebled its capacity. Now it has reached a period of consolidation. The entire paper industry is currently suffering from overcapacity. Every producer is hard pressed to preserve profit margins. Carolina is no exception, and it has called in a management consulting firm, David–John–Karen, for advice. One of the changes the consultants recommend is that Carolina adopt a materials management type of organization. The following year this recommendation is followed, and Georgina Jenkins, from a leading New England paper company, is hired as Carolina's materials manager.

One of Jenkins's first jobs as materials manager is to analyze the procedures and records in her department. She discovers that the company's single most important material, logs for the pulp mill, is controlled almost entirely by the log buyer, Alan White. Logs are purchased from dozens of small lumber mills and are also supplied by the company's own forestry department, which White treats as an outside supplier. White's procedure is to get a copy of the company's pulp-mill schedule and to determine from it what the demand for logs will be. He then places orders with his suppliers. The traffic department arranges with the railroad to have cars available to pick up logs from White's suppliers.

White keeps a separate record for each supplier. Whenever he places an order, he posts it to the appropriate supplier's record. Whan a shipment is received, White gets a copy of the receiving report and credits it against the open order. White also keeps a separate inventory record for hardwood and softwood logs. As cars come in from the suppliers, he debits this record; as they are unloaded for the logs to be cut into pulp, he credits the record. His inventory is represented by the full cars waiting in the company's switching yard.

Somewhat different systems are used by the company to control other raw materials (mostly chemicals used in papermaking and for maintenance supplies. Raw materials are stored either in the mill's yard or in a storage shed. Manufacturing makes withdrawals whenever necessary. The buyer knows from experience approximately what usage will be, and she schedules her purchases so that they will approximately equal usage. Occasionally she also makes physical checks of the stock to make certain there are no drastic fluctuations. When usage is extremely heavy, the mill's general foreman will sometimes warn her that the stock of a particular chemical is getting low. The buyer then gets on the telephone immediately and places a rush order. This is rare, however, since the buyer normally protects herself with a more than adequate safety stock. She readjusts this stock once a year, when the annual inventory is taken. Last year, the inventory indicated that she was carrying $500,000 in chemical inventories, which was an average three months' usage.

Carolina's maintenance storeroom is organized somewhat like a grocery supermarket. Whenever they need material, individual maintenance workers walk into the storeroom and help themselves to whatever they need. They record their withdrawals on a stores requisition form. The maintenance workers on the day shift simply give the form to the stores clerk, who then posts it to perpetual inventory record cards; those on the afternoon and evening shifts leave the forms in a box to be posted later by the clerk.

The clerk reorders whenever there is a stockout or when his records show that the stock has dropped to the reorder point. He calculates the reorder point by studying usage history and comparing it with the lead-time estimate he gets from the purchasing department. His reorder point is normally equal to his estimate of usage during the lead time plus a 50 percent safety allowance. Whenever there is a stockout, however, the clerk increases his safety allowance a little to try to prevent a recurrence. Stockouts do not occur too often, even though the annual physical inventory always indicates that there have been more withdrawals from stock than were ever recorded in stores requisitions; the safety stocks are more than adequate to take care of shrinkage.

When stock does drop to the reorder point, the clerk prepares a purchase requisition for the desired purchase quantity. The purchasing department then issues a conventional purchase order for the required material. The stores department gets a copy of this order, which it posts to the perpetual inventory card. In most cases, it then can forget about the order until the material is received and it posts the receiving report and move ticket to the inventory card. If there is a stockout before the material is received, the stores clerk calls purchasing and requests that the purchase be expedited. He also increases the lead time shown on his inventory card to prevent a recurrence of the stockout.

Questions

1. What improvements, if any, can be made in Carolina's materials management procedures?
2. How can control be improved or cost of paperwork reduced?

CASE 18–2. VERTOL DIVISION, BOEING COMPANY

Data-Phone system speeds order processing

John Brane, materiel director of the Vertol Division of the Boeing Company, Morton, Pennsylvania, decided to make a 30-day tour of other companies' procurement installations with his top aides in order to search for ways in which to improve his own company's techniques and procedures. He then established an "improvement board" staffed on a rotating basis with members from purchasing, outside production (subcontracting), warehousing, and various other materiel groups. The improvement board meets regularly to search for improvement procurement techniques. Its first recommendation was installation of a Data-Phone system to purchase office supplies. It was believed that this would lead to similar installations to purchase other items. The Data-Phone installation permits information to be transmitted from Vertol's EDP system over telephone lines to that of the supplier.

Brane declared, "If you have good blanket orders to begin with, you're probably ready for Data-Phone. There is nothing mysterious about the system. It's simply an ultra-efficient technique for making blanket order releases."

Al Martorell, manager of materiel, programming, and planning (one of the materiel groups reporting to Brane), points out that "all of the advantages of Data-Phone stem from its ability to transmit releases faster and more accurately. As a result of these benefits, we've reduced inventory, cut paperwork, freed the buyer from petty details, and lowered administrative expenses.

"These are impressive savings, but they're tough ones on which to hang a definite price tag. So, at least for now, we don't attempt to do so. Instead, if price, quality, service are the same among competing bids, we give the nod to the supplier equipped to plug into our Data-Phone system."

Philadelphia Stationers was Vertol's first Data-Phone connection, since it was fully equipped with a receiving set, a transmitting unit (to feed conventional orders into its automated system) and auxiliary data processing equipment. Under Vertol's setup, when an item in the stationery storeroom hits the reorder point, a stores clerk calls purchasing. One of the purchasing department clerks accumulates reorder requests and transmits once or twice a week to Philadelphia Stationers. To do this, he:

1. Dials Philadelphia Stationers' number on the Data-Phone and waits for the dial tone that indicates all is clear for transmitting.
2. Inserts Vertol's identifying master card into the IBM 1001 card reader, an adjunct to the Data-Phone.
3. Inserts each item card into the 1001, and keys in quantity required.
4. Hits the "end" button when all cards have been processed.

Whenever necessary, the clerk can establish voice communication with the supplier. An example is if he wishes to segregate certain items against a specific release number. Ordinarily, release numbers and release dates are programmed in at Philadelphia Stationers. For purchasing's records, the clerk handwrites date and quantity ordered on each item's card.

Receiving equipment at Philadelphia Stationers triggers an 026 keypunch unit to bang out duplicate IBM cards. When these cards are run through a 402 accounting machine, they produce a four-part continuous-form packing list. This list is used for stock picking and accompanies the shipment (usually within 48 hours) to Vertol.

Vertol, in turn, uses the packing list for receiving purposes. The receiving clerk signs two copies for the supplier's deliveryman, sends the third copy to the finance department, and forwards the fourth copy, with the goods, to the stationery storeroom.

EXHIBIT 1

Vendor-supplied tab cards cover every item on the blanket order for office supplies. A purchasing clerk uses these cards to transmit fast, completely accurate releases. (Unit price has been deleted from this sample.)

598

EXHIBIT 2

```
O  IVERTOL  DIVISION              20000    PACKING SLIP        O
O  BUILDING  500   01
   5TH AND UPLAND STS        PHILADELPHIA STATIONERS           O
O  CHESTER PENNA
   O                       4250 WHITAKER AVENUE • PHILADELPHIA, PA. 19124
O  15K  246518      COYLE
   ACCT COSTCODE 1525 501        PHONE     P HIL-A-MATIC S ERVICE  O
   RELEASE  65. 07 02 65      215-GA-6-9720
O                                         DIAL 426 - 5848
                                                              O
   ┌──────DESCRIPTION───────┬────┬─────┬──────────────────────┐
O  │                        │UNIT│ QTY │     ITEM CODE         │ O
   │ SHEET RING BOOK   A35P  │    │     │  465534              │
O  │  11 CODE 61026   SHEET  │PK  │  25 │  465534              │ O
   │                         │    │     │                      │
   │ CARD INDEX 5X8 HR WHT   │    │     │  188620              │
O  │  15 CODE 61907    CARD  │M   │   5 │  188620              │ O
   │                         │    │     │                      │
   │ CUSHION CHAIR BRN1012E  │    │     │  224224              │
O  │  20 CODE 63024 CUSHION  │EA  │  48 │  224224              │ O
   │                         │    │     │                      │
   │ ERASER DURALAR    555   │    │     │  258800              │
O  │  56 CODE 63551  ERASER  │GR  │   1 │  258800              │ O
   │                         │    │     │                      │
   │ BOARD CLIP 9X13   IDL   │    │     │  144525              │
O  │ 109 CODE 66039   BOARD  │EA  │  24 │  144525              │ O
   │                         │    │     │                      │
   └─────────────────────────┴────┴─────┴──────────────────────┘
                                                              O
```

Packing list, developed by the supplier's data processing equipment, serves as a receiving report on incoming shipments. The fact that this form always lists items in the same order as they appear on the original blanket order is a big help for accounting.

A key feature of this operation is that Philadelphia Stationers lists items on the packing slip in the same order as on the original blanket order. It sorts the IBM cards manually on small releases and uses automatic equipment on large ones. Vertol's finance department, consequently, need not skip from page to page of the master order to check invoice prices.

With the supplier's shelf stocks backing up the stationery storeroom so effectively, Vertol has trimmed its on-hand investment in office supplies by one third. While part of this reduction is due to conventional blanket orders (about 80 percent of office items are covered by some type of annual agreement), purchasing stresses Data-Phone's key role in shrinking the buyer-supplier communications loop.

On virtually all other Data-Phone links established by Vertol following its success with office supplies, purchasing has dealt itself out of the paper-shuffling game completely. "After six months' experience with office supplies," explains Carroll Parrish, manager of purchasing, "we started converting other blanket orders to Data-Phone. We soon had eight more. Since seven of these involve standard floor supplies like nuts, bolts, and rivets, we put the Data-Phone equipment right in the warehouse stocking the items."

"We've got about 1,500 of these supply items on Data-Phone now," Parrish continues, "and one of the orders is with a West Coast firm. We use a WATS line to make transmissions there. Or, I should say, the warehouse inventory supervisor does. We don't touch the cards in purchasing. Instead, we negotiate blanket orders annually."

When traffic from the stationery storeroom warrants, Vertol plans to install another Data-Phone there. Having the equipment in purchasing provides some decided advantages. "We use it for demonstrations to other suppliers," says Parrish, "to help sell them on the simplicity and efficiency of Data-Phone."

A significant difference between the original Data-Phone agreement covering office supplies and subsequent ones is that release cards for floor supply items are prepunched with "order quantities." On stationery orders, the clerk in purchasing keys in this information.

To make sure all stationery releases are in standard packaging units, Philadelphia Stationers ran a data processing report on all of Vertol's releases after three months on the system. Then it provided Vertol with a run-off sheet, showing item description, unit of measure, lead time for the few nonshelf items on the blanket order, unit price, package quantity, standard carton quantity, and suggested order quantity.

This sheet guides the clerk so he can amend quantities requested to the nearest standard container quantity. In addition, every month Philadelphia Stationers submits three copies of a complete analysis of all items shipped. The office supplies buyer keeps one copy for his own use, sends one to the stationery storeroom, and routes the third to procurement and material management.

Philadelphia Stationers also submits a consolidated report of usage at the end of each annual contract, or whenever Vertol requests one. The Data-Phone setup is now in its second year with the office supply house, and Vertol is very pleased with it.

Purchasing is convinced that its approach to Data-Phone—paced by the office supplies agreement—really works. No problems have arisen in the warehouse from having several vendors handle similar items by Data-Phone. Recently, for example, the inventory supervisor there sent releases on 16 items to six vendors in just eight minutes.

Currently, Vertol is considering perishable tools and maintenance supplies as likely Data-Phone candidates. Backstopped by its acquired know-how and experience with office supplies and other items, the division figures to make the switch quickly, easily, and without violating its competitive buying policies.

Questions

1. Is Data-Phone likely to limit competition among suppliers or increase it? Explain.
2. What should Vertol guard against in expanding its Data-Phone system?
3. Suppose a supplier not equipped with Data-Phone offers Vertol lower prices than a supplier equipped with Data-Phone. How would Vertol go about deciding which supplier's bid to accept?

19

Measuring materials management performance

set down a budgeture d measure [handwritten annotation]

There are four basic steps in measuring the performance of any manager or department. They are:

1. Define the limits of the job.
2. Determine the objectives to be achieved within these limits.
3. Develop a program to meet these objectives.
4. Compare progress on the program with the objectives.

The limits of the job are defined by the organization structure and policies and procedures. In previous chapters, it was noted that the ideal materials organization embraces all related materials activities: purchasing, traffic, material control, and so on. The typical objectives of the materials organization were defined as:

1. Low operating costs (i.e., low costs of acquisition and possession and low payroll costs).
2. Low prices of purchased material.
3. Minimum investment in inventory (i.e., high inventory turnover).
4. Superior supplier performance (i.e., adequate quality of purchased materials, prompt delivery, and generally favorable vendor relations).
5. Development of materials personnel.
6. Good records.

DEVELOPING THE PROGRAM

The third basic step in measuring performance—developing a program to meet objectives—was discussed in Chapter 7. The program normally would include both qualitative and quantitative goals.

Among the latter would be a detailed budget to control operating costs and specific cost-reduction and inventory management performance. Other goals are inherently qualitative, however, including those of better supplier relations, development of personnel, and good records.

The materials manager should have a program for the department to achieve these goals. In addition, he or she should require each of the key subordinates to develop programs to achieve similar goals. Authority to develop a program should be delegated to the lowest possible level in the organization. In doing this, the materials manager ensures that the efforts of everyone in the organization will be directed toward goals that are consistent with those of the whole department and of the company.

In the larger corporation, each divisional materials manager should develop his own program. Typically, he might submit a plan to the corporate materials manager once a year in which he describes his goals for the coming year. The corporate materials manager would then review and compare the plans submitted by his subordinates. Some of them he might accept without any questions. Others would have to be reviewed in some detail in order to make them consistent with department-wide goals.

Each divisional materials manager is encouraged to exercise her initiative and set standards against which her performance could be measured. She naturally would set goals for cost reduction and inventory turnover. In addition, she would encourage subordinates to control their own operating costs, budgeting themselves on travel, telephone calls, and personnel. In this plan, the materials manager would not only include how she intended to develop subordinates but also indicate—after a frank discussion of her own strengths and weaknesses with her boss—how she proposed to correct her own shortcomings.

With this approach, not only is responsibility for performance delegated to the lowest possible level, but the practice in planning is itself a management development tool. Men and women become experienced in planning and administration while they are still in junior jobs. This permits management to test their managerial ability long before they advance to levels where their mistakes can seriously hurt the organization.

The materials manager's plan is a composite of the plans of his subordinates and would also be submitted annually. If accepted by top management, it would become a standard against which the department's performance would be measured. Performance measurements of individual parts of the plan might be made annually, quarterly, monthly, weekly, or even daily. In general, performance in achieving the qualitative goals would be measured less frequently than that in achieving the quantitative goals. For example, an annual or quarterly report would usually be adequate to measure progress in personnel development. On the other hand, deviations from operating budgets might be reported monthly, while price changes often are reported weekly or daily.

The quantitative phases of performance measurement get more attention for several reasons. Among them are the following:

1. *Quantitative data are more objective.* They are based on operating statistics, whereas qualitative data reflect, in large part, the opinion of the observer. It would be hard for a materials manager to distort performance on cost reduction, where progress is measured in dollars and cents. But it would be very easy for the materials manager to exaggerate the progress he is making on such intangible goals as personnel development or improved supplier relations.

2. *Quantitative data usually change faster.* Most of the materials management goals that can only be measured qualitatively are long range in nature. Progress on them is usually so slow that it is pointless to attempt to measure it weekly or daily. On the other hand, progress on quantitative goals should be measured frequently, so that remedies can be applied immediately should performance fall short of expectations.

3. *Quantitative data are more directly related to company profits.* Top management has an immediate interest in materials management goals such as cost reduction and inventory turnover which can be measured quantitatively. Performance is directly related to day-to-day operating decisions. On the other hand, management is usually interested in qualitative goals only when it is planning for the future.

CONTROL OF OPERATING COSTS

Managements have been measuring how effectively purchasing agents and materials managers control operating costs for years. In fact, in the less progressive companies this is the only performance measurement that is applied to the materials department. The assumption is that the materials department is a service activity and should be interested primarily in providing its service at the lowest possible cost. Implicit in this assumption is the concept that the materials department is a clerical activity, and its performance should be measured in terms of how much it costs to process each purchase order, requisition, or production release. Accountants then carefully calculate the department's costs and divide them by the number of forms it processes. By this criterion, a purchasing department whose operating costs are equal to $10 for each purchase order it issues is considered more efficient than one that spends $12 per order.

This is a false concept, of course. Control of operating costs is just one objective of the materials department, and not the most important one, by any means. For example, the typical materials department can save $50 by buying materials at lower prices for every $1 and it can shave from its operating costs. And the best materials departments usually have rather high operating costs because they are willing to pay higher salaries to attract highly skilled personnel who are capable of doing an outstanding job of materials management.

Nevertheless, control of operating costs is still a fairly important objective. Were there no control, costs would soon get out of hand. Operating costs should be budgeted as part of the overall materials plan. Performance can be measured in two ways: (1) measurement of the productivity of the persons employed in the materials department with either absolute or relative standards; (2) measurement of success in controlling direct materials department expenses by comparing actual costs with budgeted costs.

Control of personnel

The materials department plan should include an estimate of personnel needed to achieve objectives. This estimate, if approved, becomes the department's personnel budget. Whenever possible, it should be based on objective criteria. For purchasing and material control jobs, the criterion may be the number of parts of a given type that a person can handle. For example, one company calculates that each buyer should be able to handle 250 complex parts and about 500 simple items; this company also needs one materials planner and two clerks for each 1,000 items that are controlled. Similar criteria can be applied to other materials activities. For example, personnel requirements in traffic, shipping, and receiving can be measured in terms of the number of shipments handled.

All the standards mentioned so far are relative. They are useful in determining personnel needs when work loads change. For example, if one buyer is needed for each 250 parts, we know that we must hire two buyers if 500 parts are added because of a new product. Absolute standards are more difficult to justify. How do we know that a buyer cannot handle 400 parts, for example, instead of only 200? For some jobs, particularly the highly skilled ones, the answer is mostly a matter of judgment. The materials manager draws on her own experience and that of her supervisors, and she may also make comparisons with companies with similar materials management problems.

Time studies.   More exact methods can be used to measure the less skilled jobs. Any job that involves doing something—as distinct from thinking about something—can be measured with conventional time study techniques. The time study engineer breaks the job into its basic components and calculates how much time it takes to perform each element at some standard of efficiency. Work standards can easily be set for such repetitive materials operations as typing purchase orders, filing various documents, processing various types of shipments and receivals, and so on. Many large corporations have made time studies of their highly repetitive materials jobs. A few even have introduced incentive pay on certain jobs. For example, one company boosted the productivity of its purchase order typists by more than 20 percent with incentive pay. Current output averages about 125 orders per typist per day.

Work sampling. It is difficult to make time studies of the less repetitive jobs, but they can be analyzed with ratio-delay, or work-sampling, studies. The first step in making such a study is to break the job into a series of simple elements that can readily be observed—walking away from the desk, talking to visitors, typing, talking on the telephone, doing nothing, and so on. Then an observer, unknown to the subject, notes the subject's activity at random intervals. Usually several thousand observations are made over a period of several months.

Accuracy of the data increases in proportion to the square of the number of observations. It is measurd with the formula

$$s = \sqrt{\frac{p(1 - p)}{n}},$$

where s is the standard deviation for an event that occurred p percent (expressed as a decimal) of n observations. For example, suppose that a buyer was attending meetings 1,000 times in the course of 10,000 observations. Thus, p obviously equals 10 percent, or 0.10.

FIGURE 19–1
Ratio-delay study of secretaries' performance

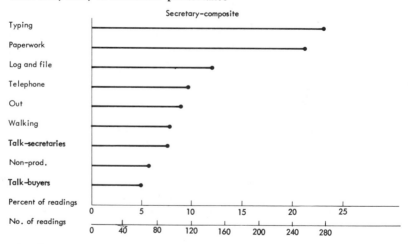

This chart shows the results of ratio-delay studies made of ten buyers' secretaries. Managers get clues to performance when they compare studies of individual secretaries to this average.

Therefore,

$$s = \sqrt{\frac{0.10(1 - 0.10)}{10,000}} = 0.003.$$

Converting to a percentage, the standard deviation is therefore 0.3 percent. Since we know that three standard deviations embrace 99.72 percent of a normal curve, we can then be more than 99 percent confident that the buyer spends at least 9.1 percent of his time attending meetings (10 percent *minus* three times 0.3 percent) and not more than 10.9 percent (10 percent *plus* three times 0.3 percent). If we made 100,000 observations, we could reduce our standard deviation to 0.03 percent, while it would be but 3.0 percent if we made just 100 observations.

Ratio-delay studies are not foolproof, but they can give clues to improvements, both in the average performance of everyone performing the job being studied and in individual performance. A large appliance firm made such a study of secretaries and buyers in its purchasing department. Figures 19–1 and 19–2 show the results. Note in Figure 19–1 that the average buyer's secretary spent 10 percent of the time on the telephone. Investigation might show either that the company was too lenient about personal calls or—as was actually the case at this appliance company—that secretaries were wasting too much time placing long-distance calls for buyers, which could be handled more efficiently by the operator on the company's switchboard.

FIGURE 19–2
Ratio-delay study of buyers' performance

This chart shows how the average buyer in a midwestern appliance manufacturing company spends her time. It is based on ratio-delay studies of ten buyers in the purchasing department.

The studies also are useful for individual comparison of performance. Figure 19–1 shows, for example, that the average secretary spent 5 percent of the time doing nothing, 10 percent away from the desk, and 7 percent talking to other clerical employees in the office. One would have little doubt as to the efficiency of the secretary who spent 10, 15, and 10 percent of the time on these activities respectively and correspondingly less on more productive (and less pleasant) jobs: typing, paperwork, and filing.

Usually there is an excellent correlation between ratio-delay studies of clerical workers and other evaluations of their efficiency. The least productive secretary will have the highest average of nonproductive time. With the more highly skilled jobs, however, this may not be true. The best buyer may spend a greater percentage of her time doing nothing than the average buyer (see Figure 19–2), who spends only 4 percent of her time engaged in no apparent activity. The reason for this, of course, is that the best buyer may be able to perform routine tasks with dispatch and devote a greater part of her time to planning and generating ideas for cost reduction and product improvement.

Control of direct costs

The materials manager rarely has any problem controlling his biggest operating expense: wages and salaries. He gets his personnel budget approved and allows for salary adjustments. His performance will inevitably be satisfactory so long as he does not grant salary increases or increase his staff in excess of the budget.

Nonsalary costs. Other expenses are harder to control. Travel and telephone expenses can easily get out of hand in a materials department, particularly if there are many unexpected quality and delivery problems with suppliers. Such expenses are heavy enough even when everything goes according to plan. Contact must be maintained with thousands of suppliers. A materials department responsible for annual purchases of $30 million may have telephone and telegraph bills that exceed $2,000 per month, and it may spend as much as $20,000 per year on travel.

Telephone and travel expenses are controlled much as personnel expenses are. A budget for each is included in the overall purchase plan. Standards are based on past experience. For example, both telephone calls and travel expenses would tend to vary with the dollar volume of purchases, the number of suppliers, and the number of employees in the department. Suppose that telephone expenses totaled $30,000 in a year when there were 100 persons in the materials department, 6,000 suppliers, and a $30 million purchase volume. Then a budget of $32,000 would not be unreasonable for a year when volume of purchases rises to $35 million, there are 110 persons in the department, and it is planned to introduce a number of new suppliers.

Most other expenses can be controlled in similar fashion. Expenses for office supplies, for example, should vary almost directly with either the number of persons employed in the materials department or the number of purchase orders and other forms being processed.

Comparison with results

Salaries and other direct costs are not ends in themselves; they are incurred to achieve results. The materials manager is concerned with both quantity and quality of the output of the staff. Quantity is easier to measure. It involves comparison of actual operating costs with tangible output: number of purchase orders issued, the rate at which requisitions are processed, stock withdrawals, receivals, and so on.

Measuring output. Many materials managers keep their finger on their departments' performance with charts that graphically measure output. For example, Figure 19–3 shows one of the operating charts

FIGURE 19–3
Performance chart

Chart measures performance in processing requisitions. Solid line shows permissible backlog (determined by comparison of requisitions on hand with department capacity). Bars show number of requisitions in various age categories.

used by I. T. T. Kellogg Communications Systems to show how rapidly the purchasing department is processing requisitions. Each week, a clerk checks all open requisitions for material that has not yet been ordered. He classifies them into four groups: those that have been in the department less than 5 days, less than 10 days, under 20 days, and over 20 days.

Of course, the object of the game is to fill all requisitions as rapidly as possible. Unfortunately the requisition load fluctuates erratically, while purchasing's ability to fill requisitions is fixed by the size of its staff. The permissible backlog is represented by the difference between purchasing's capacity to issue orders and the actual backlog. During dull periods, the permissible backlog declines and almost all requisitions can be filled within five days of their receipt in the department.

During exceptionally busy periods, the permissible backlog grows, and the age composition of open requisitions also shifts. An increasing percentage is more than five days old simply because the department has more work than it can handle. The purchasing manager can study this chart and measure how well the department is doing and, also, determine whether or not she is falling behind.

Similar charts can be constructed to measure the percentage of purchase orders on which suppliers have fallen behind in meeting delivery dates, and in processing orders. They can also be used to control operating costs.

Less valid measures. Two other commonly used measures of purchasing clerical efficiency are cost per order and cost of purchasing as a percent of the dollar volume of purchases.

The first measure is calculated by dividing the total dollar costs associated with the purchasing process by the number of orders issued. The numerator consists of the annual budgets of the purchasing department and receiving department along with that part of the accounting department which is associated with processing accounts receivable. The denominator is simply the number of orders issued each year. The "answer" that is obtained almost always suggests a cost of at least $5 per order and it may be as high as $50 per order.

While cost per order is indeed used in practice, it is not a valid measure of purchasing department clerical efficiency. The reason is obvious: *successful efforts to boost purchasing productivity usually increase cost per order*, suggesting that the department is getting less efficient. For example, suppose that an organization issues 10,000 purchase orders per year and that the clerical costs associated with the purchasing process amount to $50,000 per year. The cost per order is obviously $5 ($50,000 ÷ 10,000). Then the purchasing manager works to boost efficiency by issuing blanket orders. The number of orders declines to 6,000 and clerical costs drop to $42,000 per year. Real savings have been made. Yet cost per order increases to $7 ($42,000 ÷ 6,000)! Clearly this is not a good measure of efficiency.

The second measurement, purchasing cost as a percent of value of purchases, is more valid. Calculation is fairly simple. The numerator is the total annual operating costs associated with the purchasing process. The denominator is the annual dollar volume of purchases. Thus, if an organization has operating costs in purchasing of $100,000 per year and spends $5 million per year on purchases, then the cost of purchasing is equal to 2 percent of total purchases. Obviously, the lower the percentage figure, the greater the clerical efficiency.

This measure is certainly superior to cost per order. But it also has limitations. The major costs in purchasing are *not* clerical. They are represented primarily by the salaries of purchasing executives who do not get paid for their clerical skills but, hopefully, are more than earning their higher salaries by reducing purchase prices. In addition, the percentage on a year-to-year basis is determined by relative growth of the purchase budget relative to dollar volume. For example, if both purchase prices rise sharply and dollar volume increases, the percentage will decline. This makes the purchasing department look good when, in fact, it may not be more efficient than it was the previous year.

Also, the purchasing director does not have complete control over his own budget. He or she works within parameters that are set on a companywide basis. Thus, the budget may go up simply because the company decided to give every employee additional fringe benefits. For this reason, physical measures are usually better barometers of clerical efficiency. The purchasing director rarely sets the salaries paid typists but if they can be persuaded to work efficiently, this is a fair measure of the purchasing department's efficiency.

CONTROL OF PRICES

While it is important to measure the *quantity* of work that is being done, the purchasing manager is also interested in the *quality* of this work. She wants to know how effectively the staff is contributing to the company's profit objectives. The biggest contribution comes when costs of purchased material are reduced. Department operating costs are usually almost trivial compared with what is spent for purchased parts and materials. For example, if a typical purchasing department cut its telephone bill or its office-supply expenses by 2 percent, it might save a few hundred dollars per year. There would be no perceptible change in the company's profit margin. But if it could reduce the prices of all purchased materials by 2 percent, profits would rise noticeably. In an average manufacturing company that spends 50 percent of its sales dollar on purchased materials and earns a pretax profit of 10 percent on sales, a 2 percent reduction in purchased materials cost would boost profits by 10 percent. This leveraged effect of purchased materials cost on profits explains why price is perhaps the single most important objective in the typical materials department.

Performance in meeting the price objective can be measured in three ways: by comparing actual costs with the materials budget, by cost-reduction reports and bogies, and by price indexes.

610

The purchased materials budget

Variances. Price performance is most directly related to overall company objectives when actual costs are compared with a purchased materials budget. Most well-managed companies try to budget sales and costs at least a year ahead. Such projections help management evaluate overall performance in reaching profit and sales goals. Usually the cost department calculates standard unit material costs for each product. The materials budget is then calculated by multiplying these standard costs by proposed production volume for each product.

Performance is measured by means of variance accounts that show the difference between actual costs and budgeted costs. Variances can arise both because the unit cost of the material was different from the plan or because usage (or scrap) varied. The former is the materials manager's responsibility; the latter is the manufacturing manager's (unless extra scrap resulted from defective purchased material).

Usage versus price. An example will make this clearer to the reader who is not a cost accountant. Suppose a company uses one pound of steel in a widget. The steel costs 15 cents per pound and the company makes 1 million widgets. In theory, it should spend $150,000 for the steel to make widgets (1,000,000 × $0.15). It discovers at the end of the year, however, that it actually spent 14 cents per pound for the steel but that it somehow managed to consume 1,050,000 pounds of steel. Purchases therefore amount to 1,050,000 × $0.14 or $147,000. There are two variances from plan. Manufacturing is charged with an *unfavorable* variance for having used an additional 50,000 lbs. of material. At 14 cents per pound, this amounts to $7,000. Purchasing, in contrast, has a *favorable* variance on price of 1 cent per pound. Applied to the standard material usage, this amounts to $10,000. Subtracting manufacturing's unfavorable variance of $7,000 from purchasing's favorable variance of $10,000 gives a net favorable variance of $3,000 and, of course, actual purchase costs are indeed $147,000 instead of $150,000 as planned.

Weaknesses. Top management often likes to use the purchased materials budget to measure the materials department's performance because it is so directly related to the objectives of the business and neatly ties in the department with other company activities. However, the materials budget has serious shortcomings for performance measurement. These include:

1. *The materials budget includes only direct materials.* Yet most companies spend substantial sums for indirect materials, which should not be overlooked in cost-reduction programs.

2. *Actual costs show up in variance accounts weeks after they are incurred.* This is because of the lag between the time material is ordered and the time it is finally used after having been in inventory.

Because different items have different lead times, it is extremely difficult to reconcile the usual cost department records with purchase records. *maybe Bad cost*

3. *Variance figures rarely, if ever, show why a price changed.* Usually price increases and decreases are balanced against one another and are not segregated. In addition, cost department records often are not set up for item-by-item analysis, yet this procedure is essential for good materials management. *maybe because of a design change.*

Cost-reduction reports

For the reasons above, most materials departments maintain their own controls over cost-reduction efforts. They cannot use cost department records.

The simplest, and one of the most effective, controls over purchase cost is a daily or weekly report of price changes on purchased materials (see the sample form in Figure 19–4). The report lists each item on

FIGURE 19–4

FORM G O 120 (Rev 1/201)

WEEKLY REPORT OF PRICE CHANGES
PURCHASED PARTS AND MATERIALS
PRODUCTION ITEMS ONLY

X DIVISION — DATE 10-19-

PART NO OR MAT'L SPEC	PART NAME OR DESCRIPTION	SUPPLIER	% BUY	PURCHASE DATA						% OF CHANGE	REASON FOR CHANGE	PRESENT AVG. MO. REQ'MTS	EFFECT OF PRICE CHANGE Month
				OLD PRICE	LOT BUY	EFF DATE	NEW PRICE	LOT BUY	EFF DATE				
345675	Housing	A	100	0.275	1000	1-56	0.205	1000	10-56	+3.5	LAM	300	3.00
356305	Body	B	100	0.960	300	1-56	1.017	300	10-56	+3.8	M	100	3.70
367557	Bracket	C	25	3.10	15000	3-56	3.01	15000	9-56	-2.9	M	15000	-1350.00
370752	Cap Screw	D	100	0.43	2000	1-56	0.45	2000	10-56	+5.7	LAM	735	14.70
370941	Bolt	E	100	0.77	2000	1-56	0.79	2000	10-56	+2.8	M	1045	20.90
383610	Brace	F	70	3.63	2000	3-56	3.46	5000	10-56	-4.9	N	1000	-170.00
351226	Valve	G	100	0.57	BLKT	1-56	0.59	BLKT	10-56	+3.6	M	41108	622.16
361754	Dowel	H	100	0.205	BLKT	1-56	0.216	BLKT	9-56	+5.2	LAM	1466	16.13
534516	Cover	I	100	0.050	300	1-56	0.052	300	6-56	+3.2	LAM	25	0.05
740330	Valve	J	100	0.2902	1000	8-56	0.3250	1000	8-56	+12.0	LAM	525	18.27
737337	Fitting	K	100	0.900	10000	5-56	0.889	20000	10-56	-1.2	Q	6070	-66.77
739746	Gear	L	100	0.0095	10000	7-56	0.0092	10000	10-56	-3.2	N	4125	-1.24
35630	Plug	M	100	3.42	100/499	3-56	3.37	500	8-56	-1.4	N	300	-15.00

CODE FOR PRICE CHANGE
N - CHANGE IN MATERIAL COST
L - CHANGE IN LABOR COST
M - NEGOTIATED CHANGE
D - PRODUCT DESIGN CHANGE
S - SUBSTITUTE MATERIAL
Q - QUANTITY ONLY
O - OTHER, EXPLAIN

Courtesy Eaton Corporation

Weekly reports of changes in purchase prices help keep purchasing managers appraised of department performance on cost reduction and also expose any price increases that should be investigated.

which there is any price change, the reason for the price change, the amount of the price change, the percentage change, and the cost per month.

Each buying group normally makes its own report. Purchasing managers can use the reports both as a control and as a measure of performance. When the price for an item rises sharply, they can ask for an explanation. Similarly, when there is a sharp decrease, they may wish to know why the price was so much higher on the previous buy—or they may congratulate the buyer on a skillful job if she exercised considerable ingenuity in finding ways to reduce costs.

Cost-reduction reports can also be used to measure performance of individual buying groups. Data can be accumulated by buying group and by reason for change and compared with budgeted price changes. The reports can be used to generate a healthy spirit of competition among the various buying groups. If each group has a cost-reduction target, then each will not only carefully study the report to see what progress it is making in meeting its own bogey but also be keenly interested in the progress of other groups.

Usually the cost-reduction target is originally determined as a percentage of purchase cost for each group. Percentages are helpful because they present fewer forecasting problems. For example, a 2 percent quota would hold regardless of whether purchase volume were $10 million or $11 million, whereas an absolute quota would be easier to meet if business were slightly better than expected.

Cost-reduction quotas of 2 to 3 percent are fairly common. The targets then are translated into estimated absolute quotas, which are subject to change should actual dollar volume of purchases be different from forecasted volume. Different buying groups normally would get different quotas, both as a percentage of cost and in dollars. Ideally, the quota should reflect the cost-reduction opportunities of each group. For example, a group buying steel or other commodities where there is little price competition may have a quota of only 1 percent. If its dollar volume were $10 million, the quota would be $100,000. Another buying group might have a 4 percent quota, but its absolute quota would also be $100,000 if its dollar volume were only $2,500,000.

How is the quota determined? First, an overall quota should be set for the entire materials department. It should be based on:

1. *An economic forecast.* If the outlook is for booming business, the quota will have to be quite low, since suppliers will be operating at near-capacity levels and will not be too responsive to cost-reduction efforts. On the other hand, if business is not too good, competition among suppliers will be keen.

2. *Price forecasts for key commodities.* In many companies, a few commodities account for a large share of the volume of purchases. Predicted prices for these commodities should be taken into account

when computing overall cost-reduction quotas, using techniques discussed in Chapter 7.

3. *Past performance.* This is one of the most widely used criteria. Managers naturally like to see some improvements each year. On the other hand, buyers sometimes complain that if they succeed in reducing costs for a number of years it becomes progressively harder to meet quotas because the opportunities for cost reduction keep diminishing.

4. *Relation to company profit objectives.* Sometimes cost reduction is necessary if the company is to achieve desired profits. In some cases, top management may exert rather arbitrary pressure on its materials department to reduce costs in order to achieve these overall profit objectives.

5. *Opinions of materials personnel.* The purchasing manager and the commodities specialists know from past experience and from "feel" of the market the cost-reduction quota that can reasonably be achieved.

After an overall quota is agreed upon, individual quotas are set for each group, following the same basic criteria. Individual supervisors should have as much latitude as possible in setting their quotas. This boosts morale and stimulates effort to meet quotas, since they become bogies that the supervisor agreed were reasonable rather than targets imposed on him from above. Higher management sometimes finds, however, that it must stimulate supervisors to raise their sights in setting quotas. In some cases, supervisors try to make their jobs too easy; occasionally they are so eager to make a showing that they become overoptimistic.

Obviously, all price reductions are not the result of the buyer's efforts. Market prices drop through no effort on the buyer's part, products are redesigned to reduce cost, and so on. And price increases may reflect superior performance on the part of the buyer when they are held below the amount justified by increases in wages and raw material cost. Therefore, some evaluation of price changes is essential if they are to be good guides of purchasing performance. In a big company, this would be done by someone on the materials manager's staff, usually a purchase analyst or value analyst. In a small company, the materials manager may have to do it.

Actual performance on price reductions attributable to buyer action can be charted against the savings objective for each buying group. Figure 19–5 illustrates how one company charts price-reduction progress for each of its buying groups.

Price indexes

Although weekly or daily price change reports are useful to keep materials management informed of price actions by subordinates, they are not ideal for performance measurement. There often are hundreds

614

FIGURE 19–5
Cost-reduction comparison chart

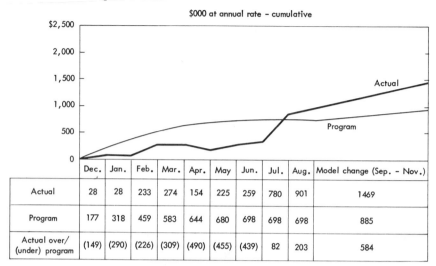

	Dec.	Jan.	Feb.	Mar.	Apr.	May	Jun.	Jul.	Aug.	Model change (Sep. – Nov.)
Actual	28	28	233	274	154	225	259	780	901	1469
Program	177	318	459	583	644	680	698	698	698	885
Actual over/ (under) program	(149)	(290)	(226)	(309)	(490)	(455)	(439)	82	203	584

Charts that compare actual cost reductions with quotas can help stimulate interest in reducing prices, in addition to serving as measures of performance.

of price changes each month, even in small companies. Tabulating and evaluating each of them from a price-change report is costly. In addition, errors are almost inevitable. Either buyers will incorrectly estimate usage in computing the monthly cost effect of the price change, or usage will change and their estimate will be inapplicable.

With a price index, on the other hand, estimates can be made with precision. In addition, they can be related directly to the cost of the company's products. There will be fewer errors and less clerical work, since a good index need contain only about 15 percent of total items.[1]

Once the overall index is established and a price-reporting system is operating, it requires relatively little effort to break up index items by buying group so that each group has its own index. This permits comparison both for performance evaluation and to generate a spirit of competition. Purchase-price indexes can also be compared with the indexes of the U.S. Bureau of Labor Statistics and other organizations.[2] For instance, an index made up primarily of metal parts can be compared with the Bureau's wholesale price index of metals and metal products.

[1] How to make and use purchase-price indexes is described in detail in Chapter 7.

[2] Many price indexes appear monthly in the *Survey of Current Business*, published by the U.S. Department of Commerce.

INVENTORY PERFORMANCE

Every materials manager strives to operate with minimum inventories, provided that in so doing he does not jeopardize achievement of other objectives (especially low prices and prompt delivery of materials to manufacturing when they are required). In some companies, inventory performance is measured simply by comparing present inventories with those of some base period.

Figure 19–6 shows how a southern textile firm measures performance in inventory management. Index numbers permit easy comparison of present inventory levels in each of its plants with inventory levels that prevailed during the base period. The lower the index number, the greater the progress that has been made in reducing stocks.

FIGURE 19–6
Inventory management performance chart

Index numbers can be useful in comparing inventory performance of various buying groups or various plants within the same company. The index number indicates the relative progress each unit has made in relation to some base period.

Though this measuring technique is simple, it can also be misleading, for it implicitly assumes that the need for inventories is constant from year to year in each plant. In most companies this would not be the case; the need for inventories would vary with the level of output. A more sophisticated approach is to set inventory standards for various levels of output and then compare actual inventories with these standards.

In general, the need for inventories does not rise in direct proportion to output. If $1 million in inventories is needed to maintain a production volume of $1 million per month, substantially less than $2 million in inventories will be needed for an output of $2 million per month. The inventory standard either can be for a specific investment or it can be measured as a rate of turnover (annual dollar volume of purchases divided by average purchased materials inventories). Whenever possible, inventory standards should be established for every subclass of inventory. Then the materials manager can compare actual performance with the standard and locate imbalances. It is possible, of course, to have too little of one class of inventory and too much of another class. Then overall turnover figures would be in line with standards, but individual turnover statistics would highlight imbalances.

Obsolescence should also be budgeted. The budget should be based primarily on past performance, but it should also reflect special conditions. For example, if obsolescence losses the previous year were unusually low because of special circumstances and higher losses will be inevitable during the current year, this should be allowed for in the budget. Otherwise materials personnel will be tempted to continue to carry inventories that should be declared obsolete. Special reports on inventory items for which there is little or no recent demand help the materials manager eliminate obsolescence.

SUPPLIER PERFORMANCE

Three major materials management objectives directly involve outside suppliers. They are adequate quality, prompt delivery, and favorable vendor relations. It is doubly important that performance in achieving these objectives be measured. It is essential not only to measurement of the materials department's performance but also to measurement of supplier performance by the materials department itself. Good buyers should regularly evaluate the performance of their existing suppliers. Not only should they visit supplier plants regularly, keep up to date on supplier finances and products, and so on, but they should try to keep objective records of supplier quality and delivery performance.

The quality objective

The purchasing department achieves its quality objective only when all supplier shipments meet standards and the cost of inspecting these shipments can be eliminated. Few purchasing departments can reach this ideal, but they can work toward it by selecting suppliers with good quality records and educating delinquent suppliers in quality procedures.

Every salesperson will maintain that the company's quality is unsurpassed. How can the purchasing manager evaluate such claims objectively? She does so by analyzing records of her own company's receiving inspection reports. She may simply keep a record of rejects in the form of percentage of total shipments received from each supplier for each basic type of material. Naturally rejects will be higher for some items than for others. What is important is the trend of rejections for a given commodity and the performance of competing suppliers on like commodities. If a vendor starts slipping on quality, the buyer first should warn it that it is falling behind its competitors. If there is no improvement, the buyer may be forced to give her next order to a different supplier.

Figure 19–7 shows the quality records of three competing suppliers. The percentage of rejections by each supplier was plotted each month. The supplier with the highest rejection rate will first be warned—and it may even be shown the chart that compares its quality record with those of its two major competitors. If it fails to improve, the purchasing manager may try to locate a fourth supplier who can deliver higher quality merchandise at the same or a lower price.

Tabulating the results. Reports such as this can rarely be made unless the company tabulates quality statistics with electronic data processing equipment. With this equipment, data from inspection reports for every shipment is keypunched on cards (see Figure 19–8). The actual quality level, determined from the inspection reports, is then compared with the acceptable quality level (AQL).

Various formulas are used to make comparisons; typical is the following quality-scoring formula used by an electronics company:

$$\text{Quality conformance} = 100 - \frac{30 \ (\text{percent defective})}{\text{Acceptable quality level}}.$$

This formula is designed to give a "passing grade" of 70 when the supplier's quality meets the standard exactly. For example, if the AQL permits a 2 percent rejection rate (i.e., two pieces out of a hundred do not meet the quality standard) and 2 percent of a supplier's shipment is actually found defective, then quality conformance = $100 - 30(0.02)/$

FIGURE 19–7
Suppliers' performance chart

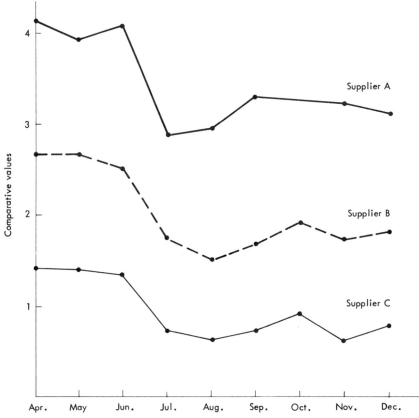

Quality performance of competing suppliers can be measured by plotting rejects as a percentage of monthly shipments. This not only permits comparison of suppliers but also indicates whether or not a poor-quality supplier is showing any signs of improvement.

0.02 = 70. Superior quality would earn the supplier a score higher than 70. Most companies would regard any score below 70 as the point where the supplier's shipments become completely unacceptable.

Quality conformance reports similar to that shown in Figure 19–9 can then be mailed to the supplier to report quality monthly. Some companies prefer not to reveal their AQL to vendors, however; they are afraid the vendor will begin to cut corners on quality and try to beat the system. Instead, they simply translate their quality tabulations into "acceptable" and "unacceptable" ratings. Vendors who get unacceptable ratings usually are invited to attend a meeting with quality control personnel to discuss ways to boost their quality.

FIGURE 19–8
EDP data on supplier performance

VENDOR NO	PT NO	TL	DATE	RPR NO	PO # CC	QTY REC	DEPT	QTY AC	NAME DEF	#	INSPECT CRIT	INSPECT MAJ	INSPECT MIN 1	INSPECT MIN 2	DEFECT CRIT	DEFECT MAJ	DEFECT MIN 1	DEFECT MIN 2
A NA NA	002 001 003																	
6468233	10-19-9				34716 61	36	335	36				7						
6672455	10-13-9			23621*	34798 61	24	335	24	160	1		7					7	
6678114	10-28-9				34721 61	17	335	17				7						
						77*		77*			•	•	21*	•	•	•	7*	•
A																		
						•		•			•	•	•	•	•	•	•	•
NA	A 087	007 001 008																
6010117	10-19-9				75568 61	36	345	36			25	7	3					
6010120	10-13-9				74400 61	12	345	12			12	7	3					
6015276	10-19-9				75568 61	36	345	36			25	7	3					
6015277	10-19-9			23665*	75568 61	36	345	34	64	2	25	7	3		1	1		
6015280	10-20-9				75568 61	36	345	36			25	7	3					
6015281	10-20-9				75568 61,	57	345	57			25	15	3					
6015282	10-20-9				75568 61	36	345	36			25	15	3					
6015283	10-20-9				75568 61	36	345	36			25	15	3					
						285*		283*			•	187*	80*	24*	•	1*	1*	'•
NA NA	A 075	003 001 004																
6010769	10-20-9				35309 74	6	345	6			6	6	3					
6010771	10-20-9				35309 74	526	345	526			50	50	50					
6011087	10-14-9			23679*	73869 74	150	345	144	33	1	25	15	3		2			
6013217	11-04-9				35309 74	50	345	50			25	7	3					
						732*		726*			•	106*	78*	59*	•	2*	•	•
A A A	100	001 000 001																
6015841	10-12-9				77629 74	475	345	475			50	35	35					
						475*		475*			•	50*	35*	35*	•	•	•	•
NA	000 001 001																	
6010844	10-16-9			23658*	35347 74	225												
						225*												

Courtesy International Business Machines Corp.

Tabulating equipment facilitates measurement of vendor quality performance. Data from inspection reports is punched on cards, and the equipment then calculates quality performance and prints the necessary reports.

Buyer quality performance. If quality ratings for each shipment from each supplier are accumulated, a computer can easily be programmed to calculate a combined vendor quality performance report for the entire materials department. This is an excellent barometer of the progress being made by the department in meeting its quality objective. The records can also be made up for individual buyers and used to measure their performance. It is not the only useful performance barometer, however.

Achievement of the quality objective affects other departments, too. When quality is poor, the operating costs of the quality control department are high, since each shipment must be carefully inspected.

FIGURE 19–9

IBM INTERNATIONAL BUSINESS MACHINES CORPORATION

FORM 920 7967 2

OWEGO, N. Y.
PLANT LOCATION

PURCHASED PRODUCT QUALITY CONFORMANCE REPORT

TO:

ABC Company	PERIOD ENDING	VENDOR NO
J. Doe QC Manager	Nov 15 19—	00000
Hometown		
New York		

THE QUALITY CONFORMANCE INFORMATION BELOW REPRESENTS IBM's EVALUATION OF YOUR PRODUCTS UPON RECEIPT

QUALITY CONFORMANCE   SHIPMENTS

THIS PERIOD	LAST PERIOD	TWO PERIODS AGO	RECEIVED THIS PERIOD	ACCEPTABLE AS RECEIVED	UNACCEPTABLE AS RECEIVED
Acceptable	Acceptable	Unacceptable	18	17	1

SHIPMENTS LISTED BELOW WERE FOUND TO BE UNACCEPTABLE AS RECEIVED. YOU WERE ADVISED OF THE RESULTS BY THE REJECTED PURCHASE REPORT INDICATED. SHIPMENTS ACCEPTED AS RECEIVED ARE EXCLUDED FROM THIS LISTING.

*INDICATES SHIPMENT RETURNED

PART NUMBER	PURCHASE ORDER NUMBER	QUANTITY RECEIVED	SAMPLE QUANTITY INSPECTED	SAMPLE QUANTITY DEFECTIVE	REJECTED PURCHASE REPORT NO	*
6000000	12345	50	25	3	54321	*

Courtesy International Business Machines Corp.

International Business Machines Corporation and other companies periodically mail reports to suppliers that indicate their quality performance. These reports can be generated easily if the company has data processing equipment and is already calculating quality performance for internal use.

On the other hand, when vendor quality standards are extremely high, it may even be possible to use purchased material on receipt with no inspection whatever.

Many companies "certify" suppliers with good quality control performance. These suppliers certify that each shipment meets the AQL, and the customer's inspectors content themselves with occasional spot-checks to make sure that the supplier's quality has not slipped below the certified standard.

When the materials department selects suppliers who meet quality standards with little inspection, it is making a considerable contribution to profits. Some companies—most notably General Electric Company—use the cost of operating and receiving inspection department as a barometer of materials management performance. The cost of shutdowns in manufacturing because of poor-quality purchased materials often can also be used legitimately as a barometer of materials management efficiency.

The delivery objective

Most shutdowns, however, result from the supplier's failure to deliver on schedule. Getting material, the most basic job in materials management, is one of the most difficult to measure objectively without data processing equipment. Records of each shipment from each supplier must be tabulated. Figure 19–10 shows how one company plots delivery performance of its suppliers. Another company uses barometers—a time rating and a quality rating—to rate its suppliers.

FIGURE 19–10
Delivery performance chart

Vendor delivery performance can be measured simply by dividing the number of times a vendor fails to keep a shipping promise by the number of shipments made. Listing the number of orders per week on the chart shows the significance of the failure. A high percentage of failures on a large number of orders is more serious than the same percentage of failures on a smaller number of orders.

622

Time and quantity ratings. The time rating is calculated by comparing the date when a shipment is actually received to the date for which it was promised. Early shipments are penalized less than late shipments, because it usually is more desirable to carry excess inventory than to risk a stockout. However, for many companies it is probably more important to detect early deliveries than late ones. The latter will be noticed anyway if they are important, but it is possible for a seller to deliver ahead of schedule without the buyer ever knowing about it. As long as everything is in order, the shipment will be processed routinely, and the company will wind up with inventory it does not really need until some weeks or months in the future. In some cases, the supplier may even wind up getting paid well ahead of schedule, resulting in cash being invested in unneeded inventory.

Scoring which takes both late and early shipments into account could be as follows:

100	Shipment received the week it was due or one week early.
80	One week late or two weeks early.
60	Two weeks late or three weeks early.
40	Three weeks late or four weeks early.
20	Four weeks late.
0	Five or more weeks late.

Partial receipts also serve as a barometer of delivery performance. A supplier who must make a lot of unscheduled extra shipments in small quantities is not doing as good a job as one who can accumulate the desired quantity and ship it according to schedule. Performance in avoiding partial shipments is measured by a quantity rating, which is calculated by dividing the number of scheduled receipts by the number of shipments actually made by the supplier.

The combined delivery performance rating is calculated by averaging the time delivery rating, weighted 70 percent, with the quantity delivered rating, weighted 30 percent.[3] For example, suppose a supplier is scheduled to make three shipments. The first shipment is two weeks early, the second scheduled shipment is received in two parts and the first part is two weeks late, and the fourth and final shipment arrives on schedule. The supplier's time delivery rating is equal to the average of individual ratings—80, 60, and 100—or 80. Since four shipments were made when three were scheduled, the quantity delivered rating is 75. The combined rating equals 70 percent of 80 and 30 percent of 75, or 78.5.

---

[3] Note that this weighting is quite arbitrary. Different companies would apply different weights, depending on what they believe to be the relative importance of the two factors.

This would not be good performance on most rating scales. The following scale is used by the New England company that devised this formula:

95–100	....	Excellent performance
90–94	....	Good
80–89	....	Fair
Under 80	....	Unsatisfactory

Once a company is set up to tabulate delivery statistics, it can use them not only to measure supplier performance but also to measure how well the overall materials department and the groups within it are doing in achieving the delivery objective. Performance of the department, of course, is equal to the combined performance of all suppliers on all shipments. Performance of individual groups within the department is calculated from statistics on the shipments for which they are responsible. With tabulating equipment, it is easy to keypunch receival cards not only with the vendor's code but also with the buyer's or expediter's code. Then it becomes a routine matter to run off not only delivery performance reports on suppliers but also on buyers, expediters, or some other organizational unit within the materials department.

Other barometers. Delivery performance statistics may be fairly difficult to compile even when a company has data processing equipment. Punched cards must be made up for each shipment, and equipment must be programmed to run off the necessary reports. This is usually practical only if delivery performance reports are a part of an overall data processing system.

Other barometers of delivery performance may be easier to use. They involve studying the effect of delivery on operations rather than analyzing the delivery statistics. When delivery performance is poor, the internal operating costs of the materials department are high. Travel and telephone costs go up, and payroll costs rise because more expediters are needed. Each is a barometer of delivery performance.

Costs also rise in manufacturing, because scheduling of production is less efficient when materials are in short supply. Shutdowns also are more frequent. Many slowdowns in manufacturing are charged to variance accounts (in companies with standard cost systems), which are designed to show why costs are higher than anticipated. If a company has a variance account for premium costs incurred on account of lack of material, this account in itself is a measure of the materials department's delivery performance. Of course, a barometer like this is not as useful as delivery statistics because its use is limited to measurement of department performance. It cannot easily be adapted to measure delivery performance of individual suppliers or buyers.

Vendor rating

The best suppliers do more than meet quality standards and ship according to schedule. They offer shorter lead times than their competitors; their prices are lower; and they offer more new products, ideas and miscellaneous services.

The combined rating. Various purchasing managers have attempted to weigh all these factors and develop numerical ratings for each of their suppliers. A supplier's price performance can be calculated by comparing the price with that of the lowest bidder on the order. A similar comparison can be made for lead time. In each case, the supplier's rating is calculated by averaging performance on a series of orders. The formulas are:

Percentage of price performance
$$= \frac{\text{Lowest price or bid (any vendor)}}{\text{Actual price}}.$$

Percentage of lead-time performance
$$= \frac{\text{Shortest lead time (any vendor on comparable item)}}{\text{Actual lead time}}.$$

Some companies consider only quality and delivery in developing composite delivery ratings. Others also take price and lead time into account. Such weighting is arbitrary and depends entirely on the materials manager's judgment of the relative importance of the various factors. One company uses the following weighting to rate its suppliers:

	Percent
Quality	40%
Delivery	20
Price	35
Lead time	5

Favorable relations. Such composite ratings may be useful as buying tools, and they also provide clues to how good a job the purchasing department is doing in terms of its objective of maintaining favorable supplier relations. But they do not tell the full story about performance on the latter objective. It shows up directly in cost-reduction reports and less directly in supplier assistance in product development. Presumably good relations help stimulate suppliers to generate helpful ideas for their customers. These result in new products or basic improvements that, while they are never reflected in cost-reduction reports, do have tremendous impact on customer profits.

Stimulating supplier R&D. Some purchasing managers operate on the theory that since their orders help support supplier research and development (R&D), they should see some of its tangible benefits. A few go so far as to ask each supplier quite bluntly what they have done for them in the past year. For example, one purchasing agent sends a letter every year to each supplier which reads as follows:

> During the year ——, our purchases from you totaled $——. We assume that you spend roughly five percent of your sales dollar on research and development. And certainly we at the ———— Company welcome your R&D efforts and believe that we have greatly benefited from them. Last year, your sales to us should have supported $—— worth of research and development. In addition, we believe that your excellent sales engineers undoubtedly made a number of tangible contributions to our success in the course of their work with our people. We would like evidence of such assistance. It is our intention to favor those suppliers who have done the most for us. Would you please give me a comprehensive report of the help you have given so that we may use it to evaluate your success as a supplier.

This purchasing agent's requests for substantiating evidence of supplier R&D have not been particularly successful. Most suppliers are unable or unwilling to provide her with evidence of how their R&D have helped her. But her principle is sound: Research and development is being paid for by every supplier's customers, and buyers should be interested in how successful it is in solving their own companies' problems.

Unfortunately, supplier research cannot always be related to customer objectives year by year, even if it is very useful over a longer term. This is just one of the reasons why evaluation of supplier relations performance is difficult. There is usually considerable lag before a successful vendor relations program shows measurable results. This year's performance in developing supplier relations may show up in cost-reduction reports or quality statistics in succeeding years. It is not possible to rely entirely on objective measures to determine whether or not the objective of favorable supplier relations is currently being achieved. The best the purchasing manager can do is to have a program and then report progress as best he can. For example, he may occasionally try to summarize the contributions that each supplier has made in suggesting new products or ideas or in helping operating personnel with their problems. This would be a barometer of past performance and might provide clues to current performance.

Carrier performance.   The vendor performance measurements described above can readily be adapted to a specialized type of supplier: the common carrier. There is some difference in objectives, of course. In most cases, the particular carrier cannot be measured on price performance, since under ICC regulations his tariffs most likely are identical with those of competitors. Quality and delivery objectives for the common carrier are essentially merged into a single service dependability objective.

There are two measures of a carrier's service dependability: time required to pick up a shipment (or to make a box car available) and time required to deliver the shipment to its destination. With electronic data processing, it is relatively easy to calculate the time required both for order processing and actual shipment of each order. Performance ratings can then be developed for each common carrier, using essentially the same techniques that have been described for purchased materials suppliers.

In addition, the traffic department may wish to monitor the quality of the carrier's service either by keeping track of damage claims or by having the consignee of the shipment fill out a short report indicating the condition in which the shipment was received. A composite rating can then be developed for each carrier. Changes in the carriers' ratings are more important in such a system than the absolute ratings themselves. For example, it would be significant if a particular carrier demonstrated either improved or deteriorating performance. But it might not be fair to compare an absolute rating of one carrier with another, just as it is not fair to compare ratings of two conventional suppliers who are in different businesses.

DEVELOPMENT OF PERSONNEL

Supplier performance is a valid measure of the performance of materials management personnel. For example, the best buyers are able to get better performance from their suppliers, and it is common practice to tabulate vendor performance by buyer. The purchasing manager must be cautious in comparing buyers on this basis, of course. The very best buyer may be assigned to a commodity group where there are inherent problems in achieving superior vendor performance. On the other hand, relative comparisons by buyer of vendor performance are perfectly valid. If the aggregate performance of a particular buyer's suppliers declines from 90 to 80, then the buyer is not doing as good a job for her company as she was before.

The concern of the materials manager should go beyond whether or not the staff is carrying out its present assignments in an efficient manner. He should also be contributing to the future strength of his company. Survival is one of the most basic objectives of any organization. To perpetuate itself and the company of which it is a part, every department should strive to develop and train future managers. Historically, the materials department has done a rather poor job on this objective. Proof of this is the minute number of chief executives who are former materials managers. For example, the author of one study of the backgrounds of chief executives in big business did not even bother to list purchasing or materials management as a department through which one could advance to become a chief executive.[4] Presumably the category "operations and production" in this study embraced materials management as well as manufacturing. Only 40 percent of the chief executives had this background (the balance came from finance, sales, legal departments, receivers in bankruptcy, personnel, and other departments), and undoubtedly practically all of them were from manufacturing or its equivalent in service companies.

More recently, the author made study of top-management's perceptions of its purchasing managers and materials managers.[5] The author discovered that only two of chief executives of 500 biggest companies, as reported by *Fortune* magazine, had backgrounds that indicated substantial experience in purchasing or materials management. While executives passed through positions in purchasing and materials management on their way to something else, the executive who was identified with these functions was not often considered a candidate for a general management position.

One of the major reasons that materials departments have done such a poor job in developing chief executives is historical. As we saw in Chapter 1, it is only quite recently that materials departments have developed enough stature and attracted enough high-caliber personnel to become logical training grounds for future top executives.

The materials department has done a better job in perpetuating itself by developing future purchasing agents and materials managers. Many, if not most, top materials managers have worked their way up through the ranks of the materials department. The materials manager should always be grooming potential replacements for each of his or her key subordinates. Personnel development is one of the most important objectives.

Unfortunately, it is not easy to measure year-to-year performance in achieving this objective. The results will be reflected in the performance of future managers, and it will be difficult, if not impossible, to trace them back to any particular period or program. The only practicable measure of year-to-year performance is to compare the materials manager's plans for achievement with those of previous years and to measure actual progress in carrying out the plans.

The materials manager is interested not only in developing future managers but also in getting the best possible performance from every person in the department. Her own performance should be measured by the success in reaching these goals. It is measured both by the

---

[4] Mabel Newcomer, "The Big Business Executive," in W. Lloyd Warner and Norman H. Martin, eds., *Industrial Man* (New York: Harper & Bros., 1959), p. 142.

[5] Dean S. Ammer, "Is Your Purchasing Department a Good Buy," *Harvard Business Review*, March–April 1974, pp. 36–43. This study was sponsored by the National Association of Purchasing Management.

628

programs she proposes for personnel development and by her ability to execute those programs.

High-potential employees

The materials manager's program should include regular appraisals of the performance and potential of every member of the materials organization. Particular attention should be given to development of the high-potential employees who are the company's future managers.

To become "high potential," an employee must not only perform well in his present job; he must also show promise of being able to perform well in jobs with substantially more responsibility. He must have the personality, intellect, and education of a manager.

There should be high-potential persons at almost every level of organization. This insures the orderly progression of competent executives that is essential to perpetuate the organization. In her annual report to top management, the materials manager should describe in some detail the progress being made by each of his high-potential employees. When there are insufficient high-potential employees, at any level in the organization, she should indicate how she proposes to fill the gap—through hiring new people, transfers, and so on.

Ideally, she should have replacements who are capable of filling any vacancies that might occur because of death, retirement, or resignation. Some managers use color-coded, phantom organization charts to help them plan. For each position, they list not only the incumbent but also his or her potential successors. Color codes indicate whether the potential successors are presently ready to handle increased responsibilities or require additional training. For example, the top candidate for promotion might carry a green color code, which indicates he or she is ready to move or without any additional training or experience. Other candidates might carry yellow color codes, indicating that they are not quite ready. The materials manager should then make certain that these candidates get the training and experience needed to qualify them for future promotion.

Developing managers

The materials manager should not assume that managers can be developed automatically, with no effect on her part. She should have a positive program designed to permit each employee to make a greater future contribution to company objectives. Included in this program would be such time-tested techniques as job rotation, special training programs, and special assignments.

Job rotation. Some materials managers deliberately rotate jobs in their department. Others prefer to make changes only when required;

they dislike going to the trouble of retraining men and women for new jobs when it is not absolutely necessary.

The former approach is the better one both for management development and for overall efficiency. People inevitably get stale on their jobs; occasional job rotation brings a fresh approach to the job and boosts morale. With a planned rotation program, the materials manager can eventually train several persons in all phases of every job in the department.

With a planned approach to job rotation, individuals are transferred from job to job not only when there is a basic need for the shift, on account of promotions, retirements, and the like, but also for the mere sake of rotation. For example, suppose there are ten buyers in a purchasing department, each specializing in some group of commodities. Buyer A might buy gray-iron and malleable castings; buyer B, permanent mold and die castings; and so on. One plan of rotation would be simply to have the buyers switch jobs; thus B might switch duties with A. With such a program, eventually every buyer would become familiar with every commodity.

Some materials managers might hesitate to follow this plan because it involves forcing a person to become immediately familiar with commodities entirely different from those he or she has handled. They prefer a more gradual approach, in which, for example, buyer A might continue to handle gray-iron castings but would swap the malleable castings for buyer B's die castings. With this type of change, neither B nor A would have to learn a brand new job all at once and, after enough of these changes each still would have learned how to buy every commodity in the department.

Special training programs. Each supervisor in the materials department should evaluate her subordinates. If there are gaps in their knowledge, she should try to fill them by means of training programs. High-potential employees should be encouraged to take special courses in night schools and take similar steps to broaden themselves. Many companies encourage such study by paying all or part of the tuition. Materials personnel should also be encouraged to participate in activities of such organizations as the National Association of Purchasing Management, the American Production and Inventory Control Society, the National Institute for Governmental Purchasing, the National Association of Educational Buyers, and various traffic clubs.

Many companies have training programs designed to give a broad overall understanding of company operations to young people fresh out of college. Figure 19–11 shows an outline of the training program of the Stromberg-Carlson Division of General Dynamics Corp. The materials department should play an active role in such companywide programs. In this way it can keep itself supplied with young high-potential employees by regularly providing jobs for a few trainees who

FIGURE 19–11
Personnel training program

Typical Program Schedule

DEPARTMENT	ASSIGNMENT	WEEKS	DEPARTMENT	ASSIGNMENT	WEEKS
ENGINEERING	General Orientation (Projects, Design, Value, Systems Engineering, Project Control, Components and Materials, Services, Mechanical Design)	2	PRODUCTION ENGINEERING	General Orientation	½
				Industrial Engineering	½
	Work Assignment (In one or more of above areas)	5		Tool Engineering	½
		TOTAL 7		Test Equipment Engineering	½
				Value Engineering	½
				Project Engineering or Assignment to one of the above areas	4½
					TOTAL 7
INSPECTION AND QUALITY CONTROL	Purchased Materials Inspection	1	PRODUCTION CONTROL	General Orientation	½
	Project Inspection	1		Material Inventory Control	1½
	Quality Control	1		Requisitioning and Scheduling	2
	Work Assignment (One of the above areas)	4		Planning and Expediting	3
		TOTAL 7			TOTAL 7
PRODUCTION	General Orientation (Organization, Labor Relations, etc.)	1	MARKETING	General Orientation	½
				Military Marketing	3
	Work Assignment (Capacity of Assistant Foreman)	6		Industrial Marketing	1
		TOTAL 7		Contracts Administration	2
				Advertising	½
					TOTAL 7
PURCHASING	General Orientation	½			GRAND TOTAL 49*
	Value Analysis and Standardization	1			
	Buying (Production)	1			
	Buying (Engineering)	1			
	Order Control	½			
	Work Assignment (One of the above areas)	3			
		TOTAL 7			

*The total of 49 weeks does not in all cases terminate the training of the individual. Depending upon the trainee's desires and qualifications and the needs of the company, the opportunity is afforded to spend two to four weeks in one or more of the following areas:

Plant Engineering
Value Engineering
Accounting
Research
General Services
Other-Operating Divisions

*Courtesy Stromberg-Carlson Division,
General Dynamics Corp.*

The materials department should participate actively in companywide training, both to recruit high-potential employees and to indoctrinate future executives in other departments in the importance of materials management. As this chart shows, two sevenths of the Stromberg-Carlson Division's training program is devoted to the materials management functions of purchasing and production control.

have completed the course. Also, trainees destined for other departments will be able to work better with the materials department if they know how it operates.

The purchasing department can make a valuable contribution to the company's sales training program. Fledgling salespersons can learn how customers react to various sales approaches either by trying them out on purchasing personnel in their own company or by actually watching supplier sales reps in action. Several companies make their sales trainees serve a short stint in the purchasing department as a buyer's assistant. They can see other sales reps at work and objectively appraise the impact of each on customers.

Special assignments.   The materials manager often can use special assignments to test subordinates. One assignment that can help develop further managers in two ways is that of organizing a training program. The subordinate who runs the training program is being developed, and the program itself helps develop others. High-potential subordinates should be tested regularly with special assignments. These may include special reports, development of new procedures, participation in various companywide activities (Community Chest drives, and so on), and various commodity studies.

GOOD RECORDS

The purchasing manager can achieve two objectives simultaneously when he assigns a high-potential subordinate to audit the department's records. He is developing personnel and he also is making certain that the department's records and procedures are satisfactory.

Many purchasing managers prefer to have their records checked by someone outside the department, however. They have the company's internal auditors make detailed examinations; a few even use outside auditing firms. Auditors are experts in checking records and in detecting deviations from standard procedures. They can be used as an independent check on the materials department, much in the same manner as they are used in the accounting department.

The internal auditor will first make a detailed review of the materials department's procedures in order to make certain that they provide adequate control. She will occasionally suggest changes that will either tighten control or cut costs. After she is satisfied with procedures, the auditor spot-checks a number of materials transactions to see if procedures have been compiled with in practice. She then notes each case in which there is some deviation or in which records are incomplete. In a materials department, she would make a special effort to be absolutely certain that business was awarded to suppliers in the best interests of the company. For example, the auditor would expect to find clear records of each supplier's bid. If the contract were not awarded to the lowest bidder, she would expect to find evidence justifying the decision.

After she checked a satisfactory number of transactions, the auditor would make a report summarizing her findings. This report would provide an impartial measure of the departments' performance in meeting its objective of having good records. This objective is especially important in the public and not-for-profit sectors of the economy. For example, the hospital purchasing manager should be able to prove that she complied with the prudent buyer while the governmental purchasing manager must prove that all applicable procurement regulations were obeyed.

COMPOSITE RATING?

We have now covered measurements of performance of all of the basic objectives of a typical materials department. One question that may arise in the reader's mind must remain partly unanswered: How does one arrive at a combined rating that shows overall performance in meeting all objectives? It would not be too difficult to calculate a combined rating. All one need do is determine the relative importance of each objective, give it a percentage weight, and then calculate some cumulative performance rating for the overall performance.

The writer believes, however, that such a combined rating would be almost meaningless. Not only is weighting of individual objectives arbitrary, but it would be necessary to combine objectives that can be measured quantitatively with those that can only be measured qualitatively. The writer believes that the only practical approach to performance measurement in materials management is to measure progress on each objective as accurately and impartially as possible. Then whoever is responsible for performance can be the judge whether or not the department's efforts were directed toward the right objectives.

Cases

CASE 19-1. CONSOLIDATED BUSINESS MACHINES CORPORATION

Measuring supplier performance

George Matheson, president of Consolidate Business Machines Corporation, is concerned about the company's choice of suppliers for sensor brushes, which are used in the company's data processing equipment. Matheson occasionally plays golf with Harold Adams, president of Adams Machine Company, one of the company's suppliers of brushes. Recently, Adams complained to Matheson that his firm has been having difficulty in getting its traditional share of Consolidated's brush business. On the last buy, Adams's firm failed to get any business, even though Adams believed he was the low bidder. Matheson tells Adams that normally he does not get into the details of procurement, but he promises to ask his purchasing manager, Joanne Howard to investigate.

The following morning Matheson calls Howard and tells her of Adams's complaint. He says he does not want to influence the company's procurement policies, but he does feel that Howard should investigate to make sure that Adams was treated fairly.

Howard discovers that Adams was indeed the low bidder on the last buy. Quotations for an order of 10,000 units were as follows:

Adams Machine Co.	$2.22
Burlington Electronics Co.	2.23
Zenith Tool & Machine Co.	2.25

Zenith and Burlington each got orders for 5,000 pieces. Zenith has done considerable development work on brushes, while Adams and Burlington have done very little. The quality and delivery records of the three suppliers on the last ten orders for the brush are shown in Exhibit 1. Consolidated's quality control department has set an acceptable quality level of 3 percent on the brush.

EXHIBIT 1

Supplier	Quantity ordered	Quantity defective	Delivery
Zenith	4,000	122	One week early
Burlington	4,000	92	One week late
Adams	3,000	120	On time
Adams	6,000	162	Two weeks late
Zenith	4,000	38	On time
Burlington	5,000	29	One week early
Adams	2,000	88	1,000 pieces on time; 1,000 pieces four weeks late.
Burlington	6,000	98	Two weeks late
Zenith	4,000	45	One week early
Adams	5,000	162	One week late

Questions

1. Is Howard justified in eliminating Adams as a supplier of brushes?
2. In what respect is the complaint from Adams justified?
3. Prepare a report for Matheson explaining the decision to eliminate Adams as a supplier; use quantitative data as much as possible to support your position.

CASE 19–2. BORG INSTRUMENTS DIVISION*

Use of bid handicaps to stimulate supplier performance

By putting a dollar sign on how well vendors do on quality, reliability, and service, Borg Instruments, a division of Amphenol Borg Electronics Corp., has taken vendor rating to its logical conclusion.

---

* The performance measurement system described is actually used by Borg Instruments, a division of Amphenol Borg Electronics Corp., but names of suppliers used in the case are fictitious.

Using a special formula, buyers convert vendors' monthly performance ratings into cash values. They add these amounts to suppliers' bids as handicaps or "fines." The poorer a supplier's performance rating, the higher the bid handicap he gets.

By using this system, the purchasing department of the Delavan, Wisconsin, maker of auto clocks and synchronous motors is able to buy on the basis of the total cost of doing business with a vendor—the sum of his quotation plus the money Borg must expect to spend to offset his lapses in quality, reliability, and service.

Because they are based on past performance, the penalties against suppliers are realistic and fair. According to Deane Grether, purchasing agent, weighting the bids of vendors is "a harsh stimulus, but it's effective because it's applied where it will do the most good."

Each month, Borg buyers rate suppliers' quality, reliability, and service. A buyer can give a vendor up to 40 points each in quality and reliability—or 10 points for each standard. The vendor can get up to 20 points for service—or 5 points per standard. A perfect score would be 100 points, which is rarely attained.

The buyer bases his ratings on facts rather than opinion. To score a vendor on quality, for instance, he goes to the supplier's inspection report form, which contains a running record on all questionable and rejected shipments. This form has previously been filled out on the basis of reports from the inspection department.

After a buyer has finished scoring a vendor, he totals the points and enters them in the summary box of a supplier evaluation report. At the bottom of the report is a table showing the penalty factors for various scores. A score of 97 points, for example, draws a penalty of 3 percent—which means that the supplier bid is to be handicapped (increased) by 3 percent.

On the reverse of the supplier evaluation report are complete explanations of Borg's rating criteria (see Exhibit 1) to ensure that all buyers use the same yardsticks in rating vendors.

The evaluation reports to to Grether for his review and signature. Afterwards, they are mailed to vendors—usually to the presidents of small companies and sales managers of large ones. They are thus sure of reaching interested and influential executives.

When a buyer has finished an evaluation report, he pulls the supplier's evaluation rating card from a file and enters the latest monthly score (see Exhibit 2). Every six months, he computes the average score and notes it on the card. The latest semiannual score determines the vendor's bid penalty.

In the Borg rating system, vendors have the right of appeal. They can express dissatisfaction with their scores and give Borg the chance to correct the infrequent scoring error. Recently, for example, a supplier protested a low quality score. When investigation proved his claim correct, the score was changed.

EXHIBIT 1

BORG INSTRUMENTS
A DIVISION OF AMPHENOL-BORG ELECTRONICS CORPORATION
DELAVAN, WISCONSIN

SUPPLIER EVALUATION REPORT

SUPPLIER _A.B.C. Co._   ATTN: _M. SELLER_   MONTH _MAY 1963_

QUALITY	1	2	3	4	5	6	7	8	9	10	Max. Grade	REMARKS
APPEARANCE/DIMENSIONAL								X			8	
SPOILAGE										X	10	
MATERIAL/PACKAGING										X	10	
DEFECT COSTS										X	10	
QUALITY RATING											38	

RELIABILITY	1	2	3	4	5	6	7	8	9	10	Max. Grade	REMARKS
DELIVERY PERFORMANCE									X		9	
ACQUISITION COSTS									X		9	
REPORTS, INFORMATION & RECORDS										X	10	
PRICE RELIABILITY										X	10	
RELIABILITY RATING											38	

SERVICE	1	2	3	4	5	Max. Grade	REMARKS
SALES PERFORMANCE					X	5	
TECHNICAL PERFORMANCE					X	5	
FINANCIAL PERFORMANCE					X	5	
MANAGEMENT PERFORMANCE					X	5	
SERVICE RATING						20	

RATING SUMMARY CHART

Item	Possible Rating	Your Rating
QUALITY	40	38
RELIABILITY	40	38
SERVICE	20	20
TOTAL	100	96

COST RATIO FACTOR	PENALTY FACTOR	COST RATIO FACTOR	PENALTY FACTOR
100	0	94	6%
99	1/2%	93	8%
98	1%	92	12%
97	2%	91	15%
96	3%	90	20%
95	5%	89	3% Ea. Pt. Below 100

	Last 6 Mos.	This 6 Mos.
COST RATIO FACTOR	97	

SIGNED _D.T. Shutter_
Purchasing Agent

(See Reverse Side for Rating Explanations)

EXPLANATION OF RATING TERMS

QUALITY RATING

1. **Appearance/Dimensional:** This refers to the over all appearance of your product, such defects as dirt, scratches, pits, bad paint, faulty plating, etc., and any defect caused by not being to print dimension.

2. **Spoilage:** This refers to costs incurred due to spoilage of materials over and above our regular inspection procedure.

3. **Material/Packaging:** This refers to any defect in the materials used in your product and poorly designed packaging or faulty packaging material.

4. **Defect Costs:** This refers to the cost incurred to Borg Instruments for premium inspection, rejections, waivers to use, specification revisions, and manufacturing losses.

RELIABILITY RATING

1. **Delivery Performance:** This refers to your ability, flexibility and performance in meeting our required delivery schedule.

2. **Acquisition Costs:** This refers to the costs incurred to Borg Instruments for expediting, telephone, telegraph, premium transportation charges, manufacturing losses, due to delinquencies and shortages.

3. **Reports, Information & Records:** This refers to your adherence in submitting all requested reports and information, and maintaining good records such as purchase order balances, engineering changes, invoices, request for quotations, cost estimates, etc.

4. **Price Reliability:** This refers to your ability to hold firm prices for at least one model year, and your completeness and reliability of your quotations.

SERVICE RATING

1. **Sales Performance:** This refers to the performance of the sales representative in calls (too little, too much), purchase order follow up, cost reduction ideas, availability and emergency help.

2. **Technical Performance:** This refers to the excellence and extensiveness of your design and development engineering, production engineering and tool engineering, as well as ability to assure quality before, during and after production.

3. **Financial Performance:** This refers to your adequacy of credit standing, cash flow, equity and working capital.

4. **Management Performance:** This refers to the scope and quality of your system, procedure and administration controls over facilities, materials, manpower, time and costs, and your ability to plan, organize, integrate and measure them effectively.

Borg instruments vendors receive a monthly supplier evaluation report which shows them how they fared in three rating categories and gives them their total score. Rating terms are fully defined on reverse side of the monthly form.

EXHIBIT 2

SUPPLIER INFORMATION & EVALUATION RECORD

ADDRESS *1001 MAIN ST.*	**CONTACT PERSONNEL**
CITY & STATE *HOMETOWN ILL.*	
TELEPHONE *HU 3 - 2100*	PRESIDENT
TERMS *2% 10 NET 30*	
F. O. B. *OUR PLANT*	*JOHN POWERS* SALES MGR.
ROUTING *TRUCK*	
DELIVERY *4 WKS*	*MIKE SELLER* ENGINEERING
D & B or NCO RATING *AAA #1*	
PRODUCTS MFGR. *STAMPINGS*	*HENRY MARKUM* QUALITY
	HARRY CHECKER PLANT MGR.
SALES REP. *JOE BROOKS*	
ADDRESS *2121 ELM ST. SUBURBIA ILL.*	*ROBERT OVERSEER* ORDER DELIVERY
TELEPHONE *CL 4 - 9981*	*RICHARD TELLER*
SUPPLIER	EVALUATION REPORT TO: *M. SELLER*
A.B.C CO	

EVALUATION RATINGS

YEAR	JAN.	FEB.	MAR.	APRIL	MAY	JUNE	6 MOS. COST FACTOR	JULY	AUG.	SEPT.	OCT.	NOV.	DEC.	6 MOS. COST FACTOR
1962	95	97	95	92	100	99	96	94	96	98	98	97	100	97
1963	96	94	100	98										

COST RATIO FACTOR	PENALTY FACTOR		COST RATIO FACTOR	PENALTY FACTOR
100	0		94	6%
99	1/2%		93	8%
98	1%		92	12%
97	2%		91	15%
96	3%		90	20%
95	5%		89 and under	3% Ea. Grade Below 100

A supplier's monthly performance scores are recorded on an evaluation rating card and are averaged for six months.

When a job is put on quote, the buyer enters all bids on a quotation record card. Then he picks up the latest ratings and penalty factors for the bidders from their evaluation rating cards. On the back of the quotation card, the buyer lists the bids and applies the proper penalty factor to each one.

To illustrate, a supplier with a semiannual average score of 94 points has a penalty factor of 6 percent. His bid is inflated by 6 percent. If this bid was $1000, it is raised to $1060. The supplier with the lowest bid will often lose the business if his penalty factor is significantly higher than those of his competitors.

Besides rewarding virtue, Borg's vendor-rating system helps eliminate marginal suppliers and is a defense against the occasional vendor who bids low to "buy" business, intending to recoup later by relaxing on quality. Monthly ratings are frequent enough to permit buyers to detect waning quality almost as soon as it develops. They can take prompt, effective action.

New vendors bidding for Borg business naturally do not have ratings and penalty factors, and it would be unfair to permit them to compete without any handicaps. Grether solved this problem by giving each new bidder the same handicap as the best established supplier against whom he is competing. New vendors thus receive a generous benefit of the doubt.

Most suppliers—especially the better ones—have praised the vendor-rating program. By introducing dollar values for quality, reliability, and service into the bidding process, the Borg system favors the good vendor and penalizes the poor one. In the meantime, scoring vendors on the major areas of their performance pinpoints their weaknesses and permits buyers to help them improve.

Has vendor rating been successful? Rod Burghoff, Borg's vice president of manufacturing, figures that the system is saving about $50,000 per year. And Grether reports that the number of suppliers with grades of 98 and better has more than doubled since the program started two years ago.

Questions

1. Suppose a Borg buyer receives three quotations on a part. The ABC Company quotes $95.00 per thousand in lots of 25,000; J. Brown Co. quotes $92.00; and R. James & Co. quotes $96.50. The part requires a four-cavity mold for which quotations from the three suppliers are $2,100, $2,050, and $1,995, respectively. It is expected that the part will continue in production at the rate of about 25,000 units per month for at least one year. Borg would like to have two suppliers and is willing to reward the best one with 75 percent of the order. Based on previous performance, ABC has earned a cost ratio factor of 94, J. Brown & Co. has 95 and R. James Co. has earned 98. Prepare an analysis of the three bids using Borg's rating system, and recommend suppliers.

2. A new supplier offers the same item at $97 per thousand. As the buyer, you investigate and discover that the supplier's reputation is excellent, but, nevertheless, you have never actually had any experience with it. Should

the new supplier be given any business? Back up your recommendation with an analysis based on Borg's evaluation system.

3. Suppose the new supplier is given the lion's share of the business and one of the established suppliers complaints. He tells you, "I agree with your rating system when you are comparing established suppliers. But I heard via the grapevine that you gave business to this fellow without having ever had any experience with him. And his price was higher than mine! The implication is that he will do a better job on quality and delivery than I do. But this just isn't true. This fellow is a competitor of mine on three other accounts and I get the biggest share of the business because my price is lower and I do at least as well on quality and delivery. You are making a decision without evidence when you favor him over me. This isn't fair."

Is the supplier's argument reasonable? How would you counter it?

CASE 19–3. CONTINENTAL AIRCRAFT CORPORATION

Choosing a new materials manager

Charles Harrington, vice president in charge of materials of Continental Aircraft Corporation, is looking for an assistant who can succeed him when he retires in two years. Harrington has three possible candidates for his job: Robert Clement, 37 years old, materials manager of the company's California Division; Alixia Dawson, 48 years old, materials manager of the Texas Missile Division; and Glenn Wilcox, 58, manager of materials research and administration on the corporate staff. Clement and Dawson report directly to the managers of their respective divisions and functionally to Harrington. Both Clement and Dawson are highly regarded by their division managers. Wilcox reports directly to Harrington and has earned the respect of everyone on the corporate staff.

Clement is a relative newcomer to Continental. He has degrees in aeronautical engineering and business administration, and he joined the company just five years ago as an executive in the customer relations department. He was appointed assistant materials manager of the California Division two years later and was made materials manager a year later. A young, aggressive executive, Clement has already racked up an enviable record at the California Division, which is the company's largest. Last year he exceeded his cost-reduction quota by nearly 20 percent and managed to keep inventories from rising, despite a 25 percent increase in division sales volume. Clement is a good leader and morale in his department is high, although he sometimes is a little impatient with others when they fail to match his fast pace.

Dawson was Clement's predecessor as materials manager of the California Division. She joined the company as an engineering trainee shortly after she received her B.S. degree. Her advancement in the organization was rapid, and she became materials manager of the California Division ten years ago. Harrington chose Dawson to take charge of materials activities at the rapidly expanding Texas Missile Division because of problems that were being encountered in producing satisfactory missiles. Before Dawson arrived, the division was plagued with both quality and delivery problems on purchased materials. Now, although costs are still much higher than Harrington believes they should be, suppliers are delivering on schedule material that meets the fantastically close tolerances required in missile manufacture.

Dawson has an excellent record for developing personnel. Clement was one of her protégés at the California Division, and other "alumni" who formerly worked for her now hold key posts both in other departments of Continental and in several outside companies. Compared with Clement, Dawson is much better at working with people, but she also has faults. Clement, in Harrington's opinion, has more imagination than Dawson, he drives both himself and his subordinates harder, and he may well have potential that will carry him beyond the position of top materials executive in some company.

Wilcox, the third candidate, is a real veteran of the company. He joined Continental 37 years ago as a draftsman, shortly after his graduation from college. His advancement has been steady if not spectacular. He has informally acted as Harrington's No. 2 man for more than ten years, and it is generally assumed that he will succeed Harrington. Wilcox has been employed strictly on staff work for the past ten years. He has spark-plugged a companywide materials training program and has done an excellent job working out ticklish policy and procedures problems. Before that, he acted as assistant materials manager under Harrington. This was a line job, since at that time all of the company's products were made by what is now called the California Division, and Harrington was its materials manager.

Questions

1. What qualities should Harrington look for in a successor?
2. Which, if any, of the three candidates should he choose?
3. When should he make his final decision?

20

Materials management organizations of the future

Even if there were no sound economic reasons for adopting materials management forms of organization, companies would probably continue to do so. One reason is simply imitation. When the time comes to make a change in organization, the chief executive is primarily concerned with what seems to work in practice, he or she is rarely eager to be organizationally innovative. This pragmatic approach was an inhibitive factor in the development of materials management as recently as the 1960s. At that time, accepted practice called for divided materials responsibility. The integrated materials organization was sufficiently esoteric so that hardly any chief executive wanted to take the risk of experimenting with one.

Now the situation is reversed. Materials management has become almost fashionable. At least one leading company in every industry has an integrated materials management set up, and chief executives have a convenient model they can copy. When they observe the XYZ Company is very successful and has materials management, their resistance to proposals that they adopt comparable organizations is overcome.

ORGANIZATION BEHAVIOR

In most cases, the chief executive would probably be too preoccupied with other problems to worry about materials management were there not pressures that encourage him to consider a change in organization. Sometimes the pressures are the product of specific materials management problems. In many cases, they are at least partly

640

contrived. Every real-life organization is a political entity in which change is far more likely to occur when some person or group has a vested interest in that change.

Sources of support

This is certainly true when a company creates an integrated materials management organization. Support for the change inevitably comes from would-be candidates for the material management position. Such support is almost automatic; the author's studies show that more than three fourths of all newly appointed materials managers are promoted from within their own organizations.[1] The director of purchases is the strongest single candidate for promotion to materials manager, followed by the production control manager in manufacturing companies. However, at least half of all newly appointed materials managers are promoted from a variety of nonmaterials management positions.[2]

While the executive who is trying to promote herself as materials manager is obviously a strong advocate of change, there is entrenched opposition to change in every organization. For every "winner" in an organizational change there may be one or more "losers"—those who will enjoy less prestige and power as a result of the change. The purchasing manager is not only the most likely "winner" in materials management if she should be chosen materials manager, she is also the most probable "loser." When a company adopts a materials management organization, it is all but inevitable that the purchasing manager will wind up one or more organizational levels lower than she was before. If purchasing reported to the general manager before the change, the very best it can expect afterward is that it will drop one level, reporting to materials management which, in turn, reports to the general manager.

But even less favorable developments are possible. A purchasing agent who reported directly to a general manager may find himself reporting to a materials manager who reports to a manufacturing manager who, in turn, reports to a general manager. In this case, not only the purchasing manager but also the production and inventory control manager and the traffic manager may find themselves effectively demoted when a materials manager is appointed.

---

[1] Based on a survey Dean Ammer made of 4,000 U.S. manufacturing companies under a grant from the American Production and Inventory Control Society. Part of the results were published in Article 3.6, "Materials Management," in the *Guide to Purchasing* of the National Association of Purchasing Management, as well as in various commercial publications.

[2] Ibid.

Timing of change

Most top managements are sensitive to the feelings of their subordinates—particularly if no overriding emergency forces them to get tough. The concept of "don't rock the boat" is tacitly accepted in almost every real-life organization. Major changes often are postponed until they can be made smoothly. Sometimes retirements or resignations provide the opportunity, as illustrated in the Gamelin case in Chapter 1. In other cases, organization changes can be grouped together so that almost everyone winds up with at least as good a job as he or she had before. For example, a purchasing manager who is downgraded by the creation of a materials manager may be promoted to purchasing manager of a larger division. In other cases, a severe recession may provide an opportunity to make changes gracefully. Reductions in staff can automatically create a need for organization changes, and materials management can be slipped in as a by-product. In some cases, the rationalization for the change may rest on even flimsier grounds.[3]

Eventually, however, every chief executive does make changes that he believes will strengthen his organization. Since the materials management organization has been widely accepted, it can be safely assumed that there is now a "backlog" of companies waiting to make the change when a strategic opportunity arises. There are also far more rational reasons for the materials management form of organization to gain wider acceptance. They are both technological and politico economic.

POLITICO-ECONOMIC CHANGE

Current politico-economic change is working to make materials management and the supply function increasingly important. Ironically, it is probably also working to reduce the number of top-ranking positions in the field. In 1950, there may have been more positions in materials management paying over $100,000 per year than there are today—even though the purchasing power of the dollar has declined by over 50 percent during that period, while the economy is twice as big. The big jobs of that time almost always carried the title of vice president—purchases. Almost every huge corporation had one. Many big companies still do, but until recently, the number seemed to shrink each year.

---

[3] In one company I know, the general manager simply announced he was filling a long-standing "vacancy" for the position of materials manager after having made an "exhaustive search" for the right person. Until this announcement, no one knew that the position existed! But presumably, since it had "always" existed, obviously no one was being reduced in status when the position was finally filled.

Decentralization

The underlying cause of a dearth of lush jobs in materials management was decentralization. In the beginning, at least, the motive for decentralization was economic: to increase efficiency. For example, until the 1950s General Electric Company had a huge, centralized purchasing operation in Schenectady, New York, headed by a vice president. Later purchasing responsibility was dispersed to individual operating departments. The purchasing manager typically reported to a materials manager who, in turn, was responsible to manufacturing. The materials management concept was also adopted at the corporate level, but so much authority had been delegated to individual operating departments that the highest ranking materials manager in the company did not have nearly as much authority or prestige as the former purchasing vice president.

Reciprocity. Other companies followed the GE example—for reasons not always related to operating efficiency. It has been deemed politic for purchasing at the corporate level to assume a low profile simply because centralized purchasing records are essential to efficient reciprocity. Reciprocity can be illegal if the Justice Department or the Federal Trade Commission can prove that it substantially lessens competition. Conglomerate corporations—which might otherwise provide a number of high-level purchasing jobs—can most easily prevent possible antitrust problems by simply not having a purchasing activity at corporate level. All buying is done by decentralized divisions and, in the absence of centralized purchase records, it becomes all but impossible to practice reciprocity on a wide scale. Other companies that still have centralized purchasing departments have been specifically enjoined by the Justice Department from maintaining corporate records of sales and purchases. Although no one likes to admit it, this action by the Justice Department eliminates a high-level purchasing function. In the process industries in particular, the chief purchasing executive was as concerned with reciprocity or "trade relations" as he or she was with more conventional purchasing activities.

While the Justice Department's antireciprocity drive has undoubtedly worked to reduce the number of top-level purchasing positions, it has probably helped accelerate the movement toward materials management. When the rules on reciprocity were free and easy, purchasing departments were sales oriented. In the paper, chemical and petroleum industries in particular, sales and purchasing were sometimes combined organizationally. When they were not, the purchasing director was often an ex-sales manager and usually played a critical role in reciprocity that informaly linked purchasing and sales, even if the combination was not part of the formal organization.

Production orientation. Former marketing-oriented purchasing departments are gradually becoming part of production-oriented materials management departments, In larger corporations, these departments occur primarily at divisional level, and there may be no corporate purchasing or materials management staff whatever. Worse yet, from the point of view of concerned materials managers, at least half of all materials managers do not report directly even to a division manager but to a second-level divisional executive—usually the manufacturing manager.

There are two basic reasons for this state of affairs, from top management's point of view:

1. A company whose purchasing department is "buried" in a materials management department which, in turn, is part of manufacturing, is less likely to be regarded as a potential antitrust offender—particularly if the organization is at divisional level.

2. The manufacturing manager may oppose creation of an independent materials management organization if this requires him to give up jurisdiction over production and material control activities. But he may welcome materials management if it is placed under his jurisdiction.

Government regulations. The Justice Department's antireciprocity stand is by no means the only government-inspired force working indirectly to spur wide adoption of the materials management form of organization. Other governmental actions are also favorable. Increasing governmental regulation of business forces top management to consult with its materials manager or purchasing manager before making major decisions. By measures both legal and unlegislated but with the force of law, the government is guiding seemingly private corporate purchasing decisions. Materials managers must work actively to develop minority suppliers and to encourage smaller vendors to attempt to compete successfully with larger ones.

In many cases, there are pressures to "buy American" even if a foreign firm offers better quality at lower prices. In addition, almost every larger corporation must keep abreast of the twists and turns of American foreign policy. At one time, for example, it was perfectly acceptable for American firms to purchase nickel from the Soviet Union, while Cuba was off limits. It mattered not that the Cubans undoubtedly sold their nickel to the USSR in order to permit the USSR to sell its nickel to the United States. While government guidance in purchasing is seldom welcomed by American business, it undoubtedly works to strengthen the purchasing organizations involved.

Full-employment economy

The by-products of the Full Employment Act of 1946 are not welcomed by most American managements either, but they, too, work to make the role of materials management more critical. This act requires the federal government to intervene in the economy to maintain full employment. The side effects of these policies are well known. They include steady inflation, historically high interest rates, and turbulent labor relations.

Inflation. One need have no forecasting ability to predict that the general price level will be higher next year than it is this year—and even higher the year after. Inflation is part of our way of life. If all prices and costs were to rise predictably at the same rate, inflation would pose no real problem for the purchasing manager. Increases in purchased materials costs would be more than offset by increases in company selling prices. Unfortunately, the rate of inflation is uneven. While selling prices of most finished goods and services eventually go up to reflect higher basic costs of material and labor, there often is a rather painful lag. This puts special pressure on the purchasing agent and materials manager who may be responsible for at least half of product costs. Increasingly, company managements are discovering that they must have a first-rate purchasing department if they are not to be caught in squeezes where company costs are rising faster than selling prices.

Interest rates. When prices are expected to go up, the logical response is to boost inventory, to stock up at a lower price. This is inhibited, however, by the high interest rates that are another by-product of successful full-employment policies. The combination of soaring prices and rising inventory carrying costs makes it imperative that a company work for optimum purchase prices and inventory levels. This is easiest to accomplish with an integrated materials management organization.

Strikes. Every employee would like to get a bigger slice of the total economic pie. Everyone also occasionally has the urge to tell off the boss. In the past, fear of unemployment worked to inhibit workers from expressing these fundamental human urges. Full employment and generous unemployment benefits take away almost all of the penalties of work stoppages. In addition, as explained below, technology gives the protesting worker a great deal more economic leverage than he or she had before. The net result is that from the worker's point of view it often pays to strike—and disruptions in supply from labor unrest seem to be increasing in frequency, especially in the English-speaking countries. This inevitably makes it more desirable for managements to have integrated materials management departments to minimize the effect of supplier strikes.

AUTOMATION AND THE SUPPLY PROCESS

It is no accident that employees in capital-intensive highly automated industries are both higher paid and far more likely to strike than their less fortunate brethren in labor-intensive, unautomated industries. The barber continues to cut hair with essentially the same tools used in 1920, but production of most other goods and services has been greatly changed by technology. Jobs that used to be done by many workers with relatively simple tools are now done by relatively few workers using very costly tools. In the factory, this process of using fewer workers and more complex machinery is called automation. But the same process of technological change has also affected most major service industries. In the hospital clinical laboratory, a $60,000 machine can perform in minutes tests that formerly required hours of a skilled medical technologist's time. Similarly, a Boeing 747 airliner is able to transport almost 20 times the number of passengers carried in the piston-engine airliners common until 1960.

Automation in manufacturing and services has greatly reduced costs. And, of course, with their relative absence of workers, automated plants look as if they should be low-cost producers, and they are. But they are not *no-cost* producers. Even though direct labor costs may have been virtually eliminated, all other costs still exist—purchased materials, administrative costs, maintenance and depreciation, interest and return on invested capital, and so on. In fact, some of these costs will be much higher in the automated plant. Its more complex equipment costs more to maintain. It also requires a greater initial investment, which means higher interest and depreciation charges.

As yet no one has built a workerless plant. But some of the highly automated plants in the electrical equipment, electronics, and auto industries provide clues as to what happens to costs when processes are automated. The following example is representative:

	Before automation	After automation
Material	$1.00	$1.02
Labor	0.38	0.04
Overhead	0.57	0.55
Manufacturing cost	$1.95	$1.61
Sales and administrative cost	0.08	0.08
Profit (to yield 20% return on investment)	0.17	0.34
Selling price	$2.20	$2.03

As expected, automation drastically reduces labor costs and also reduced total costs. Not so obvious, however are other by-products.

Overhead is practically unchanged. Although there is less indirect labor in the automated plant, what labor there is will be more highly skilled and higher priced. The greater capital investment in automated equipment raises depreciation charges and probably also general maintenance and operating costs. As a result, the composition of the overhead changes. Fixed charges (depreciation and so on) increase, while variable charges (mostly indirect labor) decrease. This makes costs more rigid.

2. Profit requirements are greater. Automation requires a bigger investment in facilities. Naturally this means that profits on each unit produced must be higher to yield the same return on investment. In the example above, a 17-cent unit profit might be adequate, at standard volume, to provide a 20 percent return on a $1 million investment in facilities. Suppose the investment in facilities increases to $2 million when production is automated. Then a 34-cent unit profit would be needed to provide a 20 percent return on investment—assuming there is no change in volume of output.

In addition, many managers believe that automated facilities should earn a greater return on investment than nonautomated facilities (although competition usually prevents this). The reason: the risks are greater with automation. In a completely unautomated plant, if a product fails to sell management can simply lay off workers and thus minimize losses. With automation, it cannot get off so easily. It is likely to be stuck with an enormous investment in equipment that is not good for much of anything except making a product that no one will buy.

3. Tighter specifications may be needed. When there are slight deviations in quality of parts and materials in a nonautomated plant, workers often are able to use the materials anyway by making minor adjustments. In a fully automated plant this might not be true. The automated equipment may not be able to compensate for off-standard materials; machines can never be as flexible as skilled human hands.[4] Inevitably, increasing automation will bring demands on suppliers to adhere more rigidly to specifications. This may raise costs of purchased materials slightly. It may also increase the probability of supply failure due to poor quality.

---

[4] I observed an excellent example of this several years ago when touring the factory of a leading manufacturer of electronic data processing equipment. Electronic control panel boards were being assembled and soldered on an automated line. The new process required just two workers to load and unload parts from the line. The old process had required more than a dozen workers, who assembled and soldered various components—capacitators, resistors, transistors, and so on—to the printed circuit panel boards. Now the job was done by machine, only the machine wasn't working when I saw it. A shipment of capacitators had arrived, and some of them had wires that had been bent slightly in packing. Were the capacitators being soldered to the board by hand, this defect probably would not even have been noticed. The workers would simply have bent the wires to make them fit when they soldered them to the panel board. With the automated setup, each capacitator with a bent wire shut down the line for 10 or 15 minutes. It jammed the magazine feed at one station in the line, and no sooner would it be unjammed by a worker when another bent capacitator would jam up another station. The problem was finally licked by packing and unpacking with special care to prevent the wires from being bent. Naturally this raised costs slightly.

4. Costs of supply failure increase. In a nonautomated plant, if a supplier fails to deliver materials of satisfactory quality the plant is shut down and the workers are sent home. This is costly enough. But in a fully automated plant, the costs of shutting down are many times greater. Since there are fewer workers, less can be saved by sending them home without pay. Substituted for the workers is a tremendous investment in equipment that goes right on depreciating, whether it is being used or not.

What happens to the costs in the example when there is a shutdown? In both the automated and the nonautomated plant, the material and direct labor costs can be largely eliminated; material is not used and workers are laid off.[5] Nevertheless, a supply failure even in the nonautomated plant can be costly. Note that the product in the example has a unit overhead cost of 57 cents when made in a nonautomated plant. Perhaps 30 cents of this is fixed or nonvariable overhead, which is incurred regardless of whether or not the product is made. In addition, the company naturally loses its 17-cent unit profit when there is a shutdown so its total loss on each unit not produced is 47 cents. If the plant has a standard volume of 1,000 units per hour, then the supply failure costs $470 per hour.

The costs of a shutdown almost double in the automated plant. The 55-cent unit overhead cost in the automated plant is a little lower than the overhead in the nonautomated plant. But much more of it—at least 45 cents—is fixed and nonvariable, incurred regardless of whether or not the plant operates. In the automated plant, the variable indirect-labor cost that was incurred for inspectors, material handlers, and so on, is replaced with nonvariable maintenance and depreciation expense needed because of the added investment in plant and equipment. As a result, the automated plant has 15 cents (45 cents minus 30 cents) more fixed and nonvariable overhead per unit than the nonautomated plant. In addition, the profit loss is greater when the automated plant shuts down. It is 34 cents instead of 17 cents, or 17 cents greater. Thus a shutdown in the automated plant results in a total additional loss of 32 cents (the 17-cent profit loss plus the 15 cents in extra fixed overhead) per unit. At standard volume of 1,000 units per hour, the supply failure in the automated plant is $320 per hour more costly than the same failure in the nonautomated plant. The total cost of the failure is $790 per hour.[6]

---

[5] This is an oversimplification. Employers incur substantial labor costs even when they lay off workers, because union contracts call for supplementary unemployment compensation. In addition, state workmen's unemployment compensation benefits are paid from taxes levied on employers in proportion to their workers' needs for such benefits.

[6] Based on 45 cents for unit fixed and nonvariable overhead in the automated plant, plus 34 cents in unit profit, multiplied by 1,000 units per hour.

5. *Probability of supply failure increases.* The extremely high cost of shutting down automated equipment is not lost on the employees who operate it. The costlier the shutdown, the greater their bargaining power. It is no accident, for example, that airline pilots are far more likely to strike than taxicab drivers. The airline pilot who strikes causes a $25 million aircraft to sit idle, and the loss to airline management for each idle plane can be several hundred thousand dollars per day. From the pilots' point of view, strikes are profitable because managements cannot afford to let their aircraft sit idle for prolonged periods, thus each strike brings new gains in wages and fringe benefits. In contrast, the owner of a taxicab loses relatively little if a driver refuses to work, and the driver has far less incentive to strike.

Thus automation in the factory and in service industries not only greatly increases the cost of supply failure but also tends to increase its probability. This unfavorable aspect of automation makes managements more conscious of the need for capable materials management personnel to minimize the effect of supply failures.

AUTOMATION IN THE OFFICE

Automation in the factory has put tremendous pressure on materials managers by increasing the costs of supply failure. The use of computers in the office relieves some of this pressure, because it allows for radically different materials management techniques.

It is also bringing substantial changes in the organization structure for materials management. Chapter 1 noted that in many companies materials activities are not unified organizationally. The typical manufacturing company has separate purchasing, traffic, and production control departments. The only person responsible for all three activities in most cases is the company's president or general manager, and often he or she is much too busy with other problems to worry much about materials management. In the typical company materials get managed if the managers of the various materials activities have learned how to work together and responsibility is divided among them quite precisely by policies, procedures, tradition, and habit.

There are at least four reasons why this approach does not work well when the computer takes over the routine tasks of materials management:

1. *Computer programs stimulate unification of materials activities.* Computer programming is extremely costly. Even fairly simple business systems require a programming investment of several thousand dollars; major systems require several man-years of work because of the many exceptions that must be allowed for in

creating the program. Programming is a problem even when cost is no object.

For this reason, it is obvious that interrelated activities such as purchasing, production control, and traffic cannot develop programs independently of one another. Materials management must be considered an integrated activity in developing a single program. This, in turn, helps break down the functional lines between departments and works to unify them organizationally.

2. *Reports from computers encourage a unified, integrated approach to materials management.* Companies rarely invest in computers simply because they want to cut clerical overhead. They are every bit as interested in another objective: to speed the flow of information needed for making decisions. Computers permit daily inventory status reports in companies that formerly were forced to use monthly reports (issued up to a month late) as a basis for materials management decisions. Such rapid reporting is useful only if management is able to use it promptly in making decisions.

This is more likely to be the case in an integrated materials department. In such an organization, one person can be delegated all the authority needed to take action on most materials problems. This is not the case in the conventional materials organization with separate purchasing, production control, and traffic departments, particularly if these departments are not even unified under a common materials manager. In such an organization, basic materials decisions can be made only after there is some consultation among individuals in the interested departments. Inevitably, this is more time-consuming than if responsibility rested with one person who is responsible for all phases of materials management for a particular item. It is also more wasteful, since it causes several persons to check similar materials problems for identical products.

3. *Personnel needs change.* The computer makes it possible to reduce sharply the number of clerical employees in materials management—especially in production control. Materials management activities that employed 200 persons in the pre-EDP period may now employ but 100. While employment for nonclerical categories increases, this is usually offset (given a constant volume of business) by reductions in clerical employees. Supervision is easier than it was before simply because there are fewer employees to supervise. In most real-life cases, this change is invisible because total office employment has tended to increase despite adoption of EDP. However, the employment gains are the product of demands that simply did not exist before. When machines take over the clerical drudgery that used to be common in most materials management activities, it becomes more feasible to group these activities under a single manager.

4. *The computer promotes centralized control.* In the pre-computer era, every production control clerk was a materials manager

of sorts. Decisions on how much to order and how much to stock were necessarily made at a rather low level in the organization. The best that top management could do was to provide broad guidelines. It could not get into the details; there were just too many of them.

Now top managers can get into as many details as they like. The computer can screen millions of bits of information and serve it up for top-management attention in bite-sized portions. An executive can sit with a CRT terminal and almost manage materials in detail. Thus, with a computer, a materials manager can interrelate all elements of job in a way that could never be done before. This has undoubtedly encouraged development of materials management organizations.

Recentralization

In fact, the computer's ability to act as a super-snoop watchdog that permits top managers to look over the shoulders of thousands of employees in hundreds of plants is causing the materials management to become more centralized. Managers still maintain that operations are decentralized. But the term decentralization has taken on a somewhat different meaning. In the past, it meant that each manager of a decentralized unit could indeed function pretty much on her own within policy guidelines set down by top management. To be realistic, it was awfully difficult for top management to keep its eye on every operation. The best that could be done was to measure performance well after the fact. The computer has changed this. The operation is still nominally decentralized. But top management knows exactly what is going on because information can be assembled and transmitted so rapidly. This makes it possible for a corporate materials manager to watch the entire process in dozens or hundreds of factories.

It is no accident that a corporation like General Motors, which invented "decentralization" about 50 years ago, now has a vice president in charge of procurement, production, and logistics. In the past, each GM division (theoretically at least) was responsible for its own materials management activities. This is still true—except that a corporate vice president has been added. Thus, the $100,000 per year positions as purchasing vice presidents that existed in the 1950s are reappearing in somewhat different form—thanks to the computer.

DEVELOPMENT OF THE PROFIT CENTER

The next logical development in materials management is to look at what the function is supposed to do and develop techniques that will naturally cause it to improve its performance. Of course, in the past, materials management activities have been regarded as "services" that help other profit centers within the company do a better job. In this respect, materials management resembles a department like maintenance which makes an indirect contribution by preventing breakdowns. Neither maintenance nor the various materials management activities have traditionally been regarded as direct profit markers. Their contribution has usually been too indirect and too difficult to measure.

Criteria for profit center

Every materials manager can improve his own performance by applying profit center techniques to the management of the department. And, in the future, the materials department may well turn out to *be* a profit center. The purpose of profit centers is to focus management's attention on the most basic objective of the business: profits. For this reason, manufacturing is almost always broken up into profit centers in big companies. Sales and engineering may also be legitimate profit centers.

Organization. A profit center is created by drawing an imaginary line around some part of the organization and arbitrarily treating it as a separate business whose manager is responsible for profits. For example, an automobile assembly plant may be a separate profit center. It may "buy" engines, bodies, and other major components from the company's own manufacturing plants or from outside suppliers. It assembles these components into complete automobiles which it "sells" to the company's sales organization which, in turn, sells to dealers. The plant "profit" represents the difference between cost and selling price.

A company's sales organization may also be considered as a profit center. It "buys" finished products at some predetermined price from the company's manufacturing organization and then resells them to company customers. Thus the marketing organization of a large manufacturer may be treated somewhat as a department store. It buys material from the factory; adds value to it with its own advertising, sales promotion, and distribution; and finally resells at a profit to the ultimate user.

Materials management can be treated the same way. It buys material from others, adds value to it in the form of distribution, and then "sells" it to the company's own manufacturing organization. The difference between the price at which material is transferred to manufacturing and the total cost of procurement represents the "profit" from materials management. This profit can be related to the capital that is employed in the materials management process.

Essential factors. Every profit center has these basic criteria: (1) value is added, (2) capital is employed productively, and (3) costs are incurred. The materials management organization in any profit or nonprofit company or institution can meet these criteria as well as a "captive" manufacturing profit center such as the Fisher Body Division of General Motors. Nevertheless, few captive materials management profit centers actually exist. One major reason is that most top managers either are not familiar with the concept or do not believe it is advantageous. Also, the application of the profit center concept implies the existence of an independent materials management organization, and this idea is not always welcome in companies where materials management is subordinate to manufacturing, finance, or some other function. The materials manager who is recognized as a "value adder" in her own right is the organizational equal of the manufacturing, marketing, and other second-level managers of the business. While few real-life materials managers head genuine profit centers, the concept is not entirely theoretical. The procurement activities of several department store chains are almost independent profit centers. They buy for a group of stores and charge them an amount that at least equals the cost of the service. The General Services Administration also buys and stores materials and supplies which it then resells at cost plus markup to other government agencies.

Profit center accounting

While top managements may not have any interest in putting the materials manager in charge of a profit center for the sake of prestige, they are sympathetic to any program designed to boost profit. The materials department can set up its own system of profit control without any formal organization changes. The end result is a profit and loss statement and a balance sheet for the materials department that resemble those of other profit centers.

Assets.   If you were a materials manager setting up a profit center system, you would first list the value of all assets under your jurisdiction. (You can get part of the data from accounting; some you may have to estimate yourself.) A medium-sized firm might have the following materials management assets:

Assets

Raw materials inventory	$1,000,000
Office equipment and floor space	200,000
Factory floor space and equipment	300,000
	$1,500,000

If yours is a manufacturing company, the purchased materials inventory would include not only direct but also indirect material. In nonmanufacturing organizations it would, of course, include only inventories of supplies and other materials not incorporated into any product. Office equipment and floor space would include the allocated share of those assets that are employed in the complete materials management process. For example, if purchasing, production control, and other materials management activities occupy 10 percent of an office building with a value of $1 million, then the value of the space these activities occupy is $10 \times \$1,000,000$, or $100,000. A similar approach is used when materials management shares factory floor space with manufacturing.

You would have no liabilities (as long as you assumed that all material in stores had been paid for), so the company's net investment in its materials management operation would be $1.5 million. Like the company's other investments, this is expected to earn a return. If it provides no economic return, then the company should liquidate it. Companies usually set target returns on capital employed. For example, the General Motors Corp. allegedly will not invest money in a project unless it promises a 25 percent return on investment.

Suppose your company has profit objectives more modest than General Motors's and is willing to settle for a 20 percent return. Then the materials management profit objective becomes 20 percent of the $1.5 million investment in materials management assets, or $300,000 per year. If you can reduce your investment, however, you can get along with less profit. Suppose, for example, that you succeed in reducing inventory investment by $200,000. This reduces total assets from $1.5 million to $1.3 million. With assets of only $1.3 million, you need earn but $260,000 per year in order to achieve management's 20 percent profit objective.

Focus on profit. So far, all you have done is draw up a theoretical balance sheet to guide you in managing materials. Nevertheless, note how this automatically helps focus your efforts on management's profit objectives and works to boost efficiency. If you occupy more floor space, buy equipment for your own use, or boost inventory, you automatically boost your department's total capital. This, in turn, boosts your profit bogey—forcing you to make 20 cents extra profit for every $1 extra investment. Conversely, you can make yourself look good by whittling down your investment, as long as this does not impair operating efficiency. You will not invest in additional facilities or inventory to provide better "service" but to make more money. This is as it should be in a competitive, profit-lean economy.

There is no way in which you can separate the return earned by assets employed in materials management from assets employed in other basic activities of the business. This is true of any "captive" profit center which does not sell its output on the open market. The reason for this, of course, is that your profit or that of any other captive profit center is heavily dependent on the price charged for goods and services. If these are sold on the open market, you can charge whatever the traffic will bear, and there is no doubt that a profit has been earned. If they are sold within the organization, there is no "free market," and the earnings of every captive profit center are at least partly suspect.

To start a captive profit center, however, it is probably reasonable to assume that it earns the same return on its capital as other profit centers in the same company earn on the capital they employ. If the company earned, for example, a 15 percent pretax return on all of the capital employed in every phase of its business, it is reasonable to assume that, in the beginning at least, materials management and every other activity in the company made this same contribution. So you arbitrarily assume that as materials manager you are neither better nor worse than any of the company's other managers, and, like them, earned a 15 percent return on the capital.

Income statement. This preliminary estimate of a target return on capital gives you a basis for pricing and creating an income statement. You incur two types of cost in the operation of your materials management profit center: cost of goods and services purchased for resale, and operating expenses. Suppose, for example, that you purchased $10 million worth of goods and services from outside suppliers last year. Total expenses associated with all materials management activities—salaries, fringe benefits, depreciation on buildings and equipment, and so forth—amounted to $300,000. Thus the total materials management effort had total costs of $10.3 million last year, exclusive of any return earned on capital. But, of course, $1.5 million of the company's capital is needed for the assets employed in materials management. If this capital has been used productively it must have earned some return, and we arbitrarily assume that this return is identical with that earned by the company's combined activities. If this overall return is 15 percent, the "profit" earned in materials management must be equal to 15 percent of the capital employed: 15 percent of $1.5 million, or $225,000. Total value added by distribution in the materials management process then becomes $225,000 plus the $300,000 of operating expenses, or $525,000. Therefore, the $10 million worth of value added by suppliers has a value of $10,525,000 by the time it is used by "customers" of the materials management department in manufacturing or other company activities.

You now have all the figures you need to construct the following income statement:

"Sales"	$10,525,000
Cost of goods sold (annual purchase volume)	10,000,000
Gross margin	$ 525,000
Expenses incurred in the materials management process	300,000
Profit earned in materials management	$ 225,000

$$\frac{\text{Materials management profit} = \$225,000}{\text{Capital employed} = \$1,500,000} = 15 \text{ percent return on capital}$$

Purpose of the profit center

So far, we have gone through what could be a meaningless exercise in bookkeeping. It has significance, however, even if we go no further. It proves rather conclusively that $1 worth of purchased material is worth more than $1 by the time it reaches the using department. Conventional accounting systems assume that there are no costs associated with each purchase and that, therefore, the using department incurs a cost that is no greater than the cash purchase price plus inbound freight. This simply is not true. Value is always added by distribution in the materials management process, and the costs of using activities are understated if they do not reflect full cost of purchased materials to the user.

This can be particularly misleading in cases where the materials management process is extremely costly. For example, the true cost of $1 worth of medical-surgical supplies delivered to a hospital nursing station may be $1.50 or even $2 by the time all materials management costs, including return on capital, are taken into account. Profit center calculations that take into account value added by materials management help shift costs to the parts of the organization where they are actually incurred. This makes for more precise financial reporting and should lead to greater overall efficiency.

Even more important, however, is the impact that a materials management profit center may have on the ways in which materials are managed. For the first time, the performance of the materials manager is directly related to the primary economic mission of the organization: to achieve maximum results with minimum resources. The efforts of the materials manager are automatically focused on economic performance.

The materials manager behaves like a business executive and works to maximize return on capital. This can be done by reducing purchase costs or operating expenses. The materials manager may also succeed in employing less capital in the materials management process, as suggested in the three simple examples given below.

1. *Inventory reduction.* The materials manager decides to cut inventories by 10 percent. She purchases smaller quantities than before and also reduces order points, thereby cutting back on safety stocks. As a result, she is able to operate with an inventory investment of only $900,000, and capital employed in materials management is reduced by $100,000 to a net total investment of $1.4 million. If we assume competent inventory management in the past, this reduction cannot be made "for free." Materials management operating expenses should go up, since shortages will occur more frequently and increased expediting will be needed.

In addition, there may be an increase in supply failures. Buck-passing is not allowed in the materials management profit center. The materials manager earns profit by guaranteeing delivery of material to users in accordance with some prearranged schedule. If material is not available because inventories are too low, then materials management must absorb any losses incurred by the using department that result from material not being on hand when needed.

Assume arbitrarily that these extra expenses and losses resulting from the cut in inventory amount to $10,000 per year. If there are no other changes in costs or revenues, this means that the "profit" earned in the materials management process declines by $10,000 to $215,000. However, this $215,000 profit is earned by an investment of only $1.4 million because inventories are $100,000 lower than before. Consequently, the return on capital is $215,000 ÷ $1,400,000, or 15.4 percent. Thus tighter inventory control has increased return on capital by 0.4 percent.

2. *Lower purchase costs.* The materials manager embarks on a campaign to reduce costs of purchased parts and materials. He believes that if he hires a specialist in cost reduction, the savings made from value analysis (see Chapter 14) will more than offset the salary and other costs incidental to the program. So he hires a value analyst, and operating costs increase by $20,000 per year. However, the value analyst succeeds in reducing purchase costs by 1 percent, so the saving is $100,000 per year (0.01 × $10,000,000). As a result, profit from materials management increases by a net of $80,000 per year. Provided there are no other changes, total profit will then be $305,000 per year, and return on capital increases to about 20 percent per year.

3. *Methods are improved.* The materials manager discovers that he can reduce payroll and other operating costs in the department by $20,000 per year if he spends $100,000 on new materials handling equipment. The reduction in operating costs increases profit by $20,000, to $245,000, but capital employed in materials management increases by $100,000, to $1.6 million. As a result, return on investment is 15.3 percent, a modest increase over the 15 percent overall return that was earned prior to the investment in new equipment.

Ground rules

If the materials manager is able to continue to make improvements in operations like those described above, return on capital will begin to increase gradually. Initially we assume that materials management earns exactly the same return as the rest of the company. At this starting point, the calculated return on capital employed in the materials management process has no real meaning. However, successive calculations of return on capital are significant. Suppose, for example, that the materials manager begins in year 1 with the same 15 percent as the rest of the company, but by year 5 she has managed to increase return on capital to 20 percent. Meanwhile, the company has made no progress in boosting overall profitability, and total return on capital continues to be exactly 15 percent. This means that over this five-year period materials management has become relatively more profitable, while other company activities have become relatively less profitable. If the ground rules for measuring profitability are correctly constructed, then this relative improvement in materials management profitability is a fair measure of the materials manager's performance.

However, tough ground rules are needed if change in return on investment is to be a valid measure of materials management performance. The exact rules would have to be tailored to fit the unique needs of each organization, but the following rules illustrate the principle.

1. *Materials management pays for all supply failures.* Losses resulting from supply failure are absorbed by materials management rather than the department that uses the purchased material. For example, suppose that late delivery of purchased materials from a supplier forces manufacturing to schedule overtime for operations that fall behind schedule due to lack of purchased material. This cost would be chargeable to materials management, not to manufacturing, even if the supply failure was more or less an act of God. For example, if an outside supplier is held up because of a fire or flood, the materials manager cannot disclaim responsibility simply because she could not anticipate the disaster. She is automatically held responsible for the performance of all outside suppliers, regardless of cause. The using departments, in effect, pay materials management to assume this responsibility so that they, in turn, can concentrate their efforts exclusively on the activities in which they specialize.

2. *Transfer prices are relatively rigid.* Materials management is a "cost plus" operation only in year 1, when a markup is added to purchased materials costs sufficient to cover both materials management operating expenses and a return on capital equal to that which is earned companywide. From then on, materials management is on its own. If a supplier increases his price, the added cost is absorbed by materials management, not by the department that actually uses the purchased material. This tough rule applies even to purchased materials whose prices cannot possibly be influenced by the materials manager. However, the rule does work both ways. If the materials manager succeeds in reducing the price paid for purchased material, the saving is *not* passed on to the user.[7] Reductions in cost auto-

---

[7] The only exception to this rule would be a case where the using department is at least partly responsible for the reduction in purchase price. Then it would naturally share in the benefit. For example, if the using department agrees to relax purchase specifications, then it would naturally benefit from the lower costs that result. On the other hand, if the cost reduction comes about simply because the purchasing department is able to buy identical material from another supplier at a lower price, then the saving need not be shared with the using department, and the transfer price to the user would not be reduced even though costs are lower.

ments, then it is only fair to consider them as part of the costs of materials management, even with failures that no reasonable person could foresee or prevent.

4. Rational risk taking is encouraged. There is some element of risk in every phase of a business. However, managements have traditionally taken substantial risks in marketing and design and avoided them in materials management. For example, a company might, in effect, take a risk at 50–50 odds when it launches some new product with a costly advertising campaign. In the same company, a purchasing manager may decline to take a chance on a new supplier, even though the odds may be 5 to 1 in favor of that supplier being as successful as the higher cost supplier than would be replaced.

In the traditional organization, the penalty for failure that is suffered by the staff executive is much greater than the reward for success. In materials management, this may mean that the saving from successful buying simply is not noticed but the failures (e.g., when the plant is shut down because of supply failure) are extremely conspicuous. It is a wonder, then, that a materials manager is willing to take any risk whatever, even when it is to the company's advantage. In the materials management profit center, in contrast, risk taking that is profitable on balance is encouraged. As long as the "winners" outnumber the "losers," the return on investment earned by materials management should increase. And, of course, this gain is not at the expense of any other activity, since materials management assumes full responsibility for supply failures.

5. Materials management can spend money to make money. In the conventional organization, materials management is treated as a cost center, not a profit center. The budget is the major tool for control and for performance measurement. When times are tough, the materials manager is expected to reduce the budget. When the outlook is rosy, top management will listen sympathetically to a materials manager's pleas for a bigger budget. Cost center control may lead the materials manager to overstaff during boom periods so that he is not badly crippled when management forces him to make cuts during periods of austerity. (The basic work load in most materials management activities is largely independent of the business cycle.)

In many cases, top management may be so preoccupied with budgetary control that it refuses to authorize materials management projects that increase profitability. For example, one manager of a materials management cost center (i.e., a conventional materials management department) requested an increase of $50,000 per year in his budget to initiate a value analysis program that promised to reduce costs by at least $200,000 per year. The materials manager's boss was sympathetic to the idea but suggested that it be tabled for a few years until the company "got back on its feet again" and could afford to take on new programs!

In the materials management profit center, the materials manager would probably still be forced to get top-management approval if he wanted to boost the operating budget. But the focus is quite different. The materials manager could point to an expected increase in profit rather than an increase in cost, and approval would be far more likely. For example, even in the toughest of times, a marketing manager may be able to hire extra salespersons provided she can convince the boss that they will earn their keep. And, of course, the manufacturing manager hires extra workers as long as customer demand provides work to do. There is no reason why the same reasoning cannot be applied to a decision to boost the materials management payroll, provided this results in a higher return on capital.

6. *Managers will develop in materials management.* At present, very few top managers begin their careers in materials management activities. For example, only two of the presidents of the 500 largest manufacturing companies have backgrounds in purchasing and, apparently, none is a specialist in production control or traffic. In contrast, marketing and manufacturing supply hundreds of top management executives. The basic reason these functions breed top managers is because their executives learn how to make basic profit and loss decisions at relatively early stages in their careers. Their counterparts in materials management, in contrast, tend to be more concerned with pleasing the real decision makers rather than making any decisions themselves. In effect, marketing and manufacturing provide an environment that makes their practitioners think like business executives; materials management activities often seem to create merely timid bureaucrats. The harsher, less sheltered environment of the materials management profit center should develop more business executives who can go on to assume top-management responsibilities.

Profit center problems

While its advantages outweigh its disadvantages, the materials management profit center is not an unmixed blessing. All types of captive profit centers—materials management or any other variety— encourage interdepartmental bickering. There is strong incentive for the profit center manager to try to look good at the expense of fellow managers. He can do this by padding his transfer prices and also by taking actions that reduce his costs at the expense of increasing costs in some other department. In the case of the materials management profit center, there might be temptation to try to cut costs by purchasing merchandise of inferior quality while maintaining the same transfer price. There would also almost certainly be difference of opinion on responsibility for stockouts. For example, if a plant suddenly ran out of material, the stockout might be blamed on the supplier, while the materials manager would claim that the plant did not have sufficient foresight to advise him of a basic change in its requirements. Well-defined ground rules could eliminate most such disputes—but not all of them.

In addition, breaking up an organization into a group of captive profit centers may create additional administrative costs. There is more bookkeeping. More time is spent negotiating transfer prices and ground rules, as well as attending to the other details of profit center administration.

Use of index numbers

Most of these intrinsic disadvantages can be avoided by using index numbers as a basis for a profit center. When this is done, a materials management department can set itself up as a profit center simply as a means of monitoring and improving its own performance. There would be no complicated bookkeeping and it would not be necessary to negotiate profit-center terms and conditions with using departments.

Two indexes needed. In the simplest case, just two sets of index numbers would be needed: purchase costs and end-product selling price. Suppose, as in the earlier example, you work for a company that has annual purchases of $10 million, materials management expenses of $300,000 per year, and employs $1.5 million worth of company capital in the materials management process. If the company earns a 15 percent return on capital, it would then be assumed that during this base year materials management will also have earned a 15 percent or $225,000 return on its capital. To recoup the $300,000 materials management expenses and earn the $225,000 profit, it is necessary to mark up purchase costs of $10 million by $525,000 or 5.25 percent, so that "sales" to using departments become $10,525,000. The $10 million spent for purchases is determined by two basic variables: physical quantities and price. Price changes can be measured with an index following the procedure outlined in Chapter 7. During this base period, the index of purchase prices is 100.0

Second-year results. The materials management profit center does not really begin to operate until the second year. During that year, suppose that:

1. Actual withdrawals of purchased materials inventories at cost plus direct purchases are $10.8 million. (This figure is easily obtainable from conventional accounting systems.)
2. Year-end inventory is up $50,000 over the previous year. No other

changes are made in materials management assets, so capital employed in materials management increases by exactly $50,000 to $1,550,000.
3. The purchase price index increases by exactly 2 percent to 102.00. The company boosts its end-product prices by exactly 1 percent.
4. Operating expenses incurred in materials management increase by exactly 5 percent, to $315,000.

From this data, you can construct a hypothetical income statement for the materials management profit center, but you first must make these adjustments:

1. Actual purchase volume must be adjusted to reflect base period purchase prices, since the materials management profit center must base its "sales" on base period rather than actual purchase prices. To do this, simply divide actual purchase volume of $10.8 million by the price index of 1.02. This indicates that volume of purchases would have been $10,588,235 had supplier prices not increased by 2 percent.

2. Applying a 5.25 percent markup to adjusted purchase volume of $10,588,235 indicates that "sales" would have been $11,144,117 had there been no change in hypothetical transfer prices charged to using departments by materials management. However, the company was able to increase its overall selling prices by 1 percent. Therefore, materials management is entitled to a 1 percent price increase. This boosts "sales" to $11,255,558.

It is now possible to calculate an income statement, as follows:

"Sales"	$11,255,558
Cost of goods sold	10,800,000
Gross margin	$ 455,558
Operating expenses	315,000
Profit	$ 140,558

Return on capital employed in materials management $= \dfrac{\$140,558}{1,550,000} = 9.03$ percent

Thus, in this example, the materials management department has permitted its costs and expenses to increase more rapidly than its revenues, and return on capital has declined to 9.03 percent. If the decline in the company's overall return has been even greater, then materials management can be assured that it is providing its fair share of support of the company. Otherwise, the materials management department should not be satisfied with its performance.

When indexes are used, the entire profit center system may take up no more space than a file folder and, since there are no genuine transactions, there is no need to involve departments other than materials

FIGURE 20–1

Sources: Data, Bureau of Labor Statistics (steel prices) and U.S. Steel (Employment and Purchased Goods and Services); chart, Annual Report to Stockholders of the U.S. Steel Corporation.

Like most other giant corporations, U.S. Steel uses indexes to measure trends of purchase prices, selling prices, and employment costs. Until 1973, the U.S. Steel purchasing department was successful in holding the advance of purchase prices to a rate slower than that at which the corporation was able to increase its selling prices. Unfortunately, purchase prices surged ahead so fast in 1974 that by 1977 the gap between purchase prices and selling prices had not been closed.

management. After she has acquired experience with this dummy system, the materials manager may suggest to top management that it be used as a basis for measurement of materials management performance and, eventually, a formal profit center may evolve.

Production versus nonproduction

In most real-life companies, the materials management profit center should be divided into two or more parts. Even in the smallest manufacturing companies, there is a substantial difference between the value added by materials management on purchases of nonproduction items and that added on production material. The 5.25 percent markup used in the example is more typical of production material. On nonproduction items it must be higher.

Inventory turnover is usually much lower on nonproduction supplies. In extreme cases, each $1 of "sales" of nonproduction supplies requires as much as 50 cents of assets. If the return on capital is 10 percent, this 5-cent profit alone creates a markup of 5 percent. In addition, the costs of operating nonproduction storerooms may be greater relative to the volume of material handled than is the case with production stores. In fact, value added by materials management for nonproduction materials may be as much as 20 percent in manufacturing companies. This is roughly equal to the markup of many industrial distributors that handle approximately the same kinds of materials. Among nonmanufacturers, storage costs may be even higher and true value added by materials management may, in extreme cases, exceed value added by the supplier.

If a materials department handles classes of material that are as widely different as production parts and nonproduction materials are in most manufacturing companies, it can measure performance on each class of material far more precisely if it sets up at least two different profit centers with markups over cost that more accurately reflect the nature of the service performed.

In some cases, of course, the materials department may perform only a buying service for the using department. It gets a requisition for the item, buys it, and the using department takes possession of it on delivery. There is no inventory carrying cost for this type of transaction, so the markup need cover only the allocated costs of making the purchase. In at least one real-life materials management profit center, the London County Council (Case 20–1), this type of transaction is performed gratis for clients and its cost is, in effect, buried in the markup applied to items that are carried in inventory.

Other materials management profit centers will no doubt find it convenient to make similar compromises between convenience and accounting precision. While each profit center must be tailored to the unique needs of the organization, the case studies that follow provide a guide to successful implementation of the profit center concept.

Case

CASE 20–1. GREATER LONDON COUNCIL SUPPLIES DEPARTMENT*

A materials management profit center in the public sector

The City of London began to expand beyond its original boundaries hundreds of years ago. By 1960, the built-up area that was then known as Greater London had an area of about 840 square miles and a population of almost 9 million persons. While Greater London is a single economic entity, it was governed in 1960 by more than 90 separate local authorities including country councils, country borough councils, and urban and rural district councils with overlapping jurisdictions.

The London Government Act of 1963 greatly simplified this structure. It created the Greater London Council, the first regional elected authority in the United Kingdom. The council is presently responsible for providing a long list of municipal services to a local government area of 610 square miles of Greater London with a population of about 7.5 million persons. The act also created the Inner London Educational Authority which consolidates the educational facilities of the 13 boroughs that comprise London's core.

The Greater London Council Supplies Department was created in 1965. It is one of the 15 specialized departments that serve the council. Of the council's 120,000 employees, approximately 2,000 work for the Supplies Department. The department provides a supply service for the council, the Inner London Educational Authority, as well as London area boroughs that wish to make use of its services. In addition, other public agencies in the London area may purchase from the department on a voluntary basis.

The department is fully self-supporting and normally makes a small profit even after making an allowance for interest on the funds it employs in the business. Its total volume of business of £46,278,932 was divided among four classes of customers:

Greater London Council	£13,337,257
Inner London Educational Authority	15,303,452
London boroughs	16,348,873
Others	1,289,350
	£46,278,932

The Supplies Department's business is classified into four basic categories: direct supply; issues from depot stocks; repair work,

---

* This case was prepared by Dean S. Ammer of the Bureau of Business and Economic Research, Northeastern University, Boston, as a basis for classroom discussion and not to illustrate either effective or ineffective handling of an administrative situation. Distributed by the Intercollegiate Case Clearing House, Soldiers Field, Boston, Mass. 02163. All rights reserved to the contributors.

sales, services; and local order contracts and joint contracts. On direct supply transactions, the Supplies Department acts as a purchasing service for the agency that needs the material. In general, direct supply is used for items where the requirements of a particular agency are unique and not shared with other agencies. The Supplies Department is responsible for buying the item and delivering it to the agency that uses it. To cover its costs, the department adds a 5 percent service charge to each purchase. However, the maximum charge for any purchase is £30, and there is a minimum fee of 25 pence. Dirct supply sales were £19,552,738.

Direct supply may not be practical for items that are used regularly by a number of agencies. In such cases, it is often more economical to purchase in large quantities and have each user draw upon the Supplies Department's inventories. The department's sales from its depot stocks amounted to £10,617,350. In general, the department tries to carry sufficient stock of each item to guarantee a 95 percent service level. According to Mr. Sam Swallow, director of the Supplies Department, "the markup over purchase cost varies by type of item but in general is designed to recoup the department's total operating costs. These costs include annual repayments of the capital cost of depot real estate and interest on the capital amounts outstanding, together with interest on stocks. Interest rates are related to the current rates at which the council borrows."

The department normally carries an inventory equal to about a three months' supply of materials that are issued from stock. Inventory naturally varies from item to item. In general, higher stocks are probably required in the United Kingdom than are needed in the United States because of the U.K.'s great dependence on imports of food and industrial raw materials. In some cases, the Supplies Department, in effect, buys food and other material by the shipload that it then issues from stores in smaller quantities.

Substantial safety stocks are sometimes needed to protect against substantial variations in usage that result from long and often erratic fluctuations in procurement lead time. As a result, a substantial increase in inventory would be essential if the department were to increase its stockout protection from its present level of 95 percent to 99 percent. The extra cost would have to be passed on to the using agencies and ultimately to the overall British economy.

The using agency normally has no contact whatever with vendors who supply material that the Supplies Department carries in stock. However, this policy simply is not practical for all purchases. For example, perishable foods are delivered directly from the vendor to the user and day-to-day contact is necessary to keep demand and supply in balance. Similarly, using agencies find it convenient to deal directly with vendors when specialized equipment breaks down and a repairman is needed immediately. The solution to problems of this sort is joint or local order contracts whose terms are negotiated by the Supplies Department on behalf of the agencies, who then deal directly with the appropriate vendors.

Joint and local order contracts amounted to £13,375,000. Major commodities included fuel and marine oil, meat, milk, gasoline, rent of Rank-Xerox copying machines, and a variety of services such as window cleaning, and laundry. While negotiation of these contracts requires a substantial effort on the part of the senior staff of the Supplies Department, it is not practical to pass on the Supplies Department's costs directly to the users because they are invoiced directly by the outside vendors and not by the Supplies Department. However, the cost of negotiating local contracts is passed on indirectly to users since the Supplies Department is self-supporting and its overall administrative costs are eventually passed through to users by a surcharge on materials on which it can take a markup.

In its fourth major activity, repair work, sales and services, the scope of the Supplies Department extends well beyond that of a conventional supply agency. The department operates a printing and bookbinding service for its client agencies that had gross sales of £1,225,357 and profit of £53,488. Advertising printing grossed an additional £349,724 with surplus of £1,824. The department also grossed £234,695 and lost £21,572 on six restaurants it operates primarily to serve employees of the Greater London Council and related agencies.

The Supplies Department also operates a motor pool and garage. It had gross income of £1,183,808 and profit of £24,594 on automotive repairs and income of £1,289,000 and profit of £14,275 from vehicle rentals. In addition, the department provides various general services such as maintenance, a central reprographic service, and office services, whose costs are mostly shared on an allocated basis.

The Supplies Department operates two major supply depots. The larger and more modern of the two is the Tottenham Hale Depot which has 288,000 square feet of space. This depot handles five major groups of materials: building materials and supplies; scientific and electrical equipment and supplies; cleaning materials, uniforms, and textiles; furniture, furnishings, and floor coverings; and food. The depot's basic function is to buy merchandise in large quantities, store it, and then deliver it to client agencies. The depot is also a processor of materials. It operates both a sawmill and a butcher shop. Basic reason for these operations is that the United Kingdom is not self-sufficient in either lumber or meat. The Supplies Department buys both of these commodities abroad in partially finished form (the lumber as timber and the meat as frozen carcasses) and then must carry on further processing before delivery to using agencies.

The Supplies Department is also responsible for disposing of surplus materials on behalf of its agency customers. Centralized surplus disposal often permits material and equipment that is surplus with one agency to be transferred to another agency which has a need for it. An important by-product of this responsibility is the school furniture repair shop at the Tottenham Hale Depot. When furniture becomes unusable, schools send it to the Tottenham Hale Depot. In some cases, the Supplies Department is not able to repair the furniture or can find no use for it. It is then sold for the best price that can be obtained. Such sales totaled £4,982. In most cases, furniture can be repaired either at the depot or by outside suppliers. Issues of repaired furniture amounted to £515,728, and the repair operation earned a profit of £6,293 after incurring internal costs £142,367 and paying outside contractors £372,050.

The Southfields Depot is older and smaller than the Tottenham Hale Depot. It has 142,000 square feet of space and is used primarily for office supplies, stationery and similar materials, as well as fuel. Like the Tottenham Hale Depot and the Supplies Department's other facilities, it maintains separate accounts for each category of business.

Exhibit 1, which shows the general stores and textile accounts at Tottenham Hale, is representative of the department's accounting system. Note that this particular account shows a surplus for the year of £45,742, after allowing for interest expense of £8,999. Also note that the accounts are limited to operating expenses and inventories. While fixed assets obviously exist, they are not accounted for in the department's annual report but are presumably treated simply as government-owned buildings.

While the department strives to make a modest profit on every account, deficits are sometimes incurred. Using agencies have fixed budgets for each fiscal year, and to permit them to stay within their budgets, the Supplies Department guarantees fixed prices for all stock items for the British April–March fiscal year. Unfortunately, the department's suppliers do not necessarily keep their prices at fixed levels. Thus, the department is often squeezed between relatively fixed prices and rising costs. This is aggravated by a rate of domestic inflation in the United Kingdom that since World War II has been consistently greater than that of the United States and most of the U.K.'s major trading partners in Western Europe.

As a result, Mr. Swallow explains that "the trading objective is to break even overall taking one year with another but to accumulate and carry forward a small surplus to safeguard the fixed prices against unexpected inflation of purchase prices or falls in demand. Part of the accumulated surplus has recently been used for repayment of some of the capital cost of the Tottenham Hale Depot and certain other items of non-recurrent expenditure."

EXHIBIT 1
London County Council Supplies Department, Tottenham Hale general stores and textile accounts (in British pounds sterling)

Stock account (in British pounds sterling) ....

Issues to other Supplies Department Depots			£ 118	
Issues to GLC and ILEA			1,583,515	
Issues to boroughs and others			1,818,354	
Total gross value of issues			£3,401,987	*(3,188,610)*
Opening stock	155,861			
Purchases	2,887,513			
		3,043,374		
Less closing stock		189,117		
Total net value of issues		2,854,257	2,854,257	*(2,673,268)*
Gross trading surplus			547,730	*(515,342)*
Clerical salaries and wages	61,000			
Operative salaries and wages	106,170			
Superannuation deficiency	5,932			
Premises	85,456			
Supplies and Services	9,527			
Office expenses	15,386			
Carriage	146,410			
Computer	44,517			
Interest	8,999			
Central expenses	18,591			
Balance transferred to Stores Surplus Account	45,742			*(+27,338)*
	547,730		547,730	

Consequently, cost reduction and value analysis are major objectives of the Supplies Department. The department maintains a laboratory at its Tottenham Hale Depot for testing materials to assure maximum value and also makes use of outside laboratories, as required. The department has been successful, in many cases, in getting greater value by purchasing on a competitive basis materials for which it has developed its own specifications. For example the department has developed a new type of work uniform for the London Fire Brigade and new designs of school and office furniture.

Unlike some American government agencies, the Supplies Department is not required to accept the lowest bid that it gets. Contracts are awarded on the basis of overall value, not exclusively on price. The department maintains its own quality control activity to monitor supplier quality and to make certain that its specifications are being met. Competitive proprietary products are also evaluated on the basis of performance and other quality characteristics. Many of the department's suppliers are in the Greater London area, since this is, of course, the economic, as well as the political, capital of the United Kingdom. However, there is no requirement that the department buy locally, although the director and other senior executives are conscious of the public relations impact of their decisions.

Questions

1. Is the GLC Supplies Department a profit center? How does it differ from a materials management profit center one might find in a private company?
2. How does the British taxpayer benefit from the GLC Supplies Department's operations? Why might a similar setup be resisted in the United States or (perhaps elsewhere in the United Kingdom)?

Index

673

This book has been set in 10 and 9 point Caledonia, leaded 2 points. Chapter numbers are 30 point Weiss Initial Number 1 and chapter titles are 18 point Caledonia. The size of the type page is 27 by 46½ picas.